Explores the multiple paths children follow to health and well-being in diverse national and international settings. It also demonstrates the connection between social and political health resources and addresses the immediate concerns of how those who care for children create the physical, emotional, and spiritual environments in which resilience is nurtured. Recommended for graduate students, academics and professionals in the human service fields.

Handbook for
WORKING
With CHILDREN
and YOUTH

Handbook for
WORKING
With CHILDREN
and YOUTH

Pathways to Resilience Across Cultures and Contexts

EDITOR
MICHAEL UNGAR
Dalhousie University

SAGE Publications
Thousand Oaks ▪ London ▪ New Delhi

For information:

Sage Publications, Inc.
2455 Teller Road
Thousand Oaks, California 91320
E-mail: order@sagepub.com

Sage Publications Ltd.
1 Oliver's Yard
55 City Road
London EC1Y 1SP
United Kingdom

Sage Publications India Pvt. Ltd.
B-42, Panchsheel Enclave
Post Box 4109
New Delhi 110 017 India

Printed in the United States of America on acid-free paper

Library of Congress Cataloging-in-Publication data

Handbook for working with children and youth : pathways to resilience
across cultures and contexts / edited by Michael Ungar.
    p. cm.
Includes bibliographical references and index.
ISBN 1-4129-0405-6 (cloth)
  1. Resilience (Personality trait) in children. 2. Resilience (Personality trait) in
adolescence. 3. Resilience (Personality trait) in children—Cross-cultural studies.
4. Resilience (Personality trait) in adolescence—Cross-cultural studies.
5. Social work with children. 6. Social work with youth. I. Title: Pathways to
resilience across cultures and contexts. II. Ungar, Michael, 1963-
BF723.R46H357 2005
362′.7—dc22

                             2004028633

05 06 07 08 09 10 9 8 7 6 5 4 3 2 1

Acquiring Editor:	Jim Brace-Thompson
Editorial Assistant:	Karen Ehrmann
Production Editor:	Sanford Robinson
Typesetter:	C&M Digitals (P) Ltd.
Copy Editor:	Linda Gray
Indexer:	Karen A. McKenzie
Cover Designer:	Michelle Kenny

CONTENTS

ACKNOWLEDGMENTS

This book wouldn't exist without the inspiration of some very special, and often ignored, individuals whom I have met during years of travel in countries like Pakistan, Malaysia, Egypt, Tanzania, Colombia, and Israel. I also owe much to children who I came to know in correctional facilities, community mental health clinics and child welfare agencies. Together these children taught me about what it takes to survive. This book, by pushing the bounds of accepted scholarship on resilience, honors their wisdom.

More practically, though, this book owes much to the world-class mentors and colleagues whom I have counted as friends these past many years and whose work has helped to inform my own. Many of them are contributors; many others continue with their work, some recognized for their contributions, others largely unrecognized. Though too numerous to name, I hope they will see in this book reflections of what they have taught me during our many discussions.

Closer to home, I would also like to acknowledge the help and patience of the research assistants and teaching assistants who have helped with the production of this work and the research projects on which it is based. These people include Linda Liebenberg, Janus Siebrits, Andrea Gregus, Anna Lee, Rhonda Brophy, Susanna Steinitz, and Nora Didkowsky, among others. I am also indebted to the editorial staff at Sage for their invaluable assistance, most notably Jim Brace-Thompson, who saw in this project an opportunity to contribute to this field of study.

Bringing this work to completion has also been greatly assisted by my family, who have joined me often in my rambles around the world in search of the inspiration for this volume. Cathy, my partner, and our two children, Scott and Meg, have always been there for me, even when commitments to writing may have meant time away from them.

Lastly, this work would never have appeared without the financial support of various granting agencies, including The Social Sciences and Humanities Research Council of Canada and the Nova Scotia Health Research Foundation, as well as supplementary funding from the Canadian International Development Agency. Well-funded research has made it possible for me to enjoy the luxury of collaborations and innovation. I am indebted to those who contribute their time and leadership to those agencies.

FOREWORD

JAMES GARBARINO

Reading through the manuscripts that constitute the chapters for this book causes me to reflect on what I have learned from almost three decades of experience as a researcher, educator, author, program consultant, and legal expert witness dealing with issues of resilience in the lives of children and youth. I have learned that human beings are indeed generally adaptive and resourceful but that resilience is not unlimited, automatic, or universal.

Under conditions of numerous serious threats experienced in hostile environments ("risk accumulation"), no child may escape unscathed, no matter how well equipped the child may be temperamentally. Every child has limits. Much is made in the scientific literature and the popular press of resilience. Although it is defined in numerous ways, resilience generally refers to an individual's ability to bounce back from adverse experiences, to avoid long-term negative effects, or otherwise to overcome developmental threats. Every one of us knows someone whose life is a testament to resilience. The concept of resilience rests on a key research finding: Although experiencing any specific negative influence increases the odds of a particular negative outcome, most children escape severe harm. I have seen and heard resilience at work in youth prisons (Garbarino, 1999), in inner-city neighborhoods and early childhood programs (Garbarino, Dubrow, Kostelny, & Pardo, 1992), in war zones and refugee camps (Garbarino, Kostelny, & Dubrow, 1991), in families (Garbarino & Bedard, 2001), and in schools (Garbarino & deLara, 2002).

However, as the concept of resilience has been promoted in ever-wider circles, there has been a parallel concern that the concept may easily be misused or misunderstood. Four such limitations are of particular importance in our conceptual toolbox as we look at the lives of children and youth coping with adversity. First, we must remember that resilience is not absolute. Virtually every youth has a breaking point. Research conducted by psychiatrist Bruce Perry on the impact of trauma and deprivation on brain development leads him to assert that kids are "malleable" rather than "resilient," in the sense that each threat costs them something.

What is more, as psychologist Patrick Tolan (1996) points out, in some environments, virtually all youth demonstrate negative effects from exposure to highly stressful and threatening environments. In his Chicago data, for example, *none* of the African American adolescent males facing a combination of highly dangerous and threatening low-income neighborhoods, coupled with abusive families, was resilient at age 15. In this case, resilience was measured by a child having completed a two-year period during which he or she was *neither* more than one grade level behind in school *nor* requiring professional mental health services to deal with psychological problems. These data, however, leave unanswered the question of how these youths perceived themselves. Some of them may well have defined their status as "normal" or "unaffected." Regardless of these self-perceptions, Tolan's data do provide a picture of their ability to cope with some important social realities of day-to-day functioning in America.

Avshalom Caspi, Terrie Moffitt, and their colleagues (Caspi et al., 2002), provide another example in research that focused on the role of a genetically based difference in crucial neurotransmitters (chemicals in the brain that influence the processing of information and arousal). When the MAOA gene is "off," the child does not have the same level of the enzyme that enables these neurotransmitters (e.g., norepinephrine, serotonin, and dopamine) than when it is "on." If children have the MAOA gene turned off *and* are abused, about 85% develop a chronic pattern of aggression, violating the rights of others, and antisocial behavior (and can be diagnosed with "conduct disorder" if one is of a clinical bent). If kids are abused and the gene is turned "on" the figure is *only* about 40%. If the gene is turned off and the child is not abused, the rate of conduct disorder is about 20% (and 20% if the gene is on and there is no abuse).

But beyond this childhood reality of almost total effect (85% of the children are diagnosable with conduct disorder), does the combination of early maltreatment and MAOA vulnerability lead to an adult life dominated by negativity? Are children resilient? An ecological perspective would predict that the answer to both questions, indeed to virtually all developmental questions, is "it depends." The effects of the childhood double whammy or the "off" gene and the experience of abuse are much less dramatic when the researchers look at whether or not an individual is convicted of a violent crime and whether or not the individual demonstrates symptoms of antisocial personality disorder in adulthood. These results seem to indicate that although the pathway into conduct disorder in childhood is almost a given for children who get the double whammy of being abused and having the MAOA vulnerability, the pathway from there into an antisocial life in adulthood is subject to other influences.

Second, we must remember that resilience in gross terms may obscure real costs to the quality of an individual's inner life. Some people manage to avoid succumbing to the risk of *social* failure as defined by poverty and criminality but nonetheless experience real harm in the form of diminished capacity for successful intimate relationships. Thus, even apparent social success—performing well in the job market, avoiding criminal activity, and creating a family—may obscure some of the costs of socially successful coping. The inner lives of

these individuals may be fraught with emotional damage—to self-esteem and the capacity for intimacy, for example. Although resilient in social terms, these individuals may be severely wounded souls.

This has long been evident in comparing the resilience of boys versus girls. Boys who succumb to the accumulation of risk have long been prone to act out in explicitly antisocial behavior (juvenile delinquency), whereas girls have been more likely to respond with self-destructive behavior and internalized symptoms such as stomachaches, nightmares, and wretchedly low self-esteem. Does this mean girls are more resilient than boys? A simple accounting of social success variables might lead us to think so. However, if we take into account the full range of harm, we can see that such an answer would be wrong. Kids adapt: for better *and* for worse.

Third, we must always be vigilant lest cultural bias and ethnocentrism cloud our assessments of resilience. Just as some individuals are socially successful yet spiritually and emotionally afflicted, so the reverse is true as well: Some individuals who are apparently social failures are actually spiritual and psychological successes. This is particularly true when there are cultural differences involved in the assessment of resilience.

Sternberg (2004) and his colleagues have provided reliable and excellent evidence that although some cognitive abilities and processes are universally part of the foundation for intelligence, social and cultural context go a long way toward defining the meaning and manifestation of competence in the real lives of children and youth. This insight has several implications for our understanding of resilience. For one thing, it highlights the importance of knowing the ecology of the child or youth so that the meaning of "competence" and "coping" used in any assessment of resilience is situationally valid. Also, it warns us against the simplistic application of standards of competence from one ecological niche to another. Rather, as Sternberg so clearly demonstrates, it impels us to see the world through the eyes of the child and youth in any effort to assess resilience. What is more, it argues for "dynamic" assessments that illuminate the child's ability to learn to demonstrate competence in new settings rather than simply taking as definitive assessments conducted at one time (and perhaps in one place). Indeed, this approach on assessment is wholly consistent with the very concept of resilience, which is not about the immediate destabilizing effects of trauma and other adverse experiences but, rather, the child's ability to learn how to move from these insults to a position of health and success (in terms that are meaningful culturally and phenomenologically).

Fourth, we must not forget that "resilient" does not necessarily mean "morally superior." The youth who demonstrates resilience has extraordinary attributes and resources that the non-resilient child does not have. Being unable to protect oneself against the accumulation of risk factors does not constitute moral turpitude. Some environments are too much for anyone, and to use the concept of resilience as a basis for moral judgment in these settings may be inappropriate and unfair. I have seen this first-hand when testifying as an expert witness in youth homicide trials. In one case, although seeking to discredit my expert testimony bearing on the role of trauma in shaping youth behavior, the prosecutor used the concept of resilience in precisely this manner. In his cross-examination, he asked why the defendant was not as successful as other kids in difficult situations. His exact words were, "What's wrong with this boy that he is not resilient?" That's not fair and it's not good science. It leads to judging and blaming in ways that are themselves unethical and bad science. The burdens imposed on children who live with violence, particularly when accompanied by an accumulation of other risk factors are sometimes too heavy for anyone to carry without psychological back breaking. Starting with compassion for this brings head and heart together. To study resilience, one should adopt a fundamental humility about oneself and one's culture and society and simultaneously a respect for the human strength of others. The chapters in this book take these four cautions seriously and offer a convincing demonstration that resilience is indeed "a many splendored thing."

REFERENCES

Caspi, A., McClay, J., Moffitt, T., Mill, J., Martin, J., Craig, I., Taylor, A., et al. (2002). Role of genotype in the cycle of violence in maltreated children. *Science, 297,* 851–854.

Garbarino, J. (1999). *Lost boys: Why our sons turn violent and how we can save them.* New York: Free Press.

Garbarino, J., & Bedard, C. (2001). *Parents under siege: Why you are the solution and not the problem in your child's life.* New York: Free Press.

Garbarino, J., & deLara, E. (2002). *And words can hurt forever: How to protect adolescents from bullying, harassment, and emotional violence.* New York: Free Press.

Garbarino, J., Dubrow, N., Kostelny, K., & Pardo, C. (1992). *Children in danger: Coping with the consequences of community violence.* San Francisco: Jossey-Bass.

Garbarino, J., Kostelny, K., & Dubrow, N. (1991). *No place to be a child: Growing up in a war zone.* New York: Lexington Books.

Sternberg, R. (2004). Culture and intelligence. *American Psychologist, 59,* 325–338.

Tolan, P. (1996). How resilient is the concept of resilience? *Community Psychologist, 29*(4), 12–15.

Introduction: Resilience Across Cultures and Contexts

Michael Ungar

Like all works on resilience, this one too is a cultural artifact, the result of a shared set of beliefs, values, and ideologies found among a group of academics, child advocates, clinicians, and other specialists who share an interest in children's unique ways of protecting themselves when growing up amid adversity. Although I share with contributors to this volume the common goal of better understanding children, our multiple standpoints make me reticent to assert that there is any one pathway to health common to children globally. Instead, I must be satisfied with a collage of competing truths, each a vibrant local account of what we have come to think we know about children's well-being. The more we dialogue across social, cultural, and linguistic barriers, the more convinced I am of a plurality of possible ways to account for children's resilience.

The best place to begin this exploration of pathways to resilience is close to home. I live on the East Coast of Canada. I am a white, heterosexual male. I earn a good income. I am able-bodied. The risks my family and I confront in our daily lives are negligible compared with those of many other families and their children living less than a mile from my home. Of course, the latchkey children across the street who come home after school to an empty house, who spend hours with video games, suffer their own risks that come with being emotionally neglected. Fortunately, as a community we have provided services and structures to, at the very least, meet these children's needs. There are schools they can attend, guidance counselors who check in on them, government-funded social workers to investigate claims of neglect against their parents. There are also community programs, perennially underfunded, but nevertheless available. There are police, doctors, and emergency services close at hand.

Farther from my home, there are children who face far different challenges. They still confront the same acute risks of my neighbors, experiencing episodes of abuse or the disruption of divorce. But their worlds provide more chronic stressors as well. For example, the African Nova Scotian communities a little north of where I live and across the harbor have experienced systematic discrimination and underservicing that have been an unfortunate part of their deep-rooted history. Their schools have historically been underfunded more than those in my neighborhood. Their access to health care is compromised by the poverty that results from prejudice. They are more likely to be the target of police checks and incarceration. These same prejudices led to the outright dislocation of the African Nova Scotian community in the 1960s to make way for a bridge over the harbor. Combined, these intrusions have taken their toll.

Of course, I could widen the circle further. I could speak about street children in other parts of my community, youth who couch surf, drift between shelters, or when weather permits, populate the streets of every major city and small town in Canada. I could go further and paint simplistic pictures from my travels in Aboriginal communities in Canada and describe the challenges they face: the legacy of residential schools that were a cultural genocide that has contributed to epidemics of substance abuse and suicide. I could move beyond my national borders and look to the United States with its structural inequities, the multiple risks of biological, psychological, emotional, and social factors confounding children's development. But why stop there? I could look overseas to the Middle East, Asia, South America, Africa, and even Eastern and Western Europe where the politics of hatred and prejudice, war, poverty, disability, and marginalization due to gender, sexual orientation, race, and ethnicity all combine to disadvantage children. I could easily paint a picture of a world of children at risk.

This monochromatic view of children and families presents us with a singular and "thin" description of children's lives. Seldom do we hear accounts from children themselves. This is unfortunate because a quieter, less articulated version of children's lives speaks of resilience. It is a much more hopeful vision, one embraced by the authors of the chapters in this volume. If we look, we can find within each population of at-risk children aspects of healthy functioning that may or may not have been overlooked.

Discovering Resilience

In the middle to late 1900s, a growing number of researchers such as Werner and Smith (1982), Rutter (Rutter, Maughan, Mortimore, & Ouston, 1979), Garmezy (1976), and Murphy and Moriarty (1976) began to structure longitudinal studies in Western contexts that found that an inconsistent and unpredictable number of children from at-risk populations presented with remarkably good mental and physical health outcomes despite the multiple disadvantages of structural, familial, and individual stressors.

That body of work has become the basis for a burgeoning field of research into resilience among children and adults. It has provided clinicians, policymakers, child advocates, and researchers a different way of thinking about populations at risk. It has shown that some individuals do survive incredible hardship and that the uniqueness of their solutions may be invisible to outsiders to those lives. However, even as we have come to notice the health to be found among at-risk individuals, our definition of this

resilience has tended to assume a minority-world bias, that of the small, privileged part of our world that lives in relative affluence in Western democracies. In particular, most resilience literature comes from the Western-trained psychological and social service community.

Within this narrow community, resilience has come to mean the individual capacities, behaviors, and protective processes associated with health outcomes despite exposure to a significant number of risks. Without risk, there is no resilience, only health of a different order. Although a good start, and a paradigmatic shift from a focus on the etiology of disease to the "etiology" of health, we have ignored the bias inherent in what we assume to be health indicators. A volume such as this, that places side by side so many different understandings of children's well-being, is a challenge to this homogenizing health discourse. This broadening of our perspective is analogous to what the theory of resilience has done to psychopathologizing discourses of well-intentioned professionals who nonetheless stigmatize at-risk populations with labels of dysfunction. This volume seeks to open to debate what is and is not a sign of health, the variety in the pathways children travel to well-being, and the theoretical and methodological challenges accounting for this plurality of perspectives internationally. This new ground can be charted, however, only because of the debt we owe to the resilience pioneers who shook us up with their vision of health hidden amid danger.

Caution is needed when speaking of resilience. The discourse of resilience can be (has been?) co-opted by proponents of a neoconservative agenda that argue if one person can survive and thrive, then shouldn't the responsibility for success be on all individuals within populations at risk to do likewise? Are services really needed, or should people themselves be expected to follow the lead of the "invulnerables" and surmount their difficult life circumstances? It is a familiar twist on the "anyone can be president" myth. It denies the very real structural constraints on children's lives. Not all children have the constellation of capacities to succeed. Much less would there be the capacity of our society as it is structured to provide places for all children if they were to succeed. After all there is only one president every four years.

More invisibly, resilience research and interventions based on a resilience framework have presented models of successful growth and adaptation that are biased toward Western conceptions of healthy functioning, ignoring the arbitrariness in their selection of outcome variables. The bulk of the resilience literature is based on a Eurocentric view of the world. This view is a product of a philosophical enlightenment that has taken place over the last 400 years during which the world became a *knowable, measurable,* and *predictable* place. Arguably, the complexity of resilience, the myriad ways individuals, families, and communities overcome adversity, cannot be so simplified as to generate a single set of principles generalizable from one contextually specific study to the next. This is not to say we cannot embrace the tools of scientific inquiry in different contexts, seeking the gold standard of external validity for each population under study. We can assert, "For this one group of people, sharing these qualities, what our research shows is likely to be true." But to go further, to speak globally, when we are bound to act only locally, requires that we overstep the bounds of reasonableness. If we learn anything from working cross-culturally, it is that to speculate on the commonality of people's experiences is to tumble into an abyss of uncertainty. Claims of external validity are now being challenged by those formerly marginalized by the process of research (minority groups, women, people with disabilities or illness). They are calling for authenticity, relevance, and the *re-presentation* of people's localized truths.

Although I might be fairly certain that what I know about health may be relevant to the neglected children who live next to me, I am less certain of the veracity of what I know about what makes a child resilient when I encounter communities further afield, such as those of Canada's First Nations or those in countries that are less economically developed, although with cultural traditions and indigenous health practices far more ancient than my own.

At a time when we are increasingly open to critical engagement between those marginalized and the elites who hold power over them, there is a need when studying resilience to understand the multiple pathways that children, their caregivers, and communities travel toward health. This book is intended to broaden our understanding of how children, youth, and the adults who care for them sustain resilience in diverse cultures and contexts. In the process, it challenges the individualizing discourse of health, showing that resilience is embedded not only in psychological factors but also in the structures that support children's access to the resources they need to sustain well-being.

A POPULAR THEORY

A burgeoning interest in the study of resilience has resulted in a fascination with lives lived well despite adversity. Television talk shows and bookstore shelves are full of tales of those who have survived well. They provide a picture of individuals who encounter any of a host of challenges and then marshal personal and social resources to overcome them. Eric Weihenmayer (2001), for example, in his biography of his life as a visually impaired mountain climber, demonstrates incredible resourcefulness and determination as he learns to conquer more and more difficult peaks, eventually reaching the summit of Mt. Everest, a metaphoric as much as a physical accomplishment. In a different vein, *The Girl in the Picture: The Kim Phuc Story* (Chong, 2000), documents the life of a 9-year-old girl badly burned during a napalm attack in Vietnam in 1974. A newspaper photo of Phuc shortly after the attack not only helped to end the war by raising awareness of what was happening but also brought her much-needed medical attention even as she was being exploited as a tool for government propaganda. Her story, too, is one of survival.

To understand these lives lived well, one cannot, however, overlook the cultural, social, and structural forces at play. Each was provided with very real resources that contributed to survival. Each had access to opportunities. Each also had the intelligence and temperament to exploit those opportunities.

A broad developmental perspective on resilience that can fully account for how children become resilient in multiple contexts and across cultures has yet to be fully articulated. A number of works from Western authors, such as Combrinck-Graham's (1995) *Children in Families at Risk*, Walsh's (1998) *Strengthening*

Family Resilience, Luthar's (2003) *Resilience and Vulnerability: Adaptation in the Context of Childhood Adversities,* and Greene's (2003) *Resiliency,* have alluded to the trajectories of at-risk children's growth and the protective factors that promote resilience. Each has contributed to our thinking about what creates healthy individuals and families. However, as helpful as these works have been, they have not demonstrated the plurality of pathways and the *cultural embeddedness* of how health is realized by children and families growing up under adversity. We need to take an approach more typical of McCubbin (McCubbin, Fleming, et al., 1998; McCubbin, Thompson, Thompson, & Fromer, 1998; McCubbin, Thompson, Thompson, & Futrell, 1999), Werner and Smith (1992, 2001), Glantz and Johnson (1999), and Johnson-Powell and Yamamoto (1997), all of whom have made more explicit the need for contextual and cultural specificity when studying, intervening, or theorizing resilience as a developmental process in at-risk populations.

The Local and the Universal

There are many branches to this unwieldy tree that makes up the field of resilience research. Fields as diverse as developmental psychology, international development, refugee studies, criminology, and child and youth care, among others, have shown an acceptance of the concept of resilience and produced bodies of literature congruent with its usage. We are now coming to understand perilous development in cultures under stress (Johnson-Powell & Yamamoto, 1997), just as we are the neurological markers of children who cope better with stress (Denenberg, 1999; Shonkoff & Phillips, 2000). However, this knowledge is seldom sufficiently contextualized to make it relevant to those whose worlds it purports to represent. Recipients of interventions based on theories unquestioningly embedded in a dominant Western psychological discourse of disease and psychopathology are routinely suspicious of concepts and interventions created by those well-intentioned "others" beyond their borders (temporal, geographic, and sociocultural) (Swartz, 1998). As Rapoport (1997) explains,

In the smaller scale societies in developing [sic] countries, the impingement of modern values has produced a spectrum of responses from reaction against what they perceive as alien to enthusiastic acceptance of what they perceive as modern and advantageous. There is still little known about how and why families respond in the way they do. Even less is known about the process of reconciling local traditional values with global values. (p. 75)

A construct as complicated as resilience requires a critical deconstruction, with special emphasis placed on the social locations of those who hold the theory to be true. What then is the value of this thing we call resilience? If it is a product of discourse, a socially and contextually specific idea that is open for interpretation by those who use it around the world, then what can it offer health professionals and researchers? How can we say anything meaningful about children's pathways through adversity that will resonate with "truth" for everyone globally if resilience remains a concept controlled by Western professionals?

These questions are answerable. In fact, if we turn to philosophers such as Hacking (1999), who has sought to understand how ideas such as health become accepted as true, we see that realities are fixed through their simple day-to-day ritualization, the everyday way in which lives are lived. Hacking illustrates his point with a critical examination of what are termed "paper crime waves," the excessive focus on a public event that exceeds the relative importance of the phenomenon to most people's lives. This media hyperbole leads people to exaggerate the occurrence of the event and gives rise to panic. In North America, we see this occurring with youth crime, which continues to decrease despite public perceptions to the contrary. Hacking cautions us, however, from treating such panics as simply social constructions. Such a simplistic and dismissive understanding, he says, overlooks the complexity of the relationships involved and the intricate power plays between individuals and institutions that sustain the definition of the problem.

Opening up the concept of resilience to a similar critique helps us to avoid simplistic explanations that all expressions of children's survival are social constructions and therefore equally valid pathways to health. Promoting such social relativism is not the intention here. A population of children at some risk may sustain health in many different ways that reflect their access to the resources they need to create health. But the views of the dominant culture, frequently that found in the minority Western world, cannot be so easily dismissed as a paper tiger. Instead, we need to move beyond the dualism, a view of resilience as all about local context or all about grand metatheories that reflect the bias of their expert proponents.

It is this same middle path that has been well charted by others such as Swartz (1998), who has examined mental health in the context of Southern Africa. To Swartz, the contextualization of mental health phenomena is essential because biomedical explanations of disorder alone are inadequate to account for people's experiences of illness worldwide. Mental health must be understood as more than an intrapsychic or psychiatric phenomenon. The difficulty will always be balancing the emic and etic perspectives of those who experience illness and those who diagnose and treat it. As Swartz observes, creating an antiracist psychiatry requires that we see beyond the empiricism of psychological theory. We need a new language that more than translates ideas across cultures but that relays differing constructions of what health means and how it is expressed. Specific to the problem of translation (in particular its failure), Swartz explains,

> If we hold the *empiricist* view, the task of translating is simply finding the appropriate words in different languages for feeling states. If on the other hand we hold the *hermeneutic/ constructionist* view, the task of translating is more complex: we have to consider the extent to which the act of translation implies the construction of a particular reality. (p. 29)

None of this, however, opens the door to a complete relativism or an overprivileging of indigenous medicine. According to Swartz (1998), mental illness does exist in developing countries, is recognized by people's communities as a sign of illness, leads to stigmatization, and cannot always be cured through the use of indigenous methods. Naïveté under the guise of

cultural sensitivity simply re-creates the dualism between the minority and majority worlds, without appreciating any shared realities whatsoever. A better balance is required.

In the chapters that follow, we move back and forth between the specific and the universal, between local knowledge and pan-global understandings. This dialogue is meant to draw a line in the sand, to find the ever-shifting place where local truths compete with global truths in a healthy dialectic. When it comes to children's survival, we need to understand their accounts of their experiences while aggregating what we know collectively to offer others at risk some signposts on an effective pathway to health. The challenge is to provide these signposts without privileging a Eurocentric understanding of resilience as universal.

Of course, some aspects of resilience are so ubiquitous as to appear universal: We agree in most cultures and contexts not to do violence to one another (except in ways justified by the need for self-defense); we agree to share food with loved ones; we form attachments; we seek power over our lives and a position of recognition in our communities. These are all essential elements of resilience that appear in global studies on health. We can assert with confidence such truths as "universal by consent" (see Leonard, 1997). We can also simultaneously strive to show tolerance for a polyocular view of the world, encouraging transcultural exchanges that help us to see the varying degrees of relevance of many of our commonly held beliefs about what makes people healthy when exposed to risk. The juxtaposition in this book of differing theories, definitions, and interventions concerned with resilience demonstrates this ambivalence between the cold certitude of the enlightenment and the free-for-all of the postmodern. If we are to understand resilience better, we must open to scrutiny what we know and how we practice based on that knowledge.

Health data are never neutral. One would, for example, hardly know that teenagers are acting more responsible sexually now than in any time since statistics have been gathered. The teen birth rate in the United States has dropped to 42.9 births per 1,000 women aged 15 to 19 (Childtrends, 2003). The drop has been seen in all racial and ethnic groups and in all regions of the United States. Furthermore, teens' self-reports of sexual activity have also declined slightly. Strange, then, that there is still a moral panic about teenagers and sexuality. Stranger still is that the rate of teen births during the 1950s and 1960s was twice what it is today, given perceptions that sexuality was more controlled during both those decades. What we fail to understand in a media awash with worry is that interventions and a widening social safety net are having the effect we anticipated. Clearly, in the context of where I live, we have the technologies required to help children grow up safer and to prevent their exposure to risk.

Is Resilience Research Flawed?

If we are to make the study of resilience a legitimate and fundable endeavor, one that can offer a counterpoint to the study of disease and psychopathology, we will need to address its shortcomings. Critics contend that the concept of resilience may be nothing more than a tautology, a simplistic way of saying that whatever makes you stronger must necessarily be good. There is also the danger of identifying resilience in individuals we have already arbitrarily designated as successful by the design of our inquiry into their lives. If, for example, a child remains in school despite population-wide risks associated with dropping out, then we might argue the child is resilient. But what does such a distinction, the laying on of the label *resilient*, add to our understanding about children and health? We already, after all, have ample theories to explain why some children drop out and why others do not.

With all the problems discussed above, it is not surprising to find some researchers abandoning the construct of resilience altogether. Tarter and Vanyukov (1999) characterize resilience as lacking heuristic value or practical usefulness because of its nonlinearity and failure to predict epigenetic trajectories through life. Their argument is ecological: "Successful or poor adjustment does not ultimately reside in some abstruse property of the person such as resilience but instead emanates from the interaction between the person's phenotype and environment" (p. 99).

Arguably, what the study of resilience as an overarching concept adds is the possibility to weave a tapestry of health-related phenomena that offers a paradigmatically different position from which to examine children at risk. Resilience researchers and clinicians look to those who succeed for clues to successful development rather than focusing on those who succumb to risk. When we investigate what makes someone strong instead of what causes weakness, we are more likely to identify that which bolsters health. Alleviating illness gets us only halfway to resilience. We might interrupt the course of a disease, but we fail to understand how individuals sustain health. This shift in focus is imperative if we are to study health rather than disorder. As Glantz and Sloboda (1999) explain, despite criticisms of resilience research, "It should not be discarded because it encourages an important focus on a real and important phenomenon" (p. 113). In our pursuit of the etiology of health, we encounter the multiple forces at play in the lives of those who survive and thrive. For example, in Canada, it is noteworthy that some children don't drop out of school when facing the combined threats of decreased job prospects or the systemic prejudice encountered by visible minorities, most notably Aboriginal and African Canadian youth. However, it is even more remarkable that children don't drop out when they must dodge bullets to get to school or resist the pull into street gangs and the money and status they bring when growing up in the poorest communities of Medellín, Colombia. Shifting our focus to health, we are given culturally embedded clues to survival strategies. Collectively, these strategies can help us understand where best to invest our limited social and financial capital.

Because good interventions and policies tend to be built on enlightened science, it has fallen to researchers to demonstrate what resilience is and how it is nurtured. The problems of arbitrariness in what is measured and what is used as health outcomes and the difficulties of accounting for social and cultural variability are all aspects of resilience research that are not insurmountable. Even the skeptics are encouraging a much-needed debate. I would agree with Glantz and Sloboda (1999) who write the following:

Unfortunately, the concept of resilience is heavily laden with subjective often unarticulated assumptions and it is fraught with major logical, measurement, and pragmatic problems. . . . We share many of these concerns. We find there is great diversity in the use of the concept; it is used variously as a quality, a trait, a process, or an outcome. We have identified few attempts to assess resilience in which measurement problems do not cloud or eclipse the findings. There is no consensus on the referent of the term, standards for its application, or agreement on its role in explanations, models, and theories. In sum, the problems and inconsistencies in measurements, findings, and interpretations in the published literature raise serious questions about the utility and heuristic value of the concept of resilience. (pp. 110–111)

These are not necessarily arguments for abandoning the term, which, as Glantz and Sloboda (1999) note, is still much needed. They do, however, push us to find a heuristically useful understanding of resilience that is helpful for comprehending the way children live their lives day-to-day.

There are many different hypotheses about what sustains resilience. Frequently, they are not well articulated, hidden beneath the fog of a dominant discourse that is more concerned with illness than health. For example, Loeber and Farrington (2000) note in their review of the factors contributing to juvenile delinquency:

Some children engage in minor delinquent acts for excitement, adventure, or other emotions common among children. For these children, offending may be considered as part of the context of child development in which youngsters learn prosocial behaviors by trial and error. (p. 742)

Although it is certain that for some of these children, these early offenses are "stepping stones in pathways to serious, violent, and chronic offending" (p. 743), for many others, these events do not predict future negative outcomes. It is intriguing that Loeber and Farrington find such problematic behaviors to be part of normative development in some contexts. The problem, as they explain, is that "currently we have few tools to distinguish between those young children who will continue with their problem behavior and those who will not" (p. 746). What is refreshing is that Loeber and Farrington can at least see the complex negotiations for health of the subjects in their study. If we are to understand healthy coping among children at risk of becoming delinquents, then we must look for patterns of health-seeking behavior that co-occur with their problems. Thus, we can see what Glantz and Sloboda (1999) mean in concrete terms when they invite us to "postulate the interaction of positive and negative influences leading to variable outcomes" (p. 114). In the case of children who act like delinquents, it is a difficult distinction to make between those who are engaged in risk-taking behaviors as a way to further their positive growth and those whose delinquency puts them on a course to more serious problems. To categorically say that risk-taking socially deviant behaviors are all bad, or all good, overlooks the variability in children's pathways to health.

An example such as this enters us into the realm of Saussure's (1978) signs and signifiers: We can no longer be entirely certain that any set of behaviors signifies either health or illness. Empiricism does not necessarily become obsolete, however. Instead, our attention is called to the contextual specificity and need to account better for the meaning those being investigated hold for the phenomena under study. The more complex and mixed method our designs, the more likely we are to achieve a theory that accounts for the multiplicity of competing understandings of health (and illness).

As Massey, Cameron, Ouellette, and Fine (1998) note in their studies with youth, at least three problems face resilience researchers: values, context, and trajectory.

Resilience researchers have suggested that resilience can be conceptualized as increased self-esteem, decreased depression, and improvements in one's social competence, sense of coherence, or sense of empowerment. These multiple indicators of wellbeing complicate a simple conceptualization of thriving. *In many cases the values implied by these indicators suggest outcomes harmonious with the lived experience of our participants, although in other cases there may be disagreement between the values of researcher and those of the researched* [italics added]. (p. 339)

In practice, one can see how these research problems get expressed in instances where children are resistant to interventions or behave in ways that challenge cultural norms. A remarkably diverse collection of studies have found that resistance is not all bad, and in fact, the children and families who challenge authority are often those who maintain health better than the passive victims of structurally exploitive educational and social welfare systems (see Ungar, 2004). Resisting hegemony has its value, although one is less likely to be seen as resilient. There is a fine balance observable in the lives of at-risk children and youth between conformity and resistance, each contributing to the definitional ceremony of becoming known as resilient to one's peers, caregivers, and community (see Bowman, 2001, for an example of how Palestinian families strengthen their collective identity through acts of resistance and personal sacrifice). Studies of lives lived well, such as those provided in this volume, highlight this tension, providing a caution to our nomothetic tendencies to categorize children without attention to the contexts in which labels are worn.

Culture and Context

The construct of resilience has relevance globally, although pathways to health must be understood as contextually specific. Take, for example, instances where children experience substantial social upheaval. In 1996, a post-Soviet Russia adopted a new set of laws to govern families that have significantly changed the relationship between children and parents and families and State institutions. In this world of ambiguity and shifting norms, there have been unforeseen challenges as both bureaucrats and professionals are reluctant to pass to parents the State powers they enjoyed before perestroika. Not surprisingly, contemporary Russian parents are also not prepared to rear their children independent of the State's sharing responsibility and authority over children (Butler & Kuraeva, 2001). From my standpoint, where the boundaries between State and family are more clearly defined, I find it difficult to understand the Russian family's dilemma. This blinder to my

Russian counterpart's more collectivist orientation would, of course, bias any research I design from my cultural standpoint that might overemphasize individualism.

But how much does any systemic risk such as that found in Russia compromise the health of children? Should it be considered a risk factor at all? Markowitz (2000) shows that despite the changes Russian children have experienced over the past decade and a half, remarkably *few* have noticed how different their lives are from that of their parents. Instead, amid the chaos, adolescents have taken up the challenge to design a life that works well for them, one that emphasizes "challenge and adventure" (p. 216). In a world of constant change, anything becomes possible. As the value placed on authority breaks down in school and community, as evidenced by the dissolution of organizations for children sponsored by the Communist party, the effect has been to leave a cultural vacuum that is more noticeable to adults than children. Yet despite the absence of these formal collectivist organizations, Russian teens still desire the same close connection to their families and a few close friends that were common a generation ago. One must therefore exercise caution assessing Russian children as more at risk now as a result of the socioeconomic turmoil experienced by their caregivers.

This trend toward greater understanding of health in context has been evolving for decades. More than 30 years ago, we saw novel approaches to studies of people's experiences that challenged racial bias. Ladner (1971) observed in her landmark study of 30 young black women:

We can observe differences between racial and social class groups regarding, for instance, the time at which the female is considered to be ready to assume the duties and obligations of womanhood. Becoming a woman in the low-income Black community is somewhat different from the routes followed by the white middle-class girl. The poor Black girl reaches her status of womanhood at an earlier age because of the different prescriptions and expectations of her culture. There is no single set of criteria for becoming a woman in the Black community; each girl is conditioned by a diversity of factors depending primarily upon her opportunities, role models, psychological disposition and the influence of the values, customs and traditions of the Black community. (p. 11)

We know that how children address the "maturity gap" (Moffitt, 1997) between their status as children and their participation in their communities as adults is an important component of how children negotiate their way to healthy adult identities. That Ladner (1971) opens to debate the cultural bias of normative behavior in *American* culture problematizes the whole notion of what is and is not measured as risk and resilience in the West. By her work, Ladner shakes the foundations of what we assume to be healthy adolescent behavior. If teenage pregnancy needs to be reconsidered as a sign of risk, then the entire psychological enterprise of arguing what is health and illness tumbles like a house of cards. What we see in its place is the tentative negotiated agreement that defines what is a healthy pathway to resilience and what is not for each specific context.

This is similar territory to that charted by other feminist authors in the late 1970s and early 1980s. Gilligan (1982) showed us the different developmental pathways for girls' moral development, and members of the Stone Center such as Surrey (1991) and Miller (1976) challenged Erikson's stage theory of development. In both cases, these authors make the distinction that what we believe about development and, ultimately, about health is influenced by the dominant culture that has privileged male ways of classifying the world as normative or nonnormative. We no longer need to think of independence and autonomy as the signs of healthy growth. Instead, if we take the lead from these feminist theorists, we see that growth in connection is a better description of how girls develop. Interestingly, this has also been shown to be an accurate description of how healthy males develop as well. Osherson (1992) found among young men an expressed desire to find connections with their fathers and children. Perhaps we must follow Ladner's (1971) lead. As she notes,

It is simply a question of whether or not the values, attitudes, behavior and systems of belief which govern the dominant white middle class

should be the criteria by which Black people, most of whom have never been allowed to assimilate into the American mainstream, should be evaluated. (pp. 267–268)

Substitute the phrase "Black people" with any other group that does not count itself among the privileged white middle class and one quickly sees the shallowness of assuming any definitive construction of healthy functioning that can be evaluated outside the context in which it is experienced. The bulk of resilience research, although itself contesting the irony of trying to say something meaningful about health from studies of illness, has avoided looking critically at how wellness is culturally embedded and expressed.

CONSTRUCTIONS OF RISK AND RESILIENCE

First things first. There is a good news story everywhere we turn. As much as professions such as social work, psychology, and psychiatry, and the general public hooked on CNN, want to imagine the world a more dangerous place, our children more at-risk than ever before, and life in general miserable, there remains much to be hopeful about. This does not minimize the staggering impact that people globally experience from HIV-AIDS, the effect of war and community-wide epidemics of violence, or the lack of human rights for the many who are dispossessed. In each instance, however, there remains an alternate story, one that is much more full of hope. There is a fine line when studying resilience: One can simply ignore the bad or, alternately, be too realistic, embedded in an empiricism that is itself biased by the numbers it reports. Instead, we may be better off to appreciate that the construction of problems is dialogical. As Houston and Griffiths (2000) have shown, at some level, risk is socially constructed, dependent for its identification on a discursive process that names what we experience as a risk to our well-being.

Take, for example, two perspectives on violence. Michael Moore's Academy Award-winning documentary *Bowling for Columbine* is a disturbing and humorous look at the culture of fear in America today, a fear that is far out of proportion to the risks people face. Instead, according to Moore, the fear that is seeded by the media and nurtured through people's collective beliefs makes Americans constantly afraid for their safety. Their response, a liberal access to guns, has ironically made the very people trying to protect themselves 10 times more likely to be killed by a firearm than in Canada and 50 times more likely than people living in Japan.

In contrast, we can examine a very different perspective on violence. Accounts from Bogotá, Colombia, one of the most violent places on earth, with homicide rates that have been as high as 4,000 per year in a city of 3 million, show that for most people the experience of violence is still a relatively rare event. Duque and his colleagues (Duque, Klevens, & Ramirez, 2003) have found that few people in Bogotá say they experience extreme forms of violence, despite very well-founded perceptions by outsiders that their communities are dangerous.

Which is the better account of the risks associated with violence? Whose view of their personal security, the American or Colombian, is the most accurate? Risk and resilience are never phenomena that are simply objective fact. They are entangled in the collective ideologies of people and their communities.

If we look closely at the risk and resilience literature, there are quiet discourses that tell a different story about the health status of at-risk populations and the unique mechanisms that promote well-being. For example, in the West, we are coming to understand that our efforts to mitigate all risk in children's lives might inadvertently be removing meaningful rites of passage through which children experience manageable risk. Perhaps we would do well to remember "that which doesn't kill you makes you stronger." Improving children's well-being is never as simple as removing risk from children's lives (Ungar, 2002).

We need to listen better. This volume is about providing a space for voices that are less often heard and, indeed, have been all but absent from discussions on resilience. Clearly, the contributors to the following chapters argue that resilience is not an individual characteristic alone. Nor is it only a process. Resilience occurs when the personal meets the political, when the resources we need for health are available so we can realize our potential. Resilience is as much a quality of my family, community, and culture as it is something inside me or a process I engage in. It is only because of a Western psychological discourse that we think more about the individual than the communal. Even when we acknowledge the agentic qualities of a child who thrives, we mustn't overlook the access that child experiences to health resources, including a collective discourse that defines the child's pattern of coping as resilient. We need a communitization of health, understanding health as a communal experience. A well-resourced community, a caring family, meaningful roles for individuals, rites of passage, social equality, and access to education and health care are some of the conditions necessary for the individual to experience health. Strictly speaking, these factors are independent of the individual. And yet, they also result from the actions of healthy individuals who provide for others who are more vulnerable.

To say "I" am resilient is to be mistaken. The *I* of which we speak is a cultural artifact, a perspective that is social and historical, relational and constructed. Instead, we might better say, "There is resilience in this child and his or her community, family, and culture." Resilience is simultaneously a quality of the individual and the individual's environment. To the extent that a child accesses communal health resources and finds opportunities to express individual resources, so too will resilience be experienced.

The implication of this way of thinking is that pathways to resilience must be adaptive and provide individuals with ways to negotiate for the health resources that are available. These resources can be diverse and include anything from attachments to others, self-efficacy, and a healthy sexual identity to safety and security and access to health care, food, and shelter. As this volume illustrates, children, youth, and adults globally enjoy differential access to these resources and exploit opportunities to overcome adversity in many different ways. However, the interplay between what is available and what is used is complicated. Simplistically, the provision of an opportunity that addresses risk is insufficient to change behavior unless the complexity of the problem and the construction of the solutions by those involved are appreciated. This may be obvious, and yet, volumes of work on program fidelity emphasize the correct implementation of programs more than their contextualization.

CONTEXTUAL SENSITIVITY IN RESILIENCE RESEARCH

Luthar, Cicchetti, and Becker (2000) make a similar point in their analysis of the field of resilience research, which according to them has become quite muddled. They argue that studies of protective processes, for example, need to be contextually sensitive to understand the nature of the protective function each plays in different settings. Protective processes are not one-dimensional but interact with the settings in which they appear. As such, a single protective process such as staying in school or remaining attached to one's family through times of crisis may either stabilize an individual's health (preventing further exposure to risks associated with dropping out or becoming a street kid), enhance his or her health (build competence, both academically and socially), be a reactive way to counter a specific threat (the more a child is in school, the less time he or she has to get into trouble), or simply be a direct and proportional response to a threatening environment (staying in school and staying connected to one's kinship network increases chances to find employment and community acceptance later in life). Any single factor associated with resilience in any particular context will protect against risk only in ways meaningful to those whose lives are affected.

We are embracing this ambiguity more often. As Kaplan (1999) notes,

A major limitation of the concept of resilience is that it is tied to the normative judgments relating to particular outcomes. If the outcomes were not desirable, then the ability to reach the outcomes in the face of putative risk factors would not be considered resilience. Yet it is possible that the socially defined desirable outcome may be subjectively defined as undesirable, while the socially defined undesirable outcome may be subjectively defined as desirable. From the subjective point of view, the individual may be manifesting resilience, while from the social point of view the individual may be manifesting vulnerability. (pp. 31–32)

The onus is on the research community, in partnership with study participants, to look closer at what is a risk factor, a protective factor, or an outcome associated with resilience (see Rutter, 2001). It is no longer good enough to arbitrarily decide the definition of these aspects of resilience without the contextualization required to authenticate the meaning of the terms with those who participate in research. Even quantitative designs can do this, although mixed-method designs that employ rigorous qualitative work may be more amenable to the task. There is reason to be cautiously optimistic that we are getting better at embracing the ambiguity of the multiple pathways people travel to health.

Take, for example, the relatively unknown work by Morgan (1998). He examined the relationship between behavioral outcomes, as measured by the level of privileges attained, and resiliency factors in residential treatment among 92 children aged 7 to 15. Hypothesizing that an internal locus of control would be related to behavior associated with resilience, Morgan found instead a null finding. There was no significant correlation between children's pattern of internality or externality, whether they behaved in ways that showed they exercised self-control or defied authority. As Morgan explains,

It seems logical to suggest that, since internal locus of control is related to more successful outcomes in resiliency studies, that it may also be related to more successful, i.e. better level scores. It must be stressed that this remains only a conjecture, however, since it seems possible to also imagine the opposite direction of this relationship, that an internal locus of control, since it may suggest more of a sense of empowerment, may cause these children to, in fact, question and rebel against a well-defined set of rules and expectations precisely because they see themselves as having more options, as being more capable of effecting change compared to those children who are more externally oriented . . . who may just simply go along with the structure of the program because they feel rather powerless to change or manipulate the system. (p. 44)

Given the lack of significant findings, Morgan (1998) listens to his data speak and concludes that "a more resilient child might actually have poorer level scores if the nature of resiliency was to cause a child to fight a system" (p. 100). In other words, the contextual specificity of the residential setting makes an attribute like internality a potential threat to resilience despite the hypothesized link between internality and resilience. Clearly, the idea that resilience is an individual characteristic is no longer tenable. A wave of new resilience researchers is showing that resilience is as much a characteristic of the environment as it is an individual's capacity to exploit opportunities in that environment (see Knox, 2000).

Take, for example, the behavior of students who cut classes. The attribution by educators might be that these are wrongful acts on the part of students. But it also may be that students are resisting a system that has failed to educate them in a way amenable to their style of learning. Fallis and Opotow (2003) talk about the incongruity between adult expectations to attend school and the boredom students who skip class say they experience: "For students, boring connotes something missing in their education, conveys a deep sense of disappointment, and casts class cutting as a coping mechanism for classes that fail to engage" (p. 108). Here again, as in earlier examples, the interplay of context, the power to define one's world (discursive empowerment), and behavior or outcomes is intricate and not always evident outside the specific context in which research takes place.

If we broaden our scope to Colombia again, we can find similar discursive resistance documented by researchers like Felsman (1989) who, based on 300 semistructured interviews with street children under 16, heard them account for ganglike behavior in nonpathologizing ways: "Although the gallada's [gangs of street youth] involvements in crime and violence must be recognized and contended with, it must first be realized that these children do not band together to fight and steal; rather, they band together to meet primary physical and emotional needs not being addressed elsewhere" (p. 66).

A host of other researchers are pushing us to redefine risk and resilience within a contextually specific discourse. Martineau (1999), for example, examined the intertextuality of resilience studies through a meta-analysis of the language used in research reports. She finds that

> obscured behind the well-meaning intentions of teaching resilience is a call for disadvantaged children and youth to conform to the behavioral norms of the dominant society (associated with social and school success) by overcoming or being invulnerable to the systemic distresses and adversities of their everyday lives. (p. 3)

This indictment of the system supports a notion of health as intricately linked to liberation. This overtly politicized understanding of resilience is neither common nor well documented. In part, this is because the dominant discourse of resilience researchers has to date been the psychologizing discourse of Western mental health researchers. Critically, Martineau argues:

> The resiliency discourse imposes prescribed norms of school success and social success upon underprivileged children identified as at risk. The effect is that non-conforming individuals may be pathologized as *non-resilient*. Emphasis remains wholly on the individual and thus, *individualism* is a dominant ideology embedded in the mainstream resiliency discourse. (pp. 11–12)

Such studies reveal that the pathways children navigate toward healthy lifestyles are far from fixed, despite discursive hegemony that tells us what is and is not normative development.

Our capacity to appreciate localized discourses of resilience has hindered our fuller understanding of how people navigate pathways to health when seriously compromised by adversity. We have tended to predetermine outcomes, blinding ourselves to the indigenous, and often everyday, occurrences of resilience. It is this more contextually sensitive, indeed everyday, understanding of resilience that is the next challenge for resilience researchers. As McCubbin and his colleagues (McCubbin et al., 1999) have explained in regard to African American families,

> Notwithstanding . . . negative realities, most minority families go on with the ordinary business

of everyday living: raising and educating their children and grandchildren, caring for the elderly and infirm, celebrating birthdays and anniversaries, attending family reunions, and finding ways to make ends meet. As deeper understanding of resiliency is sought, perhaps a closer look at the ordinary might be instructive. For many racial and ethnic minority families, the ability to do the "ordinary" is in itself an extraordinary achievement. Daily functioning amidst negative realities requires a high level of motivation, commitment, tenacity and creativity. (p. 32)

A NEW UNDERSTANDING OF RESILIENCE

If resilience is going to be understood, it is going to be a messy affair. As Genero (1998) explains,

> Studying resiliency within a context of relationships, variables such as class, gender, sexuality, and culture cannot be relegated to a background status. Nor can differences in the conceptual meaning of relationships, family, and cultural groups be ignored. . . . Although the use of both qualitative and quantitative data-gathering techniques may be desirable, it seems that an interdisciplinary, multimethod approach may generate the most exciting data. (pp. 44–45)

Sadly, this mixed-methods approach is seldom employed. Worse, we as a research community have hesitated to complicate our studies with the numerous confounding variables we would require to situate resilience within the context of each population studied.

Take for example a study by D'Abreu, Mullis, and Cook (1999) of street children in Brazil and the relationship between the quality and quantity of social support and the child's ability to adapt to street life, find food, and form attachments. Remarkably, their study found that there was no relationship between the dependent and independent variables. The results, which were based solely on quantitative data gathering, leave more questions unanswered than answered. We are left with the vaguely disconcerting thought that the research team approached its work with the certainty that they would find something without understanding

the localized constructions of the concepts indigenous to the children themselves. This openness to multiple constructions of core research terms by participants is not meant to create an epistemological vacuum typical of extreme positions in postmodernism. Not all truths will be equally privileged, but all truths may have a constituency of one and often more. The researcher who wants to understand individual and collective constructions of concepts such as resilience among marginalized populations will need to enter the world of discourse analysis. In theoretically murky spaces, the goal of inquiry must be partially consultation rather than consensus building or, perhaps worse, ethnocentric and premature generalization.

This volume is a step forward in this regard. It is an attempt to bring together well-considered arguments about what creates resilience in at-risk populations of children around the world. In one way, it seeks a tentative consensus, a tacit agreement that we can all speak about resilience as if the term is held in common. It is, of course, not. Instead, if one scratches the surface, one will find in these chapters a plurality of understandings of how we understand children's health, how we study it, and how we intervene to promote well-being amid a wide range of challenging life circumstances. The result is a pastiche, a collection of related bits brought together in a stunning collage. To bring some order to this enterprise, the book is divided into three sections, theory, research methods, and finally, practice. Each section is introduced briefly below with an overview of the chapters it contains.

Contained in this collection, then, are many perspectives not common among resilience researchers or among those who have tried to apply the concept of resilience to practice with at-risk populations across cultures and contexts. Venturing into uncharted territory has necessarily meant bringing together scholars and practitioners, advocates and community organizers, researchers and policymakers, both known and unknown, to the field. If this volume appears at moments slightly uneven in its presentation, it is because it has pulled together such a divergent group of authors under the same cover. The result is a collection of voices that have been more or less privileged. Together, however, we demonstrate that resilience is more than an individual set of characteristics. It is the structures around the individual, the services the individual receives, the way health knowledge is generated, all of which combine with characteristics of individuals that allow them to overcome the adversity they face and chart pathways to resilience.

Perhaps in the juxtaposition of our work, the embracing of our own diversity as authors, we will move a little closer to identifying something that we all hold in common, a deeper understanding of what makes children healthy when growing up facing multiple risk factors. In that moment of synergy, there is the possibility that our appreciation of our diversity will give us a glimpse of that which is universal even as we celebrate the local.

IMPLICATIONS FOR THEORY

In the first section of this volume, contributors examine how resilience is theorized and the need, if any, for change. Each chapter offers some less common perspective on the construct of resilience, pushing our conceptualization of the foundations of resilience-related research and practice. This work follows in the wake of others who have hinted at the need to look beyond the skewed, subjective bias of researchers. Take, for example, those who have challenged us to see beyond our dichotomous thinking that classifies communities as either high or low risk. Moving beyond the dichotomous thinking of inner-city human ecologies that overlook aspects of health, a number of researchers have explored the strengths of these communities, which are the direct result of the chaos people experience living there (Nelson & Wright, 1995). In such instances, the steeling effect of community stressors may actually enhance capacities that are invisible to outsiders.

Theoretically sound resilience research and interventions are similar. They must demonstrate an understanding of the warp and weave of communities that knit themselves together to achieve health. A good example was provided by Brodsky (1996) who studied 10 African American single mothers living in high-risk communities. Brodsky demonstrated that a psychological sense of community (PSOC), normally associated with measures of resilience, was in this case shown to be negatively associated with health among the women. Although interveners might bring with them as outsiders to these women's lives the belief that fostering community is a way to address the community's problems, they would actually be putting these particular women's sense of well-being more at risk because of the myopia of the theory from which they operate. Brodsky shows that the negative aspects of a PSOC far outweigh any well-intentioned outsider's positive connotation of the concept. She explains that given the atmosphere in those communities, resources, and the nature of community membership, the women in her study talked about how they maintain boundaries, avoid personal investments with others, hold common symbols of independence, and avoid emotional connections with others outside their families as strategies to protect themselves and their families from the chaos around them. It was, according to the women, a successful way to maintain health and security.

This volume strives to explore similarly different perspectives on the theory of resilience. The intention is to contribute a broader, more contextually sensitive way of conceptualizing health in at-risk populations.

The Chapters

The section begins with Boyden and Mann's (Chapter 1) global perspective on children's coping in majority-world contexts. Their work challenges our notions of what makes a child resilient, suggesting that although resilience may be a useful metaphor, we must attend far more to the specific cultural contexts in which children survive and thrive. Specifically, we must look as much at the meaning that children and their communities create for the social and developmental threats they encounter as at the political systems that do or do not meet children's needs. Boyden and Mann's extensive experience in countries as diverse as Thailand, Nepal, Tanzania, and the Balkans helps to show the plurality of understandings among children of what sustains their health under adverse circumstances.

Next, Laurie McCubbin and Hamilton McCubbin (Chapter 2) broaden our understanding of family resilience by focusing on aspects of culture and ethnic identity as important components of their family resilience model. The authors draw from research on families, trauma, and resilience and from anthropology, sociology, and feminist studies to reveal the importance of culture and ethnic identity as critical components of a relational perspective of family resilience in the face of trauma. The authors' ancestral ties to and immersion in Polynesian culture lay a foundation for their systematic study of resilience.

In the next chapter, Joyce West Stevens (Chapter 3) examines whether the notion of risk and resilience can inform our understanding of marginalized populations, specifically African American youth in inner-city communities challenged by unsafe environments, economic problems, and few social resources. Concluding that both constructs are useful, West Stevens proposes that an ecological framework that focuses attention on the intersection of persons, process, and social context will best help us to understand the lives of these marginalized youth. Learning from these youth, she shows that they can educate us as to what youth need to survive adverse environments and that youth are helped most when attributes associated with resilience are supported.

In Jane Gilgun and Laura Abrams's chapter (Chapter 4), the authors propose that resilience be understood as the expression of cultural and gendered norms. Challenging the dominance of what is and is not a sign of healthy functioning, they show through a study with violent individuals that processes associated with interpersonal violence can in some instances contribute to an "awkward but effective" way that vulnerable poorly resourced individuals experience health. Resilience is thereby understood as something individuals strive for even if their path is deviant or disordered when judged by others. In their chapter, Gilgun and Abrams analyze perpetrators' adaptations to adversity, looking at their gendered beliefs, roles, and strategies.

In the next chapter, Jacqueline McAdam-Crisp, Lewis Aptekar, and Wanjiku Kironyo (Chapter 5) provide a framework for understanding street children and their ways of sustaining resilience through nonconventional lives lived in the street. Street children in both the minority and majority world are discussed in detail, with a rich number of examples from research and interventions. McAdam-Crisp and her colleagues show both intrigue and puzzlement regarding the capacities of these children to overcome adversity. Under their scrutiny, risk chains that might be thought to compromise children (including child labor, leaving home, and even prostitution) are shown in contextually specific instances to provide some of these children with a way to survive better than they would off the street.

Ira Prilleltensky and Ora Prilleltensky (Chapter 6) move the discussion to the level of the professional intervening to promote wellness and resilience in marginalized populations, such as people with disabilities. They show that we need change in how we have understood the role of the psychologist, social worker, and other helping professionals. Interventions must necessarily be more influential in the sphere of social justice. Their argument is that wellness and resilience cannot "take hold" unless both are rooted in "socially just communities and processes." Both psychological and political influences are needed to create change at the level of individuals and their communities. To date, this critical and transformational focus has not been a large part of professional discourse by those employed to help vulnerable children, youth, and families.

In the next chapter, Cindy Blackstock and Nico Trocmé (Chapter 7) use their examination of the reasons behind the disproportionate removal of Aboriginal children from their families as a way to argue that risk to children comes from structural forces outside children's immediate families. Using data from the Canadian Incidence Study on Reported Child Abuse and Neglect, they provide evidence to support an argument that we must necessarily address structural barriers such as inequitable service access if we are to create culturally appropriate conditions for children to overcome risks associated with maltreatment.

In the last chapter of this section, Fred Besthorn (Chapter 8) advances our understanding of the conditions necessary for resilience even further. He offers a novel understanding of one aspect of resilience that has been largely overlooked by researchers: the child's inter-action with his or her natural environment. Besthorn shows that the ontological and episte-mological insularity of the human development and resilience fields, embedded as they are in Western modernity, have caused us to ignore the importance of our experiences with the natural world and their contribution to health outcomes.

IMPLICATIONS FOR RESEARCH

Achieving a more contextually relevant under-standing of resilience will require methods for research that reflect advances in health research already underway in the social sciences. Although beyond the scope of this volume to explore fully the debate over which methods are most appropriate to what kind of research, the bias of most contributors to this volume is toward some type of mixed-method approach to resilience research. The need for contextuali-zation of concepts and instruments, combined with the need for "thickly" described lives to see resilience in lives lived under adversity, makes it most likely that as valuable as quantitative approaches can be, they require a qualitative component as well (Galambos & Leadbeater, 2000). The nuts and bolts of how one actually integrates these two approaches, however, remains hotly debated (Miller & Crabtree, 2000).

Although debate continues, it appears that multiple-method designs, or at the very least the aggregated findings from studies within diverse research paradigms, both qualitative and quanti-tative, will provide the most comprehensive picture of resilience. As Tashakkori and Teddlie (2003) argue in their discussion of mixed-method approaches to research, such research

> is mixed in many or all stages of the study (ques-tions, research methods, data collection and analy-sis, and the inference process). . . . Therefore, one of the assumptions of such research is that it is indeed possible to have two paradigms, or two worldviews, mixed throughout a single research project. (p. 11)

The result is much more diversity in the data and what they can tell us. The mixed-method approach routinely combines different paradigms. It is not simply that one does a focus group, a form of qualitative inquiry, to validate an instru-ment. The researcher goes further, combining both realist or value-neutral perspectives with the value-engaged constructionist and subjec-tive position of complementary research para-digms (Greene & Caracelli, 2003). In particular, mixed-method designs are noted for their con-tribution to cross-cultural research where cul-tural distance demands researchers deconstruct their standpoint vis-à-vis research participants and the culture under study (Moghaddam, Walker, & Harré, 2003).

None of these design advances, however, lets us avoid the thorny issues that complicate resilience research when it is attentive to con-textual variation. The best these new methods do is allow us to engage more effectively in the debate. Critics from both research paradigms, quantitative and qualitative, recognize that they will have to do far more with the tools they have available if they are to adapt their methods to myriad different contexts (see, e.g., Glantz & Sloboda, 1999).

The complexity of our research is likely to get worse the better we get at documenting resilience-related phenomena. This is not a field for those who like order. It is more like reading a great epic novel where one is never, indeed if ever, quite certain what a single event means to the overall experience of a character. Further-more, if this complexity makes research difficult, the need to account for multiple constructions of health across global contexts makes it positively unwieldy. This is very similar to Cohen and his colleagues (Cohen, Cimbolic, Armeli, & Hettler, 1998) who have characterized the field of research on "thriving," principally concerned with adults who have suffered traumatic life events, as "unso-phisticated" because of the methods employed and in particular the inability of researchers who as of yet have failed to account for the variabil-ity in how participants define benefits or gains associated with health.

Under the weight of such critiques, researchers are obligated to embrace complexity and account for localized constructions of health phenomena. In this endeavor, either set of methods can become the principal tool when enhanced by the other. Far from a distant goal, such complementarity in design is now evident in many forums. As Madill and her colleagues (Madill, Jordan, & Shirley, 2000) observe, there has been a shift in tolerance for alternative epistemological orientations to research among psychologists, a shift easily seen in nursing, social work, medicine, and other disciplines as well. Maddill et al. observe that

> few psychologists today espouse a strict logical positivist in which knowledge is understood to be demonstrated through its direct correspondence with observed events and research methods modelled on those of the hard sciences. In practice, a range of post-positivist epistemologies are utilized which recognize an element of interpretation and metaphor in the production of social scientific theories and findings. (p. 1)

Interpretation? Metaphor? These are landscapes of conflict under less ideal circumstances. The contributors to this section navigate these same epistemologically troubling waters, providing bridges to collaboration across research paradigms.

The Chapters

It's appropriate, then, to begin this reflection on methods with a chapter by William Barton (Chapter 9). Barton critiques resilience research to date, acknowledging that its greatest strength has been shifting our attention to health and the ecological context in which that health occurs. However, there remain daunting methodological and theoretical challenges. Although he shows the potential value of both quantitative and qualitative methods and reviews many exemplary studies in both research traditions, he concludes that a symbolic interactionist approach to resilience is the most needed at this juncture because we still have not entirely comprehended the missing piece in most developmental theory, including resilience theory, that being the mechanism that best explains peoples' successful behavior despite exposure to risk. Quantitative designs that accomplish this have tended to be longitudinal and expensive and risk attrition in their sample. What's more, they may overlook the meaning and cultural specificity needed to understand a health-related construct such as

resilience. Although qualitative studies bring with them their own limitations, most notably a lack of generalizability (in preference for transferability and other criteria of authenticity), Barton argues we need more of them before we can carry on with quantitative work on this theme.

In the next chapter, Eli Teram and I (Chapter 10) look specifically at the contributions qualitative research can make to resilience research that is more politicized, ideological, and culturally grounded. However, as we point out, although qualitative methods offer the hope that they can make transparent the researcher's bias, perhaps preventing research from being misappropriated by neoconservatives who would have us believe resilience is something inside a child, just waiting for the child to express, qualitative research too can be problematic. Although qualitative methods might be useful to resilience research, interpretative challenges abound. The chapter concludes with an examination of how the better integration of qualitative methods can make resilience research more politically relevant and informing of public policy.

Taking a very different approach, John LeBlanc, Pam Talbott, and Wendy Craig (Chapter 11) look at the limits of epidemiological data, exploring the problems inherent in research that has tried to answer the question, "How are the world's children and youth faring with regard to their psychosocial health?" Their work highlights both the complexities and shortcomings of an epidemiological perspective, discussing the difficulties of measuring a multidimensional construct such as resilience and health. Using international data, they examine what we do know about the psychosocial health of youth while demonstrating both the strengths and limitations of the research that produced those findings.

In the next chapter, Laura Camfield and Allister McGregor (Chapter 12) explore how we research well-being in majority-world contexts. Specifically, they offer indicators of how research on well-being is seeking to integrate both objective and subjective approaches to how we understand experiences of poverty and how those experiences are reproduced. They show that it is important that we bring together a range of academic disciplines if we are to understand how people achieve a sense of themselves as *resilient,* a proxy term in Camfield and McGregor's work for *happy.* Resilience is something people create for themselves and that they rely on structures around them to create. However, there is typically a gap between people's own evaluations of their lives and what others see as their material well-being. Methodologically, Camfield and McGregor raise a number of important questions regarding the obligation of researchers to examine the nature of people's own constructions of their poverty and disadvantage. Rather than being dismissive of what these people have to say, their chapter argues people's appraisals are not the product of misinformation or poor judgment but elaborate schemes reflecting people's aspirations and strategies to survive or perhaps even thrive.

The following chapter by Linda Liebenberg and I (Chapter 13) details how one goes about researching resilience across cultures and contexts. Our experience designing and implementing the International Resilience Project, a multisite, mixed-method interdisciplinary study in 14 sites globally, provides an account of the real-world problems researchers encounter working cross-culturally. There is little, however, written to guide researchers in the specifics of how to conduct such work. In this chapter, the nitty-gritty of the perils and pitfalls of such collaborations are explored, with specific details provided regarding how to host a meeting to design a multisite study and the negotiations necessary to find consensus on how children's health should be studied.

IMPLICATIONS FOR PRACTICE

Well-considered theory regarding the nature of resilience generated from innovative and rigorous research methods can inform different practice applications. Approaching interventions to ameliorate conditions that threaten children and youth's well-being from an understanding of resilience orients clinical treatment, programming, community work, and policy initiatives in potentially novel directions. With few exceptions, however, these initiatives are seldom grouped under the heading "building resilience"

(see Ungar, 2004; Walsh, 1998). They are, nevertheless, increasingly informed by the burgeoning literature on resilience.

Practice that builds resilience is multidimensional. Resilience is not an individual trait. Huang (2003) puts it succinctly: "We need to integrate the impact of disparities into our mental health care of children." In fact, interventions that address singular dimensions of health such as self-esteem or issues of child labor can actually result in negative consequences for children. There is, for example, evidence that antibullying programs in school that show children the negative aspects of bullying actually create pro-bullying attitudes in children who feel powerless and are seeking ways to increase their self-esteem (Rahey & Craig, 2002). Sutton, Smith, and Swettenham (1999) argue that approaches to violence prevention in schools that fail to recognize aspects of health among bullies will simply not work:

> It is important to realize that some bullying children do have power, and that they can misuse this power in ways advantageous to them (in some circumstances). For some, this power takes a social rather than physical form, and such bullies are undoubtedly skilled at achieving interpersonal goals. They would probably not see their behavior as incompetent or maladaptive, and there is evidence that it often is not. (p. 133)

Although we would evidently prefer that children not bully others in their efforts to feel powerful, we cannot intervene assuming that they are incompetent. Such ungrounded, biased approaches to intervention obscure the health-sustaining behaviors of troubled children. Only when bullies are offered socially desirable outlets for their particular competencies will we see changes in their behavior. A more holistic understanding of the way children sustain health would help to avoid erroneous program design. What we now understand about resilience requires us to think more broadly about any type of interventions that address children's exposure to risk.

Once one shifts focus and understands how children in different contexts search for resilience, one understands that intended outcomes from interventions result only when our actions are grounded on the knowledge of the culture and context of those with whom we intervene. But how grounded? How specific do we need to be when we tailor interventions? There is after all a lack of homogeneity even among marginalized populations. As Dupree, Spencer, and Bell (1997) discuss in relation to self-esteem in black adolescent boys in the United States, a case-by-case and situation-specific approach is required if one is to promote resilience in children in unique circumstances. Although they speak of generic processes such as encouraging "help-seeking strategies and greater social mobility" (p. 258), which will enable many to survive in their home environments, they caution that the mistake we make is to not fully appreciate the unique constellation of resources available to support these strategies.

Because resilience is becoming an increasingly complex term to understand, problematizing our discourse on health, we see that interventions at the level of policy are as necessary as interventions targeting individuals and families. Not surprising, Queiro-Tajalli and Campbell (2003) link organizing strategies and community development with the growth in resilience among specific populations. Resilient communities mobilize to secure resources, one aspect of this mobilization being to find others who will provide mutual support and develop a movement of resistance that fosters structural change. These are lofty goals, but they are just as integral to a resilience-based approach to practice as the more immediate treatment goals of direct practice and prevention programs. As Tully (2002) writes, "There is a constant dynamic interrelationship between the development of public policy (as a response to human need), human behavior (as defined and supported by public policy), and resilience (as a positive coping mechanism related to adapting to ongoing change)" (p. 330).

When it comes to interventions, one size no longer fits all. As Crowel (2003) has pointed out, it is no longer possible to speak of evidence-based practice when we move interventions into ethnically diverse communities. Instead, we might more accurately speak only of "promising practices" that may be judged to fit with a particular population at risk.

In this section, a diverse group of authors from around the world offer their examples of interventions to build resilience with at-risk populations. The result is a pastiche of writing, varied but coherent when viewed from afar. There is much to advance our thinking here, with many different interventions advanced as multiple pathways through the swampy chaos of lives lived under adversity.

The Chapters

The section begins with work by Zahava Solomon and Avital Laufer (Chapter 14) from Israel who relate the findings of a study of responses by Jewish Israeli children to terror. Surveying almost 3,000 adolescents, aged 13 to 15, from 11 schools in Israel, Solomon and Laufer report that on the whole, Israeli teens cope well with the terror they experience, demonstrating resilience both in the way they deal with the trauma and in how they use that exposure to trauma as an opportunity for growth. Embedded in this study are many clues for those who choose to intervene with youth exposed to war and violence, including evidence that social support, ideological commitment, and religiosity all play a role in both mitigating the effects of violence and enhancing psychological growth and coping. However, as Solomon and Laufer explain, the relationship between these factors is complex, with health-enhancing effects being different for youth with different experiences and different beliefs.

The next chapter approaches the problem of intervention differently. Philip Cook and Lesley du Toit (Chapter 15) examine children's resilience when confronted with the challenge of HIV/AIDS in communities in South Africa. They discuss the Circles of Care, a community capacity-building project, as an example of culturally grounded action research and a way of supporting child and community resilience. Highlighting the fit between the project and indigenous African cultural values, beliefs, and practices, they show that children's resilience depends on the promotion of healthy human development resulting from child, peer, family, and social factors embedded in each child's social ecology.

Marion Brown and Marc Colbourne (Chapter 16) next look at a very different context and the survival strategies of youth there. They examine the experiences of lesbian, gay, and bisexual youth (LGB) who cope with homophobia and heterosexism. Brown and Colbourne show that the behaviors of this population, frequently assumed to be signs of psychic distress, mental illness, or other social problems, have seldom been recognized as the legitimate, indeed at times, only ways these youth can respond to and resist their oppression. Resilience is found when these youth manage to navigate around the prejudice they experience. Brown and Colbourne, through discussion of a youth project targeted at meeting the needs of LGB youth, provide rich examples of resilience among this population as they engage in ongoing negotiations between themselves and their environments. Despite a societal context full of problems, both structural and ideological, and precarious family environments, these youth regularly locate the personal and community resources they need to succeed.

Many of the chapters also look at families, their form and function, as one factor in the healthy development of children. Alean Al-Krenawi and Vered Slonim-Nevo (Chapter 17) report on a study of 352 Bedouin children from Israel from both monogamous and polygamous families. Theirs is an interesting story to tell, with Al-Krenawi and Slonim-Nevo hypothesizing that children from polygamous families would report more problems psychologically, socially, educationally, and within their families than children from monogamous families. Their intent is to show that different family forms affect the well-being of children differently. They show that although polygamy may once have been a family form that functioned well, the current reality of urbanization and consumerism that is changing Bedouin society seems to be making polygamous families less successful in terms of securing their children's well-being. Romanticism aside, culturally specific family forms appear to need to adapt as children's broader social environments change as well.

The theme of family functioning as a factor in resilience among children is elaborated on in the next chapter by Barbara Friesen and Eileen Brennan (Chapter 18). Friesen and Brennan explore the resilience-building mechanisms found within families and the broader ecological and specifically community contexts within which families live. Their work details the need for stable supportive communities that provide for the cultural continuity of those living there. In exploring these themes, they examine the child-community relationship, as influenced by the child-family relationship, documenting programs that build the structural conditions for resilience through quality child care arrangements, after-school and mentoring programs, and community-centered, youth development programs.

Next Kwai-yau Wong and Tak-yan Lee (Chapter 19) examine youth at risk in Hong Kong in the 1990s and report on a significant innovation in service delivery that involved the adoption of a screening mechanism in the school system for early identification and intervention. This mechanism was adapted from one used with Canadian youth. While reporting on the Understanding the Adolescent Project (UAP), Wong and Lee identify the inadequacies inherent in its theoretical framework. In particular, they explore the lack of a culture-specific dimension to the UAP. A critical read of the literature, both Western and Chinese, provides a cultural lens through which to reexamine the UAP, offering educators, social workers, and mental health counselors on the front lines with at-risk youth in Hong Kong an alternative professional discourse focused on prevention and health from a uniquely Chinese perspective.

Continuing to elaborate on this theme of resilience as dependent as much on social structures as on individual characteristics, Thomas and Menamparampil's chapter on the young people of North East India (Chapter 20) explores the complicated patterns of coping among youth who face the dual threats of poverty and armed militancy. Although their lives are difficult, youth in this remote part of India demonstrate a constellation of coping strategies aided by structural conditions that facilitate their development. In particular, Thomas and Menamparampil discuss one exemplar of community development for youth, a faith-based organization, Don Bosco, which has as its mission to educate and train youth who are marginalized. Although seldom discussed in the literature on resilience, Thomas and Menamparampil argue that faith-based organizations seed youth resilience through programs as wide ranging as literacy, peace education, vocational schools, and workshops on self-esteem.

In the next chapter, Ken Barter (Chapter 21) moves the discussion from how community agencies contribute to resilience to what government services can and should do to promote health in at-risk children. His work discusses barriers to promoting protective factors in the lives of children who receive child protection services. Barter suggests alternatives to the formal bureaucratic support provided by government systems that might better strengthen protective factors and positive outcomes for children. His work demonstrates from a Canadian perspective that an important part of marginalized children's pathways to resilience includes pathways through the formal service delivery systems mandated to protect them. His message is that we have alternatives that work, that build community, and that address the systemic barriers, such as poverty and social injustice, that affect children adversely.

As an example of alternatives to standard practices in child welfare, Nancy MacDonald, Joan Glode, and Fred Wien (Chapter 22) examine in their chapter approaches to family and children's services rooted in Aboriginal traditions in Canada. In particular, they explore custom adoptions and family group conferencing as ways of avoiding Eurocentric child welfare practices, such as adopting children out to white families, that have contributed to cultural genocide. Their work, focused on the Mi'kmaq communities of Nova Scotia, looks at how provincial, territorial, and federal levels of government in Canada have or have not changed legislation and implementation of child welfare laws to protect the rights of Aboriginal children. Their work is an example of how structures and policies (a) set the conditions to add to the risks faced by marginalized populations or (b) are designed to provide the conditions for resilience to emerge. They argue that child justice and child welfare bodies that understand the importance of using interventions that reflect traditional worldviews of Aboriginal peoples are likely to be those that are most successful in sustaining the well-being of these children.

From child welfare, we move to education. Alexander Makhnach and Anna Laktionova (Chapter 23) explore resilience among contemporary Russian youth with a special focus on both child protection and educational forces that influence children's positive outcomes in a society in transition. They review the personality characteristics found among Russian youth and families that contribute to resilience and explore the role played by communities and social institutions to strengthening qualities associated with resilience among youth. In particular, they look at how the Russian educational system is providing children and families with the interventions required to sustain them through this time of social change.

Shifting the focus back to the minority world, Mary Armstrong, Beth Stroul, and Roger Boothroyd (Chapter 24) compare the closely related constructs of systems of care and resilience. Their argument, like those of their colleagues who precede them, is that these concepts intersect. Resilience depends on structural conditions, in particular the way formal and informal systems respond to children's needs. They present a historical overview of the resilience literature and then contrast it with the similarities and differences in what we understand about systems of care for children in need. Their work points to the benefits for policymakers, planners, and researchers examining systems of care and child resilience to be aware of advances in both fields and the potential of each body of literature to inform policy, system planning, and research efforts.

Broadening our perspective further, Scotney Evans and Isaac Prilleltensky (Chapter 25) write about youth civic engagement (YCE) and its potential impact on the well-being of youth. Their argument is based on a contention that neither wellness nor resilience can be fully understood or promoted without accounting for power differentials between youth and adults and the broader social structures that adults control. However, there needs to be caution in how this engagement is undertaken. Evans and Prilleltensky explain that youth can just as easily be manipulated or cast as token agents of social control by adult-engineered systems that abuse the idealism of youth. Without a power analysis, Evans and Prilleltensky argue, YCE may pose more perils than promise.

In a very different context, these same challenges are addressed in the chapter by Toine van Teeffelen, Hania Bitar, and Saleem Habash

(Chapter 26) who detail both the adversities Palestinians face and the consequences of those adversities to the mental health of youth growing up in the Occupied Territories. Unlike many other accounts of Palestinian youth, however, this chapter examines evidence of the resilience to be found among Palestinian youth. After discussing personal, familial, and cultural resources that sustain resilience, van Teeffelen, Bitar, and Habash consider how a development organization, the Palestinian Youth Association for Leadership and Rights Activation (PYALARA), can create conditions that bolster resilience among youth. PYALARA provides both social interventions such as mentoring programs and different forms of youth-oriented media to give youth a voice in the political decision-making process.

The next chapter by Wanda Thomas Bernard and David Este (Chapter 27) examines the context within which young African Canadian males navigate through the challenges they face and the personal, family, community, and spiritual resources they use to overcome the systemic prejudice and structural disadvantage they experience. Bernard and Este examine these challenges to young African Canadian males, particularly in the areas of education and employment. They then apply Hill's (1998) resiliency model developed for African Americans to the African Canadians. Their chapter concludes with reflections on resilience collected from 30 males who discuss both their experiences of success and marginalization.

Concluding the book is a chapter by Luis Duque and his colleagues (Chapter 28) who bring us fully back to the challenge this volume addresses: What does resilience look like across cultures and contexts, and how do we promote it? In this chapter, Duque and his coauthors explore the Early Prevention of Aggression Project that was implemented in Medellín, Colombia, based on design elements from Canada and the United States. The chapter examines the challenges faced when projects in majority-world settings that seek to create the structural conditions for resilience to emerge are adapted from minority-world contexts where the bulk of the scholarship and implementation has taken place. Specifically, the chapter reviews findings from the first phases of an evaluation of

outcomes, with a special focus on how well the project was implemented and fidelity to the model when it is employed in communities far more dangerous and far less resourced than those in more economically developed nations. Far from showing that "one size fits all," the chapter shows that different settings provide children very different challenges to health that require different measures to promote resilience.

It is an appropriate place to conclude the book, with the argument for a more contextual understanding of resilience, one that acknowledges the structural, as well as the personal factors that foster resilience, demonstrated on a large scale in a context far beyond that normally discussed in the resilience literature. Combined, this and all the other accompanying chapters demonstrate the necessity for the field of resilience theory, research, and practice to broaden its focus and cultural embeddedness if it is to continue itself to "survive and thrive."

REFERENCES

Bowman, G. (2001). The two deaths of Basem Rishmawi: Identity constructions and reconstructions in a Muslim-Christian Palestinian community. *Identities-Global Studies in Culture and Power, 8*(1), 47–81.

Brodsky, A. E. (1996). Resilient single mothers in risky neighborhoods: Negative psychological sense of community. *Journal of Community Psychology, 24*(4), 347–363.

Butler, A. C., & Kuraeva, L. G. (2001). Russian family policy in transition: Implications for families and professionals. *Social Service Review, 75*(2), 195–224.

Childtrends. (2003). *Facts at a glance.* Retrieved January 18, 2005, www.childtrends.org/Files/FAAG2003.pdf

Chong, D. (2000). *The girl in the picture: The Kim Phuc story.* Toronto, Ontario, Canada: Penguin.

Cohen, L. H., Cimbolic, K., Armeli, S. R., & Hettler, T. R. (1998). Quantitative assessment of thriving. *Journal of Social Issues, 54*(2), 323–335.

Combrinck-Graham, L. (Ed.). (1995). *Children in families at risk.* New York: Guilford Press.

Crowel, R. (2003). *Improving access to care and outcomes for children from diverse racial and ethnic backgrounds and their families.* Plenary address, 16th Annual Research Conference, "A System of Care for Children's Mental Health: Expanding the Research Base," University of South Florida, Tampa.

D'Abreu, R. C., Mullis, A. K., & Cook, L. R. (1999). The resiliency of street children in Brazil. *Adolescence, 34*(136), 745–751.

Denenberg, V. H. (1999). Commentary: Is maternal stimulation the mediator of the handling effects in infancy? *Developmental Psychobiology, 34*(1), 1–3.

Dupree, D., Spencer, M. B., & Bell, S. (1997). African American children. In G. Johnson-Powell & J. Yamamoto (Eds.), *Transcultural child development: Psychological assessment and treatment* (pp. 237–268). New York: John Wiley.

Duque, L. F., Klevens, J., & Ramirez, C. (2003). Overlap and correlates of different types of aggression among adults: Results from a cross-sectional survey in Bogata, Colombia. *Aggressive Behavior, 29*, 191–201.

Fallis, R. K., & Opotow, S. (2003). Are students failing school or are schools failing students? Class cutting in high school. *Journal of Social Issues, 59*(1), 103–120.

Felsman, J. K. (1989). Risk and resiliency in childhood: The lives of street children. In T. F. Dugan & R. Coles (Eds.), *The child in our times: Studies in the development of resiliency* (pp. 56–80). New York: Brunner/Mazel.

Galambos, N. L., & Leadbeater, B. J. (2000). Trends in adolescent research for the new millennium. *International Journal of Behavioral Development, 24*(3), 289–294.

Garmezy, N. (1976). *Vulnerable and invulnerable children: Theory, research, and intervention.* Journal Supplement Abstract Service, A.P.A.

Genero, N. (1998). Culture, resiliency and mutual psychological development. In H. McCubbin, E. A. Thompson, A. I. Thompson & J. A. Futrell (Eds.), *Resiliency in African-American families* (pp. 31–48). Thousand Oaks, CA: Sage.

Gilligan, C. (1982). *In a different voice: Psychological theory and women's development.* Cambridge, MA: Harvard University Press.

Glantz, M. D., & Johnson, J. L. (Eds.). (1999). *Resilience and development: Positive life adaptations.* New York: Kluwer Academic/Plenum.

Glantz, M. D., & Sloboda, Z. (1999). Analysis and reconceptualization of resilience. In M. D. Glantz &

J. L. Johnson (Eds.), *Resilience and development: Positive life adaptations* (pp. 109–128). New York: Kluwer Academic/Plenum.

Greene, R. R. (Ed.). (2003). *Resiliency.* Washington, DC: NASW Press.

Greene, J. C., & Caracelli, V. J. (2003). Making paradigmatic sense of mixed methods practice. In A. Tashakkori & C. Teddlie (Eds.), *Handbook of mixed methods in social and behavioral research* (pp. 91–110). Thousand Oaks, CA: Sage.

Hacking, I. (1999). *The social construction of what?* Cambridge, MA: Harvard University Press.

Hill, R. (1998). Enhancing the resilience of African American families. *Journal of Human Behaviour in the Social Environment, 1*(2/3), 49–61.

Houston, S., & Griffiths, H. (2000). Reflections on risk in child protection: Is it time for a shift in paradigms? *Child and Family Social Work, 5*(1), 1–10.

Huang, L. N. (March, 2003). *Improving access to care and outcomes for children from diverse racial and ethnic backgrounds and their families.* Plenary address, 16th Annual Research Conference, "A System of Care for Children's Mental Health: Expanding the Research Base," University of South Florida, Tampa.

Johnson-Powell, G., & Yamamoto, J. (Eds.). (1997). *Transcultural child development: Psychological assessment and treatment.* New York: John Wiley.

Kaplan, H. B. (1999). Toward an understanding of resilience: A critical review of definitions and models. In M. D. Glantz & J. L. Johnson (Eds.), *Resilience and development: Positive life adaptations* (pp. 17–84). New York: Kluwer/Plenum.

Knox, L. M. (1998). *The ecology of resilience in the inner-city: Redefining resilience in the lives of high-risk inner-city youth.* Unpublished doctoral dissertation, University of Texas at Austin.

Ladner, J. A. (1971). *Tomorrow's tomorrow: The black woman.* Garden City, NY: Anchor Books.

Leonard, P. (1997). *Postmodern welfare: Reconstructing an emancipatory project.* Thousand Oaks, CA: Sage.

Loeber, R., & Farrington, D. P. (2000). Young children who commit crime: Epidemiology, developmental origins, risk factors, early interventions, and policy implications. *Development and psychopathology, 12*(4), 737–762.

Luthar, S. S. (Ed.). (2003). *Resilience and vulnerability: Adaptation in the context of childhood adversities.* Cambridge, UK: Cambridge University Press.

Luthar, S. S., Cicchetti, D., & Becker, B. (2000). The construct of resilience: A critical evaluation and guidelines for future work. *Child Development, 71*(3), 543–562.

Madill, A., Jordan, A., & Shirley, C. (2000). Objectivity and reliability in qualitative analysis: Realist, contextualist and radical constructionist epistemologies. *British Journal of Psychology, 91*(1), 1–20.

Markowitz, F. (2000). *Coming of age in post-soviet Russia*. Chicago: University of Illinois Press.

Martineau, S. (1999). *Rewriting resilience: A critical discourse analysis of childhood resilience and the politics of teaching resilience to "kids at risk."* Unpublished doctoral dissertation, University of British Columbia, Vancouver.

Massey, S., Cameron, A., Ouellette, S., & Fine, M. (1998). Qualitative approaches to the study of thriving: What can be learned? *Journal of Social Issues, 54*(2), 337–355.

McCubbin, H. I., Fleming, W. M., Thompson, A. I., Neitman, P., Elver, K. M., & Savas, S. A. (1998). Resiliency and coping in "at risk" African-American youth and their families. In H. I. McCubbin, E. A. Thompson, A. I. Thompson, & J. A. Futrell (Eds.), *Resiliency in African-American families* (pp. 287–328). Thousand Oaks, CA: Sage.

McCubbin, H. I., Thompson, E. A., Thompson, A. I., & Fromer, J. E. (1998). *Resiliency in Native American and immigrant families*. Thousand Oaks, CA: Sage.

McCubbin, H. I., Thompson, E. A., Thompson, A. I., & Futrell, J. A. (Eds.). (1999). *The dynamics of resilient families*. Thousand Oaks, CA: Sage.

Miller, J. B. (1976). *Toward a new psychology of women*. Boston: Beacon Press.

Miller, W., & Crabtree, B.F. (1994). Clinical research. In N. K. Denzin & Y. S. Lincoln (Eds.), *Handbook of qualitative research* (pp. 340–352). Thousand Oaks, CA: Sage.

Moffitt, T. E. (1997). Adolescents-limited and life-course-persistent offending: A complimentary pair of developmental theories. In T. P. Thornberry (Ed.), *Developmental theories of crime and delinquency* (pp. 11–54). New Brunswick, NJ: Transaction.

Moghaddam, F. M., Walker, B. R., & Harré, R. (2003). Cultural distance, levels of abstraction, and the advantages of mixed methods. In A. Tashakkori & C. Teddlie (Eds.), *Handbook of mixed methods in social and behavioral research* (pp. 111–134). Thousand Oaks, CA: Sage.

Morgan, R. H. (1998). *The relationship between resiliency factors and behavioural outcomes of children in residential treatment centers*. Unpublished doctoral dissertation, School of Social Services, Fordham University.

Murphy, L. B., & Moriarty, A. E. (1976). *Vulnerability, coping, and growth from infancy to adolescence*. New Haven, CT: Yale University Press.

Nelson, N., & Wright, S. (Eds.). (1995). *Power and participatory development*. London: Intermediate Technology.

Osherson, S. (1992). *Wrestling with love: How men struggle with intimacy with women, children, parents and each other*. New York: Fawcett Columbine.

Queiro-Tajalli, I., & Campbell, C. (2003). Resilience and violence at the macro level. In R. R. Greene (ed.), *Resiliency* (pp. 217–240). Washington, DC: NASW Press.

Rahey, L., & Craig, W. M. (2002). Evaluation of an ecological program to reduce bullying in schools. *Canadian Journal of Counselling, 36*(4), 281–296.

Rapoport, R. N. (1997). Families as educators for global citizenship: Five conundrums of intentional socialization. *International Journal of Early Years Education, 5*(1), 67–77.

Rutter, M. (2001). Psychosocial adversity: Risk, resilience and recovery. In J. M. Richman & M. W. Fraser (Eds.), *The context of youth violence: Resilience, risk and protection* (pp. 13–41). Westport, CT: Praeger.

Rutter, M., Maughan, B., Mortimore, P., & Ouston, J. (1979). *Fifteen thousand hours: Secondary schools and their effects on children*. Cambridge, MA: Harvard University Press.

Saussure, F. (1978). *Course in general linguistics* (C. Bally & A. Sechehaye, Eds.; W. Baskin, Trans.). London: Collins.

Shonkoff, J. P., & Phillips, D. A., (Eds.). (2000). *From neurons to neighborhoods: The science of early childhood development*. Committee on Integrating the Science of Early Childhood Development; Board on Children, Youth and Families; National Research Council & Institute of Medicine. Washington, DC: National Academy Press.

Surrey, J. L. (1991). The "self-in relation": A theory of women's development. In J. V. Jordan,

A. G. Kaplan, J. B. Miller, I. P. Stiver, & J. L. Surrey (Eds.), *Women's growth in connection* (pp. 51–66). New York: Guilford Press.

Sutton, J., Smith, P. K., & Swettenham, J. (1999). Socially undesirable need not be incompetent: A response to Crick and Dodge. *Social Development, 8*(1), 132–134.

Swartz, L. (1998). *Culture and mental health: A southern African view.* Cape Town, South Africa: Oxford University Press.

Tarter, R. E., & Vanyukov, M. (1999). Re-visiting the validity of the construct of resilience. In M. D. Glantz & J. L. Johnson (Eds.), *Resilience and development: Positive life adaptations* (pp. 85–100). New York: Kluwer Academic/ Plenum.

Tashakkori, A., & Teddlie, C. (Eds.). (2003). *Handbook of mixed methods in social and behavioral research.* Thousand Oaks, CA: Sage.

Tully, C. T. (2003). Social work policy. In R. R. Greene (Ed.), *Resiliency* (pp. 321–336). Washington, DC: NASW Press.

Ungar, M. (2002). *Playing at being bad: The hidden resilience of troubled teens.* Lawrencetown Beach, Nova Scotia, Canada: Pottersfield Press.

Ungar, M. (2004). *Nurturing hidden resilience in troubled youth.* Toronto, Ontario, Canada: University of Toronto Press.

Walsh, F. (1998). *Strengthening family resilience.* New York: Guilford.

Weihenmayer, E. (2001). *Touch the top of the world: A blind man's journey to climb farther than the eye can see.* New York: Dutton.

Werner, E. E., & Smith, R. S. (1982). *Vulnerable but invincible: A longitudinal study of resilient children and youth.* New York: McGraw-Hill.

Werner, E. E., & Smith, R.S. (1992). *Overcoming the odds: High risk children from birth to adulthood.* Ithaca, NY: Cornel University Press.

Werner, E. E., & Smith, R. S. (2001). *Journeys from childhood to midlife: Risk, resilience, and recovery.* Ithaca, NY: Cornell University Press.

PART 1

THEORETICAL PERSPECTIVES

1

CHILDREN'S RISK, RESILIENCE, AND COPING IN EXTREME SITUATIONS

JO BOYDEN

GILLIAN MANN

CHALLENGES TO CHILDREN'S WELL-BEING

Adversity comes in many forms, as a result of social or political strife, individual acts of omission or commission, environmental calamities, and many other causes. Due to their youthfulness and, specifically, their lack of social power, children and adolescents are often among the most severely affected by these adverse circumstances. Poverty, armed conflict, forced migration, family problems, environmental degradation, and exploitation, all rising to unprecedented levels, have deepened concern internationally for the protection of children[1] and for the promotion of their health and well-being.

With the nearly universal ratification of the UN Convention on the Rights of the Child (CRC), the protection of children exposed to adversity has now become one of the central priorities of childhood interventions internationally. The convention provides a comprehensive global framework for supporting children in both chronic and episodic conditions of stress. Modern policy has clearly embraced the ethical and moral view that children have a right to special consideration and that children exposed to exceptionally harsh situations merit the greatest concern. But on what terms do we extend such consideration? The logical outcome of public sector austerity and the gradual dismantling of state structures—or the absence of such

AUTHORS' NOTE: We would like to express our gratitude to the Andrew W. Mellon Foundation, which generously provided the funds that have made this chapter and the research that underpins it possible. We are also very grateful to Jo de Berry and Andy Dawes for their constructive comments on early drafts of this chapter and especially to William Myers who contributed many important insights that challenged us to become far bolder and more creative in our thinking.

structures in the first place—is that children and their families and communities cannot necessarily count on the promises made in international treaties. Moreover, due to the sheer scale of some childhood problems—for example, children in Africa orphaned by AIDS or those experiencing armed political strife—affected populations are frequently forced to rely on their own individual capacities to cope. To say this is not to exonerate callous governments that choose to ignore their responsibilities toward children, but to be pragmatic about the immediate prospects for large numbers of children and to focus policy attention on the challenges that lie ahead.

Although there are many structural and practical obstacles to the development of effective measures for children, there is evidence that shortcomings in policy and practice are also the result of erroneous conceptualization of problems and their solutions, inadequate empirical evidence to support specific interventions, and unquestioned assumptions about children's development and their relative capacities and vulnerabilities. Indeed, recent research in the social sciences and experience in dealing with children in stressful situations, as will be discussed in this chapter, are providing new insights that challenge much conventional wisdom about how to assist affected children. Because it is increasingly clear that many notions of childhood and of childhood vulnerability, development, and well-being are contextually constructed (see Ungar, 2004), serious doubt is being cast on the relevance of many traditional prescriptions for protecting children, especially interventions imposed from outside the child's social and cultural context. At the same time, new insights and ideas that could be more helpful have not been widely disseminated or evaluated.

Under increasingly difficult circumstances globally, the CRC's demand that children's best interests be a major criterion for actions concerning them has raised disturbing doubts and questions regarding how to define and deliver what is most appropriate and effective for young people. Scholars and practitioners in different parts of the world have been trying to find out what effects misfortune has on children's social, psychological, and emotional well-being and

to provide appropriate psychological and social care and support. However, child protection remains an uncertain art, beset by challenges and disputation at the methodological, conceptual, theoretical, and practical levels. The present chapter explores some of the issues and controversies pertinent to a discussion of children's vulnerability, resilience, and coping in situations of extreme hardship, highlighting problems and gaps in existing research and recommending areas for further theoretical development and field research. It makes the case for a dynamic, contextualized view of misfortune and suggests that children's experiences of adversity are mediated by a host of internal and external factors that are inseparable from the social, political, and economic contexts in which children live. It also calls for greater attention to children's own understandings of their experience. Throughout, it asserts the need for research, policy, and programmatic interventions to consider carefully the reality of children's lives in order to improve the effectiveness of interventions designed to assist them.

CHILD DEVELOPMENT, "RISK," AND "RESILIENCE" IN THE LITERATURE

In this section, we examine some of the key concepts and theories that inform discussions of development, well-being, risk, and resilience in children who are exposed to adversity. Despite the global application of these concepts, the most systematic and influential body of information on child development and well-being and on the factors that mediate risk and resilience during childhood is found in research with children in the United States and Europe.

Up until the early 1980s, scholarly understandings of child development were dominated by the work and ideas of Jean Piaget, whose emphasis was on the uniformities of children's development and the ways in which the individual child makes sense of the "generic" world (Rogoff, 1990). The Piagetian model stresses that individual children actively construct knowledge through their actions in the world. Learning takes place when a child is required to reconcile his or her expectations of the world and his or her actual experience of that world.

This constructivist approach is still important. However, in the last 25 years psychologists and anthropologists interested in child development in diverse cultural contexts have challenged Piaget's view of the child as a solitary, independent individual whose interaction with the world leads him or her to spontaneously develop general skills and strategies that can then be applied across logically similar problems (Cole, Gay, Glick, & Sharp, 1971; Rogoff, 1990). These scholars have become increasingly attracted to the sociocultural approach of Lev Vygotsky (1978) and the work of later theorists such as Barbara Rogoff (1990), Michael Cole (1996), and Jacqueline Goodnow (1990).[2] The main tenet of this more recent perspective is that all psychological phenomena originate through interpersonal interaction and hence social and cultural context provide the framework for how children learn to think, speak, and behave.

This focus on the importance of social interaction to child development is reflected in the methodology implicit in Vygotskyian theory, in which activity, rather than the individual, is the basic unit of analysis. "Activity" from this perspective includes not only the task at hand but also people, interpersonal relations, goal-directed behavior, and shared understandings. In this view, individuals are active agents in their own environment; they engage with the world around them, and in some senses, create for themselves the circumstances of their own development. The central aspect of this approach is the notion that through participation in cultural activities, and with guidance from more skilled peers, siblings, and adults, children can learn to think and to develop new skills and more mature approaches to problem solving. It is generally assumed that all communities establish ways of helping children to build connections between their current knowledge and those skills and understandings they are capable of acquiring (Rogoff, 1990).

This stress on the importance of activity, relationships, and interaction provides a useful framework within which to explore the influence of social and cultural context on child development. The ways in which children in diverse settings learn to respond to adversity and extreme hardships are critical components of this developmental process. Consciously or not, caregivers and others structure children's learning environments to support boys and girls to acquire the knowledge, skills, and experience they need to function successfully in their community. The classification of certain experiences or circumstances as "risky" or "dangerous" is thus not a straightforward, universal given. Boys and girls of different ages and different abilities in different contexts will understand and make meaning of their experiences in different ways. These understandings will be influenced not only by their individual genetic heritage and physical and biological maturity but also, and more particularly, by the social, cultural, economic, and political environment in which they live.

In assessments of the forces that undermine children's development and well-being, research in the minority world tends to focus on children who confront severe family and personal difficulties, such as recurrent ill-health, maltreatment, family separation and divorce, chronic poverty, and parental mental illness and unemployment (Garmezy & Rutter, 1983; Werner & Smith, 1998). Indeed, the death of a parent is highlighted as one of the more immediately traumatizing events for a child, linked with later psychic disorder, notably depression. This research originated in the field of psychopathology and responded initially to concerns among parents, welfare professionals, and other adults about a perceived rise in childhood problems, such as school failure, juvenile crime, and attempted and actual suicide among young people (Fraser, 1997). One of the objectives of the research was to identify factors in children's lives that increase risks for such behaviors and, insofar as these studies aimed to serve policy, establish how structural reform or service provision could prevent or reduce these risks (Garmezy, 1983). Initial concerns focused on exploring a possible correlation between stressful life experiences in children and a range of psychiatric disorders. Today, the focus for many scholars has shifted to the determination of the factors that enable children to remain competent in the face of adversity.

Although studies of children in the minority, industrialized world focus primarily on intrafamilial risk, research on young people in the majority world tends to address major societal events and situations, such as armed conflict, mass murders, famine, or mass displacement.

Such catastrophic events are generally identified in this research as being "beyond the normal" range of human experience because they cause disturbance and upheaval, not just at a personal and familial level but throughout society (Ager, 1996; De Vries, 1996). They threaten family and community coping, destroy social and cultural institutions, and distort social norms and values (De Vries, 1996). There is a particular concern that such experiences overwhelm children psychologically, undermining their development, coping, and future adaptation in adulthood.

Children's individual responses to adversity have been described in the research in terms of "risk" and "resilience." *Risk* refers to variables that increase individuals' likelihood of psychopathology or their susceptibility to negative developmental outcomes (Goyos, 1997). Some risks are found internally; they result from the unique combination of characteristics that make up an individual, such as temperament or neurological structure. Other risks are external; that is, they result from environmental factors, such as poverty or war, which inhibit an individual's healthy development. Despite the apparently devastating odds, however, not all children exposed to risks and adversities develop problems later on. In the literature, these children are deemed *resilient*. As Schaffer (1996) notes, "Whatever stresses an individual may have encountered in early years, he or she need not forever more be at the mercy of the past.... children's resilience must be acknowledged every bit as much as their vulnerability" (p. 47).

Historically, the notion of resilience entered the health sciences from applied physics and engineering, where it refers to the ability of materials to "bounce back" from stress and resume their original shape or condition. A rubber ball is an example. The term seems to have been first used in medicine to characterize the recovery of patients from physical traumas such as surgery or accidents. Somewhat later, it was adopted into psychology, first for the study of children of mentally ill mothers. It is now understood to indicate an individual's capacity to recover from, adapt, and remain strong in the face of adversity. Hence, the literature ascribes resilience to three kinds of phenomena: (a) good outcomes despite high-risk status, (b) sustained competence under threat, and (c) recovery from trauma (Masten, Best, & Garmezy, 1990).

Resilience is recognized as depending on both individual and group strengths and is highly influenced by supportive elements in the wider environment. These positive reinforcements in children's lives are often described as "protective factors" or "protective processes." They operate at different levels and through different mechanisms—individual, family, communal, institutional, and so on—and frequently correlate with and complement one another. Their effects are shown only in their interaction with risk. Although it is understood in the literature that risk and resilience are not constructed the same way in all societies, it is generally accepted that the interaction of risk and protective factors plays an important role in the social and psychological development of boys and girls in all contexts. The concepts of risk, resilience, and protective factors have now come to form the bedrock of research on children who live with adversity, although, as we argue below, they are not without their problems and limitations.

KEY MECHANISMS OF RISK AND RESILIENCE

Research has identified several processes or mechanisms at the individual, family, and wider environmental levels that have been shown to have a significant influence on risk and resilience in children. For example, a healthy, strong child is likely to be more resilient emotionally and psychologically than one who is physically weak or sick. Likewise, gender has been found to have an important effect on the way in which children respond to adversity (Werner & Smith, 1998), although the literature tends not to provide consistent patterns linking gender with coping, resilience, or vulnerability. Among other individual attributes in children, age, temperament, sense of humor, memory, reasoning, perceptual competencies, sense of purpose, belief in a bright future, and spirituality have all been found to have a significant impact on resilience (see, e.g., Bernard, 1995; Garbarino, 1999). These protective factors shape to a large extent the strategies that children use to manage stressful situations and to defend themselves against painful experiences or low self-esteem.

Some children are better able to manage stress because of disposition or temperament. Thus, protective factors such as resourcefulness, curiosity, a goal for which to live, and a need and ability to help others are largely matters of temperament and coping style. Generally, children who are able to remain hopeful about the future, are flexible and adaptable, possess problem-solving skills, and actively try to assume control over their lives are likely to be less vulnerable than those who passively accept the adversity they face (Punamaki, 1987). Socially competent children, capable of lateral thinking and problem solving can enhance their coping by identifying alternatives to their current circumstances and devising creative solutions. The capacity to engage in critical thinking can also help to shield a child from simplistic interpretations of experience that are self-defeating (Garbarino, Kostelny, & Dubrow, 1991). Personal history also influences coping (Garbarino, 1999). Children who have experienced approval, acceptance, and opportunities for mastery are far more likely to be resilient than those who have been subjected to humiliation, rejection, or failure.

The literature points not just to children's own inner resources and competencies but also to their interpersonal relationships as essential factors mediating risk and resilience. Thus, the presence of at least one supportive adult can have an enormous impact on a child's resilience (see, e.g., Ressler, Boothby, & Steinbock, 1988; Werner & Smith, 1992). Family members and significant others can play a major role in helping children interpret, "process," and adjust to, or overcome, difficult life experiences (Dawes, 1992). Acting as mentors, adults can provide models of and reinforcement for problem solving, motivation, and other coping skills (McCallin & Fozzard, 1991; Punamaki 1987; Richman & Bowen, 1997; Turton, Straker, & Mooza, 1990). Developmental psychology has long emphasized the early bonding between mother and infant and overall quality of nurture within the primary caregiving unit as absolutely fundamental to well-being, especially in younger children. Today, however, it is increasingly recognized that in many societies the mother is only one of several caregivers and that, consequently, children's attachments may be quite dispersed (Mann, 2001).

The centrality of emotional attachment to and support from a significant reference person is revealed in its absence. In the late 1990s in Sierra Leone, children who were separated from their families following abduction by the rebel forces or whose parents had been killed or deserted them during the war faced many grave difficulties. Without a caring guardian to take their side, children expressed feelings of being branded and were susceptible to discrimination and hostility. Fostering by extended family members does not always resolve their problems, as one adolescent girl emphasized:

> You have to be humble to the aunt and uncle and show them respect. You must not be proud. Because you don't have mother, you don't have father so you have no other choice but to be humble. If you do good things you never get praised—they always shout on you and put you down. (15-year-old girl, Makeni, Sierra Leone, quoted in Boyden, Eyber, Feeny, & Scott, 2004, p. 58)

Such sentiments have been commonly reported by separated and orphaned children in numerous situations, including Liberia (Tolfree, 2004), Sudan (Vraalsen, in press), Sri Lanka (Galappatti, 2002), Tanzania (Mann, 2002), Malawi (Mann, 2003a), and elsewhere. Boys and girls in these circumstances described how difficult their lives were without the love and protection provided by at least one close adult. In many villages in South Sudan, children argued that those orphaned boys and girls who live with extended families are just as vulnerable as those who live entirely without adult or family care (Vraalsen, in press).

Not only do supportive relationships with family and nonparental adults help to protect children from the negative effects of stressful situations, there is considerable evidence that social support from peers can greatly enhance children's resilience. This is clearly recognized by the Maasai, who live in an area of Kenya and Tanzania that is prone to severe drought and famine. The Maasai have a strong sense of clan, family, and community identity in which suffering is traced historically to the difficulties faced by the Maasai as a people. Traditional Maasai risk management strategies reflect a close familiarity with hunger and other hardships, such that young *morans* (teenage boys who are learning to become warriors) must always travel and eat in pairs for mutual support and protection (Boyden et al., 2004). In this context, boys learn from a young age not only the importance of teamwork and cooperation but also how to provide material, emotional, and physical assistance to peers. In addition to the confidence they build in their own ability to confront future challenges, they learn to trust that they are not alone and that others can assist them in times of need.

Positive peer relationships provide children with an arena of support outside the family in which they can experiment, develop attitudes, skills, and values, and learn to share, help, and nurture one another. These relationships become especially important during middle childhood and adolescence and both mitigate the negative effects of adversity and contribute to a child's sense of self-esteem. This process may in turn enhance the development of other protective factors, such as a sense of competence and an ability to form other meaningful relationships, empathize, and feel a sense of belonging. In short, friendships provide children, like adults, with opportunities to be themselves and to feel good about who they are—processes that help to build resilience. This truth was evident in research with children affected by HIV/AIDS in Malawi, where girls between the ages of 8 and 14 years described the opportunity to sit with friends and "share secrets" as one that made them feel "strong" and "less alone" (Mann, 2003a).

Neighborhoods and institutions such as schools and organized community groups can supplement protective factors at the individual and family levels by providing a supportive context for children. In industrialized countries, the state is fundamental in this regard, aiding children through a range of interventions, including food subsidies, housing, and social insurance. Today, specialized state-run institutions of childhood—child care and leisure centers, schools, and so on—complement the traditional roles and functions of the family. During crises, they may replace family altogether. In contrast, most poor countries do not have the resources for widespread state support to communities, families, or children living in adversity. Where high birth rates, early mortality, and educational wastage are pressing problems,

birth spacing, health, and education services take priority over social services and welfare policies. In this context, it is often a bonus if government assistance programs exist at all. Where they do, they frequently suffer heavily from underinvestment, poor outreach, high transaction costs, or corruption.

Experience demonstrates that in the absence of state intervention, child protection often relies on the mobilization efforts of civil society and participation from various community groups. These informal protective processes may include collective activities (such as joint labor on community projects or labor exchanges on farms) and institutional support (e.g., credit supplied by money lenders, remedies offered by traditional healers, or spiritual guidance provided by religious officials).

Sometimes crisis itself can lead to the development of protective processes that enhance resilience in children. In Milange, Mozambique, following the devastation of war, reconciliation and forgiveness was achieved by acknowledging and celebrating the return of former combatants, who put the war behind them by partaking in ceremonies and confessionals (Gibbs, 1994). Reconstruction was achieved through the management of everyday activities such as building houses and planting fields in which children—including former child combatants—played an integral role. The church and local healers played a major part in the reconstruction, focusing and reaffirming the process. On the other hand, in impoverished and AIDS-affected areas of southern Kenya, assistance for struggling families from the village clan committee and other sources is said to be on the decline. Whereas once there existed a broad network of neighbors and other village members to ensure that no children would go hungry, nowadays, individual or familial self-help strategies are favored over collective ones. One elderly woman recalled how at one time "a child would belong to the community." This is no longer the case, she said (Boyden et al., 2004).

THE LIMITATIONS OF EXISTING RESEARCH

Much of the literature on risk and resilience in childhood is based on longitudinal studies that cover the life span well into adulthood and amplify important individual differences between children. As such, that literature has made a major contribution to our understanding of the personal, familial, and broader environmental influences on children's well-being and development in adverse situations. In so doing, it has vital implications for children throughout the world and should be widely disseminated among practitioners and policymakers. However, even after decades of learning and experience in this field in some countries, we still do not know the extent to which these protective factors are universal across cultures. We also do not know enough about the effects on children of exposure to adversities of different kinds or the ways in which children respond to and deal with these experiences. A review of the existing research evidence on childhood adversity indicates several major shortcomings. Before commencing a discussion of some of the most significant debates and issues associated with the topic, we highlight the problems with existing research.

Limitations of Terminology. First[3], although the idea of resilience has for some purposes proven itself a useful way of imaging human ability to thrive in the face of adversity, it suffers several important limitations, both conceptual and cultural. Early writers employing the term conscientiously proposed it not as an explanation but as a temporary convenience until such time as scientific theories of natural human resistance to psychological stress could be properly formulated (Anthony, 1987). With time, however, this makeshift construct gradually came to be treated as confirmed fact by all but a few theoretical researchers. A fully featured scientific theory to explain unexpectedly positive human response to adversity still lies in the future.

As might be expected of an impressionistic metaphor imported into psychology from the natural sciences, it has been impossible to define resilience with the precision necessary to confirm it through rigorous scientific research. A variety of sometimes incompatible concepts and definitions are currently in use. The term was at first commonly characterized as a trait of individuals—children were classified as "vulnerable" or "resilient"—and much of the lay literature is still in that vein. However, as

research and careful reflection (Luthar & Cicchetti, 2000; Luthar, Cicchetti, & Becker, 2000) demonstrated this concept to be untenable, the definitional focus became both more collective, centered on families and other groupings and more abstract, portraying resilience as a "dynamic developmental process" (Yates, Egeland, & Sroufe, 2003) or the transaction between individuals and their environment. It seems increasingly clear that resilience cannot be directly observed and measured and, in fact, is only inferred from observations based on the related constructs of risk and "positive adaptation" (Luthar, 2003).

This raises the question of whether anything like resilience actually exists in nature; perhaps it is only a conceptual artifact. There is no question that some children submitted to severe stress do survive better than expected, but it is not clear that one needs a mediating factor such as resilience to explain it. This doubt is now a matter of debate. Some researchers have suggested that the issue can be tested by statistically sorting the direct effects of "protective" variables from interactions that might suggest a mediating factor (i.e., resilience). At least some analysis of this type finds that the direct, context-specific effects of protective factors can explain virtually all positive adaptation, which suggests that the notion of a general quality of resilience is superfluous (Wyman, 2003). More analysis of this type is required, but some initial findings imply that resilience is perhaps an idea we do not need to explain why some children thrive in harsh conditions and others do not.

Limited Assumptions. Second, ideas of resilience call on subthemes taken for granted in contemporary Europe and North America that are not so readily accepted by equally sophisticated intellectual systems elsewhere, including in science. A good example is the concept of self. From early on, resilience was conceived as completely or partially involving self-integration or self-organization. This, of course, requires some sort of self to be integrated or organized, perhaps the sort of core being envisaged in 20th-century Freudian or humanistic approaches to psychology. The problem is that selfhood has never been shown to exist apart from the construct of it, and other intellectually sophisticated cultures and systematic philosophies—such as Buddhism and much of Hinduism, for example—deny that self really exists. They do not deny that we experience a sense of inner self, but they consider that experience to be the most fundamental of all human illusions. There is no objective reason to consider the assertion of independent selfhood more rational than the assertion of no-self. Interestingly, some of today's leading researchers in neurology and evolutionary psychology hold to one or another version of the view that the idea of self is a sort of interpretive illusion compiled from a wide variety of neurological stimuli, perhaps originating from the entire body rather than the brain alone.

The idea of risk, as used in much of the risk-and-resilience literature, is also culturally and normatively loaded, as is the notion of *competence*, which is seen as the basis for resilience by highly influential researchers such as Garmezy and Masten. Even as used in the social science literature with a certain amount of care, these are not terms that always enjoy easy transit between cultural contexts. Even the negative conceptualization of *adversity* as hostile factors exogenous to the individual—the essential setting for the emergence of resilience—is regarded by a sizable number of non-Western cultures and philosophies as partial, short-sighted, and naive. Instead, they see connections between what we perceive and what we create. Rogoff (2003) notes that this objection is a difficult point for Westerners, including many social scientists, because schemes "separating the individual and the world are so pervasive in the social sciences that we have difficulty finding other ways to represent our ideas" (p. 49).

> Culture is not an entity that *influences* individuals. Instead, people contribute to the creation of cultural processes and cultural processes contribute to the creation of people. Thus, individual and cultural processes are *mutually constituting* rather than defined separately from each other. (p. 51)

As we argue below, there is a case to be made that adversity is as much a matter of perception as of situational fact, and many societies deliberately create painful and even potentially dangerous situations for children—such as in some rites of passage or forms of apprenticeship—to promote their development by teaching them to embrace discomfort as opportunity rather than turning it into adversity. That approach puzzles and horrifies some individuals, who might consider it abuse rather than nurture. The issue is not who is right or wrong, of course, but the degree to which the notion of resilience calls on elements of contemporary Western culture not necessarily shared elsewhere, including in the sciences. Although we use the term *resilience* here in recognition of its utility as a device for indicating a state that many of us recognize intuitively, we do not regard it as a sound theoretical construct. Indeed, we maintain that resilience may, following further enquiry, appear to be a sensible construct only in certain very limited cultural and intellectual contexts.

Limited Scholarship. A third difficulty with the risk-and-resilience research is that scholarship in this field has been limited largely to children and childhood in the industrialized, minority world. Some scholars have gone to considerable lengths in these studies to include children from diverse cultural and economic backgrounds. Nevertheless, inherent in much of the literature on risk and resilience is a view of childhood that is informed by the context of white middle-class family life, not necessarily by the very different realities that shape the lives of children in other parts of the world. The underlying assumption is that children in the minority world have grown up the "right way" and that children everywhere should be raised in the same manner—that is, in the nuclear family, with two parents, without social or economic responsibility, and so on. The implication of this assumption is that this context is the benchmark against which "healthy" childhood is measured. However, ethnographic evidence from diverse cultures suggests that there is no single, uniform approach to child rearing. Multiple developmental pathways exist throughout the world. In accordance with the insights first advanced by Vygotsky (1978), many now recognize that the well-being of children is influenced by the material, social, and cultural aspects of the specific environment in which they live, despite what the literature presumes.

The focus of this literature on the minority world and on the kinds of adversities thought to prevail in industrialized countries limits its explanatory scope. As noted, the most systematic information currently available tends to deal with often chronic personal and family problems that occur within the private domain of the home. Hence, despite the overwhelming evidence concerning the structural causes of most childhood adversities, the most extensive research on risk in childhood concerns far more immediate and personal circumstances, in particular loss of and separation from parents, especially mothers. In the majority world, children tend to face additional and sometimes far greater threats to their well-being that are not adequately addressed in this literature. For example, large numbers of children throughout the globe are routinely exposed to major societal catastrophes that affect entire communities, such as famine, forced displacement, and "ethnic cleansing." Children's responses to these and other adverse situations have been underreported in the literature and are not well understood generally.

Limited Interpretation. Finally, there is the additional problem that much of what we know about childhood experience from the research is based on adult interpretation and supposition. Most of the studies on children's vulnerability and resilience draw on researchers' preconceived ideas about what constitutes adversity or risk for children. Often, adults (parents, teachers, and others who are close to children) are used as respondents. The result is that, in many cases, we do not have accurate information on children's own perceptions. This is problematic given that there is emerging evidence that children do not share the same understanding of risk and adversity as do adults. The privileging of adult perceptions over children's experiences has sometimes meant that, in practice, resilience is conceived of more as the absence of pathology rather than the presence of personal agency in children. Thus, in many of the studies of war-affected and displaced children, resilience is tantamount to the lack of trauma or psychiatric disorder; the notion that children's own resourcefulness may promote their mental health is, in many cases, entirely foreign. In contrast, the psychological literature does envision children's personal attributes as contributing significantly to resilience, embracing

the idea of children as resourceful. Nevertheless, much of the discussion of children's competence in practice focuses on the rather passive notion of protective factors, not the idea of children actively managing and even in some instances improving their situation.

THE SOCIAL AND POLITICAL CAUSES OF RISK AND RESILIENCE

The factors that determine whether and how a person comes to experience adversity operate at numerous levels. Practical experience has shown us that there are significant disparities between groups and categories of children in terms of their exposure to risk and survival, coping, and well-being and that such disparities normally have structural causes relating to discrepancies in social power. Often, these structural threats at the macro level are transmitted through successive generations of a population, community, or family and are seldom actually within the control of the individual they affect. Caste is one structural configuration that permanently disadvantages some people, for the status, classification, and indeed, much of the fate of over 100 million *dalits* ("untouchables") in India are determined at conception and cannot be changed even after death. As a child grows up, this structural vulnerability is then compounded if the child happens to be a girl (and thereby suffers intrahousehold inequities), lives in a rural area (with limited or no access to land and basic services), and has a disability (attracting social stigma). Although each of these factors is no doubt a hindrance in terms of isolation, it is through their interaction and accumulation within the life of an individual child that he or she is rendered susceptible to developmental disruption and psychological, social, or emotional distress.

Structural disadvantage also applies at the micro level. Children who are distinguished by social attributes such as gender, ethnicity, or religion and by personal attributes such as temperament, physique, or cognitive ability tend to be valued and treated very differently within families and communities. Gender is one of the most striking and enduring examples of difference within childhood. Girls are generally stronger biologically than boys, as evidenced by their higher survival rates after birth. Yet many societies have powerful gender preferences, and these preferences have differential effects on the life chances and well-being of boys and girls. In plough agriculture in Asia and Europe, for example, there is an apparent partiality toward boys (Robertson, 1991) because daughters have to be given dowries and are "lost" to parents as a support in old age. In African hoe agriculture, on the other hand, families have good productive as well as reproductive reasons to welcome girls and good political reasons (such as perpetuation of a lineage) to want boys. In most societies where there are major distinctions, baby and young girls are at far greater risk of exposure to adversity than boys. But as children grow older, less is known about the nature and influence of the risks faced by both genders. There is an assumption in the literature that the burdens, deprivations, and dangers of girlhood are more extreme, but this assumption remains to be proven. We simply do not know enough about how boys and girls of different ages in different social, political, and cultural contexts experience and interpret risk.

During times of trouble, distinctions based on gender, ethnicity, and physical ability grow, sometimes with very serious consequences for children who are the least valued. For example, perpetuity of the social group is very important in many contexts of enduring hardship where mutual interdependence is strong and the individual cannot survive alone. In such settings, durability of the family group is commonly a greater priority than the relative well-being of individual offspring. Children in certain categories may be considered surplus to requirements and abandoned (Engle, Castle, & Menon, 1996). Recent research among displaced families in the Western Upper Nile region of Sudan has shown that disabled children are more likely than their able-bodied peers and siblings to die as a result of being left behind when families are forced to flee their villages (Vraalsen, in press). Likewise, in other extreme situations, children may be considered a good that can be exchanged or traded for income or used to forge links with political or economic allies. This practice is not uncommon in parts of Burma, where desperate families may receive money in exchange for "lending" girls as young as 12 to "employers" in Thailand. Such girls often end up working in the sex industry (Mann, 2000). Indeed, gender preference directly affects survival in some settings. In South Asia, gender discrimination is a major determinant of demographic distortion, with fewer than expected females in the population relative to males (Drèze & Sen, 1995). This pattern is linked to female infanticide, the abortion of female fetuses, and gender discrepancies in the allocation of food and health care.

Differences between groups of children often have explicitly political origins. Indeed, children's rights advocates have for some time been gathering evidence pointing to the political causes of much childhood deprivation and suffering. They have shown that the State can imperil children just as much as protect and nurture them, sometimes under the guise of protection. They have uncovered instances not just of inaction by the State but, more seriously, of acts of commission. Often, the State actively victimizes certain categories of children, as in the case of racist policies that discriminate against specific religious, cultural, or ethnic groups in the provision of services, access to resources, and so on. Hence, historically, apartheid policies in South Africa produced major disparities among ethnic groups in terms of youth and child morbidity and mortality, literacy, employment, personal security, and civil and political rights.

Variations in patterns of resilience and coping at the group level are also a function of cultural beliefs about childhood and child development. As indicated, ethnographic evidence from several parts of the world and recent research in the tradition of cultural psychology suggest that childhood is a diverse, shifting category shaped by cultural and social context. Thus, although it may be true that all children have certain basic needs and vulnerabilities in a very general sense, differentiation between societies in definitions of childhood and understandings of and approaches to child development produce very real differences in terms of children's experiences, attitudes, and behavior (Bronfenbrenner, 1986, 1996; Cole, 1992; Wilson, 1998; Woodhead, 1998, p. 17).[4] Particular societies have their own ideas about the capacities and vulnerabilities of children, the ways in which they learn and develop, and those things that are good and bad for them. These ideas affect approaches to child socialization, learning, discipline, and protection and, hence, to a significant degree, circumscribe children's adaptation, resilience, and coping (Dawes & Donald, 1994; Super & Harkness, 1986; Woodhead, 1998). In other words, the social arrangements, child development goals, and child-rearing practices of the communities in which children live play a fundamental part in determining the different capabilities and susceptibilities that children develop.

Selective neglect in the family, discrimination in the community, political oppression in national government, and pronounced inequity in international relations are all societal factors undermining children's well-being and development that policymakers have the power to do something about. The question is how to identify which groups and categories of children are the most susceptible and to find ways both of reducing risk among them and providing support to affected children. The problem is that research on risk and resilience in children seldom reveals group distinctions in a meaningful way that can be addressed by policy. On the other hand, policymakers are often reluctant to engage with issues that have political, social, or cultural roots, preferring to depoliticize adversity by defining it as a problem of family or individual pathology. The concern, then, is how research can more effectively capture these kinds of distinctions between groups and categories of children and establish their impact on children's well-being. Equally important is to identify the kinds of policies and practice that will prevent such inequities between groups of children.

BEYOND TRAUMA: THE SOCIAL EFFECTS OF ADVERSITY

We have suggested that there is a focus among some scholars on the psychological and emotional effects of highly stressful experiences. This concern with catastrophic events and situations is surely appropriate given their pernicious impact on individuals and societies throughout the world. Many label the most stressful experiences "traumatic" and link them with one specific

diagnostic category—namely, posttraumatic stress disorder (PTSD). Use of the term *trauma* is very conscious in this context, for it indicates an emotional wound or shock resulting from exposure to an event or situation that causes substantial, lasting damage to the psychological development of a person, often leading to neurosis. PTSD was first identified as a syndrome in American veterans of the Vietnam War and has subsequently been identified by the World Health Organization (WHO, 1992) as the most severe psychiatric disorder and primary stress resulting from a catastrophe.

Many find the concept of trauma useful in that it highlights how major disasters have potential to undermine children and adults psychologically (see also Solomon & Laufer's work on Israeli children in Chapter 14 of this volume). However, as we have suggested, there are numerous conceptual and methodological problems concerning the definition and measurement of life events and of psychiatric disorders (Garmezy & Rutter, 1983). For example, it is surprising to learn that of those children who suffer serious or prolonged psychological or emotional distress in conflict zones, a significant proportion have not experienced a major misfortune despite the catastrophic circumstances in which they live (Ressler, Tortorici, & Marcelino, 1992). Sometimes the most devastating situations are those involving insidious hardships and deprivations, such as constant humiliation, social isolation, or poverty related to loss of livelihood. For instance, in Dar es Salaam, Congolese refugee children between the ages of 7 and 13 years reported that discrimination and public humiliation by Tanzanian adults and children was so distressing for them that they would often prefer to remain at home than to endure the taunts of neighbors and others (Mann, 2003b). These ongoing stressors can impair the coping resources of children as well as the capacity of the community to support and protect those who care for them. Researchers looking for traumatic responses to situations identified in advance as highly stressful could miss such important subtleties.

As it happens, there has been much controversy surrounding disorders such as PTSD. A number of mental health experts do not accept PTSD as a valid diagnostic category in relation to children in particular. Some point out that it is misapplied in many situations of chronic adversity where children continue to be exposed to stress. There is nothing "posttraumatic" about their experiences. Some also argue that the symptoms associated with the syndrome do not only occur in response to major stressful life events (Richman, 1993). Others say that symptoms characteristic of the syndrome such as bed-wetting and nightmares do not constitute "sickness" but a normal physiological reaction to shock. Still others highlight that these kinds of medicalized accounts of human responses to misfortune detract from the political, economic, and social nature of much of the adversity in the world today (Bracken, Giller, & Summerfield, 1995). They are critical of medical approaches that emphasize individual psychopathology and individualized therapeutic care in clinical settings.

In fact, whatever one's views on PTSD, it is evident that this kind of diagnosis overlooks many important aspects of human experience during times of great hardship. Take, for example, the cultural bereavement experienced by many of those who are forcibly displaced by armed conflict or civil strife (Eisenbruch, 1991). Research by Armstrong, Boyden, Galappatti, and Hart (2004) with Tamil children aged 9 to 16 in the east of Sri Lanka has revealed a broad array of responses to the adverse conditions in which they live. These boys and girls have experienced displacement, armed violence, and impoverishment, loss of access to education and health care, and many other war-related risks. One of the key criteria of well-being distinguished by these children was "moving well with people," an expression used very positively with reference to a person who is hospitable, kind, polite, and generally relates well to others. The children are aware that not all their peers experience well-being and that there are boys and girls in their midst who in their view suffer impaired social and cognitive functioning. As they see it, impaired social functioning is expressed mainly in terms of solitary, antisocial behavior, symbolized by a desire to be left alone; unwillingness to play; lack of interest in, or interaction with, friends; and an inability to show affection. Cognitive functioning is judged in relation to enthusiasm for learning and sports, and attendance and performance at school.

These Tamil children explained their most frequent and distressing response to adversity as "thinking too much," a condition that can in more severe cases cause constant and intense headaches or heart pain. Most commonly, they associated this condition with the loss, disappearance, or death of a loved one or with fear of abduction and forced recruitment into the military. Other fears and anxieties—about snakebites, the proximity of armed military personnel, elephant attacks, and drowning—were similarly pervasive but seemingly less intense and did not appear to result in "thinking too much" or a somatic effect. During adversity, anxieties and fears of this nature can play a very important part in children's vulnerability as much as in their coping and resilience yet do not figure in PTSD diagnoses. Similarly, such a diagnosis says very little about children's actual functioning on a daily basis. In the Tamil areas of Sri Lanka affected by conflict, social trust outside the immediate family has been largely destroyed because neighbors have developed opposing loyalties and inform on each other to ensure their own survival. Children have few social or institutional resources to turn to for support, and mothers stand out as one of the few sources of love and protection for the young. Tamil children in the East have developed a whole host of coping mechanisms to deal with this corrosive social environment and a range of strategies to avoid abduction and other risks. These include limiting friendships to a few close and trusted peers (often cousins), restricting social visits to nearby houses, avoiding family conflict whenever possible, not discussing family problems with neighbors, being careful not to attract attention in school, staying away from school and in homes during the day; and sleeping in the forest at night. Such strategies are crucial to personal functioning.

Insofar as children in middle childhood and adolescence tend to attach a great deal of significance to personal relationships, especially to friendships with peers; social approval and acceptance among peers and in the community at large are vital factors in their well-being. It is therefore not surprising to learn that for children of this age, the experience of adversity is very much mediated by its effects on their social world. In other words, children gauge the impacts of adversity not just in terms of psychic pathology but through the constraints it puts on their social networks. Unfortunately, it transpires that children who confront adversity are often denigrated and excluded by others, as was evident in a study of child poverty in India, Belarus, Kenya, Sierra Leone, and Bolivia (Boyden et al., 2004). That study revealed that the way in which poverty undermines an individual's social interactions and relationships with others can be far more important to children than having to go without food or other commodities. Thus, in rural Bolivia, despite knowing full well that chronic shortages of water have a significant effect on livelihoods and on the survival and health of both humans and livestock, children highlighted above all the humiliation of being unable to wash and therefore being labeled smelly, dirty, and poor. These children acknowledged that frequently they are themselves the main instigators of abuses directed at others due to their poverty. In fact, one of the worst consequences of being thought of as "poor" is the associated shame, social exclusion, and susceptibility to teasing, bullying, and humiliation by peers.

CHILDHOOD ADVERSITY CONTEXTUALLY DEFINED

One of the strongest criticisms of universalized psychiatric diagnoses such as PTSD is that they seriously underestimate the differences between cultural groups in understandings of and responses to stressful events (Bracken et al., 1995). Undoubtedly, humans have a limited repertoire of responses to stressful life events, and feelings and symptoms will recur across social and cultural boundaries (Parker, 1996). Similarly, intelligence, temperament, good parenting, and family relationships early in life appear to be important contributors to resilience in all cultures and contexts. Nevertheless, children's worldview and mental health are very much influenced by local meanings given to misfortune. As we have suggested, these meanings in turn depend on other concepts—for example, ideas about causality in adversity, well-being, sickness, healing, personhood, identity, and the like (Bit, 1991; Bracken, 1998; Le

Vine, 1999; Parker, 1996; Shweder & Bourne, 1982; Summerfield, 1991, 1998). As critics of universalized diagnostic categories argue, even though certain symptoms of acute distress may occur across cultures and social groups, this does not suggest that their meaning is the same in all settings (Bracken et al., 1995; Parker, 1996). Thus, meaning is a profoundly important mediating factor in children's experiences of adversity, and yet it has been largely ignored in the literature. Indeed, it is our contention that how children respond to adversity cannot be understood without reference to the social, cultural, economic, and moral meanings given to such experiences in the contexts they inhabit.

The contextual nature of adversity is illustrated by research on child abuse and neglect across cultures conducted over 20 years ago by Jill Korbin (1981), an anthropologist. Korbin cites examples of practices such as punishments (severe beatings) to impress a child with the necessity of adherence to cultural rules and harsh initiation rites (genital operations, deprivation of food and sleep, and induced bleeding) that to many outsiders would most likely appear abusive. Indeed, some of these practices have been denounced by children's rights advocates as abhorrent. But Korbin goes on to make the sobering point that many practices in the minority world that are accepted as "normal," such as isolating infants and small children in rooms or beds of their own at night or allowing them to cry without immediately attending to their needs or desires are at odds with the child-rearing philosophies of most cultures, for whom such behaviors are likewise considered just as "abusive."[5]

Even the meaning of death varies significantly, depending on cultural and religious views about whether human existence is irrevocably constrained by the live body, which in turn hinges on ideas about the soul, reincarnation, ancestral spirits, and so on. Views about death and well-being in many parts of the world are built on the notion of congruence, not merely in the functioning of mind and body but also between the human, natural, and spirit worlds. Any or all of these dimensions may play a part in explanations of the cause of misfortune, definitions of suffering, and ways of dealing with distress. In such systems, illness and adversity are often caused by the intervention of powerful social, natural, and supernatural agents rather than individual pathology. Well-being is dependent on, and vulnerable to, the feelings, wishes, and actions of others, including spirits and dead ancestors (Lock & Scheper-Hughes, 1990). Hence, sickness is often portrayed as being caused by the witchcraft of neighbors, the forces of nature, or deities. On the other hand, spiritual and supernatural entities may also be perceived as providing protection for children and, indeed, are sometimes thought to be more effective in this regard than individual parental behavior or family circumstances (Engle et al., 1996). These kinds of beliefs sometimes account for approaches to child protection that families regard as appropriate, adaptive, and beneficial but that outsiders perceive as risky or neglectful behavior.

For example, among the Acholi in Gulu, northern Uganda, the life of an individual who has died is said to continue in the world of ancestral spirits. Many young people in the area have been abducted and made to fight by the Lord's Resistance Army (LRA). Symptoms of severe emotional and psychological distress in young former combatants are taken to indicate that they are *cen,* "mad," and have become possessed by the spirits of the people they have killed (Boyden, 2002; Jareg & Falk, 1999). Former child combatants are thought of as in some way "contaminated," and it is held that the "spirit might come out at any time," influencing the person who has been possessed to behave unpredictably or uncontrollably and possibly even to harm others. However, at the same time, because so many of these children were abducted and forcibly recruited, there is a strong will to forgive, reintegrate, and reconcile. That said, before young former abductees are accepted back into their families and communities, proof is required that they are remorseful about acts of violence they have committed and determined to mend their ways. Acceptance tends to be conditional on the performance of rites of cleansing and atonement in which the spirit leaves the body of the possessed person. It has been observed that in many cases these young people appear calmer and more controlled following reintegration.

To give another example, a study by Rousseau, Said, Gagné, and Bibeau (1998) of unaccompanied Somali boys in exile in Canada produced quite unexpected findings. These boys were found to be far more resilient than anticipated, given the many severe hardships that they had experienced. Their resilience and coping was attributed to the fact that they had already become accustomed to long periods of separation from their families and communities prior to exile. This familiarity was due to the traditional pastoral nomadic practice of sending young boys away to tend herds, a practice that enables boys to learn self-sufficiency and autonomy and to acquire status in their communities as proto-adults. Hence, in this particular context, exile and separation from family were viewed not as forms of deprivation or loss but as having certain positive attributes. This evidence suggests that the degree to which stressful situations can be defined objectively as "traumatic" or "outside the realm of normal human experience" is limited.

Phinney (1996) argues that the degree of psychological mastery children have in difficult situations to a significant extent reflects the degree to which a culture endorses active management of adversity by encouraging children to develop skills in communication, problem solving, and self-management of behavior. Thus, some societies think of misfortune as a matter of chance or fate, passively accepting and succumbing to events. Others actively train children to become resilient and to cope with unpredictable and painful situations. In the latter case, children may be encouraged to engage in activities that pose at least moderate risk to health and safety, with the aim of developing physical strength, endurance, confidence, dexterity, and self-discipline. Inuit children in Canada, for example, are taught to deal with a dangerous and often unpredictable Arctic environment, continuously tested in all spheres of knowledge and competence relating to the world around them and expected to experiment with uncertainty and danger (Briggs, 1986). They learn that the world is made up of problems to be solved: The ability to discover these problems, observe them actively and accurately, and analyze the implications of exposure to hazardous situations is a highly valued quality in Inuit society. In some African societies, learning to be resilient is institutionalized in formal rites of passage. For a male, initiation into adulthood may involve circumcision or a trial of strength, in which boys become men by passing exacting tests of performance in combat, survival, economic pursuits, and procreativity (Gilmore, 1990).

From this research and experience, it is apparent that vulnerability, resilience, and coping in children are not merely functions of health, sickness, or pathological behavioral reactions but also of beliefs and values (Gibbs, 1994; Masten et al., 1990). Dealing with distressing experiences involves making sense of those experiences; assimilating and processing fear, grief, or anger; and finding ways of adapting to, overcoming, or removing difficulties. Although these may be intensely personal processes, individuals engage with misfortune not as isolated beings but in socially mediated ways that are shared (Bracken, 1998; Kleinman & Kleinman, 1991; Reynolds-White, 1998). Crisis, suffering, grief, healing, and loss are all patterned by the social and cultural meanings they manifest. Hence,

> the "developmental appropriateness" of children's experiences, the "harmfulness" or "benefits" of their environment cannot be separated from the cultural context in which they are developing, the values and goals that inform their lives and their prior experiences of learning skills and ways of thinking. (Woodhead, 1998, p. 13)

Children grow and flourish in a whole host of different environments and under a whole variety of circumstances, and what is adaptive in child development is very much a product of these specific settings (Dawes & Donald, 1994).

CHILDREN'S EXPERIENCES: INDIRECT AND COMPLEX EFFECTS ON WELL-BEING

There is a view, prevalent in much of the global discourse surrounding child development, child protection, and children's rights, that exposure to misfortune has a direct and automatic deleterious effect on children's development and well-being. We have noted that it is common for children so exposed to be regarded as traumatized. This outlook is particularly strong in the literature on war-affected children and is

applied especially to children in early childhood, which is thought to be the most critical period of development, when children are most susceptible to harm that has long-term consequences (Schaffer, 2000).

Such a perspective seems, on the surface at least, quite compelling, for as adults, we tend to hold the commonsense view of children (especially young children) as frail and dependent. However, studies of children affected by conflict and displacement in Uganda (De Berry, 2004) and Nepal (Hinton, 2000) have shown that children exposed to many and varied risks are not all inherently vulnerable. Similarly, research from the Balkans has highlighted how vulnerability in childhood does not necessarily preclude ability (Swaine, 2004). Many children are highly adaptable and able to adjust; some show greater personal resilience even than adults (Palmer, 1983). A few authors have suggested that a minority of children can even gain socially, emotionally, or psychologically from exposure to unfavorable conditions (Dawes, 1992; Ekblad, 1993; Garmezy, 1983; Zwi, Macrae, & Ugalde, 1992). For example, in their longitudinal research with children on the island of Kauai in Hawaii, Werner and Smith (1998) found that children in families under stress who are required to attend to family needs become more committed and responsible citizens when they grow up than those raised in more secure circumstances. And in Bhutanese refugee camps in Nepal, it was discovered that, through their conscious caregiving strategies, children were able to have a significant positive impact on the psychological and emotional worlds of adults (Hinton, 2000). Indeed, there is considerable anecdotal evidence that during adversity, children, both boys and girls, often bear the prime responsibilities within the family as caregivers of incapacitated adults or younger siblings, prime earners of family income, and so on.

These kinds of findings have led many researchers and practitioners to shift the focus away from pathology and to search for the forces that might protect children from risk and promote their resilience. It is now accepted by many that the psychosocial outcome of exposure to adversity varies from individual to individual and population to population and is mediated by an array of personal, family, and broader environmental factors or processes that interact with each other in a dynamic manner. These processes produce either a heightened probability of negative outcome in children's development and well-being or prevent, or reduce, risk. The complex interplay of risk and protective factors can be observed in many cases of child labor, for example. Because children's work is often regarded as securing the transition to adulthood and because earning a wage raises an individual's status within the household, many children gain a powerful sense of independence and self-esteem from work that to expert observers is evidently menial, exploitative, and even dangerous. Thus, despite the risks, children engaged in hazardous work are likely to be buffered psychologically and emotionally if their occupation is socially valued and their work recognized as contributing to family maintenance and integration (Woodhead, 1998). On the other hand, a child whose family does not approve of his or her work or whose job is denigrated by his or her community will likely find it much harder to maintain a sense of self-worth and is at far greater risk of being overwhelmed psychologically by the experience. Thus, the value placed on children's work and the opportunities it affords have a very direct effect on coping and resilience.

Hence, children's well-being is mediated and influenced by protective processes at different levels and is highly dynamic and changeable. These processes may operate in different ways by altering exposure to risk, for example, or by reducing negative chain reactions that contribute to the long-term effects of exposure and so on (Rutter, 1987). From the child labor example, we can see that protective processes can "provide resistance to risk and foster outcomes marked by patterns of adaptation and competence" (Garmezy, 1983, p. 49).

That said, protective processes are changeable according to situation and context and can in themselves, under certain conditions, become a source of risk. This point is made by Apfel and Simon (1996), who identify a number of individual attributes in children—including resourcefulness, curiosity, intellectual mastery, flexibility in emotional experience, access to autobiographical memory, a goal for which to live, and the need and ability to help others—as contributing to their resilience. They stress how those attributes that may support well-being in some situations can, under different circumstances, have the opposite effect—they can increase vulnerability. Failure to achieve a desired goal during times of stress, for instance, can lead to loss of hope, self-reproach, and suicidal tendencies. Similarly, children who are highly motivated and driven to achieve may seem well equipped to master difficult situations. Yet these same children can feel inadequate and unsure of themselves when confronted with overwhelming circumstances over which they have no control or influence.

Thus, although many children do remain competent in the face of adversity, research and experience warn against presuming such children to be invulnerable. In fact, evidence suggests that the effects of stress are cumulative in that children who are exposed to several stressful events and circumstances are at particular risk of becoming overwhelmed emotionally and psychologically. Furthermore, children who appear resilient in the short term may not be so in the longer term, whereas children who seem more vulnerable initially sometimes grow in competence and resourcefulness (see, e.g., Rutter, 1990). Moreover, competent behavior and effective coping should not be seen as indicating high levels of self-esteem or happiness, for people who have successfully overcome adversity may still experience depression, difficulties with relationships, and so forth (Garmezy, 1993).

This evidence highlights the need to recognize that concepts such as resilience and coping should be applied with extreme caution even at the empirical level, let alone the theoretical; their use should not be taken to imply that children who appear to have adapted successfully to difficult situations suffer no ill effects. Nor should they be regarded as fixed states. The challenge in this regard is to identify ways in which resilience and coping in children can best be supported while also being mindful of the psychological and emotional costs to children and of the need to minimize these.

Children as Social Agents

Most children throughout the world are heavily reliant on the nurture and support of adults or elder siblings, without which they would fail to thrive, or perish. This fact emphasizes the virtue of making a distinction between children and adults, because such a distinction serves to protect the vulnerable and to ensure the survival and healthy development of all. Indeed, it is striking that most modern policies are based on the premise that adults are the ones best equipped to define what is good and bad for children and also the ones responsible for child protection measures. Certainly, adults have a moral obligation toward the young that includes protection against adversity. This obligation, in regard to the State at least, has now been enshrined in international law through the CRC.

Nevertheless, there is considerable evidence globally that adult society is failing children badly. Indeed, many children suffer as a consequence of actions by the very adults—parents, teachers, religious leaders, state officials—who have the greatest obligation toward them. In fact, society is structurally defined to confer on children minority status and in this way constrains their power and agency. However, conceptualizing children as helpless and dependent on adults in times of crisis is not necessarily the most effective way of supporting children's coping and resilience. This is not to deny that some children suffer long-term and highly debilitating psychological and emotional distress and that many need considerable support, specialist care, or both. It is merely to point out that children are not simply the products of adult beliefs, training, investment, and intervention but social agents in their own right. Even those children who are especially troubled can contribute to their own protection, if only in the smallest ways. For example, orphaned and separated Congolese children in Dar es Salaam reported forming alliances with kindhearted Tanzanian adults who agreed to allow the children to sleep in safety outside their homes in exchange for running occasional errands on behalf of the household head (Mann, 2003b).

Although labeling children "victims" affords an appropriate emphasis on their suffering and highlights the fact that responsibility for their misfortune lies with others, it tends to characterize children as passive and defenseless in the face of adversity. Viewing children as helpless means that their own efforts to cope are often not seen as legitimate or, indeed, even recognized at all. This lack of acknowledgment of the validity of children's own strategies can undermine their ability to act on their situation. It is vital to acknowledge that if overcoming stressful life events involves beliefs, feelings, competencies, and actions, children's own perspectives on adversity and the strategies they employ for their own protection are critical to coping and resilience. As we have stated, children do not always understand, experience, or respond to misfortune in the same way adults do. For instance, during the conflict in the Balkans, many Kosovar Albanian parents married their daughters off early so as to protect them from rape, trafficking, and other violations (Swaine, 2004). These girls, however, were unhappy with this strategy because it often resulted in their separation from cherished friends and family members at a time when they were needed most. Moreover, in many cases it restricted them to a lifetime of loneliness, domestic drudgery, and abusive or unhappy marriages. This and countless other examples show that disregarding children's perspectives can result in misplaced interventions that do not address children's real problems or concerns and may even increase their suffering.

It is now apparent that supporting children in situations of adversity requires the perspective not just that children need special protection but that they have valid insights into their well-being, valid solutions to their problems, and a valid role in implementing those solutions. Such an approach acknowledges children not merely as beneficiaries of intervention by adults or as future societal assets but as competent social actors. For adults to better understand children's perspectives, we must temper adult expertise with some humility and allow children to explain and interpret their childhoods. This is not an easy task, for adults sometimes judge children's coping strategies—being streetwise, for example, or assuming the role of freedom fighter during civil strife—to be detrimental to their well-being. But this reality implies the need for new approaches to planning and policy development that involve more effective consultation and collaboration with children. It requires their inclusion in a broad range of civic processes, especially the identification of policy need and impact, and the governance of childhood institutions. It implies also the need for research methods and methodologies that are participatory and child centered and give proper scope for children's testimony. The CRC provides for such an approach, although it is seldom translated effectively into policy and practice, which have tended to employ a far more paternalistic outlook.

If children's participation in their own protection is to become a reality, appropriate fora and mechanisms must be developed. There is considerable scope for children to become more involved in the management and implementation of existing institutions and interventions run by adults. But there is also ample opportunity for greater engagement in collective action and mutual support with peers. To suggest that children have a valid role to play in their own protection is not to imply that they should take on the full complement of adult responsibilities or that they be treated as adults. Rather, it is to argue that children should have substantially more opportunities to participate in policy and action than they do currently. It highlights the need to work alongside and "with" rather than "for" children.

CONCLUSION

In this chapter, we have argued that the term *resilience* provides a useful metaphor for the empirical observation that some children, possibly the majority, are surprisingly able to adjust to or overcome situations of serious adversity. Many of these more competent boys and girls appear to remain resourceful in the long term and to adapt well in adulthood; some even find themselves caring for younger siblings and adults more vulnerable than themselves. This quality and the factors that contribute to it are surely worthy of extensive exploration and analysis. Moreover, the ability to isolate and ameliorate risk and enhance protective factors in the life of a developing child is key to effective intervention. If we are to better protect children, we urgently require more information about what renders them vulnerable or resilient, what circumstances are amenable to intervention and change, and how best to assist them.

For interventions to effectively address the actual needs and concerns of children, this information must be grounded in both sound theory and appropriate empirical evidence from a broad range of settings. The existing research into risk and resilience in children confronting adversity goes some way toward addressing these requirements by stressing, for example, the significance of personal traits of the individual child, family circumstances, and peer and institutional support. Nevertheless, we have noted that this literature also embodies certain shortcomings, not least the fact that it makes very little use of children's own understandings and perspectives across cultures and of their active contributions to their well-being, coping, and very survival.

We suggest that given the present state of the art, use of the term resilience cannot be taken to imply a fully-fledged theory about how children deal with adversity, for the concept does not stand up to rigorous scientific interrogation, especially when translated across cultural domains. This point matters a great deal because, according to the logic laid down by Vygotsky, culture is not a mere variable in human cognition but a major generative force: It is the lens through which we view the world, learn skills in survival and coping, and interpret and respond to our experiences. If core notions like those of personhood, death, well-being, and so on vary across cultures and if these and other similar notions really do shape the way in which humans address adversities, then scholars need to develop theoretical constructs that have far greater explanatory reach globally. This may mean abandoning some of the long-cherished ideas of the social sciences, such as the dichotomous conceptualization of the individual and the world he or she inhabits. Such expanded constructs should take account of the highly dynamic and mediated nature of human responses to misfortune and the complexity of meanings attached to this experience in different contexts. What at one point in history, in one setting, and for one child may be a hazard, at another time and in another setting and for a different child may be an important stimulus to learning and competence: The factors that mediate risk and resilience may have different effects in each child at different phases during that child's life. These new constructs should also aid understanding of the effects on children of different kinds of risks, because it cannot be assumed that boys and girls deal with individual or intrafamilial adversities in the same way as they cope with major societal upheavals like war. This recognition implies a shift in emphasis away from the intrapsychic functioning of the individual, generic child and from consideration of that child as an isolated unit of analysis toward greater consideration of structural forces that mediate the well-being of whole groups or categories of children.

Thus, there is a great deal more research needed in this field, especially in majority-world contexts and with children whose lives do not conform to the image perpetuated by much of the existing literature. These children—workers, caregivers, household heads, sex workers, freedom fighters, and so on—have much to teach us in terms of broadening our understanding of well-being and coping in extremely difficult situations. Given the complexity of the issues under consideration and the diversity of children's lives in different circumstances, it is crucial that we do justice to these children's experiences and perspectives. Doing so means increasing our knowledge while avoiding simplistic policy recommendations aimed at reducing risk or enhancing protective factors. It is time to engage with the reality of children's lives in different settings and support their very different and diverse skills and capacities.

NOTES

1. For the purpose of this chapter, a child is defined in accordance with the UN Convention on the Rights of the Child as any individual below the age of 18.

2. Vygotsky articulated his ideas in the early 20th century, but North American and European researchers did not take up his ideas until much more recently.

3. We draw heavily on ideas shared with us by William Myers during personal communications for this and the following point.

4. Charles Super and Sara Harkness (1992) highlight the importance of cultural specificity through the concept of "developmental niche," which they use to explain how children's needs and development are mediated and expressed in particular ways in particular cultural and social settings.

5. As it happens, some of the most widely accepted ideas about what is detrimental and what is beneficial to children turn out to be founded on a particular ideology or set of interests and therefore have little logic in terms of children's well-being. One has only to contrast internationally promoted attitudes and assumptions toward children's labor force work with those toward children's unpaid household work to comprehend how completely modern attitudes reflect the social and historical context from which they are derived. Why is drudgery that is unpaid household work acceptable and even good for children, whereas drudgery in the paid labor force is unacceptable and bad? Just as paid and unpaid labor force work share many characteristics, so labor force work and housework are often hard to differentiate in terms of children's effort, safety and risk factors, intellectual stimulation, and hours worked. Yet in most policy, domestic work is still considered appropriate for children, whereas labor force work is not. Even if a practice was identified as abusive to children, to exhort families or communities to behave differently would not necessarily foster children's well-being. This is because, as indicated, the effects of adversity on children are determined not merely by the objective nature of an act or situation so much as by children's subjective experience of that situation.

REFERENCES

Ager, A. (1996). Children, war and psychological intervention. In S. Carr & J. F. Schumaker (Eds.), *Psychology and the developing world* (pp. 66–73). Westport, CT: Greenwood.

Anthony, E. J. (1987). Risk, vulnerability, and resilience: An overview. In E. J. Anthony & B. J. Cohler (Eds.), *The invulnerable child* (pp. 3–48). New York: Guilford Press.

Apfel, R., & Simon, B. (1996). Psychosocial interventions for children of war: The value of a model of resiliency. *Medicine and Global Survival.* Retrieved December 9, 2004, from www.ippnw.org/MGS/V3Apfel.html.

Armstrong, M., Boyden, J., Galappatti, A., & Hart, J. (2004). *Piloting methods for the evaluation of psychosocial programme impact in Eastern Sri Lanka.* Report for USAID, Oxford. Retrieved

December 9, 2004, from www.rsc.ox.ac.uk/ PDFs/ rrpilotingmethods04.pdf

Bernard, B. (1995). *Fostering resilience in children* (ERIC Digest No. EDO-PS-95). Retrieved December 9, 2004, from resilnet.uiuc.edu/library/ benard95.html

Bit, S. (1991). *The warrior heritage: A psychological perspective of Cambodian trauma.* El Cerrito, CA: Seanglim Bit.

Boyden, J. (2002, September). *Unpublished field notes: Interviews with former abducted child combatants, Gulu, Uganda.* Country Review of Uganda Programme, Save the Children Denmark.

Boyden, J., Eyber, C., Feeny, T., & Scott, C. (2004). *Children and poverty.* Part II. *Voices of children: Experiences and perceptions from Belarus, Bolivia, Sierra Leone, India and Kenya* (Children and Poverty Series). Richmond, VA: Christian Children's Fund.

Bracken, P. (1998). Hidden agendas: Deconstructing post traumatic stress disorder. In P. Bracken & C. Petty (Eds.), *Rethinking the trauma of war* (pp. 38–59). London: Save the Children Fund UK and Free Association Press.

Bracken, P., Giller, J. E., & Summerfield, D. (1995). Psychological responses to war and atrocity: The limitations of current concepts. *Social Science and Medicine, 40*(8), 1073–1082.

Briggs, J. L. (1986, September). *Expecting the unexpected: Canadian Inuit training for an experimental lifestyle.* Paper presented at the Fourth International Conference on Hunting and Gathering Societies, Ontario, Canada.

Bronfenbrenner, U. (1986). Ecology of the family as a context for human development: Research perspectives. *Developmental Psychology, 22*(6), 723–742.

Bronfenbrenner, U. (1996). *The ecology of human development: Experiments by nature and design.* Cambridge, MA: Harvard University Press.

Cole, M. (1992). Culture in development. In M. H. Bornstein & M. E. Lamb (Eds.), *Human development: An advanced textbook* (731–789). Hillsdale, NJ: Erlbaum.

Cole, M. (1996). *Cultural psychology: A once and future discipline.* Cambridge, MA: Harvard University Press.

Cole, M., Gay, J., Glick, J., & D. Sharp. (1971). *The cultural context of learning and thinking: An exploration in experimental anthropology.* London: Methuen.

Dawes, A. (1992, November). *Psychological discourse about political violence and its effects on children.* Paper presented at the meeting of the Mental Health of Refugee Children Exposed to Violent Environments, Refugee Studies Programme, University of Oxford, Oxford, UK.

Dawes, A., & Donald, D. (1994). Understanding the psychological consequences of adversity. In A. Dawes & D. Donald (Eds.), *Childhood and adversity: Psychological perspectives from South African research* (pp. 1–27). Cape Town: David Philip.

De Berry, J. (2004). The sexual vulnerability of adolescent girls during civil war in Teso, Uganda. In J. Boyden & J. de Berry (Eds.), *Children and youth on the front line: Ethnography, armed conflict and displacement.* Oxford & New York: Berghahn Books.

De Vries, M. (1996). Trauma in cultural perspective. In B. Van der Volk, A. McFarlane, & L. Weisaette (Eds.), *Traumatic stress: The effects of overwhelming experience on mind, body and society* (pp. 398–413). London: Guildford Press.

Drèze, J., & Sen, A. (1995). Gender inequality and women's agency. In J. Drèze & A. Sen (Eds.), *India: Economic development and social opportunity* (pp. 140–178). Delhi: Oxford University Press.

Eisenbruch, M. (1991). From post-traumatic stress disorder to cultural bereavement: Diagnosis of Southeast Asian refugees. *Social Science and Medicine, 33*(6), 673–680.

Ekblad, S. (1993). Psychosocial adaptation of children while housed in a Swedish refugee camp: Aftermath of the collapse of Yugoslavia. *Stress Medicine, 9,* 159–166.

Engle, P., Castle, S., & Menon, P. (1996). Child development: Vulnerability and resilience. *Social Science and Medicine, 43*(5), 621–635.

Fraser, M. W. (Ed.). (1997). *Risk and resilience in childhood: An ecological perspective.* Washington, DC: NASW Press.

Galappatti, A. (2002). *Caring for separated children: An approach from Sri Lanka.* Colombo, Sri Lanka: Save the Children Norway.

Garbarino, J. (1999, November). *What children can tell us about the trauma of forced migration.* Seminar presented at the Refugee Studies Programme, University of Oxford, Oxford.

Garbarino, J., Kostelny, K., & Dubrow, N. (1991). *No place to be a child: Growing up in a war zone.* Lexington, MA: Lexington Books.

Garmezy, N. (1983). Stressors of childhood. In N. Garmezy & M. Rutter (Eds.), *Stress, coping and development in children* (pp. 43–84). New York: McGraw-Hill.

Garmezy, N. (1993). Children in poverty: Resilience despite risk. *Psychiatry, 56*(1), 127–136.

Garmezy, N., & Masten, A. (1991). The protective role of competence indicators in children at risk. In E. M. Cummings (Ed.), *Life span developmental psychology: Perspectives on stress and coping* (pp. 151–176). Hillsdale, NJ: Erlbaum.

Garmezy, N., & Rutter, M. (Eds.). (1983). *Stress, coping and development in children.* New York: McGraw-Hill.

Gibbs, S. (1994). Post-war social reconstruction in Mozambique: Reframing children's experience of trauma and healing. *Disasters, 18*(3), 268–276.

Gilmore, D. (1990). *Manhood in the making: Cultural concepts of masculinity.* New Haven, CT: Yale University Press.

Goodnow, J. J. (1990). The socialization of cognition. In J. W. Stigler, R. A. Shweder, & G. Herdt (Eds.), *Cultural psychology* (pp. 259–286). New York: Cambridge University Press.

Goyos, J. M. (1997). *Identifying resiliency factors in adult "Pedro Pan" children: A retrospective study.* Doctoral dissertation submitted to Ellen Whiteside McDonnell School of Social Work, Barry University, Miami, FL.

Hinton, R. (2000). "Seen but not heard": Refugee children and models of coping. In C. Panter-Brick & M. Smith (Eds.), *Abandoned children* (pp. 199–212). Cambridge, UK: Cambridge University Press.

Jareg, E., & Falk, L. (1999, April–May). *Centre-based and community based psychosocial projects for war-affected children.* Draft Report for Redd Barna and Red Barnet, Save the Children Norway and Save the Children Denmark, Oslo.

Kleinman, A., & Kleinman, J. (1991). Suffering and its professional transformation: Toward an ethnography of interpersonal experience. *Culture, Medicine and Psychiatry, 15*(3), 275–301.

Korbin, J. (Ed.). (1981). *Child abuse and neglect: Cross-cultural perspectives.* Berkeley: University of California Press.

Le Vine, P. (1999, July). *Assessing "detachment" patterns and contextual trauma across cultures (trauma detachment grid).* Seminar presented at the Refugee Studies Centre, University of Oxford, UK.

Lock, M., & Scheper-Hughes, N. (1990). A critical reinterpretive approach in medicinal anthropology: Rituals and routines of discipline and dissent. In T. Johnson & C. Sargent (Eds.), *Medical anthropology: Contemporary theory and method* (pp. 47–72). New York: Praeger.

Luthar, S. S. (2003). The culture of affluence: Psychological costs of material wealth. *Child Development, 74,* 1581–1593.

Luthar, S. S., & Cicchetti, D. (2000). The construct of resilience: Implications for interventions and social policies. *Development and Psychopathology, 12,* 857–885.

Luthar, S. S., Cicchetti, D., & Becker, B. (2000). The construct of resilience: A critical evaluation and guidelines for future work. *Child Development, 71*(3), 543–562.

Mann, G. (2000). *Separated children on the Thai-Burma border: A field research report.* Unpublished paper, Refugee Studies Centre, University of Oxford, UK.

Mann, G. (2001). *Networks of support: A literature review of care issues for separated children.* Stockholm: Save the Children Sweden.

Mann, G. (2002). *"Wakimbizi, Wakimbizi":* Congolese children's perspectives of life in Dar es Salaam, Tanzania. *Environment & Urbanization, 14*(2), 115–122.

Mann, G. (2003a). *Family matters: The care and protection of children affected by HIV/AIDS in Malawi.* Stockholm: Save the Children Sweden.

Mann, G. (2003b). *Not seen or heard: The lives of separated refugee children in Dar es Salaam.* Stockholm: Save the Children Sweden.

Masten, A., Best, K. M., & Garmezy, N. (1990). Resilience and development: Contributions to the study of children who overcome adversity. *Development and Psychopathology, 2,* 425–444.

McCallin, M., & Fozzard, S. (1991). *The impact of traumatic events on the psychosocial wellbeing of Mozambican refugee women and children.* Geneva: International Catholic Child Bureau.

Palmer, O. J. (1983). *The psychological assessment of children* (2nd ed.). New York: John Wiley.

Parker, M. (1996). Social devastation and mental health in North East Africa. In T. Allen (Ed.), *In search of cool ground: War, flight and homecoming in North East Africa* (pp. 262–273). London: James Curry.

Phinney, J. S. (1996). When we talk about American ethnic groups, what do we mean? *American Psychologist, 51*(9), 918–927.

Punamaki, R.-L. (1987). Content of and factors affecting coping modes among Palestinian children. *Scandinavian Journal of Development Alternatives, 6*(1), 86–98.

Ressler, E., Boothby, N., & Steinbock, D. (1988). *Unaccompanied children: Care and protection in wars, natural disasters, and refugee movements.* New York: Oxford University Press.

Ressler, E., Tortorici, J., & Marcelino, A. (1992). *Children in situations of armed conflict: A guide to the provision of services.* New York: UNICEF.

Reynolds-White, S. (1998). *Questioning misfortune.* Cambridge, UK: Cambridge University Press.

Richman, J. M., & Bowen, G. L. (1997). School failure: An ecological-interactional-developmental perspective. In M. W. Fraser (Ed.), *Risk and resilience in childhood* (pp. 95–116.). Washington: NASW Press.

Richman, N. (1993). Annotation: Children in situations of political violence. *Journal of Child Psychology and Psychiatry, 34*(8), 1286–1302.

Robertson, A. F. (1991). *Beyond the family: The social organisation of human reproduction.* Oxford, UK: Blackwell.

Rogoff, B. (1990). *Apprenticeship in thinking.* Oxford, UK: Oxford University Press.

Rogoff, B. (2003). *The cultural nature of human development.* Oxford & New York: Oxford University Press.

Rousseau, C., Said, T. M., Gagné, M-J., & Bibeau, G. (1998). Resilience in unaccompanied minors from the north of Somalia. *Psychoanalytic Review, 85*(4), 615–637.

Rutter, M. (1987). Psychosocial resilience and protective mechanisms. *American Journal of Orthopsychiatry, 57*(3), 316–331.

Rutter, M. (1990). Psychosocial resilience and protective mechanisms. In J. E. Rolf, A. Masten, D. Cicchetti, K. Nuechterlein, & S. Weintraub (Eds.), *Risk and protective factors in the development of psychopathology* (pp. 181–214). Cambridge, UK: Cambridge University Press.

Schaffer, H. R. (1996). *Social development.* Oxford, UK: Blackwell.

Schaffer, H. R. (2000). The early experience assumption: Past, present, and future. *International Journal of Behavioural Development, 24*(1), 5–14.

Shweder, R., & Bourne, E. (1982). Does the concept of the person vary cross-culturally? In A. Marsella & G. White (Eds.), *Cultural conceptions of mental health and therapy* (pp. 158–199). Dordrecht, Netherlands: Reidal.

Summerfield, D. (1991). Psychological effects of conflict in the Third World. *Development in Practice, 1*(3), 159–173.

Summerfield, D. (1998). The social experience of war and some issues for the humanitarian field. In P. Bracken & C. Petty (Eds.), *Rethinking the trauma of war* (pp. 9–37). London & New York: Save the Children Fund UK, Free Association Books.

Super, C., & Harkness, S. (1986). The developmental niche: A conceptualisation at the interface of child and culture. *International Journal of Behavioural Development, 9,* 545–569.

Super, C., & Harkness, S. (1992). Cultural perspectives on child development. In D. Wagner & H. Stevenson (Eds.), *Cultural perspectives on child development.* San Francisco: W. H. Freeman.

Swaine, A. (with Feeny, T.). (2004). A neglected perspective: Adolescent girls" experiences of the Kosovo conflict of 1999. In J. Boyden & J. de Berry (Eds.), *Children and youth on the front line: Ethnography, armed conflict and displacement* (pp. 63–86). Oxford & New York: Berghahn Books.

Tolfree, D. (2004). *Whose children? Separated children's protection and participation in critical situations.* Stockholm: Save the Children Sweden.

Turton, R., Straker, G., & Mooza, F. (1990). The experiences of violence in the lives of township youth in "unrest" and "normal" conditions. *South African Journal of Psychology, 21*(2), 77–84.

Ungar, M. (2004). *Nurturing hidden resilience in troubled youth.* Toronto: University of Toronto Press.

Vraalsen, P. (in press). *Separated children in South Sudan: A report of a participatory study.* Nairobi: UNICEF.

Vygotsky, L. (1978). *Mind in society: The development of higher psychological processes.* Cambridge, MA: Harvard University Press.

Werner, E., & Smith, R. (1992). *Overcoming the odds: High risk children from birth to adulthood.* Ithaca, NY, & London: Cornell University Press.

Werner, E., & Smith, R. (1998). *Vulnerable but invincible: A longitudinal study of resilient children and youth.* New York: Adams, Bannister, Cox.

Wilson, E. O. (1998). *Consilience: The unity of knowledge.* New York: Knopf.

Woodhead, M. (1998). *Is there a place for work in child development? Implications of child development theory and research for interpretation of the UN Convention on the Rights of the Child, with particular reference to Article 32, on Children, Work and Exploitation.* London: Open University and Rädda Barnen.

World Health Organization. (1992). *Psychosocial consequences of disasters: Prevention and management.* Geneva: World Health Organization.

Wyman, P. (2003). Emerging perspectives on context specificity of children's adaptation and resilience. In S. S. Luther (Ed.), *Resilience and vulnerability: Adaptation in the context of childhood adversities* (pp. 293–317). Cambridge, UK: Cambridge University Press.

Yates, T., Egeland, B., & Sroufe, A. (2003). Rethinking resilience: A developmental process perspective. In S. S. Luthar (Ed.), *Resilience and vulnerability: Adaptation in the context of childhood adversities* (pp. 243–266). Cambridge, UK: Cambridge University Press.

Zwi, A., Macrae, J., & Ugalde, A. (1992). Children and war. *The Kangaroo, 1*(1), 46–57.

2

CULTURE AND ETHNIC IDENTITY IN FAMILY RESILIENCE

Dynamic Processes in Trauma and Transformation of Indigenous People

LAURIE D. MCCUBBIN

HAMILTON I. MCCUBBIN

The convergence of two generations of behavioral scientists, a psychologist and a family scientist, both of indigenous ancestry and immersed in the cultural context of their ancestors, inspired this chapter to give meaning to and advance understanding of family resilience and resilient behavior in response to trauma. In setting aside the strategy to present sweeping stereotypic generalizations about family resilience across cultures, the authors draw from ethnic identity and cultural studies in psychology, family science, feminist studies, and anthropology to explicate the dynamics of resilience in indigenous families and one of Polynesian origin. Native Hawaiian families, the indigenous people of the Hawaiian Islands in the Pacific Ocean, are viewed as a unique social context from which scientists can extract and reveal the influential role of culture and ethnicity involved in adaptation and growth, the central outcomes of the resilience process. In so doing, the authors broaden the spotlight on the central research and clinical issues in understanding and promoting resilience from a cross-cultural perspective.

Interest in resiliency in children and families has flourished in the past three decades. It is a topic of prime interest to social and behavioral scientists because of the apparent role that resilience plays in understanding both individual and family developmental transitions as well as recovery from trauma or under conditions

AUTHORS' NOTE: The authors would like to acknowledge Dr. Marilyn Ann McCubbin, Professor, School of Nursing and Dental Hygiene, University of Hawaii at Manoa, and Mrs. Ann Tom of the Center on the Family, University of Hawaii at Manoa, for their critical review and editorial comments on the chapter.

that favor personal and family deterioration or dysfunction. Predictably, knowledge about successful adaptation in the face of traumatic if not catastrophic conditions also strengthens the conceptual base needed to guide and frame both treatment- and prevention-oriented interventions for children and families at risk or those rendered dysfunctional in the face of such adversity.

Fortunately, both psychologists and family scientists have embraced the challenge of designing and conducting research that enhances the development of theories attempting to uncover the reasons why some families from different cultural and ethnic backgrounds are more resilient than others. Some families are better able to negotiate their way through both transitions and situational traumas and better able to cope, adjust, adapt, and even thrive on life's hardships, whereas other families faced with similar if not identical traumatic events give up, are easily exhausted, or deteriorate or give up altogether in the face of these difficult moments in the family's life course.

When we consider that most families do not self-destruct or even deteriorate to the point of requiring therapy or treatment and that most do recover from adversity, it seems reasonable that theories and research would be advanced to explain and predict the behaviors of these resilient families, as well as the motivators, if not the cause, of these constructive behaviors. Yet both fields, psychology and family science, are dominated by theories about failure and dysfunction and the treatment of such conditions. If we are to make a serious commitment to prevention, family preservation, and the promotion of family well-being, it seems reasonable that this agenda be driven best by research and theories that have validity in explaining why families predisposed to, vulnerable to, or assaulted by life's hardships and traumas emerge resilient, succeed, and even thrive in the process. Across cultures, the interventions, programs, and policies aimed at enhancing the well-being of families should be guided by theories and research focused on the family competencies and abilities that promote resilience.

The push for resilience research on children and families of different ethnic backgrounds and cultures has been a recent but compelling agenda. This situation is propelled by the rapid and continuous growth in the United States in the number of persons and households of different and multi-ethnic backgrounds. Data from the 2000 U.S. census, which introduced a new system of reporting race, providing a list of races and asking respondents to check all that apply, and the National Health Interview, which uses a similar system, provide ample evidence of the changing ethnic profile of the total population with increasing numbers of Asians and those of Hispanic origins. The confluence of immigrations and an increase in interethnic marriages throughout the world, including countries such as the United Arab Emirates and Kuwait in the Middle East, the Philippines, and Vietnam, to name a few, affirm the gradual but distinct emerging profile of ethnic diversity.

RESILIENCE IN FAMILIES: AN EVOLVING CONCEPTUAL FRAMEWORK

Over the past three decades, attempts to explain the variability in family behavior in response to stress have clustered around three bodies of theory building and related research. The research by Reuben Hill (1949) advanced the ABCX thesis that family resistance to the impact of stressors and avoidance of a family crisis could be explained by understanding the stressor (A), the resources available to and used by families (B), the family's definition of the stressor (C), and the outcome of family crisis (X). The research and theory building by McCubbin and Patterson (1983), nearly four decades later, focused on explaining the variability in family systems in responding to and recovering from a family crisis. To emphasize the recovery phase of family behavior, the double ABCX model of adaptation of families emerged with an emphasis on "postcrisis" factors (the ABCX model was viewed as focused on "precrisis"), such as the pile up or accumulation of life events and changes (AA); the family's rebuilding of protective resources that were depleted and the use of family recovery resources, inclusive of family coping (BB); the family's appraisal of the situation focused on balancing of demands and resources (CC); and family adaptation (XX), reflecting the outcome of family change and recovery from a crisis situation.

This model evolved into the FAAR framework, or family adjustment and adaptation response, representing the integration of the Hill ABCX and the McCubbin and Patterson double ABCX into a full model with an added focus on the family processes (McCubbin & Patterson, 1983a, 1983b). This emphasis on the dynamic processes of both adjustment and adaptation inspired family scholars to examine the role of family typologies (core family patterns of functioning) as core family competencies in shaping outcomes, adjustment, and adaptation. The typologies of *regenerative family systems* (with core strengths in hardiness and coherence), *versatile family systems* (with core strength in bonding and flexibility), *rhythmic family systems* (with core strengths in family time and routines and the valuing of both), and *traditionalistic family systems* (with core strengths in traditions and celebrations) emerged in the literature as both core *protective factors and recovery factors across the family life cycle* (McCubbin, Thompson, Pirner, & McCubbin, 1988).

The resiliency model of family adjustment and adaptation (McCubbin & McCubbin, 1993; McCubbin, McCubbin, Thompson, & Thompson, 1995), referred to in this chapter as the resiliency model, was a natural evolution of earlier theory building and research with a dedicated commitment to explaining the variability in family behavior in the course of recovery when faced with traumatic life events and catastrophes. This deliberate and planful shift in our commitment and emphasis on postcrisis and family recovery flows from the refinement in theory and research rendering clarity in distinction between protective factors and resilience (McCubbin, 2003). Beauvias and Oetting (1999) made a distinction between the two concepts by first defining protective factors as capabilities and processes that increase the chances of family prosocial behaviors and norms in the face of stressors and strains. Thus, to determine the effects of protective factors is to focus on the degree to which they foster prosocial behaviors and reduce the risks, thus avoiding a family crisis. Prosocial behavior can be considered protective when it reduces negative behaviors or symptoms such as depression or anxiety. Prosocial behavior can also be considered positive when it promotes adjustments, stability, and harmony

in functioning as well as the growth of family members.

The resilience model with its emphasis on growth in the face of trauma and crises is depicted in Figure 2.1.

By definition, the resiliency model, as well as its predecessors, is a contextualized and developmental framework; the family and family members are seen as an integral and interacting part of the larger social ecology of nature, community, society, nation, and the world, over time. In general, because the family is a system, each domain of family life has an effect on each of the other domains. From a process perspective, in crisis situations, particularly when faced with major traumas or catastrophes, the family's numerous and substantial hardships call for substantive changes in the family system, including roles, goals, value, rules, priorities, boundaries, and overall patterns of functioning. These changes are necessary to achieve balance and harmony across the domains of family functioning.

In addition, families may take advantage of a crisis situation and choose to remain imbalanced and in the state of disharmony to bring about more substantial changes in the family's patterns of functioning. New patterns of family functioning may be introduced to reestablish harmony and balance. For example, in the face of the trauma of a spouse losing a job held for 18 years, a career position the spouse expected to retire from, accompanied by a deterioration in family income and harmony, a family may struggle with the decision to have the other parent return to the work or require one or both parents to take on multiple lower-paying jobs just to survive. These changes alone will force changes in other patterns of family functioning in an effort to bring about harmony and balance. The newly unemployed spouse or significant other will be asked to take on more domestic responsibilities along with added child care responsibilities, both of which may have been the point of prior conflicts, tensions, and resentments. It is also true that an older child in the same family may be called on to take on more responsibilities at home or as a wage earner, thus pulling the child away from school, individual developmental tasks, and other social growth-producing situations and relationships.

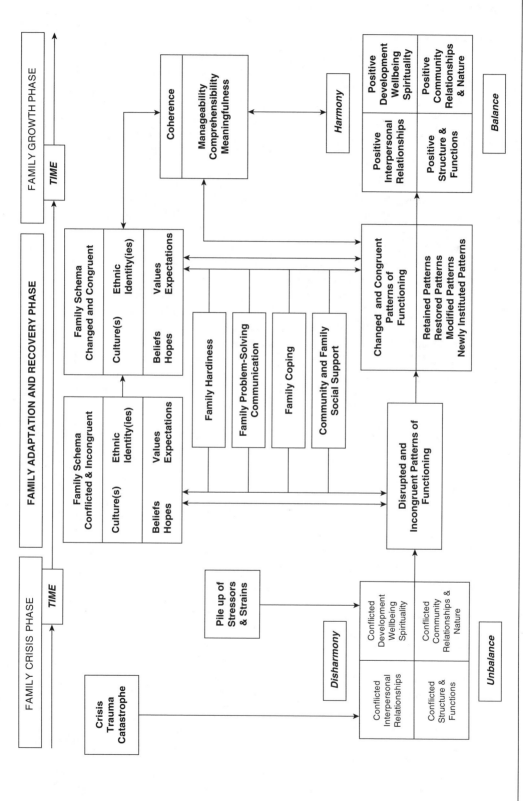

Figure 2.1   Family Resiliency Model

The family system's rules, roles, and responsibilities will in all likelihood change, which may also create additional pressures adding to the imbalance and disharmony. In situations involving this challenge to the family's internal harmonizer and thermostat—that is, the family's established patterns of functioning—the family will, in all likelihood, experience a condition of maladjustment and resulting condition of family crisis in addition to the crisis created by the initial transition of job loss.

Family crises have been conceptualized as a continuous condition of disruptiveness, disorganization, or incapacitation in the family social system (Burr, 1973) accompanied by family trial-and-error efforts to restore harmony and balance. Consistent with Reuben Hill's (1949) original definition of family crisis, within the resiliency model, a family in crisis does not necessarily carry the stigmatizing pejorative value judgment that the family unit has failed, is dysfunctional, or in need of professional treatment for such a malady. It is important to reiterate that family crises are not necessarily brought about by the family's being victimized or traumatized by events beyond its control. Families may enter into an active *process of inducing or exacerbating a crisis* to bring about transformation and changes in the family's established patterns of functioning, which some members may view as more desirable or needed. Accompanied by family efforts to change its established patterns of functioning as part of restoring balance and harmony, the system enters into the adaptation or growth phase of the resiliency model. With the presentation of core concepts of the resiliency model, and the availability of more comprehensive and complete description of the resiliency model in other publications (McCubbin, McCubbin, & Thompson, 2002), we will focus the remainder of the chapter on the key elements of the resiliency model that reveal the application of the framework to the study of families of different ethnicities, cultures, and social contexts.

FAMILY ADAPTATION
AND TRANSFORMATION

The resiliency model with its adaptation and transformation phase emerged from studies of war-induced family crises (McCubbin, Boss, Wilson, & Lester, 1980; McCubbin & Dahl, 1976), the study of families faced with chronic stressors and illnesses (Kosciulek, McCubbin, & McCubbin, 1993; McCubbin & McCubbin, 1987, 1989), the study of family transitions and changes over the life cycle (McCubbin & Lavee, 1986; McCubbin et al., 1988; Olson et al., 1983), the study of Native Hawaiian, Filipino, Asian American and African American families faced with both normative and nonnormative stressors and crises (McCubbin & McCubbin, 1988; Thompson, McCubbin, Thompson, & Elver, 1995), the study of African American families faced with relocations into foreign countries with the added risk of war (McCubbin, 1995), and the study of African American families involved in treatment programs for their sons determined to be youth offenders requiring residential treatment (McCubbin, Fleming, et al., 1995). The dynamic nature of family resilience and transformation, depicted in Figure 2.1 may be characterized in the following narrative.

Families in crisis situations are characterized, in part, by an imbalance and disharmony, a condition precipitated by a traumatic situation and fostered by the inadequacy of or the problematic nature of the family's patterns of functioning. "Families in crisis" is defined as the system's fundamental inability to *achieve balance and harmony* along four interrelated dimensions of family life: (a) interpersonal communication and emotional relationships; (b) individual member and family development, well-being, and spirituality; (c) family structure and function; and (d) community relationships and nature (McCubbin, McCubbin, & Thompson, 1996). The crisis situation pushes the family to initiate change and transformation in the family's patterns of functioning. The family's ability to bounce back and transform itself— that is, to achieve balance and harmony across its four dimensions of family life—depends on the effectiveness of the family's cluster of six core competencies:

1. The family system's competencies and ability to manage the accumulation and reduction of co-occurring or residual historic stressors and strains (e.g., initial stressor, normative transitions, situation demands, consequences of family

efforts to cope, family and social ambiguity due to the lack of experience and guidelines, or conflict with existing guidelines; conflict with new patterns of functioning that don't fit; conflicts with family norms, rules, values, and beliefs; and conflict in patterns of functioning)

2. The family system's competencies in mobilizing its member strengths and capabilities (e.g., intelligence, knowledge, personality, health, sense of mastery, self-esteem, sense of coherence, ethnic identity, and cultural practices) and its collective strengths and capabilities (e.g., organization, hardiness, communication, problem solving, traditions, celebrations, bonding, flexibility, routines, and support) to (a) rebuild those strengths that may have been diminished or that may have deteriorated in the face of trauma and its impact; (b) activate and focus its protective and recovery resources to create and implement new patterns of functioning, to change, and to stabilize old patterns; render legitimacy to the new and changed patterns; and resolve conflicts with the old patterns; and (c) maintain emotional stability during the process

3. The family system's competencies to mobilize the community strengths and resources (e.g., emotional support, esteem support, network support, altruism, honest feedback) and to cultivate, change, and improve on community resources and strengths (e.g., family and individual programs, policies, rules, guidelines, regulations, mission, and resources)—to bear on and be tailored to meet the needs of the challenged family and to aid the family in its efforts to achieve harmony with the community

4. The family system's competencies in modifying, creating, and cultivating changes in the family's schema needed to guide behaviors as well as legitimize changes in the family's patterns of functioning and, in so doing, minimize conflict, maximize congruency between the family's schema and instituted behaviors, and promote a sense of manageability, comprehensibility, and meaningfulness

5. The family system's competencies in positive problem solving and coping focused on achieving balance and harmony among the core dimensions of family life while promoting emotional stability and changes in the family's patterns of functioning and schema

6. The family's system's competencies in creating shared meaning (e.g., purpose, legitimacy, direction), as well as behavior, that will be congruent with the family's schema (e.g., ethnic identity, culture, beliefs, values, rules, priorities, expectations, relationship with nature, and convictions).

CULTURE AND RESILIENCE

In the case of ethnic minority families, the identification of resilience factors, inclusive of ethnic identity and culture, emerge as central themes of resilience research. These efforts are accompanied by a line of inquiry focused on how ethnic identity and culture, independently or in combination with other moderating or mediating factors, will have the greatest impact and value in promoting recovery.

The influence of culture on family life has been documented in the family literature. A comprehensive review by Tseng and Hsu (1991) reveals that, over time, culture has influenced family functioning in a great variety of ways: marriage forms, choice of mates, postmarital residence, the family kinship system and descent groups, household and family structure, the primary axis of family obligations, family-community dynamics, and alternative family formations (Berkner, 1972; Ishisaka, 1992; Li, 1968; Miller, 1969; Mokuau, 1992; Pelzel, 1970; Tseng & Hsu, 1986). Historically, the family has been the conduit for cultural transmission, providing a natural atmosphere for traditions, beliefs, and values to be passed from generation to generation, and it has evolved throughout the ages to keep culture and ethnic heritage alive. In turn, the family's traditions, an important element in the process of family resilience, have given families a sense of stability and support from which they draw comfort, guidance, and a means of coping with the problems of daily life.

The establishment of culture in the resilience process—that is, the recovery from trauma—has been grounded in the literature, albeit on a limited basis. To demonstrate the importance of culture to family resilience, a brief synopsis of studies of the trauma of "end-of-life decisions" would be appropriate. The end of life with its accompanying decisions, considered a traumatic family crises, offers the family scientist and clinician a vivid set of examples of the subtle but potentially profound influence of culture on family and individual resilience. For a full and expanded discussion of end-of-life decisions, the work of Gwen Yeo and Nancy Hikoyeda (2000), from which the following synopsis is drawn, deserves full review and analysis.

African Americans draw heavily from a religious doctrine that heaven is not of this earth and a transcendent soul rises to heaven on death (Mouton, 2000). This core religious belief, Lincoln and Miyama (1991) argue, emerges as a direct relationship between slavery and the notion of a "divine rescue." This deference to and dependence on a power greater than humans to relieve African Americans from the conditions of suffering is accompanied by "a belief in God's power to conquer all and a resilient hope that a miracle will happen" (Mouton, 2000, p. 74). Interestingly, studies of preference for life-sustaining care reveal that African Americans, compared with Caucasians, Hispanics and Asians, were more likely to choose life-sustaining treatment even in the face of futility or low expected quality of life.

Furthermore, African Americans appear less likely than any other ethnic group to trust health care providers, communicate treatment preference, and participate in organ donation. Levy (1985) documented how medicine proceeded with incomprehensible and seeming unethical practices in the treatment of African Americans, all justified on the notion that African Americans were inferior to Caucasians.

Hispanic families, faced with the same challenges of defining the role of religious beliefs, trust of health care providers, and choice of life-sustaining care, responded with notable differences that have implications for identifying factors in resilience and predicting family behavior. The Hispanic population is increasing significantly with about 22 million reported in 1990 and 31 million in the year 2000. The number of Hispanic elderly was expected to increase by nearly 4% each year from 1990 to the year of 2050 (U.S. Bureau of Census, 1993).

Keeping in mind that the category of Hispanics encompasses several racial subgroups—including Mexican Americans, Puerto Ricans, Cubans, Central Americans, and South Americans—we need to exercise caution in our generalizations about this group even though the members share commonalities such as language, religion, and tradition of family relations. Cuellar (1990) emphasized the importance of four cultural themes that promote resilience among Hispanics: *jerarquismo* (respect for hierarchy), *personalismo* (trust building over time based on the display of mutual respect), *espiritismo* (belief in good and evil spirits that cannot affect health and well-being), and *presentismo* (emphasis on the present and not the past or future).

A qualitative study in a rural town in northern New Mexico (Rael & Korte, 1988) revealed the common practice of holding a vigil over an older family member with a terminal illness. They believe that dead family members continue to watch over the living family members and thus are prayed to for continued support and strength. In general, the rituals support the cultural perspective that death is a natural part of the cycle of life and life is only a temporary gift from God. Talamantes, Lawler, and Espino (1995) found that older Puerto Rican, Cuban, and Mexican American women caring for a terminally ill family member depend on their faith in God to cope with the hardships of pending loss and the death of a loved one. A saying such as *Dios es Grande,* God is great, is offered as testament to the value attached to their faith in coping with illness and death. *Fe,* or spirituality, was also found to be an important coping resource among older Hispanic women. The vast majority of the respondents to a survey found that *Fe* would help in healing and coping with life's problems, such caregiving responsibilities. Mexican Americans, in a qualitative study, were concerned about God's wanting a "whole body back." They believed that the soul remained in or near the body for up to 9 days and would feel an incision or insult to the body; thus, they were more likely to limit the practice of organ donations or autopsies.

Asian/Pacific Islanders constitute a census category in the United States and thus are often treated as a unified group. In fact, more than 30 countries of origin are clustered together to form this "homogenized" grouping of races. They span over half the globe and represent literally hundreds of language and ethnic subgroups, many vastly different from one another in cultural ideology, ethnic identity, and traditions, particularly about death and death decisions. Furthermore, even within culturally defined beliefs, which have a history spanning thousands of years, there may be marked differences in those beliefs across Asian groups. For example, although Buddhist traditions are viewed as having a deep history of practice and basic doctrines are similar, there are definite differences in rituals and practices, particularly those beliefs related to reincarnation and the role of ancestral spirits. Koenig (1997) points out that Chinese and Southeast Asian Buddhists believe in the important influence of ancestral spirits, whereas Japanese American Buddhists tend to honor their ancestors but do not attribute supernatural powers to them.

"Little data are available on decision-making about death in the Native Hawaiian culture, especially outside the state of Hawaii" (Yeo & Hikoyeda, 2000, p. 119). According to Braun and Nichols (1996) current Native Hawaiian beliefs are influence by Native Hawaiian traditions as well as Christianity. As reported, some Hawaiians, particularly elders believed that talking about death will bring on death, but many Native Hawaiians make their wishes known to their *ohana* (family) and loved ones. In a study, Braun (1998) gathered end-of-life attitudes from five ethnic populations, including Native Hawaiians. It is striking that the vast majority, three fourths of the Hawaiians invited to participate in the study, refused. The few who did participate, being primarily Christians, revealed great respect for the traditional Hawaiian values of family, mutual cooperation and support, and collaborative decision making. They felt they had little control over medical decision making that affected them, which resulted in a low level of trust in physicians. Of all the ethnic groups, the Native Hawaiians were the most inclined to endorse preparation for death by making decisions about organ donations—that is, not to be organ donors: They did not believe in organ donation, for it was more appropriate to return the body to God, its maker, as it is.

Native American Indians and Alaskan Natives, two other indigenous groups, make up a small but ever-increasing component of the U.S. population. There are more than 300 federally recognized tribes, 100 state historical tribes, several dozen tribes with no formal recognition, and about 200 Alaskan Native villages (U.S. Bureau of Census, 1993). As Mason and Trible (1982) report, more than 150 languages are spoken by these diverse groups.

Recognizing that beliefs and cultural customs vary within and among Native American tribes, there is one commonality in views regarding death and dying. Native American Indians and the Alaskan Natives view death as a natural and accepted part of life; life and death are seen as a unity in a cyclical process with nature (Lewis, 1990). Lombardi and Lombardi (1982), drawing attention to the harmonious relationship between the Native American Indians and the laws of nature, report that "Native Americans thus comprehend the harmony of the endless cycle creation and re-creation: Their interred bodies return nourishment to the earth; the earth makes the plants grow; the plants feed the animals; the animals feed humanity" (p. 36).

The heterogeneity of traditional beliefs, values, and rituals can be discovered in ethnographic reports on the Lakota Sioux of South Dakota (Brokenleg & Middleton, 1993), the Tanacross Athabaskans of Alaska (Simeone, 1991), the Comanche of Oklahoma (Wallace & Hoebel, 1952), and Canadian Indians (Kaufert & O'Neil, 1991). One of the most interesting accounts reveals the beliefs of the Navajo people of Arizona, New Mexico, and Utah. The Navajo have been characterized as fearful of death and the dead, reluctant to touch the body of the dead for fear the spirit of the deceased might contaminate them. They believe that ghosts of the dead might return to their homes and harass the living to avenge past wrongs. The names of the dead are not spoken, and afterlife is an uninviting ambiguous world (French & Schwartz, 1976; Kluckhohn & Leighton, 1946).

In the contemporary context, particularly the heath care system and its emphasis on patient autonomy (i.e., patient has control over body and mind) and self-determination (i.e., the right to decide), there exists an inherent conflict with Native American values and beliefs (McCabe, 1994). The goal of recent legislation was to increase patient participation in end-of-life decision making, thus expecting agencies and professionals to fully inform the patients of the good and bad. Carrese and Rhodes's (1995) report on their qualitative study of 34 Navajo informants revealed that the traditional Navajo believe that thought and language shape reality and influence events. Thus, positive language helps to maintain or to restore health, and negative language may be harmful to the patients. The disclosure of risk, providing of negative medical information, such as the disclosure of risk in informed consent, is by definition, a contradiction to traditional Navajo ways.

Cooperation and consensus within the family system is central to the total process of end-of-life decision making in Native American and Alaskan families. End-of-life decisions are not made by the patient without consulting the family. McCabe (1994) highlighted the importance of beneficence (i.e., doing what is good for another) as central to the Navajo way of life of giving help or aid for the good of the culture without expecting anything in return. There is no hierarchical or vertical line of decision making; instead there is a horizontal line—all concerned individuals are involved.

The degree to which indigenous families are able to recover from a trauma-induced crisis, such as the loss of a loved one, depends to some degree on the cultural beliefs and values embedded in the family system and the degree to which they, in turn, shape the family's collective behavior. There is little doubt, however, that even with the diversity of beliefs and practices across ethnic groupings, particularly among indigenous peoples, cultural beliefs and practices play an important role, although with varying impact, on the family's resilience over time.

ETHNIC IDENTITY AND RESILIENCE

The concept of ethnic identity, the second key factor in explaining the variability in family resilience, deserves more in-depth consideration by both qualitative- and quantitative-oriented behavioral scientists than it has in the past. The central thesis of ethnic identity in family resilience stems from the core argument that different social categories such as race and ethnicity

shape an individual's or a family's identity as well as its social location in society. Thus, a family system that is racially coded Hawaiian in our society will usually face situations and have experiences that are significantly different from those of a family that is racially coded Asian or Caucasian. Similarly, a family that is racially coded Asian and that has ample financial and educational resources at its disposal will usually face situations and have experiences that are significantly different from a family that is racially coded as Hawaiian. The central point is that a family's identity is likely to be largely determined by its social location in a given society. In addition, identity is the formulation of a person's social, cultural, and historical matrix. Finally, a family's experience will influence, but not entirely determine, the formation of its cultural identity. Mohanty (1993) argued, "Identities are ways of making sense of our experiences." They are "theoretical constructions that enable us to read the world in specific ways" (p. 56). Moya (2000) advanced a realistic (versus postmodernism or essentialist) perspective and renders clarity to the central role of identity. She argues that an individual's understanding of himself or herself and the world will be mediated, more or less accurately, through his or her cultural identity (Moya, 2000, p. 86). She goes on to present the thesis that one's cultural identity is not fixed or absolute and is constantly being evaluated depending on the social contexts (social location consisting of race, class, gender, and sexuality) in which one lives over time:

> According to the realistic theory of identity, identities are not self-evident, unchanging, and uncontestable, nor are they absolutely fragmented, contradictory, and unstable. Rather identities are subject to multiple determinations and to a continual process of verification that takes place over the course of an individual's life through her interaction with the society she lives in. It is through this process of verification that identities can be (and often are) contested and that they can (and often do) change. (p. 84)

Ethnic identity is acknowledged as a critical component of one's sense of identity (Roberts, Phinney, Masse, & Chen, 1999). Ethnic identity focuses on attitudes and beliefs about belonging to an ethnic group, a process that evolves over time and through stages (Phinney, 1990; Tajfel & Turner, 1986). Phinney (1990, 1992) proposed three stages of ethnic identity development: (a) identity diffusion/foreclosure, characterized by lack of exploration of one's identity; (b) moratorium, which consists of exploration of one's identity; and (c) identity achievement, where one has explored in depth and made commitment to one's ethnic identity. The importance of ethnic identity for persons belonging to minority groups is established in Phinney and Alipuria's (1990) study of ethnic identity among Asian American, African American, Mexican American or Hispanic, and white American college students. African Americans scored the highest on ethnic identity search, followed by Mexican Americans, Asian Americans, and whites, respectively. Ethnic identity has greater importance for minority students than for the majority students, as predicted. Ethnic importance was significantly related to ethnic identity search overall and for the three minority groups separately; however, it was less important for whites. Ethnic importance was also significantly related to ethnic identity commitment. The study also demonstrated the possible relationship between self-esteem and ethnic identity development. This finding of a positive relationship with ethnic identity and self-esteem has been affirmed across investigations for African American and Latino adolescents. Caucasian ethnic identification was also positively related to self-esteem. It is important to note, however, when the American identity measure was given to African Americans and Latinos, there was no relationship with self-esteem (Phinney, Cantu, & Kurtz, 1997).

An investigation of 243 Native Hawaiian adolescents confirmed that ethnic identity predicted psychological well-being (self-acceptance and personal growth). The study confirmed that ethnic identity could serve as a protective factor in reducing symptoms of psychological distress and promoting well-being (McCubbin, 2003). Surprisingly, in explaining the variability in ethnic identification, the author discovered a positive correlation between the accumulation of Native Hawaiian stressors (i.e., racial discrimination) and increased ethnic identity. The pressures on Hawaiian youth, including discrimination, comparative racial backgrounds of peers, and the strong emphasis on Hawaiian language, dance, and traditions, appear to foster and deepen an adolescent's sense of Hawaiian identity. As the author concluded, the stressors raise the consciousness of youth in regard to historical discrimination, a process that may increase their sense of belonging to this social/ethnic group (McCubbin, 2003). In this investigation, ethnic identity was positively related to higher levels of self-acceptance and personal growth and to lower levels of depression and anxiety, again affirming its protective value.

FAMILY SCHEMA AND RESILIENCE

Family schema is introduced as a central dimension of family life with a function to represent the family's shared worldview inclusive of the family culture and ethnic identity. The concept of family schema has been traced to the general literature on the psychology of schemata. A family schema may be defined as a generalized structure of shared values, beliefs, goals, expectations, and priorities shaped and adopted by the family unit over time, thus formulating a generalized informational structure against and through which information and experiences are compared, sifted, analyzed, and processed. A family schema develops over time and evolves into an encapsulation of experiences that serves as a framework used to guide family behavior and patterns of functioning (Martin & Halverson, 1981; Segal, 1988). The dynamic interaction between the family schema and the family's patterns of functioning involves the family's evaluation of information leading to the acceptance or rejection of information as being irrelevant, conflictual, or congruent with the family's schema of values, beliefs, goals, expectations, and priorities. In addition, the family, guided by this analysis as a vital step in problem solving, decides on whether to introduce, change, or maintain the family's pattern of functioning. Over time, with the introduction and processing of experiences, the family unit creates a family schema that becomes self-imposed, stable, and to some degree, rigid. Not only is a family's schema highly resistant to change, but it plays a major and highly influential role in shaping and evaluating family meanings, its definition of the situation, the coping strategies employed, and the degree to which newly instituted patterns of functioning need to be cultivated to facilitate family adaptation (McCubbin & McCubbin, 1988; McCubbin & McCubbin, 1987, 1993).

Once a family schema is shaped and quietly adopted by the family system, family patterns will then be guided, if not governed, by that schema or successive schema. Once a schema is shaped, adopted, and used to interpret phenomena and to guide family behavior, there is no such thing as family functioning in the absence of a schema. The development of family schemas may be viewed as a seemingly undetectable integration of the schemata of its individual members, adopted, and employed to shape family behavior, which would be upheld and maintained as long as it is successful for the family unity and its members. The family's schema is not likely to be doubted or questioned until the family faces a crisis or a series of crisis-producing situations that place the schema or parts of the schema in question. Alternative schemas or modification in or prioritization of elements within the family's schema (e.g., values, beliefs, goals, expectations) are then introduced and tested by the family to determine their acceptability and congruency with the family's adopted behaviors. This process of testing, rejecting, substituting, and modifying a family schema may be referred to as schema transformation.

Family schemas gain their importance in family functioning by virtue of their role in guiding and legitimizing family behaviors and patterns of functioning and in the development of family meanings along with promotion of a sense of meaningfulness and comprehensibility. This aspect of family appraisal involves the creation of shared understandings and the facilitation of family resilience in the face of trauma and catastrophes. The family's meanings—shaped by the family's schema of values, beliefs, culture, ethnic identity and expectations—are often reflected in brief or meaningful phrases such as "God's will" or "God will make things *pono* (Hawaiian for making things right)" used to encourage understanding and acceptance of adversity that cannot be explained.

The crisis situation pushes the family to initiate change in and transformation of the family's schema. The family's ability to bounce back and transform itself—that is, to achieve balance and harmony—calls for changes in the family schema that will facilitate the achievement of congruency between the family's schema and the family's new patterns of functioning. Family scientists (McCubbin, McCubbin, et al., 1995) have introduced a typology of family strategies and processes involved in the family's efforts to modify its worldview and influence and legitimize the family's adopted patterns of functioning and meaning to foster family coherence (see Figure 2.1) and make family life and functioning more comprehensible, manageable, and meaningful. The typologies associated with the promotion of change and congruency with family patterns of functioning all focused on building family coherence include the following:

- **Spiritualization:** The process of framing the family crisis situation and changes in the family's patterns of functioning as part of the recovery process through an emphasis on spiritual beliefs and practices
- **Temporalization:** The process of framing the family crisis situation and change in the family's new and modified patterns of functioning as part of the recovery process through emphasizing the long- and short-term value and benefits derived from the situation
- **Naturalization:** The process of framing the family crisis situation and change as part of the family's "natural" recovery process in which the natural order of things and predictable elements of life is emphasized
- **Prioritization:** The process of framing the family crisis situation and change in the family's patterns of functioning as part of the recovery process involving a reexamination and reprioritization of values, beliefs, and expectations, which may vary from family member to family member
- **Collectivation:** The process of framing the family crisis situation and changes in the family's pattern of functioning as part of the recovery process through an emphasis on what is beneficial to the collective, the whole family, the family's relationship to the community, and

the total of relationships, with an added emphasis on the "we" as more important than the "I"

- **Culturation and multiculturation:** The process of framing the family crisis situation and changes in the family's patterns of functioning as part of the recovery process through the clarification, affirmation/reaffirmation, integration, and adaptation of the family's ethnic/multi-ethnic and cultural/multicultural history and practices

- **Acculturation:** The process of framing the family crisis situation and changes in the family's pattern's functioning as part of the recovery process grounded in the selective and strategic assimilation, modification, and adaptation of the values, beliefs, and practices of the majority group of people.

THE HAWAIIAN FAMILY: VULNERABILITY AND RESILIENCE

Scholars are reminded of the at-risk status of indigenous peoples. For example, Hawaiians are overrepresented in mortality rates of 26.4 (per 1,000) for infectious disease (versus 13 for all races), 29.0 for diabetes (versus 9.8 for all races), 46.1 for strokes (versus 35.1 for all races), 183.9 for cancer (versus 132 for all races), and 273.0 for heart attacks (versus 198 for all races) (McCubbin & McCubbin, 1997). These alarming statistics set the stage for a more comprehensive look at the survival and resilience of these indigenous people.

In an investigation of the functioning and well-being of Native Hawaiian families of preschool age children, McCubbin, McCubbin, and Thompson (1996) confirmed the importance of ethnic identity for individual family members and also as part of family schema in shaping the family's identity, as a resilience factor. Embedded in a measure of family ethnic schema (i.e., Hawaiian values, beliefs, expectation), ethnic identity emerged as a critical recovery factor in shaping the outcome of family resilience and adaptation (i.e., family well-being and functioning).

Using a path model to identify the direct and indirect influence of the resilience factor of family schema (shared ethnic identity—Native Hawaiian), the investigators (McCubbin et al., 1996) confirmed that family schema (including shared ethnic identity) was a significant and director predictor of other resilience factors of family's sense of coherence (i.e., family comprehensibility, manageability, and meaningfulness) and family problem-solving communication (i.e., high-affirming communication and low-incendiary communication). In turn, family sense of coherence (i.e., comprehensibility, manageability, and meaningfulness) had a direct and positive relationship with the resilience factors of family problem-solving communication (i.e., high-affirming communication and low-incendiary communication), the latter of which had a direct positive relationship with family adaptation (i.e., family well-being and functioning).

These findings (McCubbin et al., 1996) bring the constructs of culture and ethnic identity to center stage—as integral and vital competencies in the study of individuals and families of different ethnic and cultural backgrounds. These observations also place importance on the relatively unknown, suppressed, or ignored variable of family schema as a critical resilience factor in family life and underscore its direct and indirect bearing on the family's resilience and course of family functioning following a traumatic event. In addition, although not documented in this investigation, the findings suggest that a resilience factor may well be the family's capability and competency in modifying and transforming its schema in the process of family behavioral changes and adaptation. This proposition and principle has been advanced by Tedeschi and Calhoun (1995) as fundamental to the process of growth in the aftermath of trauma.

Family scholars engaged in the study of families under stress and family resilience share assumptions about family functioning in the face of stressors. The central commonality is that families engage in a roller-coaster course of adaptation. The course of family response and behavior over time follows a predictable pattern, beginning with the family in a stable state punctuated by the impact of a traumatic event or cluster of events that sends the family spiraling downward, reflecting family disorganization, disorientation, and dysfunction, followed by the processes of family recovery and resilience. The trajectory downward (crisis) and upward and bouncing back (resilience) depends on the family's vulnerability due to the pile up of stressors and strains and the strengths and adaptability of the family's recovery factors (i.e., individual, family, community recovery factors or competencies), the most salient of which are family hardiness, community and family social support, family coping, and family problem-solving communication. The concept of a "roller-coaster" course of adaptation is legitimized by the observation that families engage in a trial-and-error process to find the optimum "fit." In this search for fit, the family may adopt structures and behavioral changes that may not be accepted or congruent with the family's schema, thus spiraling the family downward again after a short recovery, moving the family back into a crisis state, starting the trajectory upward once again. This up-and-down cycle may repeat itself over time.

Family resilience, the process of bouncing back and adaptation following a family crisis, involves the process of restructuring and making changes in rule, boundaries, and patterns of functioning. To effect posttraumatic growth, Tedeschi and Calhoun (1995) argue that schema change will accompany the behavioral and pattern modification. Essentially, the established schema before the crisis will in all likelihood be disrupted and disorganized, producing the family's attempt to create a more useful and congruent schema (i.e., affirming and complementary to family behaviors and pattern change) that will promote the family's sense of coherence (i.e., comprehensibility, meaningfulness, and manageability). Thus, family growth, we argue, is possible because of change in schemas. Tedeschi and Calhoun (1995, p. 81) carry this point further in concluding that "growth is change in schemas" (see Figure 2.1).

The Native Hawaiian family, the *Ohana* (family) of the Kanaka Maoli or true people, for example, views resilience as a relational process. According to Marsella, Oliveira, Plummer, and Crabbe (1995) the Native Hawaiian family would best be viewed in an ecological context in which the family member (*Kamaaina*), the family unit (*Ohana*), nature (*Aina*), and the spiritual forces of the world (*uhane, akua, aumakua*) are viewed as interconnected and interdependent. The family is not only an integral part of the social fabric of society but also of the consciousness or mind of the Native Hawaiian. All these elements internal and external to the family unit are united and inseparable from the larger society, nature, and spiritual forces in the world.

Within this relational and family ecological perspective (McCubbin et al., 1996), the concept of *Lokahi* or harmony takes on a relational meaning involving the land, spiritual energy, and individuals and the family unity. A family knows, Marsella et al. (1995) argue, when *Lokahi* is achieved because the family unit experiences a general state of well-being characterized by the presence of energy (*Mana*), which is interdependent with the family unit, the individual members, the spirit, the social ecology, and nature—all as one in unity.

In the Native Hawaiian context, this ideal state may be referred to as *Pono* or *Ma'e, Ma'e*. This is the state that the family strives to achieve through seeking a balance and harmony closely related to the unity of the individual, family, nature, and the spiritual worlds. When this state is achieved, there is arguably optimum health, well-being, and functioning. McCubbin, Fleming, et al. (1995) point to the importance of culturally based resilience factors, including the placement of the "group or family" above self, investment in others through acts of altruism, commitment to conservation in the preservation of the land (*Aina*), and reverence and respect for the gods, rituals, and prayer.

Cross's (1995) sensitive portrayal of the common elements of the Hawaiians with those of the Native American families faced with trauma and oppression also underscores the importance of a relational point of view in describing the resilience in indigenous families. Only through an understanding of the holistic and complex relationship that come into play in achieving harmony do we come to appreciate that the goal of families is to thrive, not just survive. Of importance to the study of trauma and indigenous families, Cross (1995) calls our attention to the vital roles that these families play in teaching future generations about resilience and how to build these competencies for use in their futures. Families cultivate a learning environment and thus a set of learning experiences that facilitate what Cross called the sixth sense about where indigenous individuals and families are welcome and where they are not. Parents and siblings teach children to recognize the "subtle clues that spell danger." Family members interpret oppressive events from the media for young children and in so doing transmit information that cushions the assaults of the mainstream media. As adults, we learn to cope with and manage the dynamics of racial differences and pass on our strategies to our children.

In the context of family life, resilience is enhanced through the family process of self-talk and story-telling, acts through which knowledge is transmitted about managing life events and managing change. In this way, family members, young and old alike, learn proven strategies for using resources and adapting to change. In story-telling, families pass on stories of their lives, their skills, and in so doing, "we parent for resilience" (Cross, 1995). As McCubbin, McCubbin, et al. (1995) concluded, "When the family system focuses on achieving harmony, resilience is advanced by contributing to the balance among these forces" (p. 43).

CHALLENGES AND OPPORTUNITIES

Culture, by definition, is the sum total of knowledge passed on from generation to generation within a given society. Culture provides "meaning systems" in that it generally structures cognitive reality for an entire society (D'Andrade, 1984). Of importance to family resilience—the process of bouncing back from dramatic change, trauma, or catastrophe—D'Andrade (1984) affirms that culture, particularly its cultural meaning systems, has several key functions, the first of which is to enable the family within society to represent the world symbolically to its members and to persons outside of the family. In addition, culture has a constructive function of creating cultural entities that provide explanations of the world by way of rituals, scripted patterns of behavior, and rules to follow. Cultural meaning systems have both a directive function to guide persons in their behavior and a evocative function of creating rules for how to feel, by defining what a situation means. With these functions in mind, it is unequivocal that culture plays a key, although complex, role in the family's process of recovery and resilience.

Ethnic identity, gains the same prominence both for individual members and the family system, for it gives social and psychological meaning and serves as a basis for belonging to a larger group beyond the family. In the context of family resilience, ethnic identity serves to shape the "group's" sense of who they are as a collective unit in a larger society. Predictably, identity, and ethnic identity in particular give the individual and family unit a basis on which to explain behavior and interpret the social meanings of experiences. Ethnic identity plays a key role in the resilience process, for it has a significant part in shaping an individual's self-esteem and self-efficacy; it shapes the family's sense of viability and function as well as worth and confidence, all of which are essential foundations for resilience.

Even with a long history of knowledge about the anthropologist's view of ethnicity, culture, and behavior, as well as the psychologist's understanding of identity, we are novices approaching a crossroads in research and theory building to explain how culture and ethnic identity—under what circumstances and for what groups—come to promote resilience and family resilience in particular. This chapter offers but a glimpse of the elements or recovery factors that shape the resilience process. We have only scratched the surface of the dynamic processes involved and how they work together to accomplish the family's recoverability and adaptation following trauma.

One of the critical issues common to both resilience factors, culture and ethnic identity, is the reality of the proliferation of multicultural families with multicultural identities. Furthermore, culture and identities are constituted in different historical contexts. For example, the Native American living in the 1940s with the experience of World War II might experience his or her ethnic identity very differently from the Native American in the 21st century. The social cultural meanings attached to each person's ethnicity are so different as to render meaningless the project of describing one Native American in terms of the other. Consequently, in the current era of interracial marriages, cultural and ethnic identity categories may be neither stable nor internally homogeneous, thus presenting unique challenges to the theorist, research scholar, and clinicians who are called on to understand this complexity, predict behavior, prevent crises, and facilitate recovery and resilience. The decade ahead presents numerous challenges for all who have a commitment to serving families in need and promoting their growth in an era of rapid social and technological change.

REFERENCES

Beauvias, F., & Oetting, E. (1999). Drug use, resilience, and the myth of the golden child. In M. Glantz & J. Johnson (Eds.), *Resilience and development: Positive life adaptations* (pp. 101–106). New York: Plenum Press.

Berkner, L. K. (1972). The stem family and the development cycle of the peasant household: An eighteenth-century Austrian example. *American History Review, 77,* 398–418.

Braun, K. (1998). *Surveying community attitudes on end-of-life options.* Honolulu: University of Hawaii, Center on Aging.

Braun, K., & Nichols, R. (1996). Cultural issues in death and dying. *Hawaii Medical Journal, 55,* 260–264.

Brokenleg, M., & Middleton, D. (1993). Native Americans: Adapting, yet remaining. In D. P. Irish, K. F. Lundquist, & V. J. Nelsen (Eds.), *Ethnic variations in dying, death, and grief* (pp. 101–112). Washington, DC: Taylor & Francis.

Burr, W. (1973). *Theory construction and the sociology of the family.* New York: John Wiley.

Carrese, J. A., & Rhodes, L. A. (1995). Western bioethics on the Navajo reservation: Benefit or harm? *Journal of American Medical Association, 274,* 826–829.

Cross, T. L. (1995). Understanding family resiliency from a relational worldview. In H. I. McCubbin, E. A. Thompson, A. I. Thompson, & J. E. Fromer (Eds.), *Resiliency in ethnic minority families: Native and immigrant American Families* (Vol. 1, pp. 143–157). Thousand Oaks, CA: Sage.

Cuellar, J. B. (1990). Hispanic American aging: Geriatric education curriculum development for selected health professionals. In M. S. Harper (Ed.), *Minority aging: Essential curricula content for selected health and allied health professionals* (DHHS Publication No. HRS P-DV-90-4, pp. 365–413). Washington, DC: Government Printing Office.

D'Andrade, R. G. (1984). Cultural meaning systems. In R. A. Shweder & R. A. LeVine (Eds.), *Culture theory: Essays on mind, self, and emotion* (pp. 88–119). Cambridge, UK: Cambridge University Press.

French, J., & Schwartz, D. R. (1976). Terminal care at home in two cultures. In P. J. Brink (Ed.), *Transcultural nursing: A book of readings* (pp. 247–255). Englewood Cliffs, NJ: Prentice Hall.

Hill, R. (1949). *Families under stress.* New York: Harper & Row.

Ishisaka, H. A. (1992). Significant differences between Pacific-Asian and Western cultures. In J. Fischer (Ed.), *East-west directions: Social work practice, tradition, and change.* Honolulu: University of Hawaii, School of Social Work.

Kaufert, J. M., & O'Neil, J. D. (1991). Cultural mediation of dying and grieving among Native Canadian patients in urban hospitals. In D. R. Counts & D. A. Counts (Eds.), *Coping with the final tragedy: Cultural variations in dying and grieving* (pp. 231–251). Amityville, NY: Baywood.

Kluckhohn, C., & Leighton, D. (1946). *The Navaho* (Rev. ed.). Garden City, NY: Doubleday.

Koenig, B. (1997). Cultural diversity in decision-making about care at the end of life. In Institute of Medicine (Ed.), *Approaching death: Improving care at the end of life* (pp. 363–382). Washington, DC: National Academy Press.

Kosciulek, R., McCubbin, M. A., & McCubbin, H. I. (1993). A theoretical framework for family adaptation to head injury. *Journal of Rehabilitation, 59,* 40–45.

Levy, D. R. (1985). Caucasian doctors and African American patients: Influence of race on the doctor-patient relationship. *Pediatrics, 75,* 639–643.

Lewis, R. (1990). Death and dying among the American Indians. In J. K. Parry (Ed.), *Social work practice with the terminally ill: A transcultural perspective* (pp. 23–31). Springfield, IL: Charles C Thomas.

Li, Y. Y. (1968). Ghost marriage, shamanism, and kinship behavior in rural Taiwan. In *folk religion and the world view in the Southwestern Pacific.*

Tokyo: Keio University, Keio Institute of Cultural and Linguistic Studies.

Lincoln, C. E., & Miyama, L. H. (1991). *The African American church in the African American experience.* Durham, NC: Duke University Press.

Lombardi, F., & Lombardi, G. S. (1982). *Life and death: The cycle is timeless.* Happy Camp, CA: Naturegraph.

Marsella, A. J., Oliveira, J. M., Plummer, C. M., & Crabbe, K. M. (1995). Native Hawaiian (Kanaka Maoli) culture, mind, and well-being. In H. I. McCubbin, E.A. Thompson, A. I. Thompson, & J. E. Fromer (Eds.), *Resiliency in ethnic minority families: Native and immigrant American Families* (Vol. 1, pp. 93–113). Thousand Oaks, CA: Sage.

Martin, C. L., & Halverson, C. F. (1981). A schematic processing model of sex typing and stereotyping in children. *Child Development, 52,* 1119–1134.

Mason, S. M., & Trible, J. E. (1982). American Indian and Alaska Native communities. In L. R. Snowden (Ed.), *Reaching the underserved: Mental health needs of neglected populations* (pp. 143–163). Thousand Oaks, CA: Sage.

McCabe, M. (1994). Patient Self-Determination Act: A Native American (Navajo) perspective. *Cambridge Quarterly of Healthcare Ethics, 3,* 419–421.

McCubbin, H. I. (1995). Resiliency in African-American families: Military families in foreign environments. In H. I. McCubbin, E. A. Thompson, A. I. Thompson, & J. Fromer (Eds.), *Resiliency in ethnic minority families: Native and immigrant American families* (Vol.1, pp. 67–97). Thousand Oaks, CA: Sage.

McCubbin, H. I., Boss, P., Wilson, L., & Lester, G. (1980). Developing family invulnerability to stress: Coping patterns and strategies wives employ in managing family separations. In J. Trost (Ed.), *The family and change* (pp. 186–173). Västerås, Sweden: International Library Publishing.

McCubbin, H. I., & Dahl, B. B. (1976). Prolonged family separation in the military: A longitudinal study. In H. I. McCubbin, B. Dahl, & E. Hunter (Eds.), *Families in the military system* (pp. 146–176). Thousand Oaks, CA: Sage.

McCubbin, H. I., Fleming, M., Thompson, A. I., Neitman, P., Elver, K., & Savas, S. (1995). Resiliency and coping in "at risk" African American youth and their families. In H. I.

McCubbin, E. A. Thompson, A. I. Thompson, & J. Fromer (Eds.), *Resiliency in ethnic minority families: Native and immigrant American families* (Vol. 1, pp. 287–328). Thousand Oaks, CA: Sage.

McCubbin H. I., & Lavee, Y. (1986). Strengthening army families: A family life cycle stage perspective. *Evaluation and Program Planning, 9,* 221–231.

McCubbin, H. I., & McCubbin, L. D. (1997). Hawaiian American families. In M. K. DeGenova (Ed.), *Families in a cultural context: Strengths and challenges in diversity* (pp. 237–263). Mountain View, CA: Mayfield.

McCubbin, H. I., & McCubbin, M. A. (1988). Typologies of resilient families: Emerging roles of social class and ethnicity. *Family Relations, 37,* 247–254.

McCubbin, H., McCubbin, M., & Thompson, A. (1992). Resiliency in families: The role of family schema and appraisal in family adaptation to crises. In T. Brubaker (Ed.), *Families in transition* (pp. 86–100). Thousand Oaks, CA: Sage.

McCubbin, H. I., McCubbin, M. A., & Thompson, A. I. (1996). *Family assessment: Resiliency, coping and adaptation–inventories for research and practice.* Madison: University of Wisconsin System.

McCubbin, H. I., McCubbin, M. A., & Thompson, A. I. (2002). *Family measures: stress, coping and resilience.* Honolulu, HI: Kamehameha Schools.

McCubbin, H. I., McCubbin, M., Thompson, A., & Thompson, E. (1995). Resilience in ethnic families: A conceptual model for predicting family adjustment and adaptation. In H. I. McCubbin, E. A. Thompson, A. I. Thompson, & J. Fromer (Eds.), *Resiliency in ethnic minority families: Native and immigrant American families* (Vol. 1, pp. 3–48). Thousand Oaks, CA: Sage.

McCubbin, H. I., & Patterson, J. M. (1983a). The family stress process: The double ABCX model of adjustment and adaptation. In H. I. McCubbin, M. Sussman, & J. Patterson (Eds.), *Social stress and the family: Advances and developments in family stress theory and research* (pp. 26–47). New York: Haworth.

McCubbin, H. I., & Patterson, J. M. (1983b). Family transitions: Adaptation to crisis: A double ABCX model of family behavior. In D. Olson & B. Miller (Eds.), *Family studies review yearbook* (pp. 87–107). Thousand Oaks, CA: Sage.

McCubbin, H. I., Thompson, A. I., Pirner, P., & McCubbin, M. A. (1988). *Family types and strengths: A life cycle and ecological perspective.* Edina, MN: Burgess International.

McCubbin, L. D. (2003). *Resilience among Native Hawaiian adolescents: Ethnic identity, psychological distress and wellbeing.* Doctoral dissertation, University of Wisconsin–Madison.

McCubbin, M. A., & McCubbin, H. I. (1987). Family stress theory and assessment: The T-double ABCX model of family adjustment and adaptation. In H. I. McCubbin & A. I. Thompson (Eds.), *Family assessment inventories for research and practice* (pp. 3–34). Madison: University of Wisconsin–Madison.

McCubbin, M. A., & McCubbin, H. I. (1989). Theoretical orientations to family stress and coping. In C. R. Figley (Ed.), *Treating stress in families* (pp. 67–89). New York: Brunner/Mazel.

McCubbin, M. A., & McCubbin, H. I. (1993). Families coping with illness: The resiliency model of family stress, adjustment and adaptation. In C. Danielson, B. Hamel-Bissell, & P. Winstead-Fry (Eds.), *Families, health and illness* (pp. 121–143). New York: Mosby.

Miller, L. (1969). Child rearing in the kibbutz. In J. G. Howells (Eds.), *Modern perspectives in international child psychiatry* (pp. 141–162). Edinburgh, Scotland: Oliver & Boyd.

Mohanty, S. P. (1993, Spring). The epistemic status of cultural identity: On beloved and the postcolonial condition. *Cultural Critique, 24,* 41–80.

Mokuau, N. (1992). A conceptual framework for cultural responsiveness in the health field. In J. Fischer (Ed.), *East-west directions: Social work practice, tradition, and change* (pp. 118–130). Honolulu: University of Hawaii, School of Social Work.

Mouton, C. P. (2000). Cultural and religious issues for African Americans. In K. Braun, J. Pietsch, & P. Blanchette (Eds.), *Cultural issues in end-of-life decision making* (pp. 71–82). Thousand Oaks, CA: Sage.

Moya, P. (2000). Postmodernism, "realism," and the politics of identity: Cherrie Moraga and Chicana feminism. In P. M. Moya & M. R. Hamea-Garcia (Eds.), *Reclaiming identity: Realist theory and the predicament of postmodernism* (pp. 67–101). Berkeley: University of California Press.

Olson, D. H., McCubbin, H. I. Barnes, H., Larsen, A., Muxen, A., & Wilson, L. (1983). *Families: What makes them work.* Thousand Oaks, CA: Sage.

Pelzel, J. (1970). Japanese kinship: A comparison. In M. Freedman (Ed.), *Family and kinship in Chinese society* (pp. 78–191). Stanford, CA: Stanford University Press.

Phinney, J. S. (1990). Ethnic identity in adolescents and adults: Review of research. *Psychological Bulletin, 108*(3), 499–514.

Phinney, J. S. (1992). The Multigroup Ethnic Identity Measure: A new scale for use with diverse groups. *Journal of Adolescent Research, 7*(2), 156–176.

Phinney, J. S., & Alipuria, L. L. (1990). Ethnic identity in college students from four ethnic groups. *Journal of Adolescence, 13,* 171–183.

Phinney, J. S., Cantu, C. L., & Kurtz, D. A. (1997). Ethnic and American identity as predictors of self-esteem among African American, Latino and white adolescents. *Journal of Youth and Adolescence, 26*(2), 165–185.

Rael, R., & Korte, A. O. (1988). El ciclo de la vida y muerte: An analysis of death and dying in a selected Hispanic enclave. In S. R. Applewhite (Ed.), *Hispanic elderly in transition: Theory, research, policy and practice* (pp. 189–202). Westport, CT: Greenwood.

Roberts, R., Phinney, J. S., Masse, L. C., & Chen, R. (1999). The structure of ethnic identity of young adolescents from diverse ethnocultural groups. *Journal of Early Adolescence, 19*(3), 301–322.

Segal, Z. (1988). Appraisal of the self-schema construct in cognitive models of depression. *Psychological Bulletin, 103*(2), 147–162.

Simeone, W. E. (1991). The northern Athabaskan potlatch: The objectification of grief. In D. R. Counts & D. A. Counts (Eds.), *Coping with the final tragedy: Cultural variations in dying and grieving* (pp. 157–167), Amityville, NY: Baywood.

Tajfel, H., & Turner, J. (1986). The social identity of intergroup behavior. In S. Worchel & W. Austin (Eds.), *The social psychology of intergroup relations* (pp. 7–24). Chicago: Nelson-Hall.

Talamantes, M. A., Lawler, W. R, & Espino, D. V. (1995). Hispanic American elders: Caregiving norms surrounding dying and the use of hospice services. *Hospice Journal, 10*(4), 35–49.

Tedeschi, R. G., & Calhoun, L. G. (1995). *Trauma and transformation: Growing in the aftermath of suffering.* Thousand Oaks, CA: Sage.

Thompson, E. A., McCubbin, H. I., Thompson, A. I., & Elver, K. (1995). Vulnerability and resiliency in Native Hawaiian families under stress. In H. I. McCubbin, E. A. Thompson, A. I. Thompson, & J. Fromer (Eds.), *Resiliency in ethnic minority families: Native and immigrant American families* (Vol. 1, pp. 115–131), Thousand Oaks, CA: Sage.

Tseng, W. S., & Hsu, J. (1986). The family in Micronesia. In W. S. Tseng & C. A. Less (Eds.), *Culture and mental health in Micronesia.* Honolulu: University of Hawaii, John A. Burns School of Medicine, Department of Psychiatry.

Tseng, W. S., & Hsu, J. (1991). *Culture and family: Problems and therapy.* New York: Haworth.

U.S. Bureau of the Census. (1993). *We the . . . American Pacific Islanders.* Washington, DC: Government Printing Office.

Wallace, E., & Hoebel, E.A. (1952). *The Comanches: Lords of the south plains.* Norman: University of Oklahoma Press.

Yeo, G., & Hikoyeda, N. (2000). Cultural issues in end-of-life decision making among Asians and Pacific Islanders in the United States. In K. Braun, J. Pietsch, & P. Blanchette (Eds.), *Cultural issues in end-of-life decision making* (pp. 101–126). Thousand Oaks, CA: Sage.

3

Lessons Learned From Poor African American Youth

Resilient Strengths in Coping With Adverse Environments

Joyce West Stevens

Because of the many social problems in modern American society, scholars have suggested that America is a *nation at risk*. Although this claim may seem hardly credible for the richest and most powerful nation in the world, empirical data suggest that a significant number of young Americans suffer the consequences of social ills that jeopardize future possibilities for meeting the challenges of a participatory democracy. Poverty, homelessness, HIV/AIDS, child maltreatment, adolescent parenting, substance abuse, school dropout, suicide, imprisonment, delinquency, and violence have all been identified as social problems that threaten the psychological, social, and physical health of American youth and the integrity of American society (McWhirter, McWhirter, McWhirter, & McWhirter, 1998). Of special concern is that many social problems disproportionately afflict people of color. As such, the most vulnerable populations have the least social and economic resources, thereby limiting genuine prospects for social mobility. Accordingly, scholars contend that young African American males fueled by

their inability to claim a legitimate stake in society become involved in illegal drug use during early adulthood. What is more, once drug careers have developed, they are easily maintained by a drug infrastructure that promotes violence and profiteering (Gibbs, 1988; Stevens, 2001; Wallace, 1999; Wilson, 1987).

Reasonably, some scholars have therefore raised questions concerning the utility of a risk construct, suggesting that it represents a deficit model that "blames the victim" (Swadener & Lubeck, 1995). Arguably, when risks are viewed as a consequence of problems in society as a whole, there is little need to "blame the victim." Furthermore, despite adverse social conditions, some youth—perhaps all too few in such circumstances—nonetheless, do exhibit a power of endurance and competence that enables them to transcend environs replete with risks (Ford, 1994; Garmezy, 1993; Jarrett, 1995; Stevens, 1997; Wallace, 1999; Williams & Kornblum, 1985, 1994). Thus, I suggest elsewhere that resilience and risk *are* functional constructs that help clarify the intersection of social context and behavioral responses (Stevens, 2002). Given the vagaries of life, mundane circumstances are never all bad or all good but, rather, a mixture of both favorable and unfavorable conditions. Notwithstanding, I make use of the at-risk concept to refer to those circumstances that are heavily weighted on the side of being unfavorable or toxic and, as such, pose grave threats to safety and well-being. Although there are several models of risk (cumulative, additive, interactive), being at risk is ordinarily understood to indicate exposure to circumstances of harm or jeopardy in environs in which individuals and families are situated. Resilience on the other hand is achieving a good outcome from harsh circumstances as well as the management of risks to avoid misfortune or harm.

In this chapter, I suggest that the concepts of both risk and resilience have veritable utility for understanding marginalized youth in inner-city communities where many neighborhoods are characterized by unsafe environments, economic impoverishment, and depleted social resources. First, I contend that the ecological framework is a conceptual tool that brings into focus the intersection of persons, process, and social context and thus clarifies the manner in which the concepts of risk and resilience are operative in lived experience. Second, I will argue that the gravity of present-day challenges that economically disadvantaged youth face necessitates change in how we understand the nature of their achievements and strengths. Hence, I propose that practitioners can learn a great deal from resilient inner-city African American youth and their families about what is needed to succeed in adverse environments. Based on research, attributes of resilience that play a part in self-affirmation and social mobility will be discussed. Last, I suggest that youth are helped best by supporting their attributes of resilience.

RESEARCHING RESILIENCE: A CULTURAL ETHNIC STANDPOINT

The interpretation of ethnographic or qualitative data may be conducted from a standpoint epistemology—that is, from the lived experiences of the research participants themselves.

This interpretative method requires the researcher to work from the outside to the center (Collins, 1986, 1990; Denzin, 1997; hooks, 1984). A standpoint text starts from the lived experiences of those considered to be "other" or outside mainstream society. This form of reporting narrative renders data less objective and abstract (Smith, 1989). In this regard, respondents' texts reflect intersections of class, ethnicity, and gender, yielding a multivocal text. All things considered, a multivocal text is created when the researcher is located inside the cultural narrative and carries on extensive dialogue as if a member of a valued cultural group. As a researcher, it has been a humbling learning experience and a privilege to enter the lives of African American female research participants to gain knowledge of their "ways of knowing" how to cope with adverse conditions. Moreover, as an African American female, I have the privilege of being situated inside the historical cultural narrative of the "black experience"; I too am marginalized in the larger societal context as "other."

The situated experiences of ethnic outsiders are manifest concretely within a societal hierarchy distinguished by the social status of racial/ethnic devaluation and oppression. At the same time, however, my cultural ethnicity is one I share with research participants; hence, I am positioned as an "insider." Recognizably, a researcher's insider knowledge can be both an asset and a liability (Kanuha, 2000). Being all too ready with assumptions, an insider can presume to know about who research participants are and how they live their lives, minimizing an investigator's objectivity. For sure, there are limitations regarding my insider position by virtue of class and lack of personal knowledge with reference to the problems under investigation. At the same time, however, these personal characteristics could allow for objectivity and, as such, minimize bias. Indeed, the one most important lesson I learned from study participants over and over again is that resiliency exists in the direst of circumstances. Significantly, this lesson served as a caution to rethink notions of what it means to be at risk and resilient and how the two constructs operate in the lives of poor black females.

For my purposes here, qualitative and quantitative findings from research studies of economically disadvantaged inner-city black females that include studies of late-aged (17–19 years) pregnant and nonpregnant girls and early-aged (11–14 years) middle school girls provide the data for theorizing about how indigent but resilient black youth deal with adverse environments. Study samples were characterized by social indices suggesting that both groups were from impoverished environments. In the middle school study, a clinical intervention to improve school performance and adjustment was tested in a quasi-experimental design. The clinical group intervention sessions were audiotaped and used as qualitative data. Girls referred to the program displayed at-risk behaviors such as poor academic performance, excessive tardiness, absences, and school suspensions because of fights with peers. The pregnancy research was conducted to contrast and compare pregnant and nonpregnant females with regard to their self-perceptions and perceptions of the surroundings in which they lived. This research has been reported extensively elsewhere, most recently in the text *Smart & Sassy: The Strengths of Inner City Black Girls* (Stevens, 2002). Because research participants were all female, I use corresponding pronouns. As one would expect, the value of qualitative research such as this was that participants' narratives are contextualized, with the ordinary manner in which most people engage in discourse under study. Information is processed from within the multileveled social contexts in which we find ourselves grounded. The open-ended adolescent pregnancy study questionnaire that was used elicited narrative accounts about a girl's family, neighborhood, peers, and school. By doing this, stories were contextualized naturally so as to construct meaning and complexity in how I understood these girls' thinking and behavior. This process is called *contexting* (Hall, 1971).

A THEORETICAL FRAMEWORK FOR RISK AND RESILIENCE

Like others (Brunswick, 1999; Spencer, 1995), I draw on the ideas of Bronfenbrenner (1979) to consider an ecological perspective in my theorizing about at-risk social contexts, risk behaviors, and resiliency among African Americans. Briefly stated, Bronfenbrenner suggests that

an ecological system includes nested contexts within systemic domains of bio-psycho-social-historical influences that affect individual development. Namely, social contexts are the "nested contexts" of an individual's life and include a person's family, school, peers, church, neighborhood activities, and sociocultural structural conditions. The nested contexts within systemic domains are multileveled, bidirectional (reciprocal), and transactional such that the activities and persons within a given context affect the individual, who in turn has a reciprocal impact on the same social context. Consider abstractly Bronfenbrenner's systemic domains as concentric circles represented by numerical sequencing from center to outer spheres. Each circle represents a different level of abstraction: (1) ontogenetic (the individual person); (2) microsystem (family-kin, neighborhood activities, groups, and institutions); (3) mesosystem (larger community institutions, groups, and organizations); (4) exosystem (national institutions and social structures of health, welfare, business industries, financial centers, mass media); (5) macrosystem (societal attitudes and ideologies that induce structural strain); and (6) chronosystems (aspects of time, patterning of environmental events and transactions over the life course, sociocultural historical conditions, and structural strain). At this sixth level, structural strain refers to the structural barriers that block access to opportunities, privilege, and power over time. An illustrative example might be the perpetuity of "the old boys' network" of white Anglo-Saxon protestant males who have garnered prime opportunities for amassing wealth in high-status careers. Characterized by transactional intersubjective processes within contexts and between contexts, the ecological perspective is context dependent. Risk and resilience when interpreted in this light are operational within a transactional model of process and social context. What one experiences is conspicuously the result of intersubjective processes between individuals and institutions that make judgments regarding what is adaptive or maladaptive. Institutional intersubjectivity may be reflected, for example, in how well social policies and social policy formulation are tailored to meet the needs of individuals (Crossley, 1996). However, we can just as easily ignore the higher levels of policy and look only at individuals and their maladaptive lifestyles and behaviors, a position that returns us once again to blaming the victim rather than understanding the intersubjectivity of people's experiences. Individual maladaptation may manifest itself as a lack of compassion (*empathy*), a lack of a shared sense of care for others and affinity with them (*mutuality*), a seeking of *recognition* in viciously destructive behaviors, a lack of *assertion,* or the affirmation of the self through acts of violence. In this regard, it has been well documented (Anderson, 1999; Bolland, 2001; Bourgois, 1995; Ratner, 1993; Sterk, 1999) that maladaptive lifestyles (e.g., drug kingpins) pose threats (*risks*) to the quality of life in inner-city communities. This is, of course, not debatable. However, we may need to question, from an ecological point of view, the role that social forces play in making these behaviors more desirable to some populations of marginalized individuals.

Benjamin (1990) has argued that intersubjective attunements of recognition and assertion are operationalized reflexively in that they are mirrored and validated through others. Given this, I have chosen to focus this psychosocial inquiry on the following: (a) the nature of a girl's intersubjective transactions within and between social contexts; (b) the makeup of a girl's contexting or construction of meaning regarding self and surroundings; (c) the nature, content, and attitudinal perception of those social contexts in which a girl is deeply rooted; (d) the nature, content, and attitudinal perception of the social contexts in which a girl seeks to meet immediate needs; and (e) the nature, content, and attitudinal perception of the social context a girl seeks or desires to negotiate to meet future needs. Practically, this five-point query provides information that depicts portraitures about a girl's self-organization and self-regulation related to her intersubjective responses of empathy, assertion, and recognition and her attitudinal perceptions of others and various social contexts, and a girl's perception of the significance of a range of social contexts in meeting immediate needs and future goals. Perceptibly, this kind of inquiry yields rich data about risk and resiliency within the contexts of the adolescent's lived experiences. Thus, participants'

evaluative perceptions reveal judgments about favorable and unfavorable ecological conditions that lead to or inhibit the formation of resiliency.

I claim two basic assumptions that undergird my theorizing in this way. Significantly, the first assumption is the commonplace understanding that human beings by nature are relational and grounded in social context. Equally important, my second assumption is that adolescents commonly covet a relationship with an older adult—one that offers consistent emotional attunement, guidance, and direction and that validates personal and collective experiences. A practitioner, for example, often builds on this normative and expected role modeling function required by adolescents. A primary relationship with a significant adult has been empirically documented as a capacity-enhancing attribute of resilient adolescent girls. Undeniably, a practitioner's relationship with adolescents can offer an intersubjective experience of fundamental consequence. The following illustrative examples, taken from my research, explore the intersubjective world of African American girls and the interface between them as individuals and the multilevel ecology of the social and political factors that affect their well-being.

ILLUSTRATIVE EXAMPLES

Seminal ideas about person, process, and contexts begin to take hold when conducting research in an inner-city neighborhood middle school. Long hours were spent at the school. By chance, I became a participant observer, studying the varied intersubjective transactions among stakeholders (i.e., students, administrators, teachers, and auxiliary staff) that took place in the general surroundings of the school. My observations led me to understand that the school staff was generally not supportive of the girls in the study and did not see them in a good light. The girls' behaviors generated insensitive gossip among school staff, the content of which denigrated and devalued the girls. Importantly, the girls were well aware that they were viewed negatively by school personnel. The following description, illustrates how recognition, empathy, and assertion operate within two contextual fields among a group of middle school adolescent girls. The clinician who worked with the girls in the intervention study program was a social work intern.

The study girls were viewed by the school staff as displaying loud, boisterous, and brassy behaviors. Teachers complained that the girls argued and talked back to them. The girls were all given the label of conduct disorder by the school social worker, and the teachers were in agreement with this labeling. Interestingly, the girls in turn saw their teachers as not earning *their* respect, contemptuous of their scholastic efforts, and not invested in their learning. It was hard to disagree once immersed in the school ecology. Some of the teachers in the school seemed so overwhelmed by what they identified as "too many discipline problems" that their commitment to teaching was compromised by a failure to deal effectively with the many problems students presented. Likewise, the teachers were accurate in their observations of the girls as loud and argumentative. Eventually, the girls accepted responsibility for their confrontational behaviors, admitting that although their actions were defiant, it was a way they had managed to cope with feelings of being "put down." The girls questioned whether their being black was the reason they were treated disapprovingly by their teachers, who were white. From the girls' perspective, being argumentative or "speaking up" displayed self-affirmation and provided protection against feelings of powerlessness and devaluation.

In another realm, the girls used a very different set of coping strategies. In particular, they were in a quandary about what to do when adult males in their neighborhoods approached them sexually. Such advances offended the girls; unresponsive and frightened, they felt violated. What is more, the girls' unspoken disinterest provoked rude insults from the men that shocked, angered, and scared them even more. The intern helped the girls to appreciate the varied contextual complexities of their neighborhood and school. In addition, she clarified the girls' healthy need for self-affirmation (*assertion*) and their failed attempts to gain the respect (*recognition*) desired from the school setting. When engaged in this manner, the girls were willing to disclose feelings of helplessness and vulnerability and the social and personal devaluation they felt in both social contexts. As affective disclosures were acknowledged, intersubjective processes of empathy, recognition, and assertion were strengthened to the degree that self-awareness of affinity (*mutuality*) intensified the bond between them and their caregivers. Moreover, the girls had obtained from each other sympathetic understanding (*empathy*), respect (*recognition*), and affirmation (*assertion*); supported by their peer group experience, the girls enhanced their sense of self-efficacy in other social contexts. As the intern observed, in school, the girls were outspoken and seemingly self-assured, whereas in the context of their neighborhood streets, they were indeed intimidated and angered but silent.

Clearly, the girls' neighborhood presented them with multiple risks—in one case, sexual harassment and seduction by older men, in the other, a school climate that devalued them and their behavior. Through the group intervention, the girls were helped to evaluate distinctly diverse social contexts, deciding on the appropriateness of their responses within each. The purpose of the intervention was to enhance self-organization and self-regulation to aid the development of more elaborate and meaningful responses in different situations. In addition, the intent was to improve understanding of the best way to respond to varied social contexts. The intern enabled the girls to understand the need to choose different behaviors, assessing the best fit between their behavior and the demands of each context. The intern clarified the meaning of appropriate behaviors, when it was proper to turn up the verbal volume (i.e., to be self-affirming by being outspoken, blunt, candid, and loud when rejecting unwanted sexual advances) and when it was fitting and proper to turn down vocalizations (i.e., a quieter vocal style of self-affirmation in the school environment). Furthermore, clinicians empathically clarified developmental issues underlying each circumstance. For example, developmentally, adolescent girls undergo many physical changes and have many concerns about body image. Girls at this age naturally wish to be seen as attractive. The girls were confused by wishes to be sexually attractive and the anger they experienced at the vulgar lasciviousness of the older men. The social work intern validated the girls' normal developmental issues as well as pointedly expressed indignation about the "indecent behavior of the men." Observably, the girls' natural self-confidence and capacity to discern threats to their well-being were characteristics associated with resilience that were enhanced by the intern's interventions.

As this example illustrates, even though the individual is the focal point of Bronfenbrenner's (1979) ecological perspective, the person-process-context paradigm allows for a bio-psycho-social-historical systemic assessment of social contexts. The adolescent pregnancy research participants no less than the middle school intervention study participants demonstrated these same qualities of mutuality, empathy, recognition, and assertion in everyday life. One part of the adolescent pregnancy research hypothesized that nonpregnant girls are more likely than pregnant girls to develop links with their communities beyond their immediate families and peers. Such linkages are represented by engagement in church, community, employment, and educational environments. Findings supported this hypothesis. Nonpregnant girls differed from the pregnant girls at a < .05 level of significance on critical behavioral, psychological, educational, and situational variables. Unquestionably, both cohorts displayed what now are identified as resilient behaviors; however, nonpregnant girls consistently exhibited a certain individuality that demonstrated stability and hardiness in engagements with nonpeer and nonkin social contexts, such as church, social clubs, jobs, and college. Surprisingly, study results revealed that nonpregnant girls were more likely to express a strong sense of care and nurturance for others, whereas pregnant girls, although soon to be parents, were less likely to express this same care and nurturance (expressed *mutuality* and *empathy* as shared affinity with others). In view of the theoretical model set forth, it could be argued that nonpregnant girls were more likely to have sophisticated contexting experiences than their counterparts because of their involvement in varied social settings. One might conclude that the nonpregnant girls' diverse contextual experiences provided opportunities for a wide range of occurrences where intersubjective (*self-relatedness*) processes of empathy, recognition, and assertion could be played out.

Bearing in mind the distinction between the elements of a social context that includes form, intersubjectivity, and content, the adolescent pregnancy research participants provided rich qualitative data about their neighborhoods and families, including information about a vicinity's or a kin network's composition and organization, its self-relatedness (intersubjective processes), and its substance or essence (content and quality of life). Importantly, the distinction between context *structure,* context *intersubjectivity,* and context *content* is necessary because critics (Delgado, 2000; Swadener & Lubeck, 1995) of the at-risk construct mistakenly confound *form, process,* and *content.* Notwithstanding, the ecological model of context is holistic, intersectional, and transactional, making it possible to differentiate interrelated characteristics of a particular social context's elements of form, content, and process. Hence, the model can integrate the at-risk concept with specific process and, contextually, aspects of resilience and protective mechanisms. It is not a matter of either assets or risks as the more important focus for study when examining urban neighborhoods or urban families but, rather, the degree to which both are present. If a social context has a greater elemental presence of risks than assets, then it is likely that the social context poses greater dangers than protections of safety and support. On the face of it all, context elements seem equally consequential, but on closer examination, this may not be the case.

Consider for example an economically disadvantaged, single-parent family of five living in substandard rental housing (form) that flagrantly poses dangers to physical safety, yet the family is strong in its history, values, and ethos (content). In the best possible way, the discourse within the family sensitively reflects empathy, care, respect, affirmation, and affinity (intersubjectivity) among members. And yet, there is a great deal of variety in both the risks this family faces and the strengths they bring to bear on coping with their adversity. On the positive side, the eldest daughter graduated from high school, is employed part-time, and attends college and a local Catholic Church. The mother, however, collects disability and is no longer employed. Other factors that must be considered include that the family's neighborhood is ethnically homogeneous, its occupants African American.

The neighborhood lays claim to economic and social resources, most of which are liquor stores, small groceries, beauty shops and barbershops, and a local YMCA recently renovated with a gym and swimming pool. Most housing in the neighborhood is substandard with the exception of a two-floor, walk-up public housing complex. A storefront church has been conspicuously present to neighborhood dwellers with its loudspeaker service broadcasts for several years; in addition, there is an established Catholic Church that has served the neighborhood for four generations. Drug gang profiteers have commandeered two old neighborhood buildings for selling and smoking crack cocaine. Unlike the more established services just noted, this threat to the community has been a part of the neighborhood for just two years.

On the face of it, the illustration can make no claim with reference to existent risks. It does not suggest that poverty, single-parent households, or the recent infiltration of drug lords automatically mean those in this neighborhood are at risk. Although, empirically, the three demographic indices are indeed associated with neighborhood risk, descriptively, the neighborhood context element discussed thus far is one of form. What is known is a little something about physical structures of social, economic, and religious resources that are conceivably assets to the neighborhood, its families, and their children. What is not known is information about the neighborhood's substance (content), its perceptions of how neighborhood stakeholders view their environs as an identified entity, especially regarding risks and assets. Importantly, other unrevealed information is the intersubjectivity of the neighborhood, stakeholders' self-relatedness in the daily praxis of the life of the neighborhood. Although the structure of neighborhood ecologies seems transparently visible for risk and asset identification, without additional data about remaining context elements of content and intersubjectivity, a risk and asset assessment is incomplete.

DISCOVERING THE STRENGTHS OF INNER-CITY AFRICAN AMERICAN GIRLS

Often, clinician biases take place when assessing various contextual domains in which African American adolescent girls live. For example, if a girl resides in a drug- and crime-ridden neighborhood, the hazardous environment in which she lives may contextually prejudice the clinician. Thus, the clinician's assessment is likely to emphasize what may appear to be obvious social and psychological pathologies rather than the girl's less obvious strengths. Too often, African American girls' demonstrated strengths in assertively dealing with toxic inner-city neighborhoods go unevaluated altogether or are assessed negatively. But it is precisely within the self-relatedness of the nested contexts where a girl is embedded, be they hazardous or risk-free, that her strength and resilience are developed and fostered in meeting maturational challenges. Admittedly, my understanding of this subject was developed from my investigation of adolescent black girls' self-narratives and reports about themselves and the social ecologies in which they were situated. Some of what I discovered about the girls was refreshingly new information, whereas other findings simply confirmed what other studies have already told us.

Both studies referred to earlier clearly show that resilient African American girls display a personal hardiness—a focused commitment to follow events through—and a strong sense of self-efficacy. They tend to develop coping strategies that make it possible for them to achieve good outcomes despite misfortune as well as steering clear of avoidable dangerous situations (Stevens, 2002). Lest we overlook the abundant evidence, poor African American inner-city families do develop particular strategies to nurture resilient capacities in their children. Jarrett (1995) has defined such families as "defended families." Accordingly, defended families make available role models in or outside the familial network, restrict peer relationships even within the kin group, and participate in social ecologies outside neighborhood or community boundaries. Furthermore, families protect their offspring from risk environments by enculturating principled values and a future orientation. Such is the case that protected families who exhibit psychosocial strengths, have a strong work ethic, are achievement oriented, have a sense of autonomy and responsibility, and are likely to postpone birthing and marriage until vocations are established and jobs secured. Interestingly, protected families go so far as to even restrict relationships with extended family members who share similar values and behaviors. Thus, protected families are ideally situated to support their offspring in meeting developmental challenges through the use of strategies that have proved successful in supporting adolescents in at-risk environments (Hill, 1997; McAdoo, 1997).

African American adolescent girls display various discernible strengths in meeting challenges of maturation that are context dependent. These include a range of core psychological strengths, behaviors, and actions that black, poor, inner-city girls show when dealing with perceived and actual threats to safety and well-being in varied social ecologies. Specifically, resilient adolescent females are likely to do the following:

- Have strong attachments to social and religious institutions that provide communal self-relatedness—institutions that serve as havens for identity exploration and the development of leadership skills
- Select appropriate role models as a way to formulate principles and standards that will guide present and future behavior
- Demonstrate efforts in making changes in environmental situations to accommodate more positive and favorable peer affiliations
- Seek self-experiences for the development of cultural flexibility or bicultural competency when moving beyond neighborhood or community boundaries
- Confront racially devalued situations without feeling self-blame
- Assume responsibility for their behavior
- Resist collusion in racial denigration
- Discriminately appraise their social context for experiences of self-efficacy
- Exhibit a stance and attitude of candidness, courage, and assertiveness in response to racial/ethnic devaluation and life's daily hassles in general.
- Manifest a discriminating capacity in evaluating the behavior of others
- Demonstrate a capacity for care, loyalty, and nurturance in relation to others
- Have self-expectancies for social mobility to "improve one's lot in life"

The resilient attributes identified here were drawn from girls' actual experiences in living out their lives. Such traits can be strengthened and sustained when girls are served by social workers. Even though the girls who displayed the above strengths were dealing with their lives ably, they were on a journey of maturation and could benefit from services that aid in their development. To best serve girls with backgrounds similar to those in my research will require rethinking the ways in which we practice helping. Once again, bearing in mind the person-process-social context paradigm, renewed services demand working with clinical participants contextually and intersubjectively. I conclude with a brief discussion of practice implications based on the argument set forth in this chapter.

PRACTICE IMPLICATIONS

Working Contextually and Intersubjectively

Working contextually and intersubjectively, the therapist is not limited by the physical characteristics of traditional therapy (i.e., professional office space) or by the therapeutic material being subject to analytical scrutiny. Rather, development is seen in a state of fluctuation that orders complexity and informs how structure and pattern arises from many different aspects of young people's lives. Plainly, what happens inside the boundaries of the therapeutic relationship as well as what takes place peripherally becomes the playing field for therapeutic work. In the therapeutic field, both conscious and unconscious elements bear on the adolescent's past, present, organized, and organizing experiences (rigid and flexible). All such elements in this gestalt make it possible to explore unhealthy and healthy aspects of self-relatedness (Orange, Atwood, & Stolorow, 1997).

In working intersubjectively and contextually, the core strengths of African American inner-city girls delineated here can be put to effective use in the clinical relationship. For example, when doing clinical work, empirically demonstrated strength-based characteristics could be used as assessment guidelines or therapeutic goals with girls who require the building up of their capacities to meet maturational challenges more effectively. In other words, when therapeutic work is completed, a client will have developed a set of psychosocial skills to live life more fully. In particular, based on the discussion earlier, it is hoped that an adolescent girl at the end of therapy will have a more developed capacity to exercise self-efficacy appropriately in different contexts. Working intersubjectively and contextually, successful and effective clinical work strengthens the adolescent girl in a number of ways. She has a more developed capacity for self-reflection; makes pragmatic and judicious use of coping abilities; has an awareness of her gifts, talents, and strengths; and demonstrates a strengthened capacity for assessment of self and others within varied social contexts.

Social work clinical interventions take place in a relational matrix of self-relatedness, a mutually relational, culturally nuanced space where the clinician joins with the adolescent as an empathic insider. In so doing, the clinical relationship grows to be one of collaboration, and a significant piece of the clinical work becomes contexting. Recall that contexting is defined as the enhancement of the adolescent's capacity to develop meaning and complexity in thinking and behavior. Thus, the adolescent girl's self-journey within the therapeutic relationship becomes one of identity exploration and self-discovery as the clinical work addresses mutually agreed-on issues, problems, and concerns. In undertaking this learning journey collaboratively with the client, the clinician communicates to the adolescent girl quite simply the nature of the work that they will accomplish together. For instance, she or he might say,

> We can work together as we both learn who you believe yourself to be here and now—how you want to grow to be what you want to be and learning what you want for the future and how you hope to accomplish what you want. In our work together, you may experience many different kinds of feelings—anger, pain, joy—as we try to figure out answers to these questions.

Such is the case that the therapeutic journey is one where the adolescent has the opportunity to create meaning construction and meaning synthesis. The clinician and adolescent girl are engaged in a therapeutic relational matrix consisting of person-process-context.

Cultural Implications

Commonly, social workers understand the need for cultural awareness when working with different ethnicities and/or racial groups. Our contextual worlds are systemically influenced by culture. Recall my second assumption that the clinical work takes place in a relational matrix of intersubjectivity or self-relatedness, a mutually relational shared space, within a contextual field influenced by culture. This second assumption, I believe, speaks directly to issues of culture, ethnicity, and racial or cross-cultural differences. The clinician tries to understand the adolescent, emphasizing who she is and the social context that surrounds her.

Nonetheless, I wonder if social work efforts to help poor adolescents in inner-city communities are as successful as they might be. Many of the students I teach do not seek clinical jobs in inner cities. I am led to believe that many clinical social workers feel that inner-city adolescents are not necessarily good candidates for clinical work. Students complain that the many social problems in inner-city communities compromise effective clinical work. Also, most novices feel that they do not have the training and cultural competency required to work with adolescents of color. When working intersubjectively and contextually, however, such cultural competency can be achieved without extensive training. Certainly, when the clinician assumes the role of empathic insider, he or she has a cultural standpoint or some fundamental level of cultural awareness. However, even when the therapist is different from the client, creating a space for intersubjectivity through recognition that the client and clinician are contextually embedded in similar surroundings may help create a sense that they both belong to one larger community and hold much in common.

Still, when working intersubjectively and contextually, clinician biases, misperceptions (i.e., cultural, theoretical, professional, or personal) do transpire. Both anecdotal and empirical evidence suggests that in cross-race clinical dyads, practitioners with immature racial/ethnic identities themselves are not as likely to help clients achieve positive therapeutic outcomes (Carter, 1997; Helms, 1990). Obviously, when racial/ethnic biases exist, empathic failures happen. The clinician is obligated to examine why failures in empathy have occurred. Misapplication of clinical principles and human behavior theory may also result when racial/ethnic biases occur in the therapeutic relationship.

Effective clinical work demands that clinicians learn to manage tensions inherent in the nature of sameness and differences in the human condition (Dean, 2001). To be truthfully empathic, the clinician must be able to recognize difference in sameness. We like to think that empathic individuals are uniquely attuned to the mental and emotional state of another. Certainly, empathy is an imaginative process that involves mutual recognition of the other (i.e., I can perceive that the other is like myself), characterized by an attitude of care and understanding. Empathy involves both imagination and perspective taking and, thus, allows an individual to imagine himself or herself living in the context of the other.

Dean (2001) has argued, however, that cross-cultural competence, social work's standard for cultural practices, is a concept deeply flawed. She challenges social workers to adopt a postmodern view of "not knowing" and embrace a model of *cultural noncompetence*. Such a model, Dean asserts, enables the clinician to accept his or her lack of competence rather than striving to achieve a false sense of cultural competence. I agree with Dean in that the notion of cultural competence suggests a goal that is unrealizable. In my own clinical work, not knowing means I am poised, alert, and open to learning all that I can in the context of a subject-to-subject relationship. When I assume an attitude of not knowing, I am simultaneously engaged in "desiring to know." Thus, I am open to learning from myriad perspectives, one of which is the adolescent girl herself, who is, in fact, the expert witness regarding her life experiences. For that reason, I am humbled to be accepted and invited to participate in her world (Stevens, 1998). It is a world with which I want to become acquainted.

Practically speaking, absolutism, certainty, or expertness embodied in concepts of either "knowing" or "competence" applied to cultural practices infer power, dominance, and superiority, all elements of the therapeutic relationship that distance us from our subjectivity. I recognize that the objectification of clinical work belies working intersubjectively. I suggest that clinicians must have sufficient humility to enter the client's world. Understanding, acceptance, and a non-judgmental attitude—elementary components of sound clinical practice—underscore this humility (Stevens, 1998). Moreover, in desiring to know, there is a certain willingness on my part to "be known." Consequently, I can be open and (cautiously) transparent with a client.

Self-Disclosure and Engagement When Working Intersubjectively and Contextually

The clinician, when working intersubjectively and contextually, commits to the likelihood of therapist self-disclosure. Unquestionably, clinician self-disclosure has limitations, and the appropriateness of sharing personal information must be determined in advance. Clearly, the purpose of any shared material always serves the interest of the client and the therapeutic process; it stands to reason that any personal information shared should be sufficiently innocuous as to do no harm but still be of help to the client. The clinician's therapeutic position of openness, transparency, and humility reduces instances of cultural or personal bias and hence empathic failures. Not surprisingly, when empathic inquiry is sustained through clarification, interpretation, or any such therapeutic intervention, self-disclosure can advance the therapeutic work. The point to make here is that uninterrupted empathic inquiry is the crucible of working intersubjectively and contextually. Moreover, the use of nontraditional practices strengthens the clinician's role of empathic insider and offers opportunities for augmenting knowledge of the adolescent's social contexts.

REFERENCES

Anderson, E. (1999). *Code of the street: Decency, violence, and the moral life of the inner city.* New York: W. W. Norton.

Benjamin, J. (1990). An outline of intersubjectivity: The development of recognition. *Psychoanalytic Psychology, 7*(Suppl.), 33–46.

Bolland, J. M. (2001). In search of a few hundred good kids: Three months in the life of a community-based survey research study. *Families in Society, 82*(1), 76–96.

Bourgois, P. I. (1995). *In search of respect: Selling crack in el barrio.* New York: Cambridge University Press.

Bronfenbrenner, U. (1979). *The ecology of human development.* Cambridge, MA: Harvard University Press.

Brunswick, A. F. (1999). Structural strain: An ecological paradigm for studying African American drug abuse. In M. R. De La Rosa, B. Segal, & R. Lopez (Eds.), *Drugs and society: Conducting research with minority populations: Advances and issues* (pp. 5–19). New York: Haworth Press.

Carter, R. T. (1997). *The influence of race and racial identity in psychotherapy.* New York: Lexington Books.

Collins, P. H. (1986). Learning from the outsider within: The sociological significance of black feminist thought. *Social Problems, 33*(6), S14–S23.

Collins, P. H. (1990). *Black feminist thought.* Boston: Unwin Hyman.

Crossley, N. (1996). *Intersubjectivity: The fabric of social becoming.* London: Sage.

Dean, R. G. (2001). The myth of cross-cultural competence. *Families in Society, 82*(6), 623–663.

Delgado, M. (2000). *New arenas for community social work practice with urban youth.* New York: Columbia University Press.

Denzin, N. K. (1997). *Interpretive ethnography.* Thousands Oaks, CA: Sage.

Ford, D. Y. (1994). Nurturing resilience in gifted young black youth. *Roper Review, 17*(2), 80–85.

Garmezy, N. (1993, February). Children in poverty: Resilience despite risk. *Psychiatry, 56,* 127–136.

Gibbs, J. T. (1988). Young black males in America: Endangered, embittered, and embattled. In J. T. Gibbs (Ed.), *Young, black, and male in America: An endangered species* (pp. 1–35). Dover, MA: Auburn House.

Hall, E. T. (1971). *Beyond culture.* Garden City, NY: Doubleday Anchor Books.

Helms, J. E. (1990). *Black and white racial identity: Theory, research, and practice.* New York: Greenwood Press.

Hill, R. B. (1997). *The strengths of African American families: Twenty-five years later.* Washington, DC: R&B.

hooks, B. (1984). *From margin to center.* Boston: South End Press.

Jarrett, R. L. (1995). Growing up poor: The family experience of socially mobile youth in low-income African American neighborhoods. *Journal of Adolescent Research, 10*(1), 111–134.

Kanuha, V. K. (2000). "Being native" versus "Going native": Conducting research as an insider. *Social Work, 45*(5), 439–447.

McAdoo, H. P. (1997). *Black families* (3rd ed.). Thousands Oaks, CA: Sage.

McWhirter, J. J., McWhirter, B. T., McWhirter, A. M., & McWhirter, E. H. (1998). *At risk youth: A comprehensive response.* Pacific Grove, CA: Brooks/Cole.

Orange, D. M., Atwood, G. E., & Stolorow, R. D. (1997). *Working intersubjectively: Contextualism in psychoanalytic practice.* Hillsdale, NJ: Analytic Press.

Ratner, M. S. (Ed.). (1993). *Crack pipe as pimp: An ethnographic investigation of sex-for-crack exchanges.* New York: Lexington Books.

Smith, D. E. (1989). Sociological theory: Methods of writing patriarchy. In R. A. Wallace (Ed.), *Feminism and sociological theory* (pp. 34–64). Newbury Park, CA: Sage.

Spencer, M. B. (1995). Old issues and new theorizing about African-American youth: A phenomenological variant of ecological systems theory. In R. L. Taylor (Ed.), *African-American youth: Their social and economic status in the United States* (pp. 37–70). Westport, CT: Praeger.

Sterk, C. E. (1999). *Fast lives: Women who use crack cocaine.* Philadelphia: Temple University Press.

Stevens, J. W. (1997). Opportunity outlook and coping in poor urban African American late age female adolescent contraceptors. *Smith College Studies, 67*(3), 456–476.

Stevens, J. W. (1998). A question of values in social work practice: Working with the strengths of black adolescent females. *Families in Society, 79*(3), 288–296.

Stevens, J. W. (2001). The social ecology of the co-occurrence of substance use and early coitus among poor urban black female adolescents. *Substance Use and Misuse, 36*(4), 421–446.

Stevens, J. W. (2002). *Smart and sassy: The strengths of inner city black girls.* New York: Oxford University Press.

Swadener, B. B., & Lubeck, S. (Eds.). (1995). *Children and families "at promise": Deconstructing the discourse of risk.* Albany: State University Press of New York.

Wallace, J. M. (1999). Explaining race differences in adolescent and young adult drug use: The role of racialized social systems. In M. R. De La Rosa, B. Segal, & R. Lopez (Eds.), *Drugs and society: Conducting research with minority populations: Advances and issues* (pp. 21–36). New York: Haworth Press.

William, T. M., & Kornblum, W. (1985). *Growing up poor.* Lexington, MA: Lexington Books.

William, T. M., & Kornblum, W. (1994). *The uptown kids.* New York: Putnam.

Wilson, J. W. (1987). *When work disappears.* New York: Knopf.

4

GENDERED ADAPTATIONS, RESILIENCE, AND THE PERPETRATION OF VIOLENCE

JANE F. GILGUN

LAURA S. ABRAMS

Developmental psychopathologists seek to identify processes that lead to adaptive and maladaptive outcomes among high-risk groups, with the goal of contributing to interventions that can promote resilience and decrease risks (Luthar, 2003; Luthar & Cicchetti, 2000). Researchers, however, have given little attention to understanding the points of view of people who respond to their adverse life circumstances in ways that outsiders would define as maladaptive (Ungar, 2004). Soliciting the points of view of research participants helps us to understand the gendered, social, and cultural contexts to which individuals adapt. These concerns are important to human service professions that build on the premise of starting where the clients are.

This chapter is based on research with adolescents and adults, both women and men, who have experienced adversities and whose behaviors led them to involvement with the law, primarily for violent acts, which are, from almost any point of view, a maladapted outcome. In the study we discuss here, we developed a conceptual model that we applied to our analysis of two cases: an adolescent young man who was abusive to his girlfriend who was also the mother of his baby and an adult woman who engaged in sexual activities with an adolescent young woman. Our perspectives were constructivist and interpretive (Benner, 1994; Patton, 2002) in that we wanted to represent the points of view of the persons we interviewed. In our analysis, we show that the young man and adult woman view their illegal behaviors as logical and effective ways to enhance their own well-being and sometimes the well-being of loved ones, although usually they are aware that their behaviors contravene social norms and their own moral values. We contend that these views are fairly typical of people whom social and legal institutions consider "deviant" and even criminal.

The elements of our conceptual model are human agency, resilience, schema theory, gendered adaptation, feminist and masculinity theory, and gendered interpretations of female and male violence. We view these elements as interconnected and forming a viable theory of violence as gendered adaptations.

Our method is deductive qualitative analysis (Gilgun, in press a, in press b), which by definition begins with a conceptual model that researchers can put to many different uses, such as hypothesis testing, pattern matching, or as a guide to exploring poorly understood topics. Deductive qualitative analysis (DQA) is different from many other ways of doing qualitative research in that the procedures call for developing a conceptual model before entering the field. Many forms of qualitative research, taking the lead from the work of Straus and his colleagues (Charmaz, 2000; Clarke, 2003; Glaser, 1978; Glaser & Strauss, 1967; Strauss & Corbin, 1998), guide researchers toward research that begins in an open-ended, atheoretical way. DQA builds on the traditions of analytic induction (Cressey, 1953; Gilgun, in press, b; Znaniecki, 1934), a form of qualitative research that originated in the Chicago School of Sociology in the early part of the 20th century. Analytic induction begins with a loose conceptual framework but claims to be inductive, which is actually a contradiction in terms, although many of the ideas on which analytic induction is based are important to DQA as well (see Gilgun, in press b, for an extended discussion of DQA compared with other forms of qualitative research).

A WORKING DEFINITION OF VIOLENCE

For the purposes of this chapter, we contrast interpersonal violence with healthy interpersonal relationships. Mutuality, reciprocity, and the promotion of the best interests of others are widely recognized qualities characteristic of healthy relationships (Seifert, Hoffnung, & Hoffnung, 2000). Violence, on the other hand, not only bypasses mutuality and reciprocity and undermines the best interests of others, but it includes behaviors that hurt others psychologically and emotionally and often physically as well.

Individuals involved in mutual and reciprocal relationships contribute to the well-being and quality of life for others. They respect others' autonomy and freedom of choice. They provide comfort in times of stress, and they sometimes consciously give up something they want to promote the well-being of others and to nurture the continuation of the relationship. If they inadvertently hurt others, they apologize, seek forgiveness, and make efforts to repair the relationship and to change their own behaviors so as not to harm again. Such behaviors are mirror images of our concept of violence. They appear, on the surface at least, to mimic behavior we might associate with resilience.

Relationships are, of course, fraught with possibilities of hurting others, whether intentionally or not. Our definition of violence assumes differential power, which can stem from attributes such as gender, physical strength, social status, experience, age, and maturation. Ideologies, such as who is entitled to what and who has rights to do what, grow from and structure these attributes. We believe that individuals who choose to take advantage of the power they have over others have a limitless number of cultural themes and practices that they use to guide and justify their behaviors but that they transform these in individualized, idiosyncratic ways (Gilgun & McLeod, 1999). In this chapter, we look primarily at age and gender to understand how these individuals engage in processes associated with the use of interpersonal violence as an awkward but effective means of experiencing health-related phenomena.

In mutual, reciprocal relationships between generational equals, there is ongoing negotiation of issues such as understanding what the other person wants, how to reconcile differing wants and desires, and how to decide what actually does promote the well-being of the other (Gottman, 2001).

However, this is not the case in cross-generational interaction. We view older people as having particular responsibilities for recognizing and respecting generational differences, even if it means putting aside one's own powerful desires.

Nor is it the case for relationships in which there are differences in power between men and women or where violence is expressed in gender-typical ways. We view males as more likely to commit overtly aggressive acts, whether physical, verbal, or psychological—although there are exceptions, as in child sexual abuse and incest where some perpetrators insist that they act out of love and caring (Gilgun, 1995)—and for women, with some exceptions, to be more subtle and indirect in how they undermine the well-being of others (Crick, Grotpeter, & Bigbee, 2002). Even more confusing, perpetrators can experience emotional and sexual gratification from violence, often associated with a sense of power and control over others. Given these patterns, we propose that current understandings and definitions of violence are gendered—that is, biased toward more typically "male" styles of violence that connote and denote physical and verbal aggression.

Finally, we believe there can be major differences between how outsiders interpret behaviors and how the people concerned interpret their own behaviors. Professionals may have great difficulty shifting perspectives so that they can connect to and understand the points of view of clients. For example, the research and theory on which we have drawn for our analysis is based on perspectives of "outsiders"—that is, the points of view of researchers and rarely those of the researched. Insiders' views on the meaning of their behaviors, including those that outsiders view as maladaptive, will contribute to the effectiveness of interventions that professionals craft in their efforts to enhance resilience processes and decrease the effects of risks. A number of chapters in this work, for example, achieve just such a link between understanding tied to research and better-informed interventions.

Finally, contemporary thought on human agency emphasizes the idea of choice, but the range of options is restricted by the time in which people live, the settings in which they develop, and the people and ideologies to which they are exposed (Giddens, 1987). Social locations provide contexts and interpretive filters through which individuals make decisions about how to respond to challenging life circumstances (Abrams, 2003).

RESILIENCE

Resilience represents capacities for coping with, adapting to, and overcoming adversities as well as competence in developmental tasks (Masten & Coatsworth, 1998). Resilience is widely recognized as a "manifestation of positive outcomes"

after "exposure to adversity" (Luthar & Cicchetti, 2000, p. 857). People in high-risk situations and who exhibit prosocial, adaptive outcomes are said to have had the capacities to marshal sufficient resources to help them deal effectively with risks. When people do not have capacities to marshal resources in high-risk situations, then maladaptive behaviors occur, including violent acts. A person may be competent, prosocial, and well adapted in one domain, such as work, but have maladapted outcomes in other domains, such as interpersonal relationships and emotion regulation (Gilgun, 1996a, 1996b, 1999, 2002a).

Although resilience is associated with prosocial adaptations to adversities, some researchers have pointed out that definitions of competence and resilience may vary across gender, age, socioeconomic status, and ethnicity (Abrams, 2002; Burton, Allison, & Obeidallah, 1995; Ungar, 2004). For example, children who live in dangerous neighborhoods may develop adaptive coping strategies that are maladaptive in more secure settings (Garcia Coll et al., 1996), whereas people who come from backgrounds of privilege and physical security may develop a sense of entitlement that is maladaptive in other settings (Gilgun, 1996b; Gilgun & McLeod, 1999). Many young people and their parents in resource-poor environments may aspire to a "revised American dream" in their definitions of successful outcomes (Burton et al., 1995). Moreover, resilience can have a gendered component; that is, resilience processes and outcomes may be different for women and men in gendered societies.

ADAPTATION

Adaptation can be broadly defined as responses to the demands of the environment (Ashford, LeCroy, & Lortie, 2001; Siegelman & Rider, 2003). The meaning of the term encompasses the mutuality and reciprocity of interactions between people (and other organisms) and their environments (Germaine & Gitterman, 1996). Environments shape human growth and development, and human beings shape their own environments. As Germaine and Gitterman (1996) point out, all organisms require resources from their environments to survive and develop.

How individuals do this depends on the resources available to them, their capacities to respond to these resources, and the goals they value.

Adaptation is a key concept in Piaget's theory of cognitive development. Piaget's theory is constructivist in that it is based on the idea that human beings actively construct their knowledge of themselves, others, and the world. Adaptations are mediated through schemas that people construct based on their interactions with environments (Berk, 2003). Schemas can be thought of as mental representations or internalized working models that help people make sense of their experiences through assimilation and accommodation. In assimilation, individuals fit new experiences into existing schemas, and in accommodation, they modify and transform their schemas to incorporate new information.

Contemporary cognitive scientists generally have come to the conclusion that the activation of mental representations and their associated behaviors and motivations are almost entirely nonconscious. Most thoughts, emotions, moods, and behaviors occur automatically in response to a person's perceptions of environmental cues and are outside of conscious awareness (Bargh & Chartrand, 1999). These automatic mechanisms bypass conscious choice and appraisal. The cues that activate these mental representations are analogous to "buttons being pushed." According to Bargh and Chartrand (1999), "In whatever way the start button is pushed, the mechanism subsequently behaves in the same way" (p. 476).

GENDERED ADAPTATIONS

This chapter is about "gendered adaptations" to adverse circumstances. To say that human adaptation is a "gendered" process means that how individuals construct themselves, choose to act, and develop their operant worldview is influenced to varying extents by gendered schemas derived from larger social norms and expectations, stereotypes, and power relationships. This focus on gender is not intended to diminish other significant forces that shape cognitive scripts and adaptation processes, such as ethnicity and culture, class, family background, or personal experiences. Rather, with the understanding that the very meaning of violence is underscored by *gendered* assumptions (e.g., violence toward others is generally viewed as a "male" attribute, whereas violence toward the self is typically seen as a "female" attribute), we believe in the importance of analyzing perpetrators' adaptations to adverse circumstances through the lens of their gendered beliefs, roles, and strategies.

The concept of gendered adaptations draws on theories found in feminist psychology, masculinities studies, and related genres of literature. Feminist psychology, for example, illustrates how dominant societal constructs of "femininity" and expectations related to gender roles shape women's social and psychological adaptation strategies. Feminist psychologists Brown and Gilligan (1992) argue that women are socialized into a more "relational" stance than their male counterparts. This means that women are more attuned to the intricate world of human relations and that self-esteem is gained primarily by virtue of connections with others. Gilligan (1982) stated that, gradually, women learn "not only to define themselves in the context of human relationships but also judge themselves in terms of their ability to care" (p. 17). This "care" orientation continues throughout the life cycle and becomes more solidified when a woman takes on mothering roles.

According to Gilligan (1982), this emphasis on relation and care eventually becomes problematic because Western, white, Anglo-Saxon culture does not typically value or reward these traditionally female qualities. Moreover, women's socialization toward relationships as a primary gauge of self-worth sets the stage for a variety of internal conflicts for adolescent and adult women, including issues of self-doubt, authenticity, and autonomy.

Building on feminist psychology, we assume that women tend to manage processes of assimilation and accommodation of internalized messages about their gender roles and their tendencies to privilege narratives of care and relation above and beyond those of "autonomy" or "achievement." These are not merely individual scripts, but rather, they are derived from positions and discourses of masculinity and femininity that circulate through larger social arenas and institutions. Responding to adverse circumstances, women, particularly those socialized in dominant culture norms, tend to harm themselves rather than perpetrate violence or harm toward others. Turning anger or rage inward, against the self, is a traditionally gendered adaptation strategy for women.[1] A woman facing adverse economic or emotional circumstances might also draw on traditionally gendered survival skills such as selling one's body, becoming dependent, or seeking care and protection from others. The decision making that leads to these outcomes may not be based on conscious processes but may be an outcome of automatic schemas.

Women's Aggressive Behaviors

When women are aggressive toward others, there is increasing evidence that the forms the aggression takes are gendered—that is, filtered through and influenced by broader social discourses that provide constructions of "womanhood" and "femininity." For example, Crick and colleagues (Crick & Dodge, 1994, 1996; Crick et al., 2002; Crick et al., 1999) have conducted research on "female" forms of aggression, which they call "relational aggression." Focusing on school-age and adolescent girls, they defined relational aggression as behaviors that harm others through damage, or the threat of damage, to relationships or feelings of acceptance, friendship, or group inclusion. These behaviors include acts such as giving someone the "silent treatment" to punishing him or her to get one's own way, using social exclusion as a form of retaliation, or threatening to end a friendship unless the friend complies with a request (Crick et al., 1999).

These are forms of violence that are neither physically nor verbally assaultive but are, at least from perpetrators' points of view, meant to be gentle, kind, and loving. As mentioned earlier, some perpetrators of incest and child sexual abuse view their experiences in this way (Gilgun, 1995; Gilgun & McLeod, 1999). Both women and men may experience sexual behaviors with persons unable to give consent—because of age, ability, social status, and power—in these ways.

Men's Gendered Adaptations

Until recently, social theory did not directly address men's psychological development and adaptation. Rather, researchers assumed that men's psychology was the "norm" and left the gendered nature of experience unspecified. Masculinities theory, rooted in sociology and in criminology, presents understandings of gendered social and psychological adaptation that both complement and extend the feminist frame. These ideas also help to illustrate the gendered aspects of violence and the perpetration of crime.

Masculinities theory offers contextualized views of male behaviors and adaptations in its premise that there is no universal, fixed masculine identity. Rather, throughout the life course, men adopt a range of gendered and culturally patterned responses to their social environments (Connell, 1987, 1995; Goodey, 1997; Messerschmidt, 2000). Connell (1987) identified a hierarchy of possible masculinities, in which the traditionally held understanding of masculinity as the stoic, emotionally unexpressive, competitive breadwinner role assumes dominance. He called this traditional masculine response "hegemonic masculinity" and suggested that this identity has become the normative benchmark against which other masculine responses are measured. Alternative masculine responses, including more "effeminate" masculinities, homosexual, bisexual, and transgendered men, and others, become subordinated in relation to hegemonic masculinity. "Subordinate masculinities" are aberrations from the ideal and are, in many cases, negated by the dominant culture as viable or attractive masculine alternatives (Connell, 1995).

Building on Connell's construction of hegemonic masculinity, other scholars (Gilgun & McLeod, 1999; Majors & Billson, 1992; Messerschmidt, 2000; West & Zimmerman, 1987) suggest that the resources men have at their disposal for expressing their maleness play a significant role in determining their individual responses or adaptations to their social environments. In the absence of resources allowing for expression of alternate, or subordinated, masculine traits (nurturing, cooperation, nonviolent conflict resolution, etc.), men compensate with excessive demonstrations of the one form of masculinity that is most influential, obvious, and valued—hegemonic masculinity. Men whose masculine experience is limited primarily to the expression of maleness as power and aggression are unlikely to develop masculine identities that value cooperation and communication. On the contrary, their dominant gender expression is likely to fit into the framework of violence, power, and competition.

Majors and Billson (1992), for example, observed the phenomenon of subordinated masculinities in their study of African American young men and their adoption of "cool pose"— a style of behaving and speaking that for some African American men allows them to negotiate their diminished power status in relation to the dominant culture. Although the marginalization they experience as African Americans robs them of many of the opportunities and resources needed to effectively fulfill hegemonic masculine ideals of power and success, they nonetheless strive to embody these very ideals through different channels, such as aggression, or streetwise knowledge and behaviors. Thus, they assimilate and perhaps accommodate into their inner representations or schemas, representations of self, others, and how the world works based on their interpretations of their experiences and the contexts in which they live their lives.

Majors and Billson (1992), along with other masculinity theorists (Kersten, 1990; LoPresto & Deluty, 1987; Messerschmidt, 2000) identify the potential for violent or aggressive behavior as expressions of masculine scripts—which are similar to schemas—among marginalized groups of men as a means to conform to the structures of hegemonic masculinity even in their subordinated status. Anderson (1990) also suggests that violence and the perpetration of criminal acts can be seen as gendered adaptation strategies for survival in low-income communities with high rates of unemployment and social disorganization.

Men, therefore, choose from a set of gendered adaptation strategies that might vary significantly according to their available resources, their class and race positions, and their contextual frames of reference. In response to adverse circumstances or distress, men incorporate into their self-schemas values related to violence and the perpetration of crimes as a means to maintain or fulfill hegemonic male expectations— such as power, control, or making "quick money." Although women might adopt similar schemas and associated behaviors, their physical and sexual enactments of violence are typically viewed as more of a transgression of gender expectations than a conforming position, unlike the case with men.

METHOD

This is not a traditional research report, nor is it a traditional theoretical discussion but, rather, the application of a theoretical model to two cases for the purposes of illustrating how the key concepts of our model play themselves out in individual lives. This approach is characteristic of deductive qualitative analysis (Gilgun, in press a, in press b). Our goal was to show how individuals act out cultural themes and practices and even invent new ways of doing so. We developed the two cases from ethnographic life history approaches, meaning that our goal was to examine individual lives and interpretations within the contexts of social, cultural, and historical themes and practices (Chambers, 2000; Denzin, 1989a, 1989b; Goldstein, 1994). As a prime research method of the Chicago School of Sociology, a seat of interactionist theorizing, life histories are a method of choice for examining how larger social forces and ideologies, based on gender, age, and social class, influence human lives (Gilgun & McLeod, 1999; Tierney, 2000).

Gilgun's contribution to the present chapter is based on life history qualitative research she has conducted for more than 18 years with people who have had exposure to risk factors that predict violent behaviors, such as being abused and neglected in childhood, witnessing violence, espousal of violence-positive ideologies, and being discouraged from feeling and expressing emotions (Gilgun, 1990, 1991, 1992, 1994, 1995, 1996b, 1999, 2002b; Gilgun & McLeod, 1999; Gilgun, Klein, & Pranis, 2000; Gilgun & Reiser, 1990). Most had committed felony-level violence, such as child sexual abuse, physical abuse of children, woman battering, burglary, armed robbery, attempted murder, and murder and were in prison. Some of the women were convicted of felonies, but most had not. The ethnicity of the sample was European American, African American, Latino, and American Indian.

Abram's work draws on an ethnographic study of young males 14 to 17 years old incarcerated for 4 to 6 months in secure correctional facilities. That study involved both qualitative interviewing and observation. These young men were diverse in ethnicity and included white, Hmong, Native American, Latino, and African American participants. All were repeat offenders, and the majority grew up in working-class, poor, and urban environments of the Twin Cities, Minnesota. The first wave of this project involved over 100 observations and a series of in-depth interviews with 12 youthful offenders who volunteered to participate in the study. These interviews were conducted jointly by Abrams and a male research assistant (Abrams, Kim, & Anderson, in press).

Although these two studies had different goals and research questions, we found that our data complement one another in several ways. Specifically, bringing together the youth and adult perspectives on violence and resilience as gendered adaptations provides insight into useful and innovative concepts in understanding adaptation to adverse circumstances and to the development of violent and criminal behaviors.

ANALYSIS

For our analysis, we chose two cases: an adolescent young man who was in a juvenile correctional facility for physically assaulting his girlfriend and a woman who had abused her authority to engage in a sexual relationship with an adolescent young woman.

Elijah

Description

Elijah is a 16-year-old, African American male sentenced to serve 6 months in the county juvenile correctional facility for a probation violation involving a physical assault on his baby's mother, who is also his current girlfriend. His prior record includes possession of a weapon, fighting, and curfew violations. Elijah also has a history of selling and using marijuana, although he was never caught for these crimes.

Elijah was raised primarily by his biological mother and stepfather. His biological father deserted the family when Elijah was very young,

was addicted to crack cocaine, and spent time in and out of jail in Chicago. His stepfather and mother both use alcohol and marijuana openly, and his stepfather has a history of selling drugs and periodic incarceration. His older brother, whom he considered to be his closest friend, fathered five children by the age of 20 and was incarcerated for a 4-year sentence at the time of the interview. Elijah revealed that his mother and stepfather used force for discipline, including punching and whipping with a belt, but he didn't consider the behavior to be abusive.

Elijah's family lived in one of the poorest, transient neighborhoods in the metropolitan Twin Cities area. This neighborhood is known for crime, drugs, and gang activity. He claimed that his family struggled with having enough food and maintaining a stable apartment. After fathering a son at age 15, Elijah sought to make quick money by selling marijuana and having sex with older women for cash or material goods. While he involved himself in these sexual exchanges, he still maintained a primary relationship with his baby's mother, Monica, whom he still considered his "girlfriend."

On the day that he was arrested, he stated that he was upset over news of his brother's extended prison time and jealous because he saw Monica talking with a male peer at school. He said that he confronted Monica about the flirtation and she joked with him about having a crush on this other person. When they got into a verbal argument about it, the conversation escalated to a physical altercation, with Monica throwing the first punch, and Elijah proceeding to hit her and choke her until she threatened to call the police. According to Elijah, he ended up calling the police, not her. He was booked and sentenced technically for a probation violation.

Analysis

Elijah's version of his crime is imbued with several distinct and competing cognitive schemas. In his first interview (out of a series of five interviews over 6 months), he explained that he physically attacked Monica because she provoked him and disrespected him by "going for his face." Later in the same interview, he added that while he was hitting and choking her, what he was really feeling underneath it all was hurt.

Interviewer: Did you feel good when you pushed her?

Elijah: No. I was hurt. I was hurt, but I didn't really express my hurtness. I was hurt when I smacked her.

He also stated in a subsequent interview that he acted impulsively and compared his behavior with someone "who was on drugs . . . I was acting brain dead." This impulsive behavior fits into the framework of an automatic schema activated when he feels hurt or disrespected and results in the use of physical force.

At the same time that he could articulate why he used physical force against Monica, he also espouses a set of moral standards that include a strong prohibition against ever "hitting a woman." He claims that he learned these values from his mother and his stepfather. "Dad said to me, if you love a girl, don't put your hand on her." To assimilate the reality of his assault against Monica into his espoused moral frame, he convinced himself that Monica knew that he didn't want to hit her. "Each time I hit her, she knew I didn't want to hit her." Because of this overriding value, he wished that he had made a different choice and fought the "dude" that was flirting with Monica, not Monica herself. However, he made a conscious choice not to fight "the dude" because he had marijuana with him at the time. At several points during the interview series, he also talked about his ethic of treating women with respect and the importance of equality between men and women in relationships. He claimed to have a perfectly "equal" relationship with Monica because they both show each other so much love and they share the responsibility of a child. His professed morality with regard to women is a competing schema that he did not activate in the instance that he assaulted Monica.

What Elijah doesn't say explicitly but what emerged in the analysis of the transcripts was that his gender/morality schema with regard to not "hitting a woman" can be overridden by a feeling of disrespect, which, for him, automatically triggers violence. The time that he hit Monica back, he was *reacting to* being hit "in the face," which he interpreted as a sign of disrespect. Elijah described a very similar incident that occurred with a female friend a few years earlier when he hit her and pushed her "down the stairs" because she "pointed in his face" after he told her not to.

Elijah's violent responses illustrate his gendered adaptation to feelings of "disrespect" and his consistent need to prove himself or to "save face" in these interactions. This gendered version of violence, for him, works on many levels—in fights with other boys, in his drug-dealing activities, and in regard to his own beliefs about what it means to have power. In his own words, "When you have power, people pay you respect." He associates selling drugs with making oneself powerful because of the money, which also gives one respect. "I liked it [selling marijuana] cuz I was getting respect, and I liked it cuz I was getting all the money." These ideas about power and disrespect fit neatly into his contextual urban frame of reference, even though they have the potential to contradict his professed moral frame with regard to hitting a woman.

In his response to adverse family circumstances, Elijah learned to attend to his survival needs by making quick money through selling marijuana, which represents a masculinized response to adverse economic circumstances in his community. In addition, he also earned money and material goods by trading sex with older women, representing a more transgressive, or feminized gendered survival strategy. To reconcile this gender transgression, he draws a clear line between his exchanges with older women and what female prostitutes do: He doesn't negotiate money beforehand, he doesn't "pass" diseases, and he gets pleasure as well out of the sexual exchange. In this sense, he understands the exchange to be still "in his power," even though the women are older and he is bartering a service for them.

Elijah can be viewed as having resilient traits because he consistently strives to feel powerful and strong in relation to others and to meet his and his baby's material needs. Drawing on his physical strength, athletic ability, and charismatic personality, Elijah tends to craft situations to his advantage to meet his needs. According to Elijah, "It's a great feeling for you to control yourself, be power yourself than for other people to be power over you or controlling you."

His method of achieving his goal of being "on top" through fighting, sexual exchange, or selling drugs would be viewed as maladaptive from a clinical or social work perspective. However, in his social context, Elijah's willingness to go after his goals and to provide for his family can also be seen as adaptive to the circumstances that he faces and as an acknowledgment of the limited resources available to him. Appreciating Elijah's behavior as adaptive is difficult unless we look at this research through a broader social, political, and structural lens. This work makes clear the need to understand the context in which behavior occurs rather than predetermining which behaviors are and are not associated with resilience.

Caron

Description

Caron, 34, was sexually involved for 2 years with a young woman named Tina who was a member of a church youth group that Caron directed. Caron, a college graduate who had a professional career in the arts, had been married for 10 years and had no children. She worked at the church as a part-time youth leader. She had grown up in this church, where her mother had been president of the women's auxiliary for many years and where she herself had been active in youth groups in high school.

Caron had known Tina for 2 years before the sexual involvement, which began when Tina was 16. The sexual part of their relationship ended when Tina talked to a church counselor, who told the minister. The minister fired Caron and sent a letter to the congregation about the sexual abuse. Caron sought treatment with a psychiatrist who advised her to self-report her abuse to the police. She did.

The police did not bring charges because, according to Caron, Tina was 18 and Caron was seeking the therapy that social services would have recommended. Caron's husband steadfastly supported his wife. He did not know about Caron and Tina's sexual involvement until Caron was fired. He was the youth director at the church. He subsequently resigned from his job.

A year after the public disclosure of the sexual abuse, Caron and her husband invited Tina to live with them because she was having trouble at home for disobedience, staying out after curfew, and using drugs. Tina lived with the couple for several months until she returned home. Caron said there was no resumption of their sexual activity, although she remained in love with Tina.

From Caron's point of view, she and Tina both grew psychologically and emotionally through their relationship. Tina was the first person Caron was open with about her deepest thoughts and feelings. In her relationship to Tina, Caron experienced deep love, commitment, and authenticity.

Analysis

Whereas Elijah had competing schemas about how to treat women, Caron had one rock solid schema about her commitment to Tina, although she was aware that others had different views. She was unswerving in her representation of her relationship as moral. She said, "To become involved with Tina was more a moral, morally right to me, because I understood what was happening, and I felt right about it."

She knew she was contravening what "society" thought, what her church thought, what Tina's mother would think, and what her "job was telling her." She must have had a sense of what her husband would have thought because she didn't tell him. As she said, she knew "the moral stance out there is, you know, to say no." Conventional morality, according to Caron, meant "I should say no to Tina, and I should tell her to bug off and leave me alone and basically abandon her."

Furthermore, Caron believed that "not becoming involved with Tina because of someone else's feeling is not a moral stance." She said she looked very hard for reasons not to become sexually involved with Tina: "I couldn't give her enough reasons morally or enough reasons for her development to say no. I didn't find any at the time. I looked. I looked for them like crazy but I couldn't find any."

She cast this sexual relationship in terms of caring, a stereotypical female way of behaving. She recognized that she was paying the consequences, which included public exposure, firing, and her grandmother's phoning her up to tell her that she didn't want Caron to come to her funeral.

Caron viewed involvement with Tina as a courageous, caring moral act because not to be sexual with Tina would have hurt Tina emotionally. She linked her commitment to engage in a sexual relationship with Tina to her own sense of abandonment, which she saw as arising from her own mother's leaving home with a man who was not her husband when Caron was about 14. Caron said she could identify completely with Tina, whose own family was not there for her. She said that Tina wanted to be sexual with her and to turn Tina away would have hurt her. Caron said she would never hurt Tina. She linked her commitment to not abandoning Tina to her own religious beliefs:

> I didn't want to abandon her. I will take shit to king-dom come before I will bail out. . . . In some ways that is very, very strong to my religious point of view. It's very strong that you be there for people. It is very strong that that's the spiritual connection and understanding of who Jesus Christ was. He didn't bail out. He didn't go when he . . . and he didn't maybe have his self-protection up either . . . when it really comes down to the story. And so religiously and morally, it . . . it . . . yeah, that's where I'm at.

That Caron made sense of her relationship with Tina in terms of a religion and religious language in which she was steeped shows how people build their schemas and make their adjustments to their environments in terms of the resources to which they are exposed. This is an instance where an individual transformed significant religious principles and stories into guidelines for behaviors that others find deeply troubling.

Her unshakable schema not to abandon Tina appeared to be based on her interpretation of her own mother's abandonment. Caron had a difficult time stepping away from her own inner representations and seeing Tina as different. Her schema about abandonment was so strong, even in her teen years, that she was unable to reconcile with her mother. Her mother made many efforts to soften the impact of her abandonment on Caron, efforts that Caron repelled. For example, Caron's mother left a note for Caron

the night she ran off with another man. Caron could not remember the content. When she returned late at night, she woke Caron up. Caron does not remember her response. Her mother made special efforts to reconnect with Caron, such as taking her alone on a camping trip. Caron remained unresponsive.

What Caron did connect with was her mother's acts that Caron interpreted as personalized rejection. Caron clearly remembered her mother phoning her home collect while with the other man. Caron wanted to speak to her mother then but her mother hung up when the phone operator told her that the party she wished to speak to (her husband) was not there. Caron was unresponsive to her mothers' overtures for reconnection and forgiveness.

Although Elijah's assaults of women clearly fall within conventional definitions and understandings of violence, some people may have trouble labeling Caron's sexual involvement with Tina as violence. We contend that conventional definitions of violence are gendered—that is, biased toward stereotypically male behaviors. The definition of violence in this chapter, however, clearly labels Caron's behaviors as violent. There are generational and maturational differences between Caron and Tina. Caron knew Tina was dealing with many personal issues. A mature response would have been to recognize Tina's vulnerability and gently refuse her sexual advances.

Caron's responses to Tina appear to be almost the opposite of relational aggression, which Crick and colleagues (Crick & Dodge, 1994, 1996; Crick et al., 2002; Crick et al., 1999) find to be characteristic ways that girls show aggression. In her own terms, Caron sacrificed a great deal to ensure that Tina experienced inclusion, acceptance, and friendship. On the other hand, she perpetrated relationship aggression on her own mother, to whom she gave the silent treatment and whom she excluded from her life.

Because of Caron's confused schemas about abandonment, hurt, and commitment and her schemas about conventional and nonconventional moral action regarding how to care for and protect others, she was unable to use ideas about generational differences and their inherent power differentials in her decision making and subsequent interpretations of her sexual behaviors with Tina.

Caron said she sought counseling about her relationship with Tina before it became sexual. She discussed the counseling in terms of lesbianism. She made no mention about whether the counselor also brought up issues related to generational differences, power, and the vulnerability of troubled teenagers.

Caron's strong care orientation is obvious in her account. In her terms, a refusal to hurt Tina is a moral stance of caring, a stance that Gilligan (Gilligan, 1982) links to women's ways of being moral people. Caron saw the sexual relationship with Tina as part of a "whole relationship" of caring and commitment.

Her caring schema was so strong that when Tina began expressing doubts about their relationship, Caron urged Tina to go into therapy or talk to anyone she wanted about it. She was willing to risk public exposure if this is what Tina wanted. At the time of the interviews, she seemed willing and almost proud of being able to bear the consequences of expressing her love for Tina in sexual ways.

In summary, Caron was an otherwise conventional, middle-class college graduate, who had a 10-year marriage preceded by a 5-year relationship to the same man, had strong ties to her church, and was very successful in the arts community. In these areas, she was highly adapted to a secure, positive environment, whereas Elijah was highly adapted to his financially insecure, unpredictable, and sometimes dangerous environment. In the one area that others would consider maladapted—her sexual relationship with Tina—Caron herself saw in heroic terms and even mythic terms that made enormous sense to her. She implicitly linked the price she paid to the martyrdom of Jesus. She certainly would have labeled her behavior as prosocial and highly competent.

Discussion

The ideas of gendered adaptations, schemas, resilience, and our definition of violence were helpful in our analysis. We were able to see for ourselves that behaviors that outsiders might define as maladaptive, individuals themselves can define as adaptive. Both Caron and Elijah would define themselves as competent and even possibly resilient. We also saw that Caron could also fit outsiders' definitions of competent, resilient, and prosocial in her behaviors in several aspects of her functioning.

The notion of schemas contributed to our analysis. Caron had some apparently unshakable and at least partially conscious schemas about abandonment, commitment, care, and self-sacrifice. These schemas can be linked both to conventional female socialization and to Christian moral values. Although she was aware of conventional morality in regard to her behaviors toward Tina, she thought them irrelevant to her situation.

Elijah, on the other hand, did have strong values and schemas about not hurting women, but when his pride was hurt, other mechanisms took over—his schemas about what to do when disrespected. Elijah represents a lot of other men in terms of his gendered adaptations. We do not know how typical Caron is because we know little about women's ways of being violent and aggressive.

Our definition of violence, as far as we know, is novel. Although we incorporated many well-accepted ideas about power, gender, and age, we also linked violence to definitions of healthy relationships that are widely accepted as having qualities of mutuality, reciprocity, and promoting the best interests of others, all elements associated with resilient individuals. We also found that understandings and definitions of violence are gendered; that is, both denotatively in definitions and connotatively in meanings, the term *violence* evokes images of physical and verbal aggression, qualities linked to male gender roles much more than female ones. We would like to expand definitions of violence to include "female" styles of perpetrating violence, although we certainly recognize that men are much more likely to commit lethal forms of violence than women, another outcome of gendered cultural themes and practices. We hope that our definition will provoke creative discussions, new understandings, and more effective responses to violence.

We have found it challenging to drop our own schemas and link to the schemas of others, especially when their behaviors contravene our moral values. We believe, however, that researchers, practitioners, and policymakers must make these connections to others. If we don't, our responses will not be effective. Starting where clients are includes connecting to what they value. The challenge that we hope to make is to ask how social workers and other mental health care professionals can work effectively with people whose schemas and behaviors are adaptive in their own contexts but maladaptive in the larger society. How can we integrate this knowledge into our practice interventions and strategies for populations known to be vulnerable to maladaptive behaviors?

Finally, these cases illustrate how adaptation and resilience have gendered dimensions. This finding is particularly relevant for researchers who tend to conceptualize resilience as sets of universal, prosocial adaptations. Future research is needed, both qualitative and quantitative studies, to understand resilience processes for men and women, people of varying age groups, differing socioeconomic statuses, and social contexts.

NOTE

1. This theory has been shown to have several limitations for women of color and women of diverse social class backgrounds. For a review essay on this theory and its critiques, see Abrams (2002).

REFERENCES

Abrams, L. S. (2002). Rethinking girls "at-risk:" Gender, race, and class intersections and adolescent development. *Journal of Human Behavior in the Social Environment, 6*(2), 47–64.

Abrams, L. S. (2003). Contextual variations in young women's gender identity negotiations. *Psychology of Women Quarterly, 27*(1), 64–74.

Abrams, L. S., Kim, K., & Anderson, B. (in press). Paradoxes of treatment in juvenile corrections. *Child and Youth Care Forum.*

Anderson, E. (1990). *Streetwise: Race, class and change in an urban community.* Chicago: University of Chicago Press.

Ashford, J. B., LeCroy, C. W., & Lortie, K. L. (2001). *Human behavior in the social environment* (2nd ed.). Belmont, CA: Brooks/Cole.

Bargh, J., & Chartrand, T. L. (1999). The unbearable automaticity of being. *American Psychologist, 54*(7), 462–479.

Benner, P. (1994). *Interpretive phenomenology.* Thousand Oaks, CA: Sage.

Berk, L. E. (2003). *Child development* (6th ed). Boston: Allyn & Bacon.

Brown, L. M., & Gilligan, C. (1992). *Meeting at the crossroads.* New York: Ballantine Books.

Burton, L. M., Allison, K. W., & Obeidallah, D. (1995). Social context and adolescence: Perspectives on development among inner-city African-American teens. In L. J. Crockett & A. C. Crouter (Eds.), *Pathways through adolescence: Relation to social contexts* (pp. 119–138). Mahwah, NJ: Erlbaum.

Chambers, E. (2000). Applied ethnography. In N. K. Denzin & Y. S. Lincoln (Eds.), *Handbook of qualitative research* (2nd ed., pp. 851–869). Thousand Oaks, CA: Sage.

Charmaz, K. (2000). Grounded theory: Objectivist and constructivist methods. In N. K. Denzin & Y. S. Lincoln (Eds.), *Handbook of qualitative research* (2nd ed., pp. 509–535). Thousand Oaks, CA: Sage.

Clarke, A. E. (2003). Situational analyses: Ground theory mapping after the postmodern turn. *Symbolic Interaction, 26*(4), 553–576.

Connell, R. (1987). *Gender & power.* Stanford, CA: Stanford University Press.

Connell, R. (1995). *Masculinities.* London: Polity Press.

Cressey, D. (1953). *Other people's money.* Belmont, CA: Wadsworth.

Crick, N. R., & Dodge, K. A. (1994). A review and reformulation of social information-processing mechanisms in children's social adjustment. *Psychological Bulletin, 115*(1), 74–101.

Crick, N. R., & Dodge, K. A. (1996). Social information processing mechanisms in reactive and proactive aggression. *Child Development, 67,* 993–1002.

Crick N. R., Grotpeter, J. K., & Bigbee, M. A. (2002). Relationally and physically aggressive children's intent attributions and feelings of distress for relational and instrumental peer provocations. *Child Development, 73*(4), 1134–1142.

Crick, N. R., Werner, N. E., Casas, J. F., O'Brien, K. M., Nelson, D. A., Grotpeter, J. K., & Markon, K. (1999). Childhood aggression and gender: A new look at an old problem. In D. Bernstein

(Ed.), *Nebraska symposium on motivation* (Vol. 45, pp. 75–141). Lincoln: University of Nebraska Press.

Denzin, N. K. (1989a). *Interpretive biography.* Newbury Park, CA: Sage.

Denzin, N. K. (1989b). *Interpretive interactionism.* Newbury Park, CA: Sage.

Garcia Coll, C., Lamberty, G., Jenkins, R., McAdoo, H. P., Crnic, K., Wasik, B. H., & Vazquez Garcia, H. (1996). An integrative model for the study of developmental competencies in minority children. *Child Development, 67,* 1891–1914.

Germaine, C. B., & Gitterman, A. (1996). *The life model of social work practice: Advances in theory and practice* (2nd ed.). New York: Columbia University Press.

Giddens, A. (1987). *Central problems in social theory: Action, structure and contradiction in social analysis.* Berkeley: University of California Press.

Gilgun, J. F. (1990). Factors mediating the effects of childhood maltreatment. In M. Hunter (Ed.), *The sexually abused male: Prevalence, impact, and treatment* (pp. 177–190). Lexington, MA: Lexington Books.

Gilgun, J. F. (1991). Resilience and the intergenerational transmission of child sexual abuse. In M. Q. Patton (Ed.), *Family sexual abuse: Frontline research and evaluation* (pp. 93–105). Newbury Park, CA: Sage.

Gilgun, J. F. (1992). Hypothesis generation in social work research. *Journal of Social Service Research, 15,* 113–135.

Gilgun, J. F. (1994). Avengers, conquerors, playmates, and lovers: A continuum of roles played by perpetrators of child sexual abuse. *Families in Society, 75,* 467–480.

Gilgun, J. F. (1995). We shared something special: The moral discourse of incest perpetrators. *Journal of Marriage and the Family, 57,* 265–281.

Gilgun, J. F. (1996a). Human development and adversity in ecological perspective. Part 1: A conceptual framework. *Families in Society, 77,* 395–402.

Gilgun, J. F. (1996b). Human development and adversity in ecological perspective. Part 2: Three patterns. *Families in Society, 77,* 459–576.

Gilgun, J. F. (1999). Mapping resilience as process among adults maltreated in childhood. In H. I. McCubbin, E. A. Thompson, A. I. Thompson, & J. A. Futrell (Eds.), *The dynamics of resilient families* (pp. 41–70). Thousand Oaks, CA: Sage.

Gilgun, J. F. (2002a). Completing the circle: American Indian Medicine Wheels and the promotion of resilience in children and youth in care. *Journal of Human Behavior and the Social Environment, 6*(2), 65–84.

Gilgun, J. F. (2002b). Social work and the assessment of the potential for violence. In T. N. Tiong & I. Dodds (Eds.), *Social work around the world* (Vol. 3, pp. 58–74). Berne, Switzerland: International Federation of Social Workers.

Gilgun, J. F. (in press a). Deductive qualitative analysis and family theory-building. In V. Bengston, P. Dillworth Anderson, K. Allen, A. Acock, & D. Klein (Eds.), *Sourcebook of family theory and methods.* Thousand Oaks, CA: Sage.

Gilgun, J. F. (in press b). Qualitative research and family psychology. *Journal of Family Psychology.*

Gilgun, J. F., Klein, C., & Pranis, K. (2000). The significance of resources in models of risk. *Journal of Interpersonal Violence, 14,* 627–646.

Gilgun, J. F., & McLeod, L. (1999). Gendering violence. *Studies in Symbolic Interactionism, 22,* 167–193.

Gilgun, J. F., & Reiser, E. (1990). Sexual identity development among men sexually abused in childhood. *Families in Society, 71,* 515–523.

Gilligan, C. (1982). *In a different voice: Psychological theory and women's development.* Cambridge, MA: Harvard University.

Glaser, B. (1978). *Theoretical sensitivity.* Mill Valley, CA: Sociology Press.

Glaser, B., & Strauss, A. (1967). *The discovery of grounded theory.* Chicago: Aldine.

Goldstein, H. (1994). Ethnography, critical inquiry, and social work practice. In E. Sherman & W. J. Reid (Eds.), *Qualitative research in social work* (pp. 42–51). New York: Columbia University.

Goodey, J. (1997). Boys don't cry: Masculinities, fear of crime, and fearlessness. *British Journal of Criminology, 37*(3), 401–418.

Gottman, J. D. (2001). *The relationship cure.* New York: Crown.

Kersten, J. (1990). A gender specific look at patterns of violence in juvenile institutions: Or are girls really "more difficult to handle"? *International Journal of the Sociology of Law, 18,* 473–493.

LoPresto, C., & Deluty, R. (1987). Consistency of aggressive, assertive, and submissive behavior in male adolescents. *The Journal of Social Psychology, 128*(5), 619–632.

Luthar, S. (2003). *Resilience and vulnerability: Adaptation in the context of childhood adversities.* New York: Cambridge University Press.

Luthar, S., & Cicchetti, D. (2000). The construct of resilience: Implications for interventions and social policies. *Development and Psychopathology, 12,* 857–885.

Majors, R., & Billson, J. M. (1992). *Cool pose.* New York: Lexington Books.

Masten, A. S., & Coatsworth, J. D. (1998). The development of competence in favorable and unfavorable environments: Lessons from research on successful children. *American Psychologist, 53,* 205–220.

Messerschmidt, J. (2000). *Nine lives: Adolescent masculinities, the body, and violence.* Boulder, CO: Westview.

Patton, M. Q. (2002). *Qualitative research and evaluation methods* (3rd ed.). Thousand Oaks, CA: Sage.

Seifert, K. L., Hoffnung, R. J., & Hoffnung, M. (2000). *Life-span development.* Boston: Houghton Mifflin.

Siegelman, C. K., & Rider, E. A. (2003). *Life-span human development* (4th ed.). Belmont, CA: Thomson.

Strauss, A., & Corbin, J. (1998). *Basics of qualitative research: Techniques and procedures for developing grounded theory* (2nd ed.). Thousand Oaks, CA: Sage.

Tierney, W. G. (2000). Undaunted courage: Life history and the postmodern challenge. In N. K. Denzin & Y. S. Lincoln (Eds.), *Handbook of qualitative research* (pp. 537–553). Thousand Oaks, CA: Sage.

Ungar, M. (2004). *Nurturing hidden resilience in troubled youth.* Toronto: University of Toronto Press.

West, C., & Zimmerman, D. (1987). Doing gender. *Gender and Society, 1*(2), 125–151.

Znaniecki, F. (1934). *The method of sociology.* New York: Farrar & Rinehart.

5

THE THEORY OF RESILIENCE AND ITS APPLICATION TO STREET CHILDREN IN THE MINORITY AND MAJORITY WORLDS

JACQUELINE MCADAM-CRISP

LEWIS APTEKAR

WANJIKU KIRONYO

In the 1950s, children who had run away from home to the streets were classified in the DSM-III-R as having a mental disorder, a perception that focuses on a child's deficits as opposed to strengths (Demoskoff & Lauzer, 1994). Although this classification is no longer used, the idea is still prevalent that the behavior of a child that results in his or her presence on the street must be maladaptive. The media, police, courts, social workers, and the public perpetuate this sensationalist image of deviance globally (Aptekar, 2000; Le Roux, 1998; Scheper-Hughes & Hoffman, 1998). However, those of us who work with these children have a different story to tell. Since the early 1980s, a number of studies have examined the lives of street children from a strengths perspective (Aptekar, 1994; Ennew, 1994; McAdam, 1995; Norman, 2000; Panter-Brick, 2002).

There has been a growing interest in the situation of street children in both the minority and majority worlds.[1] Street children throughout the world are now readily identifiable as a group "at risk." Yet in the face of adversity, many display a great deal of resilience. In this chapter, we examine the situation of street children in the minority and majority worlds within the framework of resilience theory. Each of us has worked with street children in a variety of cultural contexts, and through these experiences, we have become intrigued and puzzled with the capacity of some of these children to overcome adversity. We have been equally curious to understand the lack of capacity among others who, in comparison, seem to have experienced fewer risks but who appear to be more vulnerable to the risks they encounter. Furthermore, we are interested in knowing the etic or emic nature of resilience theory and practice across cultures. As Poortinga (1997) states,

> Behaviour is emic, or cultural specific, to the extent it can only be understood within the cultural context within which it occurs; it is etic, or universal, in as much as it is common to human beings independent of culture. (p. 348)

For example, although street children in both minority and majority world contexts are considered to be at risk, those in the majority world seem more often to possess a sense of hope, gratitude, and resilience. Although lacking in material wealth, these children possess a wealth of strength that seems foreign to street youth in the minority world. As Aptekar (1988) notes, "These children are not the emotionally injured 'runaways' whom I had work with in North America" (p. xiii). Typically, the term *street children* conjures up images of deviant maladjusted children who suffer from a range of psychological disorders. Visible on the city streets throughout the world, street children are far from a homogeneous group. Consequently, the adversities that street children experience and the way they sustain their well-being vary globally.

To begin, then, the term street children is examined in relation to the concept of childhood, including the expectations of how children should behave and the levels of risk we assume they are competent to handle. Next, we examine the various ways street children are defined and where they are found globally. We then explore the concept of resilience as a theoretical framework for examining street children's lives. Specifically, street children who are confronted by war or high rates of AIDS in their communities (and possibly their own infection) and girls who live on the street are examined in more detail because of the unique circumstance of these children. Factors proposed to enhance or limit resilience will be highlighted and program-based solutions introduced. Research on street children in both the minority and majority worlds will be drawn on along with the authors' collective experience to explore the relationship between risk and resilience in this population. Our goal, then, is to better understand street children globally through the application of the theory of resilience to their lives. Although we advocate that each child needs to be seen in context, we hope to provide a broad enough framework for understanding resilience for those defined as street children across a variety of diverse social and cultural contexts.

THE CHILDHOOD OF STREET CHILDREN

The UN Convention on the Rights of the Child (CRC) provides a benchmark from which the situation of street children can be measured. However, there have been many reservations about a unified set of principles and its application globally because of the diverse ways childhood is understood across cultures (Aptekar & McAdam-Crisp, in press; Scheper-Hughes & Sargent, 1998). Childhood as a developmental stage is obvious by a child's physical size. Yet there is a great deal of variety regarding how children are raised and what constitutes "good" child-rearing practices (Whiting, 1963). Olson's (1981) work with Turkish people, as discussed by Ratner (1999), provides an insightful example of how our values shape what we expect of children and how children are treated.

> [Olson] traces the low incidence of child abuse to the prevalent belief that life is unpredictable and subject to the vagaries of natural and supernatural forces, which transcend human will. Since humans have neither the power nor responsibility to control, they do not seek to control their children. Nor do they set expectations for children's physical and emotional capabilities. Caretakers accept and indulge children's behaviors. As a result, most misbehaviors of children are not punished but tolerated as childish naughtiness. Thus, parents' benevolent treatment of their children is mediated by beliefs about the causes of events, the power and responsibilities of people, and the capacity of children. (p. 8)

Definitions of adolescence as a defined stage of one's childhood are also controversial across cultures. For example, the Gurage shoeshine boys seen working in the streets of Addis Ababa, Ethiopia, are an accepted norm for adolescence and not thought to be a sign of a child at risk (Veale, Adefrisew, & Lalor, 1992). Consequently, removing these children from the street would threaten their acceptance within their cultural grouping. Likewise, in East and Central Africa, it is common for rural girls to be married by the age of 14. Of course, we do not mean to imply that there are not some inherent risks with both these examples of adolescents moving quickly into adultlike roles. Instead, we wish to point out that because the concept of childhood and adolescence is not universally defined, it is equally difficult to define risk and resilience across cultures. As Black (1993) notes, "The idea of a protracted period of time in the early part of life in which youngsters enjoy special protection, nurture and dependency is relatively recent historically and largely confined to the industrialized societies" (p. 15). The concept of childhood and the value society places on this stage of development are extremely diverse; thus, so are the various ways children cope with this stage of development.

STREET CHILDREN: A DEFINITION

The term street children has been criticized as demeaning of children's experiences (Aptekar, 1988; Dallape, 1988; Hutz & Koller, 1999). Dallape (1996) notes that the term is "offensive and gives a distorted message" (p. 283). The term has been used to refer to children in a variety of circumstances, creating confusion about who these children are and what kinds of risk brought them to the streets. For years, UNICEF has referred to street children as "on" and "of" the street. Children "on" the street are those who have continual contact with their families, whereas children "of" the street have occasional contact with their families. A third category, which is the smallest, refers to children who have no contact with their families because of the death of their parent or parents, abandonment by their families, or family conflicts that necessitated the child's leaving home (Barker & Knaul, 1991; Blanc, 1994; McAdam, 1995). The first two categories account for approximately 90% of all street children, who are commonly

referred to as "working street children." Many of these children combine work and school (Lusk, 1992). The latter group is a more "pure" definition of street children, accounting for those who are potentially at the greatest risk because of the extensive amount of time they spend on the street (Aptekar, 2000; Scheper-Hughes & Hoffman, 1998). No matter how these street children are categorized, they are seen in streets throughout the world, selling candies, newspapers, magazines, and tissues, as well as begging and stealing.

Street children do not form a homogeneous group, nor do their life circumstances remain constant. Their involvement on the street varies, as does their family contact. Children may be represented in one or more categories at different times of their lives and careers in the streets. For this reason, other researchers have used their own definitions to name these youth (see Aptekar, 1988; Cosgrove, 1990; Lusk, 1992). Definitions in general can help to establish a context, but they do not fully provide a qualitative understanding of the relationship between the risk and resilience factors operating in these children's lives. They neglect to speak to the amount of time a child spends on the street, a child's source of livelihood or income, and what constitutes a responsible caregiver (Panter-Brick, 2002). Furthermore, a child's developmental stage and gender is not considered. As Kironyo notes, she has seen children in Nairobi, Kenya, as young as 2 years old on the street. The mother will sit at a corner of a shop and instruct the children who to beg from. Restrictive definitions also neglect the protective factors that can influence a child's presence on the street and decrease the cumulative effects of risk. For example, children are far more likely to stay in school if their parents value their children's education. Parents who are illiterate often do not understand the value of school. Therefore, they discourage study time because it cuts into the time children could be working on the streets and contributing to the family income.

Conventional definitions of street children also do not acknowledge a child's own interpretation of risk. In both the minority and majority world, children have a reason for leaving home and being in the streets. Although reasons may differ across cultures, it needs to be acknowledged that becoming a child of the streets is a form of coping. For example, McAdam-Crisp knew a 12-year-old girl in Addis Ababa who was living with her mother's friend because her mother had died. Prostitution was a common form of income generation in this home. The girl left, and because she had nowhere to go, she ended up in the streets. It was difficult for this girl to get services because, technically, she had a home. Leaving such an unhealthy environment would better be considered a strength and warrant services. We may wonder how often a child's sense of personal well-being is ignored as a result of well-meaning adults determining what is appropriate for the child, with decisions often dictated by strict funding criteria that identify the types of interventions available to service at-risk children. The complex realities of street life demand that children are understood as individuals within a social and cultural context that often perpetuates their existence in the streets. As in other chapters in this volume, most specifically Boyden and Mann's (Chapter 1), we, too, find it important to acknowledge children's own ways of sustaining resilience even when their choices are misunderstood by their caregivers.

STREET CHILDREN IN THE GLOBAL CONTEXT

Estimates of the number of street children vary from 30 to 170 million (Barker & Knaul, 1991). The number is expected to increase to 800 million by the year 2020 (Save the Children Canada, 2004, March 1). Of these children, 90% live in the majority world, where 50% of the population is under the age of 15. These numbers are not surprising given that poverty is one of the main factors that accounts for the number of street children in the majority world, where children on the street range in age from 5 to 18 years (Aptekar, 1988; Aptekar & Ciano, 1999; Aptekar, Maphalala, Dlamini, Makhanya, & Magagula, 1998; Ennew, 1994; Le Roux, 1996; Muchini & Nyandiya-Bundy, 1991; Veale, 1996; Veale et al., 1992). Given the complexity of the problem, an accurate count of street children is hard to determine because of their transient nature, the lack of resources to

count these children, and the lack of agreement as to what defines a street child. Furthermore, estimates of the number of street children do not include those children under the age of 5 who are on the streets, most often with their mothers. In the majority world, there are a greater number of male street children: 90% in many African countries, approximately 80% in Jamaica and other Caribbean countries, and 75% worldwide (Aptekar, 1994, 2000; Aptekar & McAdam-Crisp, in press). There are various reasons for these gender differences. Veale (1996) observed that there were no street girls in Khartoum, Sudan, because of a strong Islamic presence that makes it inappropriate for girls to work in the street. The large proportion of boys on the street in the majority world is further explained by changing family structures, along with other factors that have resulted in a great number of families headed by mothers alone. Aptekar and Ciano (1999) note that boys are socialized by their mothers to cope with the necessity of surviving in a very limited economic environment by becoming independent at a far earlier age than Western culture deems appropriate. Consequently, many boys are expected to contribute to the incomes of their families. Paradoxically, mothers teach girls how to cope with the vagaries of poverty by staying at home and learning household tasks.

Children are on the streets in the majority world for many reasons, including structural adjustment programs, rural to urban migration, changing family structures, AIDS, and civil and regional conflicts, along with problems in the immediate family, all of which contribute to the number of street children (Aptekar, 2000; Barker & Knaul, 1991; Ennew, 1994; McAdam, 1995; Scheper-Hughes & Sargent, 1998). As Kilbride, Suda, and Njeru (2000) note, "The phenomenal growth of the international economy with the demands of the global economy for competitive prices has served to pressure local markets for cheap labor, often including children as laborers" (p. 3). This, coupled with urban migration, means that many children who formerly worked in rural settings now work in the urban centers, making their work more visible.

By comparison, children in the minority world are often forced out of their homes because of a dysfunctional family environment that can include high levels of conflict; physical, emotional, or sexual abuse; and/or substance abuse (Ayerst, 1999). Although poverty may play a part in these children coming to the street, this is not always the case (Bagley, 1985; Webber, 1991). The reasons children end up in the streets are diverse, and as Webber (1991) points out, "all the partially true explanations ignore the economic, social, and moral foundation on which faltering families, failing schools, and inept social and correctional services totter" (p. 35). For these reasons, a discussion of the resilience of street children needs to incorporate the micro- and macrolevel issues that affect the social, cultural, and political circumstances of a specific environment.

STREET CHILDREN WITHIN THE FRAMEWORK OF RESILIENCE

Approaches to examine resilience have relied primarily on a systemic approach for deducing risk in relation to protective factors, an approach that assumes a predictable relationship between risk and protective factors (Ungar, 2004). As Werner and Smith (2001) note in their work, "As the number of risks factors or stressful life events increase, more protective factors were needed to counterbalance the negative aspects in the lives of those vulnerable children and to ensure a positive developmental outcome" (p. 58). This denotes a potential quantifiable relationship between the risks children face and the protective factors present in their lives. In essence, if A, B, and C are present in the face of adversity, a positive outcome will result. The inverse relationship is also true. Although this deductive approach is invaluable, there are still many questions regarding the qualitative interactions of these different factors within various cultural contexts. Kirby and Fraser (1997) express the complex nature of identifying this process:

> No single event produces a negative outcome. Rather, interactional processes shape behaviours and problems over time. The separation of risk process from risk trait remains a major challenge for practitioners and researchers who work with troubled children and who seek to design more effective social programs. (p. 13)

Examining the situation of street children globally, it is difficult to unilaterally define what might be considered protective factors for children who experience diverse sociocultural factors. In addition, there are instances where resilience occurs despite very few protective factors (Higgins, 1994). Of course, children are not invincible to continual risks that result in life-threatening or traumatic experiences or both. However, the ability to deal with adverse situations is a dynamic process that varies throughout a person's life and in relation to the various situations that he or she encounters. Consequently, a child who is resilient in one situation may not be in another.

Our approach assumes that street children have the ability to actively construct their own realities that are a reflection of their cultural values. However, we do not postulate that the culture with which a street child identifies is the same hegemonic culture that excludes them. Consider the story of a girl we will call Laura, with whom McAdam-Crisp worked in the mid-1980s in Victoria, British Columbia, Canada.

Laura's Story

Laura was a "high-risk youth" in the minority world. As a teenager, she moved between the street and various foster homes; she got pregnant and gave birth just after her 14th birthday. This was the first of four children who were either apprehended at birth or taken into care later. I began working with Laura when she was 12 until shortly after she decided to put her first child up for adoption (who had been apprehended at birth). She was just about 15 years old at the time. While she was pregnant, in an attempt to "rehabilitate" and improve the prospects for herself and her baby, I read her stories of teens who had become pregnant. This was my attempt to create an educational forum and opening for discussion between us. In response to one of these stories, Laura told me she had no idea who the father was and commented that she remembered the first time she had sex and her last partner, but all the ones in between were a blur. Laura defied the social standards of what was expected of a child of this age. Whatever Laura's abilities or more commonly discussed disabilities were, they have facilitated her coping over the years.

Now, fifteen years later, I continue to see Laura on the streets. She frequents the street kitchens and shelters and hangs out with the street people. Who am I to judge her experience as lacking in resilience? Unlike many of the other girls I worked with during my career, she is not dead. If this is used as an indicator of resilience, then she succeeded. For the most part, Laura just wanted to be able to live her life and resented being hassled by professionals.

Although a primarily social constructionist approach is taken here, a more deductive approach is not necessarily dismissed by the way we have come to understand Laura's life and the lives of other street youth. A deductive approach is drawn on, not to define hierarchical constructs of interaction, but to propose one kind of explanation for the interactions that affect children and contribute to their becoming attached to street-based lives. For example, Bowlby's (1969) work on attachment indicates that children deprived of maternal attachment are more likely to develop maladaptive behaviors in the future. Although Bowlby's theory places a great deal of emphasis on the early years, different child care practices that exist in the majority world may consequently affect a child's resilience. For example, mothers who beg in the street have their babies strapped to their backs, which may act as a psychological buffer against other risks encountered on the street. This is also observed by Werner and Smith (2001) who showed that in a group of children deemed to be high risk, those who had a consistent attachment to a primary caregiver did better in life. Furthermore, in the majority world, large, extended families provide nurturance and support for a child even if that family is homeless.

We acknowledge the presence of quantifiable indicators, such as mother-child attachment, that have been well studied in minority-world contexts that could act as protective factors, but we also acknowledge that these may not be quantifiable across cultures or between individuals. Nevertheless, the development of some guiding principles that recognize the potential intersection of quantifiable indicators and the quality of the experience for the child may help in understanding better the plight of street children and lead to the development of appropriate policies and practices.

STREET CHILDREN AND THE RISK PROCESS

Interactions of psychosocial factors within the context of culture affect the experience of street children in relation to risk and resilience. An overview of the potential risk to street children in both the minority and majority world will be discussed briefly. We then examine specific areas that pose potentially greater risk to street children. These include exposure to war, AIDS, and the special issues that affect girls.

To illustrate the confluence of factors that pose multiple risks to street children, we will use an illustration that comes from Kironyo's experience in Nairobi with a boy named Moses. Moses' story details the evolution of what we term a *risk process* for a street child and the difficulties involved in providing support to the child.

Moses' Story

A few years ago, after moving to a new neighborhood, I was approached by a small boy who asked if he could wash my car. Looking at Moses, he seemed far too small to adequately complete such a task. I agreed and watched as he quickly took a stool, stood in front of the car, and started washing. He, in fact, did a good job. Upon completion, he asked for a fee that was one quarter of what would normally be paid for such a task. Out of concern, I asked where he was from and discovered he was from the Kibera slums where he lived with his mother. He said that his father has sent him, his mother, his eight brothers, and one sister away from home after marrying a younger wife. The children moved in with their grandmother, but the father's brothers (the children's uncles) were threatened by the fact that this might result in the boy's mother and her children inheriting the grandparent's land. The family then moved to the Kibera slums, and the mother started roasting maize for income. Because the mother was unable to feed her children on her meager earnings, each was instructed to find a way to support the family. Moses was making his contribution.

I suggested that he might go to school and spoke to his mother about this option. A school placement was established. I paid the school fees for the first term, but for the second term, I gave his mother the money. This was done to allow the mother to take on the responsibility of having her child go to school. She decided that there were other more pressing priorities than the school fees. Because the school fees were not paid, Moses was sent away by the school and started doing odd jobs for my neighbors. I followed up with Moses when I saw him on the street, and he told me the money for the school fee was used to buy food and pay the house rent. He did not wish to go to school while there was no food to eat.

Later, Moses joined a group of street boys in central Nairobi whereupon his mother attempted to get him arrested and put in the Kabete remand home. While parking my vehicle in the city center, I saw a boy helping me to park and realized that it was Moses. I told him to come see me and we would discuss the issue of schooling. I found another school for him, but he said it was too far to walk.

Moses returned to the streets where he sniffed glue and petrol, a pastime often engaged in to numb the physical pain of hunger. Two years later, I met him and told him that he was welcome to visit my home. He took me up on my offer and visited regularly. To help, I found a job for him; he had learned a number of skills while in the street. Moses could construct a bicycle from scraps of metal, a chair from various scraps of wood, and make a bed out of almost anything. He was extremely creative. Through this process, he revealed to me that being in the streets was not worth the trouble because the police constantly harassed him. It is often easier for older youth to leave the street and enter the informal job market. Skills learned while on the street are useful because the informal economy is street based.

Globally, street children like Moses are exposed to a number of dangers such as beatings, rape, and sexually transmitted diseases like AIDS, along with other health problems. Those children who remain in the street are more likely to become involved in criminal activity, prostitution, and drug trafficking. However, this varies between urban settings and the way urban space is negotiated. For instance, the larger the urban setting and the greater the disparity between the rich and poor, coupled with a lack of social supports, the more risks there are to street children. A lack of social support to protect and provide for children coupled with extreme poverty in the majority world means that children are more visible in urban spaces. These children are more likely to be abducted, recruited as child soldiers, or become part of the human traffic circuit. Often, these children are maimed, because they will consequently make more money begging.

In the majority world, children can remain in the streets for many years. However, in the minority world, this is not necessarily the case. Street children in the minority world often move between various care facilities, the street, and youth detention. Often, they return to the street in reaction to the breakdown of a care arrangement, and the cycle repeats. Boys typically partake in petty crime and the selling of drugs to support themselves, often resulting in their arrest. Girls, on the other hand, are more prone to prostitution and are therefore less visible on the streets or in the justice system. In the minority world, street children are more likely to suffer from high levels of depression, suicidal tendencies, and alcohol and drug problems (Smollar, 1999).

This street cycle in both the minority and majority worlds is complicated by the concept of a risk chain, which results when a child's psychological and physical development creates vulnerabilities that in a given setting may increase the child's exposure to risk. For example, Erikson (1963) affirms a youth's need for belonging. Maslow (1954) and others have defined the need to belong as a significant process in our growth. This need provides a sense of support or enhanced community, identified in the literature as a protective factor. When a child feels disenfranchised or unconnected, he or she may gravitate toward the street to gain a sense of belonging and community through contact with informal street families. The experience on the street compels youth to rely on their street friends for support, which in turn strengthens the bonds between these children, creating a circular effect. This can result in children becoming more entrenched in street life in their efforts to survive and thrive.

That said, the concept of a risk chain might work differently in the majority world where working street children are less likely to be involved in illegal activity, drugs, or alcohol (Aptekar, 1988; Scheper-Hughes & Hoffman, 1998). In fact, these children are part of a growing urban economy that supports many of the families of the urban poor. Removing these children from the street often has negative consequences, because lack of income from the street means less money for food, medical costs, and school fees for those children who remain at home—many of whom are girls (Barker & Knaul, 1991; Boyden & Mann, 2000; McAdam, 1995). The supposed risk chain in the majority world may have a much more positive outcome because it reinforces a child's evolving self as a supportive member of the community and family.

Although those classified as working street children can become involved in deviant behavior, those who meet the purer definition of street children are more likely to be involved in deviant activities as a way of coping. As Scheper-Hughes and Hoffman (1998) note,

> Although they represent the smallest number of those who are labelled "street kids," these truly homeless children are quite visible; and because of what they have to do to defend themselves on the street, they fuel the negative stereotypes of the "dangerous" and "uncontrollable" street kids. (p. 361)

Research shows that the primary risks to street children do not come from living on the streets but from police action. In many places in the world, street children have been killed for no more than petty crimes (Aptekar, 2000; Aptekar & McAdam-Crisp, in press; Black, 1993; Ennew, 1994; Scheper-Hughes & Hoffman, 1998; Tierney, 1997). This is illustrated by the case of Simon.

The Case of Simon

Aptekar and Ciano (1999) have written about Simon, a Kenyan child, 15 years of age, who was murdered by a police reservist. He was shot five times at point-blank range, kicked into the gutter, and then spat on. He had stolen a signal lens from a parked car, nothing more. What about this boy aroused such anger? It appears that the reservist construed a scenario about street children that did not include loving parents or good character.

Simon, like street children in nearly all cultures in the world, was treated with such fury because he received the moral judgment given to those who violate the norms that cultures give to acceptable behavior for children. Street children do this by not living under the same roof as their parents, by working instead of going to school, and by assuming the right to enjoy the fruits of their work as they chose (such as consuming alcohol or drugs). Simon was a street child with loving parents, who attended his funeral. They said he was a good boy who contributed what he earned from working on the streets to his family. He often stayed at home, but even when he didn't, he kept in touch with his family. The problem was that from the perspective of the police he was viewed as a delinquent and therefore was killed. We would suggest that Simon's behavior said far more about the resilience of street children, although theories of resilience have largely overlooked the way such behavior contributes to health for the child and his or her family.

Street Children, War, and AIDS

Street children are most typically referred to as those who have suffered from prolonged deprivation or family violence at home and/or are poor and enter the streets to earn money or to escape abusive situations. This group forms the smallest cohort of street children, about 10% globally. However, the increasing number of civil and regional conflicts and the rampant spread of AIDS have changed the face of the world's street children. For example, in Rwanda, the number of children on the street increased significantly following the genocide in 1994 (Ministry of Labour and Social Affairs, 1997). Veale and Doná (2003) report that of the street children they surveyed, 87% came to the street following the genocide, and approximately 42%

of these children were living without family. This is significantly higher than the number of children who meet the stereotypical definition of a street child. Rwandan street children, like other children of war, do not have a history of living on the street. They are there because of displacement and the death of or separation from their parents (McAdam, 1997).

Similar findings were noted in a comparative study in Ethiopia, in which 20% of all children had been orphaned in the Tigray region, an area that has been affected by the civil war between Eritrea and Ethiopia over the last 30 years, compared with only 4% to 8% of children being orphans in other regions (Veale et al., 1992). Aptekar's research with those displaced from Eritrea in 1991 further illustrates this point. When Eritrea gained independence in 1991, all those who were deemed to be Ethiopian were forced to leave. Some were taken in trucks, and others left on foot for Ethiopia, a journey that required them to pass through the Danakil Depression, one of the hottest places on earth and where there is little vegetation or water. Whether they went by truck or by foot, many people witnessed the death of friends and family. Many of the survivors, young children at the time, now live on the streets in Addis Ababa, Ethiopia's capital. Are they victims of war, street children, or both? Herein lies the problem of defining these youth as street children based solely on the observation that they now live on the street. These examples illustrate that it is far more important to understand a child's attachment to the street as the result of a multidetermined process in which the outcome—street life—is an adaptation to a number of different risks and may, by necessity, be the only healthy option for the child to overcome adversity.

Despite some positives, however, a life on the street solves only some problems. It does not provide the resources to address the high rates of trauma many of these children have experienced. Many have witnessed the death of their parents, and many have also been physically wounded. Consequently, along with poverty these children may exhibit a range of behaviors such as sleep disturbances, recurring memories, and extreme sadness in relation to the trauma they have experienced. If these qualitative differences are not addressed, more extreme psychological problems

may result, such as increased aggression and other symptoms such as posttraumatic stress disorder (PTSD)[2] (for a more detailed discussion of PTSD see Solomon and Laufer's work on Israeli children in Chapter 14).

Given this risk process in which one risk piles up on another, it seems reasonable that AIDS has changed the life circumstances for many of the world's street children. For instance in 1989, ChildHope documented that Brazil had the third largest number of AIDS cases worldwide after the United States and France and that between 2% and 10% of street youth were HIV positive in San Paulo and Rio de Janeiro, Brazil; Khartoum, Sudan; and New York (Barker, 1989). Today, not only has the number of street children who are HIV positive risen, the number of children in the street who have been orphaned because of AIDS-related deaths of their parents has also risen. UNICEF (2003) reports, "Although HIV/AIDS has reached almost every part of the world, no other region has been harder hit than sub-Sahara Africa, home to nearly three quarters of the world's people living with HIV/AIDS" (p. 7). This includes approximately 11 million children under the age of 15 who have been orphaned by AIDS. Traditionally, many orphans are taken in by their extended family (UNICEF, 2003; Velis, 1995). However, the AIDS epidemic has resulted in too many orphans who cannot all be supported by their extended families. These children are often unaware of what is happening and, thus, are more vulnerable to the inherent risks associated with living on the street. Kironyo translates the words of one such orphaned youth from the Maji Mazuri Centre in Nairobi, Kenya, to illustrate this point.

I learned to survive the hard way after my mother died of AIDS before joining the Maji Mazuri Centre. I had experienced a lot of suffering by the age of 17. My mother died when I was very young. I cannot remember my age then. The problems started when she fell ill. My brother and sister went through a lot of pain, loneliness, anger as we watched our mom cough and lose weight. We did not know what she was suffering from; we only knew she was sick. We never knew our dad, nor did we have any other relatives. After mom died, we were thrown out of the shanty house we rented; we begged for food after being kicked out; the little things we owned were taken away by the landlord due to rent arrears. We used to cry a lot. I could not really comprehend what was happening. We have never been to school, even when mom was alive. We ended up on the streets. Different people in the streets frequently raped us. We did not understand what was happening to us. Other people told us their stories. I had no idea this was the same thing that was happening to me. It was difficult having to beg every day for food, and life had to go on. I had to survive. We got involved in drugs and could not control ourselves. I was preoccupied with what to eat and where to sleep, not school, as it was not a priority.

AIDS will undoubtedly change the number of children who are forced to live in the streets to survive. Both the presence of war and AIDS will influence the percentage of abandoned children who are on the street, greatly increasing their numbers over time. This growing population of abandoned children also has meant many more girls on the streets as well as boys. Thus, it has become critical to understand the risks street life poses to this group of abandoned street children without family resources, in particular for girls, who are forming a disproportionately large percentage of such street children without kinship attachments.

STREET GIRLS

An examination of the profile of street children shows the complex nature of the intersection of various factors related to gender and other risks in minority and majority world contexts. In the minority world, more girls than boys are recorded as runaways, a potential indicator of the number of street-involved youth. In Canada in 2001, 53,434 children were recorded as runaways; of this group, a total of 31,981 were girls—10,000 more girls than boys (Royal Canadian Mounted Police, 2001). Although this information is revealing, it does not necessarily provide an accurate number because many runaways return home, only to run away again and, as such, are recorded twice. Despite this fact, the greater number of street girls in the minority world is most concerning because it is an invisible

phenomenon creating a public perception that it is not a problem. The lower numbers of street girls in the public view by day is compensated for by those who have been recruited as prostitutes, most of whom are on the streets at night (Agnelli, 1986; Aptekar, 1994; Tacon, 1981). Anecdotal information in this area demands more attention, as does childhood prostitution into which girls are primarily recruited. Kim's story is just one example of the pathways to the street for girls and the prevalence of prostitution, which they must turn to for survival.

Kim's Story

I [McAdam-Crisp] met Kim in a group home in which I worked in the early 1990s in Victoria, B.C. Kim had been placed because of difficulties at home between her mom's boyfriend and herself. Kim was always doing something for the other residents in the home. She was attractive, fun to be around, and had a bright sunny disposition at the age of 15. Because this was only a transitional arrangement, Kim left the home to be placed in a more permanent arrangement. Three months later while working downtown in Vancouver, B.C., I bumped into Kim, walking along the street with a male youth. She was wearing a short black skirt and high-heeled black boots; her peaches-and-cream complexion was marred with a large scar down the side of her face. The scar, the clothing and the area were a strong indication that Kim was likely involved or becoming involved in Vancouver's prostitution circuit. I offered to help her return to Victoria and she agreed. A month later, the social worker phoned me to ask if I had heard from Kim; she was AWOL and assumed to be back on the streets in Vancouver. This is only one story of the many young girls with whom I have worked over the years who end up returning to the streets. Frequently, the draw is a boyfriend who affirms a girl's need for love and belonging. However, many of these so-called boyfriends are also pimps.

Many of these young girls have been sexually abused prior to these experiences or are soon abused on the street (Bagley, 1985).

When we look closely at the situation for girls in the majority world, the prospects of abuse are equally daunting. Girls are protected from the street for fear of sexual abuse, and if a girl is on the street, it means she has been compelled to move there against the gendered expectations of her culture. Aptekar and Ciano (1999) note in their study on gender differences among street youth in Kenya that 80% of street girls have been sexually abused. Unlike boys, these girls are not connected to their families of origin, and their time on the street is often compounded by continual sexual abuse. The story of Jocelyn, a street girl in Nairobi, Kenya, is offered as a contrast to Kim's story.

Jocelyn's Story

One evening, I (Aptekar), along with my female research partner, stopped to talk to several street boys who were living at the end of a deserted alley near an open sewer just outside the city center. They lived in two shacks they had constructed from rubble. To enter, we had to bend low to pass through the doorway. To our surprise, we found that two of the occupants were female. Jocelyn, who appeared to have just reached puberty, lay covered in rags, a jar of inhalant in her hand. Through glazed eyes, she barely greeted us. We inferred that she didn't need our attention because she was being "protected" by several of the older street boys. The next day, we returned to the site, and thanks to the skill of the female researcher (and promises of financial assistance), we were able to take Jocelyn to a center that serves street girls where she had been treated well before. Presumably, because she was cooperating with us, thus violating the behavioral expectations put on street girls by street boys, upon arrival at the center, none of her peers, some of whom she knew, greeted her. Over the next several days, we were able to get some idea of Jocelyn's background.

Jocelyn had been raised by her mother in Mathare, a large slum area on the outskirts of Nairobi. She had three older brothers. When sales of her mother's illegal beer were good, Jocelyn's brothers went to school while Jocelyn stayed at home to help with chores and her mother's business. Because her mother was not always present, she was abused several times by men who came to buy beer. Her mother, Jocelyn said, "never helped me." Over time, she began to make friends with older boys, one of whom she liked enough to accept his invitation to live with him in the alley. Before long, she was in a similar position as she had been at home. Because many of the boys found her attractive, they paid her male friend for the right to enjoy Jocelyn's "company." With nowhere to turn, Jocelyn began a habit of taking inhalants to cope. We tried to get Jocelyn's mother to help her daughter but could not locate her. We were told that she had been caught by the police and was in prison. We were eventually able to find her, but Jocelyn by that time had returned to the streets. Our forays into the alley to find her were met with increasing hostility; once she threw stones at us. The next time we looked for her, we could not gain entry to her shack and we never saw her again. The path that Jocelyn appeared to be traveling was a common one for street girls in Nairobi.

In both the majority and minority worlds, the circumstances that result in girls leaving home are different than those for boys. The risk of sexual abuse and assault on the street will often result in girls' staying home even when conditions are poor. When a girl chooses to leave home, it is often because problems have intensified. Therefore, how a girl uses street life to bolster resilience to stressors at home may be more complicated than for boys. On the street, the risks girls face may expose them to additional stressors that compound the challenges they faced at home, making it unclear if life on the street is part of a pathway to resilience or a step backward in terms of the degree of vulnerability that girls experience. Whereas in Western countries it is assumed that children are on the streets because of family dysfunction, in the majority world, this is likely to be true for street girls but not street boys.

FACTORS THAT MAY ENHANCE AND LIMIT RESILIENCE FOR STREET CHILDREN

From studying the lives of street children, we have learned that it is presumptuous to assume that a Western-style definition of risk naturally equates to a traumatic experience. As our work has shown, working street children may actually fair better than their fellow age-mates when confronted with adversity. A lack of understanding of the relationship between risk and resilience in the lives of marginalized children has often resulted in forcing these children to get off the street, an act that further jeopardizes the economic situation of their family and potentially decreases their and their families' resilience (Boyden & Mann, 2000).

Taking into account a child's subjective experience within his or her social and cultural context allows us to gain a better understanding of the intersection of risk and resilience factors associated with street life. Furthermore, just because a child is in the street does not mean that he or she is the victim of abuse or neglect, or a delinquent ready for reeducation. This is the case for both boys and girls, although the probability of risk for girls is likely higher.

An example, the story of two working street girls in Ethiopia, is illustrative of the risk and resilience factors operating in their lives at one and the same time. Although girls are at an increased risk of sexual abuse and consequently early pregnancies, neither of these girls experienced this problem. These girls were careful to remain together and never started working before 10 in the morning and left the street before dark. Furthermore, as a consequence of their time on the street and the skills they gained, these girls were later able to obtain a job at a restaurant. As Lalor (1999) comments, many girls in Ethiopia have self-imposed curfews to avoid sexual assault, decreasing their potential risks. Female street children abide by the same rules.

Viewing street children only in terms of their vulnerabilities does not do justice to the resilience of many who, in the face of adversity, have developed the ability to cope. Street children are social actors who develop a specific "microculture" that comes from balancing what they need to do to survive with the larger society's reactions to their status. Often, they do this quite successfully, much to public surprise. In fact, street children are often viewed as more resilient than their stay-at-home counterparts (Aptekar & Stocklin, 1997). In a study of street

children in Guatemala, the living conditions on the street were often better than those at home (Connelly, 1990). Studies in South Africa have noted that street children ate better and avoided the daily abuse they faced at home (Hickson & Gaydon, 1989; Scharf, Powell, & Thomas, 1986; Swart, 1990). In Brazil, street children had a higher degree of intelligence and were less likely to abuse drugs than their stay-at-home counterparts who lived in poverty (Lusk, 1992; Oliveria, Baizerman, & Pellet, 1992). Leaving home and fending for themselves on the street is seen as an indicator of resilience. In Bogotá, Colombia, street children were found to immerse themselves in a network of caring and supportive friendships (Tyler, Holliday, Tyler, Echeverry, & Zea, 1987; Tyler, Tyler, Echeverry, & Zea, 1992). These patterns hold for many street boys and girls in the majority world who have been found to have developed coping strategies that allow them to function at least as well as equally impoverished counterparts who pass less time in public view. These coping strategies include finding a niche in the economic market, which gives them sufficient income to eat and clothe themselves. They are also able to find and take advantage of programs that serve them, being sufficiently informed about their physical health to maintain their well-being, form close friendships with peers, and keep up some form of connection with their families of origin.

STREET CHILDREN: PROGRAM-BASED SOLUTIONS FOR ENHANCING RESILIENCE

With increasing awareness regarding the plight of street children, there has been a growing demand for programs that can address the needs of street children in both the minority and majority world. A key objective is to decrease the number of street children and enhance a child's potential for survival and future prospects. Services for street children are predominantly located in urban centers where street children are most often located. As an exemplar of these programs, the Undugu Society of Kenya is a well-known and well-established model for street children. This program, like many others, offers services through small primary centers that provide food, recreation, personal hygiene facilities, life skills, education, job training, and in some cases, temporary shelter. Their model provides children with services within their own environment while also facilitating supportive relationships with center staff. By providing for the children's basic needs, including a sense of belonging, these programs successfully bolster a child's resilience.

However, there are drawbacks to a model of service that provides paid relationships to adults that may be less authentic than naturally occurring relationships that have been developed on the street over an extended period of time. In the minority world in particular, the creation of trusting relationships between children and adults is complicated by a structure of formal care that often results in a child's feeling a greater sense of rejection and alienation, because the breakdown of many out-of-home placements is one of the reasons children take to the street in the first place. Coming from a background of abuse, these children are often more comfortable in the presence of peers who affirm their view of the world as a dangerous place when interacting with adults.

In the majority world, structures are different and the need for services greater. However, success may be more a matter of "anything is better than nothing" than an indication of well-run programs with adequately trained staff (McAdam, 1997). In Rwanda, following the 1994 genocide, there was a proliferation of new programs with different approaches for street children. This was also partly because many trained personnel had been killed in the genocide. Many programs succeeded. However, this was not necessarily an indication of their ability to care for children but, rather, an indication of the need for resources regardless of their quality. Often, staff members are less than adequately trained, although they may appear quite charismatic and able to engage with the youth (Ennew, 1994). Not surprisingly, such individuals also need to be carefully supervised, because they do not always have the best of intentions. As in the minority world, those who have been granted the privilege of protecting children may at times be the ones who abuse them.

Ensuring that best practices are realized and that services are tailored to the needs of the children requires that accurate data be gathered on the children to assess present and potential future risks as well as relevant protective factors. Acquiring accurate data is not easy. In the minority world, street workers in cooperation with the police often walk the streets at night to gain a more accurate understanding of who is on the streets and what they are doing. As mentioned, many street girls involved in prostitution are not on the streets during the day. In fact, they may not necessarily be on the street at night either but, instead, work out of clubs. Realizing this, McAdam-Crisp, while living in Nairobi, frequented a nightclub known for its prostitution as part of the fieldwork for her master's thesis. Young girls would come to the club, enter the washroom, and change into more seductive outfits. A woman handing out condoms in the washroom would guard their clothes for a small price. Often, there was a priest at the entrance to the club handing out information on other options available to these girls.

Many programs for these girls have been developed based on perceived rather than defined need. This is apparent in a number of programs that provide food and shelter. As mentioned before, most street children have parents and a home to go to but are on the streets because of circumstances related to their families' economic hardship. For this reason, it may be more appropriate to use a family-centered model of intervention rather than one that merely views the child individually as being at risk. For example, in the Rwandan capital, Kigali, there were significantly more services for street children than in smaller communities, which may have actually led to children's migration away from their families and into situations of greater risk. Offering a more community-based family model may help these children gain the support they need in their home communities. A family-centered approach does, however, present a number of potential problems. Although street children were reunited with their families, many children complained that their parents only took them back based on the promise of monetary benefits. Many programs provided material support, such as fixing a roof or buying a bed, as incentives for parents to accept responsibility for their children.

More positively, income-generating activities have been used to support the needs of the entire family, not just the child at risk. The development of income-generation activities has been acclaimed by many (Boyden & Mann, 2000; McAdam, 1995). However, such employment opportunities are limited. In areas where these schemes are operating, boys are traditionally trained in the area of woodwork, carpentry, and metal work and girls in hairdressing and dressmaking. Although these are all worthy endeavors to fully enhance the resilience of children, children are then expected to fend for themselves once they have completed their program. Because of a weak job market in most communities from where these children come, many are not able to get jobs, resulting in further exposure to potential risk factors. Programs that address the needs of working street children need to be designed based on a market assessment. A number of innovative programs that incorporate this have proven to be successful. For example, Peter Dalglish, the founder of Street Kids International, and others facilitated the development of a bicycle courier program for street boys in Khartoum, Sudan, in the late 1980s.

Building broader community support, including among business people, police, and politicians, has also proven to be a successful means of advocating for street children in a number of cultural contexts. In Brazil, for example, large economic shifts and the brutal death of a number of street children over the last decade have resulted in the development of a number of initiatives that involve various levels of the community (Rizzini, Rizzini, Munoz-Varga, & Galeano, 1994; Scheper-Hughes & Hoffman, 1998). These efforts focus on increasing the community awareness about the plight of street children and advocating for policy changes to secure their welfare. Many involve children in the political process, which increases children's abilities to develop successful coping strategies and a better-defined role in their communities.

Community-based models are one way of supporting street children. However, they do not fully address the needs of children who are truly orphaned, particularly girls who are on the street as a result of abuse. Although institutionalized care is often criticized regarding its overuse, it cannot be fully eliminated (Tolfree, 1995). In the minority world, a formalized structure of care is in place that includes both foster care

and group homes, in addition to an overused juvenile justice system. However, Anglin (2002) notes that these care facilities lack many of the essential elements that create a more resilient environment for children. In the majority world, because of the increasing number of children who are on the street as a result of war and AIDS, the opposite situation exists, with resilience-based models needing to develop more options for housing children. Models that promote the fostering of children in majority world contexts have been developed with some success (Doná, Kalinganire, & Muramutsa, 2001). Efforts to create an environment in which street children can enhance their resilience means creating an environment of relational elements on which children can draw as protective factors. This does not include the Westernized version of counseling as a therapeutic technique to address the trauma many street children have experienced. Such formal relationships are too hierarchical and tend to identify the adult as the one who knows all and the child as the one who is receiving knowledge. Counseling should be used as a means of facilitating growth through an interactive process that promotes the development of relationships that are more equal. In this regard, we agree with observations by Prilleltensky and Prilleltensky in this volume (see Chapter 6) that helping professionals need to become more socially and politically active in how they intervene. In the minority world, one way to accomplish this flattening of the hierarchy and involvement in the promotion of social justice is through the provision of food. As a community-based family counselor, McAdam-Crisp did most of her work with youth in restaurants and coffee shops, which provided a nurturing and a nonthreatening forum for informal counseling. Techniques such as drama, dance, and music are often more culturally appropriate for building relationships in the majority world. Kironyo has conducted monthly youth camps for the past 15 years. At these camps, youth from the Mathare valley, a large slum on the outskirt of Nairobi, learn basic life skills through a process of drama and interactive workshops. A peer-mentoring model is also used to strengthen and create relationships within the group and between group members and staff, thus promoting the group as a whole.

Often, the mothers of the children are also present at the workshop, which strengthens the family as a unit.

These initiatives show that the process of developing programs that can enhance resilience involves recruiting the appropriate staff, providing them the necessary training, and providing a venue where street children have access to their home communities and in which they feel comfortable and supported. Programs need to be community based, thus building on and strengthening the resources children already possess within their surrounding community. This needs to be coupled with educational information, such as life skills and employment training. Programs also work best when they provide AIDS education, health information, family planning, and socialization skills. Furthermore, as has been shown, an emphasis on the relational process at the core of these programs is essential to their success in mitigating risk and enhancing children's access to protective factors.

CONCLUSION

The situation of street children is a global concern. The definition of a street child is context specific, and although there are some commonalities between street children in the minority and majority world, these cannot necessarily be generalized. The growing number of these children and their distribution throughout the world demands that resources at both the international and national level be used to address both micro and macro issues that influence their lives. The way we examine street children needs to be constructive and should recognize each child's individual experience within the context of his or her environment. Presently, we know far more about street children in the minority world than their counterparts in the majority world. Therefore, arguably, we need far more research to be done on a global scale. In accomplishing this research, we will need to be sensitive to the many contextually specific conditions in which street children live. For example, as has been detailed in this chapter, there are probably more similarities in the reasons girls end up on the street globally than boys. Girls therefore are at a greater risk when living on the street but remain more invisible.

Furthermore, the term *street children* needs to be deconstructed to understand children in relation to their social and cultural contexts to better understand their ability to sustain resilience. Such knowledge, generated collaboratively, will help us to design more successful programs. This process will increase our understanding of the diverse sociocultural factors that influence resilience-enhancing processes and provide information on the generalizability of resilience theory and practices for street children globally. This information can facilitate the development of policies and practices that are inherently strength based to enhance the resilience of street children in both the minority and majority worlds.

NOTES

1. The term *minority world* refers to the Western or developed world where the minority of children live, and the *majority world* refers to children in the developing or underdeveloped world.

2. The term *PTSD* is used hesitantly because there is a great deal of controversy over its application to children; it was originally coined to describe the symptoms of American Vietnam veterans and, as such, may not be applicable for children, especially those of another culture. Aptekar notes that PTSD as listed in the *DSM-IV-R* is less likely to occur in some cultures and that, depression, phobia, and somatic complaints are more common. For this reason DESNOS (disorder of extreme stress not otherwise classified), a condition referred to in the *DSM*, may be a more appropriate term for describing the progressive psychological impact of trauma as experienced by these street children. Symptoms include difficulty modulating anger and controlling impulses, a feeling of being victimized and/or victimizing others, and an inability to trust others. Amnesia, disassociation, and somatization are common. DESNOS is considered to be more common among people who have had repeated exposure to trauma.

REFERENCES

Agnelli, S. (1986). *Street children: A growing urban tragedy.* London: Weidenfeld & Nicholson.

Anglin, J. P. (2002). *Staffed group homes for children and youth: Constructing a theoretical framework for understanding.* Leicester, UK: University of Leicester.

Aptekar, L. (1988). *Street children of Cali.* London: Duke University Press.

Aptekar, L. (1994). Street children in the developing world: A review of their condition. *Cross-Cultural Research, 28*(3), 195–224.

Aptekar, L. (2000, April). *A world view of street children in the year 2000.* Paper presented at the Program for Street Children Symposium, UNICEF, Jyvaskyla, Finland.

Aptekar, L., & Ciano, L. (1999). Street children in Nairobi, Kenya: Gender differences and mental health. In R. W. Larson (Ed.), *Developmental issues among homeless and working street youth: New directions in childhood development* (pp. 35–46). San Francisco, CA: Jossey Bass.

Aptekar, L., Maphalala, T. P., Dlamini, G., Makhanya, J., & Magagula, S. (1998). The newly emerging problem of street children in Swaziland. *Journal of Psychology in Africa, 2,* 123–141.

Aptekar, L., & McAdam-Crisp, J. (2005). Street children, a global view of. In C. B. Fisher & R. M. Lerner (Eds.), *Encyclopedia of applied developmental science* (pp. 1065–1069). Thousand Oaks, CA: Sage.

Aptekar, L., & Stocklin, D. (1997). Growing up in particularly difficult circumstances: A cross-cultural perspective. In J. Berry, P. R. Dasen, & T. S. Saraswathi (Eds.), *Handbook of cross-cultural psychology: Basic process of human development* (2nd ed., Vol. 2, pp. 377–412). Boston: Allyn & Bacon.

Ayerst, S. (1999). Depression and stress in street youth. *Adolescence, 34*(135), 567–575.

Bagley, C. (1985). Child sexual abuse: A child welfare perspective. In K. Levitt & B. Wharf (Eds.), *The challenge of child welfare* (pp. 66–93). Vancouver: University of British Columbia Press.

Barker, G. (1989). *Fact sheet on street children and AIDS/HIV.* New York: ChildHope USA.

Barker, G., & Knaul, F. (1991). *Exploited entrepreneurs: Street and working children in developing countries* (Working paper number 1). New York: ChildHope USA.

Black, M. (1993). *Street and working children: Innocenti Global Seminar summary report.* Florence, Italy: UNICEF International Child Development Centre.

Blanc, C. S. (1994). *Urban children in distress global predicaments and innovative strategies.* Florence, Italy: UN Children's Fund.

Bowlby, J. (1969). *Attachment and loss* (Vol. 1). New York: Basic Books.

Boyden, J., & Mann, G. (2000). *Children's risk, resilience and coping in extreme situations: Background paper to the consultation on children in adversity.* Oxford, UK: Refugee Studies and Centre for Child-Focused Anthropological Research.

Connelly, M. (1990). Adrift in the city: A comparative study of street children in Bogotá, Colombia and Guatemala City. In N. Boxhill (Ed.), *Homeless children: The watcher and the waiter* (pp. 129–149). New York: Haworth.

Cosgrove, J. (1990). Towards a working definition of street children. *International Journal of Social Work, 33,* 185–195.

Dallape, F. (1988). *An experience with street children.* Nairobi: Undugu Society of Kenya.

Dallape, F. (1996). Urban children a challenge and an opportunity. *Childhood, 3,* 263–294.

Demoskoff, L., & Lauzer, J. (1994). *Working with street youth: A resource manual.* Vancouver, Canada: Watari Research Association.

Doná, G., Kalinganire, C., & Muramutsa, F. (2001). *My child is yours and ours: The Rwandan experience of foster care for separated children.* Kigali, Rwanda: UNICEF.

Ennew, J. (1994). *Street and working children a guide to planning.* London: Save the Children UK.

Erikson, E. (1963). *Childhood and society.* New York: Norton.

Hickson, J., & Gaydon, V. (1989). "Twilight children": The street children in Johannesburg. *Journal of Multicultural Counselling and Development, 17,* 85–95.

Higgins, G. (1994). *Resilient adults overcoming a cruel past.* San Francisco: Jossey-Bass.

Hutz, C. S., & Koller, S. H. (1999). Methodological and ethical issues in research with street children. In M. Rafaelli & R. W. Larson (Eds.), *Homeless and working youth around the world: Exploring developmental issues* (pp. 59–70). San Francisco: Jossey-Bass.

Kilbride, P., Suda, C., & Njeru, E. (2000). *Street children in Kenya: Voices of children in search of a childhood.* Westport, CT: Bergin & Garvey.

Kirby, L., & Fraser, M. W. (1997). Risk and resilience in childhood. In M. W. Fraser (Ed.), *Risk and* resilience in childhood: An ecological perspective (pp. 10–33). Washington, DC: National Association of Social Workers.

Lalor, K. (1999). Street children: A comparative perspective. *Child Abuse and Neglect, 23*(8), 759–770.

Le Roux, J. (1996). Street children in South Africa: Findings from interviews on the background of street children in Pretoria, South Africa. *Adolescence, 21*(122), 423–431.

Le Roux, J. (1998). Is the street child phenomenon synonymous with deviant behaviour. *Adolescence, 33*(132), 915–925.

Lusk, M. (1992). Street children of Rio de Janeiro. *International Social Worker, 35,* 293–305.

Maslow, A. H. (1954). *Motivation and personality.* New York: Harper & Row.

McAdam, J. (1995). *Evaluation framework for the development of an alternative form of education for marginalized youth in developing countries: A case study Nairobi, Kenya.* Unpublished master's thesis. University of Victoria, Victoria, British Columbia, Canada.

McAdam, J. (1997). *The social reintegration of youth in difficult circumstances: Street children strategies for solutions.* Kigali: UN Development Program, Rwanda.

Ministry of Labour and Social Affairs. (1997). *Enquete sur les problemes d'integration sociale des jeunes en situation difficile dans la ville de Kigali* [Inquiry into the problems of social integration of the young people in a difficult situation in the city of Kigali.] Kigali, Rwanda.

Muchini, B., & Nyandiya-Bundy, S. (1991). *Struggling to survive: A study of street children in Zimbabwe.* Harare, Zimbabwe: UNICEF.

Norman, E. (2000). *Resiliency enhancement putting the strength perspective into social work practice.* New York: Columbia University Press.

Oliveria, W., Baizerman, M., & Pellet, L. (1992). Street children in Brazil and their helpers: Comparative views on aspiration and the future. *International Journal of Social Work, 35,* 163–176.

Panter-Brick, C. (2002). Street children, human rights, and public health: A critique and future direction. *Annual Review of Anthropology, 31,* 147–171.

Poortinga, Y. H. (1997). Towards convergence? In J. Pandey (Ed.), *Handbook of cross-cultural psychology* (2nd ed., Vol. 1, pp. 347–387). Boston: Allyn & Bacon.

Ratner, C. (1999). Three approaches to cultural psychology. *Cultural Dynamics, 11*(1), 7–31.

Rizzini, I., Rizzini, I., Munoz-Varga, M., & Galeano, L. (1994). Brazil: A new concept of childhood. In C. S. Blanc (Ed.), *Urban children in distress* (pp. 55–99). Florence, Italy: UN Children's Fund International Child Development Centre.

Royal Canadian Mounted Police. (2001). *Canada's missing children annual report.* Ottawa: National Missing Children Services. (Available at www.ourmissingchildren.ca/en/publications/2000/2001-annualrep_e.pdf)

Save the Children Canada. (2004, March 1). *Street children.* www.savethechildren.ca/en/whatwedo/isstrchi.html

Scharf, W., Powell, M., & Thomas, E. (1986). Stoller-street children of Cape Town. In S. Burman & R. Reynolds (Eds.), *Growing up in divided society: The context of childhood in South Africa* (pp. 262–287). Johannesburg: Raven Press.

Scheper-Hughes, N., & Hoffman, D. (1998). Brazilian apartheid: Street kids and the struggle for urban space. In N. Scheper-Hughes & C. Sargent (Eds.), *Small wars the cultural politics of childhood* (pp. 352–388). Berkeley: University of California Press.

Scheper-Hughes, N., & Sargent, C. (Eds.). (1998). *Small wars the cultural politics of childhood.* Berkeley: University of California Press.

Smollar, J. (1999). Homeless youth in the United States: Description and developmental issues. In M. Rafaelli & R. W. Larson (Eds.), *Homeless and working youth around the world: Exploring developmental issues* (pp. 47–58). San Francisco: Jossey-Bass.

Swart, J. (1990). *Malunde the children of Hillbrow.* Cape Town: Witwatersrand University Press.

Tacon, R. (1981). *My child now: An action plan on behalf of the children without families.* New York: UNICEF Document.

Tierney, N. (1997). *Robbed of humanity: Lives of Guatemalan street children.* Saint Paul, MN: Pangaea.

Tolfree, D. (1995). *Roofs and roots.* Aldershot, UK: Arena.

Tyler, F., Holliday, M., Tyler, S., Echeverry, J., & Zea, M. (1987). Street children and play. *Children's Environments Quarterly, 4*(4), 13–17.

Tyler, F., Tyler, S., Echeverry, J., & Zea, M. (1992). Making it on the streets of Bogota: A psychosocial study of street youth. *Genetic, Social and General Psychology Monographs, 117,* 395–417.

Ungar, M. (2004). A constructionist discourse on resilience multiple contexts, multiple realities among at-risk children and youth. *Youth and Society, 35*(3), 341–365.

UNICEF. (2003, November). *Africa's orphaned generation.* New York: United Nations Children Fund.

Veale, A. (1996). *An empirical and conceptual analysis of street children in Sudan and Ethiopia.* Unpublished doctoral dissertation, University College Cork, Cork, Ireland.

Veale, A., Adefrisew, A., & Lalor, K. (1992). *Study of street children in four selected towns of Ethiopia.* Addis Abba, Ethiopia: Ministry of Labour and Social Affairs UNICEF, Ethiopia, University College Cork.

Veale, A., & Doná, G. (2003). Street children and political violence: A socio-demographic analysis of street children in Rwanda. *Child Abuse and Neglect, 27*(3), 253–269.

Velis, J.-P. (1995). *Blossoms in the dust: Street children in Africa.* Paris: UNESCO.

Webber, M. (1991). *Street kids: The tragedy of Canada's runaway.* Toronto: University of Toronto Press.

Werner, E. E., & Smith, R. S. (2001). *Journey from childhood to midlife: Risk, resilience, and recovery.* Ithaca, NY: Cornell University Press.

Whiting, B. (Ed.). (1963). *Six cultures: Studies of child rearing.* New York: John Wiley.

6

Beyond Resilience

Blending Wellness and Liberation in the Helping Professions

Isaac Prilleltensky

Ora Prilleltensky

Resilience typically implies the ability to cope with family and social adversity (Prilleltensky, Nelson, & Peirson, 2001). Although the adversity is deplored by helping professionals, they usually limit themselves to working with the family and consider the social problems to be beyond their scope. If all of us followed this reasoning, nobody in the helping professions would enact practices that challenge injustice. Instead, we would resign ourselves to deal with the victims of injustice, hoping to steel our clients before the next blow. But an increasing number of helpers are growing uncomfortable with the idea that all they can do is react to environmental assaults—they want to prevent them. Furthermore, they want to redefine resilience as the ability to not only cope with conditions related to adversity and injustice but also to challenge their very existence.

Indeed, helping professionals are struggling to promote a social justice agenda. Counselors, psychologists, and social workers realize that their caring work is constantly undermined by conditions of injustice. At least for helpers working with marginalized populations, the injustice encountered by their clients has the power to undermine their caring work. Youth workers, for example, frequently do their utmost to empower young people and to instill in them a sense of control, only to realize early in the course of counseling that the environment in which marginalized youth live is much more powerful than the most sophisticated psychological intervention.

A growing number of professionals understand that caring in the proximal sense is insufficient in the absence of caring in the distal sense. Proximal caring is expressed within the confines of the counseling session, whereas distal caring is manifested in work to promote justice in the community. Without the latter, the former has meager chances of success. Without distal caring, in the form of challenging and changing unjust environments, proximal caring remains a humane but somewhat inadequate answer to the plight of the poor and the disadvantaged. Research has repeatedly demonstrated the effects of noxious environments on mental health (Carr & Sloan, 2003; McCubbin, Labonte, Sullivan, & Dallaire, 2003). From this perspective, promoting resilience has much to do with promoting social justice.

Helpers in the mental health field face a gap between their understanding of unhealthy environments and their ability to do something about them. Whereas the level of critique tends to be quite complex, the level of social justice practice tends to be quite embryonic. Critical psychologists, like other groups of critically oriented helping professionals in allied fields of practice, have been creating alternatives that go beyond the status quo and its critique. In this chapter, we introduce some lessons from critical psychology, a movement that promotes wellness and liberation *at the same time.* Here we recommend several steps for blending caring work with justice work in efforts to mitigate the risks that confront marginalized populations. To illustrate the application of these recommendations, we will discuss them in the context of people with physical disabilities.

There is commonality in the critique of counseling psychology put forth by Vera and Speight (2003) and Lewis, Lewis, Daniels, and D'Andrea (2003), of social work put forth by Mullaly (2002), and of psychology put forth by critical psychologists (Nelson & Prilleltensky, in press; Pare & Larner, in press; Prilleltensky & Nelson, 2002; Sloan, 2000). Vera and Speight (2003) synthesize the shortcomings of an approach that pays lip service to cultural diversity and social justice but falls short of articulating emancipatory ways to practice. They enumerate the barriers to acting, not just thinking, justly. They point out that multicultural competencies must go beyond the recognition of oppression: A caring and competent practitioner ought to enact alternatives that not only identify but also, and primarily, reduce oppression.

Helping professionals have differing degrees of critical awareness. Some of them are indifferent to how their profession promotes the societal status quo. Others, in turn, are painfully aware of how their professions blame victims for their misfortune. However mindful, the latter group is at a loss when it comes to creating alternatives. In the case of counseling, Vera and Speight perform an invaluable service for those who may be unfamiliar with psychology's support for an unjust state of affairs (Prilleltensky, 1994). They adroitly summarize the unwitting alliance between counseling psychology and the societal status quo. In this chapter, we heed their call for aligning our practice as helping professionals with the principles of social justice. We believe that progress can be made by (a) stressing the synergy of diverse values, (b) stressing the synergy between wellness and liberation, (c) learning from existing critiques within psychology and other fields, (d) promoting role reconciliation between the helping professional as healer and agent of change, and (e) adopting psychopolitical validity as a new measure for the evaluation of our social justice agenda. These five initiatives to make psychological interventions more influential in the sphere of social justice set the conditions for a broader and more contextually relevant environment in which wellness can take hold. As we will show, the roots of wellness (and resilience) are firmly anchored in the ground of socially just communities and processes.

INTERDEPENDENT VALUES

No single value is comprehensive enough to address the entire range of human needs. Therefore, we judge values such as social justice, caring and compassion, and cultural diversity on their synergistic qualities, not on their isolated merits (James & Prilleltensky, 2002; Prilleltensky, 2001). Vera and Speight (2003) correctly point out that multicultural competence without social justice is insufficient. Table 6.1 organizes human needs and values into three separate spheres of wellness and liberation: personal, relational, and collective. If we concentrate solely on relational values such as cultural diversity and democratic participation, we run the risk of neglecting both personal and collective needs. Similarly, the historical focus of psychology on self-determination and health meant that little or no attention was paid to democratic participation, cultural diversity, sense of community, or social justice (Fox & Prilleltensky, 1997). Vera and Speight are justifiably alarmed that if we concentrate on celebrating diversity without attending to power inequality and social injustice, we will undermine wellness and liberation, for they cannot exist but in the synergy created by the composite of values.

Historically, there is a propensity to concentrate on single values. Such proclivity is largely determined by dominant political and cultural ideologies. During conservative times, personal values of self-determination tend to be extolled, whereas principles of equality and justice come to the fore during progressive eras (Levine & Levine, 1992). It is our job to diagnose the mood of the times and realize what values we're missing from the equation. There is little doubt that psychology has absorbed the zeitgeist of the last three decades and concentrated on individual remedies for social maladies (Albee, 1990; Cushman, 1990; Fox & Prilleltensky, 1997; Prilleltensky, 1994; Sampson, 1983; Sarason, 1981). As Boyden and Mann show in Chapter 1, the preponderance of resilience research and theory that is focused more on the psychological development of individuals than on the social and cultural context in which individuals live exemplifies this trend. As a result, we have neglected social justice and support for marginalized communities at our peril.

However, there is also the current risk because our values extol respect for diversity above all else, even though cultural diversity cannot exist in the absence of social justice. All the values presented in Table 6.1 are codependent and interdependent. Extreme reliance on a single value undermines the existence of that very value, for it cannot thrive in the absence of others. We must be forever vigilant about what values are being privileged and what values are being ignored. There cannot be justice in the absence of compassion, and there cannot be compassion in the absence of justice. Striking a balance among values for personal, relational, and collective wellness and liberation is our most pressing task as professionals and citizens.

The values of self-determination, and social justice in particular, have been severely undermined for many people with disabilities. So long as the problems they encounter in their daily living are attributed to the impairment itself, efforts to enhance wellness are conceptualized and enacted at the individual level alone. Those who require assistance with daily living often have to fight for control over what services they will receive, their mode of delivery, and who will assist them with the most intimate self-care tasks. The inability to carry out physical tasks unassisted is often taken as deficiency in the ability to make important decisions about one's life. Combined, such threats to control threaten individuals' capacities to overcome the multiple adversities they face coping with a disability, threatening their capacity to experience themselves as both resilient (for overcoming adversity) and well (for sustaining a quality of life).

Unfair distribution of power has implications not only for how independence is defined (in primarily physical terms) but for how it is actually enacted in various medical and rehabilitation settings. Much of the work carried out by counselors and occupational and physical therapists is focused on patients' ability to independently carry out activities of daily living or to come to terms with their inability to do so. Whereas most people would prefer to be as independent as they can in self-care, it is critical that this is not regarded as necessary for autonomous adult or child functioning. I, Ora, am reminded of a patient I worked with who had to negotiate with one of his treating therapists to convince the therapist that it was pointless for the patient to attend a breakfast group that had as its goal to make him capable of preparing his own morning meal. A stroke had left this man with significant physical impairments, although his cognitive functioning remained relatively intact. It was very clear to him that he would not be attending to his own breakfast at home given the time and energy that this required of him. Given the emphasis placed on physical rehabilitation, convincing his therapist of this was no easy task. The therapist insisted the man needed to learn this skill, overlooking the man's capacity to make judgments on his own course of rehabilitation. Making such decisions on behalf of others is what truly robs people of dignity and control over their lives.

Resilience stems, in part, from the capacity and opportunity to understand the role of adversity

Table 6.1 Personal, Relational, and Collective Domains of Wellness and Liberation

Domains	Wellness and Liberation					
	Personal		Relational		Collective	
Values	Self-determination and personal growth	Health	Respect for human diversity	Collaboration and democratic participation	Support for community structures	Social justice
Definition	Promotion of ability of children and adults to pursue chosen goals in life without undue oppression	Protection of physical and emotional health and resistance to unhealthy personal, relational, and societal forces	Promotion of people's ability to define themselves individually and collectively and to resist political, ideological, and cultural domination	Promotion of fair processes whereby children and adults can have meaningful input into decisions affecting their lives	Promotion of vital community structures that facilitate the pursuit of personal and communal goals	Promotion of fair and equitable allocation of bargaining powers, obligations, and resources in society; and resistance to forces of exploitation and domination
Needs addressed	Mastery, control, self-efficacy, voice, choice, skills, growth and autonomy	Emotional and physical well-being	Identity, dignity, self-respect, self-esteem, acceptance	Participation, involvement, and mutual responsibility	Sense of community, cohesion, formal support	Economic security, shelter, clothing, nutrition, access to vital health and social services

SOURCE: Adapted from Prilleltensky and Nelson (2002).

in one's life and the role of individuals and groups to challenge systems of inequity and discrimination. Coping without challenging these systems may result in accepting the unacceptable.

WELLNESS AND LIBERATION

The helping professions have traditionally concerned themselves with wellness, health, and well-being. Under the aegis of the medical model, psychology and psychiatry conceptualized problems in living in intrapsychic terms. *Mental health, wellness,* and most recently, *positive psychology* became choice metaphors. They all conjure images of people enjoying life, worry free and healthy. This is a most worthy goal, which we fully support. But as with any single value, wellness cannot stand by itself. Unless it is supported by fairness and equality, it is bound to fall. An extensive body of research documents the ill effects of inequality and disempowerment on health and wellness (Kawachi, Kennedy, & Wilkinson, 1999; Kim, Millen, Irwin, & Gersham, 2000; Marmot, 1999). The impact of poverty, marginalization, exclusion, exploitation, and injustice is just as deleterious on the body as it is on the soul (I. Prilleltensky, 2003a). To ignore this evidence is to pretend that our psychological interventions can be potent enough to undo the damage of structural inequality—inequality often expressed in deficient health services and employment opportunities for the poor. We can afford to be humbler. Our psychological interventions are not that powerful.

Wellness is a positive state of affairs, brought about by the simultaneous satisfaction of personal, relational, and collective needs. To meet these needs, we have to attend to power dynamics operating at micro, meso, and macro levels of analysis (Nelson & Prilleltensky, in press). Thus, wellness is intricately linked to empowerment. Empowerment, in turn, does not take place only at the personal level. Relational and collective empowerment support personal empowerment and vice versa (Kieffer, 1984; Lord & Hutchison, 1993). Power equalization must take place at all these levels if wellness is to be a resource available to those

marginalized by disability and other concurrent risk factors.

Liberation needs wellness as much as wellness needs liberation from oppressive forces. Liberation, like freedom, has two aims: liberation from and liberation to (Fromm, 1960). Whereas the former strives to eliminate oppression and abuse at the personal, relational, and collective levels, the latter seeks to pursue wellness for self and others.

People with disabilities have long struggled to attain wellness and liberation at the same time. They have claimed that disability is not a personal tragedy that requires medical solutions but, rather, a social issue requiring social intervention. They have decried the medical model of disability that regarded the problem as residing solely within the disabled individual. The focus on bodily abnormality meant that medically driven solutions were called for. Treatment was designed, implemented, and evaluated by a host of professionals, with the disabled individual having little input regarding the process. What could not be cured had to be rehabilitated, and what could not be rehabilitated had to be accepted. Psychological theories focused on the need to adjust to one's misfortune and make the best of a tragic and limited life. Those who did not despair despite their disability were often perceived as being in a state of denial (Oliver, 1996; Olkin, 1999) or, more positively, resilient, to use the word in the shallowest of ways.

People with disabilities have argued that it is society, rather than the impairment itself, that is the source of their disablement. The Union of the Physically Impaired Against Segregation in 1976 declared:

> In our view, it is society which disables physically impaired people. Disability is . . . imposed on top of our impairments by the way we are unnecessarily isolated and excluded from full participation in society. Disabled people are therefore an oppressed group in society. (Barton, 1998, p. 56)

Proponents of this alternative social model of disability have demonstrated the multiple ways in which people with disabilities are socially and economically disadvantaged. Being historically excluded from mainstream schooling, many did not attain the necessary skills to further their education and make them competitive within the job market. Some encounter discriminatory attitudes and a lack of willingness to make simple accommodations within the workplace. Those who require assistive devices, attendant care, or both often come up against paternalistic policies designed to retain professional control over resources. Physical barriers have also been a source of exclusion; public spaces were historically designed with able-bodied people in mind. A shortage of affordable accessible housing and inaccessible public transportation further marginalize people with disabilities (Barton, 1998; Morris, 1993; Olkin, 1999; Oliver, 1996).

In Ora's research on women with physical disabilities and motherhood, most participants reported that they did not envision that they would lead a life similar to nondisabled peers (O. Prilleltensky, 2003, 2004a, 2004b). One participant who spent most of her childhood in an institution described the difficulty in imagining an adult life beyond that setting: "You didn't see kids there leaving, or getting married, or having kids . . . they just left and you never heard from them again" (O. Prilleltensky, 1998, p. 118). At the time of the participants' birth some four decades ago, most of their parents were encouraged to institutionalize them (although few did), were told to expect little in the way of progress and growth, and were generally painted a grim picture of life with a disability. Not surprisingly, few parents expected that their children would lead typical adult lives and some ignored or actively discouraged their daughters' emergent sexuality.

Oliver (1990), a disabled academic in the United Kingdom, was one of the first people to talk about the social versus the individual model of disability. Along with other disability activists, he argued that the very term *disability* is about exclusion and disadvantage. For example, Oliver suggested an alternative format to a disability survey conducted by the Office of Population Census and Surveys (OPCS) in the United Kingdom. Whereas the standard version focuses on the impairment as the source of limitation, Oliver's version shifts the focus to disabling barriers and attitudes. Consider the following examples:

OPCS: "Can you tell me what is wrong with you?"

Oliver: "Can you tell me what is wrong with society?"

OPCS: "Do you have a scar, blemish, or deformity which limits your daily activities?"

Oliver: "Do other people's reactions to any scar, blemish, or deformity you may have limit your daily activities?"

OPCS: "Does your health problem/disability make it difficult for you to travel by bus?"

Oliver: "Are there any transport or financial problems which prevent you from going out as often or as far as you would like?"

The political action and struggle of disabled people around the world has resulted in significant progress. No longer willing to put up with inadequate resources and professional control, people with disabilities have collectively fought for economic, legislative, and social gains. In the United States, the formation of "independent living movements" in the 1960s and 1970s has been associated with greater individual autonomy as well as more political and economic freedom (White, in press).

The legislation of the American with Disabilities Act in 1990 has ensured that many of the aforementioned gains are not contingent on people's goodwill but are enforceable by law. For example, it is illegal to discriminate against a worker based on disability status, to hold a civic gathering at an inaccessible venue, or to fail to accommodate the needs of a disabled patient at a health clinic.

Although there is still a long way to go, there is little doubt that these practical gains in legislation, economic resources, and social participation do go a long way toward the enhancement of wellness. Furthermore, the new focus on disabling societal barriers and systematic powerlessness has done much to improve the self-esteem and well-being of people with disabilities (Morris, 1993; Oliver, 1990; Shakespeare, 1998; White, in press). Combined, these changes go a long way toward creating the conditions in which people with disabilities can achieve health. These structural changes contribute to an individual's being seen by others and himself or herself as resilient. Consider the following quote of a disabled activist in the United Kingdom who describes the impact that the social model of disability has had on her life:

> My life has two phases: before the social model of disability, and after it. Discovering this way of thinking about my experiences was the proverbial raft in stormy seas. . . . For years now this social model has enabled me to confront, survive, and even surmount countless situations of exclusion and discrimination. . . . It has played a central role in promoting disabled people's individual self-worth, collective identity, and political organization. I don't think it is an exaggeration to say that the social model has saved lives. (Crow, 1996, pp. 206–207)

It is worth reexamining the concept of resilience in light of the empowering experiences of persons with disabilities. The claim can be made that Crow and other activists became more resilient precisely because they challenged the status quo and not because they learned how to cope with it. In fact, related research on empowerment demonstrates that participating in social actions enhances sense of control, a key component of resilience and mental health (Kieffer, 1984; Prilleltensky, Nelson, & Peirson, 2001).

INSULARITY AND ACTION

Helping professionals cannot afford to ignore critiques such as this that are occurring in a number of related fields. The field of critical psychology has been struggling with how to promote a social justice agenda in ways that parallel the concerns raised by Vera and Speight (2003) in counseling and by Mullaly (2002) in social work (Fox & Prilleltensky, 1997; Prilleltensky & Nelson, 2002; Sloan, 2000). Prilleltensky and Nelson (2002), for instance, proposed means of promoting a social justice agenda in psychology. They made specific recommendations for working critically in school, health, counseling, clinical, work, and community settings. Community psychology has also been highly influential in fostering social change, prevention, cultural diversity, and

empowerment for the last four decades (Nelson & Prilleltensky, in press; Newbrough, 1992, 1995; Prilleltensky, 2001; Rappaport, 1987). Disciplinary boundaries and the insularity that results sometimes prevent fruitful explorations of similar agendas.

Psychology in particular cannot afford to ignore critiques of the helping professions and the societal status quo mounted by people with disabilities (Oliver, 1990), by consumer/survivors of the psychiatric system (Nelson, Lord, & Ochocka, 2001), by sexual minorities (Kitzinger, 1997), and by other disciplines (Fox & Prilleltensky, 1997). As psychologists, our ability to see beyond our own psychological glasses is limited. Just as we need to expand our definitions of wellness to incorporate other cultural perspectives, we need to listen to critiques of psychology raised by nonpsychologists.

But the problem of insularity goes beyond critique: It affects action as well. We should heed Audre Lorde's dictum: "The master's tools will never dismantle the master's house." People with disabilities did not achieve the rights they did because of professionals. Often, it is in spite of professionals that people with disabilities and other marginalized groups make progress toward wellness and liberation (Oliver, 1990). If we are to make progress toward social justice, we need to create alliances with the people we wish to help (Nelson, Prilleltensky, & MacGillivary, 2001). Much can be learned from social movements and consumers' movements in their efforts to declassify homosexuality as an abnormality, to obtain access to pubic buildings and transportation, or to overcome the stigma of mental illness (Nelson & Prilleltensky, in press). These actions, we claim, will not materialize until counselors reconcile their roles as healers with their role as change agents.

ROLE RECONCILIATION

If helpers respond to the call for action, as we hope they do, they will pretty soon face a dilemma: how to reconcile their various roles as professional helpers on one hand and agents of social change on the other. Hitherto, we have not articulated how these two sets of knowledge, practices, and roles work in synergy for the

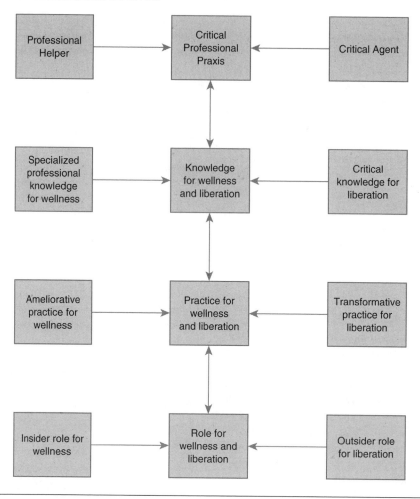

Figure 6.1   Knowledge, Practice, and Roles for Critical Professional Praxis in Mental Health Practice

SOURCE: Adapted from Prilleltensky and Prilleltensky (2003b).

promotion of wellness and liberation. Here we propose ways of melding professional and critical praxis (Prilleltensky, 2001; Prilleltensky & Nelson, 2002; Prilleltensky & Prilleltensky, 2003a, 2003b). Our challenge is to find ways of reconciling the two sets of skills and aims. From the perspective of the *professional helper*, whether a psychologist, social worker, or other helping professional, being a critical practitioner means seeking answers to three important questions:

1. How does our special *knowledge of wellness* inform our social justice work?

2. How does our *ameliorative practice* inform our transformative practice?

3. How does our *insider role* as wellness promoter in the helping system inform our outsider role as social critic?

From the perspective of the *social change agent*, the critical practitioner needs to address the following issues:

1. How does our *knowledge of inequality and injustice* inform our counseling work?

2. How does our *transformative practice* in society inform our ameliorative work in the helping system?

3. How does our *outsider role* as social critic inform or relate to our insider role?

We argue that reconciling these diverse roles would promote the dual goals of wellness and liberation, both equally important contributions to the resilience experienced by individuals and their communities. Whereas the former is the primary domain of the professional helper, the latter is the main concern of the critical change agent (Nelson & Prilleltensky, in press). Ora's work on women with disabilities and motherhood (O. Prilleltensky, 2004a, 2004b) provides some practical examples of this reconciliation of roles. For example, the professional helper informed by a critical perspective can encourage girls and young women with disabilities to explore the impact of negative societal messages pertaining to sexuality and disability. This process of conscientization can result in de-blaming and may also lay the foundation for taking a stand against oppression. At the same time, transformative work in the community can be directed at changing restrictive and oppressive concepts of female sexuality and motherhood. Narrow conceptions of motherhood limit the scope of available resources for women who are confronted with the adversity associated with having a disability. Better, we think, to understand that different types of mothering require different types of resources. An expanded notion of motherhood (to include women with disabilities) would naturally lead to a wider definition of acceptable resources.

Wellness and liberation exist in a dialectical relationship. Without liberation, many oppressed people cannot experience wellness, and without wellness, there is no superordinate goal for liberation. Our objective is to blend the two so that our various roles and skills attend to emancipation and quality of life at the same time. Figure 6.1 describes the amalgamation of knowledge, practices, and roles of the professional helper on one hand and the critical agents of change on the other.

The argument can be made that professional helpers cannot research or know in-depth all aspects of wellness and liberation. We agree that interdisciplinary research and action is vital. But it is entirely possible to have interdisciplinary research and action that supports the status quo. This is why we need critical knowledge of how power and inequality play a role in counseling and mental health (Habermas, 1971). If we were to stay at the level of individual wellness alone and were not to consider the impact of inequality, disadvantage, and oppression or were to leave these political domains to others, we would not be as effective as we might in our individual work because we would obviate the role of power in mental health. There is a need to incorporate critical insights into our daily working routine.

The type of knowledge we pursue has been well articulated by Aristotle and recently revived by Flyvbjerg (2001). *Phronesis* is the type of practical knowledge that combines scientific understanding with political wisdom. It is an applied type of knowledge that seeks understanding in context—contexts that are perpetually suffused by power differentials and inequality. What we seek, in Habermas's words, is knowledge for emancipation.

With respect to practice, we need to articulate how the various roles would be manifested in the actual day-to-day practice of helpers and community workers. Prilleltensky and Nelson (2002) and Murray et al. (2001) have proposed ways of blending the transformative role with the ameliorative task. For us, transformation refers to system change, whereas amelioration refers to individual or reformist change that leaves the sources of the problem unaffected. There are in fact many ways to advance the transformative impulse and critical knowledge in the helping professions (Prilleltensky & Prilleltensky, 2003b). Some potential avenues include the following:

- Creating awareness among colleagues about how power differentials get enacted in interactions with clients seeking counseling
- Forming research and action groups in the workplace to explore how practices may be more empowering of clients
- Increasing political literacy of community members to empower them to scrutinize the practices of helping professionals
- Establishing practices that enable participation of clients, patients, and community members in the management of human services
- Connecting with poor communities and partnering with them in raising the level of public health, advocating for more resources, protesting tobacco advertising, boycotting sexist advertising and others.

As insiders within the health and helping system, psychologists and other professionals face many barriers and limitations. Although they may be aware of many oppressive policies and practices, they may be constrained in their ability to act. Outside critics, in turn, may feel free to point to shortcomings but may not have the inside knowledge of how systems work or why some practices that may seem unnecessary from the outside may be well justified from the inside.

Whereas the pull for the professional helper is for amelioration, wellness, and the prevention of institutional unrest, the pull for the critical change agent is for transformation, liberation, and disruption of unjust practices. For critical professional praxis to emerge, these two roles need to exist in tension and synergy, not in opposition. If wellness and liberation are to emerge, we need specialized knowledge as much as political knowledge, ameliorative therapies as much as social change, and people working inside the system as much as people confronting it.

PSYCHOPOLITICAL VALIDITY

How can we make sure that our research and action live up to the ideals presented by Vera and Speight (2003), Mullaly (2002), Prilleltensky and Nelson (2002), and others? This is a question of importance to critical practitioners concerned with the promotion of social justice in the mental health field. To address this concern, I, Isaac, have recently suggested the introduction of *psychopolitical validity* as a tool for the promotion of wellness and liberation (I. Prilleltensky, 2003b, in press).

This type of validity is built on two complementary sets of factors, psychological and political: hence, *psychopolitical*. This combination refers to the psychological and political influences that interact to promote wellness, perpetuate oppression, or generate resistance and liberation. Psychopolitical factors help explain suffering and well-being. At the same time, this combination of terms denotes the need to attend to both sets of factors in our efforts to change individuals, groups, and societies. As a result, we propose two types of psychopolitical validity:

(a) epistemic and (b) transformational. Whereas the former refers to using psychology and politics in understanding social phenomena, the latter calls on both sets of factors to make lasting social changes.

We pay equal attention to psychological and political factors. Psychological factors refer to the subjective life of the person, informed by power dynamics operating at the personal, interpersonal, family, group, and cultural levels. Political factors, in turn, refer to the collective experience of individuals and groups, informed by power dynamics and conflicts of interest at the interpersonal, family, group, community, and societal levels. In both sets of factors, we emphasize the role of power in the subjective or collective experience of people and groups.

Psychopolitical validity, then, derives from the concurrent consideration and interaction of power dynamics in psychological and political domains at various levels of analyses. Hence, we can talk about psychopolitical validity when these conditions are met. When this type of analysis is applied to research, we talk about *epistemic psychopolitical validity*. When it is applied to social interventions, we talk about *transformational psychopolitical validity*. To illustrate these concepts, we refer you to Tables 6.2 and 6.3, respectively.

To understand issues of well-being, oppression, and liberation at the personal, relational, and collective domains, we turn our attention to Table 6.2. Each cell in the table refers to issues of power and their manifestation in political and psychological spheres. Needless to say, this table is not exhaustive or inclusive of all fields in the helping professions. Rather, it concentrates on the priorities of wellness and liberation, two issues we regard as crucial.

Table 6.2 may be used to guide our commitment to emancipatory research. Furthermore, it may be used as an accountability device. We can monitor the extent to which we study the priority areas described in the table. In a sense, these guidelines serve the function of a vision—a vision of what type of research we need to pursue.

Epistemic validity depends on the incorporation of knowledge on oppression into all research and action in mental health. This means accounting for power dynamics operating at

Table 6.2   Guidelines for Epistemic Psychopolitical Validity

	Domains		
Concerns	*Collective*	*Relational*	*Personal*
Well-being	Accounts for role of political and economic power in economic prosperity and in creation of social justice institutions.	Studies the role of power in creating and sustaining egalitarian relationships, social cohesion, social support, respect for diversity, and democratic participation in communities, groups, and families.	Studies role of psychological and political power in achieving self-determination, empowerment, health, personal growth, meaning, and spirituality.
Oppression	Explores role of globalization, colonization, and exploitation in suffering of nations and communities.	Examines the role of political and psychological power in exclusion and discrimination based on class, gender, age, race, education, and ability. Studies conditions leading to lack of support, horizontal violence, and fragmentation within oppressed groups.	Studies role of powerlessness in learned helplessness, hopelessness, self-deprecation, internalized oppression, shame, mental health problems, and addictions.
Liberation	Deconstructs ideological norms that lead to acquiescence and studies effective psychopolitical factors in resistance.	Studies acts of solidarity and compassion with others who suffer from oppression.	Examines sources of strength, resilience, solidarity, and development of activism and leadership.

SOURCE: Adapted from I. Prilleltensky (in press).

psychological and political levels in efforts to understand phenomena of interest. The following questions might guide the pursuit of epistemic psychopolitical validity:

1. Is there an understanding of the impact of global, political, and economic forces on the issue at hand?

2. Is there an understanding of how global, political, and economic forces as well as social norms influence the perceptions and experiences of individuals and groups affected by the issue at hand?

3. Is there an understanding of how the cognitions, behaviors, experiences, feelings, and perceptions of individuals, groups, and entire communities perpetuate or transform the forces and dynamics affecting the issue at hand?

4. Is there an appreciation of how interactions between political and psychological power at the personal, relational, and collective levels affect the phenomena of interest?

Table 6.3 integrates levels of intervention with key concerns for mental health: well-being, oppression, and liberation. This is a vision of

Table 6.3 Guidelines for Transformational Psychopolitical Validity

Concerns	Domains		
	Collective	*Relational*	*Personal*
Well-being	Contributes to institutions that support emancipation, human development, peace, protection of environment, and social justice.	Contributes to power equalization in relationships and communities. Enriches awareness of subjective and psychological forces preventing solidarity. Builds trust, connection, and participation in groups that support social cohesion and social justice.	Supports personal empowerment, sociopolitical development, leadership training, and solidarity. Contributes to personal and social responsibility and awareness of subjective forces preventing commitment to justice and personal depowerment when in position of privilege.
Oppression	Opposes economic colonialism and denial of cultural rights. Decries and resists role of own reference group or nation in oppression of others.	Contributes to struggle against in-group and out-group domination and discrimination, sexism, and norms of violence. Builds awareness of own prejudice and participation in horizontal violence.	Helps to prevent acting out of own oppression on others. Builds awareness of internalized oppression and role of dominant ideology in victim blaming. Contributes to personal depowerment of people in position of privilege.
Liberation	Supports networks of resistance and social change movements. Contributes to structural depowerment of privileged people.	Supports resistance against objectification of others. Develops processes of mutual accountability.	Helps to resist complacency and collusion with exploitative system. Contributes to struggle to recover personal and political identity.

SOURCE: Adapted from I. Prilleltensky (in press).

preferred interventions. We would show high degrees of commitment and accountability to the extent that we pursue these interventions. As a monitoring system, Table 6.3 helps to keep track of our actions. Are we intervening primarily at the personal level? Do we focus too much on oppression to the neglect of liberation and well-being? Have we neglected the collective domain?

Whereas epistemic validity refers to our understanding of psychopolitical dynamics of oppression, transformative validity demands changes toward liberation at personal, interpersonal, and structural domains. The following questions attend to transformative validity:

1. Do interventions promote psychopolitical literacy?

2. Do interventions educate participants on the timing, components, targets, and dynamics of best strategic actions to overcome oppression?

3. Do interventions empower participants to take action to address political inequities and social injustice within their relationships, settings,

communities, and states and at the international level?

4. Do interventions promote solidarity and strategic alliances and coalitions with groups facing similar issues?

5. Do interventions account for the subjectivity and psychological limitations of the agents of change?

Explicit political aims have often been advocated for but infrequently acted on in mental health. Transformative validity may serve to remind us that political literacy and social change have to be part of all interventions. We seek not only to ameliorate social conditions but also to alter the configurations of power that deprive citizens of their rights (Prilleltensky & Nelson, 2002). In so doing, we create the conditions for resilience to be nurtured and to flourish. Our worry is that we too easily psychologize the successful growth of individuals, those with or without disabilities. We have failed to investigate the conditions—social, political, and structural—that must necessarily exist to support wellness and resilience. Using the benchmarks of epistemic and transformative psychopolitical validity, we believe, offers the field of mental health (researchers and practitioners alike) a way in which to conceptually broaden the scope of their work to account for a nonindividualizing health discourse. That discourse has been thus far lukewarm to a more contextual understanding of health phenomena.

CONCLUSION

People affected with physical disabilities and psychosocial problems are better off when they demonstrate resilience as evidenced by successful ways of coping. But resilience must go beyond being a phrase limited to understanding how individuals cope with adversity. It must entail a challenge to the very structures that create disadvantage, discrimination, and oppression. This is not to pile more responsibilities on people who already experience challenges in their lives. Rather, it is a call to action for people with and without disabilities and for those who advocate with them for a more caring and just

society to create the conditions for resilience to be experienced. Their own participation, along with mental health and community workers, in challenging injustice can do much to enhance resilience. Professionals cannot stand back and hope that personal resilience will emerge from their therapeutic interventions alone. Community change, not just personal change; political change, not just psychological change; and justice, not just caring, are all urgently needed.

REFERENCES

Albee, G. W. (1990). The futility of psychotherapy. *Journal of Mind and Behavior, 11,* 369–384.

Barton, L. (1998). Society, disability studies and education: Some observations. In T. Shakespeare (Ed.), *The disability reader* (pp. 53–64). London: Cassell.

Carr, S., & Sloan, T. (Eds.). (2003). *Poverty and psychology: From global perspective to local practice.* New York: Kluwer/Plenum.

Crow, L. (1996). Including all of our lives: Renewing the social model of disability. In J. Morris (Ed.), *Encounters with strangers: Disability and feminism* (pp. 206–226). London: Women's Press.

Cushman, P. (1990). Why the self is empty: Toward a historically situated psychology. *American Psychologist, 45,* 599–611.

Flyvbjerg, B. (2001). *Making social science matter: Why social inquiry fails and how it can succeed again.* New York: Cambridge University Press.

Fox, D., & Prilleltensky, I. (Eds.). (1997). *Critical psychology: An introduction.* London: Sage.

Fromm, E. (1960). *Escape from freedom.* London: Routledge & Kegan Paul.

Habermas, J. (1971). *Knowledge and human interests.* Boston: Beacon.

James, S., & Prilleltensky, I. (2002). Cultural diversity and mental health: Towards integrative practice. *Clinical Psychology Review, 22,* 1133–1154.

Kawachi, I., Kennedy, B., & Wilkinson, R. (Eds.). (1999). *The society and population health reader: Income inequality and health.* New York: New Press.

Kieffer, C. (1984). Citizen empowerment: A developmental perspective. *Prevention in Human Services, 3*(2-3), 9–36.

Kim, J. K., Millen, J. V., Irwin, A., & Gersham, J. (Eds.). (2000). *Dying for growth: Global inequality and the health of the poor.* Monroe, ME: Common Courage Press.

Kitzinger, C. (1997). Lesbian and gay psychology: A critical analysis. In D. Fox & I. Prilleltensky (Eds.), *Critical psychology: An introduction* (pp. 202–216). London: Sage.

Levine, M., & Levine, A. (1992). *Helping children: A social history.* Oxford, UK: Oxford University Press.

Lewis, J., Lewis, M., Daniels, J., & D'Andrea, M. (2003). *Community counseling: Empowerment strategies for a diverse society.* Pacifica Grove, CA: Thomson Learning.

Lord, J., & Hutchison, P. (1993). The process of empowerment: Implications for theory and practice. *Canadian Journal of Community Mental Health, 12*(1), 5–22.

Lorde, A. (1984). The master's tools will never dismantle the master's house. In *Sister outsider: Essays and speeches* (pp. 110–113). Santa Cruz, CA: Crossing Press.

Marmot, M. (1999). Introduction. In M. Marmot & R. Wilkinson (Eds.), *Social determinants of health* (pp. 1–16). New York: Oxford.

McCubbin, M., Labonte, R., Sullivan, R., & Dallaire, B. (2003). *Mental health is our collective wealth.* Discussion paper submitted to Federal/Provincial/Territorial Advisory Network on Mental Health and Health Canada. (Available from Saskatchewan Population Health and Evaluation Research Unit)

Morris, J. (1993). *Independent lives? Community care and disabled people.* London: Macmillan.

Mullaly, B. (2002). *Challenging oppression: A critical social work approach.* Toronto, Ontario, Canada: Oxford University Press.

Murray, M., Nelson, G., Poland, B., Matycka-Tyndale, E., Ferris, L., Lavoie, F., Cameron, R., & Prkachin, K. (2001). *Training in community health psychology.* Report to Canadian Institutes of Health Research. (Available from Dr. Michael Murray, Division of Community Health, Faculty of Medicine, Memorial University of Newfoundland, St John's, Newfoundland, Canada, A1B 3V6)

Nelson, G., Lord, J., & Ochocka, J. (2001). *Shifting the paradigm in community mental health: Towards empowerment and community.* Toronto, Ontario, Canada: University of Toronto Press.

Nelson, G., & Prilleltensky, I. (Eds.). (in press). *Community psychology: In pursuit of wellbeing and liberation.* New York: Palgrave Macmillan.

Nelson, G., Prilleltensky, I., & MacGillivary, H. (2001). Building value-based partnerships: Toward solidarity with oppressed groups. *American Journal of Community Psychology, 29,* 649–677.

Newbrough, J. (1992). Community psychology in the post-modern world. *Journal of Community Psychology, 20,* 10–25.

Newbrough, J. (1995). Toward community: A third position. *American Journal of Community Psychology, 23,* 9–37.

Oliver, M. (1990). *The politics of disablement.* New York: St. Martin's Press.

Oliver, M. (1996). A sociology of disability or a disablist sociology? In L. Barton (Ed.), *Disability and society* (pp. 18–42). London: Longman.

Olkin, R. (1999). *What therapists should know about disability.* New York: Guilford Press.

Pare, D., & Larner, G. (Eds.). (in press). *Critical knowledge and practice in psychology and psychotherapy.* New York: Haworth Press.

Prilleltensky, I. (1994). *The morals and politics of psychology: Psychological discourse and the status quo.* Albany: State University of New York Press.

Prilleltensky, I. (2001). Value-based praxis in community psychology: Moving towards social justice and social action. *American Journal of Community Psychology, 29,* 747–778.

Prilleltensky, I. (2003a). Poverty and power. In S. Carr & T Sloan (Eds.), *Psychology and poverty* (pp. 19–44). New York: Kluwer/Plenum.

Prilleltensky, I. (2003b). Understanding and overcoming oppression: Towards psychopolitical validity. *American Journal of Community Psychology, 31,* 195–202.

Prilleltensky, I. (in press). The role of power in wellness, oppression, and liberation: The promise of psychopolitical validity. *Journal of Community Psychology.*

Prilleltensky, I., & Nelson, G. (2002). *Doing psychology critically: Making a difference in diverse settings.* London: Palgrave Macmillan.

Prilleltensky, I., Nelson, G., & Peirson, L. (Eds.). (2001). *Promoting family wellness and preventing child maltreatment.* University of Toronto Press.

Prilleltensky, I., & Prilleltensky, O. (2003a). Reconciling the roles of professional helper and critical agent in health psychology. *Journal of Health Psychology, 8,* 243–246.

Prilleltensky, I., & Prilleltensky, O. (2003b). Towards a critical health psychology practice. *Journal of Health Psychology, 8,* 197–210.

Prilleltensky, O. (1998). *Motherhood in the lives of women with disabilities.* Doctoral Dissertation, University of Toronto.

Prilleltensky, O. (2003). A ramp to motherhood: The experiences of mothers with disabilities. *Sexuality and Disability, 21,* 21–47.

Prilleltensky, O. (2004a). *Motherhood and disability: Children and choices.* New York: Palgrave/ Macmillan.

Prilleltensky, O. (2004b). My child is not my carer: Mothers with physical disabilities and the well-being of children. *Disability and Society, 19*(3), 209–223.

Rappaport, J. (1987). Terms of empowerment/ exemplars of prevention: Toward a theory for Community Psychology. *American Journal of Community Psychology, 15,* 121–144.

Sampson, E. E. (1983). *Justice and the critique of pure psychology.* New York: Plenum.

Sarason, S. B. (1981). *Psychology misdirected.* New York: Free Press.

Shakespeare, T. (Ed.). (1998). *The disability reader: Social science perspectives.* London: Cassell.

Sloan, T. (Ed.). (2000). *Critical psychology: Voices for change.* London: Macmillan.

Vera, E. M., & Speight, S. L. (2003). Multicultural competence, social justice, and counseling psychology: Expanding our roles. *The Counseling Psychologist.*

White, G. (in press). Ableism. In G. Nelson & I. Prilleltensky (Eds.), *Community psychology: In pursuit of wellbeing and liberation.* New York: Palgrave/Macmillan.

7

COMMUNITY-BASED CHILD WELFARE FOR ABORIGINAL CHILDREN

Supporting Resilience Through Structural Change

CINDY BLACKSTOCK

NICO TROCMÉ

"Help Me," wrote Richard Cardinal in his own blood while the 17-year-old Métis boy committed suicide after spending 13 years moving in and out of 28 foster homes, group homes, and shelters in Alberta (Obomsawin, 1986). Although Cardinal's death drew attention to the significant overrepresentation of Aboriginal[1] children in state care, 20 years later, the problem has become far more serious, with Aboriginal children representing approximately 40% of the 76,000 children and youth placed in out-of-home care in Canada (Farris-Manning & Zandstra, 2003). Although there is a lack of information on placement trends for Aboriginal children off-reserve due to variances in provincial data collection mechanisms, Department of Indian Affairs year-end data suggest that the number of status[2] Indian children living on-reserve increased 71.5% nationally between 1995 and 2001 (McKenzie, 2002). Overall, we estimate that there may be as many as three times more Aboriginal children in the care of child welfare authorities now than were placed in residential schools at the height of those operations in the 1940s (Blackstock, 2003). This is particularly concerning because information suggests that many Aboriginal children resident off-reserve continue to be placed in non-Aboriginal homes (British Columbia Children's Commissioner, 1998). Moreover, as the UN Committee on the Rights of the Child notes in its concluding remarks to Canada in 2003, Aboriginal children continue to face significant and disproportionate levels of risks in other areas, such as education, youth justice, health, and poverty. In keeping with the committee's concern for Aboriginal children, over one third of the concluding observations for Canada make specific mention of Aboriginal children (UN Committee on the Rights of the Child, 2003a).

The reasons for the disproportionate removal of Aboriginal children from their families are poorly understood. Furthermore, much of the existing resiliency literature places the child as the primary locus of analysis versus exploring the implications of cultural, community, and family resiliency as central factors. This chapter draws from a number of sources to examine some of these mechanisms. We begin by making the point that diverse Aboriginal Nations have demonstrated resiliency for thousands of years prior to the arrival of colonial powers and certainly by surviving through myriad traumas brought on by colonization. We further discuss how residential schools, out-of-community foster care, and adoptive placements have historically shaped Aboriginal communities' experience of, and relationship with, child welfare services. We then present a profile of the contemporary experience of Aboriginal children and families who come into contact with the child welfare system, through an analysis of data from the Canadian Incidence Study on Reported Child Abuse and Neglect (Trocmé et al., 2001).

We have structured our argument to demonstrate that the risks posed to Aboriginal children were, and are, often the result of structural decisions made by those outside their communities. In the process, generations of children suffered severe and long-lasting threats to their well-being, both psychologically and physically. Consistent with Aboriginal holistic approaches and structural social work theory, we believe that child, family, and community resiliency are interdependent, and thus, culturally based family interventions must be coupled with culturally based community development approaches to redress structural challenges to the safety of Aboriginal children. Finally, we discuss how culturally based community development frameworks could better address some of the current structural barriers, including inequitable service access, and the implications of systemic causal factors on child maltreatment assessment and response.

HISTORICAL CONTEXT

Carbon-dated evidence suggests that Aboriginal peoples have lived on these lands now known as Canada for over 10,500 years (Muckle, 1998), raising over 525 generations of children before child welfare and social work were even founded. These emotional, physical, cognitive, and spiritual ways of knowing and being have guided the resilient development of hundreds of generations of Aboriginal children who were healthy, proud, contributing members of society . . . living safely at home in their communities. Yet consistent with patterns of colonialism, today, this knowledge is too often viewed as ancillary to the "legitimate" knowledge of the child welfare system and to child resiliency. As the history below describes, Euro-Western-based social work in Canada frequently embodies an unearned arrogance expressed through statute, funding regimes, and social policies that directly regulate and shape the way in which Aboriginal peoples (and Aboriginal child welfare agencies) can care for their children.

The first colonists arrived on the eastern shores of what is now Canada in the 1490s. Reports indicate that initial contact between Aboriginal peoples and the colonial powers were primarily mutually beneficial because the relationship was centered on trade activity, but this rapidly changed as colonial aspirations moved to settlement, resource extraction, and the elimination of Indian peoples from the land (Royal Commission on Aboriginal Peoples [RCAP], 1996). The impacts of colonization on Aboriginal peoples cannot be underestimated. RCAP estimates that the population of Aboriginal peoples in Canada decreased 80% from the time of contact to confederation as a result of intentional and unintentional introduction of disease, bounty hunting, and starvation. Some peoples such as the Beothuck in Newfoundland became extinct. This prolific loss of life was coupled with forced displacement from traditional lands and the assignment of Aboriginal peoples to small reserves where maintenance of traditional sustenance was often not possible. The result was an erosion of communal cultural knowledge and ways of life that had sustained generations of Aboriginal children and the introduction of multi-generational grief and trauma and displacement.

Beginning in the 1800s, the government of Canada aided by the Christian churches strengthened its assimilation efforts through the operation of residential schools for Indian children (Milloy, 1999). The primary objective of these schools was to eliminate any vestige of Aboriginality, replacing it with Euro-Western culture, knowledge, and spirituality. Because Indian parents seldom voluntarily sent their children to these often distant schools, the government of Canada amended the Indian Act to force Indian parents to send their child(ren) aged 5 to 15 years to the schools. The penalty for failing to comply was incarceration and fines that often could not be paid because, typically, Aboriginal peoples were living in abject poverty. The conditions at the schools were abysmal; they were built of the cheapest possible materials, employed by untrained staff, and often overcrowded because of government financial inducements to increase enrollment. Sexual and physical abuses were prevalent as were preventable deaths from disease (Milloy, 1999). These conditions were known to the Canadian government as early as the 1890s (Milloy, 1999; RCAP, 1996). In fact, Dr. P. H. Bryce, chief medical health officer for the government of Canada, found in 1907 that the death rate at the schools from preventable disease was a shocking 24% per annum, increasing to 46% if the children were tracked over a 3-year period (RCAP, 1996.) Bryce's report was released to the government and published in the media; however, the government's response to the report was to eliminate the chief medical health officer position (RCAP, 1996). The schools continued to operate under these conditions for decades, with many schools opening cemeteries on school grounds to bury the children (Milloy, 1999).

Generations of children attended these schools. Separated from family, culture, and traditional teachings, the impact was devastating at the personal, kinship, and community levels (Fornier & Crey, 1997). Children in residential schools did not experience healthy parental role modeling and as a result had a diminished capacity as adults to care for their own children (Bennett & Blackstock, 2002). Although the schools began closing in the 1940s, it took over 50 years for the last residential school to close in Saskatchewan in 1996—making it a very recent experience for many Aboriginal people (Department of Indian and Northern Affairs Canada [INAC], 2003).

ABORIGINAL CHILD WELFARE IN CANADA

The division of constitutional powers in Canada is such that the provincial and territorial governments carry the legal mandate and responsibility for providing child welfare services (Sinclair, Bala, Lilles, & Blackstock, 2004). The provincial and territorial governments have responsibility for funding child welfare services off-reserve, whereas the federal government retains responsibility under the Indian Act to fund child welfare services provided on-reserve to status Indian children.

Up until the mid 1950s, the only "child welfare" service provided to Aboriginal families and their children was residential school placement. Advocacy efforts by social workers lead to the expansion of provincial child welfare jurisdiction on reserves. The nature and extent of child welfare services provided to Aboriginal families resident on reserves varied according to the province or territory and local practice. It was not atypical for Aboriginal children to be placed in residential schools by child welfare authorities up until the early 1970s, nor was it unusual for child welfare services on-reserve to be devoid of prevention and family support, relying instead on removal as the only response to child maltreatment (Aboriginal Justice Inquiry, 2001).

Although there are incidents where interventions by child welfare authorities were experienced as positive by Aboriginal peoples, the overall impact of child welfare involvement with Aboriginal services has been discouraging. Social workers deprived of the information, skills, and resources to address the poverty, disempowerment, multigenerational grief, and loss of parenting knowledge defaulted to a practice of mass removals known as the 60s scoop (Aboriginal Justice Inquiry, 2001). The RCAP (1996) notes Department of Indian Affairs statistics indicating that over 11,000 status Indian children were placed for adoption between the years of 1960 and 1990. This statistic does not include children for whom Indian status had not been recorded or nonstatus children. In some cases, buses were hired to remove large numbers of children from reserves, often placing them in distant non-Aboriginal families. As the removals took place, there was very little effort by child welfare authorities to address structural risk factors such as multigenerational trauma, poverty, unemployment, and substandard housing conditions, which were resulting in disproportionate rates of child abuse and neglect. There also was very little consideration of the influence of Euro-Western child welfare legislation or social workers' values and beliefs on their child welfare decision making and planning for Aboriginal children and families (Union of BC Indian Chiefs, 2002).

The 60s scoop, coupled with a growing movement within First Nations and Aboriginal communities to stem the tide of children and youth being placed outside their communities, motivated the development of First Nations[3] child and family service agencies (Blackstock, 2003). The number of First Nations child and family agencies expanded in the early 1990s when the federal government lifted a moratorium on the development of Aboriginal child agencies serving on-reserve residents and implemented a national funding formula known as Directive 20–1 Chapter 5 (with the exception of Ontario, which operates under a separate funding agreement, and agencies that had funding agreements that predated Directive 20–1). Directive 20–1 Chapter 5 (the Directive) provides funding for on-reserve child welfare services only and requires that First Nations agencies work pursuant to provincial and territorial child welfare statutes; First Nations operating under their own child welfare jurisdiction therefore are not eligible for funding under this arrangement. It is important to emphasize that the federal government will not fund services to First Nations children and families off-reserve, so many of these agencies are in the difficult position of serving only on-reserve residents, deferring off-reserve services to provincial and territorial child welfare agencies, which may or may not offer culturally based services. A further complication of the Directive 20–1 funding regime is that funding levels are not linked to the content of provincial and territorial child welfare statutes, meaning that as provinces and territories change their legislation, there is no concordant review of funding levels to ensure that adequate resources are provided to First Nations child welfare agencies to meet new statutory responsibilities. A national review conducted in June of 2000 found that, on average, First Nations child and family service agencies receive 22% less funding per child than their provincial equivalents, despite the documented higher child welfare needs on-reserve (MacDonald & Ladd, 2000).

The Directive, although facilitating the development of over 100 First Nations child and family service agencies serving on-reserve communities, has been broadly criticized for its inequitable funding levels compared with provincial child welfare providers and its emphasis on supporting child removal and placement versus allocating resources to support families and communities to safely care for their children at home (MacDonald & Ladd, 2000).

First Nations child and family service agencies have, despite the barriers, been very successful in ensuring that children are cared for in the community whenever possible, and when placement outside of community is required, steps are taken to ensure that the child has access to cultural and linguistic services and to family whenever possible. Clearly, when culturally based structural supports are provided to Aboriginal children and families at risk, significant and sustained positive outcomes in child and family well-being can be expected. Furthermore, as the practices of First Nations child and family service agencies become known, they have increasingly been recognized for the outstanding quality and innovation in service delivery. Some of these practices are discussed in detail in the chapter by MacDonald, Glode, and Wien in this volume (see Chapter 22).

In parallel to the development of on-reserve agencies, off-reserve child welfare agencies have started to develop in a number of provinces. In some cases, First Nations child welfare agencies basically extend their mandates off-reserve, whereas other agencies are developed to meet the needs of Aboriginal people living off reserves. One of the most progressive movements is the Manitoba Aboriginal Justice Inquiry Child Welfare Initiative, which allows residents of

Manitoba to choose which of four culturally based child welfare authorities they wish to be serviced by (Northern First Nations, Southern First Nations, Métis, or Mainstream). In this province where over 70% of the children in care are Aboriginal, 86% of families are choosing their culturally based authority (personal conversation with Elsie Flette, CEO of the Southern First Nations Child Welfare Authority, Winnipeg, Manitoba, February 2004). This model is very respectful of the cultural identity of clients and will be an important model to monitor over time.

A PROFILE OF ABORIGINAL CHILDREN RECEIVING CHILD WELFARE SERVICES

To date, there has been very little statistical information available about Aboriginal children and families receiving child welfare services (Blackstock, Clarke, Cullen, D'Hondt, & Formsma, 2004). The 1998 Canadian Incidence Study of Reported Child Abuse and Neglect (CIS-98) (Trocmé et al., 2001) was the first national study to examine the profile children and families coming into contact with the child welfare system. Although the scope of the 1998 study does not allow for national estimates specific to the subset of Aboriginal children, the sample of Aboriginal children included in the study nevertheless represents the best source of data currently available. The material presented in this chapter is drawn from two previous analyses of this data set (Blackstock, Trocmé, & Bennett, 2004; Trocmé, Knoke, & Blackstock, 2004). The data point to the importance of a broader conceptualization of child maltreatment, one that highlights the critical role that extended family and community supports can play in assisting children, young people, and families at risk of maltreatment.

The CIS-98 collected information directly from child welfare investigators on cases of reported child abuse or neglect. A multistage sampling design was used to track child maltreatment investigations conducted in 51 randomly selected sites, including 3 First Nations child and family service agencies, from October to December 1998. Data on Aboriginal heritage included three Aboriginal groupings: First

Nations, Métis, and Inuit. In addition, there were questions to determine if the child had status pursuant to the Indian Act and whether the parent lived on-reserve. Data on Aboriginal status were not collected in the Quebec portion of the CIS-98 ($N = 2,309$) and were missing on a further 10 cases. Because the Aboriginal status of each investigated child was determined by the status of the biological parent(s) who were living with the child, children who did not reside with a biological parent ($N = 225$) were also excluded. Finally, unsubstantiated reports ($N = 1,969$) were excluded from the analysis, leaving a sample of 3,159 cases where maltreatment had been substantiated or remained suspected.

Aboriginal Cultural Identification

Of victims of all cases of suspected or substantiated maltreatment in CIS-98 (614 of 3,149 children), 19% were Aboriginal (see Table 7.1). According to the 1996 Statistics Canada Census[4] figures, 5% of Canadians 15 years of age or younger were classified as Aboriginal, clearly indicating a possible overrepresentation[5] of Aboriginal children involved with child welfare authorities. Approximately two thirds (64%) of Aboriginal children were classified as First Nations, many of whom lived off-reserve, a distribution similar to the 1996 Census Canada estimates indicating that 69% of Aboriginal children under 16 were classified as "North American Indian." The relatively large proportion of First Nations children within the Aboriginal service population is consistent with child-in-care data from British Columbia, indicating that 87% of the Aboriginal children in care are First Nations (status and nonstatus), with Métis and Inuit children representing 12% and 1%, respectively (Ministry for Child and Family Development, 2002). Similar figures are reported in Manitoba where First Nations children are overrepresented among other Aboriginal and non-Aboriginal children in the child welfare system (Stevens, 2003).

FORMS OF MALTREATMENT

Well over half (61%) the Aboriginal cases of substantiated or suspected maltreatment primarily[6]

Table 7.1   Aboriginal Status and Visible Minority Background for Cases of Substantiated and Suspected Maltreatment, 1998 CIS[a] (*N* = 3,159)

	Number of Investigations	*Percentage of All Cases*	*Percentage of Aboriginal Cases (excluding non-Aboriginals)*
Aboriginal	614	19%	
First Nations on-reserve	120		27%
First Nations status, off-reserve	150		34%
First Nations nonstatus, off-reserve	14		3%
Métis	37		8%
Inuit	42		10%
Other	78		18%
Unsure/no answer	173		
Non-Aboriginal	2,114	67%	
Other minority	431	14%	
Total	**3,159**		

a. Unweighted sample, excludes (1) investigations in Quebec (*N* = 2,309), where aboriginal and ethnic identity data were not collected; (2) cases of children not residing with a biological parent (*N* = 225); (3) unsubstantiated investigations (*N* = 1,969); and (4) other eligible cases where Aboriginal and ethnic identity data were missing (*N* = 10).

involved some form of neglect, whereas neglect was found in only half as many non-Aboriginal cases (Table 7.2). Most cases were categorized as failure to supervise or failure to protect, resulting in either physical harm or risk of physical harm to the child. There was no differentiation between failure to protect and failure to supervise in CIS primary form of maltreatment reporting categories, so it not possible to determine what proportion of these cases were failure to protect, which suggests a more conscious decision to not meet a child's basic needs versus failure to supervise, which suggests a passive decision to neglect the child's needs.

The larger proportion of neglect cases is not surprising given the impacts of residential schools in separating children from parental and community systems of care (Earle & Cross, 2001; Indian Residential Schools Survivor Society, 2002). This, coupled with the high incidence of failure to protect or failure to supervise cases, suggests that a depoyment of resources to specifically address neglect and its related undercurrents of poverty, inadequate housing,

and substance misuse may be advised as a means of decreasing the numbers of Aboriginal children in the child welfare system. This type of investment would be consistent with First Nations' request that child welfare be positioned within a community development framework that considers some of the etiological drivers of child maltreatment, such as poverty, social isolation, racism, and socioeconomic exclusion (Blackstock, Clarke, et al., 2004; MacDonald & Ladd, 2000).

Non-Aboriginal cases were much more likely to involve physical abuse, most notably punishment-related abuse, which accounted for 35% of cases involving visible minority families and 22% of non-Aboriginal families. Sexual abuse was not noted as often in Aboriginal cases, a finding consistent with the analysis of Dr. Kathleen Earle of the secondary data from the Department of Health and Human Services archived data at Cornell University, indicating that sexual and physical abuse rates were lower for Indian and Alaskan Native children in the United States (Earle & Cross, 2001).

Table 7.2   Primary Form of Maltreatment, by Aboriginal Status, for Substantiated or Suspected Maltreatment, 1998 CIS[a] (*N* = 3,159)

	Aboriginal	*Non-Aboriginal*	*Other Visible Minority*
Physical abuse, punishment	8%	22%	35%
Physical abuse, other	8%	12%	11%
Sexual abuse	5%	10%	5%
Failure to supervise child at risk of physical harm	41%	17%	19%
Physical neglect (failure to provide adequate physical care)	7%	5%	4%
Other neglect (failure to supervise child at risk of sexual abuse, medical neglect, failure to provide treatment, educational neglect, emotional neglect, and abandonment)	11%	9%	9%
Emotional maltreatment	7%	11%	6%
Exposure to domestic violence	9%	14%	13%
Total	**614**	**2,114**	**431**

a. Unweighted sample, excludes (1) investigations in Quebec (*N* = 2,309), where aboriginal and ethnic identity data were not collected; (2) cases of children not residing with a biological parent (*N* = 225); (3) unsubstantiated investigations (*N* = 1,969); and (4) other eligible cases where Aboriginal and ethnic identity data were missing (*N* = 10).

Chi square = 244.31; *df* = 8; *p* < .001.

Child Characteristics

Aboriginal children were on average slightly younger (mean age = 7.33 years) than their non-Aboriginal counterparts (mean age = 7.93 years; *F* = 4.38; *df* = 2; *p* < .05). As reflected in Table 7.3, the greatest difference was with the larger proportion of children in the birth to 3-year-old category.

Table 7.4 presents a child functioning rating provided by the investigating social workers using a simple checklist of problems they had noted during their investigation.

Overall, there are few significant differences between the Aboriginal, non-Aboriginal, and visible minority children, with the exception of substance abuse-related birth defects and the child's own substance abuse being noted more often for Aboriginal children, and behavior problems and attending special education classes being noted less often. The higher rate of substance abuse-related birth defects among the Aboriginal children, 7%, versus 2% for non-Aboriginal

children, is consistent with reports from studies suggesting that the rates of fetal alcohol syndrome and fetal alcohol affect among Aboriginal children may be significantly higher than the estimated incidents of 1 to 3 per 1,000 live births in the population overall (Blackstock, Clarke, et al., 2004; Health Canada, 2003). The overall similarity in levels of functioning between Aboriginal and non-Aboriginal children, coupled with the significant disproportionate representation of Aboriginal children in care, suggests that child functioning may not be a significant factor informing child removal decision making. This raises the possibility that social workers are disproportionately focusing on family and community conditions as factors in removal; however, because the sample size in the present study is relatively small, this matter deserves more concentrated study.

Household Characteristics

Of non-Aboriginal families, 51% were headed by single parents, contrasted with 57%

Table 7.3   Child Age, by Aboriginal Status, for Cases of Substantiated or Suspected Maltreatment, 1998 CIS[a] (N = 3,159)

	Aboriginal	Non-Aboriginal	Other Visible Minority
Mean age	7.33	7.93	7.69
0–3 years	26%	20%	21%
4–7 years	26%	27%	29%
8–11 years	25%	26%	25%
12–15 years	24%	27%	25%
Total	**614**	**2,114**	**431**

a. Unweighted sample, excludes (1) investigations in Quebec (N = 2,309), where aboriginal and ethnic identity data were not collected; (2) cases of children not residing with a biological parent (N = 225); (3) unsubstantiated investigations (N = 1,969); and (4) other eligible cases where Aboriginal and ethnic identity data were missing (N = 10).

$F = 4.38$; $df = 2$; $p < .05$.

Table 7.4   Child Functioning, by Aboriginal Status, for Substantiated or Suspected Maltreatment, 1998 CIS[a] (N = 3,159)

		Aboriginal	Non-Aboriginal	Other Visible Minority
Developmental disability	ns	2%	3%	3%
Health condition	ns	3%	4%	4%
Substance abuse-related birth defect	$p < .001$	7%	2%	<1%
Depression or anxiety	$p < .001$	9%	12%	6%
Self-harming behavior	$p < .05$	5%	4%	2%
Behavior problem	$p < .001$	18%	25%	18%
Negative peer involvement	ns	11%	11%	8%
Violence toward others	$p < .01$	7%	9%	4%
Substance abuse	$p < .001$	7%	4%	3%
Running away (multiple incidents)	ns	4%	3%	3%
Inappropriate sexual behavior	ns	3%	4%	2%
Special education class	ns	4%	6%	6%
Irregular school attendance	$p < .001$	15%	10%	6%
Criminal/YO involvement	ns	3%	2%	2%
One or more child function concerns noted	$p < .01$	44%	46%	37%
Total		**614**	**2,114**	**431**

a. Unweighted sample, excludes (1) investigations in Quebec (N = 2,309), where aboriginal and ethnic identity data were not collected; (2) cases of children not residing with a biological parent (N = 225); (3) unsubstantiated investigations (N = 1,969); and (4) other eligible cases where Aboriginal and ethnic identity data were missing (N = 10).

Table 7.5   Household Characteristics, by Aboriginal Status, for Substantiated or Suspected Maltreatment, 1998 CIS[a] ($N = 3,159$)

		Aboriginal	Non-Aboriginal	Other Visible Minority
Age of Caregiver A (% 30 yrs of age or under)	$p < .001$	48.2	34.3	29.3
Single parent	$p < .001$	57%	51%	41%
Social assistance or other benefits	$p < .001$	59%	38%	33%
Rental housing	$p < .001$	23%	8%	16%
One move within last 6 months	$p < .001$	24%	24%	18%
Two or more moves in last 6 months	$p < .001$	21%	10%	6%
Unsafe housing	$p < .05$	9%	6%	4%
Total		**614**	**2,114**	**431**

a. Unweighted sample, excludes (1) investigations in Quebec ($N = 2,309$), where aboriginal and ethnic identity data were not collected; (2) cases of children not residing with a biological parent ($N = 225$); (3) unsubstantiated investigations ($N = 1,969$); and (4) other eligible cases where aboriginal and ethnic identity data were missing ($N = 10$).

of Aboriginal families in the sample (see Table 7.5). Of single-parent families, 90% of Aboriginal families were headed by single mothers versus 86% of their non-Aboriginal counterparts. The Canadian Mortgage and Housing Corporation reports that based on 1997 data, 1 in 5 Aboriginal families living off-reserve were headed by single parents, predominantly women, and of these, 62% were in core housing need (Canada Mortgage and Housing Corporation, 1997). This information, coupled with the higher incidence of neglect in Aboriginal communities indicated in the CIS, may partially explain why Aboriginal mothers were identified as the alleged perpetrators of child maltreatment among single-parent families in 78% of cases versus 56% for their non-Aboriginal counterparts.

Social benefits were the main source of income for 60% of Aboriginal families in the sample, contrasted with the 21% rate of non-Aboriginal families, 61% of whom had access to full-time employment. These findings are echoed by the Government of Manitoba (2000) Aboriginal and Northern Affairs report *Aboriginal People in Manitoba 2000,* examining poverty rates for off-reserve Aboriginal families, which found that 63% of Aboriginal families in Manitoba live below the poverty line and 53% of Aboriginal children live below the poverty line nationally. Poverty rates for Aboriginal children remain significantly higher (52.1%) even when contrasted with poverty rates for other marginalized groups such as visible minority children at 42.7% and children with disabilities at 23% (Anderson, 2003).

In terms of on-reserve poverty rates, Beavon and Cooke (2001) found that based on 1995 data, the average income of a status Indian on-reserve was $7,165, whereas the average income for a status Indian living off-reserve was $9,365 per annum. Overall calculations using the Human Development Index in this same study would place First Nations on-reserve alongside citizens of Brazil and Peru in terms of quality of life.

Aboriginal families in the sample were more likely to live in rental housing than their non-Aboriginal counterparts. Nearly half (46%) the Aboriginal families had moved in the last 6 months, with 21% having moved two times or more, double the rate noted for their non-Aboriginal counterparts. The instability of Aboriginal families' housing arrangements further compounds the lack of employment and high level of poverty faced by Aboriginal people in Canada. Somewhat surprisingly, investigating social workers noted only a slight, but statistically significant, difference in unsafe housing conditions of Aboriginal families and non-Aboriginal families, with Aboriginal families residing in unsafe homes in 9% of cases and

Table 7.6 Parent Risk Factors, by Aboriginal Status, for Substantiated or Suspected Maltreatment, 1998 CIS[a] (N = 3,159)

		Aboriginal	Non-Aboriginal	Other Visible Minority
Caregiver maltreated as child	p = .001	51.3%	30.6%	19.3%
Parental concerns				
Alcohol abuse	p < .001	72%	27%	15%
Drug abuse	p < .001	31%	15%	10%
Criminal activity	p < .001	21%	11%	11%
Cognitive impairment	p < .001	9%	6%	3%
Mental health problems	p < .01	25%	28%	17%
Physical health problems	ns	8%	7%	6%
Lack of social supports	ns	37%	33%	34%
Domestic violence	p < .001	37%	27%	31%
One or more parent concerns noted	p < .001	94%	73%	66%
Total		**614**	**2,114**	**431**

a. Unweighted sample, excludes (1) investigations in Quebec (N = 2,309), where aboriginal and ethnic identity data were not collected; (2) cases of children not residing with a biological parent (N = 225); (3) unsubstantiated investigations (N = 1,969); and (4) other eligible cases where Aboriginal and ethnic identity data were missing (N = 10).

their non-Aboriginal counterparts in 6% of cases. This finding is inconsistent with other studies that have found that Aboriginal families are much more likely to live in overcrowded and inadequate housing. For example, findings of a national consultation conducted by the Inuit Tapiriit Kanatami organization in 2001 indicated that 8,000 housing units were required to meet the immediate housing needs of the Inuit (Inuit Tapiriit Kanatami, 2003). In addition, a 1989 report commissioned by the Department of Indian Affairs and Northern Development notes that the number of First Nations peoples on-reserve living in crowded dwellings was 16 times the national average and that the condition of the housing was also problematic, with 38% of homes on-reserve lacking central heating (Hagey, Larocque, & McBride, 1989).

As noted by the Campaign 2000 (2003), food security is also a problem; national data indicate that Aboriginal peoples are four times as likely to report experiencing hunger than their non-Aboriginal counterparts.

Caregiver Functioning

Investigating workers completed a brief checklist identifying caregiver functioning issues that they had noted during their investigation. Of Aboriginal caregivers, 94% were reported as experiencing at least one functioning concern, compared with 73% of non-Aboriginal caregivers and 66% of other visible minority caregivers.

The problem that constituted the most frequent concern for Aboriginal families in the sample was alcohol abuse, reported for 72% of Aboriginal caregivers compared with 27% of the non-Aboriginal families and 15% of the other visible minority families. Drug abuse was noted twice as often for Aboriginal caregivers than for non-Aboriginal caregivers. The over-representation of alcohol and drug abuse in this sample is consistent with the Department of Indian and Northern Affairs report that 62% of First Nations people aged 15 and over report that alcohol abuse is a problem in their community

Table 7.7   Service Response, by Aboriginal Service Provider, for Substantiated or Suspected Maltreatment, 1998 CIS[a] (*N* = 3,159)

		Aboriginal	Non-Aboriginal	Other Visible Minority
Previously opened case (child)	*p* < .001	71%	48%	32%
Ongoing services provided	*p* < .001	55%	42%	38%
Informal placement	*p* < .001	16%	5%	5%
Child welfare placement	*p* < .001	14%	7%	13%
Application to child welfare court	*p* < .001	8%	6%	13%
Total		**614**	**2,114**	**431**

a. Unweighted sample, excludes (1) investigations in Quebec (*N* = 2,309), where aboriginal and ethnic identity data were not collected; (2) cases of children not residing with a biological parent (*N* = 225); (3) unsubstantiated investigations (*N* = 1,969); and (4) other eligible cases where Aboriginal and ethnic identity data were missing (*N* = 10).

and 48% report drug abuse as a concern (INAC, 2003).

Criminal activity by the caregiver was reported in 21% of Aboriginal homes, whereas it was reported in 11% of non-Aboriginal homes. This rate is consistent with research by Foran (1995) for Corrections Canada indicating that although Aboriginal peoples constitute 3% of the population, they compose 17% of men and 26% of women who are incarcerated.

Differences were less marked but nevertheless generally statistically significant with respect to rates of caregiver mental illness, cognitive functioning, and physical health problems. There was no significant difference in lack of social supports between Aboriginal families (37%) and non-Aboriginal families (33%). It is important to note that data regarding the cultural match of social supports were not collected in the CIS.

Ongoing Child Welfare Services

The service response, from provision of services to out-of-home placement, was dramatically different for Aboriginal children and their families. Cases of substantiated or suspected maltreatment involving Aboriginal families were significantly more likely to have been previously opened for services and more likely to remain open for ongoing services after the investigation. Over 70% of Aboriginal cases had been previously opened compared with 48% of

non-Aboriginal and 32% of visible minority cases. Ongoing services were provided to 55% of Aboriginal cases, compared with 42% of non-Aboriginal ones. The rate of admissions to formal out-of-home placements was twice as high for Aboriginal children (14% vs. 7%), and the rate of informal placement was 3 times as high. Applications to child welfare court were also higher for Aboriginal children compared with non-Aboriginal children, although they were by far the highest for other visible minority children.

FOUNDATIONS FOR A
COMMUNITY RESPONSE

So if the data indicate a need for community-based responses that address poverty, substance misuse, and inadequate housing that drive the overrepresentation of Aboriginal children in care, what resources are currently available to Aboriginal families? Unfortunately, there is very minimal data on the nature and extent of culturally appropriate services for Aboriginal families who come into contact with the child welfare authorities off-reserve. Only Manitoba has conducted a comprehensive review of services in preparation for the Aboriginal Justice Inquiry Child Welfare Initiative. Manitoba provincial data from 2003 indicate that although Aboriginal children compose

70% of the children in care in that province, Aboriginal families were benefiting from only 30% of the child welfare family support budget (personal conversation with Elsie Flette, CEO of the Southern First Nations Child Welfare Authority, Winnipeg, Manitoba, February, 2004).

Counter to a pervasive stereotype that First Nations children and families living on-reserve have enhanced access to services, the First Nations Child and Family Caring Society of Canada (Nadjiwan & Blackstock, 2003) found that First Nations families have significantly less access to child welfare-related resources in the public, corporate, and voluntary sectors. Recall that MacDonald and Ladd (2000) found that First Nations child and family service agencies receive inadequate funding for secondary and tertiary prevention services and, overall, receive 22% less funding per child than their provincial counterparts. In addition, it is atypical for a provincial or municipal government to provide any services on-reserve, thus limiting social programs to those funded by the federal government, often pursuant to population-driven funding formulas. From the corporate perspective, as demonstrated earlier in this report, Aboriginal families know poverty at levels that far outstrip the experience of other Canadians, meaning they are in less of an economic position to support their families. The concluding observations of both the UN Committee on the Elimination of Racial Discrimination (2002) and the UN Committee on the Rights of the Child (2003a, 2003b) recognize the correlation between the lack of progress in settling treaties and self-government agreements and the continued economic marginalization of Aboriginal peoples in Canada.

Nadjiwan and Blackstock (2003) built on this information by conducting a national study to determine the nature and extent of access by First Nations families to myriad social and quality-of-life supports provided by the voluntary sector in Canada, which represents over $90 billion in annual revenues. Results indicated that First Nations children and families on-reserve receive a negligible amount of service from the voluntary sector. In addition, only one First Nations child and family service agency reported receiving funds from a philanthropic foundation, with two others reporting receiving federal/provincial government money targeted for voluntary sector services.

Taken as a whole, First Nations children and their families on-reserve experience higher levels of social, economic, and cultural risk than do other Canadians and have far fewer resources. Data on socioeconomic outcomes off-reserve point to a similar pattern, although research on the degree of access to voluntary sector resources for children off-reserve requires further study. This pattern of undersupporting Aboriginal families persists despite Canada's commitments in the Statement of Reconciliation and the UN Convention on the Rights of the Child, which compels government to eradicate discrimination by giving children first call on the nation's resources.

COMMUNITY RESILIENCY AND CHILD RESILIENCY

Although it is not possible to draw a direct correlation between the overrepresentation of Aboriginal children in care and the dearth of quality-of-life and family support services on-reserve, it is very likely that a relationship exists. The argument that community resiliency is connected to child resiliency is consistent with neighborhood resource theory, which suggests that the higher the quality and degree of social supports and social capital available to a child at a community level, the better the child outcomes (Connors & Brink, 1999). Unfortunately, there is very little research on the impact of community development on child well-being in general, with most of it being conducted within the context of early childhood development (Social Development Canada, 1999). The interrelationship between community development and child maltreatment rates involving Aboriginal children is an important area for further study; it holds the promise of reducing the overrepresentation of Aboriginal children in the child welfare system through the promotion of community-based resiliency factors. Such research should respectfully reflect the resiliency embedded within Aboriginal cultural ways of caring for children, families, and communities in order to identify factors that support the safety and well-being of Aboriginal families.

Another possible influence of the community development context is how local conditions influence social worker assessment of child safety and well-being. That CIS data indicate that substance misuse, poverty, and inadequate housing appear as undercurrents to the over-representation of Aboriginal children in care is important. It can be argued that the assessment of parental neglect implies that the parent (care-giver) has some ability to change the risk factors the child experiences. It is arguably very diffi-cult for parents to influence their own poverty or poor housing without substantial and meaning-ful social aid and advocacy. Similarly, the redress of substance misuse implies a need for detox and substance misuse supports for the child and family. Research indicates a signifi-cant dearth in services for First Nations children on-reserve, and anecdotal evidence points to a significant need for families off-reserve, so it seems unreasonable to cast responsibility for addressing the causal agents of the child risk onto the families alone. This raises two impor-tant questions: (a) To what degree are parents held responsible for systemic and structural community-based challenges over which they have little or no influence? (b) To what degree is child protection social work itself prepared to meaningfully support sustainable community development approaches to reducing the drivers of maltreatment.

Increasingly, child welfare experts are sup-porting community-based interventions in child maltreatment (MacDonald & Ladd, 2000; RCAP, 1996; Saskatchewan Children's Advocate Office, 2003). The wisdom of community devel-opment approaches designed by Aboriginal communities to ensure the safety and well-being of Aboriginal children is beginning to be borne out in research. For example, research into youth suicide rates in First Nations communities in British Columbia indicates that the higher the degree of self-government (as expressed by First Nations child welfare, health, education, fire and police services, advancement in the treaty process, and women in government), the lower the youth suicide rate (Chandler & Lalonde, 2003). These findings echo the opinion of the UN Committee on the Rights of the Child Day of General Discussion on Indigenous Children (2003b) and the research of Cornell and Kalt (1992), which found that the higher the degree of self-government in Native American tribes, the higher the degree of sustained socio-economic outcomes.

Community development approaches also afford the opportunity to celebrate and leverage the resiliency founded in cultural ways of know-ing and being that sustained generations of Aboriginal children throughout the millennia and sustained them through the graphic and, we argue, ongoing impacts of colonization.

CONCLUSION

The overrepresentation of Aboriginal children in the child welfare system is a growing and complex problem rooted in a pervasive history of discrimination and colonization. Provincial and territorial child welfare authorities have made some nominal attempts to reverse this pattern of discrimination; however, the continual increase in placements points to the pressing need for bolder action at community and struc-tural levels. Aboriginal children disproportion-ately come into contact with the child welfare system because of problems associated with poverty and substance abuse, not because of higher rates of physical or sexual violence toward children. However, the likelihood of improve-ment is limited, as long as the problems are defined within the narrow scope of child protec-tion[7] systems and as long as inequitable access to social support services persists. Stronger commu-nities equipped with the governance structure and the resources to address child poverty, inadequate housing, and substance abuse are required to stem the tide of Aboriginal children coming into the child welfare system. Resilient Aboriginal communities provide the best chance for resilient, safe, and well Aboriginal children, young people, and families. In honor of Richard Cardinal's memory, we must do much better, especially now that we are beginning to under-stand some of the roots of the problem.

NOTES

1. Aboriginal describes any person who identi-fies as Métis, First Nations, or Inuit.

2. Status Indian Children refers to those children who are eligible to be registered as an Indian pursuant to the Government of Canada's Indian Act.

3. First Nations describes the original peoples of the land now known as Canada whose traditional territories were primarily between the 49th and 60th parallels longitude.

4. Available online at www12.statcan.ca/english/census01/info/census96.cfm.

5. Because the scope of the CIS-98 does not allow for precise national estimates, the comparison between the profile of children in the CIS sample and national census data should be interpreted with some caution.

6. The CIS tracked up to three forms of maltreatment for each investigated child in the sample. The primary form was defined as the type of maltreatment considered to best characterizing the major investigation concern.

7. Indeed, a growing number of jurisdictions have replaced the concept of child welfare with the narrower concept of child protection.

REFERENCES

Aboriginal Justice Inquiry-Child Welfare Initiative. (2001). *Promise of hope: Commitment to change.* Winnipeg, Manitoba, Canada: Executive Committee of the AJI-CWI. (Available online at www.aji-cwi.mb.ca/pdfs/promiseofhope.pdf)

Anderson, J. (2003, March). *Aboriginal children in poverty in urban communities: Social exclusion and the growing racialization of poverty in Canada.* Presentation to the Subcommittee on Children and Youth At Risk of the Standing Committee on Human Resources Development and the Status of Persons with Disabilities, Ottawa, Ontario, Canada. (Available on line at www.ccsd.ca/pr/2003/aboriginal.htm)

Beavon, D., & Cooke, M. (2001). *An application of the United Nations Human Development Index to registered Indians in Canada, 1996.* Unpublished paper prepared for the Department of Indian Affairs and Northern Development Canada.

Bennett, M., & Blackstock, C. (2002). *A literature review and annotated bibliography focusing on aspects of aboriginal child welfare in Canada.* Ottawa, Ontario, Canada: First Nations Child and Family Caring Society of Canada.

Blackstock, C. (2003). First Nations child and family services: Restoring peace and harmony in First Nations communities. In K. Kufeldt & B. McKenzie (Eds.), *Child welfare: Connecting research policy and practice* (pp. 331–343). Waterloo, Ontario, Canada: Wilfrid Laurier University Press.

Blackstock, C., Clarke, S., Cullen, J., D'Hondt, J., & Formsma, J. (2004). *Keeping the promise: The Convention on the Rights of the Child and the lived experiences of First Nations children and youth.* Ottawa, Ontario, Canada: First Nations Child and Family Caring Society of Canada.

Blackstock, C., Trocmé, N., & Bennett, M. (2004). Child welfare response to Aboriginal and non-Aboriginal children in Canada: A comparative analysis. *Violence Against Women, 10*(8), 901–916.

British Columbia Children's Commission. (1998). *Children's commission annual report 1996–1997.* Victoria, British Columbia, Canada: Author.

Campaign 2000. (2003). *Report card on child poverty in Ontario.* Ottawa, Ontario, Canada: Author.

Canadian Mortgage and Housing Corporation. (1997, July). Housing need among off-reserve Aboriginal lone parents in Canada. *Research and Development Highlights, Socio-Economic Series,* Issue 34. (Available online at http://dsp-psd.pwgsc.gc.ca/Collection/NH18-23-34E.pdf)

Chandler, M., & Lalonde, C. (1998). Cultural continuity as a hedge against suicide in Canada's First Nations. *Transcultural Psychiatry, 35*(2), 191–219.

Connor, S., & Brink, S. (1999). *Understanding the early years: Community impacts on child development* (Working Paper W-99–6E). Applied Research Branch, Strategic Policy, Human Resources Development Canada. (Available online at www11.sdc.gc.ca/en/cs/sp/arb/publications/nlscy/uey/1999-000092/w-99-6e.pdf)

Cornell, S., & Kalt, J. (1992). Reloading the dice: Improving the chances for economic development on American Indian reservations. In S. Cornell & J. P. Kalt (Eds.), *What can tribes do? Strategies and institutions in American Indian economic development* (pp. 1–59). Los Angeles: American Indian Studies Center.

Department of Indian Affairs and Northern Development Canada. (2003). *Backgrounder: The residential school system.* Available online at www.ainc-inac.gc.ca/gs/schl_e.html

Earle, K., & Cross, A. (2001). *Child abuse and neglect among American Indian/Alaska Native children: An analysis of existing data.* Seattle, WA: Casey Family Programs.

Farris-Manning, C., & Zandstra, M. (2003). *Children in Care in Canada: Summary of current issues and trends and recommendations for future research.* Unpublished paper prepared for the Child Welfare League of Canada for submission to the National Children's Alliance.

Foran, T. (1995). A descriptive comparison of demographic and family characteristics of the Canadian and offender populations. *Forum on Corrections Research Corrections Services Canada, 7*(2). (Available online at www.csc-scc.gc.ca/text/pblct/forum/e072/e072a_e.shtml)

Fornier, S., & Crey, E. (1997). *Stolen from our embrace: The abduction of First Nations children and the restoration of Aboriginal communities.* Vancouver, British Columbia, Canada: Douglas & McIntyre.

Government of Manitoba. (2000). Chapter 6: Labour and income. In *Aboriginal people in Manitoba 2000.* Retrieved December 15, 2004, from www.gov.mb.ca/ana/apm2000/6

Hagey, J., Larocque, G., & McBride, C. (1989). *Highlights of Aboriginal conditions 1981–2001 Part II: Social conditions.* Ottawa, Ontario, Canada: Department of Indian and Northern Affairs Canada.

Health Canada. (2003). *ECD strategy for Aboriginal children: A focus on fetal alcohol syndrome/fetal alcohol effects.* Retrieved December 15, 2004, from www.hc-sc.gc.ca/fnihb-dgspni/fnihb/cp/publications/ecd_fas_fae.htm

Indian Residential School Survivors Society. (2002). *The survivors journey.* West Vancouver, British Columbia, Canada: Author.

Inuit Tapiriit Kanatami. (2003). *Housing.* Socio-economic department, Inuit Tapiriit Kanatami. Retrieved January 5, 2005, www.itk.ca/sed/initiatives-housing.php

MacDonald, R., & Ladd, P. (2000). *Joint national policy review of First Nations child and family services joint national policy review.* Ottawa, Ontario, Canada: Assembly of First Nations.

McKenzie, B. (2002). *Block funding child maintenance in First Nations child and family services: A policy review.* Unpublished paper prepared for Kahnawake Shakotiia'takenhas Community Services, Montreal.

Milloy, J. (1999). *A national crime: The Canadian government and the residential school system*

1879–1986. Winnipeg, Manitoba, Canada: University of Manitoba Press.

Ministry for Child and Family Development. (2002). *April 2002 Month-End CF&CS Statistics: Aboriginal children in care SWISMIS statistical extract files.* Produced by Child Protection Division, Ministry for Child and Family Development, British Columbia.

Muckle, R. (1998). *The First Nations of British Columbia.* Vancouver: University of British Columbia Press.

Nadjiwan, S., & Blackstock, C. (2003). *Caring across the boundaries: Promoting access to voluntary sector resources for First Nations children and families.* Ottawa, Ontario, Canada: First Nations Child and Family Caring Society of Canada.

Obomsawin, A. (1986). *Richard Cardinal: Cry from a diary of a Métis child.* Video. Montreal, Quebec: National Film Board of Canada.

Royal Commission on Aboriginal Peoples. (1996). *The report of the Royal Commission on Aboriginal Peoples.* Retrieved December 15, 2004, from www.ainc-inac.gc.ca/ch/rcap/sg/sgmm_e.html

Sinclair, M., Bala, N., Lilles, H., & Blackstock, C. (2004). Aboriginal child welfare. In N. Bala, M. K. Zapf, R. J. Williams, R. Vogel, & J. P. Hornick (Eds.), *Canadian child welfare law: Children, families and the state, second edition.* Toronto, Ontario, Canada: Thompson.

Social Development Canada. (1999). *Understanding the early years: Community impacts on child development.* Retrieved July 31, 2004, from www11.sdc.gc.ca/en/cs/sp/arb/publications/nlscy/uey/1999–000092/page05.shtml

Stevens, H. (2003, March). *Indicators and correlates of social exclusion among Manitoba's Aboriginal working age (15–64) population.* Paper presented at the Social Inclusion Conference, Ottawa, Ontario, Canada.

Saskatchewan Children's Advocate Office. (2003). *Saskatchewan Children's Advocate 2003 Annual Report.* Saskatoon, Saskatchewan, Canada: Author.

Trocmé, N., Knoke, D., & Blackstock, C. (2004). Pathways to the overrepresentation of Aboriginal children in Canada's child welfare system. *Social Service Review, 78*(4), 577–600.

Trocmé, N., MacLaurin, B., Fallon, B., Daciuk, J., Billingsley, D., Tourigny, M., Mayer, M., et al. (2001). *Canadian incidence study of reported child abuse and neglect.* Ottawa, Ontario: Health Canada.

Union of BC Indian Chiefs. (2002), *Calling forth our future: Options for the exercise of indigenous people's authority in child welfare.* Retrieved December 15, 2004, from www.ubcic.bc.ca/docs/UBCIC_OurFuture.pdf

UN Committee on the Elimination of Racial Discrimination. (2002). *Concluding observations of the Committee on the Elimination of Racial Discrimination: Canada.* Geneva, Switzerland: UN Office of the High Commissioner for Human Rights.

UN Committee on the Rights of the Child. (2003a). *Concluding observations of the Committee on the Rights of the Child: Canada.* Geneva, Switzerland: UN Office of the High Commissioner for Human Rights.

UN Committee on the Rights of the Child. (2003b). *Day of general discussion on the rights of indigenous children: Recommendations.* Geneva, Switzerland: UN Office of the High Commissioner for Human Rights.

8

Beetles, Bullfrogs, and Butterflies

Contributions of Natural Environment to Childhood Development and Resilience

Fred H. Besthorn

Although childhood development begins in family, neighborhood, and community, childhood experience is also centered in a specific place, geography, and natural setting where children begin the process of exploration and discovery. The *earth* for most children is their first real home. It is the place where they first realize awe, surprise, and even danger. In this chapter, I explore the health-enhancing role that contact with and an appreciation for natural environment can play in the lives of those children who struggle to live good lives amid great adversity. I argue that nature can be one of the most important resources for nurturing resilience in even the most at-risk children. Unfortunately, for many children, growing up in a world fecund with plants, animals, and exquisite landscapes is now far more the exception than the rule.

The chapter presents both the theoretical and empirical literature that discusses the relationship between nature, childhood development, and resilience. Empirical and theoretical evidence is offered to support the conceptual perspective that natural settings, vegetative life, and all manner of wild and domesticated animals can have a significant impact on the prosocial development of children.

Resilience and the Human Experience

From ancient mythological accounts of personal courage and collective resolve to more modern media portrayals of grit in the midst of hardship, human history is replete with stories of individuals overcoming adversity and even thriving in the midst of calamity and misfortune. Clearly, human resilience has played an important role in shaping our history and the way we have storied our relationship with a difficult and sometimes harsh environment. Only within the last few decades has a rigorous research agenda evolved seeking to clearly specify how resilience is demonstrated and how it may be nurtured in diverse settings to enhance the well-being of children and adults (Fraser, 1997; Glantz & Johnson, 1999; Greene, 2002; McCubbin, Thompson, Thompson, & Futrell, 1999; Norman, 2000; Rutter, 1987; Ungar, 2002, 2004; Walsh, 1998; Werner & Smith, 2001; Wolin & Wolin, 1993).

The early derivation of resilience comes from the engineering and construction trades and suggests the capacity of a substance to recover its original shape after having been deformed under extreme stress. It carries the idea of pliability, elasticity, and malleability of a substance or form. A plastic container that is crushed and then immediately springs back to its original shape is an example of a resilient material. This definition fits very well with the current use of the term in the study of human growth and competent development that posits *resilience* as a general term used to describe attitudes, behaviors, and environmental circumstances that help people adjust to or blend with obstacles to living.

According to Vanistendael (1998), resilience is the capacity to do well in a socially acceptable way when faced with adversity. This implies two important ingredients: (a) the capacity for resistance against the forces of destruction or annihilation—the capacity to protect one's personal integrity under severe pressure—and (b) the capacity to construct and maintain a positive life experience and worldview in spite of difficult circumstances. Norman (2000) more simply suggests that resilience is "successful adaptation under adverse conditions" (p. 8). A bit more specifically, Norman adds that resilience refers to those "factors and processes enabling sustained, competent functioning in the presence of major life stressors" (p. 8).

Resilience is not a homogeneous concept. Numerous authors have distinguished between various kinds and levels of resilience and have attempted to look at the various phases or stages of resilience. Fraser (1997) has classified resilience into three main categories:

Overcoming odds: A child attains positive outcomes despite high-risk status. For example, a child mired in the cycle of poverty and family violence that has very few available resources and faces a multitude of risks overcomes the odds when he or she triumphs over misfortune and leads a satisfying life.

Sustained competence under stress: Here, the focus is on coping skills and the ability to "bounce back" despite various stressful situations. Children from high-conflict families who are able to cope with various stressors and maintain their internal and external equilibrium are examples of this type of resilience.

Recovery from trauma: Individuals who recover well from trauma are those who are able to find significance in a traumatic experience and continue their life meaningfully. Survivors of war, riots, natural disasters, accidents, concentration camps, or imprisonment who are scarred by the experience, but not devastated, are examples of this type of resilience.

Resilience research began in earnest in the early 1970s after researchers discovered, somewhat surprisingly, that many adults thrived in later life despite their high-risk childhood (Luthar, Cichetti, & Becker, 2000). One of the most groundbreaking of the early research efforts was that undertaken by Werner and Smith in the 1970s (as cited in Werner & Smith, 2001). Werner and Smith conducted a longitudinal study of the development of over 600 Hawaiian children exposed to a variety of risk factors, including prenatal stress, chronic poverty, family discord, and parental psychopathology. They found that almost one third of these high-risk children grew into competent, confident, and caring young adults. These individuals were classified as resilient. It was also discovered that most of the high-risk youths who developed serious coping problems in adolescence could be described as resilient by the time they reached the age of 30. It thus became apparent that resilience is not a fixed attribute but rather a dynamic characteristic that may emerge even after poor outcomes are evident at an earlier age.

Early resilience research tended to focus on risk factors that were predictive of negative outcomes (Haggerty, Sherrod, Garmezy, & Rutter, 1998). Risk or vulnerability represents a heightened probability of negative outcomes based on the presence of one or more risk factors. These may include genetic, biological, behavioral, and sociocultural factors; personal characteristics, attitudes, or temperament; and demographic conditions. Smith and Carlson (1997) have defined risk factors as those circumstances that increase the likelihood that a child develops an emotional or behavioral disorder compared with children from the general population. *Risk traits* are certain predispositions in an individual that heighten the vulnerability to negative outcomes; *contextual effects* are environmental factors conducive to higher risk. These effects can be direct or indirect and they can be both proximal and distal (Greene & Conrad, 2002). For instance, poverty directly affects children by lowering their access to survival resources such as food, shelter, and security while indirectly affecting them by placing parent(s) under such constant strain that they cannot adequately respond to the child's needs. Links between different risk factors often occur, creating risk chains. Again, poverty often coincides with parental unemployment, family breakdown, high-parental stress, lower educational attainment, and a complex mix of other factors (Smokowski, 1998). As I will show, these now conventional understandings of risk and resilience factors are equally relevant (although as yet largely unexplored) in our understanding of how a child's *natural environment* either mitigates risk by providing resources for resilience or, in the absence of contact with a health-enhancing natural world, contributes to a child's vulnerability.

The decade of the 1980s brought a gradual shift of focus in resilience research from risk factors predictive of negative outcomes to protective factors and processes that tend to lead to positive outcomes (Greene, 2002). This conceptual change is not static. That is, protective factors are not a fixed set of attitudes or behavior but, much like risk factors, complex processes involving both personal and environmental factors and the interaction between them (Norman, 2000). In addition, protective factors also interact with risk factors, either reducing or increasing the probability of negative outcomes. According to Greene and Conrad (2002) protective factors can be categorized in three primary ways. First, there are protective factors of personal disposition such as self-esteem and self-efficacy. A second protective factor involves qualities of the family environment such as familial warmth and domestic cohesion. Finally, there are protective factors in the social environment such as social support, opportunities to exhibit skill and to have competence recognized, and reliance on religious or spiritual supports.

The resilience approach offers an increasingly sophisticated conceptual framework that can explain the dynamics of adversity and responses to it, thus guiding interventions with children living with hardship. It is a dynamic concept that reflects a finely tuned balance between stress and coping and suggests developmental characteristics that are responsive to improvement over time through successful experiences with positive protective and supportive factors. I suggest that in conceptualizing these protective processes and factors, we have overlooked the role played by children's natural environment.

NATURE DEVELOPMENT AND RESILIENCE

As has been suggested, the last number of years has seen an increasing volume of research on the topic of resilience in both children and adults. In this same period of time, there has also been a growing body of research documenting the extent to which human relationships with the natural world affect childhood development and children's ability to cope with stressful life situations. Unfortunately, the preponderance of the developmental literature focuses on how changes in childhood and their adaptive capacities are influenced by a combination of internal experience and contextual and cultural variables (Besthorn, 2002c). Resilience research has also focused primarily on how to enhance these same potential protective factors. However, to more fully understand both childhood development and resilience, a third consideration becomes necessary: Changes in children's experience and sociocultural environments require a thoughtful consideration of the physical and biological environment encountered by children (Cobb, 1977; Heerwagen & Orian, 2002; Searles, 1959). It is possible to enrich the dialogue around resilience that includes the perspective of the child's ecological and earth-based worldview. A child's experience of nature is thus recommended as an essential and irreplaceable dimension of physical, cognitive, and emotional development and for successful adaptation under adverse conditions.

A Theoretical Framework: Biophilia

A logical starting point in considering the impact of nature contact in childhood development and a child's ability to adapt to adverse life situations is to review a recently emerging theoretical construct: biophilia, the theory suggesting that the human need to connect with nature is associated with genetic predispositions and deeply engrained biological processes. This construct aims at developing a set of principles to help explain an emerging body of evidence supporting an ecological-evolutionary perspective on human development and resilience.

People of diverse cultural and historical backgrounds have long held that natural settings are good for the mind, body, and spirit (Besthorn & Saleebey, 2004). Around the world, millions of people gaze out a window at a simple scene of trees or tend a small garden and feel a deep sense of wholeness. At any given moment, a child picks up a cherished pet or marvels at the wonder of an ant colony and feels connected and often less frightened and more loved. In 1984, evolutionary biologist and Harvard Distinguished Professor E. O. Wilson concluded after a generation of research and observation that these phenomena and countless others like them furnish compelling evidence of what he called the *biophilia hypothesis.* Wilson and other biophilia theorists assert that human beings not only derive aesthetic benefits from connecting with nature but that humans have an instinctive, genetically predisposed need to *deeply affiliate* with natural settings and life forms. Wilson (1993) contends that the need to affiliate with nonhuman organisms and ecosystems is innately biological and intensely emotional. The human responses to these affiliations have complex benefits that not only enhance emotional and physical well-being but are also critical to adaptation to environmental factors and critical to the survival of the human species.

Evidence of this biologically determined need to affiliate with and experience nature has persisted throughout premodern and modern cultures (Kellert, 1997). This inclination to affiliate with nature is more than an aesthetic sensibility

or emotional support mechanism. It is, according to biophilial theorists, integral to healthy human development (Kellert, 1997). The essence of biophilia is that human beings have a need—*a biological imperative*—to connect with nature to maximize their potential and lead productive, fulfilling lives. The foundation idea of this ecological-evolutionary perspective is that current neural capacities and response patterns have evolved as a result of past species responses to environmental contingencies.

Biophilia theory is still in an emerging stage of development. Nevertheless, researchers from diverse fields such as architecture, landscape design, psychology, biology, genetics, child development, geography, and evolutionary science are beginning to critically examine and detail both the limits and possibilities of this promising interdisciplinary impulse. Wilson (1984), as one of the progenitors in the fields of evolutionary psychology and sociobiology, has led the way in these efforts by asserting that humans developed in a coevolutionary manner. In other words, genetic predispositions arose within natural settings and local contexts; as a species, human beings have been intimately tied to a variety of natural environments. Cultures, too, developed over time, in part, as a response to local, natural conditions. These dual dynamics—culture and natural environment—have played a far more pivotal role in human development and adaptation than previously thought. Other eminent scientists and scholars, including Stephen Kellert, Professor of Forestry and Environmental Studies at Yale University, and Robert Ulrich, Professor of Architecture at Texas A&M, also continue to verify from a growing number of cross-cultural studies that our eon's old *affiliation* with nature conferred advantages in our species' survival throughout history (Kahn, 1997, 1999). From this evidence, it seems clear that people continue to need and value nature precisely because of the genetically encoded *adaptive benefits* it has conferred on us physically, emotionally, and intellectually (Kellert, 1997).

For nearly all of human history, people lived in hunter-gatherer groups. Survival depended on their familiarity with all aspects of their physical, natural surroundings (Besthorn, 2001, 2002a, 2002c; Besthorn & McMillen, 2002).

Over millions of years, a kind of biocultural evolution progressed wherein genetics and culture evolved simultaneously. Propensities for certain behaviors (culture) were spread by natural selection if they bestowed adaptive advantage and, thus, the ability to reproduce successfully (natural selection). Wilson (1993) explains: "A certain genotype makes a certain behavioral response more likely and the response enhances survival and reproductive fitness . . . the genotype consequently spreads through the population and the behavioral response grows more frequent" (p. 33). Thus today, an intriguing body of new research suggests that when given the option, people routinely choose landscapes such as water views or eminences near water from which park or parklike land can be viewed. This is probably an important remnant of the fact that all natural selection is "about adaptation to changing *local* environments" (Gould, 1996, p. 139).

Nature and Childhood Development

If certain natural settings have promoted and currently reflect evolutionary survival, and if the biophilia connection to these natural places exists as hypothesized, then these same constituent places should still show evidence of continuing to nurture human development. Ulrich (1993) and Kellert (1997) analyzed over 100 studies that had shown that exposure to natural areas, especially those with savanna-like properties, have a powerful impact on the development of children and adults. They concluded that the postulated biophilia relationship does, in fact, exist even if not yet fully explicated. Indeed, minimal contact with nature and other-than-human beings, such as looking out a window or having a pet, has a profoundly positive impact on human physiology, psychology, self-awareness, and metaphysical connections, which is often disproportional to the amount or degree of exposure to these natural domains (Herzog & Bosley, 1992; Kahn, 1997).

Nature has historically been experienced by children as a template or model to better interpret and manage the tensions and uncertainties of childhood (Carson, 1998). The symbolic depiction of natural world as teacher, guide, protector, and sustainer is perhaps as old as the human species itself (Cornell, 1979; Hart, 1979; Jung, 1964; Levi-Strauss, 1966; Moore, 1986). Shepard (1996) notes that profound knowledge, understanding, and sense of self can be drawn from natural phenomena. There is really nothing like experience with nature to aid the child in the unraveling of his or her own unique developmental tasks. Speaking of late childhood and adolescent development Shepard notes that adolescence

> is a preparation for ambiguity, a realm of penumbral shadows. Its language includes a widening sensitivity to pun and poetry. Appropriate to its psychology is attention to the zones between categories, zones that have their own animals. The borders from which obscenity and taboo arise are figured in creatures that embody a sense of overlapping reality: the insects that crawl between two surfaces, the owl flying at dusk, the bat that seems to be both bird and mammal. The adolescent person is a marginal being between stages of life, on the shifting sands of an uncertain identity. In this respect his [sic] symbols are changeling species: the self-renewing, skin-shedding snake, the amphibious frog that loses a tail and grows legs, and the caterpillar that metamorphoses into a butterfly. (p. 5)

Increasingly, theorists are suggesting that direct and indirect experiences with nature exert a significant impact on the cognitive, affective, and evaluative (values/ ethical) maturation and development of children (Altman & Wohlwill, 1978; Derr, 2001; Kaplan & Kaplan, 1989; Kahn, 1997, 1999; Kellert, 2002; Nabhan & Trimble, 1994; Ratanapojnard, 2001; Sobel, 1993). Although the body of literature is still small and systematic, study of the nature-development construct is just now beginning to emerge in a sustained manner; it is, nonetheless, quite apparent that researchers from diverse disciplines are taking very seriously the potential of this new avenue of study. One cannot help but wonder if the relative paucity of published material up to this point reflects a modern, Western society so estranged from its natural origins that it fails to even recognize our species' basic and fundamental dependence on nature as the most indispensable and elemental condition of human growth, psychological development, and ongoing well-being. In general, the Western psychological discourse has not adequately accounted for all the myriad ways people's mental health is sustained.

A child's experience of nature encompasses a complex array of emotions, cognitions, and value orientations. The natural world is an unfailing and indefatigable source of stimulation for children. It provokes pleasure and enthusiasm but also a sense of danger and even terror. One may ask correctly what is it that stimulates and retains children's attention to the natural world to the degree that it appears to exert such a significant effect on childhood development. Although this question raises a plethora of issues beyond the scope of this chapter, several tentative observations are at least suggested. Sebba's (1991) comprehensive research studying the memories of adults and children around early experiences with nature and Kellert's (2002) review of children's experience with nature offer salient assistance. Sebba (1991) notes that the especially compelling dimension of nature is that "the stimuli of the natural environment . . . assault the senses at an uncontrolled strength" (p. 416). Children are fully immersed, even in large, supposedly *de-natured* urban areas, by a cacophony of sounds, panoply of sights, a bouquet of smells, and a bristling array of tactile stimuli from the natural world. These sensory stimuli are unavoidable whether explicitly recognized or not. In addition to the diversity and variability of the natural world, Sebba also suggests, "The natural environment is characterized by a continual change of stimuli (over time or across area)" (p. 417). Compared with the artifactual or built environment, nature is characterized by variability, which "requires alertness and attention" (p. 417). A child is not only confronted by continuous and often unpredictable change in nature, but these changes challenge the entire sensory capacities of children, necessitating a broad range of flexibility and problem-solving responses.

Sebba (1991) also emphasizes that children experience the natural environment as a place "from which life springs and one which exerts forces that cause inanimate objects to move" (p. 417). Thus, nature is teeming with life and life-enduring features and phenomena. This

recognition is arguably the most powerful, intense, and meaningful attraction of the natural world for developing children. "Nature is intrinsically and qualitatively different" (Kellert, 2002, p. 140) from anything the child sees or hears in the human-built world, no matter how well constructed or virtually sophisticated these artificial contrivances may be. Nature for the child signifies life, death, and rebirth; riots of distinctive and unique organisms that move, grow, reproduce, and soften and that apparently feel, think, and communicate (Besthorn, 2002a, 2002b; Besthorn & Canda, 2002; Besthorn & Saleebey, 2004; Kellert, 2002). As psychiatrist Harold Searles (1959) observed almost 50 years ago, nature offers children a simplicity, stability, and coherency often lacking in the human world. For the child, "the non-human environment is relatively simple and stable, rather than overwhelmingly complex and ever shifting . . . and generally available rather than walled off by parental injunctions" (p. 117).

The following is a description of a client's recollection of a childhood experience, taken from my own practice that illustrates the many aspects of the role of nature in a child's development. She said,

> I remember being on an overnight camping trip with my Girl Scout troop. My best friend and I awoke very early, at predawn, and snuck out of our tent to "go on an adventure." When we emerged from the tent, the whole world was a misty, mysterious place, and we were drawn to a nearby ravine that was totally shrouded in morning fog. We had to scoot down the steep bank on our bottoms, scraping our hands and elbows on the way down. Once there, we felt that we were in a secret and somewhat dangerous place, full of messages to be discovered, and that only we would know how to interpret signs sent especially to us from some unknown source. We did indeed find meaning in the shape of split-open walnut shells and hollows in trees and stones that lay buried beneath mossy ferns. We lost our sense of ordinary time as each moment was imbued with immediacy and excitement and timelessness. When we emerged from the ravine some time later—dirty, wet, and flushed with energy—we were surprised to find that we had missed breakfast and that the adult leaders had been frantically

looking for us. Although acting appropriately remorseful, we laughed in secret conspiracy when later alone, marveling at our bravery and defiance during a time in our young lives when the actions and rules of adults left us often feeling inadequate, wrong, and somehow "tamed." It is a favorite memory of mine to this day.

The whole experience gave this client a sense of power and mastery—both within the natural world and within the world of adults. Both the client and her friend came from "dysfunctional" families that did not support their development in a healthy way but, rather, forced them into developing *false selves* that learned to read the social environment and act accordingly. By going off on their own and tapping into the mysteries of the natural world, it made them feel special and gifted and in charge of their own lives—at least for that brief amount of time. They relished "being in trouble," doing something that girls weren't supposed to do, and defying the rules of adults. The natural world seemed to be hearing their cry, "Here I am, here's who I am, and here's what I want to be," and supported and nurtured the unique being that lived within them.

Nature and Resilience

Orr (2002) has observed that the reigning political and economic ideology has drastically shifted the emotional and developmental life of children from direct encounter with nature to experiences of an ever abstract and more symbolic nature, from routine and daily tangency with animals to contact with things and devices, from immersion in a community of beings to isolated and alienated individualism, from direct experience with essential reality to abstractionalism and virtual reality, and from a relatively slow pace of observation and husbandry to an accelerated pace marked by accumulation and consumption.

Published research explicating the connection between children's experience with nature and a child's ability to adapt to chaotic environments is small and fragmentary. However, the intense connection that stressed and traumatized children have with special places in nature is no furtive enterprise. Work has been going on for

some time. But although the paucity of systematic and rigorous research suggests caution in accepting premature conclusions and the need for future scientific study, there is a growing body of literature investigating the origins and protective functions of children's direct and indirect experiences with the natural world. Kahn (1999), for example, has concluded that children, especially those subject to the great stresses associated with modern culture and the growing number of dyspeptic families, are nurtured and strengthened through contact with the natural world even when these encounters may be infrequent and fragile. Bixler and Floyd (1997), Chawla (1997), Harvey (1990), Katcher and Wilkins (2000), Lawrence (1993), Lundberg (1998), Margadant-van Arcken (1984), Nabhan and Trimble (1994), Nixon (1997), Pyle (1993, 2000), Redefer and Goodman (1989), Sobel (1993), and Taylor, Kuo, and Sullivan (2001) have all explored in varying degrees the restorative and remedial properties of the *geography of childhood and the nature of nonhuman connections.* They detail their research with rich descriptions of making forts, finding refuge, avoiding hostile conspecifics, foraging, feeding, escape, discovery, and unadorned communicative and relational encounters with living beings, beginning with insects such as beetles and butterflies and progressing upward through a sentient matrix of bullfrogs, snakes, mice, domesticated animals, and an occasional *wild* creature.

Published research also indicates that children develop rich and varied conceptualizations and supports from the natural world. And they seem to do so across cultures even in physically remote and economically harsh and ecologically truncated urban and industrial settings. Kahn (2002) reports on four studies conducted in Alaska, an inner-city African American community in Houston, a remote part of the Brazilian Amazon region, and in Lisbon, Portugal, that sought to discover both the developmental influences and protective processes associated with children's nature experiences. Although fine-grained data summary is impossible here, it is important to note that the researchers found remarkably similar values and protective factors associated with nature experiences across culturally diverse locations (see Herzog,

Herbert, Kaplan, & Crooks, 2000). This, of course, does not prove the intercultural connection between nature experiences of children and developmental pathways leading to resilience, but it does suggest a clear relationship and fertile ground for future study.

Establishing familiarity with nearby natural environments and becoming constructive and creative in co-managing these settings, provides a wealth of opportunities for children to generate a sense of autonomy, independence, self-esteem, self-efficacy, and self-sufficiency—all long known to be important protective factors in resilience research. In a more recent major study, Kellert and Derr (1998) looked at over 700 participants in several outdoor challenge programs. After assessing the data from both a retrospective and longitudinal investigation of past and recent participants, they concluded that the respondents' experience with nature in these structured settings had a profound influence on their lives. A vast majority indicated that the experience "had greatly enhanced their self-confidence, self-concept, and capacity to cope with adversity and challenge" (Kellert, 2002, p. 137). Over two thirds also reported sustained improvement in self-esteem, initiative, decision-making and problem-solving abilities, and interpersonal skills and relationships. Katcher (2002) and Katcher and Wilkins (1993, 1998, 2000, 2001) also report on fascinating controlled clinical trials, correlational studies, and clinical case histories on the use of animals in therapeutic education with children suffering from autism, developmental learning disorders, attention deficit hyperactivity disorder, conduct disorder, oppositional defiant disorder, and severe emotional disturbances. The researchers conclude that therapeutic animal education decreased aggression and negative social attribution and increased cooperative behavior and social competence and affiliation.

The aforementioned studies and a spate of earlier works (Guttmann, Predovic, & Zemanek, 1985; Hendy, 1984; Perin, 1981) support the findings of Sebba's (1991) study of adults and their early reminisces of experiences with the natural world. Sebba's findings led her to make the compelling concluding statement that despite the heterogeneous nature of the study participants in terms of sex, age, character, and the cultural and family environments in which they grew up, "96.5% of them indicated the outdoors was the most significant environment in their childhood" (p. 400). These are powerful words and conclusions about a domain of life and personal and collective experiences that are too often lacking in how we understand the way children develop and the way they respond to difficult life situations. Sebba's observations correspond very well to the eloquent reflections of Rachael Carson (1998), arguably America's first and most renowned ecologist and environmental ethicist:

> A child's world is fresh and new and beautiful, full of wonder and excitement. . . . What is the value of preserving and strengthening this sense of awe and wonder, this recognition of something beyond the boundaries of human existence? Is the exploration of the natural world just a pleasant way to pass the golden hours of childhood or is there something deeper? I am sure there is something much deeper, something lasting and significant. . . . Those who contemplate the beauty of the earth find reserves of strength that will endure as long as life lasts. There is symbolic as well as actual beauty in the migrations of the birds, the ebb and flow of the tides, the folded bud ready for the spring. There is something *infinitely healing* [italics added] in the repeated refrains of nature. (pp. 54, 100)

The significant, and what seems indispensable, importance of children's experience with nature and nonhuman others has been strongly inferred from both the theoretical and empirical literature. At this point in modern Western history, with the ongoing decline of biodiversity and habitats to support rich and diverse ecosystems, the critical question seems less about whether nature is important to children's development and resilience and more about whether modern society can provide sufficient quantity and quality of opportunities for childhood experiences of the natural world. Pyle (1993) calls this insipient loss of direct connection with nature the *extinction of experience*. It may be that as our megacities, burgeoning suburbs, and alienated citizenry forsake their natural heritage we will lose our *deeper* awareness, appreciation, and sensitivity regarding nature and retreat into an ever closed-off world of human artifice and impoverished relationships. One cannot help but ponder the long-term impact and consequences "of having so many traditional symbols of awe, wonder, and beauty in nature become ubiquitous signs of rarity, loss and decline" (Kellert, 2002, p. 141).

CONCLUSION

This chapter concludes with a fair degree of hesitancy and diffidence. Although it contains no summary of original research, its review of theoretical formulations and extant empirical data, albeit yet quite sparse and not fully conclusive, provides tentative support for the belief that children's developmental pathways and their ability to respond successfully to difficult tasks in living are significantly enhanced by varied and sustained contact with natural places and their dynamic processes. The more sobering conclusion is that a range of trends in the developmental and resilience literature, and in the ontological and epistemological insularity associated with the modern capitalist project in general, seems to have suppressed our direct experience of the natural world and the ability of professional practitioners and researchers to analyze its influence on a range of developmental and recuperative constructs and processes.

The advances made in our understanding of nature and children have tremendous implications for the many fields that work with childhood development and resilience issues. The implicit assumptions about the character of development that *de-privileges* the child's ability to contemplate natural systems with cognitive, emotional, and affective profundity and to use his or her full complement of resources for healing and nurturing must be reconsidered. Children bring interpretive frameworks that they use to make sense of their lives that may not always correspond well to accepted knowledge. Their intuitive theories, communication patterns, affinity networks and coping strategies, understood and fostered in the context of the natural environment, are not always consonant with the prevailing worldview. The hope is that we in the adult and professional world can radically change not only our minds and our hearts but also our behaviors to transform the way we have come to view nature and its importance to us. If we can find a way to heal our estrangement from the earth, then perhaps, we can begin to incorporate all the values and lessons of the natural world as an essential core of children's lives.

REFERENCES

Altman, I., & Wohlwill, J. (Eds.). (1978). *Children and the environment.* New York: Plenum Press.

Besthorn, F. H. (2001). Transpersonal psychology and deep ecological philosophy: Exploring linkages and applications for social work. In E. R. Canda & E. D. Smith (Eds.), *Transpersonal perspectives on spirituality in social work* (pp. 23–44). Binghamton, NY: Haworth Press.

Besthorn, F. H. (2002a). Expanding spiritual diversity in social work: Perspectives on the greening of spirituality. *Currents: New Scholarship in the Human Services, 1*(1), 44–61. Retrieved December 17, 2004, from www.fsw.ucalgary.ca/ currents/articles/index.htm?m=fred_besthorn/be sthorn_main.htm&i=fred_besthorn/besthorn_ index.htm

Besthorn, F. H. (2002b). Natural environment and the practice of psychotherapy. *Annals of the American Psychotherapy Association, 5*(5), 19–22.

Besthorn, F. H. (2002c). Radical environmentalism and the ecological self: Rethinking the concept of self-identity for social work practice. *Journal of Progressive Human Services, 13*(1), 53–72.

Besthorn, F. H., & Canda, E. R. (2002). Revisioning environment: Deep ecology for education and teaching in social work. *Journal of Teaching in Social Work, 22*(1/2), 79–102.

Besthorn, F. H., & McMillen, D. P. (2002). The oppression of women and nature: Ecofeminism as a framework for an expanded ecological social work. *Families in Society: The Journal of Contemporary Human Services, 83*(3), 221–232.

Besthorn, F. H., & Saleebey, D. (2004). Nature, genetics and the biophilia connection: Exploring linkages with social work values and practice. *Advances in Social Work, 4*(1), 1–18.

Bixler, R., & Floyd, M. (1997). Nature is scary, disgusting, and uncomfortable. *Environment and Behavior, 29,* 443–467.

Carson, R. (1998). *The sense of wonder.* New York: Harper Collins.

Chawla, L. (1997). Growing up in cities: A report on research underway. *Environment and Urbanization, 9,* 247–251.

Cobb, E. (1977). *The ecology of imagination in childhood.* New York: Columbia University Press.

Cornell, J. (1979). *Sharing nature with children.* Nevada City, CA: Dawn Publishing.

Derr, V. (2001). *Growing up in the Hispano homeland: The interplay of nature, family, culture, and community in shaping children's experiences and sense of place.* Doctoral dissertation, School of Forestry and Environmental Studies, Yale University.

Fraser, M. W. (1997). *Risk and resilience in childhood.* Washington, DC: NASW Press.

Glantz, M., & Johnson, J. (1999). *Resilience and development: Positive life adaptations.* New York: Plenum Press.

Gould, S. J. (1996). *Full house: The spread of excellence from Plato to Darwin.* New York: Harmony Books.

Greene, R. R. (Ed.). (2002). *Resiliency: An integrated approach to practice, policy, and research.* Washington, DC: NASW Press.

Greene, R., & Conrad, A. (2002). Basic terms and assumptions of resiliency. In R. Greene (Ed.), *Resiliency: An integrated approach to practice, policy, and research* (pp. 29–62). Washington, DC: NASW Press.

Guttmann, G., Predovic, M., & Zemanek, M. (1985). The influence of pet ownership on non-verbal communications competence in children. In *The human-pet relationship* (pp. 58–63). Vienna: Institute for Interdisciplinary Research on the Human-Pet Relationship.

Haggerty, R., Sherrod, L., Garmezy, N., & Rutter, M. (1998). *Stress, risk and resilience in children and adolescents: Process mechanisms and interventions.* London: Cambridge University Press.

Hart, R. (1979). *Children's experience of place.* New York: Knopf.

Harvey, M. (1990). The relationship between children's experiences with vegetation on school grounds and their environmental attitudes. *Journal of Environmental Education, 21,* 9–15.

Heerwagen, J., & Orian, G. (2002). The ecological world of children. In P. Kahn & S. Kellert (Eds.), *Children and nature: Psychological, sociocultural, and evolutionary investigations* (pp. 29–64). Cambridge: MIT Press.

Hendy, H. (1984). Effects of pets on the sociability and health activities of nursing home residents. In R. Anderson, B. Hart, & L. Hart (Eds.), *The pet connection* (pp. 430–437). Minneapolis: University of Minnesota.

Herzog, T. F., & Bosley, P. J. (1992). Tranquility and preference as affective qualities of natural environments. *Journal of Environmental Psychology, 12,* 155–157.

Herzog, T., Herbert, E. Kaplan, R., & Crooks, C. (2000). Cultural and developmental comparisons of landscape perceptions and preferences. *Environment and Behavior, 32,* 323–346.

Jung, C. (1964). *Man and his symbols.* Garden City, NJ: Doubleday.

Kahn, P. (1997). Developmental psychology and the biophilia hypothesis: Children's affiliation with nature. *Developmental Review, 17,* 1–61.

Kahn, P. (1999). *The human relationship with nature.* Cambridge: MIT Press.

Kahn, P. (2002). Children's affiliations with nature: Structure, development, and the problem of environmental generational amnesia. In P. Kahn & S. Kellert (Eds.), *Children and nature: Psychological, sociocultural, and evolutionary investigations* (pp. 93–116). Cambridge: MIT Press.

Kaplan S., & Kaplan, R. (1989). *The experience of nature.* New York: Cambridge University Press.

Katcher, A. (2002). Animals in therapeutic education: Guides into the liminal state. In P. Kahn & S. Kellert (Eds.), *Children and nature: Psychological, sociocultural, and evolutionary investigations* (pp.179–198). Cambridge, MA: MIT Press.

Katcher, A., & Wilkins, G. (1993). Dialogue with animals: It's nature and culture. In S. Kellert & E. Wilson (Eds.), *The biophilia hypothesis* (pp. 173–200). Washington, DC: Island Press.

Katcher, A., & Wilkins, G. (1998). Animal-assisted therapy in the treatment of disruptive behavior disorders. In A. Lundberg (Ed.), *The environment and mental health* (pp. 193–204). Mahwah, NJ: Erlbaum.

Katcher, A., & Wilkins, G. (2000). The centaur's lessons: Therapeutic education through care of animals and nature study. In A. Fine (Ed.), *The handbook on animal assisted therapy: Theoretical foundations and guidelines for practice* (pp. 153–178). New York: Academic Press.

Katcher, A., & Wilkins, G. (2001). *The centaur's lessons: The companionable zoo method of therapeutic education based upon contact with animals and nature study.* Chicago: PAN-ATA Press.

Kellert, S. (1997). *Kinship to mastery.* Washington, DC: Island Press.

Kellert, S. (2002). Experiencing nature: Affective, cognitive, and evaluative development in children. In P. Kahn & S. Kellert (Eds.), *Children and nature: Psychological, sociocultural, and evolutionary investigations* (pp. 117–151). Cambridge: MIT Press.

Kellert, S., & Derr, V. (1998). *National study of outdoor wilderness experience.* New Haven, CT: Yale University School of Forestry and Environmental Studies.

Lawrence, E. (1993). The sacred bee, the filthy pig, and the bat out of hell: Animal symbolism as cognitive biophilia. In S. Kellert & E. Wilson (Eds.), *The biophilia hypothesis* (pp. 301–341). Washington, DC: Island Press.

Levi-Strauss, C. (1966). *The savage mind.* Chicago: University of Chicago Press.

Lundberg, A. (Ed.). (1998). *The environment and mental health.* Mahwah, NJ: Erlbaum.

Luthar, S., Cichetti, D., & Becker, B. (2000). The construct of resiliency: A critical evaluation and guidelines for future work. *Child Development, 71,* 543–562.

Margadant-van Arcken, M. (1984). "There's a real dog in the classroom?" The relationship between young children and animals. *Children's Environmental Quarterly, 1,* 13–16.

McCubbin, H., Thompson, E., Thompson, A., & Futrell, J. (1999). *The dynamics of resilient families.* Thousand Oaks, CA: Sage.

Moore, R. (1986). *Childhood's domain: Play and space in child development.* London: Croom Helm.

Nabhan, G., & Trimble, S. (1994). *The geography of childhood.* Boston: Beacon Press.

Nixon, W. (1997). How nature shapes childhood. *Amicus Journal, 19*(2), 31–35.

Norman, E. (Ed.). (2000). *Resiliency enhancement: Putting the strengths perspective into social work practice.* New York: Columbia University Press.

Orr, D. (2002). Political economy and the ecology of childhood. In P. Kahn & S. Kellert (Eds.), *Children and nature: Psychological, sociocultural, and evolutionary investigations* (pp. 279–303). Cambridge: MIT Press.

Perin, C. (1981). Dogs as symbols in human development. In B. Fogle (Ed.), *Interrelations between pets and people* (pp. 68–88). Springfield, OH: Charles C Thomas.

Pyle, R. (1993). *The thunder tree: Lessons from an urban wildland.* Boston: Houghton Mifflin.

Pyle, R. (2000). *Walking the high ridge: Life as field trip.* Minneapolis, MN: Milkweed Press.

Ratanapojnard, S. (2001). *Community-oriented biodiversity environmental education: Its effects on knowledge, values, and behavior among rural fifth and sixth grade students in northeastern Thailand.* Doctoral dissertation, School of Forestry and Environmental Studies, Yale University.

Redefer, L., & Goodman, J. (1989). Brief report: Pet-facilitated therapy with autistic children. *Journal of Autism and Developmental Disorders, 19,* 461–467.

Rutter, M. (1987). Psycho-social resilience and protective mechanism. *American Journal of Orthopsychiatry, 57,* 316–331.

Searles, H. (1959). *The nonhuman environment.* New York: International Universities Press.

Sebba, R. (1991). The landscapes of childhood: The reflections of childhood's environment in adult memories and in children's attitudes. *Environment and Behavior, 23,* 395–422.

Shepard, P. (1996). *The others: How animals made us human.* Washington, DC: Island Press.

Smith, C., & Carlson, B. (1997). Stress, coping and resilience in children and youth. *Social Service Review, 71,* 231–256.

Smokowski, P. (1998). Prevention and intervention: Strategies for promoting resilience in disadvantaged children. *Social Service Review, 72,* 337–364.

Sobel, D. (1993). *Children's special places: Exploring the role of forts, dens, and bush houses in middle childhood.* Tucson, AZ: Zephyr Press.

Taylor, A., Kuo, F., & Sullivan, W. (2001). Coping with ADD: The surprising connection to green play settings. *Environment and Behavior, 33,* 54–77.

Ulrich, R. (1993). Biophilia, biophobia and natural landscapes. In S. Kellert & E. Wilson (Eds.), *The biophilia hypothesis.* Washington, DC: Island Press.

Ungar, M. (2002). *Playing at being bad: The hidden resilience of troubled teens.* Toronto, Ontario, Canada: Potterfield Press.

Ungar, M. (2004). *Nurturing hidden resilience in troubled youth.* Toronto, Ontario, Canada: University of Toronto Press.

Vanistendael, S. (1998). *Growth in the muddle of life: Resilience-building on people's strengths.* Geneva: International Catholic Child Bureau.

Walsh, F. (1998). *Strengthening family resilience.* New York: Guilford Press.

Werner, E., & Smith, R. (2001). *Journey from childhood to midlife: Risk, resilience and recovery.* Ithaca, NY: Cornell University Press.

Wilson, E. O. (1984). *Biophilia.* Cambridge, MA: Harvard University Press.

Wilson, E. O. (1993). Biophilia and the conservation ethic. In S. Kellert & E. Wilson (Eds.), *The biophilia hypothesis* (pp. 31–41). Washington, DC: Island Press.

Wolin, S. J., & Wolin, S. (1993). *The resilient self: How survivors of troubled families rise above adversity.* New York: Villard Books.

PART 2

METHODOLOGICAL CHALLENGES IN RESILIENCE RESEARCH

9

METHODOLOGICAL CHALLENGES IN THE STUDY OF RESILIENCE

WILLIAM H. BARTON

Among the many existing definitions of resilience, those of Masten (1994) and Richman and Fraser (2001), considered together, may be the clearest and most comprehensive. Masten (1994) defines resilience as "successful adaptation despite risk and adversity" (p. 3). She further states that resilience refers to successful adaptation either (a) in the presence of high risk, (b) despite stressful experiences, or (c) in recovery from trauma. In summarizing several definitions of resilience, Richman and Fraser (2001) note that "resilience requires exposure to significant risk, overcoming risk or adversity, and success that is beyond predicted expectations" (p. 6). Moreover, most resilience scholars agree that resilience is not just a characteristic of an individual but "occurs at the nexus of high risk and exceptional resources, whether these resources are personal or environmental in nature" (p. 6).

Resilience, then, may be thought of as an ecologically contextualized set of patterns, each involving "successful" adaptation in the face of some "adversity." The cumulative research to date has suggested that such successful outcomes are aided by combinations of general and specific protective factors at intraindividual, interpersonal, organizational, and societal levels, much as earlier research suggested that poor developmental outcomes resulted from combinations of general and specific risk factors at multiple levels. The goal of resilience research appears to be to specify what protective factors are necessary to counter or buffer exposure to various risk conditions for individuals who possess various combinations of assets and vulnerabilities.

Science, at least the dominant Western paradigm of inquiry, seeks explanations for natural phenomena—explanations in the form of theories depicting lawlike causal relationships between predictors and outcomes. These theories, in turn, are built on postulated hypothetical relationships among theoretical constructs, which are then tested via observations. Those hypotheses that withstand such tests become part of the accepted web of theoretical explanation. So it would seem straightforward to scientifically explore the phenomenon of resilience as is being attempted in this volume. Such studies would delineate determinants of, or pathways to, resilience. Because resilience is viewed as a good thing, the determinants or pathways discovered could inform policies and practices designed to promote more resilience than might otherwise occur without such interventions. After all, isn't that how scientific knowledge has led to dramatic decreases in the incidence of numerous diseases in recent decades?

Focusing on resilience instead of, or in addition to, pathologies has had several positive effects on policy and practices in education and the human services. It has produced greater awareness of and respect for people's strengths, and directed attention away from merely trying to change individuals toward addressing a more ecological constellation of influences on behavior. Alas, a closer look at the concept of resilience reveals daunting methodological and theoretical challenges. This chapter attempts to describe these challenges by looking first at how resilience became a salient focus for research in the latter part of the 20th century, reviewing several major studies of resilience, discussing the strengths and limitations of the many methodologies applied, and in the end, questioning the basic utility of the concept of resilience as a focus for systematic inquiry. However, because I do not wish to throw out the baby with the bathwater, the chapter concludes with a potential way to reframe the conceptual territory and promote a continuing, multimethod agenda of research that can help promote healthy developmental outcomes.

OUR EMERGING INTEREST IN RESILIENCE OVER TIME

Resilience is a relatively recent concept in the arena of human development and social services, having evolved from an earlier focus on social problems. This evolution had three major influences:

1. Theoretical and empirical advances in understanding that a variety of social problems appeared to be determined by a common set of multiple risk and protective factors (e.g., Dryfoos, 1990; Hawkins, Catalano, & Miller, 1992);

2. The recognition that some individuals appeared to thrive despite sharing the characteristics and conditions of those who exhibited serious social problems (e.g., Anthony, 1987; Rutter, 1985; Werner & Smith, 2001);

3. The "strengths perspective" in social work (e.g., Saleebey, 1997) and related movements in other helping professions that encouraged helping professionals to build on clients' strengths or assets rather than focusing exclusively on problems or deficits.

Resilience, then, became the other side of the coin of personal and social problems. New research questions emerged as researchers sought to understand the causes and correlates of positive developmental outcomes.

Focus on Social Problems

Throughout much of the 20th century, social researchers focused on social problems, seeking to discover the etiological determinants of phenomena such as child abuse, mental illness, crime and delinquency, and substance abuse. They paid particular attention to youth, because such conditions frequently appeared first during childhood or adolescence. This body of research seemed based on the assumption that pinpointing the causal determinants of poor developmental outcomes would permit well-intentioned professionals to design policies and programs that prevented, countered, or buffered the effects of such determining factors, thereby either preventing the onset of the social problems or treating those who exhibited them.

Entire human service bureaucracies have evolved around each of several social problems—mental health, special education, child welfare, addictions services, corrections, and so on. Each is staffed with a particular group of specially trained professionals, draws on a separate body of research literature to inform its policies and practices, has established definitional rules (e.g., diagnoses) to determine who is "eligible" to receive its services, taps dedicated funding streams for resources, and provides particular "interventions" designed to prevent or treat the specific social problem.

The similarities of this approach to traditional medical practice are obvious, and the dominant approach to human services may be called the "medical model." At its extreme, this approach detects and defines deficits and treats them in isolation. Not surprisingly, without attention to ecological context (the whole person-in-the-environment), these treatments are often unsuccessful. Coming from their specific research traditions and practice backgrounds, human service professionals in all arenas have begun to recognize the limitations of this "silo" approach and have converged to embrace a more ecological approach, as described in the next sections.

Risk and Protective Factors

Much of the impetus for this more ecological approach to social problems came from those studying the etiologies of major problems affecting youth—delinquency, violence, substance abuse, school dropout, and teenage pregnancy. In the 1990s, researchers suggested that there were overlapping causes and correlates of these diverse youth problems (Dryfoos, 1990; Hawkins, Catalano, & Miller, 1992). The social development model of Hawkins, Catalano, and Miller (1992) combined aspects of control theory (Gottfredson & Hirschi, 1990; Hirschi, 1969) and social learning theory (Akers, 1985) to provide a conceptual framework encompassing an array of risk and protective factors that combined in various ways to promote either healthy or problematic developmental outcomes. The policy and practice implications were clear—attempts to address a specific youth problem alone would be less effective than community-based prevention initiatives aimed at reducing risk and enhancing protection. The *Communities That Care* model (Hawkins, Catalano, & Associates, 1992) is a resulting blueprint for community mobilization for prevention.

Kirby and Fraser (1997) provide a concise yet thorough summary of what has been learned about risk and protective factors at multiple levels. At the level of individual psychosocial and biological characteristics, risk factors include gender (males are at higher risk) and biomedical problems, whereas protective factors include an "easy" temperament, high intelligence, high self-esteem, and a sense of efficacy and competence. Family, school, and neighborhood level risk factors include child abuse, interparental conflict, parental pathology, and poor parenting. Examples of corresponding protective factors are social support, the presence of caring and supportive adults, a positive parent-child relationship, and effective parenting. Finally, at the most macro level, risk factors include poverty, racial discrimination, and limited opportunities for education, employment, or both, whereas protective factors include the presence of many opportunities for education, employment, growth, and achievement (Kirby & Fraser, 1997, p. 20). There is evidence that the effect of these risk and protective factors on youth outcomes is cumulative (Pollard, Hawkins, & Arthur, 1999).

Overcoming the Odds

At about the same time, another set of researchers, most from the fields of mental health and education, became interested in persons who appeared to be thriving despite having characteristics and being in situations that would normally be associated with pathological outcomes. Children with a mentally ill parent are at risk for developing mental illness themselves, but Anthony (1987) noticed that some did not. Similarly, growing up poor in disorganized neighborhoods places children at risk for poor educational outcomes and delinquency, but a series of studies (Furstenberg, Brooks-Gunn, & Morgan, 1987; Gordon & Song, 1994; Long & Vaillant, 1989; Luthar, 1991) showed that some children were able to escape such dire predictions. Although many children who are abused become abusive themselves as adults, not all do (Egeland, Jacobvitz, & Sroufe, 1988). A landmark, longitudinal study by Werner and colleagues (Werner, Bierman, & French, 1971; Werner & Smith, 1977, 1982, 1992, 2001) followed a birth cohort of children from the Hawaiian island of Kauai until age 40 (so far), examining patterns of risk and protective factors associated with developmental outcomes at various ages. The methods and results of this study will be discussed in more detail in a later section of this chapter, but it is mentioned here because it has framed much of the current interest in resilience research.

The Strengths Perspective

Recognizing the limitations of the medical model approach to social problems, some writers began to promote an alternative paradigm, known as the *strengths perspective* (Saleebey, 1997; Weick, Rapp, Sullivan, & Kisthardt, 1989). The basic premise of this approach is that people possess inherent strengths, or assets, that hold the key to their ability to cope with stress and trauma. Instead of diagnosing deficits and prescribing treatment to address them, strengths-based therapists help clients identify and build on their capacities. Such strengths include not only internal attributes but also supports from the natural social environment. Thus, an important aspect of strengths-based practice is the identification and mobilization of natural social support.

The strengths-based approach is rapidly finding adherents across a broad spectrum of service arenas. Among the most notable extensions are system-of-care, wraparound models of service delivery for children and families experiencing challenges in multiple arenas (Burchard, Bruns, & Burchard, 2002; Goldman, 1999; Stroul & Friedman, 1986; VanDenBerg & Grealish, 1996). In sharp contrast to the medical model approach, wraparound models engage the child and family members as partners in service planning, emphasize cultural competence, mobilize teams of professional and nonprofessional supports, and tailor intervention plans to individual needs and strengths. Of relevance to this discussion, wraparound services are based on an explicitly ecological model of behavior and draw directly on the risk and protective factor research to enhance resilience.

In sum, concern with social problems led to research into specific etiological pathways producing the problems and to the proliferation of targeted, categorical services to treat them. Over time, the overlap between etiological pathways to various problematic outcomes became apparent, along with dissatisfaction with the relative ineffectiveness of many categorical service delivery models. The search for common pathways promoted more interest in prevention, accompanied by attention to those who appeared to succeed despite being at high risk for failure. These latter persons have become the focus of research into the pathways to resilience, accompanied by an increase in human service professionals' attention to and respect for the strengths in persons. As Nash and Fraser (1997) note,

> The epidemiological literature yields three very useful ideas. To understand social and health problems more fully, we should focus on the distribution of wellness in addition to the distribution of problems and disorders in large groups and populations, attempt to identify potential causal agents, and produce knowledge that is practical, in that it can be used in the design of services. (p. 34)

METHODOLOGICAL VARIATIONS

A variety of methods have been used in the study of resilience. Quantitative approaches include cross-sectional and longitudinal surveys. Qualitative approaches include ethnographic and phenomenological studies. Each has its strengths and weaknesses, and none alone can claim to produce definitive conclusions. This is amply evident in the chapters that make up this volume.

Criteria for assessing the quality of quantitative studies are well known. These include the clarity of the research questions, theoretical soundness of the hypotheses being tested, adequacy of model specification, reliability and validity of measures, objectivity of data collection procedures, internal validity of the research design (e.g., use of control groups), external validity of the design (or generalizability resulting from the sampling strategy), confidence warranted in the results (often based on statistical significance), and the extent to which the researcher's interpretations match the data (Grinnell, 2001).

Because qualitative methods are inherently subjective, objective quality standards such as validity and reliability have little meaning. Guba and Lincoln (1989) and Marshall (1990), among others, have proposed standards of "trustworthiness" and "authenticity" for judging the merits of qualitative research. The trustworthiness of qualitative research is enhanced by (a) *credibility* (prolonged engagement, persistent observation, peer debriefing, member checks), (b) *transferability* (thick description allowing the reader to determine if there are parallels between the situation described and others), (c) *dependability* (a careful audit trail of the researchers' process and decisions), and (d) *confirmability* (data, interpretations, and outcomes based on the perspectives and contexts of those being studied rather than of the investigator) (Guba & Lincoln, 1989). The authenticity of qualitative research refers to its (a) *fairness* (in representing all relevant constructions in a setting and in openly negotiating the recommendations and subsequent actions resulting from the research) and (b) *ontological, educational, catalytic,* and *tactical authenticity* (improving the level of understanding among study participants, both of their own situation and that of others, stimulating action, and empowering participants to act) (Guba & Lincoln, 1989, pp. 245–250).

Cross-Sectional Surveys

Studies using cross-sectional surveys identify a sample generally representative of some population, or they may identify a sample because its members exhibit a particular developmental outcome (perhaps also using a control group matched on relevant demographic characteristics). Survey items attempt to measure each respondent's exposure to the array of risk and protective factors gleaned from the literature and then look for associations between these factors and developmental outcomes. The advantages of cross-sectional surveys are their relatively low cost and quick completion time and the ability to collect information from large numbers of respondents, thus increasing the statistical power of analyses. Depending on the sampling strategy used, findings from these studies may be widely generalizable. An example is Resnick et al.'s (1997) report of findings from the first year of the Add Health survey of a nationally representative sample of 11,572 students in Grades 7 through 11. Results showed a number of general and domain-specific stressors and protective factors associated with a variety of adolescent health risk behaviors (e.g., emotional distress, suicidality, substance use, sexual behavior).

Cross-sectional surveys, however, cannot provide a strong examination of causality. For example, an association found between a developmental outcome such as school success and the presence of a positive relationship with one or more parents might be interpreted as evidence that the positive relationship was a protective factor contributing causally to the positive school outcome. However, the child's success in school could just as easily be interpreted as one factor contributing to the positive relationship.

Most survey studies are variable centered. That is, the analysis examines the relationships among variables, such as risk and protective factors and developmental outcomes. As Magnusson and Bergman (1990) caution, interpreting results from this approach is susceptible to the ecological fallacy. That is, the various relationships among variables in the aggregate may say little about how they operate within individuals. Magnusson and Bergman use an alternative, person-centered approach that seeks to identify categories of persons, based on distinctive clusters of predictors, and then examines differences in outcomes among groups. Their Stockholm study followed a cohort of 545 sixth-grade boys into adulthood, identifying eight types based on varied clustering of overt adjustment problems at age 13 and using adult records of criminality, alcohol use, and psychiatric care as outcomes.

Researchers at the University of Washington (Whitney, Herrenkohl, Tajima, & Huang, 2004) are exploring the use of another person-centered approach called "mixture model analysis" in studying the relationship between multiple risk factors, delinquency, and school failure. Mixture modeling includes latent profile analysis, a data reduction technique like factor analysis that identifies latent subclasses of individuals through an iterative, goodness-of-fit analysis. In their study, Whitney et al. identified three classes of risk based on six major risk indicators (IQ, socioeconomic status, child maltreatment, domestic violence, and Child Behavior Checklist measures related to early behavior problems and early risk of school failure). The highest risk group's profile included very low SES, indication of domestic violence and child abuse, low IQ, and indications of early behavior problems and early risk of school failure. The low-risk group, as would be expected, scored high on measures of SES and IQ, low on domestic violence and abuse, and low on indicators of early childhood problems. The medium-risk group resembled the low-risk group on most indicators, except for lower SES and IQ. In terms of outcomes, the high-risk group had much higher levels of delinquency, school dropout, and other indications of school problems than did the low-risk group; the medium-risk group's outcomes fell in between (Whitney et al., 2004).

Longitudinal Cohort Studies

A better methodology for teasing out causal influences is the prospective, longitudinal study. Examples include the Kauai study mentioned previously (e.g., Werner & Smith, 2001), the Berkeley and Oakland cohorts studied by Clausen (1993) and Elder (1999), the Baltimore study (Furstenberg et al. 1987), and Vaillant and associates' (Long & Vaillant, 1989; Vaillant, 1977, 1983; Vaillant & Milofsky, 1980; Vaillant & Vaillant, 1981) follow-up of the control group from the Glueck and Glueck (1968) study of factors related to delinquency. Such studies can identify risk and protective factors as they appear and look for associations with developmental outcomes measured years later. Taken together, these studies have demonstrated the importance of parental education and supportive adults outside the family along with internal characteristics such as personal industry and planfulness in overcoming risks associated with growing up in poverty and multiproblem families.

Werner and her colleagues' Kauai study (Werner et al., 1971; Werner & Smith, 1977, 1982, 1992, 2001) is notable for the multiple sources of data, multiple waves of data collection, and high retention rates. Beginning by examining records of demographic, prenatal, and perinatal data of Kauai's 1955 birth cohort ($N = 837$), Werner et al., to date, have collected extensive follow-up information from and about these individuals at ages 2, 10, 18, 31/32, and 40, using interviews with the subjects and their parents, teachers, and significant others as well as observations of public health nurses and official records of involvement with the courts and mental health systems.

Of particular importance in this study is the subsample of individuals determined to be at high risk from birth and early childhood due to physical complications, poverty, and family dysfunction. Although some members of this high-risk group displayed more childhood and adolescent problems in school and the community, others did not. Furthermore, even most of those who experienced difficulties in adolescence had achieved some level of success by midlife. The wealth of longitudinal data on this resilient subsample has enabled Werner et al. to develop detailed path models relating protective factors and stressful life events to quality of adaptation and psychological well-being at age 40 (Werner & Smith, 2001). Describing the full details of these models, which differ slightly for males and females, is beyond the scope of this chapter—suffice it to say that they articulate the interplay between protective factors within the individual (e.g., temperament, self-efficacy) and outside sources of support and stress as predictors of developmental outcomes at midlife. As an aside, although the path coefficients and indications of significance are given, the total explained variance is not, so it is unclear how much is left unexplained by the models.

Although prospective, longitudinal studies have provided the richest quantitative data about resilience, they are not without their limitations. Important practical limitations include the relatively high cost and length of time involved. During the many years from the design of a study to the wave of data collection measuring midlife or later developmental outcomes, unanticipated theoretical or measurement advances might occur that could render aspects of the design obsolete. As the years go by, the likelihood of attrition increases so that the cohort sample left at midlife may be quite different from the original cohort in key characteristics (the Kauai study, however, is exceptional in its good retention rates). The generalizability of longitudinal cohort studies may be questioned beyond the specific location and historical context of the cohort used.

Qualitative Studies

Unlike quantitative studies that measure a large number of variables across many persons and seek to explain relationships among these variables, qualitative studies attempt to provide a "thick description" (Geertz, 1973) of a setting through in-depth engagement with a small number of persons. Varieties of qualitative methods used in the study of resilience have included interpretive phenomenology (Gilgun, 1999), grounded theory (Gordon & Song, 1994), and narrative constructionism (Ungar, 2001c). In each method, primacy is given to participants' subjective meanings of experiences, and theory evolves from identifying patterns derived from a process of comparing and contrasting their accounts.

Recent books by Maruna (2001) and O'Brien (2001) explore qualitatively the experiences of male British ex-prisoners and urban American female ex-prisoners, respectively, as they return to their communities after years of incarceration. Such individuals are at extremely high risk for reoffending and returning to prison; recent estimates suggest that nearly two thirds of released prisoners are rearrested within 3 years (Beck, 2000). Those ex-offenders who do succeed meet the definition of resilience. Maruna's (2001) study suggests that those men who succeed are able, with social support, to reframe aspects of their identity. O'Brien (2001) highlights the importance of the successful woman's own motivation and strengths as well as support from family and friends. Of particular interest is the challenge that both books pose toward the human services establishment. Traditional resilience research might suggest that ex-offenders could be helped by a well-functioning aftercare program, including case management with coordination of a range of services to meet individual needs—that is, to bolster protective factors in the presence of risk. However, participants in both studies expressed considerable skepticism in regard to service professionals, often viewing them as additional agents of social control. They viewed informal social supports and their own motivation as more helpful. Such insights would be less likely to emerge from quantitative studies than from qualitative studies in which investigators truly listen to the voices of the participants.

Similarly, Ungar's (2001c) qualitative study of high-risk youths in out-of-home placements challenges the very definition of resilience outcomes. In most conventional studies, out-of-home placement in correctional or treatment facilities would serve as an indicator of an unsuccessful developmental outcome (at least at that point in time). Several of the youth in Ungar's study, however, viewed placements positively, as an escape from the perils of the street and as a structured environment in which to pursue educational or other positive goals. In a sense, then, these youths could be considered resilient, having discovered an effective way of coping with their life situations. Using this insight, Ungar recommends that service providers help high-risk youths develop identity narratives that draw on a resilient interpretation of their past and present. Continuity of this resilient self-construction after release is believed to help youths feel empowered to make better choices rather than repeating the cycle of deviance (Ungar, 2001c).

Despite the nuances and challenges to conventional wisdom brought by qualitative studies such as those mentioned above, qualitative studies generally have reinforced and deepened the findings from quantitative studies. There is converging evidence regarding the key protective factors that appear to promote resilience in the presence of a variety of risks and across several distinct population groups, mostly in the United States and Europe. Taken together, this evidence combines the reliability, validity, and generalizability of the various quantitative methods with the trustworthiness and authenticity of the qualitative methods, at least to some extent. Such convergence promotes confidence in the general findings of resilience research, because the strengths of each method help to address the limitations of the others (McGrath, 1982). This same complementarity between methods is evident in this volume, with both quantitative and qualitative researchers represented.

Conclusions

Potentially Fatal Limitations of Resilience Research

Accepting for the moment that the concept of resilience is meaningful, viable, and researchable, the challenges in conducting such research are still daunting. The sheer multiplicity of potential risk and protective factors and the possible relationships among them (reciprocal, conditional, etc.) places strains on the most complex multi-variate, quantitative models. When one introduces time as a variable—that is, that certain processes may apply only at certain times, have lagged effects, or both—another layer of complexity emerges. The richest approach would appear to be the prospective, long-term, longitudinal design (e.g., Werner & Smith, 2001). Even this design has its limitations, including attrition, cost, and sheer length of time required to produce definitive findings.

Perhaps the most serious limitation of resilience research, however, is conceptual. Rigsby's (1994) assertion, echoed to some extent by Bartelt (1994) and Tolan (1996), that resilience is a "quintessentially U.S. concept" (Rigsby, 1994, p. 85) is difficult to refute. The notion of defying the odds, exceeding expectations, overcoming adversity, and the like fits well with an individualistic society's competitive ethos. Rigsby (1994) identifies several underlying assumptions of this ethos, that

> everyone should strive to get ahead . . . ; the arena of competition . . . is . . . open, fair, and accessible to all . . . one can always get oneself together and reenter the competition; [and] disadvantages that affect one's chances of success are individual and can be overcome with individual effort. (p. 97)

As he further states, "In the United States we value and celebrate 'resilience' and recoil from failure or defeat. Our commitment to achievement and success is so strong that we sometimes label lack of success 'pathology'" (p. 87).

Rigsby is not alone in suggesting that resilience is a culture-bound concept. Richman and Fraser (2001) state,

> Of course, problems arise when researchers and practitioners attempt to agree on what constitutes *significant* risk and *successful* outcomes that are *beyond predicted* expectations. For adaptations to be classified as resilient, should the outcomes be *highly* successful adaptations or can they be adaptations and outcomes that are at the level of social *competence* and *functionality?* For example, does a high school student who is identified as "at risk" of school failure have to graduate at the top of his/her class to be considered "resilient"? Or is graduation from high school significant? (p. 6)

How, then, can researchers adequately operationalize the key constructs in a resilience study? Who defines the dependent variable (success), and at what level must it appear to be considered as an indicator of resilience? An etic definition imposed by the researcher permits a nomothetic design and analysis but is susceptible to the culture-bound criticism above. An emic definition provided by the "subjects" in the research may be more meaningful but may not provide the generalizable data needed for robust theory development.

Finally, notwithstanding the challenges mentioned so far, interpreting the results of resilience research is inherently ambiguous. Despite the insistence of Rutter (2001) and others that resilience is not the same thing as the acquisition of social competence or positive mental health, it is not clear that factors typically identified as resilience enhancers are different from those that simply promote positive developmental outcomes in the presence *or* absence of high risk, stress, or trauma. The recent emphasis by researchers and practitioners on positive youth development echoes much of the resilience literature in identifying "assets" at multiple levels that are correlated with or predict healthy developmental outcomes (Connell, Gambone, & Smith, 2001; Eccles & Gootman, 2002; Hamilton & Hamilton, 2004; Pittman, Irby, & Foster, 2001; Scales & Leffert, 1999). So, for example, if resilience researchers purport to observe some persons who "succeed" in the presence of risk factors that would normally predict "failure" and then identify some "protective factors" correlated with success, does this really indicate "resilience"? One could just as easily conclude that the predictive model was misspecified, that had a more complete predictive model been used that incorporated the protective factors, the results would not have "exceeded expectations."

Reframing the Concept of Resilience

The definitional ambiguities in the study of resilience may ultimately render methodological quibbles moot. Research, both quantitative and qualitative, has identified a set of risk and protective factors combining in various ways at various times producing adaptive or maladaptive developmental outcomes. Knowing all this, however, does not permit us to predict an individual's developmental outcomes with much certainty. Perhaps that's as good as it gets. Acknowledging the limitations of stress research, Rutter's (1994) comments apply to resilience research as well:

> Far too much research into psychosocial risk factors has been content to stop at the point of identifying risk variables. There is no shortage of data on such variables and we know a good deal about the identification of risks. What we know much less about is how these risk mechanisms operate. Inevitably, that means that we are in a weak position when designing interventions to prevent or treat disorders. (p. 365)

Perhaps the current attention to resilience as a universal concept is misplaced. As noted above, all the related concepts—for example, risk factors, protective factors, vulnerability, assets, "successful" outcomes, and so on—are culturally and individually relative at least to some extent. Qualitative researchers (e.g., Gilgun, 1999; Gordon & Song, 1994; Ungar, 2001a, 2001b, 2001c) explicitly acknowledge this relativity and argue that such concepts function phenomenologically rather than mechanically. Herein may lie the key to transcending the limitations of most resilience research.

Most developmental theories, and their accompanying programs of research, are positivistic and mechanistic, seeking to fit "reality" into multivariate, usually linear combinations of predictors and outcomes. Despite occasional nods to the possibilities of reciprocal effects, these models do not, and probably cannot, "explain" much of the variance in outcomes. For the most part, they ignore the role of individual agency or choice, relegating this along with many other unmeasured influences to the catchall "error variance."

Symbolic interactionism (Blumer, 1969) offers a theoretical lens that may permit a fuller understanding of developmental pathways. A key concept of symbolic interactionism is the socially constructed, dynamic self-concept (Cooley, 1927; Mead, 1934; Turner, 1968). Symbolic interactionism's notion of a relational self has been further elaborated by Gergen (1994), who views identity as a constructionist narrative.

One way to begin to grasp this perspective is via an analogy. Consider group improvisation in music or theater. The physical context provides certain cues that elicit or constrain certain actions, the social context provides cues as to what actions are acceptable, the personal context provides a repertoire of abilities and previously learned actions, and the confluence of influences in the moment unleashes the improvisers' imaginations. Aesthetically satisfying improvisation usually requires that the improvisers have some background knowledge of the relevant language (be it musical, verbal, or nonverbal). The physical and social setting provides both opportunities and constraints on what is possible or normatively desirable to enact. Within such parameters, the actors or musicians are free to choose a wide range of actions. Of course, each action elicits reactions from the others present, and each individual considers such feedback in deciding what to do next. Note that the same individuals, in the presence of different companions or on a different stage at a different time, might perform quite differently. Note, too, that individuals learn certain patterns that seem to work in particular situations or with particular persons, and these patterns become part of the behavioral repertoire to be summoned when deemed appropriate in the future.

According to symbolic interactionism, social behavior is just such a series of improvisations, or iterative attempts at negotiated meaning. Social reality is thus constructed on the fly, as it were, grounded in the cultural context of language (verbal and nonverbal) and individuals' reference to themselves as socially constructed, dynamic selves. It is the dynamic, socially evolving self-concept, as understood from symbolic interactionism, that may be the missing piece of most developmental theory, including resilience theory—that is, the mechanism through which the multiple personal and environmental characteristics are mingled together to influence behavior. For it is the actor (whose current definition of self encapsulates intraindividual characteristics, prior social learning, and current motivational state) who interprets the environmental context, imagines the array of possible actions and their likely consequences, and chooses to act. The consequences of action are then interpreted by the individual, who may adjust his or her self-concept accordingly. No wonder positivistic, mechanistic models cannot explain much of the variance. Most of the variance is "in the moment" as the individual negotiates meanings and makes choices, not *determined* by a set of risk and protective factors, although such factors are indeed important as elements of the setting constraining the choice of possibilities.

Driving home one evening while struggling with the stress of finishing this chapter, my resilience increased as I heard a radio interview with Dr. Jeremy Groopman concerning his recent book, *The Anatomy of Hope: How People Prevail in the Face of Illness* (2003). His basic thesis is that "hope," defined as an envisioned pathway to a positive outcome, is a critical factor in people's abilities to defy the odds of terminal medical prognoses. Among his examples was a man with lymphoma who appeared to be without hope, because his point of reference was a military colleague who had died of cancer. When he went to his first chemotherapy appointment, the nurse seated him next to another lymphoma patient who was well on the road to recovery. As the two became acquainted, the new patient began to develop hope, now that his frame of reference was someone in a similar situation who was recovering. What Groopman calls a change in frame of reference may be thought of as a change in "possible selves" (Markus & Nurius, 1986)—that is, the patient could now imagine himself as a cancer survivor. His ensuing actions indeed placed him on a path to recovery, and his outcome could be considered "resilient."

Possible selves, introduced by Markus and Nurius (1986), are "those elements of the self-concept that represent what individuals *could* become, *would like to* become, or are *afraid of* becoming" (Oyserman & Markus, 1990a, p. 112). Possible selves provide a psychological link between identity and motivation. If one can imagine oneself in a particular end state, one is motivated to either achieve it (if it is a subjectively desirable end state) or avoid it (if it is undesirable). In a series of studies, Oyserman (Oyserman & Markus, 1990a, 1990b; Oyserman & Saltz, 1993; Oyserman, Terry, & Bybee, 2002)

examined the relationship between possible selves and delinquency and the potential value of altering at-risk youths' involvement in school by intervening to provide additional, prosocial, possible selves. The link to resilience is apparent—opportunities for individuals to imagine positive end states, with or without the presence of risk or adversity, can elicit motivation to behave in ways that make achievement of those end states more likely. The value of protective factors, or salutogenic factors more generally, may be that they provide or encourage such opportunities.

Thus, resilience as a concept may be largely irrelevant, although continued attention to strengths and the ecological interplay of forces at various levels may be highly valuable. In this regard, the international research agenda of Ungar and Liebenberg (Chapter 13 in this volume), with its emphasis on mixed-method research, is well positioned to make a major contribution to our understanding of the patterns and meanings of developmental outcomes in a variety of cultural contexts. As Rigsby (1994) notes, "What we really want to understand are the processes of human development in different times and places, for individuals with varying risks and assets, and for individuals developing in a variety of social contexts" (p. 91). What needs to be studied is how people make choices under various conditions. How do individuals vary in the perceived opportunities and constraints of a given set of environmental conditions? Can these perceptions be changed, for example, by introducing additional "possible selves" that expand the range of perceived adaptive responses to certain risky or stressful conditions? Can the environment be modified to introduce opportunities for imagining additional "possible selves?" How are adaptive responses perceived by others, and how do the others' perceptions, in turn, affect the self-concept of the original actor, perhaps shaping subsequent behavior (the classic research on teacher expectancy effects, Rosenthal & Jacobson, 1968, comes to mind)? Much of this research, at least initially, will have to be qualitative. It remains to be seen whether quantitative approaches other than expensive longitudinal designs can add much to a contextualized understanding of the factors that contribute to resilience.

REFERENCES

Akers, R. L. (1985). *Deviant behavior: A social learning approach* (3rd ed.). Belmont, CA: Wadsworth.

Anthony, E. J. (1987). Children at high risk for psychosis growing up successfully. In E. J. Anthony & B. J. Cohler (Eds.), *The invulnerable child* (pp. 147–184). New York: Guilford Press.

Bartelt, D. W. (1994). On resilience: Questions of validity. In M. C. Wang & E. W. Gordon (Eds.), *Educational resilience in inner-city America: Challenges and prospects* (pp. 97–108). Hillsdale, NJ: Erlbaum.

Beck, A. J. (2000, April). *State and federal prisoners returning to the community: Findings from the Bureau of Justice Statistics.* Presentation to the First Reentry Courts Initiative Cluster Meeting, Washington, DC.

Blumer, H. (1969). *Symbolic interactionism: Perspective and method.* Berkeley: University of California Press.

Burchard, J. D., Bruns, E. J., & Burchard, S. N. (2002). The wraparound approach. In B. J. Burns & K. Hoagwood (Eds.), *Community treatment for youth: Evidence-based interventions for severe emotional and behavioral disorders* (pp. 69–90). New York: Oxford University Press.

Clausen, J. A. (1993). *American lives: Looking back at the children of the Great Depression.* New York: Free Press.

Connell, J. P., Gambone, M. A., & Smith, T. J. (2001). Youth development in community settings: Challenges to our field and our approach. In P. L. Benson & K. Pittman (Eds.), *Trends in youth development: Visions, realities, and challenges* (pp. 291–307). Boston: Kluwer Academic.

Cooley, C. H. (1927). *Social processes.* New York: Scribner's.

Dryfoos, J. G. (1990). *Adolescents at risk: Prevalence and prevention.* New York: Oxford University Press.

Eccles, J., & Gootman, J. A. (Eds.). (2002). *Community programs to promote youth development.* Board on Children, Youth, and Families, Division of Behavioral and Social Sciences and Education, National Research Council and Institute of Medicine. Washington, DC: National Academy Press.

Egeland, B., Jacobvitz, D., & Sroufe, L. A. (1988). Breaking the cycle of abuse. *Child Development, 59,* 1080–1088.

Elder, G. H., Jr. (1999). *Children of the great depression.* Boulder, CO: Westview Press.

Furstenberg, F. F., Jr., Brooks-Gunn, J., & Morgan, S. P. (1987). *Adolescent mothers in later life.* New York: Cambridge University Press.

Geertz, C. (1973). *The interpretation of cultures.* New York: Basic Books.

Gergen, K. J. (1994). *Realities and relationships: Soundings in social construction.* Cambridge, MA: Harvard University Press.

Gilgun, J. F. (1999). Mapping resilience as process among adults with childhood adversities. In H. I. McCubbin, E. A. Thompson, A. I. Thompson, & J. A. Futrell (Eds.), *The dynamics of resilient families* (pp. 41–70). Thousand Oaks, CA: Sage.

Glueck, S., & Glueck, E. (1968). *Delinquents and non-delinquents in perspective.* Cambridge, MA: Harvard University Press.

Goldman, S. K. (1999). The conceptual framework for wraparound: Definition, values, essential elements, and requirements for practice. In B. J. Burns & S. K. Goldman (Eds.), *Systems of care: Promising practices in children's mental health* (1998 Series: Vol. 4, pp. 27–34). Washington, DC: American Institutes for Research, Center for Effective Collaboration and Practice.

Gordon, E. W., & Song, L. D. (1994). Variations in the experience of resilience. In M. C. Wang & E. W. Gordon (Eds.), *Educational resilience in inner-city America: Challenges and prospects* (pp. 27–43). Hillsdale, NJ: Erlbaum.

Gottfredson, M., & Hirschi, T. (1990). *A general theory of crime.* Palo Alto, CA: Stanford University Press.

Grinnell, R. M., Jr. (2001). *Social work research and evaluation: Quantitative & qualitative approaches* (6th ed.). Itasca, IL: F. E. Peacock.

Groopman, J. (2003). *The anatomy of hope: How people prevail in the face of illness.* New York: Random House.

Guba, E. G., & Lincoln, Y. S. (1989). *Fourth generation evaluation.* Newbury Park, CA: Sage.

Hamilton, S. F., & Hamilton, M. A. (Eds.). (2004). *The youth development handbook: Coming of age in American communities.* Thousand Oaks, CA: Sage.

Hawkins, J. D., Catalano, R. F., & Associates. (1992). *Communities that care: Action for drug abuse prevention.* San Francisco: Jossey-Bass.

Hawkins, J. D., Catalano, R. F., & Miller, J. Y. (1992). Risk and protective factors for alcohol and other drug problems in adolescence and early adulthood: Implications for substance abuse prevention. *Psychological Bulletin, 112,* 64–105.

Hirschi, T. (1969). *Causes of delinquency.* Berkeley, CA: University of California Press.

Kirby, L. D., & Fraser, M. W. (1997). Risk and resilience in childhood. In M. W. Fraser (Ed.), *Risk and resilience in childhood: An ecological perspective* (pp. 10–33). Washington, DC: NASW Press.

Long, J. V. F., & Vaillant, G. E. (1989). Escape from the underclass. In T. F. Dugan & R. Coles (Eds.), *The child in our times: Studies in the development of resiliency* (pp. 200–213). New York: Brunner/Mazel.

Luthar, S. S. (1991). Vulnerability and resilience: A study of high-risk adolescents. *Child Development, 62,* 600–616.

Magnusson, D., & Bergman, L. R. (1990). A pattern approach to the study of pathways from childhood to adulthood. In L. N. Robins & M. Rutter (Eds.), *Straight and devious pathways from childhood to adulthood* (pp. 101–115). Cambridge, UK: Cambridge University Press.

Markus, H. R., & Nurius, P. (1986). Possible selves. *American Psychologist, 41,* 954–969.

Marshall, C. (1990). Goodness criteria: Are they objective or judgment calls? In E. G. Guba (Ed.), *The paradigm dialog* (pp. 188–197). Newbury Park, CA: Sage.

Maruna, S. (2001). *Making good: How ex-convicts reform and rebuild their lives.* Washington, DC: American Psychological Association.

Masten, A. S. (1994). Resilience in individual development: Successful adaptation despite risk and adversity. In M. C. Wang & E. W. Gordon (Eds.), *Educational resilience in inner-city America: Challenges and prospects* (pp. 3–25). Hillsdale, NJ: Erlbaum.

McGrath, J. (1982). Dilemmatics: The study of research choices and dilemmas. In J. McGrath, J. Martin, & R. Kulka (Eds.), *Judgment calls in research* (pp. 69–102). Beverly Hills, CA: Sage.

Mead, G. H. (1934). *Mind, self, and society.* Chicago: University of Chicago Press.

Nash, J. K., & Fraser, M. W. (1997). Methods in the analysis of risk and protective factors: Lessons from epidemiology. In M. W. Fraser (Ed.), *Risk and resilience in childhood: An ecological perspective* (pp. 34–49). Washington, DC: NASW Press.

O'Brien, P. (2001). *Making it in the "free world": Women in transition from prison.* Albany: State University of New York Press.

Oyserman, D., & Markus, H. R. (1990a). Possible selves and delinquency. *Journal of Personality and Social Psychology, 59*(1), 112–125.

Oyserman, D., & Markus, H. R. (1990b). Possible selves in balance: Implications for delinquency. *Developmental Psychology, 10*(2), 764–771.

Oyserman, D., & Saltz, E. (1993). Competence, delinquency, and attempts to attain possible selves. *Journal of Personality and Social Psychology, 65*(2), 360–374.

Oyserman, D., Terry, K., & Bybee, D. (2002). A possible selves intervention to enhance school involvement. *Journal of Adolescence, 25*(3), 313–326.

Pittman, K., Irby, M., & Foster, T. (2001). Unfinished business: Further reflections on a decade of promoting youth development. In P. L. Benson & K. Pittman (Eds.), *Trends in youth development: Visions, realities, and challenges* (pp. 3–50). Boston: Kluwer Academic.

Pollard, J. A., Hawkins, J. D., & Arthur, M. W. (1999). Risk and protection: Are both necessary to understand diverse behavioral outcomes in adolescence? *Social Work Research, 23*(3), 145–158.

Resnick, M. D., Bearman, P. S., Blum, R. W., Bauman, K. E., Harris, K. M., Jones, J., Tabor, J., et al. (1997). Protecting adolescents from harm: Findings from the National Longitudinal Study on Adolescent Health. *JAMA, 278*(10), 823–832.

Richman, J. M., & Fraser, M. W. (2001). Resilience in childhood: The role of risk and protection. In J. M. Richman & M. W. Fraser (Eds.), *The context of youth violence: Resilience, risk, and protection* (pp. 1–12). Westport, CT: Praeger.

Rigsby, L. C. (1994). The Americanization of resilience: Deconstructing research practice. In M. C. Wang & E. W. Gordon (Eds.), *Educational resilience in inner-city America: Challenges and prospects* (pp. 85–94). Hillsdale, NJ: Erlbaum.

Rosenthal, R., & Jacobson, L. (1968). *Pygmalion in the classroom.* New York: Holt, Rinehart & Winston.

Rutter, M. (1985). Resilience in the face of adversity: Protective factors and resistance to psychiatric disorders. *British Journal of Psychiatry, 147,* 598–611.

Rutter, M. (1994). Stress research: Accomplishments and tasks ahead. In R. J. Haggerty, L. R. Sherrod, N. Garmezy, & M. Rutter (Eds.), *Stress, risk, and resilience in children and adolescents: Processes, mechanisms, and interventions* (pp. 354–385). Cambridge, UK: Cambridge University Press.

Rutter, M. (2001). Psychosocial adversity: Risk, resilience and recovery. In J. M. Richman & M. W. Fraser (Eds.), *The context of youth violence: Resilience, risk, and protection* (pp. 13–41). Westport, CT: Praeger.

Saleebey, D. (1997). *The strengths perspective in social work practice* (2nd ed.). New York: Longman.

Scales, P. C., & Leffert, N. (1999). *Developmental assets: A synthesis of scientific research on adolescent development.* Minneapolis, MN: Search Institute.

Stroul, B. A., & Friedman, R. M. (1986). *A system of care for children & youth with severe emotional disturbances.* Washington, DC: CASSSP Technical Assistance Center, Center for Child Health and Mental Health Policy, Georgetown University Child Development Center.

Tolan, P. H. (1996). How resilient is the concept of resilience? *The Community Psychologist, 29*(4), 12–15.

Turner, R. H. (1968). The self-conception in social interaction. In C. Gordon & K. J. Gergen (Eds.), *The self in social interaction* (pp. 93–106). New York: John Wiley.

Ungar, M. (2001a). Constructing narratives of resilience with high-risk youth. *Journal of Systemic Therapy, 20*(2), 58–73.

Ungar, M. (2001b). Qualitative contributions to resilience research. *Qualitative Social Work, 2*(1), 85–102.

Ungar, M. (2001c). The social construction of resilience among "problem" youth in out-of-home placement: A study of health-enhancing deviance. *Child & Youth Care Forum, 30*(3), 137–154.

VanDenBerg, J. E., & Grealish, E. M. (1996). Individualized services and supports through the wraparound process: Philosophy and procedures. *Journal of Child and Family Studies, 5*(1), 7–21.

Vaillant, G. E. (1977). *Adaptation to life.* Boston: Little Brown.

Vaillant, G. E. (1983). *The natural history of alcoholism.* Cambridge, MA: Harvard University Press.

Vaillant, G. E., & Milofsky, E. S. (1980). Natural history of male psychological health, IX: Empirical evidence for Erikson's model of the life cycle. *American Journal of Psychiatry, 137,* 1347–1359.

Vaillant, G. E., & Vaillant, C. O. (1981). Natural history of male psychological health: X. Work as a predictor of positive mental health. *American Journal of Psychiatry, 138,* 1433–1440.

Weick, A., Rapp, C, Sullivan, W. P., & Kisthardt, W. (1989). Towards a strengths model for social work practice. *Social Work, 34*(4), 350–354.

Werner, E. E., Bierman, J. M., & French, F. E. (1971). *The children of Kauai.* Honolulu: University of Hawaii Press.

Werner, E. E., & Smith, R. S. (1977). *Kauai's children come of age.* Honolulu: University of Hawaii Press.

Werner, E. E., & Smith, R. S. (1982). *Vulnerable, but invincible: A longitudinal study of resilient children and youth.* New York: McGraw Hill.

Werner, E. E., & Smith, R. S. (1992). *Overcoming the odds: High risk children from birth to adulthood.* Ithaca, NY: Cornell University Press.

Werner, E. E., & Smith, R. S. (2001). *Journeys from childhood to midlife: Risk, resilience, and recovery.* Ithaca, NY: Cornell University Press.

Whitney, S. D., Herrenkohl, T. I., Tajima, E. A., & Huang, B. (2004, January). *The application of mixture model analysis in the study of multiple risk factors for delinquency and school failure.* Paper presented at the Society for Social Work and Research Conference, New Orleans, LA.

10

QUALITATIVE RESILIENCE RESEARCH

Contributions and Risks

MICHAEL UNGAR

ELI TERAM

The emergence of research with a focus on enhancing the capacities of at-risk children, youth, and families has contributed to the reframing of mental health issues in terms of resilience rather than psychopathology. Although this research is noteworthy for its attempt to understand the pathways to survival of children confronted with life's greatest adversities, it has failed to challenge our thinking about youth and the labels they carry. Thus, we continue to distinguish between successful and unsuccessful youth, thereby violating them through methodologically flawed and contextually irrelevant interpretations of their worlds. Our universal version of the lives of children facing multiple risks continues to be guided by a dominant culture deeply imbued with the perspective of a Western psychological discourse—one that arbitrarily designates some children as healthy and others as deviant, dangerous, delinquent, and disordered based on the perceived social acceptability of children's behavior.

Two frequently noted shortcomings in studies of resilience are yet to be adequately addressed. The first is the arbitrariness in the selection of outcome variables, with standardized testing more appropriate for discovering the etiology of illness than the building blocks of health. The second is the limited attention paid to the social and cultural contexts in which resilience occurs, with an implicit assumption that all children have access to the requisite resources for achieving the type of functioning that signifies successful coping as decided by the dominant culture. Thus, for example a well-known scale for assessing health phenomena in children (Epstein & Sharma, 1998) includes questions about individual children's "hobbies" and "favorite vacations." This remarkably insular series of questions speaks more to the commonplace in middle-class American culture than to the lived experience of a global community of children. The questions carry the implicit message that a child who has interests and a family with leisure time is healthier than those who do not.

These issues alert us to the fact that resilience research, like all social science research, is conducted within political, ideological, and cultural arenas. Although in some areas the message about desired research topics and outcomes is explicit, in others it is ambiguous and masked by the acceptable rhetoric of the day. In this regard, the adoption of progressive ideas by conservative governments can be disarming. Thus, for example, neoconservatives have adopted the concept of community revitalization to justify the elimination of social services because they create dependency and do not let people and communities look after themselves. Resilience researchers face similar risks of having their ideas interpreted and used in ways they have not intended.

In this chapter, we argue that although qualitative resilience research is most suitable to consider contextual issues and youth's own accounts of their pathways to health, the essence of its methodology presents unique interpretive challenges. Our argument unfolds in four parts. After first pointing out the shortcomings of current resilience research, we next discuss the contributions of qualitative methods to the study of resilience, highlighting their incorporation of context and the voices of youth in the development of professional practice and social policy. In the third section, we examine the perils of interpreting or misinterpreting qualitative studies and their perceived lack of credibility. In the final part, we explore how qualitative researchers can address these issues by making both their methods and their findings more politically relevant to those who use research as the basis for decision making and intervention.

A CRITIQUE OF CURRENT RESILIENCE RESEARCH

Definitional ambiguity of terms such as *risk factors, protective mechanisms, vulnerability,* and *resilience* has produced a large and inconsistent set of variables to study the health-seeking life trajectories of children and youth growing up facing adversity or trauma. Debate about what is and is not resilience continues to plague this worthwhile field of research (Anthony & Cohler,

1987; Cairns & Cairns, 1994; Fraser, 1997; Glantz & Sloboda, 1999; Luthar, 1993). Typical of many of her colleagues, Masten (2001) defines resilience as a "class of phenomena characterized by *good outcomes in spite of serious threats to adaptation or development*" (p. 228). The term resilience refers to both a child's state of well-being (as in he or she *is resilient*) and to the characteristics and processes by which that well-being is achieved and sustained (as in he or she *shows resilience to* a particular risk) (Gilgun, 1999).

This ambiguity has been accompanied by an arbitrary selection of outcome measures and lack of contextual specificity in the design of studies. Combined, these two problems have made generalization of findings across sociocultural contexts difficult (Masten, 2001; McCubbin et al., 1998; Silbereisen & von Eye, 1999). As Richman and Fraser (2001) note,

> Resilience requires exposure to significant risk, overcoming risk or adversity, and success that is beyond predicted expectations. Of course, problems arise when researchers and practitioners attempt to agree on what constitutes *significant* risk and *successful* outcomes that are *beyond predicted* expectations. (p. 6)

Similarly, Cohen, Cimbolic, Armeli, and Hettler (1998) characterize studies of thriving after or during a crisis as "unsophisticated," noting methodological problems with "the variability in participants' subjective definitions of terms such as *benefits* or *gains*" whereas "reliance on researchers' definitions of growth might introduce bias associated with their model of adjustment and value system" (p. 325). Skepticism regarding self-reports of thriving have led to the validation of these accounts through corroboration from victims' significant others, use of control analyses that compare responses on other instruments administered before and after a crisis, or by using control groups to compare scores on adjustment-related measures.

As we shall see, quantitative researchers have not been oblivious to the arbitrariness of the resilience construct and have attempted to deal with it through the refinement of measures, the expansion of data collection to include more contextually relevant variables, and the use of more powerful tools of analysis. Nevertheless, in only a few instances have complementary qualitative methods been employed (see, e.g., Boehnke, 1999; Graham, 2001; Graham & Rockwood, 1998; Hauser, 1999; Kaplan, 1999; Luthar & Zigler, 1991; Magnus, Cowen, Wyman, Fagen, & Work, 1999; Nesselroade & McCollam, 2000; Rutter, 2001; Thoits, 1995; Yellin, Quinn, & Hoffman, 1998). Thus, the efforts to deconstruct the arbitrariness of what is and is not a good outcome have fallen short of broadening our understanding of resilience.

The reluctance of authors to present the voices of youth and their unique communities in a way that is appreciative of who they are and how they survive has meant that we have been particularly unsuccessful in sustaining a child-focused understanding of their lived experiences. With the myopia of the controlled study, we have classified children based on the selection criteria of adults, despite the growing evidence that resilience and other health-related phenomena are heterogeneous in their manifestation. For example, signs of health in one domain of a child's life may not correlate with healthy functioning in another (Luthar, Cicchetti, & Becker, 2000), and resilience in one setting may mask problems in another. As Galambos and Leadbeater (2000) recognize, there is a need for "studies of resilience in contexts of adversity" (p. 289). Although more advanced quantitative techniques can capture some of the multidimensional and shifting patterns of resilience, Galambos and Leadbeater note the increasing need for qualitative data in research with children and adolescents.

However, true to their bias, the response of quantitative researchers to the problem of arbitrariness in their designs has been to simply do more of the same. A case in point is Nesselroade and McCollam (2000), who offer the following observation regarding processes in developmental research:

> Depictions of occasion-to-occasion and age-to-age average changes and the stability of rank order (e.g., as in using test-retest correlation coefficients), interesting though they may be from a descriptive point of view, can point to process in only limited ways. In many cases, the measurement occasions are begun, spaced, and end arbitrarily

and the descriptions they afford of what is transpiring are just as arbitrary. (p. 295)

Despite the obvious need for methodological diversity, Nesselroade and McCollam's response to this shortcoming is a call for "more powerful methods of measurement, analysis, and modeling" (p. 295). Nowhere do they suggest the complementarity of qualitative designs that facilitate the participation of youth in research and challenge assumptions of homogeneity.

The exclusion of youth voices has rendered quantitative research incapable to explain the marginal discourses they may find among youth. For example, Sutton, Smith, and Swettenham (1999) had no satisfactory way to explore further the troubling finding of their quantitative study that bullies may not be as incompetent as we have suspected. They write:

> It is important to realise that some bullying children do have power, and that they can misuse this power in ways advantageous to them (in some circumstances). For some, this power takes a social rather than physical form, and such bullies are undoubtedly skilled at achieving interpersonal goals. They would probably not see their behaviour as incompetent or maladaptive, and there is evidence that it often is not. (p. 133)

Such findings would not be surprising if we attend to the voices of children themselves.

Children cannot only help us understand these findings but also explain the ineffectiveness of the interventions employed to correct their behaviours. For example, Salmivalli's (Salmivalli, 2001; Salmivalli, Kaukiainen, Kaistaniemi, & Lagerspetz, 1999) quantitative work in Finland using a peer-led school intervention to address bullying found through postintervention testing that participants showed at best ambivalence about bullying and at worse that pro-bullying attitudes actually *increased* among boys. If we are to move beyond the confusion such findings reveal, we must adapt qualitative methods that can capture the alternate perspectives of children themselves (see, e.g., Lightfoot, 1992).

The need for methodologies that include the voices of youth is even greater when it comes to studies in non-Western societies. Painter (2001) argues against the use of standardized instruments in cross-cultural research where cultural differences are further accentuated by the microcultures of children. He notes that the methodological imperative in psychology to conceive of social phenomena as objects of study and a lack of appreciation for how social representations differ across cultures raise questions about the validity of any investigation of another culture that does not start from a method indigenous to those studied.

Arguably, it is not that such research cannot be done but that the problem of studying children's health outside Western contexts is frequently one of design. Cooke and Michie (2002) note the need to pay particular attention to cultural variation and the thorny issue of cultural relevance: "The cross-cultural generalizability and validity of risk assessment methods may founder if the relevance of responses to questionnaires or interviewers varies across cultures" (p. 242). Add to this the problem of cultural norms concerning children's self-disclosure, the inappropriateness of testing methods, translation issues, and variable levels of literacy, and one quickly realizes the questionability of any data gathered across cultures without using participatory research designs with indigenous or culturally anchored methods (Hughes & Seidman, 2002; Israel et al., 2003).

We can also inadvertently export our cultural biases through our research, imposing them on others by seeking explanations for people's experiences in terms that are relevant mostly to the outsiders conducting the study. To continue with the theme of bullying, Ohsako (1998), in his look at peer-to-peer interactions among school-age children, notes that the majority world lacks both a language and perspective of children to discuss this form of violence. For research on children to be truly inclusive, we must pay attention to the "different socioeconomic or sociocultural backgrounds and different developmental stages of both industrialized and developing countries" (p. 359). A recent article by the Zimbabwean researcher Mpofu (2002) recounts the different meanings of early-onset aggression for youth in his country. It is highly improbable, he says, that such patterns are equivalent to those found among their counterparts in economically developed countries.

Yamamoto and his colleagues (Yamamoto, Silva, Ferrari, & Nukariya, 1997) take a similar stance when they look critically at the transcultural study of children's mental health. For them,

> The science of transcultural child mental health . . . focuses not only on child and adolescent psychopathology from a cultural viewpoint, but also on the many ways that culture can facilitate optimal child development in the family and society in which the child happens to be raised. (pp. 36–37)

Noting the need to contextualize our understanding of mental disorders in children, Yamamoto fully realizes the controversy that arises when one thinks of disease as a cultural construct. Nevertheless, cross-cultural studies openly question even commonsense Western notions such as adolescent independence. For example, work by Indian scholars has shown that children in India prefer to spend time with their families, even during adolescence, and that street youth continue to both respect and enjoy their family's presence in their lives even while living independently at a young age (Larson, Verma, & Dworkin, 2002; Sharma & Sharma, 1999). Neither pattern would be easily accounted for by Western psychological theories of child development or attachment.

CONSIDERING CONTEXT AND YOUTH VOICES THROUGH QUALITATIVE RESEARCH

Clearly, we require methodologies that can engage with children, their caregivers, and their elders in ways that promote their constructions of health. To be relevant, these methodologies must also demonstrate an awareness of the contextual factors that restrain children's choices for health. As Flyvbjerg (2001) argues, the problem of relevance in social science can be addressed by anchoring the research in the context studied and by getting "close to the phenomenon or group whom one studies during data collection, and [remaining] close during the phases of data analysis, feedback and publication of results" (p. 132). Although there is much work to be done before we reach such ideals, some resilience researchers have demonstrated how qualitative methods can move us in the right direction.

Participatory research with youth to co-construct a definition of resilience may reshape our thinking about this construct. For example, youth naively labeled as deviant, dangerous, delinquent, and disordered have argued that resilience is the outcome from negotiations between individuals and their environments to maintain a self-definition as healthy (Ungar, 2002, 2004b). In other words, resilience is not something that can be arbitrarily designated beyond due consideration given to the relative power of the one doing the defining and the one being defined (see Fine, 1994). To summarize the words of participants in a recent study we conducted, "'Sticks and stones may break our bones, but names will really hurt us'" (Ungar & Teram, 2000, p. 229). Defined this way, resilience becomes a question of one's degree of discursive empowerment. If I am convinced I am healthy despite the adversity I face, and I am capable of convincing others of my health status, then I am healthy.

In line with this definition, children's health-seeking behaviors can be better understood when explored through their own eyes. A poignant example is the intelligibility of children's pathways into and out of care as part of their strategy to protect against risk (Garbarino, 2001; Ungar, 2001b). A recent qualitative study employing in-depth interviews with 43 youth who had experienced multiple out-of-home placements found that high-risk youth

> talked about their behaviours before, during and after placement as efforts to construct a self-definition for themselves as resilient. These constructive efforts resisted the problem-saturated identities imposed on them both by their communities and caregivers while residents/clients/ wards/patients. Contrary to what caregivers believe, youth see themselves as exercising a great deal of control (but not exclusive control) over several aspects of the placement process. They argue that they influence when they "get put inside," the way they "survive inside," and the way they cope when "going home." At each juncture, youth say they use placement as a way to negotiate continuities and discontinuities in their identity

> constructions in order to co-create the most powerful and health-enhancing identity available from the resources they have at hand. (Ungar, 2001b, pp. 143–144)

A process of institutionalization as negotiation for health resources is not typically what we imagine occurring among high-risk children. These findings have practical implications for the way we organize institutional resources. As Ungar, Teram, and Picketts (2001) argue, institutions can provide meaningful support for young offenders if they are framed as an extension of the community. As such, youth and their communities can use institutions flexibly when a temporary respite is required for either or both.

Seeing the world through the eyes of youth can help us gain a new understanding of what we consider signs of disordered behavior. Using a triangulated research design, Hunter and Chandler (1999) collected data, both quantitative and qualitative, from 51 tenth-and eleventh-grade vocational students. They observed that

> resilience to [the participants] meant being insular, disconnected, self-reliant, self-protective with no one to depend on or trust but themselves . . . . These findings suggest that resilience meant something very different to these adolescents than what the Resiliency Scale was measuring. Being resilient was not having a healthy sense of self, a strong sense of self-worth, or the ability to connect and trust others. Being resilient meant surviving. (p. 245)

Felsman (1989) reported similar findings about the way youth negotiate for health resources. Based on 300 semistructured interviews with children under the age of 16 in Colombia he concluded, "Peer support is directly tied to survival itself" (p. 66). In fact,

> Although the gallada's [gangs of street youth] involvement in crime and violence must be recognized and contended with, it must first be realized that these children do not band together to fight and steal; rather, they band together to meet primary physical and emotional needs not being addressed elsewhere. (p. 66)

Such discoveries are typical of qualitative methods that have promoted lengthy engagement with participants, their files, or key informants, discovering health-related patterns that might not otherwise be obvious to outsiders (Gilgun, 1996, 1999; Rodwell, 1998; Silverman, 2000; Strauss & Corbin, 1990).

In addition to lengthy engagement with youth and their inclusion in the research process in a way that *re-presents* their voices, qualitative researchers have also paid explicit attention to context. For Johnson-Powell and Yamamoto (1997),

> A comprehensive assessment requires information from the school, the parents, significant family members, and the child; and it must also include the cultural factors related to the psychosocial environment, the cultural identity, and the cultural explanation or meanings given to the child's symptoms or behavior. The cultural assessment then becomes an essential part of the diagnostic process. (p. 350)

In practice, this implies a research design like the one used by Dupree, Spencer, and Bell (1997). Building on Spencer's (1995) phenomenological variant of ecological systems theory, Dupree et al. challenged culturally inappropriate assumptions such as those regarding the prevalence of suspected deviance in African American communities. Instead, they urge us to see children's behavior as meaning different things in different cultural contexts. For example, to see resilience among African American youth and families, notably the healthy aspects of how children are raised in "fatherless" homes (a biased perspective at best), we need to look beyond outcomes. Rather than blaming parents for what may be highly adaptive coping strategies among their children, we have to appreciate children's experiences of their oppression, living situation, and other broad social forces.

Such appreciation is demonstrated in Flom's (2002) qualitative research with a group of 15 adolescents attending a day treatment program at a state mental health facility in the United States. Flom highlights the "resilience aspirations" of the participants who hold clear hopes for a better future and a critical perspective on the service gaps they experience, despite the problems they face and their precarious mental health status. These aspirations are in contrast to the individualized claims of psychopathology found in these youth's clinical records and among the professionals who provide them with care. Within Flom's account of these adolescent voices, there is recognition that health is resource dependent. As Huang (2003) says, "We need to integrate the impact of disparities into our mental health care of children" (see also Caputo, 1999).

Qualitative research provides an effective way to achieve this integration because it thickly describes the lives of children, especially those from culturally diverse backgrounds who may be doubly marginalized by both age and social address. Moreover, although offering these thick descriptions, qualitative research does not attempt to claim grand generalizations. As Rodwell (1998) explains,

> If the findings transfer, it is the responsibility of the reader of the inquiry report to make that determination, since it is only the reader, not the inquirer, who can be familiar with the time and context in which transfer of the findings might be possible. (pp. 31–32)

The qualitative researcher "can provide only the thick description necessary to enable someone interested in making a transfer to reach a conclusion about whether transfer can be contemplated as a possibility" (Lincoln & Guba, 1985, p. 316).

Issues of relativism and contextual specificity are even more relevant when we broaden our perspective beyond economically developed regions and look to economically developing regions such as our inner cities, the remote North, and overseas to people living in the majority world. A Eurocentric perspective dominates and presupposes that what we think we know about health in others, especially children, is relevant to their lives. However, as Klevens and Roca (1999) found in their exploration of life histories of 46 young men from high-risk families in Bogata, Colombia, the common epidemiological predictors for violence were not sufficient to explain their behaviors. Hence they "chose qualitative methods for data collection and analysis to avoid imposing foreign variables and hypotheses in this new context and to allow new variables to emerge from the data" (p. 313).

Far from an argument for unhampered relativism, the deconstruction of children's points of view by employing qualitative research methods is meant to politicize our understanding of resilience. What is health and who decides? Social sciences philosopher Ian Hacking (1999) has argued that too often we divorce our conversations about social constructions from the factual social locations in which discourses operate. The unmasking of hidden discourses of resilience among high-risk children and youth is based on the unequivocal belief that children's lives are lived with purpose even when it appears that purpose runs counter to the conventions of good behavior dictated by the children's caregivers (Ungar, 2004a, 2004b). The bias to psychopathologize the behavior of children has been our way to control our fear of them as they challenge established norms (Lesko, 2001). When we fail to listen to children's own stories, we are likely to miss important details of their thriving. What Ungar (2001a) called "narratives of resilience" are in fact healthy self-constructions hidden beneath chaotic behaviors in resource-poor environments.

Clearly, qualitative researchers are equipped to discover these narratives and offer an alternative discourse about youth and their problems. Exemplary qualitative study of childhood resilience and the factors contributing to health outcomes have shown that individuals, families, and communities hold very specific understandings of their health based on their social locations (Gilgun, 1999; Klevens & Roca, 1999; Taylor, Gilligan, & Sullivan, 1995; Ungar & Teram, 2000). To those studies already mentioned, one can also add Schofield's (2001) study of children's resilience following placement by state authorities in a nonkin family. Taking a life span perspective, Schofield interviewed 40 adults aged 18 to 30 who had been in out-of-home placement an average of 7 years during their childhoods. Hauser's (1999) work has tracked a similar population of at-risk children over 20 years. Work by Todis and her colleagues (Todis, Bullis, Waintrup, Schultz, & D'Ambrosio, 2001) followed 15 adolescents over 5 years as they made the transition from incarceration back to their communities and

found as well that youth can survive incredible displacements when there is continuity in their care and attachments as they perceive it. Related work by De Antoni and Koller (2000) examined the lives of Brazilian street children and their myriad ways of surviving by creating attachments to each other in the absence of caring adults. Finally, two psychoanalysts from Israel, Apfel and Simon (2000) used unstructured interviews to examine the lives of 10 Israeli and 10 Palestinian children thematically around issues of health and coping. As these examples combine to show, such cross-cultural perspectives abound in the qualitative resilience literature for what should now be obvious reasons.

THE PERILS OF QUALITATIVE RESEARCH

As the preceding discussion demonstrates, qualitative inquiries have much to offer for our understanding of resilience-related phenomena and the discoveries of health among those we assume to be unhealthy. However, the voices of marginalized youth can be disturbing; as a result, the implications of qualitative resilience research may be misinterpreted or disregarded. If we want to be relevant and have an impact on professional practice and social policy, we have to explain the implications of our findings clearly to those we want to influence. Otherwise, we risk that the messages children trust us to deliver will not be accepted or, even worse, distorted to serve an agenda that is neither ours nor that of the youth whose cause we want to advance.

One of the most difficult challenges faced by qualitative researchers is the practical implications of reframing resilience by valuing youth's own understanding of this construct. Clearly, children who resist the hegemony of the neutered Disney-like norms imposed on them that strip away hyperactivity, adventure, risk-taking, and uniqueness are unlikely to convince others that their resistance is a disguised form of resilience. Thus, as Massey, Cameron, Ouellette, and Fine (1998) observe, "Valuing social competence and compliance over expressions of personal agency would bias who gets the label *resilient* toward those most likely to conform, overlooking those most likely to critique" (p. 339).

Similarly, Martineau (1999) points out that

> obscured behind the well-meaning intentions of teaching resilience is a call for disadvantaged children and youth to conform to the behavioral norms of the dominant society (associated with social and school success) by overcoming or being invulnerable to the systemic distresses and adversities of their everyday lives (p. 3) . . . The resiliency discourse imposes prescribed norms of school success and social success upon underprivileged children identified as at risk. The effect is that nonconforming individuals may be pathologized as *non-resilient*. Emphasis remains wholly on the individual and thus, *individualism* is a dominant ideology embedded in the mainstream resiliency discourse. (pp. 11–12)

Professionals accustomed to certain typologies and interventions, and policymakers who follow the lead of these professionals, are bound to resist a new resilience discourse. Unfortunately, researchers have not always been consistent in presenting a clear alternative. A case in point is the contrast between Martineau's critique of the emphasis on individualism and her complaint, along with Massey et al., that social agency and nonconformity are being pathologized or overlooked as an indication of resilience. We doubt that criticizing the emphasis on individualism is going to take us too far when we want to emphasize the unique patterns of resilience exhibited by youth. Clearly, qualitative resilience research is about individuals and personal agency in its many forms. If we accept that, we can more effectively point out the connections between the choices made by youth and the contexts for making these choices. The point of the new resilience discourse is to highlight these connections, emphasizing that unless these contexts are changed, youth will continue to be resilient in ways that may not conform to society's norms. Qualitative research, as we know, is most effective for contextualizing behaviors and processes.

Highlighting these connections does not mean an endorsement of the choices young people make but an understanding that under certain circumstances their options are limited. Given the socially unacceptable nature of some of the attitudes and behaviors discovered by qualitative resilience researchers, this point must be emphasized. Otherwise, our message to professionals and policymakers will be inconsistent or misinterpreted. Ironically, the risk of misinterpretation is intensified the more we highlight the health and resilience that underlie behaviors that are socially unacceptable or deemed unhealthy. Although these arguments represent youth perceptions about resilience and health-seeking behaviors and offer an alternative to the dominant psychopathologizing discourse, carried to the extreme, it may offer policymakers a way out of their obligations to address the needs of youth. If youth in trouble are indeed as healthy and resilient as some researchers (e.g., Ungar, 2002, 2004b) suggest, why not leave them alone to pursue whatever forms of happiness and health they desire? Such an argument can reinforce the tendency to spend government resources on controlling youth who commit crimes rather than on prevention and treatment programs (for Canada, see, e.g., Rains, Teram, & Toutant, 2001). After all, the argument can be, "Your thick qualitative evidence that these youth are not weak, destitute, and helpless is compelling, so why not let them continue to fend for themselves?" Within current neoconservative thinking, this line of misinterpretation of well-meaning research is quite plausible.

We therefore have to come to terms with the contradiction between respecting youth's definitions of resilience and health and our understanding that to gain full citizenship in society, some of these definitions must shift toward common norms, however defined. An extreme postmodernist stance suggesting that youth are healthy as long as they perceive themselves as such and convince others that they are will not advance the interests of youth. The agenda of portraying youth as healthy and resilient, in spite of appearances that suggest otherwise, would not be weakened by a reminder that this is so within the context of their poorly resourced environments.

As Garbarino (2001) found in his examination of youth violence among inmates at a maximum-security juvenile detention center,

> All acts of violence express a need for justice. . . . Such behaviors may be warped and distorted and difficult to fathom from the outside, but if we dig deeply enough and listen openly enough, we may hear of the need to restore justice by personally

acting on the feelings of shame that come from being rejected, denied, abused, and deprived. (pp. 84–85)

If our goal is to help children move toward prosocial behaviors, an understanding of their behavior as motivated by a search for health, and part of their negotiations with others to be seen as healthy, will put us in a better position to intervene effectively.

The implication of this line of reasoning is that within a better-resourced context these youth's definition of health and well-being is bound to move closer to that of mainstream society. Unless we explicitly highlight this point, the relevance of qualitative research with at-risk youth will be questionable. Moreover, researchers (quantitative or qualitative) who criticize the behaviors of "problem" youth without investigating their access to resources and limited life opportunities will appear more authentic and relevant to policymakers and program developers.

In this vein, one can look at Hemmings's (2000) work on the "hidden corridor curriculum" among high school students. Hemmings explores the unofficial curriculum within high schools, both inside the classroom and in the hallways, finding among students an alternate set of values to cope with their disenfranchisement. Instead of conceding some intelligibility to these choices, as we would expect from a qualitative researcher who appreciates context, Hemmings does the opposite, arguing,

> Most [of the adolescents] were cut off from middle-class modes of economic advancement, and deeply divided along racial and gender lines. They were profoundly alienated, and adapted to their circumstances by constructing what can be aptly described as a youth culture of hostility. (p. 3)

Hemmings's conclusions are puzzling. Being marginalized, whose expectation is it that these youth will create something other than a culture of hostility? Their hostility, rather than appreciated for the power it may bring (one can only speculate given that the data cannot and should not be generalized), is described by Hemmings as a "crude rendition of this discourse formed in response to chronic joblessness. This rendition rejected legitimate middle-class modes of economic advancement, and instead emphasized

the rapid acquisition of money and all that money could buy through illicit means" (p. 5). One might wonder what Hemmings expects youth to do when confronted with systemic disadvantage and middle-class norms for consumption? If not for illicit activities, how else would these marginalized youth find access to the resources necessary to compete on an equal footing with their more fortunate peers? The front-and-center position of the researcher's voice is unfortunate in this case. We learn little about the pathways these youth must travel to health through impoverished environments and everything about a community that admonishes them for doing what they must to achieve the same goals as set for youth who are more privileged.

The last thing youth in trouble need is qualitative researchers entering their world to unconditionally condemn it. Notwithstanding their position regarding conformity and traditional measures of success, qualitative researchers need to better understand the important contribution they can make to the well-being of youth—highlighting the multiple contexts that underlie children's lives and their accounts of the phenomena under inquiry. In this regard, caution is needed. Whereas Hemmings's approach blames the victims of oppression for their not measuring up, at the other end, a superficial reading of Ungar's work as promoting unconditional acceptance of children's definitions of health and resilience is just as likely to prevent the integration of troubled youth into their communities. It is important that we make efforts to connect children's behaviors to the realities of their worlds. When qualitative researchers fail to make these connections, by ignoring either poorly resourced environments or society's standards of success, they neglect one of the important contributions they can make: helping children have a voice in the political process that determines the allocation of health resources.

MAKING QUALITATIVE RESEARCH POLITICALLY RELEVANT

The fit between qualitative methods and the study of phenomena in which one must account for the contextual specificity of the construct under investigation is well established. Such inquiry may, however, be risky amid the maze of confusion occurring when qualitative inquiry takes place in settings that are less familiar with these methods (Ungar, 2001c). As Miller and Crabtree (2000) write in regard to their experience doing qualitative research in biomedical clinical contexts,

> Successfully entering the biomedical world as a qualitative clinical researcher requires a many-eyed *model of mediation.* Qualitative clinical researchers need to learn the discipline of seeing with three eyes: the biomedical eye of "objectivity," the inward searching eye of reflexivity, and a third eye that looks for the multiple, nested contexts that hold and shape the research questions. (p. 611)

One way of juggling these multiple ways of seeing is through participatory action research. Minkler and Wallerstein (2003), proponents of community-based participatory health research, point to the need for all research to be grounded in the communities being studied and reciprocal in its collection and dissemination of data. In this way, power is shared between the researcher and the researched, a particularly challenging thing to accomplish with children. Not to give the illusion of utopia, we prefer to think of this sharing in ways similar to those proposed by Cheatham and Shen (2003). For them, "Dealing explicitly with issues of power [in community-based participatory research] does not mean that power is always equally shared but rather that power dynamics are not hidden and that efforts at democratizing power take place to the extent possible" (pp. 318–319). With an emphasis on process, long-term vision, a focus on community and strengths, participation, and capacity, their model of research is more likely to capture the localized health discourses of disadvantaged children.

However, when using these participatory research methods, there is a risk that the outcomes, and the voices of the children the research purports to represent, can be marginalized because these methods do not fall in line with the conventions of "legitimate research." As Kemmis and McTaggart (2000) argue,

> In most action research, including participatory action research, the researchers make sacrifices in methodological and technical rigor in exchange for more immediate gains in face validity: whether the evidence they collect makes sense to *them, in their contexts.* For this reason, we sometimes characterize participatory action research as "low tech" research: It sacrifices methodological sophistication in order to generate timely evidence that can be used and further developed in a real-time process of transformation (of practices, practitioners, and practice setting). (p. 591)

Recognizing this problem, Schachter, Teram, and Stalker (2004) designed a study that amplified the voices of participants (survivors of childhood sexual abuse) not only through their participation in empowering research processes but also by ensuring that the ideas they generate will be well received by the gatekeepers of professional knowledge. To address the imbalance between the expertise accorded to clients and that of professionals and ensure that survivors' knowledge was not discredited, they integrated traditional grounded theory and participatory action research methods (Teram, Schachter, & Stalker, in press). This approach ensured that the findings were sufficiently credible to have significant impact on those the participants were trying to influence.[1]

The approach used in the demonstration project examining resilience across cultures discussed in Chapter 13 attempts to achieve a similar balance between participation and credibility. Combining quantitative and qualitative methods in a way that considers both their philosophical and technical differences, as suggested by Morgan (1998), is one important feature of the International Resilience Project. Studies that are sensitive to cross-paradigm issues in their design share the advantages of a deeper engagement with the data and the potential to demonstrate that the results are not idiosyncratic to the method used.

Integrating qualitative and quantitative methods and employing them rigorously are not sufficient for making research relevant and empowering for youth.

Although the use of conventional research procedures facilitates validity claims based on the "quality of the craftsmanship," establishing "communicative and pragmatic validity" requires attention to the meaningful participation by youth and careful consideration of context. Kvale (2002) offers a distinction between these types of validity as a way of extending the conception of validity in the social sciences. Communicative validity refers to testing the validity of knowledge claim through a dialogue, whereas pragmatic validity focuses on the relevance of the knowledge for generating action and change.

Although participatory action research is equated with inclusive knowledge generation processes and the remedy of power inequities (Gaventa & Cornwall, 2001), it may not always be effective as an exclusive approach. Collaboration between youth and researchers to determine research questions and methodologies does not instantly erase the power differences between the two groups (for recent discussions of this issue, see, e.g., Gaventa & Cornwall, 2001; Low, Shelly, & O'Connor, 2000; Regehr, 2000). Unlike professionals, youth and, for that matter, most client groups, do not have an institutionalized group identity, with a body of knowledge and authority to help construct this identity. Thus, youth are not considered "expert witnesses," and the evidence they provide to inform professional practice can be easily disregarded as impressionistic, idiosyncratic, and subjective. As Ray and Mayan (2001) argue, "The public audience is purposefully excluded and discredited in the creation and utilization of evidence in health care" (p. 51).

To successfully deliver the message of youth to professionals and policymakers, we must facilitate communicative processes between those most informed about a particular problem and those who have to address it.

Academics are well positioned to mediate between the two groups and respond to the unmet needs of disadvantaged groups by taking on research that aims at social improvement (Greenwood & Levin, 2000). Such research does not have to make sacrifices in methodological and technical rigor or ignore participative and inclusive processes. The critique of participatory action research as being partisan and partial and as lacking objectivity and rigor is well documented. Although qualitative researchers in general, and action researchers in particular, are working hard to redefine objectivity, validity, and rigor, they are mainly talking to each other. As suggested by Gaventa and Cornwall (2001),

Empowerment through knowledge means not only challenging expertise with expertise, but it means expanding who participates in the knowledge production process in the first place.... When the process is open to include new voices, and new perspectives, the assumption is that policy deliberation will be more democratic, and less skewed by the resources and the knowledge of the more powerful. (p. 71)

If the message of youth is to be accepted by professionals and influence practice and social policy, it must not only be participatory and inclusive but also constructed through research processes that are considered legitimate and credible.

NOTE

1. One of the study's reports is on the list of key references for the national physiotherapy competency exam and in the Canadian Medical Association's InfoBase for clinical practice guidelines.

REFERENCES

Anthony, E. J., & Cohler, B. J. (Eds.). (1987). *The invulnerable child.* New York: Guilford.

Apfel, R. J., & Simon, B. (2000). Mitigating discontents with children in war: An ongoing psychoanalytic inquiry. In A. Robben & M. M. Suarez-Orozco (Eds.), *Cultures under siege: Collective violence and trauma* (pp. 102–130). New York: Cambridge University Press.

Boehnke, K. (1999). Is there social change? Photographs as a means of contrasting individual development and societal change in the new states of Germany. In R. K. Silbereisen & A. von Eye (Eds.), *Growing up in times of social change* (pp. 31–50). New York: Walter de Gruyter.

Cairns, R. B., & Cairns, B. D. (1994). *Lifelines and risks: Pathways of youth in our time.* Cambridge, England: Cambridge University Press.

Caputo, T. (1999). *Hearing the voices of youth: A review of research and consultation documents.* Ottawa, Ontario: Health Canada.

Cheatham, A., & Shen, E. (2003). Community based participatory research with Cambodian girls in

Long Beach, California: A case study. In M. Minkler & N. Wallerstein (Eds.), *Community-based participatory research for health* (pp. 316–331). San Francisco, CA: Jossey-Bass.

Cohen, L. H., Cimbolic, K., Armeli, S. R., & Hettler, T. R. (1998). Quantitative assessment of thriving. *Journal of Social Issues, 54*(2), 323–335.

Cook, D. J., & Michie, C. (2002). Towards valid cross-cultural measures of risk. In R. R. Corrado, R. Roesch, S. D. Hart, & J. K. Gierowski (Eds.), *Multi-problem violent youth: A foundation for comparative research on needs, interventions and outcomes* (pp. 241–250). Burke, VA: IOS Press.

De Antoni, C., & Koller, S. (2000). Vulnerability and resilience. A study with adolescents who had suffered intrafamilial maltreatment. *PSICO, 31*(1), 39–66.

Dupree, D., Spencer, M. B., & Bell, S. (1997). African American children. In G. Johnson-Powell & J. Yamamoto (Eds.), *Transcultural child development: Psychological assessment and treatment* (pp. 237–268). New York: John Wiley.

Epstein, M. H., & Sharma, J. M. (1998). *Behavioral and emotional rating scale (BERS).* Austin, TX: PRO-ED.

Felsman, J. K. (1989). Risk and resiliency in childhood: The lives of street children. In T. F. Dugan & R. Coles (Eds.), *The child in our times: Studies in the development of resiliency* (pp. 56–80). New York: Brunner/Mazel.

Fine, M. (1994). Working the hyphens: Reinventing self and other in qualitative research. In N. K. Denzin & Y. S. Lincoln (Eds.), *Handbook of qualitative research* (pp. 70–82). Thousand Oaks, CA: Sage.

Flom, B. L. (2002). Just don't shut the door on me: Aspirations and resilience characteristics of adolescents in day treatment (Doctoral dissertation, University of Minnesota, 2002). *Dissertation Abstracts International, 62*(10-B), 47–82.

Flyvbjerg, B. (2001). *Making social science matter.* Cambridge, England: Cambridge University Press.

Fraser, M. (Ed.). (1997). *Risk and resilience in childhood: An ecological perspective.* Washington, DC: NASW Press.

Galambos, N. L., & Leadbeater, B. J. (2000). Trends in adolescent research for the new millennium. *International Journal of Behavioral Development, 24*(3), 289–294.

Garbarino, J. (2001). Making sense of senseless youth violence. In J. M. Richman & M. W. Fraser (Eds.), *The context of youth violence: Resilience, risk, and protection* (pp. 83–95). Westport, CT: Praeger.

Gaventa, J., & Cornwall, A. (2001). Power and knowledge. In P. Reason & H. Bradbury (Eds.), *Handbook of action research* (pp. 70–80). London: Sage.

Gilgun, J. F. (1996). Human development and adversity in ecological perspective: Part 1. A conceptual framework. *Families in Society, 77*(7), 395–402.

Gilgun, J. F. (1999). Mapping resilience as process among adults with childhood adversities. In H. I. McCubbin, E. A. Thompson, A. I. Thompson, & J. A. Futrell (Eds.), *The dynamics of resilient families* (pp. 41–70). Thousand Oaks, CA: Sage.

Glantz, M. D., & Sloboda, Z. (1999). Analysis and reconceptualization of resilience. In M. D. Glantz & J. L. Johnson (Eds.), *Resilience and development: Positive life adaptations* (pp. 109–128). New York: Kluwer Academic/Plenum.

Graham, J. (2001). If meaning counted: Measuring e/affect in antidementia therapies. *Gerontology, 47*(Suppl 1), 572–573.

Graham, J., & Rockwood, K. (1998). Treatment expectations for Alzheimer's disease: The ACADIE study. *The Gerontologist, 38*(1), 99.

Greenwood, D. J., & Levin, M. (2000). Reconstructing the relationships between universities and society through action research. In N. K. Denzin & Y. S. Lincoln (Eds.), *Handbook of qualitative research* (2nd ed., pp. 85–106). Thousand Oaks, CA: Sage.

Hacking, I. (1999). *The social construction of what?* Cambridge, MA: Harvard University Press.

Hauser, S. T. (1999). Understanding resilient outcomes: Adolescent lives across time and generations. *Journal of Research on Adolescence, 9*(1), 1–24.

Hemmings, A. (2000). The "hidden" corridor curriculum. *High School Journal, 83*(2), 1–10.

Huang, L. N. (2003, March). *Improving access to care and outcomes for children from diverse racial and ethnic backgrounds and their families.* Plenary address, 16th Annual Research Conference, "A System of Care for Children's Mental Health: Expanding the Research Base," University of South Florida, Tampa.

Hughes, D. L., & Seidman, E. (2002). In pursuit of a culturally anchored methodology. In

T. A. Revenson, A. R. D'Augelli, S. E. French, D. Hughes, E. Seidman, M. Shinn, & H. Yoshikawa (Eds.), *Ecological research to promote social change: Methodological advances from community psychology* (pp. 243–255). New York: Kluwer.

Hunter, A. J., & Chandler, G. E. (1999). Adolescent resilience. *Image: Journal of Nursing Scholarship, 31*(3), 243–247.

Israel, B. A., Schulz, A. J., Parker., E. A., Becker, A. B., Allen, A. J. III, & Guzman, R. (2003). Critical issues in developing and following community-based participatory research principles. In M. Minkler & N. Wallerstein (Eds.), *Community-based participatory research for health* (pp. 53–76). San Francisco, CA: Jossey-Bass.

Johnson-Powell, G., & Yamamoto, J. (Eds.). (1997). *Transcultural child development: Psychological assessment and treatment.* New York: John Wiley.

Kaplan, H. B. (1999). Toward an understanding of resilience: A critical review of definitions and models. In M. D. Glantz & J. L. Johnson (Eds.), *Resilience and development: Positive life adaptations* (pp. 17–84). New York: Kluwer/Plenum.

Kemmis, S., & McTaggart, R. (2000). Participatory action research. In N. K. Denzin & Y. S Lincoln (Eds.), *Handbook of qualitative research* (2nd ed., pp. 567–605). Thousand Oaks, CA: Sage.

Klevens, J., & Roca, J. (1999). Nonviolent youth in a violent society: Resilience and vulnerability in the country of Colombia. *Violence and Victims, 14,* 311–322.

Kvale, S. (2002). The social construction of validity. In N. K. Denzin & Y. S. Lincoln (Eds.), *The qualitative inquiry reader* (pp. 299–325). Thousand Oaks, CA: Sage.

Larson, R., Verma, S., & Dworkin, J. (2002). Adolescent's family relationships in India: The daily family lives of Indian middle class teenagers. In J. J. Arnett (Ed.), *Readings on adolescence and emerging adulthood* (pp. 133–141). Upper Saddle River, NJ: Prentice Hall.

Lesko, N. (2001). *Act your age: A cultural construction of adolescence.* New York: Routledge Falmer.

Lightfoot, C. (1992). Constructing self and peer culture: A narrative perspective on adolescent risk taking. In L. T. Winegar & J. Valsiner (Eds.), *Children's development within social context* (Vol. 2, pp. 229–245). Hillsdale, NJ: Erlbaum.

Lincoln, Y. S., & Guba, E. G. (1985). *Naturalistic inquiry.* Beverly Hills, CA: Sage.

Low, J., Shelley, J., & O'Connor, M. (2000). Problematic success: An account of top-down participatory action research with women with multiple sclerosis. *Field Methods, 12*(1), 29–48.

Luthar, S. S. (1993). Annotation: Methodological and conceptual issues in research on childhood resilience. *Journal of Child Psychology and Psychiatry, 34*(4), 441–453.

Luthar, S. S., Cicchetti, D., & Becker, B. (2000). The construct of resilience: A critical evaluation and guidelines for future work. *Child Development, 71*(3), 543–562.

Luthar, S. S., & Zigler, E. (1991). Vulnerability and competence: A review of research on resilience in childhood. *American Journal of Orthopsychiatry, 61*(1), 6–22.

Magnus, K. B., Cowen, E. L., Wyman, P. A., Fagen, D. B., & Work, W. (1999). Correlates of resilient outcomes among highly stressed African-American and white urban children. *Journal of Community Psychology, 27*(4), 473–488.

Martineau, S. (1999). *Rewriting resilience: A critical discourse analysis of childhood resilience and the politics of teaching resilience to kids at risk.* Unpublished doctoral dissertation, University of British Columbia, Vancouver, BC.

Massey, S., Cameron, A., Ouellette, S., & Fine, M. (1998). Qualitative approaches to the study of thriving: What can be learned? *Journal of Social Issues, 54*(2), 337–355.

Masten, A. S. (2001). Ordinary magic: Resilience processes in development. *American Psychologist, 56*(3), 227–238.

McCubbin, H. I., Fleming, W. M., Thompson, A. I., Neitman, P., Elver, K. M., & Savas, S. A. (1998). Resiliency and coping in "at risk" African-American youth and their families. In H. I. McCubbin, E. A. Thompson, A. I. Thompson, & J. A. Futrell (Eds.), *Resiliency in African-American families* (pp. 287–328). Thousand Oaks, CA: Sage.

Miller, W., & Crabtree, B. F. (2000). Clinical research. In N. K. Denzin & Y. S. Lincoln (Eds.), *Handbook of qualitative research* (2nd ed., pp. 607–631). Thousand Oaks, CA: Sage.

Minkler, M., & Wallerstein, N. (2003). Introduction to community-based participatory research. In M. Minkler & N. Wallerstein (Eds.), *Community-based participatory research for health* (pp. 3–26). San Francisco, CA: Jossey-Bass.

Morgan, D. L. (1998). Practical strategies for combining qualitative and quantitative methods: Applications to health research. *Qualitative Health Research, 8*(3), 362–376.

Mpofu, E. (2002). Types and theories of aggression in an African setting: A Zimbabwean perspective. *International Society for the Study of Behavioural Development Newsletter, 2*(42), 10–13.

Nesselroade, J. R., & McCollam, K. M. (2000). Putting the process in developmental processes. *International Journal of Behavioral Development, 24*(3), 295–300.

Ohsako, T. (1999). The developing world. In P. K. Smith, Y. Morita, J. Junger-Tas, D. Olweus, R. Catalano, & P. Slee (Eds.), *The nature of school bullying: A cross national perspective* (pp. 359–375). New York: Routledge.

Painter, D. (2001). Social representations and aggression: On culture and the psychology of violence. In J. M. Ramirez & D. S. Richardson (Eds.), *Cross-cultural approaches to aggression and reconciliation* (pp. 205–213). Huntington, NY: Nova Science Publishers.

Rains, P., Teram, E., & Toutant, C. (2001). Young offenders: Balancing control and treatment. Special issue introduction. *Canadian Journal of Community Mental Health, 2(2),* 5–9.

Ray, L. D., & Mayan, M. (2001). Who decides what counts as evidence? In J. M. Morse, J. M. Swanson, & A. J. Kuzel (Eds.), *The nature of qualitative evidence* (pp. 50–73). Thousand Oaks, CA: Sage.

Regehr, C. (2000). Action research: Underlining or undermining the cause? *Social Work & Social Sciences Review, 8,* 194–206.

Richman, J. M., & Fraser, M. W. (2001). *The context of youth violence: Resilience, risk, and protection.* Westport, CT: Praeger.

Rodwell, M. K. (1998). *Social work constructivist research.* New York: Garland.

Rutter, M. (2001). Psychosocial adversity: Risk, resilience and recovery. In J. M. Richman & M. W. Fraser (Eds.), *The context of youth violence: Resilience, risk and protection* (pp. 13–41). Westport, CT: Praeger.

Salmivalli, C. (2001). Peer-led intervention campaign against school bullying: Who considered it useful, who benefited? *Educational Research, 43*(3), 263–278.

Salmivalli, C., Kaukiainen, A., Kaistaniemi, L., & Lagerspetz, K. M. J. (1999). Self-evaluated self-esteem and defensive egotism as predictors of adolescents' participation in bullying. *Personality and Psychology Bulletin, 25*(10), 1268–1278.

Schachter, C. L., Teram E., & Stalker, C. A. (2004). Integrating grounded theory and participatory research to develop sensitive practice with childhood sexual abuse survivors. In K. W. Hammell & C. Carpenter (Eds.), *Qualitative research in evidence-based rehabilitation* (pp. 77–88). Edinburgh: Harcourt.

Schofield, G. (2001). Resilience and family placement: A lifespan perspective. *Adoption & Fostering, 25*(3), 6–19.

Sharma, N., & Sharma, B. (1999). Children in difficult circumstances: Familial correlates of advantage while at risk. In T. S. Saraswathi (Ed.), *Culture, socialization and human development: Theory, research and applications in India* (pp. 398–418). Thousand Oaks, CA: Sage.

Silbereisen, R. K., & von Eye, A. (Eds.). (1999). *Growing up in times of social change.* New York: Walter de Gruyter.

Silverman, D. (2000). *Doing qualitative research: A practical handbook.* Thousand Oaks, CA: Sage.

Spencer, M. B. (1995). Old issues and new theorizing about African-American youth: A phenomenological variant of the ecological systems theory. In R. L. Taylor (Ed.), *Black youth: Perspectives on their status in the United States* (pp. 37–70). Westport, CT: Praeger.

Strauss, A., & Corbin, J. (1990). *Basics of qualitative research: Grounded theory procedures and techniques.* Newbury Park, CA: Sage.

Sutton, J., Smith, P. K., & Swettenham, J. (1999). Socially undesirable need not be incompetent: A response to Crick and Dodge. *Social Development, 8*(1), 132–134.

Taylor, J. M., Gilligan, C., & Sullivan, A. M. (1995). *Between voice and silence: Women and girls, race and relationship.* Cambridge, MA: Harvard University Press.

Teram, E., Schachter, C. L., & Stalker, C. A. (in press). The case for integrating grounded theory and participatory action research: Empowering clients to inform professional practice. *Qualitative Health Research.*

Thoits, P. (1995). Identity-relevant events and psychological symptoms: A cautionary tale. *Journal of Health and Social Behavior, 36*(1), 72–82.

Todis, B., Bullis, M., Waintrup, M. Schultz, R., & D'Ambrosio, R. (2001). Overcoming the odds:

Qualitative examination of resilience among formerly incarcerated adolescents. *Exceptional Children, 68*(1), 119–139.

Ungar, M. (2001a). Constructing narratives of resilience with high-risk youth. *Journal of Systemic Therapies, 20*(2), 58–73.

Ungar, M. (2001b). The social construction of resilience among problem youth in out-of-home placement: A study of health-enhancing deviance. *Child and Youth Care Forum, 30*(3), 137–154.

Ungar, M. (2001c). The unapologetic qualitative social work researcher: A critical look at research methods and questions. *Social Work and Social Sciences Review, 9*(2), 17–24.

Ungar, M. (2002). *Playing at being bad: The hidden resilience of troubled teens.* East Lawrencetown, Novia Scotia: Pottersfield Press.

Ungar, M. (2004a). A constructionist discourse on resilience: Multiple contexts, multiple realities among at-risk children and youth. *Youth and Society, 35*(1), 341–365.

Ungar, M. (2004b). *Nurturing hidden resilience in troubled youth.* Toronto, Ontario, Canada: University of Toronto Press.

Ungar, M., & Teram, E. (2000). Drifting towards mental health: High-risk adolescents and the process of empowerment. *Youth and Society, 32*(2), 228–252.

Ungar, M., Teram, E., & Picketts, J. (2001). Young offenders and their communities: Reframing the institution as an extension of the community. *Canadian Journal of Community Mental Health, 20*(2), 29–42.

Yamamoto, J., Silva, J. A., Ferrari, M., & Nukariya, K. (1997). Culture and psychopathology. In G. Johnson-Powell & J. Yamamoto (Eds.), *Transcultural child development: Psychological assessment and treatment* (pp. 34–60). New York: John Wiley.

Yellin, E. M., Quinn, M. M., & Hoffman, C. C. (1998). Heavy mettle: Stories of transition for delinquent youth. *Reaching Today's Youth, 4*(2), 4–8.

11

PSYCHOSOCIAL HEALTH IN YOUTH

An International Perspective

JOHN C. LEBLANC

PAMELA J. TALBOT

WENDY M. CRAIG

In this chapter, we will address the question, "How are the world's children and youth faring with regard to their psychosocial health?" Although at first glance this question is straightforward, it requires careful dissection and definition. There are no universally accepted definitions of psychosocial health, nor are there standard ways of measuring this concept even in one culture at one point of time. Measuring change in psychosocial health requires definitions that hold their meaning over time and across cultures. Such measurements of health over time and across cultures are most amenable to epidemiological methods with emphasis on (a) generalizability, the extent to which sample results can be extrapolated to the population of interest; (b) reliability, the extent to which repeated measures yield the same result; and (c) validity, the extent to which measures actually measure what they purport to measure. Qualitative methods deliver rich data but do not aim to find results that can be generalized to a population from which the research participants are a particular sample.

First, we will discuss psychosocial health and our choice of positive youth development as a conceptual model for psychosocial health. Second, we will discuss the difficulties inherent in measuring the multidimensional concept of psychosocial health across cultures. Third, we will highlight measures of psychosocial health in youth using national and international data and comment on the strengths and limitations of these resources. Finally, we will suggest potential directions for future research to assist with tracking changes in psychosocial health of children and youth. Through this work, we demonstrate that despite many studies and theories to explain children's well-being, we actually have done little globally that allows us to either track *health* phenomena or compare *health* outcomes associated with resilience across child populations. The bulk of the work in this area of epidemiology has been related to documenting the prevalence of disease and disorder. An epidemiological approach to documenting health factors, although holding promise to deepen our understanding of the risks and resilience factors affecting children, still requires further development and much wider application if it is to inform theory and intervention.

One factor that facilitates optimal development of children in the face of adversity is superior psychosocial health. In this context, psychosocial health can be defined as a broad group of psychological assets that insulate "at-risk" youth from, or buffer the effects of, adverse life circumstances. As other chapters in this volume show, this state of psychosocial health is one component of resilience. These intrinsic psychosocial assets are shaped by the person's environment and express themselves through that environment. In a recently published book on child well-being, Eccles et al. noted that the changing social and cultural climate in the United States has been marked by a substantial increase in the number and variety of risk factors that young people are exposed to (Eccles, Templeton, Barber, & Stone, 2003). In light of this changing social milieu, the assessment and enhancement of psychosocial health in youth is of paramount importance.

CHALLENGES IN DESCRIBING DISEASE AND HEALTH

In 1946, the World Health Organization (WHO) defined health as "a state of complete physical, mental and social wellbeing and not merely the absence of disease or infirmity" (WHO, 1946). This definition is unchanged to the present, and although other definitions of health exist, it remains one of the most succinct and useful. There is broad consensus on definitions of specific physical and mental illnesses. There has been a century-long evolution behind the almost universally accepted and used International Classification of Diseases, now in its 10th revision (ICD-10) (WHO, 1992). ICD-10 specifies diagnostic criteria for almost all physical and mental conditions. With respect to mental illness, it disagrees only in minor details with the other widely used manual, the *Diagnostic and Statistical Manual of Mental Disorders* (*DSM-IV-TR*) (American Psychiatric Association, 2000).

Our focus is on psychosocial health, those aspects of well-being related to one's intrinsic psychological state and one's relationships with other human beings and social institutions. Psychosocial health has been defined negatively as the absence of negative characteristics of illness and positively as the presence of self-efficacy, cognitive abilities, social skills, healthy emotional states, and resiliency. Unfortunately, ICD-10 and other disease classification systems do not address positive constructs of well-being and development, and there are no analogous classification systems for psychosocial health or even agreement as to its essential components. An investigator who wishes to measure positive psychosocial health must construct a definition that pertains to his or her specific work and risk missing domains believed to be important by other investigators. Consequently, comparison of psychosocial health causal factors, correlates, and outcomes across studies is subject to bias and opinion as readers attempt to reconcile results based on different definitions.

This lack of agreement with respect to characteristics of psychosocial health compounds difficulties with respect to its measurement. First, should psychosocial health be measured by functional indicators (e.g., rates of participation in social life, employment, marriage, relationships with others)? Second, to what extent should psychosocial health measures reflect intrinsic characteristics of attitudes and belief, confidence, competence, or feelings of self-worth? Third, should psychosocial health be depicted by both positive and negative measures, so-called asset-based and risk-based approaches? A comprehensive assessment of psychosocial health could include all the above but should do so without being unwieldy and with appropriate attention to weighting of different elements. Current descriptions of psychosocial health, then, including the present chapter, require clear specification of the theoretical framework and tools used to assess it.

POSITIVE YOUTH DEVELOPMENT AS A CONCEPTUAL MODEL FOR PSYCHOSOCIAL HEALTH

Our intention here is to highlight positive characteristics about an individual and his or her relationships rather than risk behaviors, such as substance abuse or aggression. This focus is not to diminish the importance of risk-based assessments. Understanding of risk factors for poor outcomes and high-risk behaviors has been, and will continue to be, critical to the development and evaluation of effective prevention programs. However, compared with asset-based assessments (i.e., measures of positive attributes), risk-based measures tend to address psychosocial health by measuring the *absence* of negative characteristics rather than the *presence* of positive characteristics. To date, asset-based assessments are much less common than risk-based assessments. An effective asset-based perspective includes questions that reflect the strengths that youth possess, such as engagement in one's community, degree of closeness to others, and degree of sharing and helping behavior. Thus, this perspective identifies traits in children and youth that reflect optimal psychosocial health. A comprehensive definition of psychosocial health would necessarily be multidimensional, with measures that reflect underlying constructs, function, and both positive and negative states and traits. We need commonly accepted definitions of psychosocial health and its underlying constructs as well as reliable and valid tools to measure these. With few exceptions, those concerned with assessing the psychosocial health of children and youth have had to blaze their own trail forward.

The Positive Youth Development Model of Psychosocial Health

The quantitative assessment of psychosocial health of youth requires, first, that researchers, policymakers, and professionals who work with youth agree on most elements that constitute psychosocial health and, ideally, a model that ties these elements together. Two such formulations include the 40 developmental assets promoted by the Search Institute and the "positive youth development" (PYD) model. The Search Institute is an American nonprofit organization that conducts research, publishes findings, and hosts conferences that support the healthy development of children and adolescents. It has developed a framework of 40 positive youth development assets, 20 of which are considered internal to the young person and are considered to reflect positive internal growth and development and 20 that reflect positive and nurturing experiences derived from the world in which youth live. The internal assets fall into four categories: commitment to learning, positive values, social competencies, and positive identity.[1]

Since the mid 1990s, many researchers have formulated the (PYD) conceptual framework, which stresses the support of youth before problems arise rather than responses to existing crises, such as delinquency, substance abuse, violence, unintended pregnancy, school truancy, and others (Catalano, Berglund, Ryan, Lonczak, & Hawkins, 2002). The PYD perspective is that of the "person-in-environment" in which youth development depends on intrinsic characteristics; socializing influences of family, peers, and other relationships; and the standards and values of a youth's community and culture (Bronfenbrenner, 1979). Accordingly, the healthy and successful development of young people is realized through the adaptive regulation of person-context relations. Thriving youth exhibit not only the absence of negative behaviors but also the presence of positive development (Lerner, 2002, 2004). A popular and parsimonious conceptualization of PYD is the "five Cs": Competence, Confidence, Character, social Connection, and Caring or compassion (Eccles et al., 2003; Roth & Brooks-Gunn, 2003a, 2003b). These Cs are regarded as healthy outcomes, just as characteristics antithetical to these five attributes (e.g., negative self-regard, abusive or manipulative social relationships, and the absence of integrity) are examples of unfavorable outcomes. Youth who exhibit these characteristics of positive development tend to possess an orientation to Contribute to their community. Lerner has called this the "sixth C" of positive youth development (Lerner, 2002, 2004), although contribution to the community is also seen as a manifestation of caring.

Resilience is an important concept within the PYD framework that is not explicitly captured within the five Cs. Resilience has been defined as "patterns that protect children from adopting problem behaviors in the face of risk" (National Research Council & Institute of Medicine, 1996). Youth who possess positive characteristics in the face of past or present adversity can contribute much to our understanding of how to promote positive youth development in adverse circumstances. Ideally, we would like to describe not only characteristics of positive youth development but also environmental characteristics, both nurturing and destructive, in which that development occurs. Such knowledge of environmental characteristics can lead to the development of effective prevention programs that affect the environment as well as the youth within that environment. Catalano et al., (2002) reviewed 25 youth development programs that met criteria for being "effective" with respect to altering at least one PYD construct. Although resilience was discussed in 12 of these programs, it was in the text of the evaluation with no clear description of how it was actually measured.

The Catalano et al. (2002) review illustrates the lack of defined, universally agreed-on, quantitative measures of resilience. Studies that could provide that information must simultaneously measure psychosocial health and functioning as well as risk and protective factors for psychosocial health. They must include at least one follow-up assessment to establish a temporal relationship between putative factors and outcomes. Many of the resilience measures that have been developed and used in longitudinal studies have been developed using adult respondents, with one notable exception—the Resiliency Scale of Jew, Green, and Kroger (1999). The measurement of trends in resilience would require the use of a standardized instrument such as the Child and Youth Resilience Measure being developed by Ungar and his colleagues (see Chapter 13, this volume) or the resiliency assessment and evaluation protocol from Resiliency Canada.[2] Later chapters in this volume address this very issue by examining practices related to promoting resilience.

In summary, assessing positive psychosocial health remains elusive and is in marked contrast with clinical disease outcomes where there are international standardized instruments, such as the ICD mentioned above, or instruments that focus on a specific condition, such as the Beck Depression Inventory (Beck, Ward, Mendelson, Mock, & Erbaugh, 1961). A strong advantage of the PYD model with its five Cs (and the sixth C of a young person's contribution to community) is that it is parsimonious, backed by empirical evidence (Catalano et al., 2002), and therefore can serve as a strong theoretical foundation to guide the development of more focused, reliable, and valid assessment tools.

Ideal Qualities of Instruments Designed to Measure Positive Youth Development

Constructs such as "competence" that are seen as fundamental characteristics of PYD must be measured with instruments that meet several requirements. The most important is the establishment of validity. Validity is commonly partitioned into content, construct, and criterion validity (Fletcher, Fletcher, & Wagner, 1996, pp. 22–23). Content (also known as "face") validity implies that the domain of interest is adequately captured by the individual items in an instrument. Construct validity implies that a measure is capturing to some extent the underlying, and unmeasurable, psychological construct or characteristic. By definition, there is no gold standard in this case; one must rely on agreement with other accepted measures of the underlying construct. For example, there is no single description or measure of intelligence; rather, there exist general (or broad-band) and specific (or narrow-band) measures that focus on specific cognitive, executive, knowledge, and memory skills. There is potential confounding in the measurement of the underlying construct and its manifestation, especially when measured simultaneously as in cross-sectional surveys. For example, is competence the outcome of someone who is psychosocially healthy, or is competence an intrinsic quality that results in psychosocial health? Measurement of competence through evaluation of cognitive and emotional abilities does not distinguish which is the underlying construct and which is its manifestation. Criterion validity implies that the proposed measure correlates with an external, accepted, and measurable criterion, called a "gold standard." For example, visual confirmation of a wound infection can be confirmed by growing an organism in a laboratory from a sample taken from the wound. The criterion or gold standard for self-administered questionnaires that ask youth about their involvement in community activities would be the assessment of actual attendance records for these activities. Unfortunately, such gold standards for characteristics such as competence or caring are rare.

To be useful, a valid measure must also be (a) reliable, the extent to which a measure repeatedly administered will yield the same result; (b) responsive, the extent to which the measure changes when that which is measured changes; and (c) meaningful or interpretable. For example, a score of 65 on an instrument that measures caring must be interpretable to the user and not be an arbitrary number with no point of reference. Comparisons over time imply that measures and concepts of mental health conditions must have relatively stable meanings over time. Over a few years, descriptions of mental health conditions are unlikely to change substantially. However, one study that spans 40 years illustrates change in understanding and measurement of mental health conditions. The Stirling County study, a landmark mental health survey conducted in Atlantic Canada in 1952, 1970, and 1992, demonstrated the change in language used to describe depression. The phrase used exclusively in the 1952 survey was "poor spirits." In the two later surveys, "feeling low and hopeless" was added. The prevalence of poor spirits decreased in 1992 in spite of unchanging prevalence of depression over the 40-year study period, whereas the prevalence of feeling low and hopeless increased. The investigators attributed this change in the rate of poor spirits to a change in language describing depression (Murphy, Laird, Monson, Sobol, & Leighton, 2000).

SOURCES OF PSYCHOSOCIAL HEALTH DATA

Instruments to Measure Psychosocial Health

Currently, no instrument measures all attributes of positive youth development with known reliability and validity. However, many narrow-band instruments focus on one of the five Cs separately, such as the Harter Social Competence Scale (Harter, 1982) and the Eisenberg Empathy Scale (Zhou, Valiente, & Eisenberg, 2003). In terms of broad-band instruments that assess psychosocial health comprehensively, the Search Institute has developed survey instruments that assess 40 developmental assets at different ages.[3] The UK Strengths and Difficulties Questionnaire (SDQ) contains 25 questions, phrased both positively and negatively, that assess the following domains: emotional symptoms, conduct problems, hyperactivity/inattention, peer relationship problems, and prosocial behavior. Although primarily designed as a screening instrument for mental health conditions, it has the virtue of assessing strengths such as prosocial behavior in addition to difficulties (Goodman, 2004). By design, these broad-band instruments will tap into more than one domain of psychosocial health, but there is no consensus as to the relative importance of these domains and the ability of individual questions to reflect a particular domain. Consequently, youth who perceive themselves as high or low in one particular domain may see themselves quite differently in terms of their overall psychosocial health.

As in the case of clinical assessment tools, self- versus third-party reports or observations provide different information and require different resources. Many of the five Cs assessed in large surveys use self-administered instruments because these are feasible and much less expensive than using other sources of information, such as assessments by educators, family members, and friends. Use of these instruments also facilitates comparisons over time and across countries that would be difficult to obtain any other way. However, self-administered tools do have limitations. First, research participants must have a certain level of cognitive and literary skills to successfully complete the instrument, and the instrument has to be tailored to target age groups. As a result, the number and content of the items are limited compared with multi-informant designs in which many data can be collected from observers of young and cognitively impaired participants. Second, responses from self-administered instruments may be biased if respondents have an inflated view of their own psychosocial health or are in a state of denial about major underlying disorders. Respondents may not be entirely truthful; for example, high-risk behaviors may be underreported. Such bias may be less important when comparing across countries or over time in the same country because the biases will likely be in the same direction and have similar magnitudes. For example, respondents in most countries or time periods may underreport high-risk sexual behavior, but if respondents in two surveys being compared underreport to the same degree, the biases will cancel each other out. Unfortunately, it is extremely difficult to execute studies that measure bias and its variation across time and place and that can therefore measure the magnitude (or lack thereof) of such biases. Third, information from self-reports lacks the rich detail of a personal interview because practical limits to instrument size restrict the number of questions that can address important domains.

On the other hand, self-report questionnaires can provide valuable insights into respondents' self-perceptions and relationships with friends and family that might not be forthcoming through observation or interview. As well, single-informant data can be supplemented by information obtained through interviewing respondents, their peers, teachers, and families and through linking data with available routinely collected data, such as school disciplinary reports or records of participation in community activities. Examples of public sources of routinely collected data come from the education system (standardized academic achievement scores, school completion rates, truancy, disciplinary referral, and suspension rates), the health system (mental health diagnoses, intentional injuries, suicide), social services (child maltreatment and foster home placements), and the justice system (property damage and violent crime rates). However, the advantages of data being readily available and having large representative samples must be balanced against the variable quality of the measures themselves, the predominant focus of most routinely collected data on risks rather than assets, and the confounding of the measurement of the characteristic with the response of the system. For example,

violent crime rates reflect the interaction between the actions of those convicted; the social definition of the crime itself, which can vary over time; and the response of the justice system, which can alter the resources targeted to particular crimes depending on political and public needs.

Formally Administered Serial Cross-Sectional Surveys

Formally administered serial cross-sectional surveys, although costly and difficult to fund long-term, allow one to specify content, control quality, and characteristics of the study sample that facilitate generalizability. To allow comparisons over time, however, they should contain the same core questions and should use a similar sample selection protocol. The Youth Risk Behavior Surveillance System (YRBSS) developed by the Centers for Disease Control (CDC) in the United States is a well-known example. Starting in 1991, a questionnaire concerning substance abuse, sexuality, violence, and other risk factors has been administered every 2 years to a nationally representative sample of secondary school students (CDC, 2004).

Challenges in Assessing Change Over Time

Addressing the question, "How are youth faring over time?" requires different approaches depending on whether one wants to follow the same cohort as its members develop over time or compare cohorts of the similar ages at different points in time. In several longitudinal surveys, such as the Dunedin project (Caspi, Moffitt, Newman, & Silva, 1996), the Pittsburgh Youth Study (Loeber et al., 2001), and the Montréal Longitudinal Survey (Nagin & Tremblay, 2001), cohorts have been followed for a decade or more. Although providing excellent insight about social development and relevant causal and correlational factors, these studies do not provide insight into whether youth in general are better or worse in, say, the year 2004 versus the year 1994. This question requires the use of common measures applied to similar cohorts at different times. None of these studies assembled new cohorts while continuing to collect data on already recruited, and aging, cohorts.

The Canadian National Longitudinal Survey of Children and Youth is an excellent example of a cross-sequential survey with a longitudinal component in which core questions have been constant from 1994 to the present. Because a subsample of participants are followed longitudinally and new participants are enrolled every 2 years, researchers are able to describe age, period, and cohort effects and to describe changes in prevalence of risk behaviors over approximately one decade of data collection (Human Resources Development Canada, 2001).

Comparisons Across Countries and Cultures

Comparison across countries and cultures provides a different set of challenges, including assumptions that characteristics such as confidence and competence have similar meanings in different cultures and that instruments can be translated accurately enough to allow for such comparisons. For example, the authors of the 1993–94 report from WHO's Health Behaviour in School-Aged Children Survey (HBSCS) note that some concepts translate well, such as smoking or brushing your teeth, but psychosocial concepts such as loneliness and depression can be impossible to translate (King et al., 1996). Even when the translation itself is literally accurate, cultural differences may well influence answering of certain questions because of strong cultural taboos against certain activities or different perceptions of relationships between individuals, families, and communities. Comparisons of country-to-country data require careful assessment of the differences in beliefs and practices among the relevant cultures.

In summary, single-informant, cross-sectional surveys provide insights into psychosocial health over time and across countries that cannot be feasibly obtained in any other way even if these insights are incomplete and possibly biased. We therefore present data from several large epidemiological studies that compare the five Cs of positive youth development across countries and over time.

MEASURES OF POSITIVE YOUTH DEVELOPMENT AMONG THE WORLD'S YOUTH

Methodology

The criteria for selecting studies were that (a) they be population or school based, (b) they assess assets relevant to PYD, (c) they are focused on preadolescents and adolescents, (d) they are repeated over time, and (e) each cycle or wave uses similar sampling methodology and at least some constant core questions. We searched the electronic databases PsycInfo, the Web of Science, and the U.S. National Library of Medicine, using general Internet search engines to find these databases.

Table 11.1 lists the principal available studies that address psychosocial health in youth. The first, WHO's HBSC, assesses psychosocial health broadly and in several countries. Starting in 1983 and repeated every 4 years, 11-, 13- and 15-year-old students in approximately 30 countries completed questionnaires dealing with school, relationships with parents and peers, psychosocial resources, physical health and activity, nutrition, injury, and substance use.[4] Because of its standardized questions, use since 1983, and international scope, this survey is by far the most useful in providing insights into psychosocial health across cultures and over time.

The second source is the Youth Risk Behavior Surveillance System (YRBSS) from the American CDC (2004) described above. Its core questions do not address assets related to PYD, although some participating jurisdictions have added their own questions. For example, 12 U.S. states supplemented the risk-based questions of the 2003 national survey with at least one question that addressed PYD (Kann, 2004). In 2001, the Vermont Department of Health added questions that dealt with positive attributes such as academic competence, participation in the community, and volunteerism (Department of Health, 2001). These positive attributes are reported here. The third source is the Canadian National Longitudinal Survey of Children and Youth (NLSCY), which as of 2000–01 included 27,000 children followed longitudinally and 9,500 households sampled

(Text continues on page 176)

Table 11.1   Sources of Data for Assessing Psychosocial Trends in Children and Youth

Survey Name & Description	Design Attributes	Measures of Positive Youth Development	Strengths & Limitations
Health Behaviour in School-Aged Children (HBSC) – WHO (www.hbsc.org/publications/reports.html) 11-, 13-, & 15-year-old students 36 nations **Content:** school experience, relationship with parents, relationship with peers, psychosocial resources, physical health, physical activity, nutrition, injury, substance use	• Cross-sectional survey • Cluster sampling strategy • Self-administered questionnaire • 1983–4, 1985–6 cycle & every 4 years thereafter	**Competence:** student perception of personal academic achievement **Connection:** to family members **Confidence:** items such as "I feel confident making friends" as well as items about body image, self-confidence, acceptance by peers and teachers	**Strengths** • Excellent for tracking secular trends because the same core questions have been used repeatedly over past 20 years **Limitations** • In-school sample excludes early school leavers and underrepresents youth with poor attendance • Unknown response bias due to dependence on a single self-administered questionnaire • Cross-sectional design does not permit examination of causal relationships
Youth Risk Behavior Survey – CDC (www.cdc.gov/HealthyYouth/yrbs/index.htm) Students in Grades 9–12 United States: national, state, and local surveys **Content:** physical activity, nutrition, injury, violence, substance use, risky sexual behaviors, mood	• Cross-sectional • Cluster sampling • Representative • Self-administered questionnaire • 2-year cycles beginning in 1991	None, although one can determine rates for absence of negative factors such as dysthymia, violent or risky behavior **Vermont 2001 survey only:** Academic **competence**, participation in community activity and volunteerism	**Strengths** • Vermont 2001 state questionnaire added several questions about assets **Limitations** • No specific core questions about assets • In-school sample excludes early school leavers and underrepresents youth with poor attendance • Unknown response bias due to dependence on a single self-administered questionnaire • Cross-sectional design does not permit examination of causal relationships

Survey Name & Description	Design Attributes	Measures of Positive Youth Development	Strengths & Limitations
National Longitudinal Survey of Children and Youth – Canada (www.statcan.ca/english/sdds/4450.htm) In 2000/01, 27,000 children followed longitudinally and 9,500 households with cross-sectional profiles. Children from birth through adolescence. Started in 1994 with approximately 23,000 children in 13,000 households. Informants: parents/guardians, youth age 11 and up, school staff **Content:** school experience, family formation & background, expectations for future, relationships, risky behaviors, sexual behaviors, health & health practices, living environment, hope for the future	• Longitudinal & cross-sectional (new birth cohort added at each cycle) • Nationally representative sample • 2-year cycles beginning in 1994	**Competence:** perception of academic ability **Connection:** questions about quantity and quality of friendships, quality of family relationships, involvement in community activities **Confidence:** self-esteem, body image, self-efficacy **Caring:** volunteerism, sympathy for others, help someone who is hurt or who is having difficulty with a task	**Strengths** • Household sample captures early school leavers and youth with poor attendance • Not limited to self-report data only—youth, parents, teachers, and school principals supply information • Longitudinal design allows for examination of causal pathways **Limitations** • Poor compliance rate for school staff informants
National Longitudinal Survey of Youth 1997 – US Dept. of Labor (http://stats.bls.gov/nls/nlsy97.htm) 9,000 individuals 12–16 years of age by December 31, 1996 United States	• Longitudinal • Nationally representative sample and an oversample of African American and Hispanic youth	**Competence:** objective measures of academic achievement such as SAT, ACT, AP, PIAT, and school grades; plans for future education (i.e., college, university, etc.)	**Strengths** • Sample not school based, thus captures early school leavers and youth with poor attendance • Includes questions about home and school environment, which enables researchers to establish a context within which respondents are developing

(Continued)

173

Table 11.1 (Continued)

Survey Name & Description	Design Attributes	Measures of Positive Youth Development	Strengths & Limitations
Content: standardized achievement tests; school experience; employment history; family formation & background; expectations for future, attitudes about relationships, social systems, & religious experience; risk behaviors' sexual behaviors; health & health practices; living environment; major life events	• Interviewed annually • First cohort assembled in 1979, second in 1997	**Connection:** items about relationships with parents and participation in organized religion, organized sports, clubs, and extracurricular activities **Caring:** volunteerism	**Limitations** • Only two cohorts sampled
National Longitudinal Survey of Adolescent Health (Add Health) (www.cpc.unc.edu/projects/addhealth) Students in Grades 7–12 United States **Content:** relationship with peers, psychosocial resources, expectations for future, health & health service use, mental health, sexual health & behavior, physical activity, nutrition, injury, violence, delinquent behavior, substance use, risk behavior, runaway	• Longitudinal & cross-sectional • Stratified sampling • Self-administered in-school questionnaire, in-home follow-up interview, parent questionnaire, & school administrator questionnaire • 3 waves: 1994–5, 1996, & 2001–2	**Competence:** items assessing academic competence (grades in English, science, math, history, social studies, and language arts) and social competence **Connection:** items about quality of relationships with parents, relationships with siblings and peers, participation in extracurricular activities, and feelings of belonging at school **Confidence:** items about liking self, feeling proud of self, and having good qualities	**Strengths** • Not limited to self-report data only—youth, parents, and school administrators supply information **Limitations** • In-school sample excludes early school leavers and underrepresents youth with poor attendance

Survey Name & Description	Design Attributes	Measures of Positive Youth Development	Strengths & Limitations
Monitoring the Future (www.monitoringthefuture.org) Students in Grades 8, 10, & 12; college students; and young adults The European School Survey Project on Alcohol and Other Drugs – (ESPAD) is modeled after this survey and takes place in 30 European countries. It can be accessed via this Web site. **Content:** Substance use, beliefs & attitudes about substances & substance use	• Longitudinal & cross-sectional • Multistage random sampling • Self-administered questionnaire	None	**Strengths** • Mixed design allows for the examination of secular trends, developmental trajectories, and causal pathways • Design allows for the separation of age, period, and cohort effects • Items periodically updated such as to reflect current drug scene while maintaining original core items • Over 25 years of data **Limitations** • Focus is solely on substance use and related issues • In-school sample excludes early school leavers and underrepresents youth with poor attendance

cross-sectionally through surveys conducted every 2 years starting in 1994 (Human Resources Development Canada, 2001). As described in the table, it does have many questions related to positive youth development such as competence, connection, confidence, and caring, but these are not available in summary documents and would have required primary analyses of the data sets. Although aggregate data can be downloaded, investigators who wish to conduct individual-level analyses must apply for permission to do so and are restricted to conducting their analyses inside carefully controlled data centers situated in major Canadian cities. The fourth source is the American National Longitudinal Survey of Youth, a nationally representative sample of 9,000 individuals aged 12 to 16 (U.S. Department of Labor, 2004). It follows two cohorts annually, the first one having been assembled in 1979 and the second in 1997. It has questions dealing with competence, connection, and caring. A major strength is that it is not school based and therefore it captures early school leavers and youth with poor attendance. The fifth source is the American National Longitudinal Survey of Adolescent Health, known informally as Add Health (UNC Carolina Population Center, 2004). This survey sampled cohorts of students in Grades 7 to 12 three times between 1994 and 2002. It has several questions dealing with competence, connection, and confidence. A major strength is that it is not limited to self-reports but gathers data from parents and school administrators.

The Monitoring the Future project (Johnston, O'Malley, Bachman, & Schulenberg, 2003) is an example of an excellent study that unfortunately focused solely on risk behaviors. It has used the same core questions for 25 years, and a new cohort is recruited every few years and then followed longitudinally. A European version, known as the European School Survey Project on Alcohol and Other Drugs (ESPAD) has been administered in 30 countries (Johnston, Bachman, O'Malley, Schulenberg, & Wallace, 2004). Both the American parent and its European offspring focus solely on attitudes toward and use of licit and illicit substances by adolescents; neither survey measures relevant attributes of positive youth development.

We chose the HBSC reports as our primary source of data because only these reports gave both international and cross-sectional data collected over several years. All other surveys were limited to only one nation (NLSCY to Canada, YRBS to the United States). We used the HBSC whenever possible and used the other surveys only when a specific "C" was not addressed in the HBSC. Stating results for the approximately 30 participating countries would have created verbose tables and figures, and the results are available from the original report. We therefore concentrated on countries that were representative of regions and that participated over several years. Canada and the United States were both selected to represent North America, Greece for Mediterranean countries, Israel for Middle Eastern countries, Russia for Asian countries, Scotland for the United Kingdom (there were no results for England in 1993/4 survey), Portugal alternating with Spain for southern European countries (neither country participated in all surveys), Switzerland for Western Europe, and Sweden for Scandinavia. Unfortunately, there were no participating countries from Africa, Asia (excepting Russia), Oceania, or Central and South America in either HBSC international report that we cite.

For each survey, we selected specific questions that addressed four of the five Cs of PYD: competence, connection, confidence, and caring. We did not cover character because it was not addressed in any of the surveys. For the HBSC, we created a graph or table for each selected question that contained the percentage responses during the 1993–94 survey (King, Wold, Tudor-Smith, & Harel, 1996) and the 1997–98 survey (WHO, 2000).

Results

Competence

The first of five Cs of psychosocial health is *competence*, which can be defined as possessing the intellectual, social, and behavioral skills necessary to successfully navigate through life (Lerner, Fisher, & Weinberg, 2000). In this section, we will examine international and temporal trends, using a number of available indicators that tap into the concept of competence.

Intellectual competence is an important component of psychosocial health that is commonly assessed through measures of literacy, numeracy, and knowledge. Academic competence influences the future of youth through its close association with academic placement and later academic and career opportunities (Plank & MacIver, 2003). Unfortunately, this important aspect of youth development has not been well measured by the major nationally representative surveys mentioned above. For example, the HBSC survey includes questions about students' perceptions of their academic success, but it does not include objective measures of academic competence such as grades and high school completion. However, trends in science and mathematics performance have been monitored in approximately 50 countries in a survey that began in 1995 and repeated every 4 years. This is known as the Trends in International Mathematics and Science Study (TIMSS) (International Association for the Evaluation of Educational Achievement [IEA], 2003). A report from the U.S. National Center for Health Statistics summarized changes from 1995 to 1999 in Grade 8 mathematics and science achievement for 23 countries. For mathematics, only 4 countries had statistically different results across time; 3 countries showed an improvement (Canada, Cyprus, and Latvia), and 1 country experienced a decline (the Czech Republic). Similarly, for science outcomes, 18 of the 23 countries reported no change; Canada, Latvia, Lithuania, and Hungary reported increases; and Bulgaria reported a decline (U.S. Department of Education, 2000).

Competence is defined as the skills required to initiate and maintain social relationships. The HBSC asks young people if it is easy or difficult for them to make new friends. Cross-national results from the 1993–94 and 1997–98 HBSC surveys indicate that regardless of age, sex, or nationality, the majority of youth found it easy or very easy to make new friends. Spanish youth fared best in the 1993–94 survey, with no less than 90% of males and at least 85% of females reporting that they made new friends easily (Table 11.2). Spanish results were not available for the 1997–98 survey. In 1997–98, Portugal had the highest proportion (≥ 85%) of youth reporting a sense of competence in initiating new friendships. With respect to temporal trends, the proportion of youth who reported that it was easy or very easy to initiate new friendships was similar in 1993–94 and 1997–98. Russia, however, was an exception; the proportion of Russian youth who found it easy or very easy to form new friendships increased substantially from 14% in 1993–94 to 22% in 1997–98. An increase also occurred among Swiss males, with the proportion rising from 61% in 1993–94 to 78% in 1997–98. The sex differences for making new friends were relatively small (< 10%) for all countries and both surveys.

Connection

The second C of healthy psychosocial growth is *connection*—a feeling of belonging. Important connections in the lives of youth include those with parents, peers, school personnel, and members of the greater community. Trends in young people's connectedness in each of these arenas will be discussed, drawing on data collected through the HBSC survey.

A feeling of connectedness with one's family fosters an environment in which young people can comfortably discuss their problems with one or both parents. A core question of the HBSC survey, reported in Table 11.3, assesses the ease with which young people feel they can "talk about things that really bother them" with their parents. The majority (> 60%) of youth regardless of age, sex, or nationality indicated that they were able to discuss problems with their mothers. However, the proportion of young people who held the same belief about their fathers was much lower, especially among females. For example, Israel ranked highest for the proportion of 13-year-old females who could easily or very easily discuss things that bothered them with their mothers (88%) and with their fathers (63%). For 13-year-old boys, Israel was second only to Sweden for the proportion of youth who could easily discuss problems with either parent. These proportions were much less divergent than those for 13-year-old females, with 89% of boys reporting ease discussing issues with mothers and 77% with fathers.

The proportion of young people who felt they could discuss their problems with either parent

Table 11.2   Percentage of 13-Year-Olds Who Answered That It Was "Easy" or "Very Easy" to Make New Friends: By Sex, Age, and Nationality

Country	The Health of Youth: A Cross-National Survey (1993–94)		Health and Health Behavior Among Young People (1997–98)	
	Males	Females	Males	Females
Canada	80	82	81	81
Greece	—	—	83	83
Israel	87	85	82	81
Portugal	—	—	89	89
Russia[a]	60	64	69	73
Scotland	83	81	82	85
Spain	91	85	—	—
Sweden	85	82	86	86
Switzerland	76	81	79	77
United States	—	—	84	86

a. Includes only St. Petersburg and district.

declined with increasing age (King et al., 1996). At least 80% of 11-year-old males and females reported that they could easily or very easily talk about problems with their mothers. By 15 years of age, the majority of these proportions fell to 60% to 70%. The trend among fathers was similar.

We compared changes from 1993–94 to 1997–98. For most countries, the proportion of youth who felt it easy to discuss problems with their parents remained stable over time for both males and females—no difference exceeded 10% except for Israeli students. Among Israeli youth, there was a sharp decline in the proportion of young people who could easily discuss things that bothered them with their mothers, especially among 13-year-olds. Among this age group, the proportion dropped from 89% to 78% for males and from 88% to 76% for females for the 1993–94 and 1997–98 surveys respectively (Table 11.3).

There were no substantial sex-related differences for the proportion of youth who felt it easy to very easy to discuss their problems with their mothers—no difference exceeded 10%. However, the same was not true of the proportion of youth who reported it was easy or very easy to discuss things that bothered them with

their fathers. Here, the proportions were higher for males than females. The largest difference was found in Russia, where 70% of boys found it easy to consult with their fathers compared with 48% for girls (Table 11.3).

Peers. As children develop into adolescents, their connectedness to their parents tends to wane, whereas their connections with peers take on added importance (Larson & Richards, 1991). Friendship provides a context for social and emotional growth (Newcomb & Bagwell, 1995). For the majority of countries that participated in the 1993–94 HBSC, at least three quarters of the youth reported having two or more close friends (Figure 11.1). In Sweden, for example, a minimum of 90% of 11-, 13-, and 15-year-old males and females indicated that they had at least this number of friendships. These high proportions are not unique to Sweden; Canada, Israel, and Scotland reported similar figures. Moreover, these values are remarkably consistent across age and sex. For Spain and Russia, however, the proportion of youth with two or more close friends is somewhat lower, and it differs slightly across the sexes. The proportions of Russian males who

Table 11.3 Percentage of 13-Year-Olds Who Felt It Was "Easy" or "Very Easy" to Discuss Problems With Their Parents: By Sex, Age, and Nationality

Parent	Country	*The Health of Youth: A Cross-National Survey (1993–94)*		*Health and Health Behavior Among Young People (1997–98)*	
		Male	*Female*	*Male*	*Female*
Mother	Canada	73	71	75	73
	Greece			76	75
	Israel	89	88	78	76
	Portugal			80	78
	Russia[a]	80	74	77	72
	Scotland	74	77	79	82
	Spain	84	82		
	Sweden	90	88	83	85
	Switzerland	77	79	78	74
	United States			72	70
Father	Canada	58	41	65	43
	Greece			63	39
	Israel	77	63	73	59
	Portugal			64	49
	Russia[a]	70	48	65	47
	Scotland	61	46	69	53
	Spain	69	51		
	Sweden	79	61	75	59
	Switzerland	66	51	66	45
	United States			65	46

a. Includes only St. Petersburg and district.

indicated that they had at least two close friends ranged from 73% to 83% for the three age groups (11, 13, & 15 years), whereas the corresponding proportions for females ranged from 65% to 72%. In Spain, the proportion of males who reported having two or more friends was the lowest of the 25 participating nations, with 75%, 72%, and 69% of 11-, 13-, and 15-year-olds positively endorsing this item. The corresponding proportion for 11-, 13-, and 15-year-old Spanish females were 64%, 65%, and 64%, respectively.

Although the overwhelming majority of youth in most nations reported having two of more close friends, far fewer indicated that they spent time after school with their friends 4 or 5 days per week (Table 11.4). In most cases, these proportions were below 50%, especially among females. For the most part, more males than females reported spending time after school with their friends at least 4 days per week. Sometimes these differences were small (< 10%), but in a few nations the difference was considerable. For example, in Sweden the proportion of males who indicated that they spent time with their friends after school at least 4 days per week exceeded that of females by 10% at ages 11 and 13 and by 21% at age 15.

Surprisingly, there was little change across age groups or over time. Again, Sweden is the exception. For the 1997–98 survey, the proportion of 11-year-old males who reported socializing with their friends after school 4 or 5 days a week exceeded that of 13-year-olds by 9% and 15-year-olds by 11%. The corresponding proportion for 11-year-old females exceeded that of the 13-year-olds by 15% and that of the 15-year-olds by 20%. From the 1993–94 to the 1997–98 survey, there was a 17% drop in the proportion of 15-year-old Swedish males who reported spending time after school with friends on 4 or 5 days each week.

The perception of school as a "nice place to be" dropped as age increased. As well, there was substantial country-to-country variation with, for 15-year-old females, a high of 62% in

Canada versus a low of 15% of students in Russia affirming school as a positive part of their lives. Student perceptions in Sweden were similar and were substantially above mid-ranking countries such as Israel and Scotland (Figure 11.2).

Confidence

Globally, Spanish students fared the best among the 25 participating countries with regard to self-confidence. The highest proportion of male students in all three age groups and the highest proportion of 11- and 13-year-old female students indicated that they "always felt confident" (Figure 11.3). Among the six nations selected for cross-national comparison, all showed a pattern of declining self-confidence

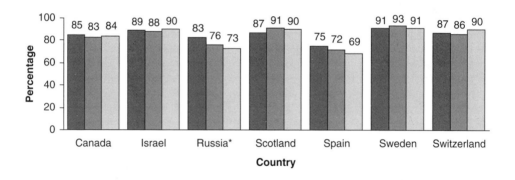

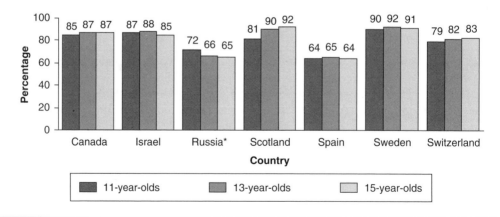

Figure 11.1 Percentage of Male (a) and Female (b) Students Who Indicated That They Had At Least Two Close Friends: By Age and Nationality (1993–94)

SOURCE: Adapted from *The Health of Youth: A Cross-National Survey* (King, Wold, Tudor-Smith, & Harel, 1996).
*Includes only St. Petersburg and district.

Table 11.4 Percentage of 13-Year-Olds Who Spent Time With Friends After School on 4 to 5 Days of the Week: By Sex, Age, and Nationality

Country	*The Health of Youth:* *A Cross-National Survey (1993–4)*		*Health and Health Behavior* *Among Young People (1997–8)*	
	Male	*Female*	*Male*	*Female*
Canada	45	36	39	28
Greece	—	—	39	32
Israel	44	45	41	39
Portugal	—	—	41	37
Russia[a]	42	36	40	34
Scotland	52	39	48	42
Spain	53	42	—	—
Sweden	41	31	33	24
Switzerland	—	—	28	23
United States	—	—	36	33

a. Includes only St. Petersburg and district.

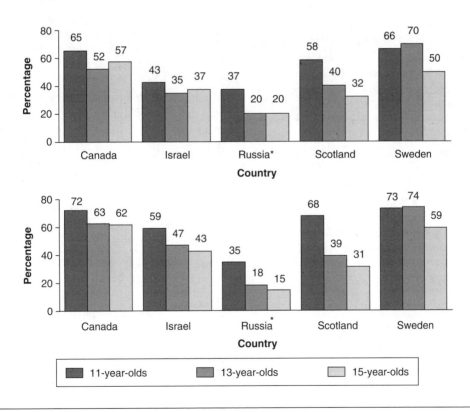

Figure 11.2 Percentage of Male (a) and Female (b) Students Who Indicated That Their School Was a Nice Place to Be: By Age and Nationality (1993–94)[a]

SOURCE: Adapted from *The Health of Youth: A Cross-National Survey* (King, Wold, Tudor-Smith, & Harel, 1996).

a. Not measured in Spain or Switzerland.

*Includes only St. Petersburg and District.

Table 11.5 Percentage of Canadian Students by Sex, Grade, and Year Who Positively Endorsed Items Related to Psychosocial Health

		Grade 8		
Item	*Sex*	*1990*	*1994*	*1998*
Protective factors				
Felt "very happy" about their life	M	—	—	42
	F	—	—	33
Felt "very healthy"	M	—	—	44
	F	—	—	30
Had self-confidence	M	74	77	74
	F	54	61	62
Liked themselves	M	82	87	87
	F	68	73	73

with increasing age. This pattern held for both sexes but was more striking among females. For example, in Spain, the proportion of always-confident females dropped from 62% at age 11 to 33% at age 15, whereas the proportion of always-confident males decreased only from 68% to 52%. In Canada, the proportion of always-confident female students declined from 35% at age 11 to a mere 14% at age 15; however, the corresponding drop for male students was only from 47% to 30%. Another pattern consistent across all nations was that the proportion of always-confident male students exceeded that of female students, and this disparity increased as age increased.

Canadian boys liked themselves more than Canadian girls and had substantially higher perceptions of self-confidence. Rates of self-confidence and "liking themselves" increased from 1990 to 1998 for both boys and girls (Table 11.5).

Caring

The 2001 Vermont Youth Risk Behavior Survey (Department of Health, 2001) asked students about serving their community to make it a better place to live. Rates of participation were approximately 50% of students devoting at least 1 hour per week and 15% to 20% of students devoting at least 3 hours per week (Figure 11.4). There was little difference between students from Grades 8 through 12.

Connectedness

The 2001 Vermont Youth Risk Behavior Survey reported student participation in non-athletic clubs or organizations outside of school. From Grade 8 through Grade 12, approximately 30% of students spent at least 1 hour per week and 12% to 14% at least 3 hours per week in a non-athletic club or organization not affiliated with their school (Figure 11.5). The percentage of students who felt valued by their community dropped steadily from 52% for 8th graders to 45% for 11th graders and then jumped to 54% for 12 graders (Figure 11.6). The increase in Grade 12 may have occurred because many students who did not perform well during secondary school might have dropped out before reaching their graduation year.

DISCUSSION AND STEPS FORWARD

The state of psychosocial health of children in surveyed countries, as captured in single-informant surveys, is mostly positive but with some areas for concern. Most youth felt that they could make new friendships easily, most had two or more close friends, and most could talk to their parents about problems that arose. Only in Spain did the majority of 11-, 13- and 15-year-olds always feel confident, and in Sweden, exactly 50% of 11-year-olds always felt confident. Self-confidence dropped substantially

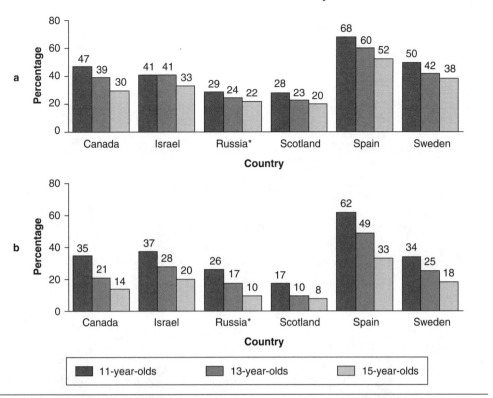

Figure 11.3 Percentage of Male (a) and Female (b) Students Who Indicated That They "Always Felt Confident": By Age and Nationality (1993–94)

SOURCE: Adapted from *The Health of Youth: A Cross-National Survey* (King, Wold, Tudor-Smith, & Harel, 1996).

*Includes only St. Petersburg and district.

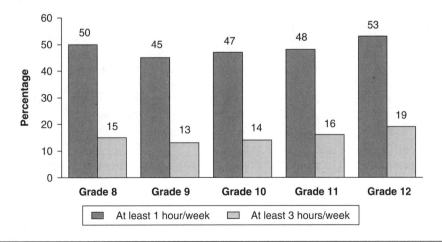

Figure 11.4 Percentage of Students Who Served Their Community to Make It a Better Place to Live

SOURCE: Adapted from *The 2001 Vermont Youth Risk Behavior Survey* (Department of Health, 2001, p. 84).

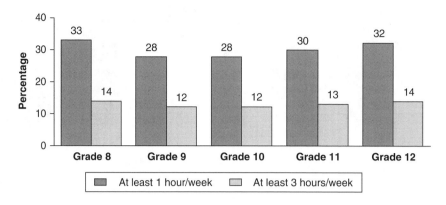

Figure 11.5   Percentage of Students Who Participated in a Nonathletic Club or Organization Outside Their School

SOURCE: Adapted from *The 2001 Vermont Youth Risk Behavior Survey* (Department of Health, 2001, p. 83).

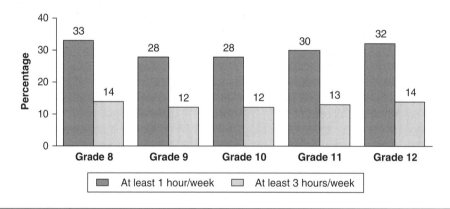

Figure 11.6   Percentage of Students Who Felt Valued by Their Community

SOURCE: Adapted from *The 2001 Vermont Youth Risk Behavior Survey* (Department of Health, 2001).

with increasing age in all countries, including Spain and Sweden. In most countries less than half of the students felt connected to their schools, and in Russia particularly, less than 20% of students felt connected. At least for the state of Vermont, in the United States only a small proportion of students participated in voluntary community activities. Throughout surveyed countries, differences between males and females were small except for perceptions of self-confidence, where it was substantially lower for females and decreased from age 11 through 15. With respect to levels of comfort discussing problems with parents, male and female youth had similar rates for mothers. For

fathers, however, males had substantially higher rates of comfort.

Our opportunities for comparing similar cohorts at different points in time were very limited and consisted largely of comparing youth in 1993–94 with youth in 1997–98 with the exception of one Canadian publication of HBSC data that included data from 1989–90, 1993–94, and 1997–98 cohorts. Country-to-country variations were large, and country rankings varied considerably depending on the question being asked. In general, youth from Europe and North America scored better on most questions than Israel and Russia. Differences across the 4-year period of time available were small. Not surprisingly, no single data source could provide insights into the psychosocial health of youth around the world. Finally, data were not available from countries in South America, Asia, and Africa, which limits the scope of this international comparison.

The Five C's: What Is and What Is Not Measured in Large Surveys

With respect to the five Cs of positive youth development, we did find information with respect to intellectual and social competence; connection to parents, peers, and schools; confidence; and positive self-regard. In a few surveys, caring was measured indirectly by asking youth to report on volunteer community. Character was not measured in any of the surveys, perhaps because the many questions required to capture this construct adequately would significantly increase the size of these general survey tools. Not surprisingly, resilience was not measured in any of the studies listed in Table 11.1. This measurement requires assessment of psychosocial health and assessment of preceding or concurrent adversity, a difficult task. In general, there were more data on behaviors and actions than on underlying personal characteristics and traits.

Moving Ahead: The Quantitative Measurement of Psychosocial Health

Widely accepted quantitative measures of psychosocial health will be useful both on an individual and aggregate basis. On the individual level, such measures will provide a means to assess strengths and weaknesses in various domains such as academic and social competence and self-confidence. These can guide education and mentoring, and for those youth who are dysfunctional, these can complement measures of mental illness, such as measures for depression or anxiety. Psychosocial health measures can also be used to assess response to programs or health interventions and alter those programs if they are not achieving desired results. On an aggregate level, psychosocial health measures can be used to compare the psychosocial health of a population with a contemporaneous population or a past one. On a grander scale,

measures of psychosocial health reflect to some extent the human and social capital of a society—that is, the resources within the members of that society that facilitate social and economic development (World Bank, 1997). A standardized quantitative assessment will allow members of a society to balance the benefits of certain societal choices or policies against a potential negative impact on social capital.

What are the steps to achieving standardized measures of psychosocial health? The first step is one of definition; there must be wide consensus among researchers, policymakers, and the general public as to the elements of psychosocial health deemed to be essential. The PYD model discussed here has found wide, but by no means universal, acceptance. As discussed, the Search Institute has a framework of 40 youth development assets that partially overlap with the PYD elements. Specific instruments that measure the elements of their particular models have been developed, and this development will likely continue for the near future.

Beyond agreement on a common core of constructs, there must be consensus on comparable sampling methodologies, questionnaires, interview techniques, and number of informants. Otherwise, researchers will invent their own instruments for their studies. This will lead to a plethora of studies and surveys that are compared only with great difficulty.

Psychosocial health in youth requires the development of questions that are age dependent. Empathy is likely a different attribute in a 6-year-old compared with empathy in a cognitively and emotionally mature 15-year-old. It requires different methods of measurement, and possibly, it reflects a different underlying construct.

Although there is broad agreement on elements deemed important to PYD, such as competence, caring, and the other Cs, there is as yet no accepted model that specifies the extent to which these reflect truly fundamental characteristics as opposed to being manifestations of underlying and as yet poorly described characteristics. Such a model should also specify the relative importance of such underlying characteristics. For example, can a youth who is competent and caring but is not confident to be considered healthy from a psychosocial point of view? Must one have all these characteristics to some degree, or could one or two be missing as long as the other characteristics are strongly present? How will one decide the criteria against which such characteristics will be assessed? These criteria could rely on (a) "structural" features—for example, the extent to which a youth feels healthy, competent, and compassionate; (b) "functional" features—for example, the assessment of activities that reflect psychosocial health such as interaction with peers, family, and others; engagement in the community; avoidance of risky activities; making moral and just choices; or (c) some combination of structural and functional. Who will decide? Should such a model suffice for all the world's youth, or must models be culture specific and recognize that emphasis on characteristics may differ from culture to culture?

Fortunately, groups of researchers have been working to achieve consensus in describing and measuring psychosocial health. For example, the resilience instrument with its contextualized development through qualitative methods being validated by Ungar and his colleagues (Chapter 28 this volume; Ungar, Lee, Callaghan, & Boothroyd, in press) is an example of such an approach. Evidently, as the above review demonstrates, much more still needs to be done.

Additional studies are required to better define psychosocial health and its measurement and to compare levels of psychosocial health with other measures of health and functioning in society. Although longitudinal studies lasting many years will continue to provide data about the natural course of psychosocial health, short-term cross-sectional and case-control studies can provide the data needed to illustrate that different levels of psychosocial health predict different levels of functioning in society. Small and quickly executed cross-sectional studies would facilitate the field-testing of many items and provide data for multivariate analyses to identify the most meaningful items for many different informants. Longitudinal studies with larger sample sizes would allow for the assessment of reliability and validity, especially predictive validity because at least some short-term outcomes (e.g., gaining employment, becoming married) should occur before the study ceases. The fruit of such studies will be in systematic reviews, meta-analyses, and consensus conferences

that provide the impetus for the development of a widely accepted model of psychosocial health. Finally, a commonly accepted model of psychosocial health will allow for the accumulation of evidence from randomized controlled trials. These trials must use common measures to assess interventions that aim to improve psychosocial health.

NOTES

1. See the Search Institute Web site at www.search-institute.org.

2. Summary available online at www.resiliencycanada.ca/aboutus.htm.

3. See surveys at www.search-institute.org/surveys.

4. See the HBSC Web site at www.hbsc.org.

REFERENCES

American Psychiatric Association. (2000). *Diagnostic and statistical manual of mental disorders* (4th ed., text rev.). Washington DC: Author.

Beck, A. T., Ward, C. H., Mendelson, M., Mock, J., & Erbaugh, J. (1961, June). An inventory for measuring depression. *Archives of General Psychiatry, 4*, 43–63.

Bronfenbrenner, U. (1979). *The ecology of human development: Experiments by nature and design.* Cambridge, MA: Harvard University Press.

Caspi, A., Moffitt, T. E., Newman, D. L., & Silva, P. A. (1996). Behavioral observations at age 3 years predict adult psychiatric disorders. Longitudinal evidence from a birth cohort. *Archives of General Psychiatry, 53*(11), 1033–1039.

Catalano, R. F., Berglund, M. L., Ryan, J. A. M., Lonczak, H. S., & Hawkins, J. D. (2002). Positive youth development in the United States: Research findings on evaluations of positive youth development programs. *Prevention & Treatment, 5*(Article 15). Retrieved December 21, 2004, from http://journals.apa.org/prevention/volume5/pre0050015a.html

Centers for Disease Control. (2004). *YRBSS: Youth risk behavior surveillance system—United States, 2003.* Retrieved October 11, 2004, from www.cdc.gov/HealthyYouth/yrbs/index.htm

Department of Health, Division of Alcohol and Drug Abuse Programs. (2001). *The 2001 Vermont Youth Risk Behavior Survey.* Retrieved September, 19, 2004, from www.healthyvermonters.info/adap/pubs/2001/yrbs2001.shtml

Eccles, J., Templeton, J., Barber, B., & Stone, M. (2003). Adolescence and the emerging adulthood: The critical passage ways to adulthood. In M. H. Bornstein, L. Davidson, C. L. M. Keyes, & K. A. Moore (Eds.), *Well-being: Positive development across the lifespan* (pp. 383–406). Mahwah, NJ: Erlbaum.

Fletcher, R. H., Fletcher, S. W., & Wagner, E. H. (1996). Abnormality. In *Clinical epidemiology: The essentials* (3rd ed., pp. 57–64). Baltimore: Williams & Wilkins.

Goodman, R. (2004). *SDQ: Information for researchers and professionals about the Strengths & Difficulties Questionnaires.* Retrieved December 22, 2004, from www.sdqinfo.com

Harter, S. (1982). The perceived competence scale for children. *Child Development, 53*(1), 87–97.

Human Resources Development Canada. (2001). *National longitudinal survey of children and youth (NLSCY).* Retrieved October 11, 2004, from www11.hrdc-drhc.gc.ca/pls/edd/NLSCY.lhtml

International Association for the Evaluation of Educational Achievement. (2003). *Trends in international mathematics and science study.* Retrieved October 11, 2004, from http://isc.bc.edu/timss2003.html

Jew, C. L., Green, K. E., & Kroger, J. (1999). Development and validation of a measure of resiliency. *Measurement and Evaluation in Counseling and Development, 32*(2), 75–89.

Johnston, L. D., Bachman, J. G., O'Malley, P. M., Schulenberg, J. E., & Wallace Jr., J. M. (2004). *Monitoring the future: A continuing study of American youth.* Retrieved October 11, 2004, from www.monitoringthefuture.org

Johnston, L. D., O'Malley, P. M., Bachman, J. G., & Schulenberg, J. E. (2003). *Monitoring the future: National results on adolescent drug use. Overview of key findings, 2003.* Bethesda, MD: National Institute on Drug Abuse.

Kann, L. K. (2004). *2003 high school site-added questions to the Youth Risk Behavior Surveillance System.* Unpublished manuscript, Atlanta, GA.

King, A., Wold, B., Tudor-Smith, C., & Harel, Y. (1996). *1993/94 international report: The health of youth:*

A cross-national survey. Retrieved October 11, 2004, from www.hbsc.org/publications/reports.html#Internationalreports

Larson, R., & Richards, M. H. (1991). Daily companionship in late childhood and early adolescence: Changing developmental contexts. *Child Development, 62*(2), 284–300.

Lerner, R. M. (2002). *Concepts and theories of human development* (3rd ed.). Mahwah, NJ: Erlbaum.

Lerner, R. M. (2004). *Liberty: Thriving and civic engagement among America's youth.* Thousand Oaks, CA: Sage.

Lerner, R. M., Fisher, C. B., & Weinberg, R. A. (2000). Toward a science for and of the people: Promoting civil society through the application of developmental science. *Child Development, 71*(1), 11–20.

Loeber, R., Farrington, D. P., Stouthamer-Loeber, M., Moffitt, T. E., Caspi, A., & Lynam, D. (2001). Male mental health problems, psychopathy, and personality traits: Key findings from the first 14 years of the Pittsburgh Youth Study. *Clinical Child and Family Psychology Review, 4*(4), 273–297.

Murphy, J. M., Laird, N. M., Monson, R. R., Sobol, A. M., & Leighton, A. H. (2000). A 40-year perspective on the prevalence of depression: The Stirling County study. *Archives of General Psychiatry, 57*(3), 209–215.

Nagin, D. S., & Tremblay, R. E. (2001). Parental and early childhood predictors of persistent physical aggression in boys from kindergarten to high school. *Archives of General Psychiatry, 58*(4), 389–394.

National Research Council & Institute of Medicine. (1996). *Youth development and neighborhood influences: Challenges and opportunities, summary of a workshop,* Retrieved December 22, 2004, from www.nap.edu/books/0309056497/html/index.html

Newcomb, A. F., & Bagwell, C. L. (1995). Children's friendship relations: A meta-analytic review. *Psychological Bulletin, 117*(2), 306–347.

Plank, S. B., & MacIver, D. J. (2003). Educational achievement. In M. H. Bornstein, L. Davidson, C. L. M. Keyes, & K. A. Moore (Eds.), *Well-being: Positive development across the lifespan* (pp. 341–354). Mahwah, NJ: Erlbaum.

Roth, J. L., & Brooks-Gunn, J. (2003a). What exactly is a youth development program? Answers from research and practice. *Applied Developmental Science, 7*(2), 92–109.

Roth, J. L., & Brooks-Gunn, J. (2003b). What is a youth development program? Identification of defining principles. In R. M. Lerner, F. Jacobs, & D. Wertlieb (Eds.), *Promoting positive child adolescent and family development: A handbook of program and policy innovations* (Vol. 2, pp. 197–223). Thousand Oaks, CA: Sage.

World Bank. (1997). *Expanding the measure of wealth: Indicators of environmentally sustainable development.* Retrieved December 22, 2004, from www-wds.worldbank.org/servlet/WDSContentServer/WDSP/IB/1997/06/01/000009265_3971113150949/Rendered/PDF/multi_page.pdf

Ungar, M., Lee. A. W., Callaghan, T., & Boothroyd, R. (in press). An international collaboration to study resilience in adolescents across cultures. *Journal of Social Work Research and Evaluation.*

U.S. Department of Education, National Center for Education Statistics. (2000, August). *Pursuing excellence: Comparisons of international eighth-grade mathematics and science achievement from a U.S. perspective, 1995 and 1999. Initial findings from the Third International Mathematics and Science Study—Repeat* (Statistical analysis report. NCES-2001–028). Retrieved December 22, 2004, from http://nces.ed.gov/pubs2001/2001028.pdf

U.S. Department of Labor. (2004, July). *The NLSY97.* Retrieved October 11, 2004, from http://stats.bls.gov/nls/nlsy97.htm

UNC Carolina Population Center. (2004). *Add Health: The National Longitudinal Survey of Adolescent Health,* from http://www.cpc.unc.edu/projects/addhealth

World Health Organization. (1946, June). *Preamble to the constitution of the World Health Organization.* Paper presented at the International Health Conference, New York.

World Health Organization. (1992). *International statistical classification of diseases and related health problems.* Retrieved September 9, 2004, from www.who.int/whosis/icd10

World Health Organization. (2000). *1997/98 international report: Health and health behaviour among young people.* Retrieved October 11, 2004, from www.hbsc.org/downloads/Int_Report_00.pdf

Zhou, Q., Valiente, C., & Eisenberg, N. (2003). Empathy and its measurement. In S. J. Lopez & C. R. Snyder (Eds.), *Positive psychological assessment: A handbook of models and measures* (pp. 269–284). Washington, DC: American Psychological Association.

12

RESILIENCE AND WELL-BEING IN DEVELOPING COUNTRIES

LAURA CAMFIELD

ALLISTER MCGREGOR

The study of international development has historically been concerned with the material wealth of nations. Where it has focused on the *people* of developing nations, it has tended to be concerned with what they lack in material terms. This is hardly surprising; a feature of our modern and wealthy world is the persistence of extreme poverty and widening global inequality. The publication of the first Human Development Report by the United Nations Development Programme (UNDP) in 1990 was an important signal to academics and practitioners in international development to pay more attention to development's human dimensions, as was the adoption of the UN Convention on the Rights of the Child in 1989. Although there has been much progress in this direction, this chapter seeks to stimulate further debate over how we can conceptualize and study "human development."[1] In particular, it considers how a notion of human development that recognizes the importance of the interplay between the material and cognitive dimensions of people's well-being might contribute to our understanding of resilience in populations at risk globally.

The Research Group on Wellbeing in Developing Countries (WeD) at the University of Bath is carrying out detailed empirical research in four developing countries whose per capita incomes range from $668 to $6,402 per annum (2002 figures, US $ at purchasing power parity).[2] These compare to an average of $34,142 and $23,509 per annum for the United States and the United Kingdom, respectively. However, these figures tell us remarkably little about how people struggle, survive, and even thrive in these different developing country contexts. The research employs a conception of well-being that seeks to encompass the material, relational, and cognitive dimensions of development. It conceives of people as constrained but active agents, involved in the ongoing social and cultural construction of well-being for themselves and their communities. We argue that this broadening of our conception of human development can provide us with a means of better understanding the persistence of "ill being" (or the more narrowly defined condition of "poverty") in many countries of the developing world.

In researching the experiences of men, women, and children in developing countries, it is hard not to be struck by the contrasts of hardship and happiness. Their resilience amid what most people in the industrialized North would regard as extremely difficult conditions is remarkable. This observation is supported by some counterintuitive results from international surveys of people's happiness and satisfaction with life. For example, the World Values Survey for 1999–2001 reports that Nigeria, which the UNDP ranks as one of the bottom 25 countries for human development, placed at the top of world rankings for "happiness" (Inglehardt, Basañez, Díez-Medrano, Halman, & Luijkx, 2004). Nearly 70% of the Nigerian population reported that they were "very happy." Similarly, Bangladesh, once stigmatized as "the basket-case of international development," frequently affected by environmental disasters, and categorized by Transparency International (2003) as the most corrupt country in the world, averaged a happiness score of 6 out of 10 in surveys carried out in the 1990s (Veenhoven, 2001/2002), putting it ahead of Turkey and Greece. A study with young people in 42 countries (Oishi, Schimmack, Diener, & Suh, 1998) found that although there may be great variation in the way happiness is defined and bounded, it is considered universally important; in fact only 1% of respondents to the survey claimed they had never thought about it. The respondents' ratings of the importance of happiness on a scale of 1 to 7 fell within a narrow spectrum, ranging from an average score of 5.45 in Tanzania to 6.78 in Argentina, suggesting that it is an important and potentially measurable aspect of people's experience.

We do not want to be swept up by the wave of current academic enthusiasm for "happiness" research (Layard, 2003; Oswald, 2003; Veenhoven, 2001/2002); it seems evident, however, that although people in the poorest countries can experience material hardships and deprivations, their lives are not permanently blighted by misery. This simple observation opens up a large field of conceptual debate and empirical investigation that has previously not been addressed in a systematic and multidisciplinary way. In this chapter, we explain how we seek to understand the apparent resilience of people in economically developing countries

and how this connects with our exploration of the day-to-day efforts of people in these countries to construct their well-being. The nature of the relationships between material conditions and the subjective dimensions of well-being; the effect of these on people's own definitions of what they need, expect, and aim toward; and the extent to which people feel their aspirations are satisfied represent distinctive and central areas of inquiry for the WeD Research Group.

THE GAP

The field of development studies has not engaged extensively with psychology, and although interesting comparisons have been made at the national level demonstrating the effect of income on subjective well-being (e.g., Cummins, 2000; Diener & Biswas-Diener, 2002), psychology has done relatively little work with people living in poverty. An exception to this is a recent study by Biswas-Diener and Diener (2001), which empirically investigates the question, "Are the extremely poor of the world miserable, and if not why not?" To answer this question, the researchers explored the extent to which people in Calcutta who were living in slum housing or on the streets or who were working in the commercial sex trade evaluated their lives "as a whole" as satisfactory ("global life satisfaction") or expressed satisfaction with particular areas of their life ("domain-specific life satisfaction") in areas such as friendship or morality. Their conclusion was that although these groups were slightly less satisfied overall than middle-class comparison groups (because of the strong correlation between global life satisfaction and objective income), satisfaction with individual areas of life was uniformly positive. This was particularly evident in the area of "social relationships." The authors conclude:

> The participants in this study do not report the kind of suffering we expect. Rather, they believe they are good (moral) people, they are often religious . . . and they have rewarding families. . . . They have satisfactory social lives and enjoy their food. (Biswas-Diener & Diener, 2001, p. 348)

The findings of this study illuminate a generic problem for the social sciences that manifests itself in a variety of forms across the different disciplines. The problem is what appears to be "the gap" between people's observed condition, usually labeled "objective" (also connoting universal, quantifiable, scientific, unbiased, etc.), and their personal or "subjective" evaluation of it (local, qualitative, unscientific, biased, etc.). All the disciplines in the social sciences have extensive literatures and sophisticated constructions that seek to explain the gap. In political economy and sociology, this debate has revolved around notions of false consciousness and concepts of power (Lukes, 1986); in economics, it has been dealt with in terms of irrational behavior, market failure, or a lack of information (see Bardhan, 2001, for a review); in psychology, there are expanding literatures on "adaptation" and "response shift" (see Cummins, 2002a Sprangers & Schwartz, 1999). Across all the disciplines, the gap tends to lie at the heart of a deeply contested area of debate. Outside academia, such gaps are more usually implicitly, or explicitly, explained in terms of "ignorance" or "stupidity." The shift from the rather benign notion of the "noble but uneducated" peasant has often been blurred in some of the cruder discourses of development practice, where it is not uncommon to find poor people being treated as lacking the intelligence to make the "correct" decisions.

We recognize the possibility that there may be no uncontested explanation of such phenomena (Lukes, 1986), but we nevertheless argue here that a better understanding of the gap between observed objective condition and subjective evaluation must draw on all the disciplinary debates. Thus, there is a role for analyses of power, of the information or referents that people draw on, and of the underlying psychological processes. The combination of insights that these analyses yield is important.

There is a further alternative and important way in which this same problem is framed. Currently, within development studies and social anthropology, there is renewed interest in the mismatch between "our" (the economically developed world's) idea of the good life and "theirs" (the developing world) (see Alkire, 2002; Clark, 2000, for reviews). One way in which this debate is taken forward is in terms of "local" and "universal" understandings of well-being. In development studies, the participation movement has sought to strengthen the local by giving "voice to the poor" (Narayan, Chambers, Shah, & Petesch, 2000), but thus far, this work has focused more on how people can overcome their predefined poverty than on how they themselves define well-being and understand the processes that support or impede it (White & Pettit, 2004). Social anthropology has long dealt with the tensions between the etic and the emic but has not extensively explored how this relates to well-being or any policy regimes concerned with poverty. In psychology, Markus and Kitayama (1991), Christopher (1999), and writers from the subdiscipline of "cultural psychology" (e.g., Shweder, 1993) have been prominent voices in the challenge to "universalist" tendencies, stressing the need to embed concepts and analysis in local cultures and constructions.

From a policy perspective, however, it is clear that both universal and local understandings will be a necessary part of our knowledge base, if policy is to be effective from its formulation to its implementation. Because the agreement on the Millennium Development Goals or MDGs (see UNDP, 2002) has made the eradication of poverty perhaps the major global policy challenge for the 21st century, it behooves any academics working in this area to explore the relationship between universal and local conceptions of well-being.

QUALITY OF LIFE AND SUBJECTIVE WELL-BEING

Before we can discuss the challenges of combining objective and subjective perspectives in a study of well-being in developing countries, it is necessary to map out some of the main contributions to the subjective well-being literature. Currently, there are two main approaches to researching subjective well-being. First, there is the quality-of-life (QoL) school, which developed along two distinct paths (represented by the membership organizations, the International Society for Quality of Life Research [ISOQOL] and the International Society for Quality of Life

Studies [ISOQOLS]). The key philosophical division between the organizations is whether members concur with most "health-related quality of life" researchers that "the term 'quality of life data' should be used . . . only in connection with data about people's subjective feelings about life" (Nord, Arnesen, Menzel, & Pinto, 2001, p. 3)—the approach of ISOQOL— or take the approach of "social indicators" researchers who include objective measures (both self-reported and external)—the approach of ISOQOLS.

Second, there is the subjective well-being (SWB) approach from social psychology, which uses subjective well-being as both an indicator (made up of satisfaction with life as a whole and "hedonic balance" or happiness) and a goal. This also includes "positive psychologists" (who attempt to develop individual psychological health and fulfillment) and "economists of happiness" (who treat happiness as the paramount indicator of utility—e.g., Frey & Stutzer, 2002; Oswald, 2003). Remarkably, although there is creative interaction between the social indicators and SWB approaches, the powerful and well-funded health-related QoL approach appears to have had little influence on either (see Michalos, 2004). We first discuss the health-related QoL approach and then explore the social indicators and SWB approaches together, acknowledging the considerable overlap in terms of methods and personnel.

QoL Research

As just noted, QoL research has developed along two distinct paths. The first, and the one that we mainly deal with here, has been dominated by social and health psychology and has focused predominantly on subjective perceptions of quality of life (possibly in reaction to the medical reliance on clinical measures such as blood pressure). It is usually described as "health-related quality of life." The second is identified with the "social indicators movement" (made up of economists, sociologists, and psychologists) and tends to look at both subjective and objective dimensions of quality of life. Despite this important philosophical difference, the methods used to produce the measures of quality of life are very similar; both

approaches to QoL work originated in the social indicators research in the mid-1970s (e.g., Andrews & Withey's "General Well-Being Scale," 1976). The separation occurred because of the ways in which the concept of quality of life was taken up and strongly adopted in health sciences and in health care circles (Ager, 2002), which has enabled it to become increasingly psychometrically and methodologically sophisticated (e.g., "item response theory," item "banking" for computer administration, etc.).

Health-Related QoL Research

Research and writing on QoL measures has grown exponentially over the past decade. This has been funded by national health services, international agencies, pharmaceutical companies, and the U.S. health insurance industry. MEDLINE, the main index for medical papers, first used the phrase "quality of life" as a heading in 1975. Since then, tens of thousands of papers have been published, nearly 18,000 between 2000 and 2003 alone, and there has been a proliferation of study groups, conferences, and special journal issues. This remarkable growth is linked to increasing cost consciousness in medicine, risk management by health care providers, and the desire for more sensitive measures to compare treatments for chronic illness.

Although there are some "global" QoL measures that ask people directly to make a numerical assessment of their quality of life (e.g., the EuroQoL thermometer; Kind, 1996), the majority are "profile" measures that ask the respondents to judge their quality of life across a range of separate areas or "domains" (e.g., the WHOQOL-100; WHOQOL Group, 1995). These scores can then be analyzed either separately or in aggregate form. The main distinction between different profile measures is their provenance—specifically, whether the domains of importance and the questions that address them were selected from population focus groups or interviews, or by "expert consultation" and reviews of existing measures. Furthermore, these measures have typically not been global (in the North-South sense) in their design, in that they tend to be compiled by researchers in developed countries and are less influenced by the views of researchers and other stakeholders in developing nations.

Broadly speaking, however, three types of QoL measure are currently used in health care:

1. "Generic" measures, which can be used in sick and healthy populations, cover all conditions, and are brief and relatively easy to translate (e.g., the MOS short form 36-item health survey or SF-36; Ware & Sherbourne, 1992)

2. "Disease-specific" measures, which are generated from interviews with people with particular conditions and clinicians who specialize in these conditions and are appropriate only to that condition (e.g., the Multiple Sclerosis Impact Scale-29 item; Hobart, Lamping, Fitzpatrick, Riazi, & Thompson, 2001)

3. "Individualized" measures, which reverse the expert-subject relationship that dominate the first two types of measures. Individual respondents specify the areas of life that are important to them and evaluate their performance in those domains (e.g., the SeiQoL; O'Boyle, McGee, Hickey, O'Malley, & Joyce, 1992; and the Patient-Generated Index or PGI; Ruta, Garratt, Leng, Russell, & MacDonald, 1994).

Although disease-specific measures are popular with patients and clinicians because the questions are obviously relevant, generic measures are more widely used because they express outcomes in a standard numerical format. This makes them more suited for health care decision making and other bureaucratic purposes. Scores from the generic instruments make it possible to compare the quality of life of people with different conditions and thus also make it possible to compare the value of different treatments. As such, these measures fit well with techniques in public policy making, which are intended to contribute to more efficient resource allocation. However, individualized measures are also becoming increasingly influential within medicine because they place the patient more at the center of the analysis. Technically, they have high "face" and "content" validity and directly address the changes that are important to patients (for a useful review, see Joyce, O'Boyle, & McGee, 1999).

There are some very obvious attractions to thinking about the applicability of these approaches to measuring quality of life in international development. Development policies from governments and international agencies are interventions in people's lives, often justified by the claim that they are intended to improve people's quality of life. However, similar pressures operate on development policymakers and practitioners as on health professionals. They are required to make choices between types of intervention and to justify these decisions in terms of outcomes and the efficiency of resource allocation (see Ireland, McGregor, & Saltmarshe, 2003). To put it crudely, development practitioners are often found asking where they will get "the best bang for their buck" or, more precisely, where their budgets can be allocated most efficiently in terms of their objective to eradicate poverty. Generic measures are attractive because they are bureaucrat-friendly instruments and fit well with the range of cost-benefit techniques familiar to development policymakers. Individualized QoL measures are, however, becoming more attractive because of the current openness among development practitioners to being more people centered. As such, it would be possible to see these being adapted to play roles such as establishing local priorities in local-level planning systems or warning where poorly designed interventions might have negative consequences for the quality of life of the different individuals they are intended to benefit.

There are, of course, reservations about the simplistic transfer of such instruments to developing-country contexts and for development purposes. Not least among these is the fundamental criticism that measures of health-related quality of life have tended to pay insufficient attention to their conceptual foundations. As some critics have put it, their authors have focused much more on their "psychometric properties" than on their philosophical underpinning (Keedwell & Snaith, 1996; Ziebland, Fitzpatrick, & Jenkinson, 1993). This, combined with the "pragmatism of clinical practice," means that

> many [QoL] measures make no reference to the concepts that they are trying to measure. . . . It is

rather like possessing a thermometer and knowing that it is intended to identify patients with a fever but not knowing that what it actually measures is temperature. (Wilkin, Hallam, & Doggett, 1992, p. 18)

In these approaches, quality of life tends to be used as a holistic concept—namely, what individuals feel about their lives when they evaluate them as a whole. However, it is argued that this is not necessarily what these QoL measures assess, because they are biased toward "physical function" as the most concrete and generalizable aspect of health (e.g., Leplege & Hunt, 1997). In a regression analysis of mean happiness scores from 11 QoL surveys carried out by Michalos (2004), it was found that satisfaction with health was never the strongest predictor of happiness, and in 5 of these, it failed to qualify for the final regression due to lack of statistical significance. Although self-reported health (measured with the SF-36) accounted for 4% of explainable variance in happiness scores, this was entirely due to the scores on the mental health domain.

Although many health care professionals now recognize the importance of social and environmental factors, underlined by many population and patient surveys (e.g., Bowling, 1995; McDowell & Newell, 1987), health-related QoL researchers have found it difficult to include these in their measures. This is due both to the challenges of measuring intangible or social aspects of people's experiences and to resistance from powerful stakeholders. For example, valued aspects of life such as feeling a sense of identity or belonging are unlikely to be included for the pragmatic reason that these aspects of the human condition tend not to be affected by medical interventions.[3]

Finally, since QoL measures have generally been developed to address problems in wealthy and capitalist societies, many of the normative reference points for functional scales may be irrelevant. The inevitable individualism of these QoL measures has also come in for criticism. It is argued that this strong underpinning philosophy may affect their comprehensibility in societies that operate with different models of the person (e.g., what is characterized as internal or external to a person). At a more basic level, the material points of reference will often be suspect. For example, the majority of the functional items in one French blindness scale (e.g., Can you drive a car? Can you see street lamps?) needed to be reworked so they could be used in Francophone Mali (Do you know which way is east [necessary to establish orientation for prayer]? Do you fall into holes?) (Leplege & Marquis, 1999). But problems of translation go beyond vocabulary to the tacit models underlying the measures and can be interpreted as power in action in scientific practice. Following Lukes (1986), it is apparent that the crude imposition of models developed in one type of society on others with significant cultural and material differences runs the risk not only of setting the agenda in terms of what quality of life is to encompass but also of shaping the very ways in which the concept can be thought about in the first place (see Chapter 13 for a discussion of an international resilience project that has attempted to address this problem).

The veteran QoL researcher Hunt (1999) observes ironically that

the ethnocentricity of assuming that a measure developed in, say, the USA, or England, will be applicable (after adaptation) in pretty much any country or language in the world . . . is highlighted if one imagines the chances of a health questionnaire developed in Bali, Nigeria, or Hong Kong being deemed suitable for use in Newcastle, Newark, or Nice. (p. 230)

Perhaps for the reasons explored above, or what Veenhoven (2000) describes as their "domination by psychometricians, who focus . . . on factor loadings, reliability issues and inter-test correlations" at the expense of a "clear answer to the question of what these measures actually measure" (pp. 19–20), many researchers from social indicators or economic backgrounds prefer to measure outcomes such as subjective well-being and life satisfaction directly, either through global questions or scales. We describe these next.

Subjective Well-Being

Subjective well-being is commonly defined as a subjective measurement that combines the presence of positive emotions and absence of negative emotions ("hedonic balance") with overall satisfaction with life (Diener, 1984). It is usually investigated using standard global questions about happiness (equated with hedonic balance) and life satisfaction,[4] which are a routine part of international data sets[5] (collated for comparative purposes in the World Database of Happiness[6]). The global questions are often combined with psychological measures of these concepts—for example, the Satisfaction With Life Scale (Diener, Emmons, Larsen, & Griffin, 1985) and the Bradburn Affect Balance Scale (Bradburn, 1969).

Subjective well-being, like quality of life, is often seen as a vital "missing measurement" because it is perceived to combine the cognitive (satisfaction with life) and emotional (happiness) aspects of subjective experience. In fact, some "economists of happiness" characterize it as "the ultimate utility" or an incarnation of Aristotle's "summum bonum" (Hirata, 2001). The presence of longitudinal international data on people's reports of their subjective well-being has also enabled interesting theorizing on topics such as the marginal utility of increased national income (e.g., Easterlin, 2004) and the effect of political change in South Africa and the former Russian republics (e.g., Inglehardt & Klingemann, 2000; Moller, 2001).

However, as with measures of quality of life, we need to acknowledge a number of critiques of "global" (single question) and profile measures of subjective well-being before we can consider their place in the exploration of well-being in developing countries.

Global Questions

Despite the evident value of international data sets, there are some issues relating to the equivalence of the data collection methods and the reliability of global questions. For example, the way the questions were phrased and ordered (so-called order effects[7]) and the choice of response scales were not uniform across countries and time periods, which may have affected responses. In addition, global questions are more prone to biases from mood (Diener, 2000; Schwarz & Strack, 1991), timing (Redelmeier & Kahneman, 1996), or social desirability

(Diener, Suh, Lucas, & Smith, 1999; Diener, Suh, Smith, & Shao, 1995; Oishi, Diener, Lucas, & Suh, 1999) and may be simply very difficult to answer sensibly (Antaki & Rapley, 1996).

Global questions are usually phrased in terms of life satisfaction rather than happiness because this is thought to be a more "cognitive" (and thus scientific) measure of subjective well-being than happiness; however, some cultures find it difficult to get a meaningful response to questions phrased in these terms. For example, the coordinator of a project investigating well-being in the United Kingdom stopped asking people how satisfied they were because the word sounded "dead" and provoked responses such as, "Well, I mustn't grumble" (drawing on a valued national stereotype about never complaining) (personal communication, Nic Marks, July, 2003,). Similarly, site visits by teams from the WeD ESRC Research Group in Thailand and Peru to pilot potential questions found that the concept becomes less useful in situations where people have little control or choice in the areas that matter to them (i.e., their only option is satisfaction) and unhelpfully evokes Western discourses of voluntarism and consumer power.

Although the term *life satisfaction* is used as though it were universally meaningful, this doesn't mean it has the same meaning universally: Kilian's review of "patient satisfaction" studies in the United Kingdom described how being satisfied with a treatment can encompass feelings of resignation and helplessness and a belief that the treatment is useless (Kilian, Lindenbach, Lobig, & Angermeyer, 1999). Recent psychological research (Schimmack, Diener, & Oishi, 2002) also suggests that a personality "trait-level" propensity to be satisfied with life is a more important determinant of life satisfaction scores than objective life circumstances, which may reduce its utility as an indicator. This is an interesting addition to the studies of identical and nonidentical twins carried out by Hamer (1996) and Lykken and Tellegen (1996) that measured the happiness of twins raised apart and together and concluded that up to 80% of the stable differences in life satisfaction were heritable. Less than 3% of variance was explained by socioeconomic status, educational attainment, family income, marital status, and religious commitment. For these reasons, Felce (1997) argues, "Far from being the subtle indicator of QoL that it is often assumed to be, satisfaction may be an unresponsive indicator, sensitive only to gross and immediate changes in life conditions" (p. 127).

Profile Measures

Bearing in mind the problems with global questions described above, some researchers have tried to measure subjective well-being using a measure with multiple, independent domains, but as with QoL measures, these often bear little resemblance to the initial definition or are extremely culturally specific. For example, the six factors in Ryff's (1989) measure of subjective well-being (self-acceptance, personal growth, purpose in life, positive relations with others, autonomy, happiness, and environmental mastery) reflect its development as part of a North American project looking at resilience in older adults. Christopher (1999) suggests that Ryff's choice of autonomy (or internal control) reveals the individualism of the society the measure was developed in; in other societies, secondary control through acceptance and harmonization is more common. Similarly, her assumption of a self that was "always already" (not constituted through relations with others) and can exist outside society is specifically Western, as is the implicit rejection of "conformity" (or "pro-solidarity behavior" as it might be more positively described).

Markus and Kitayama (1991) also argue that subjective well-being cannot be studied cross-culturally because its definitions are culturally rooted "moral visions." They maintain that the concept is less relevant to societies they define as "collectivist" (using Triandis's bipolar classification system; Kim, Triandis, Kagitcibasi, Choi, & Yoon, 1994) because it is founded in individual judgments. This argument is not universally accepted (the unemployment rate for psychologists would be much higher if it were), and researchers exploring the subject in Southeast Asia, Russia, and Eastern Europe[8] have found some interesting national variations in the way people's judgments of subjective well-being are constructed. For example, self-esteem and self-consistency apparently correlate more strongly with life satisfaction in individualist than in collectivist societies (Diener & Diener, 1995; Suh, 2000), satisfaction with freedom is less predictive of subjective well-being in collectivist societies, and individualists are more likely to use emotions than norms to judge life satisfaction (Oishi et al., 1998). These national differences are paralleled among ethnic groups in the United States (Diener & Suh, 1999) and do not appear to be attributable to language (Ouweneel & Veenhoven, 1991; Larson & Shao, 1993).

A problem with all holistic measures such as the QoL and SWB ones described above is that we do not currently understand how the scores from individual domains (e.g., social relationships) are combined into an overall evaluation of subjective well-being, either by the researcher or by the respondent in answer to a global question about the quality of his or her life. We cannot even be sure that people's thought processes follow this type of rationality where the flow of experience is chopped into domains that can then be quantified and recombined.

Lack of Correlation With Objective Measures

There is also a more profound "problem," which is that subjective perceptions of life satisfaction or happiness (at least, those expressed in response to a direct question from a researcher) rarely correlate with objective assessments of people's material circumstances. Cognitive explanations for this include psychological processes such as adaptation, "response shift" (Sprangers & Schwartz, 1999), "positive cognitive biases" (Cummins & Nistico, 2002) (part of Cummins's homeostatic theory of subjective well-being, 2000, 2002), and the "psychological immune system" (Gilbert, Pinel, Wilson, Blumberg, & Wheatley, 1998), some of which are described later in this chapter. Of course, lack of correlation with objective measures doesn't necessarily mean that subjective measures are less reliable, just that they measure something different. Even if subjective quality of life does derive from an incomplete or distorted perception of reality, as the theory of false consciousness suggests, it is still real to the people who experience it and forms a basis for actions that shape people's external realities.

An example of this would be the role of self-enhancing biases, which protect our confidence and self-esteem by convincing us that good things are more likely to happen to us than to others. Interestingly, if we act with this expectation, they often do.

To summarize, although people's subjective quality of life is obviously important, both on an experiential level and as one of the conditions for their actions, it is extremely difficult to measure. All the measures reviewed earlier in the chapter have a number of problems, which relate to their original purpose and the context of their development. Measures of subjective well-being and quality of life can fragment people's accounts of their experience or reduce them to a single indicator; in addition, measures of health-related quality of life tend to focus on physical function, which is only one aspect of our concept of well-being. The meaning of global questions is often opaque, especially if they are phrased in terms of satisfaction, and they are also prone to bias and may be difficult to answer sensibly. A common concern for scales of subjective well-being is that it is not always clear what is being measured, nor is the source of the material being used. Questions can also be culture bound, making the process of translation for use in other contexts more than merely technical. This has not been resolved by international comparative research on subjective well-being because it usually involves classifying societies as "individualist" or "collectivist," which doesn't acknowledge the multiplicity of discourses available to individuals in particular societies.

Despite these problems, however, we feel that measures of subjective well-being offer something valuable and novel to research on resilience in resource-poor environments, particularly because the question of what these measurements mean can be partially addressed with cognitive debriefing techniques and individualized measures, which enable discussion of the thought processes behind the numbers. Having explored some of the problems with measures of subjective well-being that make it more difficult to make statements about people's resilience, we will now look at the cognitive and social explanations for why people survive and thrive in "aversive environments" globally.

COMBINING PSYCHOLOGICAL AND SOCIAL EXPLANATIONS OF RESILIENCE

> Psychologists from Freud to Festinger have described the artful measures by which the human mind ignores, augments, transforms and rearranges information in its unending battle against the affective consequence of negative events. (Gilbert et al., 1998, p. 619)

> Our mental reactions to what we actually get and what we can sensibly expect to get may frequently involve compromises with a harsh reality. The destitute thrown into beggary, the vulnerable landless laborer precariously surviving at the edge of subsistence, the over-worked domestic servant working round the clock, the subdued and subjugated housewife reconciled to her role and her fate, all tend to come to terms with their respective predicaments. The deprivations are suppressed and muffled in the necessity of endurance in uneventful survival. (Sen, 1984, pp. 21–22)

As we have already noted, mean scores from measures of subjective well-being and subjective quality of life are uniformly high across country and population groups. A meta-analysis by Cummins (1995) of the subjective well-being literature found mean satisfaction scores of between 70% to 80% in Europe and America and 60% to 80% SM (percentage of scale maximum) in Africa, which fell within a very narrow range (two standard deviations from the mean). This phenomenon was observed by Brickman as early as 1978 when he described interviews with people who had been severely incapacitated by accidents or who had won the lottery and a control group who had experienced neither (Brickman, Coates, & Janoff Bulman, 1978). Brickman found that there was no significant difference in happiness between people who had won the lottery and the control group, and little between the control group and the people who had been severely incapacitated, who still rated themselves as happier than average. This supports Headey and Wearing's (1988) finding that "in nearly all countries that have been studied, almost all sections of the community rate their subjective wellbeing above the mid-point of scales" (p. 497).[9]

Thus, we return to the issue of explaining the gap, or how it is that subjective well-being appears to vary so little between countries and people where there are gross differences in the material conditions that people experience. In psychology, explanations have been sought in genetics (Lykken & Tellegen, 1996), personality (Costa, McCrae, & Zonderman, 1987), and various conscious and unconscious processes—for example, "positive illusions" (Taylor & Brown 1988), "global positivity bias" (Schwarz & Strack, 1991) (rating global areas higher than specific ones), and "selective evaluation"[10] (Taylor, Wood, & Lichtman, 1983). It is argued that the purpose of these mechanisms is to "regulate" self-esteem by sustaining a "sense of relative superiority" (Tesser, 2001; see also Headey & Wearing, 1988). They operate alongside longer-term processes such as "adaptation" and "response shift" (Blumberg & Golembiewski, 1976; Schwartz & Sprangers, 1999; Sprangers & Schwartz, 1999). If we are to understand resilience, with all the subjectivity and perceptual variation that has been overlooked in assessments of who is surviving and thriving and who is not, then we must begin to examine critically the mechanisms and processes by which people sustain views of themselves as healthy, and therefore resilient, even when others would "objectively" categorize them as vulnerable or unhealthy based on particular understandings of how one *should* respond to exposure to adversity. We will now selectively review some of the discussions of these key processes and look at the ways in which cognitive and social explanations are interwoven in them.

The "Focusing Illusion"

The concept of the "focusing illusion," as advanced by Schkade and Kahneman (1998), addresses the differences between the "outsider's view" and the feelings and interpretations of the subjects of observation. Following experiments that asked students to assess the happiness of paraplegics, Schkade and Kahneman concluded that "the less you know about paraplegics, the worse off you think they are" (p. 340). In their article on poor people in Calcutta, Biswas-Diener and Diener (2001)

recognize the significance of this concept. They note that in a study of this kind, it means that "easily observed and distinctive differences" may be given more weight in their assessment of people's quality of life than these would have in the subject's own reality. The authors conclude that "it is apparent that while the poor of Calcutta do not lead enviable lives, they do lead meaningful lives. They capitalize on the non-material resources available to them and find satisfaction in many areas of their lives" (p. 349).

The need to take account of what poor people have and are able to do rather than focus on their deficits has already been acknowledged in recent approaches to understanding the dynamics of poverty and of surviving and thriving in developing countries (see Lawson, McGregor, & Saltmarshe, 2000).

The focusing illusion has profound implications for how we study people's experiences of poverty and ill-being in developing countries, and Schkade and Kahneman (1998) highlight it as a significant potential source of research bias. It suggests that external researchers are poorly equipped to judge what people are experiencing and will focus on obvious and measurable differences, which may have little effect on subjective judgments of quality of life. This is particularly true where the experiences are unfamiliar, and the point is reinforced by the human tendency to underestimate how quickly people adapt.

"False Consciousness"

The gap between poor people's accounts of their experiences and those of external observers has been a rich ground of debate in the social sciences. It is explored by Nobel prize winner Amartya Sen (1999) in his meditations on poverty, where he expresses concern that people's perceptions of how they are doing "can be easily swayed by mental conditioning or adaptive expectations" (p. 62), leading to the "scandalous" situation where, "If a starving wreck, ravished by famine, buffeted by disease, is made happy through some mental conditioning (say, via the 'opium' of religion), the person will be seen as doing well on this mental states perspective" (p. 188).

In support of this, he cites evidence from a postfamine health survey of widows in India that suggested significant disparities between self-reports and external observations (Sen, 1984, p. 309). He also appeals to a form of the false consciousness argument by stating that people's accounts are shaped by wider social, cultural, and political structures and as such cannot always be taken as "true" reflections of their experience or satisfaction with it.

The debate over the place of the concept of false consciousness in the social sciences is, however, a long and weary one. In 1975, Scott described the false consciousness argument as an inadequate or even obstructive analytical device in the study of developing countries and their peoples. He notes that "when perceptions of workers or peasants (assuming these can be accurately gauged), whom the (class) theory tells us are exploited, fails to accord with their 'objective situation' they are said to be in a state of false consciousness" (p. 491).

Lockwood (1981) expresses similar concerns to Scott as a more general and fundamental criticism of Marxist theory. He argues that this flaw in its theory of action lies at the heart of crises in contemporary Marxist theories of social class. As he notes,

> In general, social theory has found only two main ways of explaining deviations from rational action. The first, an integral part of utilitarian thinking, relies heavily on the concepts of "ignorance" and "error." In other words, irrational action is seen to be due either to the actor's inadequate knowledge of the facts of the situation or to his imperfect understanding of the most efficient, that is, scientifically rational, means of attaining his ends. (p. 441)

As we have suggested, this is not enough to help us understand what poor people do to cope with and struggle out of their poverty. Their knowledge, their goals, their strategies all constitute important elements in an explanation of their resilience in adverse conditions and are also the key to making policy interventions relevant for poverty eradication.

Agency and Structure

In establishing the conceptual ground for his own study of "The Experience of Poverty" in West Bengal in India, Beck (1994) reviews a well-known and heated debate between social historians E. P. Thompson and Perry Anderson. Thompson emphasizes a bottom-up perspective on the contribution of the working classes to the creation of history and thus focuses on interpretations of the experiences of the poor, whereas Anderson criticizes this approach for failing to take adequate account for the structural determinants of the experience. As Giddens (1987) notes in reviewing the debate, the main problem is the extremity of their respective positions at either end of the agency-structure debate. Whereas Thompson understates the significance of structures in constraining and shaping individual agency, Anderson threatens to overstate structure to the extent that we end up with "seriously deficient accounts of action" (Giddens, 1987, quoted in Beck, 1994, pp. 38–39)

The combination of social and cognitive contributions to the study of the gap between objective and subjective well-being requires a recognition that structure and agency each have a range of dimensions and effects. These include not only the objective but also the relational, cognitive, and affective. Thus, agency is determined not only by the physical capacity of an individual but by the extent to which that is supported by relationships with others and their own perceptions of the extent to which they can exercise agency. Although we acknowledge the inseparability of agency and structure embodied in the notion of "structuration" employed here (see Giddens, 1976), we can also recognize that structures enable and constrain in a range of different ways. These include restricting options physically (e.g., poor infrastructure limiting access to markets or health and education facilities) and socially (e.g., community rules restricting the access of some members of the community to natural resources) and by limiting the range of what can be thought (e.g., cultural limitations on the prospect of women challenging the decisions of males).

"Response Shift"

Response shift is the psychological equivalent of false consciousness or what economists term "adaptive preferences." The concept has been particularly investigated within health-related,

QoL measurement (Schwartz & Sprangers, 2000; Sprangers & Schwartz, 1999) to explain subdued responses to medical interventions and unexpectedly high levels of quality of life among people with disabling conditions. Response shift represents a change in the meaning of the respondent's evaluation of subjective well-being or quality of life. It results, Sprangers and Schwartz argue, from three processes: a change in internal standards (recalibration),[11] a change in the person's values (reprioritization of values), and a redefinition or reconceptualization of quality of life. Upward and downward comparisons appear to be the main way of achieving this shift (Michalos, 1985; Suls & Wheeler, 2000), but other coping mechanisms—for example, seeking support from social networks—may also be involved.

Response shift provides another explanation for the findings of Gilbert et al. (1998) who demonstrated experimentally that people overestimate the duration of their affective reactions to both happy and sad events and return to their previous state within a much shorter time period than they predicted. There are some conditions, however, that people never adapt to, as Cummins (2000) acknowledges in the concept of "homeostatic defeat." The death of a husband (Stroebe, Gergen, Gergen, & Stroebe, 1996) or child is one, although the anthropologist Scheper-Hughes (1993) suggests that in areas of high infant mortality, mothers can protect themselves by not becoming emotionally attached to a child until it reaches a certain age or distancing themselves from children who appear sickly.

Social Comparison

Social comparison (or "rivalry") is also becoming an important concept for contemporary economists in their forays into the field of subjective well-being. Kahneman and Tversky (1984) note that all human judgments are relative to the "frame" in which they are made and that an important part of this frame is the performance of others, which is established through social comparison (see Parducci, 1995). In other words, social comparison is one way that people get a sense of how they're doing and manage feelings of stress or anxiety. The general

view is that comparisons can be made in three directions: downward, which generally has a bolstering effect; laterally, through affiliation, which can make people feel more secure; and upward, which can increase self-esteem and motivation, or reduce them, if people feel their situation cannot be changed. Taylor et al. (1983) and Wood, Taylor, and Lichtman (1985) observed the cheering effect of downward comparison among the husbands of female breast cancer patients who even invented "mythical men" (men who were not giving their wives the support that they were) to compare themselves with!

Kahneman and Tversky (1984) introduce a further dimension of comparison with the proposition that people tend to evaluate outcomes as changes, not states. People make comparisons over time, both forward toward the future (how things might be) and backward (how things used to be). For example, according to Kahneman and Tversky, people will judge what it is like to be destitute by imagining what it is like to become destitute. This adds the further distortion of the focusing illusion, where from their present position people may overstate the impact of the change by misconstruing what it is to be destitute.

Already, the notion of comparison is complex, and it is made less straightforward still by the fact that empirical studies show no certain direction of comparison. This is because people have multiple identities, which leads to shifts in who their comparator groups might be, and also because people make strategic choices about the types of information they attend to in making their judgments (e.g., depressed people don't always compare downward). Earlier theories about "forced comparisons" (where reference groups are dictated by proximity) have been disproved by studies showing that rich people or nations are not happier if their neighbors are poorer (Diener, Sandvik, Seidlitz, & Diener, 1993; Diener et al., 1995).[12] This may be because judgments of satisfaction come from comparisons with a number of standards, including past experience, expectations, and ideals (Michalos, 1985; Sirgy et al., 1995). But what is clear is that whoever people are comparing themselves to, a comparison gap makes them feel unhappy.

The "Comparison Gap"

The importance of the "comparison gap" highlights the potential significance of inequality for perceptions of subjective well-being. Where there is considerable and evident inequality, this may have a significant effect on the subjective well-being of others within the same area. But it also highlights the question of who people are able to compare themselves with. In this respect, the choice of comparisons may be constrained by norms, traditions, or aspects of culture. A recent study by Graham and Pettinato (2002) using data from Peru and Russia focuses on the ways in which comparisons work within communities and nation-states. Although they confirm that "after a certain absolute level of basic income—relative income differences matter more than absolute ones" (p. 128), they then observe that this differs for those located at different trajectories in the income distribution. Intriguingly, they note that "differences are more important for those in the middle of our distribution than for either the very wealthy or the very poor" (p. 129). They also note the increasing significance of international comparisons for some groups.

Michalos has been one of the foremost voices in this area of study. Testing his multiple discrepancy theory[13] (Michalos, 1985) in over 18,000 students from 39 countries, he demonstrates that among this population at least, the comparison gap is the strongest correlate of life satisfaction, happiness, and satisfaction with health (Michalos, 1991). The results of these and other studies later prompted him to suggest that

in so far as policy makers are primarily interested in voters' satisfaction with their health rather than with voters' health itself (because net satisfaction drives voting behaviour more than health drives voting behaviour), they might reap greater benefits by manipulating voters' perceived discrepancies rather than improving their health. (Michalos, 2004, p. 65)

However, this is not news to politicians and "spin doctors" who have produced many examples of the "you've never had it so good" style of political campaign. Nor has this been overlooked by academics in other disciplines (consider, e.g., Keynes with his emphasis on moral suasion in his discussions of economic policy options). It may, however, be something that contemporary neoclassical economists and their market-loving political adherents have partially forgotten.

THE HOMEOSTATIC THEORY OF SUBJECTIVE WELL-BEING: AN ATTEMPT AT SYNTHESIS

Robert Cummins (2002a has made a gallant attempt to bring many strands of the SWB and psychology literature together in his "homeostatic theory of subjective well-being." This proposes that SWB indicators such as happiness and life satisfaction are maintained by a "dispositional brain system" that keeps each person's well-being within a narrow, positive range. The system consists of (a) an "unconscious, constitutional component," dominated by the two personality factors of extroversion and neuroticism, and (b) a conscious "buffering system," consisting of self-esteem, perceived control, and optimism,[14] which filters the impact of environmental events.

Although the unresponsiveness of subjective well-being seems to make it a poor indicator (see Felce, 1997), Cummins (2002b) argues that "the fact that it is generally predictable and stable enhances its usefulness . . . because the values for subjective QoL can be referenced to a normative range [which] is homeostatically maintained" (p. 264), making it the best way of identifying an "aversive environment." He even suggests it could "yield substantial new understanding concerning human resilience" by enabling us to ask, "What are the conditions that produce homeostatic defeat?" and "What are the personal and instrumental resources that defend against such defeat?" (p. 264).

THE WeD APPROACH AND PRELIMINARY INSIGHTS

One of the key elements of the WeD conceptual framework is the resource profiles approach (RPA). This approach has been developed over the years by academic staff and research students at the University of Bath as a means of exploring how individuals and households deploy different types of resources in their struggles to survive and thrive. The approach broadens the notion of resources from that conventionally employed in economics and operates with five categories of resource (material, human, natural, social, and cultural), each of which have material, relational, and symbolic dimensions (McGregor, 2000). This framework is useful in helping us understand the repeated observations that where individuals or households are working with few material and human resources (where they are experiencing what is objectively defined as poverty—low incomes, low levels of nutrition, education, or skills), the significance of the social and cultural resources they are able to deploy becomes all the greater (McGregor, 1994; Wood, 2003). Where households are materially poor, they may adopt "survival strategies" that involve investing scarce human or material resources not directly in the production of food or income but in social relationships (see Wood, 2003) or in forms of cultural status (see Lawson et al., 2000). This way of conceiving of and analyzing resources fits well with both the work of Cummins (2000, 2002) and the study by Biswas-Diener and Diener (2001) in that both emphasize the diversity of resources that people use to maintain resilience and the significance of nonmaterial resources in aversive environments.

A major challenge of the first phase of the WeD fieldwork has been to integrate approaches to subjective well-being with the RPA. In each of the four study countries (Bangladesh, Ethiopia, Peru, and Thailand), we have selected at least four rural and two urban communities in which to carry out detailed and intensive fieldwork over an 18-month period. Preliminary fieldwork in all of the countries has built up community profiles for each of the rural communities being studied. The community profiles have provided an overview of some of the basic parameters of the communities selected—their demography and social, political, and economic structures— and also begin to offer some insights into the ways in which people think about well-being.

The fieldwork seeks to achieve two things in its first phase:

1. To establish what resources individuals and households have and how these are distributed within the communities

2. To explore what people themselves in these communities consider to be important in their own definition of well-being

The first of these two objectives is addressed using a specifically designed survey instrument (the Resources and Needs Questionnaire or RANQ), which is applied where possible to all households in the selected communities. Using the RPA categories, it provides a means of establishing what people objectively "have" at their disposal and then allows further purposive subsampling for more detailed qualitative fieldwork, which will explore what people can then "do" with these resources. The second objective focuses on the subjective dimensions of the research, and in this, we begin with a more inductive phase, going back to the foundations of the conceptual debates about quality of life and subjective well-being. As indicated earlier in the discussion, there is concern, first, that as measures of quality of life have become more psychometrically sophisticated, they may have lost touch with what they are actually measuring and second, that specific notions of subjective well-being may not be cross-culturally applicable. To address both concerns, the WeD integration of subjective well-being begins with a more inductive approach, exploring what people in these communities report as being important to them and how they make judgments about these matters.

This involves the use of individual semistructured interviews, focus groups, and also experimentation with and adaptation of individualized QoL approaches (e.g., Ruta, 1998). The latter fit well with this phase of the WeD research because they are designed both to "elicit the value system of individual respondents and to quantify quality of life using this elicited system" (Browne, McGee, & O'Boyle, 1997, p. 742). The feasibility of individualized QoL measures has been tested by a small number of pilot exercises in Ethiopia and Bangladesh, which found that people in Ethiopia who completed the measure "visibly enjoyed" allocating coins to indicate their priorities and were "amused and pleased" by the outcome (Bevan, Kebede, & Pankhurst, 2003). The use of these methods in the initial phase of the WeD research is one means by which the research investigates whether subjective quality of life is simply the extent to which "the hopes of an individual are matched and fulfilled by experience" (Calman, 1984, pp. 124–125), which would suggest that development interventions should focus on adjusting people's expectations rather than on their material conditions because these have a greater influence on their reality.

The community profiling work that has been carried out in Ethiopia offers us preliminary insights into some of the factors that people themselves consider important for their resilience in their particular circumstances. It also illustrates how these factors can be seen as consistent with, and provide further validation for, the multidimensional approach to resources described above. The WIDE (Wellbeing and Ill-Being Dynamics in Ethiopia) was a scoping study carried out as part of the preparation for the main phases of the WeD fieldwork. It is an individually interview-administered questionnaire, which is structured around eight modules and which elicits open-ended answers. Four hundred men and women were interviewed in 20 rural sites, most of which have been subject to periodic study by the Ethiopian researchers over the last 15 years.

From the answers, we get a sense of what different kinds of resources matter for people's sense of well-being in this context. The inquiry has produced a number of examples of individual "coping strategies" with objective, relational, and subjective dimensions. When people were asked how they cope with bad times, the use of comparisons was evident. For example, one woman's response combined comparisons with her own past and the present experiences of others: "She remembers her good times and (that other) people suffer more than her." The responses to the questions illustrate a wide and diverse range of resources that are important in the struggle to cope with adversity. Spiritual responses are noted as important for many of the respondents, and three other dimensions of the RPA are also strongly highlighted.

Human Resource Dimensions. In its conception of human resources, the RPA has sought, alongside

Sen's (1985, 1999) capability approach, to broaden out what in individuals is to be considered as contributing to their struggle to secure their state of well-being. Here, we go beyond those aspects normally dealt with in "human capital" approaches (looking at labor power, levels of education or skills, and health condition) to look at some of the characteristics or traits of individuals that may result in their being more successful than others in achieving their desired state of well-being. Although the development literature has flirted with what could be considered to be "cross-over" traits,[15] such as entrepreneurialism, some of the SWB literature draws us closely into more personal characteristics. Here we can begin to explore what types of human characteristics are considered valuable in particular cultural contexts. The WIDE responses particularly emphasize those characteristics that relate to making social relations work well within both the household and the wider community. Traits considered necessary for men and women to live well include being sociable, generous, and hospitable ("the way she celebrates the feasts"); being "communicative" ("having a bright face"); being industrious, neat, and clean; being respectful rather than proud or insulting; and being practical and a good "administrator" of home and family.

Social Resource Dimensions. The human resource responses give a strong indication of the importance of social relationships for the respondents to the WIDE. These are further amplified in responses that emphasize appropriate behaviors within both the family and community. The responses indicate that in these Ethiopian communities, quality of life is closely related to the quality of family relationships and social networks and that the role each member of the household plays in sustaining this is clearly defined. For example, a husband should "eat with his family on time," be "proud of and love his wife" and have "good relations with family," while a wife should "feed children in a good way," "live in peace and happiness" and foster "peaceful and respectful relation in the home." The household as a whole should also contribute by maintaining a "feeling of kinship" with the community, "support(ing) relatives and other kinsmen" and "assist(ing) others in time of problems."

Cultural Resource Issues. Finally, coffee features in a significant number of responses, reflecting its cultural importance in the Ethiopian context. As one respondent reported, his way of coping with adversity was as follows:

> "I order my wife to serve a coffee (a good one) and enjoy it with my neighbors."

This quote captures the relational and symbolic importance of the preparation and consumption of coffee in Ethiopian rural life. This is true even for the very poorest, to the extent that not having anyone to drink coffee with practically defines what it is to be poor, lonely, or socially excluded.

CONCLUSION

This chapter has offered some indications of how contemporary research on well-being in developing countries is seeking to integrate both objective and subjective approaches to our understanding of how poverty is experienced and reproduced. It argues that it is necessary to bring together contributions from a range of different academic disciplines if we are to understand the resilience that many people in developing countries demonstrate from day to day. "The gap" between people's own evaluations of their lives and what others perceive as their material poverty, requires constructive explanation and not simple dismissal as a product of misinformation or poor judgment. After all, like the rest of us, materially poor people have just got to get on with their lives. They have to avoid Cummins's (2002) homeostatic defeat. However, if policymakers are intent on eradicating poverty—or to put it another way, on assisting people in impoverished circumstances—they cannot formulate their schemes and interventions ignorant of the views and aspirations of men women and children in these circumstances and the strategies they adopt to simply survive or perhaps even thrive.

NOTES

1. Human development approaches use indicators such as literacy and mortality rather than economic outcomes such as increases in gross national product (e.g., the UNDP's Human Development Index [HDI]).

2. In ascending order of per capita income, Ethiopia, Bangladesh, Peru, and Thailand (see www.welldev.org.uk). The purchasing power parity measure makes incomes comparable by taking account of the cost of goods in each country.

3. In the creation of the Multiple Sclerosis Impact Scale-29 item (Hobart, Lamping, Fitzpatrick, Riazi, & Thompson, 2001) where there were statements that the researchers did not think related to quality of life (e.g., reactions to diagnosis), these were excluded from the first draft of the measure. Subsequently, items related to "coping with multiple sclerosis" and the "positive impact of multiple sclerosis" were excluded as "irrelevant" given the "treatment" orientation of the instrument, although they were obviously relevant to the lives of the people who generated them.

4. For example, "On the whole, are you very satisfied, fairly satisfied, not very satisfied, or not at all satisfied with the life you lead?"

5. For example, the World Values Survey (http://wvs.isr.umich.edu), the Eurobarometer (http://europa.eu.int/comm/public_opinion), and the South African General Household survey (available at www.statssa.gov.za).

6. See www.eur.nl/fsw/research/happiness.

7. "Order effects" are a problem where preceding questions focus respondents' attention on particular definitions of well-being, causing them to evaluate their experience in those terms (e.g., how much money they have or, in one experiment with students, how many dates they had had in the past month; Schwarz, 1996).

8. Mainly from the research groups of Diener or Ryan and Deci, both part of the emergent "positive psychology" movement in the United States (see the Gallup Positive Psychology Center www.gallup.hu/pps).

9. See Edgerton (1996) for a review of this literature.

10. "The point is, of course, that everyone is better off than someone as long as one picks the right dimension" (Taylor, Wood, & Lichtman, 1983, p. 30).

11. See also Carver (2000) who suggests that the affect system is continuously calibrated, causing

those who experience repeated negative affect to become less demanding, whereas those who experience repeated positive affect become more so.

12. However, there are "context effects." For example, Strack, Schwarz, Chassein, Kern, and Wagner (1990) observed that the presence of a person with disabilities in the room caused people to report higher subjective well-being, and questionnaires can also have a normative effect where response alternatives shape responses by providing information about the typical distribution of a characteristic in the population (Schwarz, 1996).

13. Michalos (1985) identified six discrepancies between "self now" and "others now," "self past best," "self expected by now," "self expected in future," "self deserves," and "self needs." These discrepancies, along with demographic variables, income, self-esteem, and social support, influence "perceived self now/wants" and produce "net satisfaction."

14. The three "positive illusions" (described by Taylor & Brown, 1988) that are the key to sustaining good mental health.

15. By "cross-over," we mean a trait that is cognitive but has been studied by disciplines other than psychology; for example, entrepreneurialism is dealt with by both management studies and economics (for development studies, see MacClelland's, 1961, work on "n-ach").

REFERENCES

Ager, A. (2002). "Quality of life" assessment in critical context. *Journal of Applied Research in Intellectual Disabilities, 15*(4), 369–376.

Alkire, S. (2002). Dimensions of human development. *World Development, 30*(2), 181–205.

Andrews, F., & Withey, S. (1976). *Social indicators of well-being: Americans' perceptions of quality of life.* New York: Plenum Press.

Antaki, C., & Rapley. M. (1996). "Quality of Life" talk: The liberal paradox of psychological testing. *Discourse and Society, 7,* 293–316.

Bardhan, P. (2001). Distributive conflicts, collective action and institutional economics. In G. M. Meier & J. E. Stiglitz (Eds.), *Frontiers of development economics: The future in perspective* (pp. 269–298). Oxford, UK: Oxford University Press.

Beck, T. (1994). *"The rich don't help the poor, and they never did": Power and the poorest. The experience of poverty. Fighting for respect and resources in village India.* London: Intermediate Technology.

Bevan, P., Kebede, K., & Pankhurst, A. (2003). *A report on a very informal pilot of the Person Generated Index© of Quality of Life in Ethiopia.* Unpublished manuscript, ESRC Research Group, Wellbeing in Developing Countries, Swindon, UK.

Biswas Diener, R., & Diener, E. (2001). Making the best of a bad situation: Satisfaction in the slums of Calcutta. *Social Indicators Research, 55,* 329–352.

Blumberg, A., & Golembiewski, R. T. (1976). *Learning and change in groups.* Oxford, UK: Penguin.

Bowling, A. (1995). A survey of the public's judgments to inform scales of QOL. *Social Science & Medicine, 41,* 1411–1417.

Bradburn, N. M. (1969). *The structure of psychological well-being.* Oxford, UK: Aldine.

Brickman, P., Coates, D., & Janoff-Bulman, R. (1978). Lottery winners and accident victims: Is happiness relative? *Journal of Personality and Social Psychology, 36*(8), 917–927.

Browne, J. P., McGee, H. M., & O'Boyle, C. A. (1997). Conceptual approaches to the assessment of quality of life. *Psychological Health, 12,* 737–751.

Calman, K. C. (1984). QOL in cancer patients a hypothesis. *Journal of Medical Ethics, 10,* 124–127.

Carver, C. S. (2000). On the continuous calibration of happiness. *American Journal on Mental Retardation 105,* 336–341.

Christopher, J. C. (1999). Situating psychological well-being: Exploring the cultural roots of its theory and research. *Journal of Counseling & Development, 77,* 141–152.

Clark, D. A. (2000). *Concepts and perceptions of development: Some evidence from the Western Cape* (Working Paper 88). Cape Town: University of Cape Town, South Africa Labour and Development Research Unit.

Costa, P. T., McCrae, R. R., & Zonderman, A. B. (1987). Environmental and dispositional influences on wellbeing: Longitudinal follow-up of an American national sample. *British Journal of Psychology, 78,* 299–306.

Cummins, R. (1995). On the trail of a gold standard for subjective well-being. *Social Indicators Research, 35,* 179–200.

Cummins, R. (2000). Personal income and subjective well-being: A review. *Journal of Happiness Studies, 1,* 133–158.

Cummins, R. (2002a). Normative life satisfaction: Measurement issues and a homeostatic model. *Social Indicators Research, 64,* 225–256.

Cummins, R. (2002b). The validity and utility of subjective quality of life: A reply to Hatton & Ager. *Journal of Applied Research in Intellectual Disabilities, 15,* 261–268.

Cummins, R., & Nistico, H. (2002). Maintaining life satisfaction: The role of positive cognitive bias. *Journal of Happiness Studies, 3,* 37–69.

Diener, E. (1984). Subjective well-being. *Psychological Bulletin, 95*(3), 542–575.

Diener, E. (2000). Subjective well-being: The science of happiness and a proposal for a national index. *American Psychologist, 55,* 34–43.

Diener, E., & Biswas-Diener, R. (2002). Will money increase subjective well-being? *Social Indicators Research, 57,* 119–169.

Diener, E., & Diener, C. (1995). The wealth of nations revisited: Income and quality of life. *Social Indicators Research, 36,* 275–286.

Diener, E., Emmons, R. A., Larsen, R. J., & Griffin, S. (1985). The Satisfaction With Life Scale. *Journal of Personality Assessment, 49*(1), 71–75.

Diener, E., Sandvik, E., Seidlitz, L., & Diener, M. (1993). The relationship between income and subjective well-being: Relative or absolute? *Social Indicators Research, 28,* 195–223.

Diener, E., & Suh, E. M. (1999). National differences in subjective well-being. In D. Kahneman & E. Diener (Eds.), *Well-being: The foundations of hedonic psychology* (pp. 434–450). New York: Russell Sage.

Diener, E., Suh, E. M., Lucas, R. E., & Smith, H. E. (1999). Subjective well-being: Three decades of progress. *Psychological Bulletin, 125,* 276–302.

Diener, E., Suh, E., Smith, H., & Shao, L. (1995). National differences in reported subjective well-being: Why do they occur? *Social Indicators Research, 34,* 7–32.

Easterlin, R. A. (2004, May). *Diminishing marginal utility of income? A caveat* (Working Paper 5). University of Southern California Legal Working Paper Series. University of Southern California Law and Economics Working Paper Series. [Available at http://law.bepress.com/usclwps/lewps/art5]

Edgerton, R. B. (1996). A longitudinal ethnographic research perspective on quality of life. In R. L. Schalock & Siperstein, N. (Eds.), *Quality of life: Vol. 1. Conceptualization and Measurement* (pp. 839–890). Washington, DC: American Association on Mental Retardation.

Felce, D. (1997). Defining and applying the concept of quality of life. *Journal of Intellectual Disability Research, 41*(2), 126–135.

Frey, B. S., & Stutzer, A. (2002). What can economists learn from happiness research? *Journal of Economic Literature, 40,* 402–435.

Giddens, A. (1976). *New rules of sociological method.* London: Hutchinson of London.

Giddens, A. (1987). *Social theory and modern sociology.* Cambridge, UK: Polity Press.

Gilbert, G. T., Pinel, E. C., Wilson, T. D., Blumberg, S. J., & Wheatley, T. P. (1998). Immune neglect: A source of durability bias in affective forecasting. *Journal of Personality and Social Psychology, 75,* 617–638.

Graham, C., & Pettinato, S. (2002). *Happiness and hardship: Opportunity and insecurity in new market economies.* Washington, DC: Brookings Institution Press.

Hamer, D. H. (1996). The heritability of happiness. *Nature Genetics, 14*(2), 125–126.

Headey, B., & Wearing, A. (1988). The sense of relative superiority: Central to well-being. *Social Indicators Research, 20,* 497–516.

Hirata, J. (2001). *Happiness and economics: Enriching economic theory with empirical psychology.* Unpublished master's thesis, Maastricht University, Maastricht, The Netherlands.

Hobart, J., Lamping, D., Fitzpatrick, R., Riazi, A., & Thompson, A. (2001). The Multiple Sclerosis Impact Scale (MSIS29): A new patient-based outcome measure. *Brain, 124*(5), 962–973.

Hunt, S. (1999). The researcher's tale: A story of virtue lost and regained. In C. R. B. Joyce, C. A. O'Boyle, & H. McGee (Eds.), *Individual quality of life: Approaches to conceptualization and assessment* (pp. 225–231). Amsterdam, Netherlands: Harwood Academic.

Inglehart, R., Basañez, M., Díez-Medrano, J., Halman, L., & Luijkx, R. (Eds.). (2004). *Human beliefs and values. A cross-cultural sourcebook based on the 1999–2002 values surveys.* Mexico City: Siglo XXI Editores.

Inglehardt, R., & Klingemann, H. D. (2000). Genes, culture, democracy, and happiness. In E. Diener &

E. M. Suh (Eds.), *Culture and subjective well-being* (pp. 185–218). Cambridge: MIT Press.

Ireland, M., McGregor, J. A., & Saltmarshe, D. (2003). Challenges for donor agency country level performance assessment: A review. *Public Administration and Development, 23,* 419–431.

Joyce, C. R. B., O'Boyle, C. A., & McGee, H. (1999). *Individual quality of life: Approaches to conceptualization and assessment.* Amsterdam, Netherlands: Harwood Academic.

Kahneman, D., & Tversky, A. (1984). Choices, values and frames. *American Psychologist, 39,* 341–350.

Keedwell, P., & Snaith, R. P. (1996). What do anxiety scales measure? *Acta Psychiatrica Scandinavia, 93,* 177–180.

Kilian, R., Lindenbach, I., Lobig, U., & Angermeyer, M. C. (1999). The subjective meaning of psychiatry outpatient care for the quality of life of people with chronic schizophrenia: A qualitative analysis [Abstract]. *Quality of Life Research, 8*(7), 576.

Kim, U., Triandis, H. C., Kagitcibasi, C., Choi, S. C., & Yoon, G. (Eds.). (1994). *Individualism and collectivism: Theory, method, and applications* (Cross-Cultural Research and Methodology Series, Vol. 18). Thousand Oaks, CA: Sage.

Kind, P. (1996). The EUROQOL instrument: An index of HRQOL. In B. Spilker (Ed.), *Quality of life and pharmacoeconomics in clinical trials* (2nd ed., pp. 32–47). Philadelphia: Lippincott-Raven.

Larson, R., & Shao, L. (1993). Culture and contentment: Is the path of happiness universal? *Hiroshima Forum for Psychology, 15,* 47–48.

Lawson, C. W., McGregor, J. A., & Saltmarshe, D. K. (2000). Surviving and thriving: Differentiation in a peri-urban community in Northern Albania. *World Development, 28*(8), 1499–514.

Layard, R. (2003, March). *Happiness: Has social science a clue?* Lionel Robbins Memorial Lectures 2002/3, London School of Economics. Retrieved January 4, 2005, from http://cep.lse.ac.uk/events/lectures/layard/RL030303.pdf

Leplege, A., & Marquis, P. (1999, November). *Workshop on cross cultural issues in HRQOL.* Paper presented at the International Society for Quality of Life Research conference, Barcelona, Spain.

Leplege, R., & Hunt, S. (1997). The problem of QOL in medicine. *Journal of the American Medical Association, 278,* 47–50.

Lockwood, D. (1981). The weakest link in the chain? Some comments on the Marxist theory of action. In R. I. Simpson (Ed.), *Research in the sociology of work* (Vol. 1, pp. 435–481). Greenwich, CT: JAI Press.

Lukes, S. (1986). *Power.* Oxford, UK: Basil Blackwell.

Lykken, D., & Tellegen, A. (1996). Happiness is a stochastic phenomenon. *Psychological Science, 7*(3), 186–189.

MacClelland, D. C. (1961). *The achieving society.* Princeton, NJ: Van Nostrand.

Markus, H. R., & Kitayama, S. (1991). Culture and the self: Implications for cognition, emotion, and motivation. *Psychological Review, 98*(2), 224–253.

McDowell, I., & Newell, C. (1987). *Measuring health.* Oxford, UK: Oxford University Press.

McGregor, J. A. (1994). Village credit and the reproduction of poverty in rural Bangladesh. In J. Acheson (Ed.), *Anthropology and institutional economics* (pp. 261–281). Washington, DC: Society for Economic Anthropology, University of America Press.

McGregor, J. A. (2000). *A poverty of agency: Resource management amongst poor people in Bangladesh.* Paper presented at the Plenary Session of European Network of Bangladesh Studies Workshop, University of Bath, England, April 1998. 2000 draft retrieved January 4, 2005, from http://staff.bath.ac.uk/hssjam/povertyofagency.pdf

Michalos, A. C. (1985). Multiple discrepancies theory MDT. *Social Indicators Research, 16,* 347–413.

Michalos, A. C. (1991). *Global report on student well-being: Vol. I. Life satisfaction and happiness.* New York: Springer.

Michalos, A. C. (2004). Social indicators research and health related quality of life research. *Social Indicators Research, 65*(1), 27–72.

Moller, V. (2001). Happiness trends under democracy: Where will the new South African set-level come to rest? *Journal of Happiness Studies, 2*(1), 33–53.

Narayan, D., Chambers, R., Shah, M. K., & Petesch, P. (2000). *Voices of the poor: Crying out for change.* New York: Oxford University Press for the World Bank.

Nord, E., Arnesen, T., Menzel, P., & Pinto, J. (2001, January–June). Towards a more restricted use of the term "quality of life." *Quality of Life Newsletter, 26,* 1–28.

O'Boyle, C., McGee, H., Hickey, A., O'Malley, K., & Joyce, C. R. B. (1992). Individual QOL in patients undergoing hip replacement. *Lancet, 339,* 1088–1091.

Oishi, S., Diener, E. F., Lucas, R. E., & Suh, E. M. (1999). Cross cultural variations in predictors of life satisfaction: Perspectives from needs and values. *Personality and Social Psychology Bulletin, 25,* 980–990.

Oishi, S., Schimmack, U., Diener, E., & Suh, E. M. (1998). The measurement of values and individualism-collectivism. *Personality and Social Psychology Bulletin, 24*(11), 1177–1189.

Oswald, A. (2003). The macroeconomics of happiness. *Review of economics and statistics, 85,* 809–827.

Ouweneel, P., & Veenhoven, R. (1991). Cross national differences in happiness: Cultural bias or societal quality? In N. Bleichrodt & P. A. Drenth (Eds.), *Contemporary issues in cross cultural psychology* (pp. 168–184). Amsterdam: Swets & Zeitlinger.

Parducci, A. (1995). *Happiness pleasure and judgment: The contextual theory and its applications.* Hillsdale, NJ: Erlbaum.

Redelmeier, D. A., & Kahneman, D. (1996). Patients' memories of painful medical treatments: Realtime and retrospective evaluations of two minimally invasive procedures. *Pain, 66*(1), 3–8.

Ruta, D. A. (1998). Patient generated assessment: The next generation. *MAPI Quality of Life Newsletter, 20,* 461–489.

Ruta, D. A., Garratt, A. M., Leng, M., Russell, I. T., & MacDonald, L. M. (1994). A new approach to the measurement of QOL. The patient-generated index. *Medical Care, 32*(11), 1109–1126.

Ryff, C. D. (1989). Happiness is everything, or is it? Explorations on the meaning of psychological well-being. *Journal of Personality and Social Psychology, 57*(6), 1069–1081.

Scheper-Hughes, N. (1993). *Death without weeping: The violence of everyday life in Brazil.* London: University of California Press.

Schimmack, U., Diener, E., & Oishi, S. (2002). Life satisfaction is a momentary judgment and a stable personality characteristic: The use of chronically accessible and stable sources. *Journal of Personality, 70*(3), 345–384.

Schkade, D. A., & Kahneman, D. (1998). Does living in California make people happy? A focusing illusion in judgments of life satisfaction. *Psychological Science, 9*(5), 340–346.

Schwarz, N. (1996). *Cognition and communication: Judgmental biases, research methods and the logic of conversation* (John M. MacEachran memorial lecture series). Mahwah, NJ: Erlbaum.

Schwarz, N., & Strack, F. (1991). Evaluating one's life: A judgment model of subjective well-being. In Strack, F., Argyle, M., & Schwarz, N. (Eds.), *Subjective well-being: An interdisciplinary perspective. Vol. 21. International series in experimental social psychology* (pp. 27–47). Elmsford, NY: Pergamon Press.

Schwartz, C. E., & Sprangers, M. A. (1999). Methodological approaches for assessing response shift in longitudinal health-related quality of life research. *Social Science & Medicine, 48*(11), 153–148.

Schwartz, C. E., & Sprangers, M. A. (2000). *Adaptation to changing health: Response shift in quality-of-life research.* Washington, D.C.: American Psychological Association Books.

Scott, J. C. (1975). Exploitation and rural class relations: A victim's perspective. *Comparative politics, 7,* 489–532.

Sen, A. (1984). *Resources, values and development.* Oxford, UK: Blackwell.

Sen, A. (1999). *Development as freedom.* New York: Knopf.

Shweder, R. A. (1993). *Thinking through cultures: Expeditions in cultural psychology.* Cambridge, MA: Harvard University Press.

Sirgy, J. M., Cole, D., Kosenko, R., Meadow, L. H., Rahtz, D., Cicic, M., Xi Jin, G., et al. (1995). A life satisfaction measure: Additional validational data for the congruity life satisfaction measure. *Social Indicators Research, 34*(2), 237–259.

Sprangers, M. A. G., & Schwartz, C. E. (1999). Integrating response shift into health-related quality of life research: A theoretical model. *Social Science & Medicine, 48,* 1507–1515.

Strack, F., Schwarz, N., Chassein, B., Kern, D., & Wagner, D. (1990). Salience of comparison standards and the activation of social norms: Consequences for judgements of happiness and their communication. *British Journal of Social Psychology, 29*(4), 303–314.

Stroebe, M., Gergen, M., Gergen, K., & Stroebe, W. (1996). Broken hearts or broken bonds? In D. Klass, P. R. Silverman, & Nickman, S. L. (Eds.), *Continuing bonds: New understandings of grief* (Series in Death Education, Aging, and Health Care, pp. 31–44). Philadelphia: Taylor & Francis.

Suh, E. M. (2000). Self: The hyphen between culture and subjective well being. In E. Diener & E. M. Suh (Eds.), *Culture and subjective well being* (pp. 185–218). Cambridge: MIT Press.

Suls, J., & Wheeler, L. (2000). A selective history of classic and neo-social comparison theory. In J. Suls & L. Wheeler (Eds.), *Handbook of social comparison: Theory and research* (Plenum Series in Social/Clinical Psychology, pp. 3–20). Dordrecht, Netherlands: Kluwer Academic.

Taylor, S. E., & Brown, J. D. (1988). Illusion and well-being: A social psychological perspective on mental health. *Psychological Bulletin, 103*(2), 193–210.

Taylor, S. E., Wood, J. V., & Lichtman, R. R. (1983). It could be worse: Selective evaluation as a response to victimization. *Journal of Social Issues, 39*(2), 19–40.

Tesser, A. (2001). On the plasticity of self-defense. *Current Directions in Psychological Science, 10*(2), 66–69.

Transparency International. (2003). *Transparency International corruption perceptions index 2003.* Retrieved March 2004, from www.transparency.org/cpi/2003/cpi2003.en.html

UN Development Programme. (2002). *Millennium development goals.* Retrieved January 4, 2005, from www.un.org/millenniumgoals

Veenhoven, R. (2000). Freedom and happiness: A comparative study in forty four nations in the early 1990s. In E. Diener & E. M. Suh (Eds.), *Culture and subjective well being* (pp. 185–218). Cambridge, MA: MIT Press.

Veenhoven, R. (2002). *Average happiness in 68 nations in the 1990s, World Database of Happiness, Rank report 2002/1.* Retrieved date March 2004. www.eur.nl/fsw/research/happiness

Ware, J. E., & Sherbourne, C. D. (1992). The MOS short form 36-item health survey (SF-36): Conceptual framework and item selection. *Medical Care, 30,* 473–483.

White, S., & Pettit J. (in press). Participatory approaches and the measurement of human wellbeing. In M. McGillivray (Ed.), *Measuring human wellbeing.* Oxford, UK: WIDER/Oxford University Press.

WHOQOL Group. (1995). The World Health Organisation Quality of Life assessment (WHO-QOL): Position paper from the World Health Organisation. *Social Science & Medicine, 41,* 1403–1409.

Wilkin, D., Hallam, L., & Doggett, M. (1992). *Measures of need and outcome for primary care.* Oxford, UK: Oxford University Press.

Wood, G. (2003). Staying secure, staying poor: The Faustian bargain. *World Development, 31*(3), 455–473.

Wood, J. V., Taylor, S. E., & Lichtman, R. R. (1985). Social comparison in adjustment to breast cancer. *Journal of personality and social psychology, 49*(5), 1169–1183.

Ziebland, S., Fitzpatrick, R., & Jenkinson, C. (1993). Tacit models of disability underlying health status instruments. *Social Science & Medicine, 37*(1), 69–75.

13

THE INTERNATIONAL RESILIENCE PROJECT

A Mixed-Methods Approach to the Study of Resilience Across Cultures

MICHAEL UNGAR

LINDA LIEBENBERG

Typically, studies of resilience have employed designs that integrate established test instruments with demonstrated reliability and validity from studies of mental and social functioning. Few of these instruments, and the studies that use them, account sufficiently for their Eurocentric bias when working in high-risk environments. Furthermore, researchers have made only limited attempts to understand the contextual variability of health resources such as family structure, financial security, or even exposure to violence. Combined, social and cultural factors shape the meaning a child attaches to his or her experience of risk factors. With these concerns in mind, the International Resilience Project (IRP) was developed. This multinational project seeks to effectively deal with long-standing problems in resilience research and resolve the apparent contradictions between the demands for contextual specificity and construct validity across settings. Findings from the research are intended to demonstrate that culturally sensitive methods can generate helpful information on children's resilience that inform policies and direct interventions across the diverse contexts in which children grow.

This chapter will describe how the IRP was developed and implemented across 14 different cultures and contexts, highlighting the problems and concerns that have arisen and how these were dealt with. It is an exploration of the seldom-discussed aspects of children's mental health research: the daily details of making multisite, mixed-methods research work in real-world practice settings.

Two frequently noted shortcomings that plague much of the resilience research are addressed in the research design of the IRP: (a) the arbitrariness in the selection of outcome variables and (b) the challenge of accounting for the social and cultural context in which resilience occurs. It is our belief that this research design successfully addresses these shortcomings and produces a unique research protocol and set of instruments that are useful internationally. The 11-phase process that guides the IRP includes design components that integrate qualitative and quantitative research methods, fostering a convergence between research paradigms (Ungar, Lee, Callaghan, & Boothroyd, in press). In this regard, our work is an attempt to address some of the shortcomings in resilience research that Barton identifies in Chapter 9 of this volume. Methodological diversity built into the IRP has ensured that the research we are doing is contextually relevant while also being adaptable enough to accommodate differences across each research site. In this regard, we have reached consensus as an international team regarding what we hold in common as well as the methods required to explore our differences.

Cultural and Contextual Sensitivity in Resilience Research

Decontextualized findings generalized across populations are unlikely to demonstrate construct validity for participants from different cultures. We are unable to know for certain if what we think we are measuring as researchers is what participants mean for us to learn when the tools of research are used without a lengthy process of matching them to the cultural nuances of those being studied. For example, it has been shown that Latino children are best protected from multiple stressors, even school violence, by the use of disciplinary measures that keep children in school (Morrison, Robertson, Laurie, & Kelly, 2002). For this population, suspensions exacerbate the risks they face by putting the highest-risk children in unstructured settings and conveying to them the message that they don't belong at school. An argument against disciplining Latino children with unstructured forms of punishment may have much to do with related findings that less, rather than more, parental supervision than commonly found among non-Latino white samples has been associated with positive outcomes in Latino youth (Morrison et al., 2002).

Arguably, without understanding the context and culture in which behavior occurs, there can be little authoritative comment made on findings related to resilience and the structures that help to create health (Newton, Litrownik, & Landsverk, 2000; Pollard, Hawkins, & Arthur, 1999).

We are learning that even when we account for cultural differences, we can blind ourselves to the real factors at play in children's lives, their culture being only one small part of a matrix of environmental conditions. Take for example Magnus, Cowen, Wyman, Fagen, and Work's (1999) study of the correlates of resilience found among highly stressed African American and white urban children. Based on data collected for the Rochester Child Resilience Project, findings were analyzed for fourth-through sixth-grade urban children. Magnus et al. hypothesized that different factors among the African American children and the white children would identify those who were either resistant to stress or affected negatively by stress. It was thought that social problem solving, coping skills, perceived competence, and self-esteem would differentiate stress-resistant (SR) and stress-affected (SA) African American children much more than whites. For white children it was thought that locus of control, realistic control, and self-rated adjustment would be the discriminating variables. Of the final sample of 125 children, it was found that in fact racial differences *could not account for differences* between SR and SA children. There were simply more similarities than differences among these *urban* children of both races.

These results are instructive. We become just as blinded by ideology when as researchers we assume cultural uniqueness as when we assume sameness. It is just as likely that at-risk populations share characteristics because of common experiences related to class, colonialism, and other forms of oppression. Similarly, resilience is complex because it reflects how each culture negotiates with and integrates aspects of the dominant culture, in most cases a Western capitalist, socially democratic tradition. We see exactly this tension in Al-Krenawi and Slonim-Nevo's discussion of the traditional polygamous family structure and its negative impact on children's mental health among Bedouin-Arabs of the Negev who in recent years have settled in urban environments (see Chapter 17). As Rapoport (1997) has discussed, we know little why some families or individuals reconcile their traditional practices with those of the dominant culture. There can be a wide spectrum of possible responses, which can and frequently do include "enthusiastic acceptance of what they perceive as modern and advantageous" (p. 75). Research works best when participants are able to educate researchers and help them become aware of how research contributes to or resists cultural hegemony.

A growing awareness of the need to diversify our research is leading to innovation in design and research questions that are more relevant to understanding the dynamics of people in environments. Guerra (1998) notes,

> It is . . . important to study further how risk and protective factors together with accompanying developmental processes vary as a function of other key characteristics such as gender, culture, and social class. This requires a more sophisticated operationalization of "sociocultural context" that goes beyond a checklist of ethnicity, a 5-point social class rating index, or a simple contrast of males versus females. (pp. 399–400)

Coming from a prolific scholar concerned with the measurement of risk, Guerra's admonishment for greater methodological diversity cannot be taken lightly.

By making use of mixed methods, the IRP has been specifically designed to account for contextual and cultural issues in the study of resilience. A mixed-method design addresses the need for greater specificity in how we link protective factors with the risks they mitigate (Guerra, 1998; Luthar, Cicchetti, & Becker, 2000). Our work reflects that of others who have noted the same shortcomings in health-related research. Cooke and Michie (2002), for example, note that the relevance of questionnaires and interview guides designed outside the culture they are to be used in often makes them of little use. After all, "There may be variations in the relevance, significance or psychological meaning of behaviors across cultures. Cultural factors may influence the significance of responses even to a deceptively simple set of questions" (p. 212). Add to these problems the issues surrounding the cultural norms regarding self-disclosure and the appropriateness of Western models of research, confounded further by translation problems of key constructs (such as resilience), and one is in murky waters indeed with regard to theory generation.

AN ARGUMENT FOR MIXED METHODS

Various quantitative designs are plagued by issues that compromise their findings. Prospective longitudinal studies concerned with person, environment, and time may be best to account for all three dimensions, although they are logistically challenging and expensive and tend to focus on samples that share too much in common. Variable-centered studies, according to Barton (2002), are not much better, susceptible as they are to the "ecological fallacy in aggregate analyses" (p. 103). The cumulative profile of risk and resilience is hidden in whatever model the researcher chooses to help understand the data. As Barton warns,

> All quantitative designs face the issue of model specificity. That is, to what extent is error variance due to incomplete specification? Since resilience is often inferred from the error variance of multivariate risk-prediction models, it is impossible to determine if the error really reflects resilience or if a better-specified model would have explained more of the variance. (p. 103)

There are any number of such drawbacks to resilience research that relies solely on one method or another. We would agree with Banks and Pandiani (2001) who argue that "Today, data are everywhere" (p. 204) but that we lack efficient means to mine it, in particular to aggregate data across service delivery systems to reflect children's experiences of health and social interventions. The result is that although we might be able to find what we need to understand children's lives as they are lived in different contexts, there are many barriers to accessing this data, and the data we do find are seldom sufficiently robust to answer all our questions quantitatively. Researchers rely mostly on sophisticated analyses of data that are often beyond the capacity of most researchers to employ (Zaslow & Takanishi, 1993). Similarly, other statistical tools available, such as accelerated longitudinal designs and general growth mixture modeling, used to capture the complexity of children's lives in different contexts, are able to discern relationships between variables to such an extent that the complexity of the findings that can be generated by computer analyses are beyond our capacity to understand or apply. Although these statistical methods may allow us to investigate chaos as it is lived, we are missing the theory to explain what we can describe numerically. There is a dire lack of well-understood theory on which to base an analysis of potential findings. We may have placed the cart before the horse, with an abundance of statistically significant correlations but little theory grounded in people's experiences on which to base our analysis. A mixed-methods approach may provide a better balance between the quality and quantity of our findings.

Qualitative studies may help, but as Barton (2002) asserts, by themselves they "cannot yield a complete picture of the complex relationships among risks, protective factors, and outcomes" (p. 104). Their value, however, lies in their contribution to our understanding of people's symbolic interactions, deepening our understanding of what is taking place between the sequential measurement of people's lives over time. Qualitative work animates people's narratives and their meaning that would otherwise remain invisible (Nelson, Laurendeau, Chamberland, & Peirson, 2001; Swenson & Kolko, 2000). Unfortunately, there has been a tendency to dismiss the potential contribution from qualitative methods among risk and resilience researchers (Ungar, 2001, 2003). Nonqualitative users of mixed-method designs have routinely promoted the perception that qualitative results must be treated as tentative until they are confirmed by quantitative research (Morgan, 1998). Arguably, this is largely a matter of perception. There is nothing about these designs that implies that qualitative research is inadequate or incomplete; instead, the argument should be that quantitative methods have a different set of strengths that can, in some cases and for some purposes, add to what is achieved through qualitative research alone.

Without a qualitative component however, there is a danger that many findings remain detached from the context in which they were generated. The definition, after all, of what is a good outcome for any child, is highly specific. Furthermore, definitions of resilience and the indicators of health associated with it are not static but embedded in the discursive "to-ing and fro-ing" of knowledge elites whose ideas are challenged or supported when dialoguing with research participants. For this reason, there is, according to Gilgun (1999), a need to operationalize our definitions, to be specific about what we as researchers think are behaviors associated with the outcomes we nominate as "good."

No matter what their potential, the tools we use to gather data are only as good as the data with which we choose to work. When we are not overwhelming ourselves with data, we are likely to unduly limit the data we gather in order to answer manageable questions that may nevertheless be completely meaningless for the population under study.

A recent report from the U.S. National Institute of Mental Health (2001) regarding child and adolescent mental health cites "discipline insularity" as a major threat to our "prospects for gaining a deeper understanding of the complexities of child and adolescent mental illnesses" (p. 5). In combining the quantitative tradition in resilience research with a qualitative component, the IRP's investigation of the phenomenon of resilience is necessarily broad and multidisciplinary. Employing a number of different methods has created a dovetailed design rather than a stepwise progression in which, as is typically the case, qualitative methods are considered exploratory and quantitative techniques are used to confirm hypotheses. Within a relational research context that is attentive to how different groups define their worlds and successful growth in them (more routinely the type of data that qualitative methods generate), one can see the need for a mixed-methods approach to the study of resilience. Only then are we likely to weave a rich tapestry of detail that is able to capture a person's pattern of growth and survival. Arguably, an interdisciplinary, culturally diverse and mixed-method approach is the one most likely to generate this tapestry of workable and authentic results.

There is evidence, for example, in research related to resilience, that each domain studied can produce varying degrees of healthy outcomes (Luthar et al., 2000). Children's normal development does not proceed at an even pace, with advances in one life domain not necessarily congruent with growth in another. Thus, the anomalous findings of high self-esteem among street youth and bullies who have low academic achievements, addictions, or impulsivity are not as incongruous as they may seem at first (Massey, Cameron, Ouellette, & Fine, 1998; Sutton, Smith, & Swettenham, 1999). Understanding resilience requires methods that can produce comprehensive theory that encompasses a broad ecology of health factors. The need for methodological diversity is more apparent when we look specifically at pathways through life rather than outcomes alone (Rogler & Cortes, 1993).

THE IRP RESEARCH PROCESS[1]

Getting Started

IRP team members were brought together who could bring methodological and cultural expertise to the study of resilience from around the world. Research sites were chosen based on the criteria of maximizing variability: Each had to be significantly different from the next. Sites for the IRP include Halifax, Canada; Winnipeg, Canada (with both Aboriginal and non-Aboriginal youth); Sheshatshiu, Labrador in northern Canada; Tampa, south Florida, United States; Medellín, Colombia; East Jerusalem, Palestinian Occupied Territories; Tel Aviv, Israel; Hong Kong, China; Moscow, Russia; Imphal, India; Serekunda, The Gambia; Moshi Tanzania; and Cape Town, South Africa. Our hypothesis was not to demonstrate what resilience means to every culture but, instead, to develop the tools to conduct research sensitively across many different cultures recognizing differences in how health among children is understood.

Sites were suggested by members of the research team or through the authors' personal contacts. In many cases, it took several tries until an appropriate research site was found in a specific geographic or cultural setting. Given that some sites, such as those in Africa, were underresourced to start with, there was much interest but no surplus capacity to assist with a research project, even if it would bring useful information on children and their survival strategies. Ultimately, sites with some latent capacity, interest in the topic, and desire to link with partners internationally were those most interested in joining the project. Those that were overwhelmed by day-to-day demands found it difficult to commit to participating. Only a nominal stipend, of about $3,000 Canadian dollars, was paid to each site for the data collection activities. One participant from each site was also provided two trips to Halifax as part of the research team. A listserv established through a free hosting service (Yahoo) and a Web site (www.resilienceproject.org) has kept the team in communication.

Working across cultures to conduct research is complicated. Add to this the limits of financial resources and one sees ideals of good practice tested when/while managing the day-to-day exigencies of getting the work done. Accomplishing this is easier when researchers look to local communities as a source of research capacity. For example, researchers who examined child labor in Nepal (International Union of Anthropological and Ethnological Sciences, 2002) found that it was necessary to maintain strong relationships with the children's communities and include them, and the children themselves, as co-researchers. This approach placed value on the expertise of the study's outside researchers while still supporting Nepalese practitioners to conduct the study. Much the same approach was used in the IRP, with local researchers and frontline professional staff assuming responsibility for their portion of the work.

Getting Together

In March 2003, team members from around the world met together in Halifax, Canada, to finalize the research design. With the help of a professional facilitator, general consensus was reached on a pilot design for the research. The meeting was also an opportunity to create a sense of teamwork and increase understanding of each other's culture, the challenges youth face, and appropriate research methods.

With only two and a half days together, the team maneuvered quickly through a three-stage process that emphasized dialogue and interaction within a flexible structure. During Phase 1, "Sharing and Understanding," team members got to know each other and the multiple contexts for the research. Phase 2, "Dialogue on Methods," focused on five key topics that were the building blocks for the research design. These sessions were structured to provide a range of activities that would make dialogue less hierarchical, quieting Western voices and offering space for non-Western researchers to express their perspectives. Phase 3, "Research Design Development," provided a structured process through which the group worked toward a consensus on the specifics of the research design. Although consensus was not reached on all details, a general framework for the IRP was established that was later finalized through electronic comment on a report summarizing this first meeting.

Phase 1: Sharing and Understanding

The international research team devoted itself to a critical deconstruction of the ethnocentric barriers that confound the study of health. Racial and ethnic variation was sought as an essential part of the research to strengthen the construct validity/authenticity (depending on one's research paradigm) of the concept of resilience as it appears in different settings. To achieve this, a member of the team from each research site presented a 15-minute review on his or her cultural and research context. Each discussed the most significant challenges faced by youth in local agencies/settings/communities and some of the most common factors that help youth cope with the adversities they face. Presenters were asked to include some type of audiovisual component that allowed team members to see and/or hear from youth in each setting (some of which can be viewed on the IRP Web site). Representatives brought photos and digital video clips that showed the rest of the team the settings in which youth around the world are growing up, and still others included cultural artifacts used by people in their communities. All provided statistical and phenomenological data on youth at risk. Presenters also attempted to define the construct

of resilience from the perspective of those in their communities.

The value of contextualized understanding is emphasized by much of the cross-cultural research literature from the fields of social work, anthropology, critical psychology, medical anthropology, psychiatry, and medicine (see, e.g., Johnson-Powell & Yamamoto, 1997; Sue & Sue, 2003; Tseng & Streltzer, 1997). This literature endorses consideration of cultural contexts in research design. As Dupree, Spencer, and Bell (1997) explain, we have mistakenly tended to assume homogeneity both *among and between* members of dominant and marginalized populations. This assumption, as noted by Massey et al. (1998) in their discussion of adults who thrive despite adversity, contributes to a

> disagreement between the values of researcher and those of the researched . . . valuing social competence and compliance over expressions of personal agency would bias who gets the label resilient toward those most likely to conform, overlooking those most likely to critique. (p. 339)

By embracing cultural variability, the team avoided the imposition of artificial dichotomies (i.e., "ethical" vs. "unethical"; "resilient" vs. "nonresilient") typical within a Northern, or Eurocentric, health research discourse. Through these discussions, team members not only became aware of the staggering challenges confronting youth around the world but also that, fundamentally, the ability to *cope* and the ability to *hope* seem to form the basis of cross-cultural understandings of resilience.

Phase 2: Dialogue on Methods

Five questions, negotiated through electronic discussions prior to the Halifax meeting, guided Phases 2 and 3:

1. Who do we study?

2. Which domains (areas of people's lives) do we study that will be common to all sites? Which domains will be unique to different sites?

3. What are the best qualitative and quantitative research practices appropriate to this study?

4. What are the ethical challenges we will face (and possible solutions)?

5. What will be returned to the participants and their communities who become involved in this research?

Topic 1: Who Do We Study?

To decide who we would study, the team split into three small groups, each with a flip chart and marker. At the center of a piece of paper, a circle was drawn, representing a silo holding the sum of information we hoped to learn through this research. The group was then asked to draw stick figures, labeling the key informants who would hold the information we were looking for. These key informants were then positioned on the page with those who were thought most important placed closest to the silo. Each group reported back to the entire team who they thought were the three most important key informants. A large-group discussion followed, reflecting on the results, the interconnections between groups, and implications for the study.

These discussions highlighted the need to consider the responsibilities and developmental crises that youth face, the transitions being made from one developmental stage to another, and the age at which these occur. Given the complexity of developmental trajectories across cultures (e.g., the timing at which children take responsibility for themselves, make a meaningful contribution to others, or become sexually active), team members ultimately felt it best to *allow each site to determine the age of the youth who were to be invited to participate in the study.* The specific age would be decided through discussions with elders and children at each site. Final selection of children globally included those aged 11 through 19, with each site limited in their selection to children spanning a 3-year time frame (i.e., 11–13, 14–16, etc.).

Although it was generally agreed that youth who are "doing well" and those who are "not doing well" should be sampled and that both males and females should be worked with, concern was voiced about determining who is a youth "at risk." The issue of timing was also raised: Is the determination of being at risk an a priori or post hoc decision? Questions concerning whether we speak with youth who self-identify

as being resilient or those who are struggling were also raised. One practical suggestion was to match those who are not doing well with controls in their communities who are doing well based on the advice of a local advisory committee established in each site to oversee the research. For example, youth in the Halifax site who were in residential treatment facilities were matched with youth in community sports teams, whereas in Colombia we sampled both children who are in school and those who leave school to join gangs. There was some concern among the team, however, that these categories were too rigid, because children may do well in one area of their lives and not others. To resolve all these issues, it was decided to emphasize variability along a continuum of risk exposure based on recommendations of each site's advisory committee.

Discussions also highlighted the need to include adults in the study. Many risk-taking behaviors are adult defined rather than youth defined, and it was evident that we would need to find ways of balancing the two definitions of what is and is not appropriate behavior for a young person. It was also believed that adults provided a valuable source of information about how to overcome challenges retrospectively. It was therefore decided to include adults in focus groups at each site. These adults would be either individuals who had been identified as being resilient themselves or people who work with youth in risky environments and may therefore have something important to say about resilience based on their experiences.

Topic 2: What Domains Do We Study?

To understand resilience, we agreed prior to the first meeting that we would focus on a small number of common aspects found among youth, their families, and communities that promote resilience (although each community has had the opportunity to study aspects of resilience unique to their setting). Several factors were identified via a premeeting survey completed by team members. Team members were asked to rank, in order of importance to this study, domains commonly found in the literature. External protective factors such as a good school, secure attachment to caregivers, and meaningful participation, as well as internal resources such as self-efficacy, self-esteem, problem-solving ability, a future orientation, and good communication were all suggested as possible domains to study in order to understand resilience. Those items ranked highest were brought to the March meeting for further discussion.

To gain greater clarity on the domains to be studied, the larger team once again split into three small groups (the composition of which was varied from the first exercise), each being given a set of colored index cards with the highest-ranked domain titles typed on them. Cards were sorted by teams into three categories: Yes (the domain should be included in the study), Maybe, and No (the domain is not important to the study). Each group was asked to place no more than 12 cards in the Yes pile with the option to include three more topics of their own choosing written on blank cards. Groups had 30 minutes to reach consensus on the topics to be included. A large-team discussion was then held to reflect on the results from each subgroup. During this discussion, domains were also gathered under four headings: individual, interpersonal, community, and culture.

In discussing the many factors that could potentially affect resilience, two concerns were expressed. First, the group was troubled by how to combine factors while still ensuring that each factor was not so broad in scope that it failed to say anything meaningful about youth. Second, many of the cultural items did not translate well into English from non-English-speaking sites. Interestingly, among the items made available electronically (based on the literature) before the March meeting, cultural factors were all but invisible. Most notable in the final sort of items, however, was the number of items that emerged related to cultural considerations. The final sort of items, combined for redundancy and repetition, identified 32 items that were thought most important to the study of resilience. These items, listed by category, included the following:

Culture

1. Affiliation with a religious organization

2. Youth and their family are tolerant of each others' different ideologies, beliefs (such as gender roles)

3. Cultural dislocation and a change (shift) in values are handled well

4. Self-betterment (betterment of the person and community)

5. Having a life philosophy

6. Cultural/spiritual identification

7. Being culturally grounded: knowing where you came from and being a part of a cultural tradition, which is expressed through daily activities

Community

8. Opportunities for age-appropriate work

9. Exposure to violence is avoided in one's family, community, and with peers

10. Government plays a role in providing for the child's safety, recreation, housing, jobs when older

11. Meaningful rites of passage with an appropriate amount of risk are accessible

12. Community is tolerant of high-risk and problem behaviors

13. Safety and security needs are met

14. Perceived social equity

15. Access to school and education, information, learning resources

Relationships

16. Quality of parenting meets the child's needs: The family is emotionally expressive and parents monitor the child appropriately

17. Social competence

18. Having a positive mentor and role models

19. Meaningful relationships with others at school, home, perceived social support, peer group acceptance

Individual

20. Assertiveness

21. Problem-solving ability

22. Self-efficacy (a sense of control over one's world)

23. Being able to live with uncertainty

24. Self-awareness, insight

25. Perceived social support

26. A positive outlook, optimism

27. Empathy for others and the capacity to understand others

28. Having goals and aspirations

29. Showing a balance between independence and dependence on others

30. Appropriate use of or abstinence from substances such as alcohol and drugs

31. A sense of humor

32. A sense of duty (to others or self)

Although an endless number of possible constructs could be identified as contributing to resilience, the 32 domains that were agreed on by the team were thought relevant to each of the cultural contexts in which the research is taking place. In addition, all carry with them, in one context or the other, theoretical support. For example, questions related to rites of passage as integral to children's healthy development (#11), finds support in a number of cultures. Schmidt (1999) has shown that opportunities to experience challenge are a component of resilience in Western cultures. Similarly, Swartz (1998) talks about the same importance of rites of passage among families in Southern Africa. And Markowitz (2000), in her study of Russian youth coming of age postperestroika, found that many youth had lost opportunities to participate in youth groups that previously provided socially acceptable rites of passage. Findings such as these are sufficiently generic to hint at their applicability across cultures.

Topic 3: What Are the Best Qualitative and Quantitative Methods for Studying Health Phenomena?

The team next shared stories of best practices that might be integrated into the IRP. We were looking for examples of research methods that could work across disciplines, across cultures, and be used collaboratively with researchers and community leaders from different theoretical orientations. Specifically, we sought approaches to research that could include elements of both qualitative and quantitative work.

To tap the expertise of those in the group with diverse methodological expertise, team members were divided into two groups—those with experience working qualitatively and those with experience working quantitatively. Individuals were asked to reflect on what they felt is the most promising research tool or methodology they have seen in the last few years that could be applicable to this particular study.

Specifically, to conduct *quantitative* research, it was agreed that we would need to find ways to account for the voices of youth themselves in the design of the study's questions. In this regard, we followed the lead of Gilgun (1996) (a member of the IRP) and others who note the need to develop research protocols and measures that better account for the implicit, although unintended, cultural and contextual bias of researchers and for the instruments they use (Blankenship, 1998; Hauser, 1999; Martineau, 1999). Therefore, rather than simply seeking consensus on the factors to be studied, the design preferred by the team opens for debate competing definitions of the construct of resilience each time it is studied. Qualitative methods are used to contextualize the quantitative instrument. Specifically, it was agreed that in the design of an instrument to measure resilience, we would begin by interviewing both youth and adults in each community to ascertain what questions should be asked to understand resilience (or a term that meant something similar) locally. Because we would require a semi-structured interview tool to accomplish this, it was proposed that a conceptually driven interview skeleton be created and distributed to all the sites. This became an interview guide for field researchers. The sites conducted interviews, derived as many questions as possible from the interviews, and collectively, finalized a single unified instrument. The Child and Youth Resilience Measure (CYRM), as the instrument came to be known, was then returned to each research site to be piloted.

Creating the CYRM from site-specific questions proved a challenging exercise in cross-cultural negotiation. Questions suggested by different sites were combined, then edited to simplify language, avoid redundancy, and ensure that they were framed positively. Some questions were split into two new questions when they addressed more than one issue or required clarification. For example, "Are you proud of your nationality?" is included in the CYRM but was felt to be too specific to stand alone. The question, "Are you proud of your ethnic background?" was therefore added.

In still other cases, issues raised by one site may have been culturally inappropriate for another. Questions relating to sexual identity and relationships came most from the two Canadian sites, with one recommended by focus group participants in Moscow. Questions included the following:

- Do you see yourself as physically attractive?
- Are you comfortable with your level of sexual activity?
- Are you comfortable with your sexual identity?
- Are you aware of your own sexual orientation?
- Do you feel you have to have sex to belong?
- Do you have to cope with sex?
- How does sex affect how you cope?
- How does your sexual orientation affect how you cope?
- Do your parents restrain your wishes regarding sexual relations?

From this group of questions, we decided to address two in the CYRM: "Are you aware of your own sexual orientation?" and "Do your parents restrain your wishes regarding sexual relations?" To make the questions make sense in a variety of cultures and languages they were reworded to read, "Are you comfortable with how you express yourself sexually with others?" and "Do your parents respect your wishes regarding sexual relations?" After accepting that we very possibly had questions that would translate well, we were now faced with examining whether the questions would move across cultures. How could we hope to make the CYRM acceptable, for example, in conservative Muslim and Christian communities with questions such as these? Discussions surrounding the wording of the questions resulted in variations ranging from "Are you comfortable with how you express yourself intimately with others?" to "Are you comfortable with how you express yourself in close relationships with others your own age?" Similarly, the question relating to parents went from "Do your parents respect how you express yourself intimately with boys and girls?" to "Do your parents respect how you express yourself intimately/ sexually with boys and girls?" although this question made us want to ask "Do you express yourself sexually with other boys and girls in front of your parents *at all?*" Finally, after many consultations, the team decided to include on the CYRM "Are you comfortable with how you express yourself sexually?" and "Do your parents respect how you express yourself sexually?" Neither question carries a specifically heterosexist bias, nor does either question introduce ideas of sexual orientation that may be unfamiliar to many youth in non-Western countries where discussion about sexual orientation is less common.

It was often very challenging to make the questions work and still express their original meaning. For example the word *camaraderie* was replaced with "you feel part of a group when you are with your friends," eliminating what could be misunderstood (we were told) as militant undertones. Similarly, the suggested phrase "express protest against" was felt to be too hostile and was replaced with *disagree*.

Site-specific questions generated from the initial community consultations, but that were not included on the final version of the CYRM because of their specificity to one site or another, could be included in site-based administrations of the international instrument. Those intending to replicate this study or use the measures and protocols that were developed would therefore require this period of contextualization to modify the CYRM to fit each community setting. Although this challenges the external validity and cross-site reliability of the research, our compromise position has resulted in uniquely tailored and more valid representations of health phenomena.

It was noted by members of the IRP that the quantitative methods we would be using would have to be merged with other aspects of the research to ensure that each context in which the instrument is administered is fully appreciated.

An iterative qualitative process was therefore chosen to occur alongside the quantitative. The IRP team decided that a variety of qualitative methods would work best and that each site could then choose specific qualitative "tools" to gather their data. It was suggested that these techniques include techniques such as exploring sociohistorical backgrounds, ethnographies, the use of culturally appropriate forms of disclosure such as sharing circles or story-telling, developing games to stimulate conversation, making use of images or short vignettes to elicit responses, the sharing of cultural artifacts, and so on.

To effectively guide all these activities a core set of "catalyst" questions were used in all sites that were devised to create consistency in the data collected and facilitate cross-site comparisons. These questions included the following:

Child and Youth Resilience Measure

- What would I need to know to grow up well here?
- How do you describe people who grow up well here despite the many problems they face?
- What does it mean to you, to your family, and to your community when bad things happen?
- What kinds of things are most challenging for you growing up here?
- What do you do when you face difficulties in your life?
- What does being healthy mean to you and others in your family and community?
- What do you do, and others you know do, to keep healthy—mentally, physically, emotionally, and spiritually?
- Can you share with me a story about another child who grew up well in this community despite facing many challenges?
- Can you share a story about how you have managed to overcome challenges you face personally, in your family, or outside your home in your community?

Field researchers were required at each site to administer the instrument and conduct the qualitative aspects of the research. Similar studies, such as that by Laverack and Brown (2003) who studied workers in Fijian workshops, have demonstrated the success and value of inviting local people to act as researchers. With regard to administering the quantitative instrument consistently, it was recognized that there would be problems with how to train field workers at each site. Techniques to accomplish this are, however, available (see Daiute & Fine, 2003).

Topic 4: What Are the Ethical Issues Related to This Research?

Team members were asked to consider the most important ethical challenges that would face researchers globally and offer suggestions to resolve them. Once again, the team split into small groups. Group members were asked to share case examples of important ethical issues they have faced in a research study relevant to this work and how they addressed each. Among the most common issues identified were confidentiality and safety, obtaining consent, coercion, ethics reviews locally, and the benefits to each participating community.

Confidentiality and Safety. Confidentiality and safety concerns need to be discussed at the local level if a study like this is to succeed. It became apparent to team members that Western research contexts offer far different constraints on research than in the majority world. For example, soliciting more individual, personal stories, the team has had to pay attention to the dangers of personal disclosure. In cases where there is good reason for people to fear for their safety, as in instances of war or gang or tribal conflict, personal disclosure may compromise one's neutrality or inadvertently make it seem one is colluding with outsiders to the community.

Obtaining Consent. Numerous contextual variations with regard to obtaining consent were noted by the team. It was strongly felt that there needed to be the option of requiring only verbal consent in many sites. Furthermore, the inability to always obtain parental consent needed to be recognized despite Canadian standards in this regard. It also became challenging to ensure that enough information was shared with study participants to allow them to make an informed consent without overwhelming them with pages of ethically sound, but inaccessible, statements. The tendency of Western institutions to demand lengthier and lengthier disclosures by researchers prior to consent was thought to be unworkable by many team members in all research settings.

Coercion. Concern was raised regarding the interview process involving younger children who often feel compelled to continue with an interview, even if they are told that they can stop at any time. In some cultures, children and youth would not see it as their right to refuse participation even as they are making the transition to more adultlike status. The formality of the research process can create social expectations for compliance.

Review of the Research Locally by an Ethics Board. In many research sites, rigorous review by an ethics review board has not been possible. In several settings, such structures do not exist. It was decided that at the very least, advisory committees would discuss a dozen key topics with regard to ethics and document the community's response as a way of auditing the project at the local level. These topics included the following:

1. Can people be hurt in any way from taking part in this research?

2. Have people agreed to the research?

3. Do they fully understand what they are agreeing to do and what happens to the information that they provide?

4. Do they understand who sees the information that they provide?

5. Do they understand what the information will be used for?

6. Do they understand that they can leave the study at any time?

7. Are there places where people can go if they feel uneasy or upset during the research?

8. Who do they go to for support?

9. Who can they talk to about how they were treated during the research?

10. Is there a local person (most likely on the advisory committee) who can speak with them confidentially?

11. What will be given back to the community?

12. What can people expect to be gained from taking part in the research?

Each community has provided answers to each of these questions whether through a formal or informal ethics review.

Communities Benefit From Their Participation. The need for participation to be experienced at the local level was emphasized by team members. Some partner communities have a history of being "researched to death" and therefore needed it made very clear how information was to be interpreted and who would have ownership of the research results. We have had to consider what we could give the participants for their time, not only monetarily but also what we could promise in the future in terms of tangible benefits to them and their communities. We also needed to consider what services we could offer, if any, after individual interviews and when the research is done. Several researchers expressed concern that the IRP would generate expectations in their communities that the project was going to offer programs to solve the problems youth face. Clearly, this was not possible; however, results are being returned to each community in an appropriate form to help decision makers address children's health issues.

Topic 5: What Are the Constraints and Opportunities We Are Likely to Encounter During This Research?

As the final topic of discussion in preparing our research design, we again divided into groups, this time representing each research site. Team members were asked to identify the site-specific obstacles and opportunities they anticipated encountering when attempting the research. Although much of this discussion revisited issues already identified, these smaller groups provided a forum to raise new questions that needed to be addressed by the entire team. For example, the issue was raised of whether to sample different cultures in settings with more than one cultural group. It was decided that where possible, such plurality in sampling design would be beneficial. Response bias was also anticipated to be a problem in certain contexts where youth, unfamiliar with standardized questions, were likely to try to give the "correct" answer. In some contexts, the use of open-ended qualitative methods was thought inappropriate because youth would not feel comfortable disclosing personal information. Such fears have been addressed in the flexible design that was created, allowing, for example, a large number of qualitative data collection techniques and ensuring researchers provide more detailed instructions to participants when completing the CYRM.

Phase 3: Research Design Development

After completing Phases 1 and 2, the group was ready to move toward making decisions regarding specific design features of the research. In groups of approximately 10, team members pulled together a comprehensive methodology that links qualitative and quantitative research paradigms and the roles of various stakeholders. Each small group then presented to the larger group its research template. Similarities and differences were discussed and a tentative consensus was reached on how to proceed.

Finalizing the Research Process: Perils and Pitfalls

The Fieldwork Documents. Following the Halifax meeting, a research model was completed, with final details being negotiated electronically. It was a struggle to ensure that the methodology was, on one hand, standardized while, on the other, flexible enough to accommodate the cultural diversity present in the study.

A manual to guide the research was developed. It was designed to be accessible to all site researchers, avoiding academic research jargon. Furthermore, because many site-specific researchers do not speak English as a first language, the document had to be easy to read and affordable to translate. The manual we developed is divided into two sections. The first gives an introduction to the project; outlines the goals; describes the people involved, including participants; and provides contact details for the project leaders. The second section gives a detailed description of the 11 phases of the research process. Flowcharts were created detailing each phase as a quick overview of what would need to be done. Flowcharts were accompanied by written explanations of each phase. Use was also made of icons throughout to indicate the various people involved, making it easier for various team members to easily identify and distinguish their roles from others on the team.

Accompanying the research manual is a toolbox of qualitative methods, providing layman's descriptions of various means of gathering data. Once again, the toolbox had to be written in a way that would make it accessible to team members whose first language was not English as well as to less experienced site researchers. Descriptions of methods had to provide enough detail so that fieldwork would be carried out effectively, yet at the same time, we had to prevent descriptions from becoming too cluttered with detail. Neither did we want our suggestions to inhibit creativity. We emphasized that researchers at each site use methods that would generate data effectively given unique cultural contexts.

A fieldwork checklist was also created. This two-page grid allowed site researchers to track their progress. This grid contained administrative details, such as submitting research agreements, invoices, and ethics reviews to the principle investigator as well as relevant contact details. A suggested time line was also included. Small details such as this surprised us with the amount of time they consumed for their development and the complexity involved in ensuring that every site completed *all* the steps involved in the research process.

Ethics Reviews. Even with a spirit of cooperation and sincere intent by the host Canadian institution's research ethics board, the complexity of conducting this research and the flexibility required to work with marginalized young people worldwide demanded a lengthy process of negotiation to pass the required ethics review. Five submissions were completed before approval was secured. Comments by the REB were helpful, although most difficult of all was getting permission to proceed without a guarantee that signed consent would be required in all sites. Instead, a compromise was found in which a witness would attest to the fact that the research had been explained to the youth and informed consent had been given verbally.

Efforts were made to keep the consent forms simple, although Western research bias still made the forms long and in places cumbersome with detail.

Agreements. To maintain professional working relationships, we drafted agreements between each site and the host Canadian institution, outlining how fieldwork would be funded and what was expected of researchers at each site. Although we began with a straightforward document, legal requirements at the host institution created a highly technical, extremely complex document loaded with legal jargon. The demands made on the project by the university administration and our knowledge of the realities confronting each research site resulted in another lengthy process of negotiation and revision (very similar to that of obtaining ethics approval). It was eventually agreed that sites could submit invoices of their anticipated expenditures in order to advance them funds, that ethics reviews could be entered into a preestablished template by advisory committees, and that the agreement's language could be simplified and much of our original format be included in the final version. Our experience highlights the importance of clarifying university administration requirements in the early stages of project planning.

What We Have Learned

Although complex, the methodological challenges we confronted as a team in designing the IRP have provided opportunities to examine the requirements for cross-cultural research with children. In particular, we have come to understand better the challenges to methodological rigor and the difficulties in ensuring that children and their communities benefit from participation in multisite research. We believe that the dual emphasis on qualitative and quantitative data collection both addresses the need for contextual variability across sites and provides opportunities for children and communities to have a greater voice in the research process, ensuring that findings are reliable and valid, authentic and trustworthy. Most important, our work, like that of Jones and Kafetsios

(2002), among others, is demonstrating how to accommodate diverse perspectives on health phenomena. Jones and Kafetsios, for example, studied 337 children on both sides of the Bosnian conflict, examining their mental health as it relates to exposure to the war. Most significantly, they found that although the quantitative instruments they used met the standards for internal consistency and discriminant validity, a large number of participants in their study were shown through clinical interviews and other qualitative assessments to not have the mental health problems testing identified. Furthermore, test instruments proved poor at distinguishing children who were doing well from those who were not doing well, once lengthy interviews were conducted with the children in their homes and community settings using qualitative data-gathering techniques.

Jones and Kafetsios (2002) speculate that it was the particular context in which their research took place, normative in terms of high levels of exposure to violence and resulting trauma that made it impossible to simply parachute in measures that were designed to evaluate non-war-affected children. As they explain, "High levels of symptoms do not necessarily equal psychiatric disability. They may reflect a norm for that population, or a temporary adjustment to the stresses of war" (p. 1060). The narrative discussions with the children that followed administration of the test instruments proved insightful, helping the researchers distinguish between those who were stress affected and those who were stress resistant.

Our design has also sought to address the increasingly vocal calls for greater benefits for children and their communities when they participate in research. A recent report from the Save the Children Task Group for the UN Special Study on Violence (Laws & Mann, 2003), coauthored by Laws and Mann (see Chapter 1 for related work by Boyden and Mann), views children's active participation in research as fulfilling the goals of the UN Convention on the Rights of the Child. The convention stipulates that children have a right to be heard and to participate in decisions that affect them. We believe the reciprocity and mixed methods of the IRP are in keeping with the spirit of the convention.

Clearly, our experience tells us that there is a need for culturally sensitive mixed-method designs when working across multiple research sites. However, there is little to guide us as researchers in the specifics of how to conduct such work. This chapter has provided the kind of nitty-gritty detail often missing when we write about international collaborations. By elaborating on some of our challenges and solutions, we hope to have contributed to a much larger discussion of how to conduct this kind of research. However, we humbly concede we still find ourselves with more questions than answers.

NOTE

1. The IRP began with funding from the Social Sciences and Humanities Research Council of Canada with the purpose of demonstrating that it was possible to conduct multisite, mixed-methods resilience research across cultures in a contextually sensitive manner. Additional funding was later received from the Nova Scotia Health Research Foundation to extend the scope of the research.

REFERENCES

Banks, S. M., & Pandiani, J. A. (2001). Using existing databases to measure treatment outcomes. In M. Hernandez & S. Hodges (Eds.), *Developing outcome strategies in children's mental health* (pp. 203–220). Baltimore, MD: Brookes.

Barton, W. H. (2002). Methodological square pegs and theoretical black holes. In R. R. Greene (Ed.), *Resiliency: An integrated approach to practice, policy, and research* (pp. 95–114). Washington, DC: NASW Press.

Blankenship, K. M. (1998). A race, class, and gender analysis of thriving. *Journal of Social Issues, 54*(2), 393–404.

Cooke, D. J., & Michie, C. (2002). Towards valid cross-cultural measures of risk. In R. R. Corrado, R. Roesch, S. D. Hart, & J. K. Gierowski (Eds.), *Multi-problem violent youth: A foundation for comparative research on needs, interventions and outcomes* (pp. 211–220). Burke, VA: IOS Press.

Daiute, C., & Fine, M. (2003). Youth perspectives on violence and injustice. *Journal of Social Issues, 59*(1), 1–14.

Dupree, D., Spencer, M. B., & Bell, S. (1997). African American children. In G. Johnson-Powell & J. Yamamoto (Eds.), *Transcultural child development: Psychological assessment and treatment* (pp. 237–268). New York: John Wiley.

Gilgun, J. F. (1996). Human development and adversity in ecological perspective, Part 1: A conceptual framework. *Families in Society, 77*(7), 395–402.

Gilgun, J. F. (1999). Mapping resilience as process among adults with childhood adversities. In H. I. McCubbin, E. A. Thompson, A. I. Thompson, & J. A. Futrell (Eds.), *The dynamics of resilient families* (pp. 41–70). Thousand Oaks, CA: Sage.

Guerra, N. G. (1998). Serious and violent juvenile offenders: Gaps in knowledge and research priorities. In R. Loeber & D. P. Farrington (Eds.), *Serious and violent juvenile offenders: Risk factors and successful interventions* (pp. 389–404). Thousand Oaks, CA: Sage.

Hauser, S. T. (1999). Understanding resilient outcomes: Adolescent lives across time and generations. *Journal of Research on Adolescence, 9*(1), 1–24.

International Union of Anthropological and Ethnological Sciences. (2002). *Studies of integrated holistic programmes with children and youth: Child labour in Nepal.* New York: IUAES.

Johnson-Powell, G., & Yamamoto, J. (Eds.). (1997). *Transcultural child development: Psychological assessment and treatment.* New York: John Wiley.

Jones, L., & Kafetsios, K. (2002). Assessing adolescent mental health in war-affected societies: The significance of symptoms. *Child Abuse and Neglect, 26,* 1059–1080.

Laverack, G. R., & Brown, K. M. (2003). Qualitative research in a cross-cultural context: Fijian experiences. *Qualitative Health Research, 13*(3), 333–342.

Laws, S., & Mann, G. (2003). *So you want to involve children in research?* Stockholm, Sweden: Save the Children.

Luthar, S. S., Cicchetti, D., & Becker, B. (2000). The construct of resilience: A critical evaluation and guidelines for future work. *Child Development, 71*(3), 543–562.

Magnus, K. B., Cowen, E. L., Wyman, P. A., Fagen, D. B., & Work, W. (1999). Correlates of resilient outcomes among highly stressed African-American and white urban children. *Journal of Community Psychology, 27*(4), 473–488.

Markowitz, F. (2000). *Coming of age in post-soviet Russia.* Chicago: University of Illinois Press.

Martineau, S. (1999). *Rewriting resilience: A critical discourse analysis of childhood resilience and the politics of teaching resilience to "kids at risk."* Unpublished doctoral dissertation, University of British Columbia, Vancouver, BC.

Massey, S., Cameron, A., Ouellette, S., & Fine, M. (1998). Qualitative approaches to the study of thriving: What can be learned? *Journal of Social Issues, 54*(2), 337–355.

Morgan, D. L. (1998). Practical strategies for combining qualitative and quantitative methods: Applications to health research. *Qualitative Health Research* [Electronic version], *8*(3), 362–376. (Available at http://proquest.umi.com)

Morrison, G. M., Robertson, L., Laurie, B., & Kelly, J. (2002). Protective factors related to antisocial behavior trajectories. *Journal of Clinical Psychology 58*(3), 277–290.

National Institute of Mental Health. (2001). *Blueprint for change: Research on child and adolescent mental health.* Bethesda, MD: Author.

Nelson, G., Laurendeau, M., Chamberland, C., & Peirson, L. (2001). A review and analysis of programs to promote family wellness and prevent the maltreatment of preschool and elementary-school-aged children. In I. Prilleltensky, G. Nelson, & L. Peirson (Eds.), *Promoting family wellness and preventing child maltreatment: Fundamentals for thinking and action* (pp. 220–272). Toronto, Ontario, Canada: University of Toronto Press.

Newton, R. R., Litrownik, A. J., & Landsverk, J. A. (2000). Children and youth in foster care: Disentangling the relationship between problem behaviors and number of placements. *Child Abuse and Neglect 24*(10), 1363–1374.

Pollard, J. A., Hawkins, J. D., & Arthur, M. W. (1999). Risk and protection: Are both necessary to understand diverse behavioral outcomes in adolescence? *Social Work Research, 23*(3), 145–158.

Rapoport, R. N. (1997). Families as educators for global citizenship: Five conundrums of intentional socialization. *International Journal of Early Years Education, 5*(1), 67–77.

Rogler, L. H., & Cortes, D. E. (1993). Help-seeking pathways: A unifying concept in mental health care. *American Journal of Psychiatry, 150*(4), 554–561.

Schmidt, J. A. (1999). *Overcoming challenges: Exploring the role of action, experience, and opportunity in fostering resilience among adolescents.* Unpublished doctoral dissertation, University of Chicago.

Sue, D. W., & Sue, D. (2003), *Counseling the culturally diverse: Theory and practice* (4th ed.). New York: John Wiley.

Sutton, J., Smith, P. K., & Swettenham, J. (1999). Socially undesirable need not be incompetent: A response to Crick and Dodge. *Social Development, 8*(1), 132–134.

Swartz, L. (1998). *Culture and mental health: A southern African view.* Cape Town, South Africa: Oxford University Press.

Swenson, C. C., & Kolko, D. J. (2000). Long-term management of the developmental consequences of child physical abuse. In R. M. Reece (Ed.), *Treatment of child abuse* (pp. 135–154). Baltimore: Johns Hopkins University Press.

Tseng, W., & Streltzer, J. (Eds.). (1997). *Culture and psychopathology: A guide to clinical assessment.* New York: Brunner/Mazel.

Ungar, M. (2001). The unapologetic qualitative social work researcher: A critical look at research methods and questions. *Social Work and Social Sciences Review, 9*(2), 17–24.

Ungar, M. (2003). Qualitative contributions to resilience research. *Qualitative Social Work, 2*(1), 85–102.

Ungar, M., Lee. A. W., Callaghan, T., & Boothroyd, R. (in press). An international collaboration to study resilience in adolescents across cultures. *Journal of Social Work Research and Evaluation.*

Zaslow, M. J., & Takanishi, R. (1993). Priorities for research on adolescent development. *American Psychologist, 48*(2), 185–192.

PART 3

INTERVENING ACROSS CULTURES AND CONTEXTS

14

ISRAELI YOUTH COPE WITH TERROR

Vulnerability and Resilience

ZAHAVA SOLOMON

AVITAL LAUFER

S ince September 2001, the long Israeli-Palestinian conflict has taken an increasingly bloody turn with the armed Palestinian uprising called the El-Aqsa Intifada. This uprising-become-war has been fought in populated areas, largely against civilians. In areas of Israel within the internationally accepted 1967 borders, suicide bombers have exploded themselves in buses and bus stops, restaurants and shopping malls, discotheques, wedding halls, and other crowded places. In the disputed areas beyond the 1967 line, Israelis have been murdered in their homes or shot as they drove on the roads. Since the violence began, hundreds of Israelis have been killed and thousands injured, some permanently disabled. All segments of the Israeli population, have been exposed to terror, whether directly in their own person or through the injury or death of

friends, family, or neighbors or indirectly, through the ceaseless media coverage of the attacks, foiled attacks, threats of attacks, and funerals. One outcome of the violence has been a pervasive undercurrent of danger and insecurity alongside the normal routine of life, which has been maintained.

Like the rest of the population, Israeli children have been under constant threat and their lives disturbed. Figures collected by B'tselem,[1] the Israeli information center for human rights in the occupied territories, show the devastating toll these children pay. Children under the age of 18 made up about 18% of all those killed at the time our study was conducted, in the spring of 2002.

This chapter relates the findings of a study on the responses of Jewish Israeli children to the terror. The study was carried out in May and

AUTHORS' NOTE: This study was supported by the Adler Research Center, Tel-Aviv University.

June of 2002. It so happens that the months of March and April of that year were particularly horrendous. There were almost daily terror attacks while the Israeli Army was still taking a largely defensive pose, trying, without much success, to prevent attacks and, in some cases, carrying out punitive actions. The violence against Israelis peaked with the suicide bombing of a hotel dining room during the Passover celebration, where children, parents, and grandparents had come together for the holiday. Dozens of people were killed, and many were seriously injured.

Almost 3,000 (2,999) adolescents aged 13 to 15, from 11 schools in Israel, were surveyed. The schools were in four areas, which differed in their level of exposure to the terror attacks:

1. Areas within the green line where there had been no terror attacks

2. Areas within the green line where there had been terror attacks

3. Areas in Judea and Samaria that had relatively few terrorist attacks

4. Areas of Judah and Samaria and the Gaza Strip where there were many terrorist attacks.

In the first three areas, we randomly chose one secular and one religious high school. In Zone 4, which has no secular schools, we chose two religious schools.

The gender distribution of our sample was 42.2% boys and 57.8% girls. Their age distribution was as follows: 35.5% were 13 years old, 36.5%, were 14, 26.9% were 15, and 1% were 16. All the children were Jewish. With respect to religiosity, 0.7% identified themselves as ultraorthodox, 39.0% as religious, 27.4% as traditional, and 32.9% as secular. With regard to economic status, 0.6% classified it as very low, 4.3% as low, 70.4% as similar to that of their friends, 20.4% as above that of their friends, and 4.3% as very high.

The aims of the study were (a) to assess the level and type of exposure to terror-induced traumatic events among Israeli youth during the El Aqsa Intifada, (b) to assess the pathogenic (e.g., Posttraumatic Stress Disorder) and salutogenic effects (psychological growth and resilience) resulting from exposure to terror, and (c) to examine the role of social support, ideology, and religion in both pathogenic and salutogenic outcomes.

PATHOGENIC EFFECTS OF EXPOSURE TO WAR

Prolonged exposure to political violence has been implicated in a host of psychiatric problems and disorders among children and adolescents (e.g., Papageorgiou et al., 2000; Thabet, Abed, & Vostanis, 2002). Studies carried out on children and adolescents in conflict areas as far apart as Ireland, Rwanda, the Middle East, and the former Yugoslavia point to somatic problems (Llabre & Hadi, 1994); truncated moral growth (Ferguson & Cairns, 1996); attention, memory, and learning problems (Qouta, Punamäki, & El-Saraaj, 1995a; Saigh, Mroueh, & Bremner, 1997; Walton, Nuttall, & Nutall, 1997); nightmares and sleep problems (Baker, 1990; Punamäki, 1998; Ronen & Rahav, 2003; Walton et al., 1997); depression (Hadi, 1999; Papageorgiou et al., 2000; Zivcic, 1993); and anxiety (Milgram & Milgram, 1976; Vizek-Vidovic, Kutervac-Jagodic, & Arambasic, 2000) as resultant pathologies. Studies on Palestinian, Lebanese, and Israeli children show increased risk for behavioral problems such as disobedience, violence, and risk taking (Baker, 1990; Garbarino & Kostelny, 1996; Punamäki & Suleiman, 1990; Ronen & Rahav, 1992; Qouta, Punamäki, & El-Sarraj, 1995b; Zahr, 1996).

The most common and conspicuous psychological disturbance among individuals exposed to traumatic events is Posttraumatic Stress Disorder (PTSD). The symptoms include recurrent and intrusive recollection of the traumatic event, psychic numbing with markedly diminished interest in activities, feelings of detachment and constricted affect, fear of repeated trauma and renewed anxiety resulting in hypervigilant or avoidant behavior, decline in cognitive performance, startle reactions, and persistent feelings of guilt disproportionate to any realistic responsibility for having caused harm. Among children, the clinical picture is somewhat different. Nightmares and reliving the past through compulsive play are the most common manifestations of posttrauma in children of war. The nightmares of traumatized children, which initially reflect the direct content of the trauma, become more generalized over time, for example, in dreams of fighting monsters or of rescuing others (American Psychiatric Association [APA], 1994). Attempts to master the situation and the anxiety it provokes are reflected in behaviors that repeat the themes of the trauma. Such behaviors can be maladaptive, especially if they cause children to place themselves in life-threatening situations. Among adolescents, traumatization may lead to self-destructive and antisocial behaviors, such as substance abuse and acting out through violence and sex.

Although some of these symptoms and problematic behaviors may be adaptive or functional in the short term, they may cause severe distress and become maladaptive in the long run. Psychic numbing, for example, may at first help children keep their fear and sorrow at bay, and hypervigilence may ensure the alertness that is essential for survival in a war zone. If such behaviors continue after the threat is over, however, they become dysfunctional. Psychic numbing limits the child's capacity to trust and to form and maintain intimate relationships. Hypervigilence makes it difficult for the child to relax, enjoy life, and channel his or her psychic energy into growth-enhancing daily activities.

Very high rates of PTSD have been reported among young people exposed to a variety of war related-stresses. Over 70% of Kuwaiti youth exposed to the Iraqi incursion showed moderate to extreme posttraumatic responses (Nader, Pynoos, Fairbanks, Al-Ajeel, & Al-Asfour, 1993). Among Palestinian children aged 9 to 18 whose homes had been shelled, 59% reported such symptoms (Thabet et al., 2002). Of Bosnian children aged 6 to 16, 41% reported clinical levels of posttraumatic symptoms (Allwood, Bell-Dolan, & Husain, 2002). In a previous study by our group, over half (53.1%) of the Israeli youngsters exposed to multiple incidents of terror reported moderate to very severe posttraumatic symptoms, and 20.5% met the criteria for PTSD (Solomon & Lavi, in press).

To examine levels of PTSD in our sample, we used the CPTS-RI (Child Posttraumatic Stress Reaction Index; Frederick & Pynoos,

1988). This is a self-report questionnaire that assesses the severity of posttraumatic stress in young people. It contains 20 statements of symptoms consistent with *Diagnostic and Statistical Manual of Mental Disorders (DSM-IV)* (APA, 1994) criteria for PTSD and that reflect the three symptom categories: intrusion, avoidance, and hyperarousal. The sum of all the items represents the global symptom score (GSS), which can range from 0 to 80. The GSS can be divided into five levels of symptom severity: 0 to 11 (doubtful), 12 to 24 (mild), 25 to 39 (moderate), 40 to 59 (severe), 60 to 80 (very severe).

Our findings show that 26.5% of the subjects reported mild posttraumatic symptoms, 10.1% moderate symptoms, 4.0% severe symptoms, and 0.7% very severe symptoms. Comparison to other war zones is problematic because of differences in social context and levels of exposure, as well as in research tools. It may be noted, however, that studies of Palestinian, Kuwaiti, Eritrean, and Bosnian children and adolescents report that between 43% and 73% of them suffered from moderate to clinical levels of PTSD (Farwell, 1999; Macksoud & Aber, 1996; Nader et al., 1993; Smith, Perrin, Yule, Hacam, & Stuvland, 2002; Thabet et al., 2002; Thabet & Vostanis, 1999).

The lower percentage of Israeli youths suffering from posttraumatic symptoms may be attributed to the relative stability of life in Israel. It may also offer clues to the mechanisms that enhance resilience in children when exposed to war. In particular, the children continued to go to school fairly regularly and their parents to their jobs despite the violence. The government remained stable and, aside from occasional strikes, government services continued as before. In addition, the economic situation of most of our subjects was, by their own reports, satisfactory. In the other regions studied, social crisis, poverty, and sometimes societal disintegration constituted added stresses that may have contributed to the development of posttraumatic symptoms (Allwood et al., 2002; Walton et al., 1997). In fact, a study of children in Northern Ireland found that children who lived in economically well-off areas functioned better under terror than their poorer peers (Muldoon & Trew, 2000).

SALUTOGENIC
EFFECTS OF EXPOSURE TO WAR

Not all children are negatively affected by the adversity and stress related to exposure to violence. More than half (58.3%) the respondents in our study did not meet the criteria for PTSD. Moreover, several researchers have recorded positive effects of traumatic events on children and adolescents exposed to violent political conflicts. These include prosocial behavior (Macksoud & Aber, 1996; Saric, Zuzul, & Kerestes, 1994), elevated self-esteem (Baker, 1990), and greater well-being (Bachar, Canetti, Bonne, Denour, & Shalev, 1997). These findings support the salutogenic approach postulated by Antonovsky and Bernstein (1986) who contend that stressful events may have salutogenic, or positive, outcomes as well as pathogenic ones.

One salutogenic outcome of stress is psychological growth, marked by significant changes for the better in self-image, worldview, and relations with others as a result of exposure to a traumatic incident (Tedeschi, 1999). In a study of students, Tedeschi and Calhoun (1996) found that 60% of those who had experienced a negative event showed posttraumatic growth. Furthermore, those who experienced serious incidents showed more growth than those who had experienced only moderately negative incidents. Park and colleagues reported similar findings (Park, Cohen, & Murch, 1996).

In the last few years, researchers have also found evidence for posttraumatic growth in adults following exposure to traumatic events (Lev-Wiesel & Amir, 2003; McMillen, Smith, & Fisher, 1997; Park et al., 1996; Tedeschi & Calhoun, 1996), including war (Powell, Rosner, Butollo, Tedeschi, & Calhoun, 2003). Nonetheless, posttraumatic growth has received considerably less attention than the negative outcomes of traumatic exposure. Even less is known about posttraumatic growth in children and adolescents than in adults.

We tried to determine whether Israeli children exposed to the daily terror of the El-Aqsa Intifada experienced posttraumatic growth. Posttraumatic growth was assessed via a modified version of the PTGI (Posttraumatic Growth Inventory) developed by Tedeschi and Calhoun (1996). The original questionnaire contains 21 items divided into five categories, each representing a different dimension of posttraumatic growth: new possibilities, relating to others, personal strength, spiritual change, and appreciation of life. For this study, we introduced two additional dimensions: feelings of responsibility (8 items, such as "I feel that my family relies on me") and feelings of connection to community (4 items, such as "I feel more connected to Israel"). The full-study questionnaire contains 33 items. For each, respondents were asked to indicate how much change they experienced as a result of their exposure to the terror. The reliability of the modified questionnaire was $\alpha = .94$.

Although very few respondents (1.9%) reported very high levels of posttraumatic growth, a quarter (24.6%) reported high levels, and almost half (47.9%) reported some growth, albeit low. Only just over a quarter of respondents (25.6%) reported no growth.

Moreover, our findings show that posttraumatic growth was significantly correlated with posttraumatic symptoms ($r = 0.4$, $p < 0.001$, $n = 2,254$), with children who reported more growth reporting more symptoms. In other words, the likelihood of growth increased with the number of symptoms. This finding is consistent with the positive correlations found between growth and posttraumatic symptoms among child Holocaust survivors and among students who had experienced traumatogenic events (Lev-Wiesel & Amir, 2003; Tedeschi & Calhoun, 1996).

These findings support Antonovsky and Bernstein's (1986) claim that positive outcomes may appear along with negative ones following trauma. They also raise the question of whether posttraumatic symptoms and posttraumatic growth may be two aspects of the same phenomenon. Because the correlation was not all that strong, the answer seems to be that they are two related outcomes of trauma rather than part of a single outcome. The relation between the two outcomes may be similar to that found by Waysman, Schwarzwald, and Solomon (2001) between negative and positive outcomes of war captivity among former Israeli prisoners of war. According to these authors, whereas the negative effects of trauma express themselves mainly as psychological symptoms, the positive effects are manifested in the person's worldview, self-esteem, and relation to one's surroundings.

The coexistence of pathology and growth in the same individual attests to the complexity of the human psyche. It shows that for all the suffering trauma may cause, it does not necessarily destroy a person's ability to develop and grow.

This connection notwithstanding, as researchers committed to the well-being of people, whether children or adults, it is incumbent on us to try to learn as much as we can about the factors that may attenuate posttraumatic distress and those that may promote posttraumatic growth. The next section examines variables having to do with Israeli youth's exposure to the traumatic events of the second intifada, as well as their social support, ideological commitment, and religiosity.

Exposure Variables

According to the *DSM-IV* (1994), PTSD may develop when a person experiences, witnesses, or is confronted with an event or events that involve actual or threatend death or serious injury, or threat to the physical integrity of the self or others. As suggested by this wording, exposure need not be direct for PTSD to develop. To be sure, many studies have found that children's risk of developing posttraumatic symptoms rises with their level of exposure (Garbarino & Kostenly, 1996; Macksoud & Aber, 1996; Qouta et al., 1995a; Thabet & Vostanis, 1999) and with proximity or psychological closeness to victims (Schwartzwald, Weisenberg, Waysman, Solomon, & Klingman, 1993). However, research suggests that persons not directly exposed can also develop stress responses. Studies conducted after the terror attack on the Twin Towers in New York, for example, identified a high level of distress among persons living outside New York City and its environs (Cohen-Silver, Holman, McIntosh, Poulin, & Gil-Rivas, 2002; Schlenger, Caddell, Ebert, Jordan, & Batts, 2002).

In addition to exposure, the *DSM-IV* (1994) stipulates that for PTSD to develop, the person must experience feelings of fear, helplessness, or horror. In this connection, several studies have found that the subjective experience of an event, as manifested in feelings of threat, is the most significant predictor of posttraumatic stress symptoms (Dyregrov, Gupta, Gjestad, & Mukanoheli, 2000; Gavrilovic, Lecic, Knezevic, & Priebe, 2002). In light of these findings, we examined both objective exposure, as gauged by the number of terror incidents the children experienced, and subjective exposure, as gauged by the fear they felt at the time of the incident.

To assess the subjects' objective exposure to terror, we used Lavi's (2004) exposure-to-war-and-terror questionnaire. The questionnaire contains 17 statements covering different kinds of terror incidents. Two examples: "Stones were thrown at a car in which an acquaintance was traveling." "I was injured in a terror attack." Respondents were asked to mark the incidents they had experienced. Objective exposure was calculated as the total number of terror incidents the respondent marked, such that scores could range from from 0 to 17. This scale provides both a numerical measure, which can be used to answer the research questions, and a general picture of the types of incidents to which young Israelis were exposed. For more specific and personal pictures, we also asked the study participants an open question: to relate the terror event that most upset them.

The numerical findings show that in the first year and a half of the intifada, over 70% of the study participants experienced one or more terror incidents, whereas some 30% were not exposed to any terror incident. Around a quarter experienced four or more incidents, either to themselves or to friends or relatives. It must also be pointed out that the vast majority of those who were not exposed to the terror themselves or through family or friends were fully cognizant of the terror, through the daily reports on TV, radio, and in the printed press.

The most prevalent incidents reported were knowing a person who had been killed (37.5%) or injured (30.4%). Next in magnitude were stones thrown at a relative (20.6%) and a relative injured in a terror attack (17.5%). Smaller proportions reported losing a close relative in a terror incident (11%), having been shot at (4%), and having been injured themselves (1.6%). These levels of exposure are as high as, and even higher than, the levels reported by children in other war zones—for example, Croatia (Vizek-Vidovic et al., 2000) and Lebanon (Macksoud & Aber, 1996)—and in some earlier studies of children in our region (e.g., Slone & Hallis, 1999).

This intensity contrasts with the fact that the intifada is generally not regarded as a war but only as a "rebellion."

The personal incidents the respondents related give a sense of how closely the terror touched them: "I was on the way to the shopping mall when there was an attack there." "I missed an attack by only half an hour." "My sister lives just next to a place where there've been lots of attacks." "A friend and I were looking for our parents just after an attack, and we couldn't reach them by cell phone." "I was shocked when my grandfather was in a terror attack." "I ran away from someone I thought was a terrorist." "A tire blew in a bus we were riding, and we all thought it was a terror attack." Examination of the responses to the open question indicates that most of the respondents related to events they saw on television (e.g., the Park Hotel attack on the first night of Passover; the Twin Towers attack) and were more concerned about the safety of others, particularly family members, than their own.

Significant positive correlations were found between objective exposure (number of terror incidents) and both posttraumatic symptoms ($r = .22$; $p < 0.001$; $n = 2,256$) and posttraumatic growth ($r = .28$; $p < 0.001$; $n = 2,968$). Both increased with the degree of objective exposure. The more acts of terror to which the respondents were exposed, the greater both their growth and their posttraumatic symptomatology. These findings are consistent with previous findings linking level of exposure to posttraumatic symptoms (Garbarino & Kostelny, 1996; Macksoud & Aber, 1996; Qouta et al., 1995a; Schwartzwald et al., 1993; Thabet & Vostanis, 1999) and the severity of the traumatic event to growth (Tedeschi & Calhoun, 1996; McMillen et al., 1997).

Subjective exposure was gauged by the respondents' feelings of fear. For each terror event to which they were exposed, the respondents were asked to indicate the level of fear they felt at the time, on a 4-point scale, ranging from 1 (*not frightened*) to 4 (*very scared*). Subjective exposure (henceforth referred to as "fear") was calculated as the mean level of the respondent's answers ($M = 2.07$; $SD = 0.90$).

The teens' fear thus varied with the nature of the terror incident. Of the 17 terror incidents

queried, the 3 most frightening ones, evoking intense fear, were those in which a relative died ($M = 2.79$) or was shot at ($M = 2.56$) or was injured ($M = 2.47$). The respondents rated shots fired at themselves as the sixth most frightening terror incident ($M = 2.38$). Incidents that were only somewhat frightening included stones being thrown at an acquaintance's car ($M = 1.58$), shots fired at an acquaintance ($M = 1.95$), and stones being thrown at a car in which the respondent was riding ($M = 1.96$).

In other words, the incidents that evoked the greatest fear were those that threatened the lives and safety of close relatives. Such incidents evoked greater fear even than incidents that threatened the respondents themselves. These findings are consistent with findings among Palestinian adolescents (Lavi, Levinovski, Dekel, Ginzburg, & Solomon, 2002), whose major worries were for their loved ones much more than for themselves. The key place of worry for relatives is also consistent with findings showing that various forms of war-related psychological stress (e.g., posttraumatic symptoms, anxiety, and depression) in young people tend to be stronger when the traumatic event involves loss of or separation from parents (Chimienti, Nasr, & Khalifeh, 1989; Macksoud & Aber, 1996; Zvizdic & Butollo, 2001) or displacement from home (Ajdukovic & Ajdukovic, 1998; Chimienti et al., 1989; Kuterovac, Dyregrov, & Stuvland, 1994; Zivcic, 1993). These findings show how greatly injury to their protected environment threatens youngsters' well-being and peace of mind.

Contrary to expectations, the adolescents' level of fear was only weakly linked to their objective level of exposure ($r = .087$; $p < 0.001$). The weak association, however, is consistent with Thabet's (Thabet et al., 2002) findings suggesting that indirect exposure can produce more fear than direct exposure.

It is worth noting that Israeli society is relatively small both in terms of land area and population size. By augmenting both the potential for victimization and the emotional identification with the victims, this small size may intensify the impact of the terror on those who do not experience it directly. Along similar lines, several studies that examined the role of the media, especially television, in exposing children to traumatic incidents such as the *Challenger* shuttle disaster (Terr et al., 1999), the Twin Towers attack (Schuster et al., 2001), and the Iraqi invasion of Kuwait (Nader et al., 1993) showed that learning of a traumatic event through the media could cause fear and posttraumatic symptoms even among children who lived in unaffected areas. Similarly, in our study, when the respondents were asked to describe the most frightening events that they had experienced, many reported horrific scenes that they had watched on television.

Significant positive correlations were found between fear and both posttraumatic symptoms ($r = .35$; $p < 0.001$; $n = 1,673$) and psychological growth ($r = .31$; $p < 0.001$; $n = 2,082$). The greater the fear, the more symptoms and the more growth the respondents were likely to report. Moreover, fear is more strongly correlated with the two outcome variables than is objective exposure.

The finding that fear was more strongly related to posttraumatic symptoms than objective exposure was similarly reported in an earlier study of children in Israel (Weisenberg, Schwarzwald, Waysman, Solomon, & Klingman, 1993), as well as in studies of children in Rwanda (Dyregrov et al., 2000) and Yugoslavia (Gavrilovic et al., 2002). These findings provide empirical support for Lazarus, DeLongis, Folkman, and Gruen (1985) who claim that subjective appraisal plays a significant role in coping with stressful events and that it is the interpretation of the event, rather than exposure per se, that determines its psychological outcome.

Finally, objective and subjective exposure explained under a fifth of the variance in both posttraumatic symptoms and growth. This relatively low explained variance indicates that exposure to traumatic events is not the only factor that accounts for these outcomes. This means that it is important to consider other variables that may explain children's behavior after exposure to trauma. In the next part of this chapter, we report findings on the role of social support and two forms of ideology—ideological commitment and religiosity—in relation to posttraumatic symptoms and growth. Each of these factors appears frequently in studies of resilience across cultures and is discussed in other chapters in this volume as well.

Social Support

Social support and positive social relationships are widely recognized as facilitating adjustment to stress and adversity. Among adults, social support derived from intimate relationships that make the individual feel loved, valued, and cared for has consistently been documented as having beneficial effects on coping with adversity (Sarason, Sarason, & Pierce, 1995). The very expectation that such support will be forthcoming has been shown to facilitate coping with stressful life events, because people who expect to receive support from their families and significant others cope better than those who do not (Andrews, Tennant, Hewson, & Schonell, 1978).

Similar findings have been obtained among children. Studies of a group of Israeli teens caught in a disastrous bus-train collision during a school trip that killed 12 of their classmates (Milgram & Toubiana, 1996) and of Israeli children threatened by missile attacks (Itskowitz, Zeidner, & Klingman, 1994) have shown that social support from family members had positive effects on their coping. A study of Israeli children during the 1991 Gulf War showed that the expectation of receiving social support was positively associated with adjustment and negatively associated with passivity and distress (Zeidner, 1993). Studies among Palestinian children showed that supportive parents (Punamäki, Qouta, & El Sarraj, 1997) and family cohesion (Punamäki, Qouta, & El-Sarraj, 2001) enhanced children's resilience during and in the aftermath of political violence.

Along similar lines, social support from the community has also been shown to have positive effects on adjustment. Israeli children living in the closely knit collective society of the kibbutzim showed lower rates of anxiety following repeated exposure to bombardment than did comparable children living in a less cohesive community (Ziv & Israeli, 1973). Similarly, among children who lost their father in war, those who had supportive ties within their community suffered less distress and adjusted better than similar children who lacked supportive ties (Lifschitz, 1978).

Not only is the availability of social support important but so too is the ability to seek it. In fact, Sarason et al. (1995) posit that people seek help selectively, turning first to those who had helped them in similar situations in the past and then, if that help proves ineffective or unforthcoming, going to others in their social network.

Milgram and Toubiana's (1996) study of the teens involved in the above-mentioned bus-train collision found that seeking help was directly associated with level of distress: Teenagers who were more distressed sought help from many sources—not only family and friends but also professionals such as teachers and counselors. Follow-up 9 months later showed that support had a positive effect and facilitated coping.

These findings demonstrate that support is derived from different social ties. Similarly, our current study examined social support from various sources, using the Support Persons Scale (Milgram & Toubiana, 1996). Study participants were presented with the question "If you want to share your feelings in the aftermath of a terror attack, is there anyone you can turn to?" followed by a list of 10 possible sources of social support (father, mother, brother or sister, other relative, teacher, headmaster, rabbi, professional—e.g., psychologist, counselor, etc.). The youth were asked to indicate on a 4-point Likert scale the extent to which they felt they could turn to each person. Factor analysis yielded three groups of supporters: family (Cronbach's α .75); professionals (e.g., teachers, counselors; Cronbach's α .78), and friends (one item). Level of support was categorized as low (below 2.5) or high (2.5 and above).

In addition, connection to the community was assessed using the Neighborhood Cohesion Scale (Buckner, 1988). This is a 6-item self report measure in which participants rate their agreement with statements on a 4-point Likert scale (e.g., I feel connected to my neighborhood; the neighbors in our community are nicer than in other places). The original scale has good psychometric properties. Cronbach's alpha for the current study was .82. Subjects were divided into two groups: those reporting a low sense of connectedness (below 2.5) and those reporting a high sense of connectedness (2.5 and above).

The findings showed that children who felt that they could turn to the various sources of social support exhibited more distress than those who did not. Those who felt they could talk with their family about their feelings after terror attacks reported higher mean symptomatology ($M = 13.87$ vs. $M = 11.57$, respectively; $t(1,387.35) = -4.05$, $p < 0.001$).

Those who felt they could share their emotions with their friends had higher levels of symptomatology than those who did not ($M = 13.76$ vs. $M = 11.96$, respectively; $t(2,162) = -3.10$, $p < 0.01$). In the same vein, the teens who felt they could turn to a professional reported higher levels of PTSD ($M = 16.77$ vs. $M = 12.70$, respectively; $t(301.01) = -4.42$, $p < 0.001$).

Finally, the respondents who endorsed a strong sense of connectedness to their community showed higher levels PTSD ($M = 13.74$ vs. $M = 12.03$, respectively; $t(2,162) = -2.97$, $p < 0.01$).

In short, our findings suggest that social support does not moderate the pathogenic effects of war. Similar conclusions can be drawn from findings reported by Walton et al. (1997) in their study of children exposed to traumatic events in the civil war in El Salvador. Both sets of findings suggest, however, that although social support may generally be effective during adversity, it is not always effective under extreme and prolonged traumatic circumstances that occur during war. Alternatively, symptom levels may have influenced readiness to seek help and talk to others about distress. That is, the more distress participants felt, the more they were inclined to seek help and share their feelings with potential support providers.

Of particular interest is the finding that links posttraumatic symptoms with seeking professional help. The explanation that most readily comes to mind is that the more distressed persons feel, the more likely they are to seek professional help. If we consider the Sarason et al. (1995) model, it may be that the informal social network no longer meets the needs of highly distressed persons, leading them to seek help from formal sources of support. Alternatively, findings may be explained by the possibility that individuals in treatment are more aware of their distress than those who are not and more willing to report it. A study of traumatized Israeli soldiers who had psychological treatment suggests that treatment raised their awareness of their problems and may even have exacerbated their distress (Solomon et al., 1992).

Less is known about the role that social support plays in psychological growth. Our findings show that the young people who were inclined to share their feelings about terror with family members, friends, and professionals reported higher levels of growth in all but one of the dimensions (new opportunities) assessed than those who tended to keep their feelings to themselves. Moreover, those who reported a strong sense of connectedness to their communities also reported higher levels of growth than did those who reported less connectedness. In other words, the findings show that the readiness to seek social support is associated with psychological growth after trauma, even though it is not associated with reduced psychological distress.

Henderson (1977) claims that the benefit of social support as a resource does not stem from its existence but rather from its adequacy in meeting the individual's specific needs in time of adversity. One can speculate that social support has a differential effect on PTSD than on psychological growth because the two represent independent entities.

In summary, the role of social support in moderating PTSD and enhancing psychological growth here was limited. We turn now to a similar examination of the protective role of ideology and religion in the face of terror.

Ideological Commitment

Studies show that political conflicts increase group cohesion while increasing suspicion and hatred of the enemy. Studies of Israeli children (Chen-Gal, 2001; Gutman, 1992) found that children who lived in communities that were hit by terror expressed more hatred and stronger desire for revenge than did children who lived in less troubled areas. Studies of Palestinian youngsters (Punamäki, 1987) found that the more political violence they were exposed to, the more they supported war and retaliation against Israel.

An explanation for increased hostility toward the enemy in time of threat is offered by the terror management theory (Becker, 1973, 1975). According to this theory (Greenberg et al., 1990), our awareness of human vulnerability and mortality leads to the development of cultural institutions that provide order and meaning

and thereby ensure literal or symbolic immortality. The protective effect of culture is especially salient when awareness of human vulnerability and death is augmented, as it is in wartime. Under such circumstances, people tend to cling to their cultural beliefs, or ideology, with the result that they embrace those who are similar (the in-group) and reject those who are dissimilar (the out-group). Greenberg et al. (1990) have shown that reminding people of what they are most afraid of increases group favoritism and the rejection of out-group members.

The observations of Bruno Bettelheim (1961) on survival in the Nazi concentration camps in which he had been incarcerated are in line with these contentions. Bettelheim observed that those inmates who had strong ideological or religious convictions were best able to maintain their human dignity and persevere. Their ideology or religious commitment was a sustaining force that gave meaning to the barbarities inflicted by the Nazis and enabled those incarcerated to endure their extreme suffering. Inmates lacking in such conviction were more vulnerable to despair and less able to withstand the torture and humiliation, because they could not make any sense of it. The importance of ideology as a sustaining force is also attested to by the proclivity of leaders in all sorts of battles to galvanize their followers around one ideology or another.

Nonetheless, there are few studies of the role of ideology in maintaining mental health under stress. Most of the few that have been carried out support Bettelheim's observations. Punamäki's (1996) study of Israeli children exposed to terror showed that children with strong ideological commitment suffered less anxiety, depression, and distress than those with weak commitment. Punamäki concluded that ideology can serve as a psychological shield and defend children from the detrimental effects of traumatic events. In a similar vein, Kostelny and Garbarino (1994) and Punamäki et al. (2001) found that Palestinian adolescents with high ideological commitment, manifested in a willingness to engage in political demonstrations with the risk of death for their national cause were more resilient than those without such commitment. Especially interesting is a cross-cultural comparison that found that ideologically committed youngsters (i.e., militant Black Muslims in Chicago, militant Hamas supporters in the West Bank, and "extreme Zionists," fanatic supporters of a greater Israel), suffered least from distress related to armed conflict (Garbarino, Kostelny, & Dubrow, 1991). On the other hand, Slone, Lobel, and Gilat's (1999) study of Jewish children in various parts of Israel found no association between ideology and coping.

The difference in findings may be related to the studies' different operational definitions of ideology. The studies that found that ideology augmented psychological resilience (Kostelny & Garbarino, 1994; Punamäki et al., 2001) measured ideological commitment by the willingness to take action—that is, active commitment; the study that did not find that ideology increased resilience (Slone et al., 1999) measured it intellectually—that is, passive commitment—in terms of a right-wing political position and especially an unwillingness to return disputed territories.

Our study operationalized ideology as both active and passive commitment to any political view (whether right or left) and measured it by employing a specially designed ideological commitment questionnaire. The questionnaire consists of 20 statements with which respondents rated their agreement on a 4-point Likert scale, ranging from 1 (*strongly agree*) to 4 (*do not agree at all*). Factor analysis yielded three factors: (a) practical commitment (e.g., "I'm willing to participate in demonstrations"), with $\alpha = 87$; (b) ideological conviction (e.g. "I'm convinced that I'll still hold my current political views when I'm older"), with $\alpha = .68$; and (c) intolerance of other political views ("I think there are some political views that shouldn't be heard"), with $\alpha = .72$. The first factor, practical commitment, was deemed to represent active commitment; the second two, ideological conviction and intolerance, were deemed to represent passive commitment. A global score consisting of the mean of all the items was calculated, and three levels of ideological commitment were defined: low (1–2), medium (2–4), and high (4 and above).

Findings show that the teens who reported stronger ideological commitment tended to endorse more posttraumatic symptoms ($M = 22.28$ for high committed, $M = 14.19$ for medium committed, and $M = 9.24$ for less committed; $F[2, 2163] = 63.52$, $p < 0.001$). Here, too, the correlate of PTSD was the same as that for psychological growth. Those with high ideological commitment endorsed more psychological growth in all dimensions than did their less committed peers. They reported feeling more personal strength, greater appreciation of life, more new possibilities, relating better to others, and greater spiritual change (for the global growth score: $M = 2.54$ for high committed youth, $M = 2.16$ for medium committed, and $M = 1.72$ for low committed; $F[2, 2971] = 185.13$, $p < 0.001$).

Ideology in Israel may well be associated both with place of residence and likelihood of exposure to terror. In particular, persons living in settlements in the disputed territories may be more likely than those living elsewhere both to affirm strong ideological commitment and to be exposed to terror attacks. To assess the unique contribution of ideology, beyond that of exposure, to the variance of posttraumatic symptoms and psychological growth, we performed a linear regression. The findings show that ideological commitment makes a significant contribution to the explained variance in both these outcomes, above and beyond exposure. Specifically, the two passive factors, ideological conviction and intolerance of other political views, contributed to the explained variance of posttraumatic symptoms, whereas the active factor, practical commitment, contributed to the explained variance in psychological growth.

We also sought to determine the relationship of each of the ideological commitment factors to the outcome variables. Our findings showed that the conviction and intolerance factors, which define ideological rigidity, were positively correlated with posttraumatic symptoms ($\beta = .11$, $p < 0.05$ for conviction and $\beta = .14$, $p < 0.01$ for intolerance). Those who endorsed a high level of intolerance to opposing political views and those who showed high levels of conviction tended to report more posttraumatic symptoms than did their more tolerant and less convinced peers. Was there any relation between intolerance and conviction and growth? Interestingly, those who showed high practical commitment were more inclined to show psychological growth.

Stein (2001) argues that the role of ideology in children's coping depends on the interaction between ideological principles and reality. It may be that adolescents who have strong ideological convictions that they see are not implemented experience greater distress when they are exposed to terror events.

These findings are also consistent with previous findings (presented above) that suggest that active manifestations of ideological commitment are salutogenic, whereas passive manifestations are not. They also support the widely held view in the literature on coping and adjustment that active coping is more effective than passive coping (Punamäki & Puhakka, 1997). Action in the name of ideology may be considered a form of active coping.

It is also possible that more traumatized individuals may express more ideological conviction and intolerance in an effort to improve their psychological state by finding a firm anchor in their beliefs. Along similar lines, the higher ideological conviction and intolerance can be derivatives of the anger and hostility that often arise from trauma.

Finally, ideological commitment may enhance coping by making suffering meaningful as suggested by Bettleheim (1961), Punamäki (1996), and others.

Religious Conviction

Religious faith is widely believed to be an important inner resource in coping with adversity. The tendency of people to turn to religion in times of trouble may be illustrated by the finding of a national survey of a representative sample of American adults following the September 11, 2001, Twin Towers attack. A full 90% of those queried stated they turned to religion to help them cope (Schuster et al., 2001).

Whether religion can attenuate the pathogenic effects of terror is not entirely clear from the extant research, but two Israeli studies suggest that it can. Soraski's (1996) study of religious, traditional, and secular Jews residing in the disputed territories found that the religious settlers exhibited greater resilience in the face of political violence and threat than did nonreligious settlers. A study conducted by our research group (Solomon & Berger, 2004) found that ultra-orthodox volunteer rescue workers (ZAKA) were highly resilient to posttraumatic effects even in the face of repeated exposure to the exploded, fragmented corpses of persons killed in suicide attacks. Similarly, a positive association was found between religiosity and positive patterns of coping among Muslin adult war refugees from Kosovo and Bosnia (Ai, Peterson, & Huang, 2003). On the other hand, a study of young people exposed to the civilian war in Sarajevo found that religion was positively associated with PTSD (Durakovic-Belko, Kulenovic, & Dapic, 2003). There are also studies showing that believers are more sensitive to the negative effects of family stressors (e.g., Strawbridge, Shema, Cohen, Roberts, & Kaplan, 1998) and may adopt maladaptive passive styles of coping (Pargament et al., 1992).

The present study compared the number of PTSD symptoms of the religious, traditional, and secular study participants, based on self-definitions of their religiosity. The comparison showed that the religious teens were more likely to have higher PTSD levels than their less religious peers ($M = 14.87$ for ultra-orthodox adolescent, $M = 14.28$ for religious youngsters, $M = 14.20$ for traditional youth, and $M = 10.99$ for secular ones; $F[3, 2134] = 10.29$; $p < 0.001$). At the same time, the more religious youngsters also tended to report more psychological growth in all dimensions ($M = 2.17$ for ultra-orthodox adolescent, $M = 2.22$ for religious youngsters, $M = 2.05$ for traditional youth, and $M = 1.80$ for secular ones; $F[3, 2920] = 69.49$; $p < 0.001$).

Investigations into the role of religion in many areas of life, including well-being and physical health, have yielded inconsistent findings (Hackney & Sanders 2003). The inconsistency has been attributed to both differences in the way that religiosity was measured in the different studies and in the way in which religiosity is held or manifested. According to Allport and Ross (1967) religious persons can be inclined either to an "intrinsic religious orientation" or an "extrinsic religious orientation." In an intrinsic orientation, religion itself—or spirituality—is the goal; in an extrinsic orientation, religion is largely a means to another end (e.g., social status, security). Several studies have linked intrinsic religious orientation with well-being and extrinsic orientation with high levels of anxiety and low self-esteem (Bergin, Masters, & Richards, 1987; Pargament et al., 1992). We thus hypothesized that the study participants with a more intrinsic religious orientation would be helped by their religiosity, whereas those with a more extrinsic religious orientation would not.

To assess religious orientation, we used the revised Religious Orientation Scale (Gorsuch & McPherson, 1989), which distinguishes between intrinsic and extrinsic religious orientations. The scale contains 14 statements rated on a 6-point Likert scale ranging from 1 (*to a great extent*) to 6 (*not at all*). The original scale has three subscales: intrinsic, extrinsic/personal, and extrinsic/social. The questionnaire was translated into Hebrew and then translated back into English. Factor analysis yielded three factors that were different from the original factors obtained among Christian subjects. The first was religion as a lifestyle (e.g., "I try to live my life according to my religious beliefs"), which reflects the extent to which persons live by their religious values ($\alpha = .90$). This factor represents an active dimension of religiosity and resembles intrinsic orientation. The second was religion as a social value (e.g., "I attend synagogue because I enjoy meeting people") ($\alpha = .78$). This is similar to a social extrinsic orientation. The third was religion as defining identity (e.g., "It is not so important to me what I believe in as long as I am a moral person"). This can be considered a passive intrinsic dimension ($\alpha = .69$). In addition, a mean score was calculated and three levels (low, medium, and high) of religious commitment were defined.

Results showed that religious lifestyle was positively associated with psychological growth ($\beta = .21$, $p < 0.001$), whereas religion as social value was related to posttraumatic symptoms ($\beta = .09$, $p < 0.05$). Religion as a source of identity had no association with posttraumatic symptoms or with growth. These findings suggest that religious commitment should not be seen as a single entity. Like ideological commitment, it is a multifaceted concept. Religious lifestyle seems to be empowering and conducive to growth. Religion as social value, in contrast, may further pressure youths and contribute to their distress.

Some researchers claim that religion serves as a cognitive scheme that helps in the interpretation of, and gives meaning to, negative experiences (Koenig, 1995; McIntosh, Silver, & Wortman, 1993). Intrinsic religion—that is, profound religious belief—enables the believer to make sense of, and find meaning in, adverse experiences and thus facilitates coping (Park & Cohen, 1993; Park, Cohen, & Herb, 1990). Extrinsic religious orientation, which reflects an external social obligation, does not provide meaning and thus does not help in coping and may, rather, exert additional stress (Pargament et al., 1992).

In sum, the findings show that trauma can lead to seemingly opposite outcomes in the same child. There is no doubt that terror and war are potent pathogenic agents that can cause great psychological distress. The very same conditions, however, can also foster emotional growth, manifested in increased caring for others, appreciation of life, sense of new possibilities, personal strength, and spiritual enrichment. In fact, growth and suffering seem to go hand in hand: the more of one, the more of the other.

The study does, however, have several limitations. One is the associational nature of most of the findings so that causality cannot be determined with certainty. A second is that because it is being carried out in Israel, questions can be raised about the generalizability of its findings. Here, however, we may note both that most of the findings are consistent with those of previous studies and that terror is a local phenomenon, which can only be studied in the locations where it occurs. Unfortunately, Israel is a prime site. For deeper understanding, we urge comparative studies. Finally, the third limitation of the study is that it does not follow the adolescents into adulthood. We thus do not know what latent effects the terror may have.

RELATING NEGATIVE REACTIONS TO TRAUMA AND GROWTH

For the most part, the same factors that were implicated in the adolescents' PTSD were also implicated in their growth. The higher their exposure, the more symptoms they had as well as the greater their growth. Both objective exposure (measured by number of incidents the respondents were exposed to) and subjective exposure (measured by their level of fear) were related to these outcomes. Fear, however, was considerably more strongly related. Fear may be understood in two different ways: one as reflecting the real danger of the incidents to the individual, the other as the subjective interpretation that the adolescents gave to the incidents. The first is suggested by the tendency of incidents that threatened the lives of close relatives to evoke more fear than "less dangerous" incidents, such as stones being thrown at a friend's car. The second is perhaps suggested by the lack of statistically significant association between fear and exposure (e.g., number of incidents).

The workings of the factors associated with the teens' coping with the terror are somewhat more complex. The readiness to seek social support from intimates was unrelated to PTSD and only weakly related to psychological growth. Ideology and religiosity both seem to have had beneficial effects on young people's coping, but different parameters seem to have contributed differently to symptoms and to growth. Overall, strong ideological commitment was associated both with more PTSD symptoms and with more growth. However, when the impact of place of residence was taken into consideration, ideological conviction and intolerance contributed more to the variance in PTSD, whereas active, practical commitment contributed more to the variance in growth. Similarly, the more religious adolescents tended both to suffer from more PTSD symptoms and to enjoy more psychological growth than did their less religious peers. Here, religion as social value was related to posttraumatic symptoms, whereas religious lifestyle was associated with psychological growth.

The findings also indicate that, on the whole, Israeli teens cope well with the terror they experience, demonstrating a large measure of resilience despite their long exposure. About 15% of our subjects suffered from moderate to severe posttraumatic symptoms, which probably warrant professional intervention. The vast majority, however, seem to handle the wave of terror without untoward effects. It must be kept in mind, however, that should the terror continue, the figures may change, and more young people may suffer its deleterious effects. This is all the more likely given that indirect exposure, through TV and other media, may also give rise to anxiety and ensuing symptoms of trauma.

Our findings that practical ideology and religious lifestyle are associated with posttraumatic growth suggest that it might be helpful to encourage young people in traumatogenic situations to take up meaningful activities and to practice their religion. At the same time, we must keep in mind that rigid ideology and social religiosity may have adverse consequences and should be discouraged.

NOTE

1. See www.btselem.org.

REFERENCES

Ai, A. L., Peterson, C., & Huang, B. (2003). The effect of religious-spiritual coping on positive attitudes of adult Muslim refugees from Kosovo and Bosnia. *International Journal for the Psychology of Religion, 13,* 29–47.

Ajdukovic, M., & Ajdukovic, D. (1998). Impact of displacement on the psychological wellbeing of refugee children. *International Review of Psychiatry, 10,* 186–195.

Allport, G. W., & Ross, J. M. (1967). Personal religious orientation and prejudice. *Journal of Personality and Social Psychology, 5,* 432–443.

Allwood, M. A., Bell-Dolan, D., & Husain, S. A. (2002). Children's trauma and adjustment reactions to violent and non-violent war experiences. *Journal of the American Academy of Child and Adolescent Psychiatry, 41,* 450–457.

American Psychiatric Association. (1994). *Diagnostic and statistical manual of mental disorders (DSM IV).* Washington, DC: Author.

Andrews, G., Tennant, C., Hewson, D., & Schonell, M. (1978). The relation of social factors in physical and psychiatric illness. *American Journal of Epidemiology, 108,* 7–35.

Antonovsky, A., & Bernstein, J. (1986). Pathogenesis and salutogenesis in war and other crises: Who studies the successful coper? In N. A. Milgram (Ed.), *Stress and coping in times of war: Generalizations from the Israeli experience* (pp. 52–65). New York: Brunner/Mazel.

Bachar, E., Canetti, L., Bonne, O., Denour, A. K., & Shalev, A. Y. (1997). Psychological wellbeing and ratings of psychiatric symptoms in bereaved Israeli adolescents: Differential effect of war vs. accidents related bereavement. *Journal of Nervous and Mental Disease, 185,* 402–406.

Baker, A. M. (1990). The psychological impact of the intifada on Palestinian children in the occupied West Bank and Gaza: An exploratory study. *American Journal of Orthopsychiatry, 60,* 496–505.

Becker, E. (1973). *The denial of death.* New York: Free Press.

Becker, E. (1975). *Escape from evil.* New York: Free Press.

Bergin, A. E., Masters, K. S., & Richards, P. S. (1987). Religiousness and mental health reconsidered: A study of an intrinsically religious sample. *Journal of Counseling Psychology, 34*(2), 197–204.

Bettelheim, B. (1961). *The informed heart.* New York: Free Press.

Buckner, J. C. (1988). The development of an instrument to measure neighborhood cohesion. *American Journal of Community Psychology, 16*(6), 771–791.

Chen-Gal, S. (2001). *Social support as moderator of the relationship between exposure to political violence and distress.* Unpublished masters thesis, Tel-Aviv University, Tel-Aviv, Israel.

Chimienti, G., Nasr, J. A., & Khalifeh, I. (1989). Children's reactions to war-related stress: Affective symptoms and behavior problems. *Social Psychiatry and Psychiatric Epidemiology, 24*(6), 282–287.

Cohen-Silver, R., Holman, E. A., McIntosh, D. N., Poulin, M., & Gil-Rivas, V. (2002). Nationwide longitudinal study of psychological responses to September 11. *Journal of the American Medical Association, 288,* 1235–1244.

Durakovic-Belko, E., Kulenovic, A., & Dapic, R. (2003). Determinants of posttraumatic adjustment in adolescents from Sarajevo who experienced war. *Journal of Clinical Psychology, 59*(1), 27–40.

Dyregrov, A., Gupta, L., Gjestad, R., & Mukanoheli, E. (2000). Trauma exposure and psychological reactions to genocide among Rwandan children. *Journal of Traumatic Stress, 13,* 3–21.

Farwell, N. (1999). After liberation: Psychological well-being of Eritrean youth. *Dissertation Abstracts International Section A: Humanities and Social Sciences, 59*(8-A), 3208.

Ferguson, N., & Cairns, E. (1996). Political violence and moral maturity in Northern Ireland. *Political Psychology, 17*(4), 713–725.

Frederick, C., & Pynoos, R. S. (1988). *Child Posttraumatic Stress Reaction Index.* University of California, Los Angeles, Neuropsychiatric Institute and Hospital.

Garbarino, J., & Kostelny, K. (1996). The effects of political violence on Palestinian children's behavior problems: A risk accumulation model. *Child Growth, 67,* 33–45.

Garbarino, J., Kostelny, K., & Dubrow, N. (1991). What children can tell us about living in danger. *American Psychologist, 46*(4), 376–383.

Gavrilovic, J., Lecic, T. D., Knezevic, G., & Priebe, S. (2002). Predictors of posttraumatic stress in civilians 1 year after air attacks: A study of Yugoslavian students. *Journal of Nervous and Mental Disease, 190,* 257–262.

Gorsuch, R. L., & McPherson, S. E. (1989). Intrinsic/extrinsic measurement: I/E–Revised and single-item scales. *Journal for the Scientific Study of Religion, 28*(3), 348–354.

Greenberg, J., Solomon, S., Veeder, M., Pyszczynski, T., Rosenblatt, A., Kirkland, S., & Lyon, D. (1990). Evidence for terror management theory II: The effects of mortality salience on reaction to those who threaten or bolster the cultural worldview. *Journal of Personality and Social Psychology, 58,* 308–318.

Hackney, C. H., & Sanders, G. S. (2003). Religiosity and mental health: A meta-analysis of recent studies. *Journal for the Scientific Study of Religion, 42,* 43–55.

Hadi, F. A. (1999). Predicting psychological distress in children. *Journal of the Social Sciences, 27,* 73–87.

Henderson, S. (1977). The social network, support and neurosis: The function of attachment in adult life. *British Journal of Psychiatry, 131,* 185–191.

Itskowitz, R., Zeidner, M., & Klingman, A. (1994). Children's affective reactions to the Gulf War. *Psychologia: Israel Journal of Psychology, 4*(1–2), 170–181.

Koenig, H. G. (1995). Religion as cognitive schema. *International Journal for the Psychology of Religion, 5,* 31–37.

Kostelny, K., & Garbarino, J. (1994). Coping with the consequences of living in danger: The case of

Palestinian children and youth. *International Journal of Behavioral Development, 17,* 595–611.

Kuterovac, G., Dyregrov, A., & Stuvland, R. (1994). Children in war: A silent majority under stress. *British Journal of Medical Psychology, 67*(4), 363–375.

Lavi, T. (2004). *Palestinian children exposed to political violence: Situational variables and personal constructs as moderators of the pathogenic effects of exposure to extreme political violence.* Unpublished Ph.D. dissertation, Tel Aviv University, Tel Aviv, Israel.

Lavi, T., Levinovski, L., Dekel, R., Ginzburg, K., & Solomon, Z. (2002, June), *Both sides of the fence: Palestinian and Israeli children exposed to the intifada.* Paper presented at the annual Trauma Coalition Conference, Petah Tikva, Israel.

Lazarus, R. S., DeLongis, A., Folkman, S., & Gruen, R. (1985). Stress and adaptational outcomes: The problem of confounded measures. *American Psychologist, 40,* 770–779.

Lifschitz, M. (1978, June). *Growing up without a father.* Paper prepared for presentation to the second International Conference on Psychological Stress and Adjustment in Time of War and Peace, Jerusalem.

Lev-Wiesel, R., & Amir, M. (2003). Posttraumatic growth among Holocaust child survivors. *Journal of Loss and Trauma, 8,* 229–237.

Llabre, M., & Hadi, F. (1994). *Anxiety, Stress and Coping: An International Journal, 7,* 217–228.

Macksoud, M. S., & Aber, J. L. (1996). The war experience and psychosocial growth of children in Lebanon. *Child Growth, 67,* 70–88.

McIntosh, D. M., Silver, R. C., & Wortman, C. B. (1993). Religion's role in adjustment to negative life events: Coping with the loss of a child. *Journal of Personality and Social Psychology, 65,* 812–821.

McMillen, J. C., Smith, E. M., & Fisher, R. H. (1997). Perceived benefit and mental health after three types of disaster. *Journal of Consulting and Clinical Psychology, 65,* 733–739.

Milgram, N., & Toubiana, Y. H. (1996). Children's selective coping after a bus disaster: Confronting behavior and perceived support. *Journal of Traumatic Stress, 9*(4), 687–702.

Milgram, R. M., & Milgram, N. A. (1976). The effect of the Yom Kippur war on anxiety level in Israeli children. *Journal of Psychology, 94,* 107–113.

Muldoon, O. T., & Trew, K. (2000). Children's experience and adjustment to political conflict in Northern Ireland. *Peace and Conflict: Journal of Peace Psychology, 6,* 157–176.

Nader, K. O., Pynoos, R. S., Fairbanks, L. A., Al-Ajeel, M., & Al-Asfour, A. (1993). A preliminary study of PTSD and grief among the children of Kuwait following the Gulf crisis. *Journal of Clinical Psychology, 32,* 407–416.

Papageorgiou, V., Frangou, G. A., Lordanidou, R., Yule, W., Smith, P., & Vostanis, P. (2000). War trauma and psychopathology in Bosnian refugee children. *European Child and Adolescent Psychiatry, 9*(2), 84–90.

Pargament, K. I., Olsen, H., Reilly, B., Falgout, K., Ending, D. S., & Van Haitsma, K. (1992). God help me (II): The relationship of religious orientations to religious coping with negative life events. *Journal for the Scientific Study of Religion, 31*(4), 504–513.

Park, C., & Cohen, L. H. (1993). Religious and nonreligious coping with the death of a friend. *Cognitive Therapy and Research, 17,* 561–577.

Park, C., Cohen, L. H., & Herb, L. (1990). Intrinsic religiousness and religious coping as life stress moderators for Catholics versus Protestants. *Journal of Personality and Social Psychology, 59,* 562–574.

Park, C., Cohen, L. H., & Murch, R. L. (1996). Assessment and prediction of stress-related growth. *Journal of Personality, 64,* 71–105.

Powell, S., Rosner, R., Butollo, W., Tedeschi, R. G., & Calhoun, L.G. (2003). Posttraumatic growth after war: A study with former refugees and displaced people in Sarajevo. *Journal of Clinical Psychology, 59,* 71–83.

Punamäki, R. L. (1987). *Childhood under conflict: The attitude and emotional life of Israeli and Palestinian children* (Research report No. 32). University of Tampere, Tampere Peace Research Institute, Finland.

Punamäki, R. L. (1996). Can ideological commitment protect children's psychosocial wellbeing in situations of political violence? *Child Development, 67,* 55–69.

Punamäki, R. L. (1998). The role of dreams in protecting psychological wellbeing in traumatic conditions. *International Journal of Behavioral Growth, 22,* 559–588.

Punamäki, R. L., & Suleiman, R. (1990). Predictors and effectiveness of coping with political violence among Palestinian children. *British Journal of Social Psychology, 29,* 67–77.

Punamäki, R. L., Qouta, S., & El-Sarraj, E. (1997). Models of traumatic experiences and children's psychological adjustment: The roles of perceived parenting and children's own resources and activity. *Child Development, 68*(4), 718–728.

Punamäki, R. L., & Puhakka, T. (1997). Determinants of children's coping with political violence. *International Journal of Behavioral Development, 21*(2), 349–370.

Punamäki, R. L., Qouta, S., & El-Sarraj, E. (2001). Resiliency factors predicting psychological adjustment after political violence among Palestinian children. *International Journal of Behavioral Development, 25,* 256–267.

Qouta, S., Punamäki, R. L., & El-Sarraj, E. (1995a). The impact of the peace treaty on psychological well-being: A follow-up study of Palestinian children. *Child Abuse and Neglect, 19,* 1197–1208.

Qouta, S., Punamäki, R. L., & El-Sarraj, E. (1995b). The relations between traumatic experiences, activity, and cognitive and emotional responses among Palestinian children. *International Journal of Psychology, 30,* 289–304.

Ronen, T., & Rahav, G. (1992). *Children's behavior problems during the Gulf War.* Paper presented at the Ministry of Education Conference on Stress Reaction of Children in the Gulf War, Ramat Gan, Israel.

Ronen, T., Rahav, G., & Rosenbaum, M. (2003). Children's reactions to a war situation as a function of age and sex. *Anxiety, Stress and Coping: An International Journal, 16*(1), 59–69.

Saigh, P. A., Mroueh, M., & Bremner, D. (1997). Scholastic impairments among traumatized adolescents. *Behavior Research and Theory, 35,* 429–436.

Sarason, I. G., Sarason, B., & Pierce, G. R. (1995). Stress and social support. In S. E. Hobfoll & M. W. de Vries (Eds.). *Extreme stress and communities: Impact and intervention* (pp. 179–197). New York: Kluwer Academic/ Plenum.

Saric, Z., Zuzul, M., & Kerestes, G. (1994). War and children's aggressive and prosocial behavior. *European Journal of Personality, 8,* 201–212.

Schlenger, W. E., Caddell, J. M., Ebert, L., Jordan, B. K., & Batts, K. R. (2002). Psychological reactions to terrorist attacks. Findings from the Hationa Study of Americans' reactions to September 11. *Journal of the American Medical Association, 288,* 2684–2685.

Schuster, M. A., Stein, B. D., Jaycox, L. H., Collins, R. L., Marshall, G. N., Elliott, M. N., Zhou, A. J., et al. (2001). A national survey of stress reactions after the September 11, 2001, terrorist attacks. *New England Journal of Medicine, 345,* 1507–1512.

Schwartzwald, J., Weisenberg, M., Waysman, M., Solomon, Z., & Klingman, A. (1993). Stress reactions of school-age children to the bombardment by Scud missiles. *Journal of Abnormal Psychology, 102,* 404–410.

Slone, M., & Hallis, D. (1999). The impact of political life events on children's psychological adjustment. *Anxiety, Stress and Coping: An International Journal, 12,* 1–21.

Slone, M., Lobel, T., & Gilat, I. (1999). Dimensions of the political environment affecting children's mental health. *Journal of Conflict Resolution, 43,* 78–91.

Smith, P., Perrin, S., Yule, W., Hacam, B., & Stuvland, R. (2002). War exposure among children from Bosnia-Hercegovina: Psychological adjustment in a community sample. *Journal of Traumatic Stress, 15*(2), 147–156.

Solomon, Z., & Berger, R. (2004). Coping with the aftermath of terror: Resilience of Zaka body handlers. In Y. Danieli, D. Brom, & J. Sills (Eds.), *The trauma of terrorism: Sharing knowledge and shared care, an international handbook.* Binghamton, NY: Haworth Maltreatment & Trauma Press.

Solomon, Z., & Lavi, T. (in press). Israeli youth in the second intifada: PTSD and future orientation. *Journal of the American Academy of Child and Adolescent Psychiatry.*

Solomon, Z., Shalev, A., Spiro, S. E., Dolev, A., Bleich, A., Waysman, M., & Cooper, S. (1992). Negative psychometric outcomes: Self-report measures and a follow-up telephone survey. *Journal of Traumatic Stress, 5,* 225–246.

Soraski, H. (1996). *The relationship between values and coping with stress among religious and secular Jews.* Unpublished master's thesis, Bar-Ilan University, Ramat Gan, Israel.

Strawbridge, W. J., Shema, S. J., Cohen, R. D., Roberts, R. E., & Kaplan, G. A. (1998). Religiosity buffers effects of some stressors on depression but exacerbates others. *Journals of*

Gerontology: Series B. Psychological Sciences and Social Sciences, 53B: S118–S126.

Stein, E. (2001). *Children's reactions to the stressful situation aroused by the intermediate phase of the peace process.* Unpublished doctoral dissertation, Bar-Ilan University, Ramat Gan, Israel.

Tedeschi, R. G. (1999). Violence transformed: Posttraumatic growth in survivors and their societies. *Aggression and Violent Behavior, 4,* 319–341.

Tedeschi, R. G., & Calhoun, L. G. (1996). The Posttraumatic Growth Inventory: Measuring the positive legacy of trauma. *Journal of Traumatic Stress, 9,* 455–471.

Terr, L. C., Bloch, D. A., Michel, B. A., Shi, H., Reinhardt, J. A., & Metayer, S. (1999). Children's symptoms in the wake of challenger: A field study of distant-traumatic effects and an outline of related conditions. *American Journal of Psychiatry, 156,* 1536–1544.

Thabet, A. A. M., Abed, Y., & Vostanis, P. (2002). Emotional problems in Palestinian children living in a war zone: A cross-sectional study. *Lancet, 359,* 1801–1804.

Thabet, A. A. M., & Vostanis, P. (1999). Posttraumatic stress reactions in children of war. *Journal of Child Psychology and Psychiatry and Allied Disciplines, 40*(3), 385–391.

Vizek-Vidovic, V., Kutervac-Jagodic, G., & Arambasic, L. (2000). Posttraumatic symptomatology in children exposed to war. *Scandinavian Journal of Psychology, 41,* 297–306.

Walton, J. R., Nuttall, R. L., & Nuttall, E. V. (1997). The impact on the mental health of children: A Salvadorian study. *Child Abuse & Neglect, 21,* 737–749.

Waysman, M., Schwarzwald, J., & Solomon, Z. (2001). Hardiness: An examination of its relationship with positive and negative long term changes following trauma. *Journal of Traumatic Stress, 14*(3), 531–548.

Weisenberg, M., Schwarzwald J., Waysman, M., Solomon, Z., & Klingman, A (1993). Coping of school-age children in the sealed room during Scud missile bombardment and postwar stress reactions. *Journal of Consulting and Clinical Psychology, 61,* 462–467.

Zahr, L. K. (1996). Effects of war on the behavior of Lebanese preschool children: Influence of home environment and family functioning. *American Journal of Orthopsychiatry, 66,* 401–408.

Zeidner, M. (1993). Coping with disaster: The case of Israeli adolescents under threat of missile attack. *Journal of Youth and Adolescence, 22,* 89–108.

Ziv, A., & Israeli, R. (1973). Effects of bombardment on the manifest anxiety levels of children living in the kibbutz. *Journal of Consulting and Clinical Psychology, 40,* 287–291.

Zivcic, I. (1993). Emotional reactions of children to war stress in Croatia. *Journal of the American Academy of Child and Adolescent Psychiatry, 32,* 709–713.

Zvizdic, S., & Butollo, W. (2001). War related loss of one's father and persistent depressive reactions in early adolescents. *European Psychologist, 6*(3), 204–214.

15

Overcoming Adversity With Children Affected by HIV/AIDS in the Indigenous South African Cultural Context

Philip Cook

Lesley du Toit

T his chapter examines children's resilience against the background of the devastating effects of HIV/AIDS on children and their communities in South Africa. Specific attention is focused on the Circles of Care: Community Capacity Building project and its culturally grounded action research methodology as an intervention supporting child and community resilience. This strategy is presented in the context of indigenous African cultural values, beliefs, and practices as a basis of support for children's resilience by promoting healthy human development at the level of the child, his or her peers, the family, and the social structures making up each child's local social ecology.

For 5 years, the Child and Youth Care Agency for Development (CYCAD), a South African nongovernmental organization (NGO), has been working in partnership with the University of Victoria's International Institute for Child Rights and Development (IICRD) to identify and reinforce community and cultural assets in supporting child and family resilience. The project, titled Circles of Care: Community Care and Support for Children Affected by HIV/AIDS[1] has developed and piloted a model of community capacity building that supports traditional African community structures and local government in reinforcing child resilience both through local capacity building and through bottom-up, rights-based advocacy. In doing this, the project applied the "Triple A" participatory research process in which children, women's groups, local community leaders, and traditional elders collectively *assess* the local situation of children's vulnerability before *analyzing* this information using principles from the Convention on the Rights of the

Child (CRC). The final step in this process involves an *action* stage in which local resources are built on to bridge the gaps between children's needs and the resources available to them. In addition, building bridges also means building relationships and action plans with child rights "duty bearers" from local government as well as reinforcing traditional African governance systems supporting children.

This chapter presents the results of the Circles of Care Triple A process in the context of the project's community interventions in several municipal areas located in three *Sotho*-speaking municipalities in South Africa's Free State province. The chapter concludes with a discussion on the lessons learned from this experience in light of current thinking on resilience with particular attention paid to issues of contextual approaches to supporting children's resilience in South African settings highly affected by HIV/AIDS.

Background

The world is currently witnessing one of the greatest human calamities of all time in the AIDS pandemic. The disease has cut the largest and deepest human swath across the countries of sub-Saharan Africa, where the majority of the world's 40 million persons now infected by HIV/AIDS can be found.

Among the countries most affected by this disease, South Africa is experiencing the crushing burden of having the highest number of persons living with AIDS of any country in the world. In 2003, this accounted for 5 million persons out of a total population of 43 million. The number of orphans expected to result from this high level of mortality is expected to reach 2 million or more by the year 2010 (UN Children's Fund, 2003). Not surprisingly, government policy and programming have been unable to keep pace with the scale of this epidemic and the burden it has placed on communities, families, and above all, children.

Children are born into this world dependent on adult-based circles of care. Research on human development now conclusively shows that for infants to reach their maximum human potential, they need a basis of physical, emotional, cognitive, and social supports (Shonkoff & Phillips, 2000). Different cultures weave the strands of these supports together in different patterns that have evolved in response to the local natural and human-made environment. However, in general, it is safe to say that all children have basic and similar needs. These include stable, loving relationships; proper nutrition; positive role models; and socially and culturally constructed pathways to help transition through the various stages of childhood and adolescence to become mature adults ready to participate in society and parent the next generation (Myers, 1992). Key to this process is the need for children to interact with their world and have access to diverse opportunities to participate and learn from adults in community and culture, in developing a sense of control, self-efficacy, and a positive sense of self and collective identity.

Perhaps the most insidious aspect of HIV/AIDS, then, is the capacity of the disease to sever those human bonds and social ties that children need to survive and thrive. Across Southern Africa, and now particularly in South Africa, we are witnessing not only the reversal of development trends but also the very destruction of age-old patterns of traditional family, community, and social supports for children. In taking those members of society who are most crucial for children's immediate developmental needs (e.g., parents, relatives, teachers, nurses, social workers), AIDS slowly unravels the delicate web of relationships children need.

The role of local government and civil society organizations in finding responsive and innovative ways of rebuilding these circles of care is critical to ensuring the reversal of this negative development trend and reweaving child-centered webs of relationship. Of particular importance is the need to bridge the gap between policy and practice related to child protection and development at the level of local government and communities most affected by HIV/AIDS. This needs to involve identifying and building on local capacity in partnership with families, community leaders, and above all, children and young people.

It is a terrible irony that this most recent of human pandemics has taken root in the very cradle of humanity. Southern Africa contains some of the oldest social traditions of the human family. Better understanding and building on traditional Africa values, beliefs, and practices supporting children remains an untapped well of collective human potential that should be drawn on to address the social aspects of HIV/AIDS and the crushing poverty that fuels and accompanies this disease.

LOCATION OF THE PROJECT

The Circles of Care project is presently located in several municipal areas in the three Free State municipalities of Maluti-A-Fophong, Welkom, and Sasolberg. Each municipal area contains anywhere from three to nine communities governed by locally elected councils. These councils sit periodically to hear local complaints, and they are frequently the first line of informal dispute resolution for many community issues prior to someone's formally approaching the municipal governance structures.

Unemployment is extremely high for the adult population in all these municipalities, creating an underlying and pervasive systemic level of poverty that colors almost every aspect of children's needs and vulnerabilities. The unemployment for youth is close to 90%; this in itself creates vulnerability and serious social problems for the area. Poverty, HIV/AIDS, and sexual and physical abuse are the main factors causing extreme vulnerability to children in this area. Of the child population, we estimate that 80% or more are vulnerable because of poverty even without other factors such as HIV/AIDS and child abuse (which has been identified by the communities as one of their main problems).

CIRCLES OF CARE: REINFORCING RESILIENCE IN THE AFRICAN CONTEXT

Innovative, participatory child-centered research strategies that seek to better understand the individual and collective dimensions of poverty and AIDS in relation to children's well-being are needed to inform community and local government responses to the social and cultural roots and results of the disease. Combining the best and most socially grounded research practice in

child development, community empowerment, good governance, and human rights with a culturally sensitive approach to working in the collective African context will be crucial to bridging the gap between creative policy and innovative, responsive practice in regard to HIV/AIDS.

The Circles of Care project aims to bridge this gap by building on the inherent resilience, or coping capacity, of children and their families and communities (Fraser, 1997). Many current interventions targeting children affected by HIV/AIDS apply a deficit model in which risks associated with HIV/AIDS, and the social dysfunction associated with the disease, are the center of attention. The Circles of Care project draws on current resilience theory by focusing on ways in which children and their communities successfully cope in the face of adversity. Factors that promote children's resilience under conditions of adversity have been identified in a number of studies (Donald, Dawes, & Louw, 2000; Garmezy, 1993; Garmezy, Masten, & Tellegen, 1984; Werner & Smith, 1982). Factors that promote resilience and protect children from negative outcomes include capacities that are part of the child's physical and psychological makeup as well as features of the social ecology in which the child lives.

Garmezy et al. (1984) and Donald et al. (2000) outline three models that explain how resilience operates. The first is a *compensatory model.* In this model, a particular positive influence neutralizes the impact of other stresses on a specific outcome such as educational achievement. For example, in a community with high levels of unemployment, the parents may still be very supportive of their child's academic work at school. Their attention and support for their child's study therefore "compensates" for the stresses that would otherwise be expected to affect his or her school performance.

The second model is the *challenge model.* Here the child's exposure to a moderate amount of stress acts to strengthen his or her ability to cope with difficulties at later points in life. This model explains the findings that children who have been exposed to adversity and have learned to cope well are likely to feel more competent in coping with future difficulties. In the present context, this might indicate that some children exposed to moderate amounts of stress resulting from high levels of poverty, HIV/AIDS, or both in their community would develop coping skills that would enable them to deal with other threats such as abuse and neglect.

The third case is the *protective factor model.* A protective factor is a process that interacts with a risk factor in reducing the probability of a negative outcome. Protective factors work by moderating the effect of exposure to risk and by modifying the response to risk factors. For example, in many studies of the impact of traumatic experiences on children, it has been found that the presence of at least one stable and supportive caregiver can "protect" or "buffer" the child, thereby reducing the risk that the child develops serious problems later in life (Cairns, 1996). An example of this in the present context would be a youth worker who intervenes to provide ongoing support for a child orphaned by HIV/AIDS, thus reducing the affects of isolation and marginalization on the child.

Although some studies have focused particular attention on the African context of child resilience (Donald et al., 2000; Nsamenang & Dawes, 1998; Ramphele, 1993), there still exists a dearth of research examining the social construct of resilience in non-Western cultural settings. Each of these three resilience models was therefore examined in this way in the specific African context of the Circles of Care project using the Triple A methodology. To better understand the role of culture as a determinant of children's resilience, particular attention was paid to ways in which the local South African cultural context mediated resilience.

CIRCLES OF CARE: PROJECT GOALS

Circles of Care is a comprehensive project focused primarily on vulnerable children and youth[2] and aimed at achieving the following broad goals:

    a. To develop and refine a particular model of community care that reinforces the resilience, or coping capacity, of vulnerable children and youth (and their families and communities), as well as *local government,* thereby enabling families, communities, and municipalities to

take responsibility for the care and protection of their vulnerable young people

    b. To provide practical guidelines for local government and community leaders on how to further support this reliance—guidelines that result from the participatory research process and that are based mainly on the voices of children and youth

    c. To identify and reinforce unique African values, beliefs, and practices supporting coping and healthy human development

    d. To establish one South African province as a setting for a best-practice initiative and all other areas as learning sites

    e. To enable provincial, local, and traditional systems of governance in at least 8 to 10 municipal areas to replicate the model and processes

The fundamental concept of the Circle of Care is that local governments, in partnership with communities, form an invisible "circle of care" around their most vulnerable citizens (particularly children and youth, but not excluding women and older people where this seems a natural part of the work). Children's rights become known and respected by integrating them into every facet of local government and community life. The CRC and African Charter are used as the framework or lens through which the model is developed and applied. Key to supporting resilience is that within these circles, vulnerable children and youth are safe, have their basic needs met, experience growth and achievement, participate in all aspects of community life that concerns them, respect and enjoy their environment, are educated, and thrive.

To accomplish these goals, we employ *participatory research* that uses the Triple A method to hear and reinforce the agency of children and youth (and their families and communities) with respect to their coping needs, vulnerabilities, rights, strengths and dreams. These methods also allow us to capture and feedback their voices in a manner that builds the capacity of communities and local governments to understand people's needs, engage in decision-making processes with young people, and take active steps in the protection, care, development, and survival of vulnerable children and youth. It will further influence and facilitate the development and implementation of comprehensive guidelines and policies for the care and protection of vulnerable children and youth.

TRIPLE A METHODOLOGY

To stimulate the growth of these Circles of Care in each community, we employ the Triple A method, which aims to strengthen the resilience of vulnerable children. The Triple A method is itself not unique to Circles of Care and was pioneered by UNICEF in Tanzania in the 1970s. However, it was later refined by the IICRD to include more culturally grounded approaches in a participatory research project in Malawi addressing issues of community support for orphans and vulnerable children in the context of matrilineal and patriarchal cultural communities (Cook, Ali, & Munthali, 2000). In the Circles of Care project, the method was further adapted to specifically build on South African traditional and municipal levels of governance.

The Procedures

As noted earlier, the Triple A approach is a participatory research and community development tool used to *assess* strengths and weaknesses in the care and support of orphans and vulnerable children so that local facilitators can work with a community to *analyze* this information to create and carry out a plan of *action* that fills the gaps in the lives of these children by building on local strengths or assets at the level of the child, the family and community, social institutions, and cultural values, beliefs, and practices.

This plan of action is first used to help mobilize local resources (personal, family based, cultural, economic, natural) to respond to locally identified children's needs that are most likely to reinforce resilience. The plan is also used to help communities liaise more effectively with their local government in efforts to better channel government resources to fill the gaps in service that communities cannot cover or for which they are not responsible. Local community-based organizations (CBOs), international NGOs, and

international agencies (e.g., UNICEF) can all play a role in this process. In this way, the Triple A was applied in the Circles of Care project to building local capacity for vulnerable children and their families and communities.

Specifically, the Triple A process involves various sectors of a community identified through a preliminary series of key informant interviews and mapping of resources. Representatives from each sector are then invited to become involved in a development approach supporting the rights of vulnerable children. These local groups (e.g., children, women, men, traditional leaders) become the focus groups that carry out the Triple A cycle.

Key Informant Interviews

The first step in preparing for the beginning of the Triple A process is to carry out select key informant interviews. These interviews are carried out with local traditional leaders, children's advocates, NGOs, and government representatives connected to children (e.g., health care workers, social workers, teachers, agricultural extension workers, etc.). The process and information collected in the interviews serves to inform local traditional and government leaders about the process of the Triple A and gather specific information relevant to children affected by HIV/AIDS.

Community Mapping

Following the key informant interviews, a general community assessment is conducted with representatives from various sectors of the community. The community assessment usually takes the form of at least one community-mapping workshop and a study of documents. Community asset mapping is a rapid rural appraisal tool that has been successfully applied in various situations where children at risk to assess local assets—strengths or social resources, including support networks. Asset mapping is grounded in the asset-based approach of Kertzmann and McKnight (1993). It is a multiple-use tool that allows children to engage through an asset-mapping process and researchers to gain asset data. Asset mapping has been successfully used with other groups of vulnerable children in the African context (Veale, 2000). The asset-mapping approach is a critical step in identifying local resilience and forms the basis of planning for the implementation of the Triple A participatory research. The information from the key informant interviews is then included to provide a comprehensive "map" of the community.

One large component of the mapping process is to identify sources of social support available to vulnerable children. Typically, obvious social supports identified in the asset mapping are institutions such as schools or health clinics, yet in many cases, vulnerable children, especially children traumatized by HIV/AIDS, do not access these social services. Social mapping can help identify less obvious supports, as well as focusing on damaged supports, emergent supports, and less "tangible" cultural supports, such as rituals and the natural and supernatural world of the child.

The Triple A Components

Following the mapping process, focus group discussions are facilitated by someone familiar with the local community who understands the cultural context of those living there. The CRC guiding principles are used to help focus groups address key children's issues. These include survival, development, protection, and participation. Young people are encouraged to participate, using various age-appropriate means of expression: for example, (a) focus group discussions, (b) local games, (c) culturally rooted drama, and (d) artwork.

In this research, cultural considerations are addressed by the following:

- Carrying out key informant interviews with traditional and cultural leaders prior to using the Triple A approach
- Meeting in culturally "safe" and appropriate places and times for each group
- Finding a common language that bridges children's rights and local expressions supporting children's well-being (e.g., dignity, respect)

The process of the Triple A approach should help with the following:

- Identify child, family, community, and cultural strengths that can be drawn on to fill the gaps

in the local Circles of Care and support for vulnerable children

- Facilitate a sense of ownership and responsibility in families and communities, identifying and applying local resources in support of vulnerable children
- Assist communities and local government to work together more efficiently and effectively in caring and supporting AIDS-affected and other vulnerable children
- Identify mutual roles and responsibilities of families, communities, and government in supporting the rights of children affected by HIV/AIDS
- Better understand and reinforce traditional African practices supporting children
- Effectively tie rights-based interventions to community development strategies
- Meaningfully involve young people in this process

A DEVELOPMENTAL-RIGHTS-BASED APPROACH TO PROMOTING RESILIENCE

The three resilience models discussed earlier build on research that has shown that many youth problems have common antecedents (Dryfoos, 1990). A developmental approach emphasizes the investment in young people's assets and protective factors rather than focusing on specific problems. We believe it is a more effective method for addressing youth's problems. Similarly, a developmental approach sheds light on the context of children's lives, emphasizing the importance of connectedness, participation, and strategic partnership as effective strategies for overcoming youth challenges (Rajani, 2001). This is in keeping with a rights-based approach that emphasizes people as subjects of rights and underscores the participatory importance of self-realization of rights.

Some of the advantages of promoting child and youth participation include the following:

- Participation is itself a part of development and is therefore both a means and an end to healthy growth.
- Young people can make a valuable contribution to society.
- Participation builds community programs' effectiveness and sustainability.

- Participation fosters learning, builds life skills, and enables self-protection.
- Young people's participation builds civil society and strengthens democracy (Cook, Blanchet-Cohen, & Hart, 2004).

A bottom-up, Triple A–informed, rights-based approach was applied during the Circle of Care project to better appreciate local understanding and attitudes toward children's rights and to build supports for children's rights. The rights-based approach ensures that all human beings, *including children,* have equal opportunity to realize their full developmental potential. When working with children affected by HIV/AIDS, the rights approach promotes the concept that all children—regardless of age, gender, race, religion, ethnic status, or any other difference—have basic rights and deserve a life with security and dignity. Rights-oriented programs are not based only on responding to specific "needs"; rather, they address all aspects of a child's life. They depend on holistic and inclusive social support measures being implemented by children's duty bearers (governments, NGOs, communities, families) while involving children as active "claim holders" (Knutson, 1997).

In our work, we found that by employing a Triple A model of research, which itself was guided by this rights-based approach to children, helped us to proceed in a way that was congruent between our methods and what we hoped to achieve. Arguably, the Circle of Care is an attempt to create a community concerned about improving children's lives through their expression of their rights. The participatory nature of the methodology ensures that children are part of the process of inquiry into their lives and the development of interventions; this is itself a core value expressed by the CRC and operationalized through the rights-based approach.

In theory, this approach should promote children's resilience by identifying assets that can compensate for stresses in a vulnerable child's life as well as strengthening relationships that will buffer and protect the child. Finally, it was thought that the self-protective skills learned through the participatory process would help enable children to cope with additional and future threats in their local environments.

Mapping Rights in the Context of Local Risk and Resilience

Although these notions of rights are frequently assumed to be "universals," their applicability to the "small" spaces of children's lives, particularly in non-Western contexts, remains unclear. The project therefore applied the Triple A method to "map" local perspectives on children's rights from the point of view of children themselves as well as from their guardians and other key informants to assess the cultural "fit" of the CRC with local values, beliefs, and practices affecting children. Following are examples of variables included in this mapping:

- Local child-rearing practices
- Opportunities for children's participation in matters affecting them
- Barriers to children's well-being
- Acceptance of concepts of children's dignity and the value attached to childhood, in comparison with the value placed on other persons (e.g., women, adults in general, elders)

Specifically, three different steps were used to apply a rights-based approach as a framework for intervention. All three relied on a bottom-up approach that builds on local assets. The steps included the following:

- Identifying unmet basic needs of children
- Identifying the cause of the problem
- Identifying people, organizations, or systems that have duties to respect, protect, and facilitate and fulfill these needs

It is important to note that as we proceeded through each step, interventions and strategies based on the analysis of our findings as they emerged were intended to accomplish the following:

- Empower caregivers, communities, local organizations, and government to meet their obligations
- Empower children to participate in realizing their rights
- Promote child supportive cultural practices
- Mobilize advocacy networks to influence various levels of government to avoid actions and

omissions that result in the violation of children's rights

In recognition that children vary greatly in how they can participate, we used a number of tools to facilitate participation in the Circles of Care project:

- Role play and drama
- Games
- Artwork (drawing, painting, collage, etc.)
- Mapping and modeling
- Interviews

The tools worked only to the extent that we created a safe environment for children's participation in the research. Guided by this principle, successful implementation of the research involved the following:

- Finding a physical place where children feel safe and comfortable
- Encouraging both listening and speaking
- Allowing children to answer as many questions as they wanted
- Affirming cooperation
- Encouraging curiosity, games and play, and various forms of self-expression
- Inviting a respected traditional leader or trusted person in the community to act as a resource on cultural issues and help support follow-up to the discussion and other activities

In the context of children affected by HIV/AIDS, a rights-based approach such as this creates an environment where children can be heard. It also makes children aware of the obligation placed by participants (both adult and child) on local government and all involved in the lives of these children (including international relief agencies) to assume their responsibilities in protecting and promoting the rights of children affected by the widespread impact of HIV/AIDS at the level of the child, family, community, and society. It also implies addressing the rights of all children involved (e.g., girls, children of vulnerable groups such as children with a disability, and orphans).

In addressing the rights of these children, the rights approach views rights as indivisible and interdependent. Thus, no one right is seen

as more important than another, and action to realize these rights must simultaneously address various groups of rights (e.g., AIDS protection programs should also consider children's long-term protection and psychosocial needs). Finally, a rights-based approach advocates for outcomes that meet the standards set forth in the CRC while suggesting a process that involves children and their guardians as stakeholders in this process. In doing so, it builds on children's natural resilience and coping strategies. It therefore sets the stage for involving children and their natural support systems (both natural and human) as action-oriented advocates rather than as helpless victims.

THE SOCIAL ECOLOGY OF CHILDREN'S RIGHTS AND HIV/AIDS

The diagram presented in Figure 15.1 represents a "developmental child rights framework" that draws on the social ecology of childhood developed by Urie Bronfenbrenner (1979) and that can be used to discuss and implement a rights-based approach.

The figure places each child at the center of a series of concentric, nested circles representing differing layers of support networks. The child's basic human developmental needs are represented in the inner physical, emotional, cognitive, and social quadrants. The next level addresses support for the child's family. This is composed of various family patterns, including nuclear, extended, fragmented, alternative guardians, and other immediate primary care providers of children.

The next level includes the community and the child's natural and human-made environment. It is recognized that each child's development will take various routes based on each child's "developmental niche." This system is composed of cultural values influencing children's development, specific child-rearing patterns, and the environmental conditions influencing variations in healthy growth and development.[3] The environment includes things such as the presence or absence of child-friendly community structures (e.g., play spaces, safe housing, availability of fresh drinking water), as well the direct impact of the local natural environment

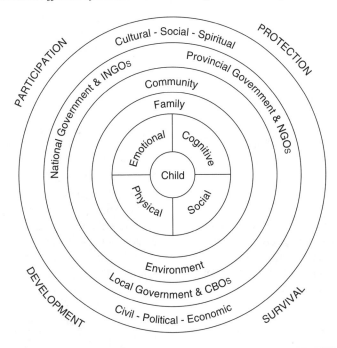

Figure 15.1   The Social Ecology of Children's Rights

(e.g., rural farming community, peri-urban community dependent on labor migration, and urban communities) on children's development (for more on environmental contributions to resilience, see Chapter 8 in this volume).

Moving further from the center, the next level addresses the roles of various forms of government, including local, provincial or state, national, and regional as well as the presence or absence of alternate forms of governance (e.g., NGOs, both domestic and international) and civil society. The final level of the diagram represents the presence of local and national values that are either supportive or nonsupportive of children's civil, political, social, economic, and cultural rights as well as the role of spiritual beliefs influencing children's physical and moral development.

The four guiding principles of the CRC are portrayed on the outside of the diagram and represent cross-cutting themes that emerge in each of these levels that are either strengths or weaknesses in these systems insofar as they promote a rights-based approach. For example, cultural attitudes restricting open discussion of

HIV/AIDS with young people discriminates against these children's right to access the information they need to make safe choices about their own and others' safety. It is also inimical to their survival and healthy development and often does not allow them meaningful participation in expressing their opinions in matters relating to their safety as well as the security of their peers and other family members.

Typically, stronger links between the constituents found at each layer represented in Figure 15.1 results in children having healthier connections through positive relationships with their human and natural environment, which in turn leads to greater resilience and healthier individual and community development. Conversely, in situations of extreme social and political upheaval resulting from HIV/AIDS, these protective relationships are broken down by community stigma and silence surrounding AIDS and by the sickness and death of adults in positions of care and support for children. This results in death or injury of care providers and loved ones, debilitated social service structures such as schools and hospitals, lack of safe places for children, and risky and antisocial behavior that weakens or destroys adolescents' healthy relationships with care providers and cultural traditions. These relationships, when optimal, have the potential to foster positive self-esteem and powerful identities.

In keeping with the African Charter on the Rights and Welfare of the Child and Article 30 of the CRC (a child's right to language, culture, and religion), the Circle of Care project emphasizes the need to build on positive culture strengths. One of the key components of the project is the emphasis placed on building on local cultural beliefs, values, and practices supporting children's healthy development. This involves working closely with local traditional leaders and other persons with cultural expertise on children's issues such as traditional healers.

ENHANCING CHILD AND YOUTH PARTICIPATION

Responses to children affected by AIDS should address the needs of children of all ages, including infants, young children, adolescents, and youth. In addressing these needs, a child rights-based approach requires that children affected by HIV/AIDS be viewed as subjects of rights and not passive recipients of care and support. This is often an especially challenging notion for many programs oriented toward a welfare-based approach more likely to respond to children in ways that make them into passive victims.

In contrast, the Circles of Care approach to supporting vulnerable children in the context of building stronger communities seeks to involve children in meaningful dialogue and action in identifying gaps and needs, as well as helping locate local resources, including the active participation of young people as action-oriented agents of change.

The CRC recognizes the importance of participation across the child's life span. This is supported by child development theory that speaks to the importance of children's capacity to safely explore and interact with their environment as key criteria in healthy human development.

In children's infancy and early development, creative play is an especially important component of participation. As the child grows, socialization

becomes a central focus of participation. These social skills are further refined during adolescence when children actively experiment with and explore social rules and continue the process of developing a personal identity and self-image in relationship with other children and key adults. This process is largely determined by cultural socialization practices and is a constantly evolving process, with children themselves more frequently defining the shape and form their growth takes through their own rituals of participation.

We believe the key to promoting dialogue on children's participation lies in supporting the meaningful involvement of young people in discussing issues relevant to them in a safe environment that promotes children's expression while also including the voice of families, key community representatives, and traditional leaders with expertise and knowledge on social balance and harmony. This is especially important to bear in mind when working with AIDS-affected children, for these children need both (a) the positive structure of community and culture to help create a healthy sense of belonging and self-esteem *and* (b) the opportunity to work with adults in shaping cultural norms to better support their changing needs and those of other vulnerable children.

It is also important to be aware of the great diversity that exists between young people both at different ages and across different subgroups. Often, participation strategies assume that a small group of young people represent the voice of all of their colleagues, whereas in fact the variation in children's perspectives is often as great as among adults. These variations can be due to age differences, rural-urban disparities, socioeconomic gaps, and cultural diversity. Care needs to be taken to ensure representation across these diverse groups of children.

RESULTS OF CIRCLES OF CARE PROJECT: THE EROSION OF CHILDREN'S NATURAL SUPPORTS FROM HIV/AIDS

As a precursor to identifying and building on local strengths supporting resilience, participants in the Triple A assessment identified a range of direct negative consequences arising from poverty and HIV/AIDS that seriously affect children's survival, protection, and full and healthy development. Using the model of social ecology, the negative factors that erode children's natural supports at the traditional, community, and family level can be grouped under a number of topics.

First, the focus group discussions in all communities identified a weakening of supports for children at both government and traditional cultural levels. At the national and provincial government level, people complained that not enough was being done to specifically address the needs of vulnerable children. For example, participants frequently complained that many children were still not allowed to attend school if they did not have a school uniform or could not pay school fees, even though this exclusionary practice is now illegal in South Africa.

Second, although participants clearly want some form of social security, they were critical about the lack of access to the national child support grant for which they were eligible and the lack of monitoring of the granting process. Participants described how this frequently leads to the most vulnerable children not receiving the benefits of the grant, because these funds are often used by parents and extended family members to purchase alcohol, clothing, or other non-child-related items. A particularly disturbing trend was also described in which women, some in their teenage years, were forced by men (husbands, partners, or boyfriends) to have three or more babies in order to receive the income from the child support grant of R120 per month (approximately $17 US).

Third, participants described how the lack of government education programs on AIDS prevention resulted in continued risky sexual behavior, stigma toward those people living with AIDS, and denial of the affects of AIDS in the community.

Participants related the direct affect this had on children who were affected by these secondary threats. These children were described as suffering from a lack of community action to help those who were ill or orphaned, as well as from the inability of communities to adequately discuss prevention measures with young people.

Fourth, discussions with both children and traditional leaders were surprisingly similar in identifying the weakening of the traditional *Sotho* supports for children. Specific traditions that were said to be disappearing included the following:

- Birth ceremonies protecting the mother and young child
- Initiation ceremonies conducted correctly for boys and girls
- Cultural restrictions on sexual activity between youth
- Community sanctions against divorce and extramarital sex
- The role of traditional elders and other community leaders in advising couples experiencing marital difficulties
- Support for abandoned and orphaned children through the intervention of relatives and elders

Fifth, focus group participants in all communities identified a worsening of the overall situation for children and their families over the past 10 years. Although a few improvements were noted, such as better water access and the construction of low-cost new homes under the Rural Development Program (RDP), the general picture was bleak. Examples of this worsening situation included the following:

- Increased poverty
- Rising unemployment and a return to the community of unemployed from other parts of the country
- Lack of alternate jobs for unemployed persons
- Higher costs for basic food stuffs such as *mealies*
- Reduction in nutrition
- Rising rates of crime associated with alcohol and drug abuse
- Increase in prostitution
- Increased sexual and physical abuse of children and youth

Focus group participants were particularly concerned about the harmful affects of poverty and HIV/AIDS at the family level in all municipalities over the past 10 years. It was often difficult to distinguish the separate effects of poverty and HIV/AIDS, because these two factors were clearly perceived to be interlinked. For example, greater unemployment in the mine sector resulted in more young men without jobs returning to families or remaining unemployed in the community. This in turn was thought to lead to greater alcohol abuse and prostitution (because wives and daughters without support from the husband or other male relative were forced to support themselves and their families by exchanging sex for food or other favors). Both factors then resulted in greater HIV infection. Similarly, AIDS-related sickness and death in families were described as leading to a dramatic decrease in mean family income because family resources were drained by payment for medicines and funeral expenses.

IDENTIFYING ESPECIALLY VULNERABLE CHILDREN

Community focus group participants in Maluti-A-Phofeng, Welkom, and Sasolberg were asked to identify especially vulnerable groups of children. All assessments of these groups were discussed and analyzed using the CRC themes of survival, protection, development, and participation. After applying a content analysis of the data using these four themes as guiding principles, participants and facilitators identified a number of key issues.

Vulnerability Across the Life Span

Vulnerability was described according to the age of a child. After collectively analyzing data from the three municipalities, the leading causes of vulnerability associated with poverty and HIV/AIDS were described by adult focus groups (women, caregivers, and local leaders) as follows:

0 to 2 Years

- Pregnant mothers' drinking leads to fetus mortality and harm to the fetus, causing children to be born with a disability.
- Parents use the child support grant to purchase alcohol instead of food.
- Young infants are frequently left alone while parents are looking for work or when sick.
- Orphans who lose their parents in infancy are particularly vulnerable to abuse.
- The lack of proper parenting leads to stunted development.
- Unemployment results in lack of nutritious food.

3 to 10 Years

- Children are unable to attend school because of lack of school fees.
- Parents are either sick or drinking, and children are unsupervised and at risk of abuse or rape.
- Children cannot concentrate in school because of hunger.
- Many parents are in their teens and as such have their own "childhood" needs to meet and cannot care for a baby or young child.

11 to 17 Years

- Shortage of constructive activities for children to engage in leads to antisocial behavior.
- Breakdown of initiation ceremonies restricts natural transition of boys and girls from childhood to adulthood.
- Vulnerable youth often drop out of school and engage in risky behavior (e.g., drinking and unprotected sex) and are more at risk of contracting HIV/AIDS.
- Poverty among youth causes boys to engage in crime and girls in prostitution.

18 to 25 Years

- Few jobs following school matriculation result in even higher rates of unemployment among youth.
- Stigma and a culture of silence surrounding HIV/AIDS creates difficulties for youth to engage in constructive dialogue with their parents and elders on issues of sexuality, safety, and self-protection.

CHILDREN DEFINING THEIR OWN VULNERABILITY

Issues of vulnerability specifically identified and discussed by the children in their focus groups were similar to those raised by adult informants. However, some differences are evident. Children noted they are most vulnerable for these reasons:

- Some children are neglected because they live with grannies who have only pensions as support and cannot look after them properly.
- Children with a disability are abused and often do not attend school.

- Some children use drugs to help them forget the pain of parents dying.
- Very young children are raped.
- Children who live with adults who are not relatives are beaten or raped.
- Some children get "hurt" inside by abuse.
- Local businesses use orphans and pay them nothing or only a little food.
- Children coming from broken marriages do not get enough love.
- Children living alone without any parents or other adults are especially vulnerable.
- Children are fearful of initiations because of lack of safeguards and protection.
- Children are not cared for by adults and are forced to play in dangerous areas such as busy streets and polluted *dongas* (ditches).
- Children and youth have no access to positive human values (e.g., love, peace, and integrity).

VULNERABILITY AS DEFINED BY TRADITIONAL LEADERS

Issues of vulnerability specifically identified by the elders during focus groups include these concerns:

- Traditional leaders feel that their role in society has been marginalized by the government and modern notions of human rights and democracy. There is already a "gap," as they put it, between the community, government/politics, and traditions, and they feel that an emphasis on child rights (and possibly on human rights) have contributed to some of these splits. This gap has affected the role of parents and traditional leaders. Children and youth have become isolated because people "are divided" in their interests. The chiefs feel that cultural traditions and values have been eroded and devalued (e.g., initiation ceremonies, ways of controlling and teaching girls and boys).
- Schools are promoting children's rights in ways that reduce children's responsibility and undermine the authority of leaders.
- The issue of rights is controversial. Traditional leaders (elders) feel that these rights restrict them because they were able to discipline children as they wished before and are now unable to do this. *Ubuntu*,[4] or community support, is also affected. For example, when

children exercise their perceived "right" to come home late, parents feel disempowered and the leaders feel very worried.

- In many cases, fathers are not at home—many have left or gone to seek employment—and the mother alone is left in charge. In the past, mothers would have brought their concerns to the chiefs but this no longer happens and has resulted in children's vulnerability not being brought to the attention of traditional leaders.
- The elders believe that the issue of AIDS is being addressed in an unhelpful manner. Outsiders did not take into account the tribal governance structures and traditional ways of healing. For example, one of the paramount chiefs in QwaQwa used to have responsibility to manage and help prevent such health crises. However, the government did not turn to him for leadership in this regard. As a consequence, traditions that might prevent the spread of HIV/AIDS are no longer practiced. One focus group noted that, traditionally, a wife may not use her father-in-law's name and may not touch the father-in-law or his clothes. It was felt that this prevents sexual intercourse between the woman and the father-in-law.
- Before a marriage, the chief used to give advice and guidance. Young women or men, it was said, never had sex outside marriage. Now the chiefs feel that women tell the young girls about sex, making it impossible for the chiefs to give this counsel. In the perception of the elders, these approaches have caused traditions that might have prevented the spread of disease to be "taken away."
- Initiations are no longer run by traditional leaders (some are carried out by children, and many are carried out by people who conduct them as a business); the lack of traditional regulation of initiation ceremonies (particularly for boys) results in injuries, HIV infection (through the use of unsterilized razors for circumcision), and death.

GENDER ISSUES AND VULNERABILITY

In general, parents in all communities expressed love and affection for their children regardless of gender. Many parents were gravely concerned about the situation of both boys and girls in their communities, particularly in regard to the pressures from poverty that resulted in neglect and abuse of children, and the terrible toll that AIDS was having in breaking the bonds between children and their parents, families, and communities.

Girls were perceived to be at greater risk from the effects of HIV/AIDS and poverty than boys from infancy onward. There were many examples of strong, confident young women who participated in the focus groups and other Circles of Care activities. However, overall, girls were perceived to be more vulnerable to being forced to trade sex for food, money, and housing, whereas vulnerable boys engaged in criminal activity to meet their survival needs. Child rape, mostly of girls although also of young boys, was thought to be very prevalent across South Africa and was widely reported and discussed in all focus groups.

Girls also described being emotionally abused by teachers much more than boys. Some teachers apparently ask that girls go and clean their houses during the day. More disturbing, in some instances, girls described being sexually coerced by teachers.

Both girls and boys described a tendency for their vulnerable peers to engage in drug and alcohol abuse, which further fueled the cycle of both AIDS and poverty. Elders noted an increase in drug and alcohol abuse among youth and also indicated that more girls seemed to be engaging in drug abuse than in the past.

Boys reported resorting to violence and crime in response to personal exposure to abuse and lack of love as a child, extreme poverty and unemployment, and lack of opportunities and community activities for young people.

In discussions with both boys and girls, anti-social activities such as crime and prostitution were seen as part of a vicious cycle of vulnerability that young people entered. Focus group discussions with boys and girls also revealed a distrust of adults in positions of authority (e.g., social workers, police) and hesitancy about turning to them as potential sources of support. The criminal justice system was described as further driving this cycle of vulnerability through its emphasis on punishment rather than rehabilitation.

TRIPLE A ACTIONS: STRENGTHENING CHILD AND COMMUNITY RESILIENCY

The Triple A methods are part of a praxis of both reflection and action. As such, actions resulting from the focus groups with adults included the following:

- Establishing vegetable gardens to feed young people infected and affected by AIDS and their families
- Teaching children, parents, and extended family members to keep and maintain a garden
- Teaching parenting skills and basic supports for young children
- Recreational work with youth at risk
- Establishing an inexpensive community-based crèche (day care) for infants and young children left alone while their parents are at clinics, looking for work, or working
- Traditional cultural clubs for adolescents to strengthen cultural ties

Actions resulting from the focus groups with children included the following:

- Raising awareness in families and communities about the rights of vulnerable children affected by HIV/AIDS
- Inviting orphans home for a meal on a regular basis
- Collecting and dispensing clothes and shoes to children excluded from school due to lack of uniforms
- Establishing cultural "clubs" to encourage vulnerable children's participation in their community and culture

THE TRIPLE A: CRITICAL REFLECTIONS ON PROMOTING RESILIENCE IN THE CONTEXT OF HIV/AIDS

One of the primary messages to emerge from this research is that a simple, low-cost participatory research intervention such as the Triple A can be an effective tool in supporting children living in the darkness of HIV/AIDS and poverty. In particular, the methodology allowed for the identification and creation of local assets required to sustain coping in vulnerable children and youth. The process of carrying out the steps of the Triple A enabled poor beneficiaries, including children, to gather and apply local knowledge as metaphoric protagonists in the drama of their lives. Although local governance structures were frequently unresponsive to this process, or in some instances even opposed to community participation in support of vulnerable children, there was nevertheless considerable success in applying a bottom-up, developmental approach to supporting the rights of children affected by HIV/AIDS and poverty. A discussion is required, however, to critically reflect on the results of this research in terms of its ability to inform debate on resilience at the level of the child and of community and local governance.

At the level of the child, the research indicated that, to some degree, children participating in local discussions on their rights in the context of poverty and HIV/AIDS resulted in greater self-efficacy, increased self-esteem, and increased capacity for local agency in promoting the rights of vulnerable children. A central theme that emerged from the discussions with young people was that the very act of *collectively discussing* their situations in a safe environment, in the company of trusted, supportive adults, was itself healing for children. This underscores the power of personal narrative as a restorative tool in supporting children's capacity for making sense of their own self-identity in reinforcing individual resilience in the midst of the darkness of HIV/AIDS.

This wasn't the case for all children involved in this process, however, and in certain cases, some children were clearly overwhelmed by the adversity in their communities. As other authors writing on resilience have discussed (Garbarino, 1999), some children are so loaded for risk factors that local interventions of this nature will still have no success in reinforcing *any* of the three models of resilience. These children surely existed in each of the communities involved in this project, and there were a number of tragic testimonials of young participants who fell victim to crime, prostitution, or other forms of social isolation *in spite of* the research and other interventions.

At the level of the community, the Triple A approach seemed to also be a useful tool for locating and reinforcing local supports for vulnerable children. Indeed, the Triple A appeared to support the notion that *child and youth individual self-efficacy* reinforced *collective adult self-efficacy.* One of the significant challenges of the Circles of Care project, however, was the lack of support from some local municipal governments. Although local communities clearly proved their abilities at responding to the needs of vulnerable children, this wasn't always reciprocated by local government service providers responsible for vulnerable children, their families, and their communities.

Ultimately, the Triple A, although successful as a grassroots, participatory research tool that reinforced children's resilience in the context of HIV/AIDS, still requires the support of meaningful and effective child rights legislation and policy to bridge local gaps in the realization and respect for children's rights. In the context of HIV/AIDS in sub-Saharan Africa, this will likely not come about through legal advocacy procedures alone but will also require the community-driven, restorative practice demonstrated by both children and traditional African elders in the Circles of Care communities. This partnership is evidence of a unique quality of resilience that is a testimony to the age-old strengths of the collective African culture and the contemporary power of the African child's own capacity for regeneration.

NOTES

1. The present project focused on children *affected* by HIV/AIDS as opposed to children *infected* with HIV/AIDS. The primary child participants in the research therefore included orphaned children or children made vulnerable from other secondary aspects of the AIDS pandemic such as poverty, breakdown in family and community caring capacity, or the reduction of services to children due to death or illness of professionals working with children, such as teachers, nurses, and social workers.

2. Vulnerable children and youth are defined in terms of this project as those young people between the ages of 0 and 18 years who are made vulnerable as a result of HIV/AIDS or poverty.

3. See Super and Harkness (1984) for a full discussion of the notion of "development niche."

4. *Ubuntu* is originally a Zulu term that means "I am a person because you are a person, I am because you are." This value once underpinned most African cultures in South Africa. It meant that everyone was related to everyone else and all were there to support each other. This includes a collective value system where children in the community can be fed, clothed, disciplined, or supported by anyone from their community. No child would be simply left to go hungry. Similarly, no child would have been left to "misbehave" without being chastised. Tribal courts also played a role in this collective approach to holding everyone accountable for everyone else. Although this value is not gone from people's traditional sense of identity, it has been eroded over many years through the imposition of Western individualism and customs imposed by past South African governments and missionaries.

REFERENCES

Bronfenbrenner, U. (1979). *The ecology of human development: Experiments by nature and design.* Cambridge, MA: Harvard University Press.

Cairns, E. (1996). *Children and political violence.* Oxford, UK: Blackwell.

Cook, P., Ali, S., & Munthali, A. (2000). *Starting from strengths: Community care for vulnerable children in Malawi.* Unpublished manuscript, University of Victoria, British Columbia.

Cook, P., Blanchet-Cohen, N., & Hart, S. (2004). *Children as partners: Child participation promoting social change.* Victoria, British Columbia: University of Victoria, International Institute for Child Rights and Development.

Donald, D., Dawes, A., & Louw, J. (2000). *Addressing childhood adversity.* Cape Town, South Africa: David Philip.

Dryfoos, J. (1990). *Adolescents and risk: Prevalence and prevention.* New York: Oxford University Press.

Fraser, M. (1997). *Risk and resilience: An ecological perspective.* Washington, DC: NASW Press.

Garbarino, J. (1999). *Lost boys: Why our sons turn violent and how we can save them.* New York: Anchor Books.

Garmezy, N. (1993). Children in poverty: Resilience despite risk. *Psychiatry, 56*(1), 127–136.

Garmezy, N., Masten, A., & Tellegen, A. (1984). The study of stress and competence in children: A building block of development psychopathology. *Child Development, 55*(1), 97–111.

Kertzmann, J., & McKnight, J. (1993). *Building communities from the inside out.* Chicago: ACTA.

Knutson, K. (1997). *Children: Noble causes or worthy citizens.* Aldershot, UK: Arena.

Myers, R. (1992). *The twelve who survive: Strengthening programming of early childhood development in the third world.* New York: Routledge.

Nsamenang, A., & Dawes, A. (1998). Developmental psychology as political psychology in sub-Saharan Africa: The challenge of Africanization. *Applied Psychology: An International Review, 47*(1), 73–87.

Rajani, R. (2001). *Promoting strategic adolescent participation.* New York: UNICEF.

Ramphele, M. (1993). *A bed called home: Life in the migrant hostels of Cape Town.* Cape Town, South Africa: David Phillip.

Shonkoff, J., & Phillips, D. (Eds.). (2000). *From neurons to neighborhoods: The science of early childhood development.* Washington, DC: National Academy Press.

Super, C., & Harkness, S. (1984). The developmental niche: A conceptualization at the interface of child and nature. *International Journal of Behavioral Development, 4,* 545–569.

UN Children's Fund. (2003). *Africa's orphan generations.* New York: Author.

Veale, A. (2000). Dilemmas of community in post emergency Rwanda. *Community, Work and Family, 3,* 233–239.

Werner, E., & Smith, R. S. (1982). *Vulnerable but invincible: A longitudinal study of resilient children and youth.* New York: McGraw-Hill.

16

Bent But Not Broken

Exploring Queer Youth Resilience

Marion Brown

Marc Colbourne

W hy is it relevant to include a chapter on lesbian, gay, and bisexual (LGB)[1] youth in a text on resilience? What are the reasons for drawing a connection between the lives of LGB youth and the theories of resilience? In most ways, after all, regardless of where they live, queer youth are just like heterosexual youth: They come from all ethnic, religious, and socioeconomic backgrounds, and they share the same skills, interests, and physical attributes (Savin-Williams, 2001). They grow up both within and outside of families of origin, they navigate popular culture demands and peer dynamics, they cope with disappointments and uncertainties, and they prepare for their futures. Yet the contexts within which these developmental experiences occur are fundamentally different.[2] So are the challenges LGB youth face. A few examples follow:

- In 1999, Canadian Justice Minister Anne McLellan promised "necessary changes" to the *Criminal Code* to protect gays and lesbians under hate propaganda laws "in the coming months." No changes have yet occurred.[3]

- In November 2001, Aaron Webster, a young gay man, was beaten to death in Vancouver. Lesbians, gays, bisexuals, and transgendered people are excluded from federal hate propaganda laws, making it legal to promote hatred against our communities.

- In April 2002, the Durham Catholic School Board in Ontario denied Marc Hall the right to bring his same-sex partner to his high school graduation dance. The Ontario Supreme Court upheld his right to do so, and Marc did take his partner to the prom.

- On November 27, 2003, Canadian Alliance MP Larry Spencer claimed there is a "well-orchestrated . . . conspiracy" in Canada designed to seduce and recruit young boys. He advised that homosexuality should be recriminalized ("Egale Calls on Alliance Party," 2003).

- The headline of a letter to the editor published in the *Abbotsford Times,* in the Fraser Valley of British Columbia recently read: "If we allow gay marriage, is legal rape next?" (MacQueen, 2004, p. 30)

- Youth riding on the Lesbian, Gay and Bisexual Youth Project float in the 2004 Pride Parade in

Halifax, Nova Scotia, were taunted by a group of spectators; after the parade, a female member of the Youth Project was punched in the face by one of the male spectators.

This chapter begins with a review of the sociopolitical context in contemporary North American society as it relates to homophobia and heterosexism, then moves to an exploration of significant challenges faced by LGB youth in an effort to locate how this population creates and enacts resilience. Resilience herein is defined as an ongoing process of engagement between self and community, consisting of series of interactions and reflections that contribute to surviving adversity and living well (Ungar, 2004). The Lesbian, Gay and Bisexual Youth Project, located in Nova Scotia, is highlighted as an example of programming that opens spaces for young people to experiment with and experience ways to cope with threats to them that result from their sexual orientation. The life stories of young people involved with the Lesbian, Gay and Bisexual Youth Project are woven throughout this chapter, connecting salient points in the literature with the lived experience of youth.

HOMOPHOBIA AND HETEROSEXISM

Any discussion of the lives of LGB youth must necessarily begin with analysis of the context of homophobia and heterosexism that has been and continues to be pervasive around the world. The challenges faced and particular coping strategies chosen by LGB youth do not result from individual pathology or deficiency but, rather, have to do with oppressive societal conditions associated with heterosexism and homophobia. By context, then, we mean the social and political conditions surrounding the lives of young LGB people that bring with them unique meanings and consequences to those lives. At the same time, we recognize that both homophobia and heterosexism are themselves human creations, or constructions, borne of particular, prevailing, and legitimized belief systems, or dominant ideologies. In this chapter, the concepts of context and construct are closely linked, given that the societal *contexts* within which LGB youth live are comprised of societal *constructs*.

A term coined by the psychologist George Weinberg in the late 1960s, *homophobia* is generally defined as the irrational fear and hatred of gay, lesbian, and bisexual people, their behaviors, choices, and lives (Weinberg, 1972). It has also been taken to include any belief system that supports negative myths and stereotypes about same-sex attraction and couples (Mihalik, 1991). The reported intent of this definition was to remove stigma from the LGB person and, rather, pathologize the person holding the antigay attitudes and beliefs. However, there have been difficulties with the concept since the outset.

Some researchers, notably psychologists, assert that to use the *phobia* suffix implies a psychological condition, which is not primarily the case here. Others have argued that, given the ideological and societal context that supports misinformation about, exclusion of, and intolerance toward LGB persons, there is little irrationality about these negative attitudes and beliefs. Indeed these attitudes and beliefs are reinforced in myriad ways, and use of the term homophobia, given its focus on individual thoughts and feelings, diverts attention from a necessary macroanalysis of institutional and systemic prejudice toward LGB persons.[4] Unlike classic phobias, homophobia has some basis in a logic that has been construed and constructed and that has a distinct political agenda (Eliason, 1995). Expressions of homophobia range along a continuum from attitudes of exclusion and intolerance to verbal targeting and harassment to physical manifestations of assault and murder. Rather than the personal opinions of a subset of the general population, the prevalence and meanings of homophobia have profound social significance and intersect in complex ways with patriarchy, sexism, and heterosexism.

Heterosexism refers to institutionalized and cultural homophobia: the legitimization of prejudice on the basis of nonheterosexual orientation through overt social practices and systems and covert social mores and customs (Appleby & Anastas, 1998; Herek, 1984, 2000; Pharr, 1988; Sanders & Kroll, 2000). Dominant ideologies regarding sexual expression, behavior, and identity assert the preference of heterosexuality over other alternatives. Beyond social mores and customs, heterosexism refers to the legitimized enforcement of compulsory hetero-sexuality[5] and bestows entitlement and social acceptance on all those who correspond with its expectations. Heterosexism is the unspoken and unconscious assumption, for example, that my neighbor is heterosexual unless and until demonstrated or articulated otherwise; homophobia is the feeling of disgust on my hearing that, indeed, she is lesbian. Heterosexism ensures that there are no "checks and balances" on the many potential expressions of homophobia. In ways both explicit and implicit, it allows a culture of sexual prejudice to continue without threat.

Roots of Homophobia and Heterosexism

The meanings and implications among hetero-sexism, homophobia, patriarchy, and sexism are overlapping and expansive, and they all begin with recognition of the use of power and control to establish and maintain dominant ways of thinking.[6] A sociopolitical analysis suggests that, in Western thought, power is embedded within the notion of hierarchy; that is, power of one idea, person, or thing *over* another, resulting in oppression and "othering" of the entity on the lower end of the hierarchy. Oppression, the core concept of which is "press," is both outcome and process: It consists of collective personal experiences located in the structures that determine and maintain a particular ordering of societal relationships. "Something pressed is something caught between or among forces and barriers which are so related to each other that jointly they restrain, restrict or prevent the thing's motion or mobility" (Frye, 1983, p. 2).

Oppression is at the same time overt, blatant, and unmistakable, as well as insidious, covert, and easily overlooked. "It is organized violence at the top that permits individual violence at the bottom" (Weick & Vandiver, 1982, cited in Dalrymple & Burke, 1995, p. 15). It is the manifestation of an ideology so pervasive that for the dominant, at least, it can go unrecognized, both as process and as outcome. Ideology, political systems, and economic structures form a powerful triumvirate of social control.

This weblike system of restraint and immobility requires classification into easily discernible categories and the ordering of such categories within a hierarchy that confers superiority and inferiority. Domination allows for a systematic valuing of human worth, wherein the powerful are bestowed with the positioning and authority to include or exclude based on this determination. Privileges and normative expectations are ascribed according to one's role within the hierarchy, and the perpetuation of the hierarchy is made feasible through the development of social systems that see such ordering as natural and, in Christian cultures, God given. Exclusion inherently necessitates othering, the designation for those who are deemed without merit for inclusion.

It has been suggested that the social system within which children first learn about differential access to power, which is the gravity for societal values, is in the family home (hooks, 1984). It is here that children learn about status, voice, representation, relationships, and positioning relative to power, as well as the manifestations and consequences of choices that comply with or contradict uses of dominant discourses of power.

> It is in this form of the family where most children first learn the meaning and practice of hierarchical, authoritarian rule. Here is where they learn to accept group oppression against themselves as non-adults, and where they learn to accept male supremacy and the group oppression of women. Here is where they learn that it is the male's role to work in the community and control the economic life of the family and to mete out the physical and financial punishments and rewards, and the female's role to provide the emotional warmth associated with motherhood while under the economic rule of the male. Here is where the relationship of superordination-subordination, of superior-inferior, or master-slave is first learned and accepted as "natural." (hooks, 1984, p. 36)

Within this analysis, two relationships begin to emerge more clearly. First, there is a conceptual and practical relationship between hetero-sexism, homophobia, and sexism. The family system described above indicates the subtle yet pervasive reinforcement of compulsory hetero-sexuality, gender role distinction, and the risks of nonconformity within this paradigm. Where heterosexism is the ideology and homophobia the system of thoughts, behaviors, and attitudes keeping it the paradigm in place, patriarchy is the ideology of male supremacy and control, and sexism is the system of thoughts, behaviors, and attitudes maintaining the paradigm's prevalence (Pharr, 1988). The conceptual and practical overlap between heterosexism, homophobia, and sexism is exemplified through the hate speech directed toward males that equates acting "like a girl" or in conventionally feminine ways, with being gay (Plummer, 2001; Tolman, Spencer, Rosen-Reynoso, & Porche, 2003). Both being perceived as gay and perceived as femalelike are considered the ultimate insult for boys and men and evidence of failure to adhere to compulsory heterosexuality, which is a cornerstone of patriarchy, and thus these must be met with swift and mighty derision.

Sexism is the principle underlying this configuration: elaborate cultural, societal, and economic structures designed to denigrate the female under male superiority (Frye, 1983; Pharr, 1988). Same-sex affection and attraction practically (if not ideologically) reject such a notion, therefore inherently challenging the bases on which society is meant to maintain itself: patriarchy, heterosexuality, and sexism. hooks (1984) asserts that sexism is the site of domination experienced by most people, either as oppressor or oppressed, and that we experience it before we know or experience other oppressions. Ideologies of sexuality and gender are woven within and around sexism: Expectations for gender roles and heterosexual activity are communicated overtly and covertly and are the ways and means through which girls and boys learn the values, beliefs, and customs of conventional masculinity and femininity. Some say that to be heterosexual is to meet the basic expectation of gender socialization, given that, from the outset, regardless of the other characteristics one has, choices one makes, and behaviors one engages in, if one does not conform with being heterosexual, one is already violating the dominant discourse of gender (Appleby & Anastas, 1998).

Unlike other social prejudices, homophobia and heterosexism are most often first learned in the family home. Contrast, for example, that experiences and awareness of racism and classism are generally first encountered on entering the outside social world (Blumenfeld, 1992). Home can remain, then, a haven to which to return for a sense of shared identity, culture, and meaning, a place to combat the ignorance, hostility, hatred, and violence prevalent in the wider community. No such comfort is ensured in the home of LGB youth, who include this divergence in family identity as a significant source of distress and isolation (Flowers & Buston, 2001).

THE CENTRALITY OF CONTEXT

Analysis of this societal landscape is critical to understanding the context within which LGB youth live their lives and must precede discussion of the risk factors faced and coping strategies employed by this population. A research focus on alcohol and drug abuse, suicide, self-harm, and prostitution, devoid of analysis of the societal context of heterosexism, homophobia, patriarchy, sexism, and the call to comply with conventional and narrow gender expectations dangerously and inappropriately pathologizes and segregates LGB youth. Being LGB is not inherently reflective of psychic distress, mental illness, or other social problems, yet LGB people have often been "studied" as a problematic population, on the basis of engagement in the above-named behaviors. Alternately, LGB youth have been subsumed within the heterosexual youth population out of ignorance. Neither approach is cognizant of, nor responsive to, the myriad ways through which LGB youth resist oppression and enact their resilience.

Much as we recognize and assess evidence of the many societal constructs that marginalize and oppress LGB young people as central themes in our analysis, we are wary of casting these features as nonnegotiable and rigid in their impact on society's citizens. Young LGB people's lives inform us on a daily basis that these structures are not irrevocably fixed. At the same time as acknowledging and fully appreciating their weight, we need to appreciate the lived reality that LGB youth can and do act to transform their situations as a marginalized group and maneuver for better positions on a daily basis. Every day, LGB youth find ways to overcome the structural obstacles that permeate society, as the stories included here attest. Thus, although there is much to critique and dominant ideology and discourse is indeed pervasive, there is also much to celebrate. The effects of structural inequalities do not necessarily saturate the daily lives of young LGB people.

Some theorists posit that young LGB people are growing up in a social climate less oppressive than earlier generations, with qualitative data suggesting that some LGB youth consider themselves more alike than dissimilar to their non-LGB peers (Eccles, Sayegh, Fortenberry, & Zimet, 2003). Furthermore, the diversity of life experiences within this and any other population means that experiences of life obstacles, ideologies, and societal structures necessarily vary from person to person, according, minimally, to ethnicity, class, and gender (Savin-Williams, 2001). There is great diversity among this population, and we are wary not to invoke an essentialized "community" of LGB youth. We do not assume that what difficulties one faces, all will face, and in the same manner.

Homogenizing of the LGB population has occurred on three notable levels. First, subsumed under a macro youth narrative, there has been the homogenization that all young people, variously aged between 12 and 19 years, are considered to be developmentally progressing at the same time and speed, regardless of the social locations of race, class, and sex. Early research and modular development theories of identity formation during adolescence exemplify this trend (see, e.g., Erikson, 1963, 1968). Second, studies that compare LGB youth with heterosexual youth imply through their design that the two populations are distinct. Such research wrongly labels youth as LGB or as questioning or same-sex attracted, which may or may not connote homosexual orientation (Savin-Williams, 2001). Third, studies related to LGB youth have frequently applied findings of studies with gay boys to lesbian girls, erasing the implications of sex and gender.

Finally, we resist the draw to characterize the lives of LGB youth as fully knowable and reducible to discrete variables revealed for our examination, although much of the literature is organized in this way. Although there can be great understanding facilitated, solidarity achieved, and comfort generated through the predictability and certainty available by quantifying the rich experiences of people's lives, in so doing we run several risks.

First, the task of categorizing or labeling a person is vulnerable to making one-dimensional a multidimensional life and assuming a fixed rather than fluid identity. There are some who assert that affixing any category as well as abbreviating that category is to further oppress the LGB person, for that which we choose to name becomes prioritized, and the choice is inherently political.

> To be "gay" means belonging to a class of individuals who are subject to hate crimes, prejudice and stereotypes. . . . it is to be expected that some adolescent might choose to describe not their sexual identity but their sexual desires or attractions (e.g., "I'm attracted to women"). (Savin-Williams, 2001, p. 11)

As a parallel point, many researchers have asserted that sexual identity and same-sex attraction are evolutionary phenomena and that traditional identity development models, including coming-out models (see, e.g., Cass, 1979; Troiden, 1989), suggest a linear progression and causal relationships that are not useful for spiral, reflective learning and living processes. Although we have surveyed the literature and we include life story vignettes, and we hope that this exploration is helpful in understanding the layers of richness that may contribute to resilience among LGB youth, we fully embrace that there is no one way to "live well" within one's environment.

HETEROSEXISM AND HOMOPHOBIA: WHERE THEY CAN LEAD

Expressions of homophobia and heterosexism stigmatize, isolate, and thereby traumatize LGB youth during critical stages of their development (Bagley & D'Augelli, 2000). Correspondingly, many LGB youth speak of their adolescence as a time filled with anxiety, isolation, and fear. Experiences of homophobia and heterosexism put LGB youth at risk for dropping out of school, suicide, drug and alcohol abuse, physical and verbal abuse, homelessness, and prostitution (Bagley & Tremblay, 1997; D'Augelli, Pilkington, &

Hershberger, 2000; Grossman, 1997; Remafedi, Farrow, & Deisher, 1991; Remafedi, French, Story, Resnick, & Blum, 1998; Savin-Williams, 1994; Uribe & Harbeck, 1992).

Because homophobia and heterosexism continue to be largely unchallenged in contemporary society, LBG youth frequently face overt discrimination without intervention from others. The Gay, Lesbian, and Straight Education Network's (GLSEN) survey of LGB and transgender students across the United States reported that 83% had been verbally harassed and 42% had been physically harassed in school, with 84% of high school students hearing the words *faggot* or *dyke* in the classroom frequently or often (GLSEN, 2001). Concluding their study, they assert that despite the benefits of sexual diversity education, schools remain reluctant to address lesbian and gay issues, particularly in curricula aimed at youth aged 12 to 16 years (GLSEN, 2001). Another American study concurred with these findings, with 86% of the students reporting that school officials "rarely or never" challenged this type of harassment (Peters, 2003). The international group Human Rights Watch reported in 2001 that the public school system in the United States had repeatedly and uniformly failed to protect LBG and transgender students (Human Rights Watch, 2001). Correlated with this abuse and lack of validation from school staff, LGB, transgender, and questioning youth are 2 to 5 times more likely to drop out of school than their heterosexual counterparts (*Nuggets,* 1998).

The heightened rate of suicide among LGB and bisexual youth has been well documented in the literature (see, e.g., Bagley & Tremblay, 1997; D'Augelli et al., 2000; Remafedi et al., 1991; Remafedi et al., 1998). Gibson (1989) found that in the United States, lesbian and gay youth make up between 30% and 60% of all completed youth suicides. In Canada, a study at the University of Calgary found that LGB youth are 13.9 times more likely to commit suicide than heterosexual youth (Bagley & Trembley, 1997). Factors including social isolation, lack of affirming and validating support services, alienation from family and friends, and gender nonconformity have been noted as contributing to this heightened suicide risk. D'Augelli et al. (2000) assert that "gender atypical" males

encounter more physical and verbal abuse related to their suspected sexual orientation than do males who conform more closely to society's concept of masculinity and are therefore better able to "hide." Remafedi et al. (1991) and Remafedi et al. (1998) have linked gender nonconformity and subsequent homophobic abuse to an increased risk of suicide.

The predominance of research supports the notion that most LGB youth are aware of their sexual orientation early in their adolescent development, with many self-identifying by the age of 16 (Ryan & Futterman, 1997). However, many of these young people do not disclose their orientation to others until later in their lives because of fear of stigmatization and harassment. This is particularly true in the case of disclosure to family members (D'Augelli, Hershberger, & Pilkington, 1998). Research has shown that the majority of these young people face mistreatment by family members after their sexual orientation is disclosed. As a result, many are either forced to leave home by their family or choose to leave because of safety concerns (Savin-Williams, 1994). There are corresponding elevated levels of homelessness among this population: conservative estimates indicate that 25% to 40% of homeless youth are LGB (Ryan & Futterman, 1997). It is anticipated, however, that this percentage is significantly lower than the reality because many of these young people choose to "mask" their orientation out of fear of further stigmatization (Ryan & Futterman, 1997). There is also evidence of some LGB youth turning to work in the sex trade at least initially as a means of economic support and finding a place to belong (Banks, 2001; Tremble, 1993).

Several studies have highlighted the incidence of substance abuse among LGB young people. LGB youth may turn to use and abuse drugs and alcohol for varied reasons, including managing stigma and shame, denying same-sex feelings, or as a defense against ridicule and violence (Garofalo, Wolf, Kessel, Palfrey, & DuRant, 1998; Orenstein, 2001; Ryan & Futterman, 1997).

A critical factor to consider in understanding the experiences of LGB youth is the relative lack of responsive and affirming services available. Because of the social alienation and stigmatization experienced, many do not feel safe in accessing health or social services and, as a result, do not seek support in dealing with the concerns discussed above (Babineau, 2001). Youth who do attempt to circumvent these barriers and access services are often met with additional homophobia and heterosexist assumptions on the part of the service provider. Not only can this combination of experiences prevent the youth from accessing safe and supportive services, it often contributes to overall feelings of hopelessness and alienation (Babineau, 2001).

The above examples are included here not for the purposes of underscoring a message that being LGB is hazardous to physical, emotional, and psychological health, for this is not the case (Savin-Williams, 2001). Rather, their relevance is in highlighting that negative effects emanate from lack of support and resources, externalized homophobia, internalized homophobia, self-concealment of sexual orientation with the requisite alterations in behavior, and the stresses of coming out in an often hostile environment (Banks, 2003).

LOCAL STORIES OF LIVING WELL

The sociopolitical context of heterosexism and homophobia, the foundations on which they are built, and their manifestations, have been discussed above. Given this context and these consequences, we need to ask some questions: Is there such a thing as queer resilience? Are there resilient characteristics or experiences held or faced by LGB youth and unique negotiations between LGB youth and their environments that may encourage resilience? Are there programs and services or support that can nurture latent resilience in LGB youth? If there are such programs, what can be learned from them?

To approach these questions, we sought the voices of LGB youth regarding their definitions and experiences of resilience. We used both interviews conducted as part of our clinical work with these youth and research specifically on the theme of resilience. All the youth were members of the Lesbian, Gay and Bisexual Youth Project ("the Youth Project") of Halifax, Nova Scotia, Canada. Their stories are included here. This method of data collection was chosen given

the imperative to isolate the concept of queer resilience according to the language and lived realities of queer youth themselves. We begin, however, with an explanation of the scope of services provided by the Youth Project as a way of demonstrating the context that must necessarily be established if LGB youth are to be given the opportunities to advance socially, academically, and psychologically unhindered by the barriers imposed on them because of their sexual orientation.

THE YOUTH PROJECT: CREATING A CONTEXT FOR RESILIENCE

In spite of the specific and daunting impediments detailed above, the daily lives of LGB youth inform us consistently of perseverance, courage, and commitment to self-worth. Expressions of this resilience have been witnessed through the Youth Project, which was begun in November 1993 as a field placement for a bachelor of social work student at the Maritime School of Social Work, Dalhousie University. The Youth Project was conceived and developed to meet needs of LGB youth that were then unmet by other youth-serving organizations. Initially, the Youth Project was composed solely of two support groups, both for individuals 25 years of age and under—one for gay and bisexual men, the other for young lesbian and bisexual women. For several years, it was run fully by volunteers and supported in-kind by Planned Parenthood Nova Scotia. Incorporated as a nonprofit society in Nova Scotia in 2002, the Youth Project is an independent, charitable organization society governed by a board of directors and a youth board of directors, with a provincial mandate and staffed by two full-time employees and numerous volunteers.

The mission of the Lesbian, Gay and Bisexual Youth Project is "to make Nova Scotia a safer, healthier, and happier place for lesbian, gay, bisexual and transgendered youth through support, education, resource expansion and community development" (www.youthproject.ns.ca). One of its key features is the involvement of youth at all levels of the organization, as reflected in the board governance structure. In addition to reserved seating on the board of directors, the youth board is composed of youth aged 25 years and younger who have accessed the programs and services of the Youth Project. Together, these boards are responsible for all aspects of the agency, including budget and policy development, service implementation, and personnel/volunteer issues. This coleadership ensures that the services being offered meet the needs identified by youth themselves, and as a result, services are continually evolving to meet the dynamic needs of the youth accessing the Youth Project.

Over the past decade, the programs and services offered by the Youth Project have grown into three service areas: support services, education services, and social opportunities. Over the years, countless stories and experiences have been shared. Many are captured here in an effort to explore queer resilience in ways that may expand understanding of the broader resilience construct.

Support Services

Support Services offered at the Youth Project include confidential individual and family counseling, safe housing, HIV testing and pre- and post-HIV test counseling, the facilitation of a province-wide Ally identification program, and biweekly support groups. The counseling service is offered free of charge to young people and their families, with referrals primarily made by self, family members, and school personnel and contact occurring in the youth's home community, across the province. Although most youth access the support services for issues directly relating to sexual orientation, many access counseling for a variety of other issues. They speak of choosing the Youth Project because the mandate makes clear that barriers due to homophobia and heterosexism will not be encountered. Jade, age 17, says this of her experience visiting the Youth Project:

> After that first time coming down here, I left here thinking, "Wow, a whole house, a whole place"; they come in and do workshops and are like a guiding hand, so many resources. . . . I had never seen people so out, and this whole house, you know, all the gay stuff, I hadn't seen that before . . . it was something new and I liked it, so I just kept coming back, like all the time, and I would read about it, and ask around.

A component of the Youth Project, the Safe Home Program, addresses the reality that young LGB people experience homelessness as a result of feeling unsafe, at risk, or not supported in their home living environments, a situation generally precipitated by the severe isolation and, often, by violence provoked by the prevalence and expressions of homophobia. Homeless by this forced choice or by the actions of family members, LGB youth find that the Safe Home Program provides supportive living environments through which to complete educational goals, develop a positive sense of self, and gain skills necessary to make a healthy transition to adulthood. Robert's story is typical of many youth who participate in the Youth Project out of the necessity to deal with threats to their well-being:

> Robert was 16 when he first contacted the Youth Project, referred by a psychologist he was seeing to help cope with the homophobia experienced in his rural community. Robert was being taunted by his classmates and threatened on a daily basis after he was "outed" to his school by his best friend. One day Robert was chased home from school by five classmates. When they caught him, they shot him numerous times with a pellet gun. Robert no longer felt safe in his community and moved into the Safe Home Program. He stayed in the program for 9 months during which time he completed high school and became employed.

The literature is replete with accounts from LGB youth who say that fear of homophobia prevents them from trying to access support from teachers, guidance counselors, physicians, and other adults in their lives. The Ally Card program was developed by the Youth Project to identify affirming and inclusive individuals whom young people can approach for support. An ally is someone who accepts, appreciates, and celebrates LGB youth—someone of any sexual orientation who commits to work alongside the Youth Project to eradicate the discrimination and fear that LGB youth experience.

Following a screening process, the Youth Project provides a card for display, thus helping to identify safe spaces for LGB youth. In return, the ally is called on to be active within a network of supports and resources throughout the province.

In addition to the above efforts, one of the bedrocks of the Youth Project is the provision of biweekly support group meetings for LGB and transgendered youth. Groups are held in Halifax, a community of 300,000, and in rural communities throughout the province. These groups provide opportunities for youth to come together for education and peer support as directed by the expressed needs of the youth who attend them. Facilitation is provided through trained adult volunteers.

Tamryn started coming to the support meetings when she was 15 years old. At first she didn't speak much, but slowly she began to form connections with other group members. After coming to the meetings for about a year, she brought her mother into the Youth Project to meet the staff and volunteers. Her mother thanked the staff and volunteers, saying that Tamryn had changed dramatically since coming to the meetings. Her grades had returned to the A level they had been prior to her coming out, and she was no longer depressed. Both Tamryn and her mother attributed these positive changes to connections she had made with peers at the support meetings.

Education Services

The Youth Project provides several services to young LGB and transgendered people to facilitate reaching educational goals. These services include advocacy within the education system, free tutoring, support, and information in decision making with regard to postsecondary education, job search skill development, and an on-site school program.

As discussed above, LGB youth have reported feeling unsafe and not validated within their community school environments. As a result, many choose to drop out of school, despite identifying school as an important aspect of their lives (Peters, 2003). The Safe Classroom program began in 2002 as an alternative school environment for LGB and transgendered youth.

This structured day program facilitates the completion of high school credits in a classroom setting with the support necessary to return to a mainstream school environment or graduate from high school through an off-site collaboration between the Youth Project and a local school board. The Youth Project also provides an annual bursary to a LGB or transgendered youth pursuing postsecondary education.

Chris had transferred to three different schools in one academic year because of the homophobia he faced from his classmates. He heard about the Youth Project Safe Classroom program from friends and applied. In his meeting with the Youth Project Education Coordinator, it was realized that he only had four courses to complete in order to graduate. He enrolled in the classroom program and completed his courses and obtained his high school diploma. He is now taking a year off and working before deciding what postsecondary institution he will attend.

Education services also include community education workshops on homophobia and heterosexism and their effects on LGB youth. Interactive workshops and professional development training are conducted in a range of environments, including junior and senior high schools, youth-serving organizations, and university classes. Topics range from creating safer school environments to meeting the counseling needs of LGB youth. There are also educational opportunities, either group or individual, to gain information on a variety of topics, including safer sex practices, spirituality, healthy relationships, coming-out issues, and any other topic identified by the youth. As one youth commented after a school presentation, "Thanks so much; that was the first time I've heard anyone say that what I experience every day [the homophobia] is wrong."

Social Opportunities

Queer youth often face extreme isolation. Given the prevalence of homophobia and heterosexism, many do not have the opportunity to socialize with other youth, and when they do, these experiences may bring with them yet more fear of violence and intimidation. The Youth

Project recognizes that isolation is one of the key factors contributing to the risk-taking behaviors of LGB youth, behaviors that may expose the youth to great danger and exploitation. Thus, the project facilitates drug- and alcohol-free safe social opportunities as a central aspect of its programming. Examples of activities include biweekly drop-in nights; movie nights; barbecues; Pride Week activities; dances, including an annual Queer Prom; and annual summer and winter retreats. Retreats range in duration from 3 to 6 days and are held in areas across the province and in other provinces as well. The duration and nature of the retreats allows youth from rural areas to attend and creates a powerful opportunity for socializing in an environment that is affirming and validating.

> During a retreat that was held in Montreal during Pride Week, Bobby, who was about 23 years old, was found sitting on a curb. One of the facilitators sat down and asked him what was wrong. He looked up and with tears streaming down his face said, "This is the first time I ever felt I truly belonged . . . anywhere. . . . The first time."

UNDERSTANDING QUEER RESILIENCE

The lives of queer youth present rich examples of resilience when their well-being is seen as the result of ongoing negotiations between themselves and their environments. Despite a societal context laden with structural and ideological challenges and family environments often precarious with regard to acceptance and validation, queer youth regularly locate the personal and community resources to maximize their life opportunities. How does this happen?

Peirson, Laurendeau, and Chamberland (2001) assert, "Protective mechanisms (conditions, circumstances, characteristics of person or environment) serve to enhance the potential for resilience" (p. 58). These features can be found at the levels of the individual, family, and gay and ally community. This section explores our emerging thoughts on a pattern of queer youth resilience that reflects both the constraints and opportunities to be found in the current societal context, the literature, and the stories of youth as heard through the Lesbian, Gay and Bisexual Youth Project. We identify key components that contribute to experiences of living well.

Invoking the language of "protective factors" requires a few provisos. First, we note that our intention is not to suggest these are binary characteristics, representing either "good" or "bad" traits. Furthermore, we accept that there can be no distinction that a young person either *has* or *does not have* these characteristics; they exist along a continuum and within each person to a greater or lesser degree. In addition, we are not suggesting that these features are not available also for straight youth; they are not "gay" characteristics. At the same time, these features do seem to combine in unique ways in the lives of LGB youth to produce experiences of queer resilience.

Truth in Being

To begin, there is in the literature documented evidence of a sense of entitlement that queer youth carry that contributes to their belief that they deserve to express truth in their being. There is a prerogative, or a right, to feel fulfilled in life and a corresponding choice to manage appropriately what Lance, a 16-year-old project participant calls "the sexual orientation stuff." Associated with this entitlement is a sense of personal agency covertly evidenced through the stories youth tell about themselves. These stories are full of accounts of forward momentum and an action orientation toward self-acceptance and making the choices required to be "out" as LGB. Rob, age 17, asserts,

> Coming out, to me, was a lot more than just affirming my own sexuality. It was saying, "This is who I am and I don't care about what others think." I know that is about my sexuality, but it changed every dynamic of my life—*every* dynamic. One morning it just clicked and it was like, "You don't deserve this at all. . . . these people don't know you." Not even my parents, they don't know me; very few people know me. If I don't get respect and validity, I don't deal with that person. It's like, "Hello, I know what I'm talking about. I know who I am."

> When I came out, that's when I started to give myself some respect and validity and when I came

out, that's when I started to look at everyone else and said, "Well if I can give it to myself, then they can too." When I came out I started to give myself respect, and the more respect I gave myself, the more I got. . . . not letting people walk all over me, standing up for myself, stuff like that.

There is evidence that youth who have familiarity or experiences with autonomy and self-reliance may be prepared to work with the isolation or "covering up" that is required of many youth who have not yet come out. Although they may not *enjoy* the self-reliance or might not have sought it out otherwise, familiarity with being on one's own in some area of one's life is reported as one of the experiences of queer youth that may be linked with resilience features on the individual level. Jade shares her thoughts:

I think if you can overcome the adversity of, you know, being a target, when you are gay or lesbian or bisexual growing up, it lends itself to resilience. You know, if you can overcome that, then you can overcome a lot of other things because you have been through that adversity already and you have tackled, you know, isolation and unacceptance and being alone. . . . If you have to go through all of that conflict, then that would build you. And people grow up being targeted even if no one knows—you are still affected by all those messages.

I guess my resiliency comes with just constantly separating what I do and where I work and who I am from my family and my relatives. . . . I guess they're proud of me, and I have this fear that that would go away . . . that's going to all stop if they find out, so I keep it away.

Experiences of youth who are participants in the Youth Project also suggest there is a personal orientation toward rejecting the negativity and myths promoted by heterosexism and homophobia. This rejection seems to parallel a theme, heard throughout the Youth Project stories, of being true to oneself and seeking to be true in relationships with others. Carmella notes, "The word *normal* is bullshit anyhow. . . . it's a place in Idaho. There are 14,000 normal people, that's all."

Miguel, age 29, captures the quest for living true to oneself when he says,

Coming out was the most difficult, the most painful time of my life but also the most liberating, crazy time . . . but the alternative [to not coming out] was worse. I couldn't achieve or live my life in the closet. . . . I was doing up my resume and listing all this great stuff, and I looked at it and went, "None of this is mine. . . . this is all what other people want me to be." I needed to be true to myself but also true to my relationships. I was so afraid I would lose my family, but more important there was no bright future. Coming out looked more real. . . . I could start negotiating stuff. And I remember . . . the good stuff about coming out. All of a sudden I was so light.

Family Characteristics

In theorizing family characteristics that contribute toward resilience, we note that there are overlaps between community and family. In addition, although most often, family stories refer to the youth's family of origin, we recognize that not infrequently a young person's family of choice is the family they refer to when they speak of their experiences with their families. Families that respond in a welcoming and affirming manner to the coming out of their children necessarily contribute to family-related resilience among LGB youth (Savin-Williams & Dube, 1998). This experience has not been well documented in the literature, nor was it present in the stories heard through the Youth Project, which may be indicative of its relative lack of frequency. More often, one or two family members may be aware and may be conditionally supportive, as opposed to there being full-family acceptance and celebration of the youth's sexual orientation (Mallon, 1999). Organizations such as Parents and Friends of Lesbians and Gays (P-FLAG) may be more accessible to youth than their own families. Jade, age 17, recalls,

When I was younger I wanted to join P-FLAG, like before I came out to myself. I just wanted to be involved and be around families that were okay with it all. I don't really know why.

Some youth suggest that when issues around same-sex relationships and intimacy remain invisible, the youth experience marginal freedom from myths and stereotypes they may otherwise be subjected to in family contexts. This is, however, a precarious situation. Invisibility can be a mask for intolerance. As one participant noted, an absence of discussion about sexual orientation issues can potentially limit *mis*information and hostility, which may in turn limit internalized homophobia among an LGB youth. Jessica notes,

> My family never said anything homophobic; they didn't say anything at all. So although I didn't receive any accurate information about being lesbian, I also didn't have to navigate a load of antilesbian stereotypes and myths.

Gay and Ally
Community Characteristics

The wider community can play a role in either hindering or supporting the positive identity formation of queer youth. Communities hold the promises of exclusion and violence as well as promises for inclusion and acceptance. As Bernice, a transsexual character in the film *Priscilla, Queen of the Desert* says, "I don't know if the ugly walls of suburbia are put up to keep *them out* or to keep *us in.*"

The vitality of the Youth Project, expressed by its members, rests firmly on the platform of its community features and its role in breaking the isolation, loneliness, and fear experienced by many queer youth. Locating and securing the means to break social isolation, accessing the gay and ally community, and sharing identity are cornerstones in naming protective features that contribute to resilience. Twenty-three year old Carmella shares that

> once you're in the gay community, it's like family. It helped me form relationships, kept me from being lonely and afraid. . . . it connected me to other people. If I hadn't identified with the people I identified with, I don't know what would've happened.

Having a peer group with whom one feels accepted for one's core identity is an empowering experience, one that offers validation and a safe space to be one's self. When one lives outside the boundaries of what is socially accepted, youth tell us that there is more room

for self-expression. When one finds in that same space beyond conventionality like-minded people, then the LGB youth may be more likely to encounter encouragement and positive feedback for however she or he wants to be identified. Locating and securing safe places to explore one's identity and its meanings is critical to fanning the embers of resilience.

> Matthew was 17 when he attended his first Youth Project retreat, held in Montreal during Pride Week. At the beginning of the retreat, Matthew said he didn't feel comfortable participating in the parade that would happen at the end of the week because he didn't want anyone to know he was gay. Five days later, as the group prepared to leave for the parade, Matthew came dancing out of the cabin where the youth were staying dressed in full drag and yelling that he was ready for the parade!

As such stories demonstrate, finding a gay or ally community often brings access to information that can counteract the messages of heterosexism and homophobia found in the larger community. Role models play an important part in gaining this access. Jade explained, in regard to her own experience,

> Some people come here [the Youth Project] and have no friends whatsoever because they are gay or not accepted, and they find, like, good role models here. Some of the older staff are gay people who are successful, and they are helping kids who are insecure in who they are, and young gay kids can see these people who are successful in their relationships and they see it is not impossible. . . . "I can have that, I can have a good relationship. I can get married if I want to." They provide that here. At school they may be called a freak or a fag, and here they are accepted and people like you for who you are, and people can sympathize with what you've gone through because people have gone through it themselves.

MORE STORIES ARE STILL TO BE TOLD

The iterative and interactive relationships between self, family, and the gay and ally community suggested here make up an initial step in theorizing queer resilience. There are yet more layers to be revealed through yet more stories and experience. To reach a conclusive statement in this discussion seems not only unlikely but also inappropriate. Sexual orientation and expression are fluid social categories, concepts continuously negotiated and renegotiated in multiple contexts.

As evidenced throughout this chapter, queer youth resilience is realized within a society predicated on homophobia and heterosexism. Professionals working in this field can become allies with LGB youth in this work in ways that encourage and nurture this resilience. We suggest a few guiding principles for this work based on the narratives of those youth with whom we have spoken:

1. Do your own work first. Commitment to the social justice agenda of being an ally in this work comes more easily after we have sorted through our own assumptions, biases, experiences, concerns, and hopes. Queer youth cannot be expected to burden themselves with helping us to work through our issues.

2. Read about heterosexual privilege and consider its effects in your life. Read "first voice" material from LGB people about their experiences of heterosexism and homophobia. Let feelings of discomfort be part of the journey.

3. Continue to expand the space for queer youth to explore their sexual orientation in affirming and validating environments. Get involved in your local community by joining programs such as the Youth Project, which exist around the world, or by starting new ones. Safe spaces can blossom in just about any community.

4. Heed the call to confront and challenge the homophobia and heterosexism that exist in our society, in private and public. Protest can happen in many forms, from marching in pride parades to articulating our refusal to join in ridicule of LGB people when it happens in social circles. Read stories to the children you know that have same-sex character pairings, or at the least, question openly the predominance of the Cinderella story and its derivatives. Find your voice somewhere on the continuum and practice its expression.

Efforts such as these can help create a healing context for young people who must navigate the conditions of heterosexism and homophobia and the resulting oppressions. All the ingredients required for resilience are available within LGB youth and our communities. Making choices to intentionally season and simmer those ingredients can yield a rich broth of health and happiness for everyone committed to a more just and caring world.

NOTES

1. The politics of language deserve mention in our choices of words throughout this chapter. Although it is not our intention to blur the distinctions of lesbian, gay, and bisexual identity or to depersonalize identity, we have chosen for simplicity of reading to abbreviate our language to LGB. Alternately, we use the term *queer* for the same population.

2. A note on the parameters of this chapter: Transgendered youth are not included in this chapter given the distinction adopted that transgender relates to gender orientation and not sexual orientation. Beyond this, there are additional layers to societal context, including intolerance when there is discrepancy between biological sex and gender expression. These different expressions of intolerance require closer examination that is beyond the scope of this chapter.

3. Retrieved from http://www.egale.ca, June 28, 2004.

4. This debate is simplified here; however, the interested reader is directed to Herek (2000) for discussion and inclusion of other terms (e.g., *homonegativity, homohatred,* and *sexual prejudice*) as alternatives.

5. The term *compulsory heterosexuality* was first articulated by Rich (1981), capturing the analysis that heterosexual activity is more than a pervasive and persistent scripted behavior; it is a political (rather than natural) social institution and tool required by patriarchy to maintain itself.

6. Given the parameters of this chapter, intersections among race and class relative to those noted are not explored here. The reader is directed to the resources of hooks (1984) and Collins (1990) for this exploration.

REFERENCES

Appleby, G. A., & Anastas, J. W. (1998). *Not just a passing phase: Social work with gay, lesbian and bisexual people.* New York: Columbia University Press.

Babineau, N. (2001). *Access denied: Lesbian, gay and bisexual youth and the health care system: A resource for service providers.* Halifax, Nova Scotia, Canada: Lesbian, Gay and Bisexual Youth Project.

Bagley, C., & D'Augelli, A. R. (2000). Suicidal behavior in gay, lesbian and bisexual youth. *British Medical Journal, 320,* 1617–1618.

Bagley, C., & Tremblay, P. (1997). Suicidal behaviors in homosexual and bisexual males: Evidence from a random community study of 750 men aged 18 to 27. In C. Bagley & R. Ramsay (Eds.), *Suicidal behaviour in adolescents and adults: Research, taxonomy, and prevention* (pp. 177–195) Brookfield, VT: Avebury.

Banks, C. (2001). *The cost of homophobia: Literature review of the economic impact of homophobia in Canada.* Saskatoon, Saskatchewan, Canada: Rochon Associated.

Banks, C. (2003). *The cost of homophobia: Literature review on the human impact of homophobia in Canada.* Saskatoon, Saskatchewan, Canada: Rochon Associated.

Blumenfeld, W. J. (1992). *Children, families and homophobia.* Boston: Beacon Press.

Cass, V. C. (1979). Homosexual identity formation: A theoretical model. *Journal of Homosexuality, 4,* 219–235.

Collins, P. H. (1990). *Black feminist thought: Knowledge, consciousness, and the politics of empowerment.* Boston: Unwin Hyman.

D'Augelli, A., Hershberger, S., & Pilkington, N. (1998). Lesbian, gay and bisexual youth and their families: Disclosure of sexual orientation and its consequences. *America Journal of Orthopsychiatry, 68,* 361–372.

D'Augelli, A., Pilkington, N., & Hershberger, S. (2000). *The mental health impact of sexual orientation victimization of lesbian, gay and bisexual youth in high school.* Unpublished manuscript.

Dalrymple, J., & Burke, B. (1995). Some essential elements of anti-oppressive theory. In J. Dalrymple & B. Burke (Eds.), *Anti-oppressive practice: Social care and the law* (pp. 7-21). Buckingham, UK: Open University Press.

Eccles, T. A., Sayegh, M. A., Fortenberry, J. D., & Zimet, G. D. (2003). More normal than not: A qualitative assessment of the developmental experiences of gay youth. *Journal of Adolescent Health, 32,* 137–139.

Egale Calls on Alliance Party to Permanently Expel MP Larry Spencer from Caucus [Press release]. (2003, November 27). Retrieved July 14, 2004, from www.egale.ca/index.asp?lang=E&menu=2003&item=776

Eliason, M. (1995). Attitudes about lesbians and gay men: A review and implications for social service training. *Journal of Gay and Lesbian Social Services, 2*(2), 73–90.

Erikson, E. (1963). *Childhood and society.* New York: Norton.

Erikson, E. (1968). *Identity, youth and crisis.* New York: Norton.

Flowers, P., & Buston, K. (2001). I was terrified of being different: Exploring gay men's accounts of growing up in a heterosexist society. *Journal of Adolescence, 24*(1), 51–65.

Frye, M. (1983). *The politics of reality: Essays in feminist theory.* New York: Crossing Press.

Garofalo, R., Wolf, R. C., Kessel, S., Palfrey, J., & DuRant, R. H. (1998). The association between health risk behaviors and sexual orientation among a school-based sample of adolescents. *Pediatrics, 101,* 895–902.

Gay, Lesbian and Straight Education Network. (2001). *The 2001 national school climate survey: Lesbian, gay, bisexual and transgendered students and their experiences in schools.* New York: Author.

Gibson, P. (1989). *Secretary's task force on youth suicide report.* Washington, DC: U.S. Department of Health and Human Services.

Grossman, A. (1997). Growing up with a "spoiled identity": Lesbian, gay and bisexual youth at risk. *Journal of Gay & Lesbian Social Services, 6*(3), 45–56.

Herek, G. (1984). Beyond "homophobia": A social psychological perspective on attitudes toward lesbians and gay men. *Journal of Homosexuality, 10*(1/2), 1–21.

Herek, G. M. (2000). The psychology of sexual prejudice. *Current Directions in Psychological Science, 9*(1), 19–22.

hooks, b. (1984). *Feminist theory: From the margin to the center.* Boston: South End Press.

Human Rights Watch. (2001). *Hatred in the hallways: Violence and discrimination against lesbian, gay, bisexual and transgender students in U.S. schools.* New York: Human Rights Watch.

MacQueen, K. (2004, March 29). Mrs. and Mrs. in a gay mecca. *Macleans Magazine,* p. 30.

Mallon, G. P. (1999). Gay and lesbian adolescents and their families. *Journal of Gay and Lesbian Services, 10*(2), 69–88.

Mihalik, G. J. (1991). Homosexuality, stigma, and biocultural evolution. *Journal of Gay and Lesbian Psychotherapy, 1*(4), 15–29.

Nuggets: News, notes and findings from the ADAP Program Compliance & Analysis Unit. (1998). [Survey]. Burlington, VT: Vermont Department of Health, Office of Alcohol and Drug Free Programs.

Orenstein, A. (2001). Substance use among gay and lesbian adolescents. *Journal of Homosexuality, 41*(2), 1–15.

Peirson, L., Laurendeau, M., & Chamberland, C. (2001). Context, contributing factors, and consequences. In I. Prilleltensky, G. Nelson, L., & L. Peirson (Eds.), *Promoting family wellness and preventing child maltreatment* (pp. 41–123). Toronto, Ontario, Canada: University of Toronto Press.

Peters, A. (2003). Isolation or inclusion: Creating safe spaces for lesbian and gay youth. *Families in Society, 84*(3), 331–337.

Pharr, S. (1988). *Homophobia: A weapon of sexism.* Inverness, CA: Chardon Press.

Plummer, D. (2001). The quest for modern manhood: Masculine stereotypes, peer culture and the social significance of homophobia. *Journal of Adolescence, 24*(1), 15–23.

Remafedi, G., Farrow, J. A., & Deisher, R. W. (1991). Risk factors for attempted suicide in gay and bisexual youth. *Pediatrics, 87,* 869–875.

Remafedi, G., French, S., Story, M., Resnick, M., & Blum, R. (1998, January). The relationship between suicide risk and sexual orientation: Results of a population based study. *American Journal of Public Health, 88,* 57–60.

Rich, A. (1981). *Compulsory heterosexuality and lesbian existence.* London: Onlywomen Press.

Ryan, C., & Futterman, D. (1997). *Lesbian and gay youth: Care and counselling.* Philadelphia: Hanley & Belfus.

Sanders, G. L., & Kroll, I. T. (2000). Generating stories of resilience: Helping gay and lesbian youth and their families. *Journal of Marital and Family Therapy, 26*(4), 433–443.

Savin-Williams, R. C. (1994). Verbal and physical abuse as stressors in the lives of lesbian, gay male and bisexual youths: Associations with school problems, running away, substance abuse, prostitution, and suicide. *Journal of Consulting Clinical Psychology, 62,* 261–269.

Savin-Williams, R. C. (2001). A critique of research on sexual minority youths. *Journal of Adolescence, 24*(1), 5–13.

Savin-Williams, R. C., & Dube, E. M. (1998). Parental reactions to their child's disclosure of a gay/lesbian identity. *Family Relations 47*(1), 7–13.

Tolman, D. L., Spencer, R., Rosen-Reynoso, M., & Porche, M. V. (2003). Sowing the seeds of violence in heterosexual relationships: Early adolescents narrate compulsory heterosexuality. *Journal of Social Issues, 59*(1), 159–178.

Tremble, B. (1993). Prostitution and survival; Interviews with gay street youth. *Canadian Journal of Human Sexuality, 2*(1), 39–45.

Troiden, R. R. (1989). The formation of homosexual identities. *Journal of Homosexuality, 17*(1-2), 43–73.

Ungar, M. (2004). *Nurturing hidden resilience in troubled youth.* Toronto, Ontario, Canada: University of Toronto Press.

Uribe, V., & Harbeck, K. (1992). Addressing the needs of lesbian, gay and bisexual youth: The origins of Project 100 and school-based intervention. In K. Harbeck (Ed.), *Coming out of the classroom closet: Gay and lesbian teachers and curricula.* Binghamton, NY: Haworth Press.

Weinberg, F. (1972). *Society and the healthy homosexual.* New York: St. Martins Press.

17

Psychosocial Functioning of Children From Monogamous and Polygamous Families

Implications for Practice

Alean Al-Krenawi

Vered Slonim-Nevo

Polygamy and the Well-Being of Children

Polygamy is defined as "a marital relationship involving multiple wives" (Kottak, 1978, cited in Low, 1988, p. 189). Polygamy may serve as a reproductive strategy by which men increase the number of their offspring but reduce the level of investment in each child (White, 1988). In addition, polygamy can be practical economically by increasing the family's labor force as well as its power and prestige (Ware, 1979). Therefore, polygamy is often found in social systems in which human resources are particularly important in contrast to other resources, such as land and private property. When the latter are most important, a monogamous nuclear family structure tends to be the rule (*Macmillan Dictionary of Anthropology,* 1986, p. 228). Thus, in Western societies, where there is less need for working

hands, the polygamous family may be weak and experience economic and social difficulties (Al-Krenawi, Graham, & Izzeldin, 2001).

Several studies carried out in different countries in the Middle East and Africa show that children of polygamous families may suffer from emotional, behavioral, and physical problems; a more negative self-concept; lower school achievement; and greater difficulties in social adjustment than children in monogamous families (Al-Krenawi & Lightman, 2000; Cherian, 1990; Eapen, Al-Gazali, Bin-Othman, & Abou-Saleh, 1998; Owuamanam, 1984). It has also been found that adolescents are less accepting of polygamy than adults (D'Hondt & Vandewiele, 1980; Dorjahn, 1988), objecting mainly to the economic difficulties and lack of communication among children of different wives. The study discussed in this chapter examines the impact of polygamous marriage on the psychological, social, and educational functioning of Bedouin-Arab children in the south of Israel. On the basis on previous studies, we hypothesized that children from polygamous families would report more psychological, social, familial, and educational functioning problems compared with children from monogamous families. Our intent in reporting our results in this volume is to broaden the discussion of different family forms and their impact on the well-being of children. We examine in our discussion the implications of our findings for our understanding of risk and resilience among children being raised in culturally specific family forms.

THE BEDOUIN-ARABS

Bedouin-Arabs, although part of the Arab people, are a distinct linguistic, political, and geographic entity. Like other traditional Arab societies, the Bedouin society is a "high-context" culture, in which the collective takes precedence over the individual, and continuity and stability are valued over change (Al-Krenawi & Graham, 1997; Hall, 1976). Its social structure is patriarchal and gender segregated. Men lead the household and dominate the polity and economy. Women's physical and intellectual capacities are generally devalued (Al-Sadawi, 1985; Chaleby, 1985; El-Islam, 1983).

In the course of the last few decades, as a result of globalization and other factors, Bedouin society has been undergoing a rapid and unremitting process of modernization. This process has been characterized by major economic, political, social, and value changes that have undermined traditional Bedouin culture and pose a threat to Bedouins both as individuals and as a group. Inevitably, the process has created myriad new and unfamiliar challenges and problems that the society lacks the experience and skills to cope with. Thus, even as the changes wrought by modernization penetrate all aspects of Bedouin life, a great part of the society strives to preserve the familiar and protect its religion and culture.

One of the major changes is the steady sedentarization of the Bedouin, who were traditionally a seminomadic people. In Israel today, virtually all the 130,000 Bedouin-Arabs inhabiting the Negev, Israel's southern region, live in villages—56% in officially recognized villages where they receive government services and 44% in unrecognized villages, where there are very few services for them to access (*Statistical Year Book of the Negev Bedouin,* 2004). The transition to permanent villages of both types has led to a loss of traditional employment (e.g., herding, agriculture), leaving the Bedouin without necessary skills to find adequate employment in modern society (Al-Krenawi, 2001).

As one might expect, the progressive sedentarization of the Negev Bedouin has made polygamy much less economically worthwhile and sustainable than in the past. However, polygamy is still prevalent and largely accepted in Bedouin society in the Negev, among the young and the educated as well. Precise figures are unavailable, but estimates are that approximately 20% of all Bedouin Arab marriages in the Negev are polygamous.

The persistence of polygamy among the Bedouin-Arabs of the Negev has a variety of interrelated reasons, the major one, perhaps, is that Bedouin society places a premium on large family units, whether at the level of the nuclear family, the *hamula* (or clan), or the tribe. There is a particularly emphasis on having many sons. Because the Bedouin-Arabs were historically a warrior people, the larger the tribe, the more powerful it was and the higher its status (Marks, 1974). On the level of the individual and family, a person's status, economic security, and potential for personal development continue to be based on family belonging. Socially and psychologically then, polygamy and the large families it enables are still associated with power and prestige (Al-Krenawi, 1998, 1999). Thus, although no longer either an economic necessity or in keeping with the dominant culture of those they have settled alongside, many Bedouin-Arabs have continued to choose this culturally specific family form. The question, then, is whether this type of family actually contributes to children's well-being? This is an important point to consider because it opens the possibility that nonconventional forms of family, if appropriately supported by the cultures in which they appear, may in fact contribute greatly to the well-being of family members, most notably the children. The Bedouin-Arabs of the Negev provide us with a unique opportunity to witness a family form that many societies have abandoned while also demonstrating whether such minority patterns of family attachment may in fact bolster children's health.

Polygamy occurs for any number of reasons. Although the economic and social status argument discussed above is frequently the reasons for polygamy, another reason is anchored in the institution of "exchange marriage" in Arab society. In such a marriage, which is fairly common in Bedouin society, two men marry one another's sisters. Should one of the men take a second wife, the other will most likely be pressured by his family of origin to follow suit, to maintain symmetry between the two family structures.

A third motive for polygamy is the perceived inadequacies of the man's wife. It is viewed as acceptable and even appropriate for a man to take a second wife if the first wife is not fertile, if she has not borne him sons, if she becomes physically or mentally ill, or if she does not gratify his sexual needs (Al-Krenawi, Graham, & Al-Krenawi, 1997). Polygamy, under these circumstances, protects the wife from the highly adverse consequences of divorce in Bedouin society.

Polygamous wives may live together in the same house or separately, where each wife lives with her children in a different home. A senior wife is defined as any married woman who is followed by another wife in the marriage. A "junior wife" is the most recent wife joining a marriage (Chaleby, 1985). Many societies award senior wives a high status, with power over the other wives, exclusive privileges, and strong influence with the husband (Broude, 1994). In Bedouin society, however, the first wife has a lower status than subsequent wives (Al-Krenawi et al., 1997) because the first marriage, which is usually at a very young age, is generally the product of parental matchmaking, in which partners are chosen for political and economic reasons (Al-Haj, 1987; El-Islam & Abu-Dagga, 1992). Second, third, and fourth marriages are products of choice, however, in which the man may select his wife for love. As a result, subsequent wives often receive preference in the distribution of the husband's economic resources, social support,

and attention (Al-Krenawi, 1998; Al-Krenawi et al., 1997).

Al-Krenawi (2001) found that first wives in polygamous marriages in Bedouin-Arab society in the Negev suffered from low self-esteem, loneliness, and other emotional problems more than did monogamous wives. He and his colleagues also found that Bedouin-Arab children of polygamous marriages suffer from a variety of behavioral problems, psychosocial difficulties, and low school achievement compared with children from monogamous families (Al-Krenawi et al., 1997; Al-Krenawi & Graham, 2001; Al-Krenawi & Lightman, 2000). But although these studies provide a preliminary picture of the many difficulties faced by wives and children in polygamous Bedouin families, they are limited in both size and scope. Moreover, they did not take into account the possible intervening role of other variables, in particular the family's economic status and family functioning, both of which have been found to be associated with children's adjustment in a wide variety of areas.

Studies consistently show that living in poverty has negative implications on children's physical and mental health, academic achievement, and behavior and that it affects interpersonal relationships within the family (Montgomery & Carter-Pokras, 1993; Starfield, 1991; Weinger, 1998). Findings indicate that children living in poverty tend to reveal higher rates of depression, social avoidance, low self-esteem, and serious behavioral disorders than do children in more affluent families (Leadbeater & Bishop, 1994) and that long-term poverty is associated with increased risk of dropping out of school, juvenile delinquency, and crime (Korenman, Miller, & Sjaastad, 1995).

Family dysfunction, a concept that has been studied only in monogamous families, has been shown to have negative implications for children's adjustment, quite similar to those of poverty. Findings show that children from dysfunctional families tend to do poorly in school, have higher dropout rates than children from better-functioning families, and are at a higher risk of drug abuse, criminality, and a variety of psychological and psychiatric symptoms (Boettcher, Billick, & Burgert, 2001; Bradley, 2001; McDermott, McKelvey, Roberts, & Davies, 2002). To date, however, we have little idea whether family dysfunction in polygamous families, if the term can be defined at all in that context, affects children. In fact, it might be hypothesized that because polygamy avoids divorce and the possible poverty that results, children in polygamous households where there is parental discord may still fare better than monogamous households that break up, as is the cultural norm.

Therefore, the current study takes into account the possible impact of the family's economic status and functioning on the psychosocial condition of children living in a polygamous or a monogamous family structure. The focus, however, is not only on detecting problems in children, although this has been the thrust of most investigations into polygamy. We have approached the topic with the assumption that children must lose out in such family structures. Researchers in the area of developmental psychology now emphasize not only risk factors and vulnerability but also the concept of "individual resilience" as a protective factor in helping children cope with stressful life events and situations (Greenbaum & Auerbach, 1992). Furthermore, the salutogenic perspective, as discussed in the psychological literature (Antonovsky, 1987, 1993, 1998) suggests that stressful events and conditions are a normal part of human experience. As opposed to the pathogenic perspective that emphasizes the negative side effects of stressful events and life conditions, the salutogenic perspective stresses the advantages of overcoming challenges. Moreover, positive outcomes (empowerment, a sense of meaningfulness) may result from transcending difficult situations. Thus, research conducted under a pathogenic model concentrates on negative symptoms and outcomes (e.g., the negative consequences to children of being raised in a polygamous household), whereas research conducted with the salutogenic perspective searches for positive outcomes—that is, how individuals and families may overcome stressful life events and conditions (e.g., how does the polygamous household help to buffer children from negative life events and stress?) (Sagy & Antonovsky, 1998; Waysman, Solomon, & Schwarzwald, 1998). In the study discussed next, we do not abandon the pathogenic model because we want to find out what social and psychological difficulties children in polygamous families might experience. At the same time, however, we try to interpret

our findings not only in light of what is wrong in polygamous families but also in light of what occurs in these families that enables children to survive and flourish in such a familial structure.

METHOD

Sample

The sample consisted of 352 children: 174 from monogamous families and 178 from polygamous families. This is a representative sample of both polygamous and monogamous families in the Negev (for more details, see Al-Krenawi & Slonim-Nevo, 2003). Both groups were fairly evenly divided between boys (47% in the polygamous group; 50% in the monogamous group) and girls (53% in the polygamous group; 50% in the monogamous group). Their ages ranged between 13 and 15 (mean = 14.05; $SD = 0.83$). All the fathers in the polygamous families had two wives.

Data Collection

Data were collected during school hours with permission of the school authorities and the children. Children who could read and write received a self-report questionnaire in Arabic, containing closed questions selected from standard research instruments. Arabic-speaking students were present while the questionnaires were being answered in order to respond to questions when needed. Arab students interviewed those children who were unable to read and write.

Research Instruments

In addition to sociodemographic factors, we used standardized scales to assess the main independent and dependent variables of the study (for details on the properties of each scale, see Al-Krenawi & Slonim-Nevo, 2003).

Academic Achievement. The children's academic achievement was assessed using the average of the pupils' grades in four subjects—English, Arabic, Hebrew, and arithmetic—over a period of three semesters. The children's school grades were taken from the school files.

Social Functioning. Social functioning was measured by a standard measure assessing peer group relationships (Hudson, 1982). The measure consists of 25 questions, and scores range from 0 to 100. Those who score below 35 are within the norm, whereas those who score above 35 apparently have problems with their social functioning skills. The level of internal reliability of the scale in the current sample was high (Cronbach's alpha = 0.89; $N = 256$).

Psychological Functioning. Scales included the following:

1. Self-esteem: The Rosenberg (1979) Self-Esteem Scale consists of 10 items, and ranges from 1 to 4; higher scores indicate higher self-esteem. The level of internal reliability of this scale in the current study was moderate (Cronbach's alpha = 0.62; $N = 317$).

2. Mental health: The Brief Symptom Inventory (BSI) measures psychiatric symptomatology (Canetti, Shalev, & Kaplan-De-Nour, 1994; Derogatis & Spencer, 1982). It consists of 53 self-report items that elicit perceptions of symptoms during the last month. It has nine dimensions of mental functioning, and in addition, the scale provides a general severity index (GSI), a positive symptom distress index (PSDI), and a positive symptoms total (PST). All scales range from 0 to 4, with higher scores indicating more mental health problems.

The reliability of the subscales among the Bedouin-Arab children in the current study was as follows: *somatization*: alpha = 0.73, $N = 309$; *obsession-compulsion*: alpha = 0.73, $N = 302$; *interpersonal sensitivity*: alpha = 0.59, $N = 326$; *depression*: alpha = 0.74, $N = 320$; *anxiety*: alpha = 0.48, $N = 320$; *hostility*: alpha = 0.69, $N = 312$; *panic* (phobic anxiety): alpha = 0.65, $N = 315$; *paranoid ideation*: alpha = 0.64, $N = 331$; *psychotism*: alpha = 0.67, $N = 323$; all items together: alpha = 0.94, $N = 185$.

Father-Child and Mother-Child Relationships. This was assessed using the Hudson (1982) measure of father-child and mother-child relationships, as perceived by the respondent. Both scales contain 25 items, scores range from 0 to 100, with higher scores indicating a more problematic relationship with the father. The internal reliability among the Bedouin-Arab adolescents in the current study was adequate (father-child: Cronbach's alpha = 0.71, $N = 242$; mother-child: Cronbach's alpha = 0.84, $N = 265$).

Perceived Family Functioning. The McMaster Family Assessment Device (FAD), developed by Epstein, Baldwin, and Bishop (1983), was used to assess overall perceptions of family functioning. In this study, we used the 12 items that assess the family's general functioning as perceived by the respondents. The scale ranged from 1 to 4, with higher scores indicating more problems. The level of reliability of the scale in the current study was relatively low (Cronbach's alpha = 0.50; $N = 302$). Therefore, results should be interpreted cautiously.

It should be noted that all research instruments were translated into Arabic by a professional translator who was fluent in both Arabic and English and then independently translated back into English for accuracy of translation.

RESULTS

Sociodemographic Characteristics

Table 17.1 presents the sociodemographic characteristics of the participants in both groups. The results show that the children of the monogamous families have significantly more educated parents than those of the polygamous ones, although in both groups, the parents' education level is quite low. Similarly, although there is a high rate of unemployment in both groups, the children in the polygamous families are more likely than those in the monogamous families to have unemployed parents (the biological mother and the father). In addition, although both groups have large families, children from polygamous families have many more siblings (approximately five more in this study) than those from monogamous families. The perceived economic situation of the polygamous child's family is also worse, with 62% of the children of monogamous families, but only 45% of those of polygamous families, reporting that their family's economic situation was good and several times as many children from polygamous families reporting that their family's economic situation was poor.

Table 17.1   Sociodemographic Characteristics (%, means, standard deviation, and chi-square)

	Whole Sample (N = 352)	Polygamous (n = 178)	Monogamous (n = 174)
Gender			
Male	49%	47%	50%
Female	51%	53%	50%
Age	M = 14.05	M = 14.17	M = 13.93
	SD = 0.85	SD = 0.83	SD = 0.80
Father's years of education**	M = 7.62	M = 6.99	M = 8.19
	SD = 4.15	SD = 4.20	SD = 4.04
Mother's years of education**	M = 5.11	M = 4.20	M = 6.05
	SD = 4.40	SD = 4.20	SD = 4.40
Father's employment**			
Unemployed	48%	56%	39%
Employed	52%	44%	61%
Retired	8%	10%	5%
Mother's employment			
Unemployed	88%	90%	85%
Employed	12%	10%	15%
Type of family			
Polygamous	51%		
Monogamous	49%		
Number of siblings		M = 13.37	M = 8.30
(excluding the participant)***		SD = 5.26	SD = 2.77
Economic situation***			
Good	53%	45%	62%
Nearly good	40%	44%	35%
Not good/not good at all	7%	11%	3%

*$p < 0.05$; **$p < 0.01$; ***$p < 0.001$.

Psychosocial and Familial Functioning

Table 17.2 presents the psychological, social, and familial functioning of both groups. The results indicate that adolescents from polygamous families showed significantly more psychological distress than their monogamous peers. Specifically, they reported more somatization, obsession-compulsion, depression, interpersonal sensitivity, hostility, phobic anxiety, paranoid ideation, and psychosis. Their GSI, PSDI, and PST were all higher than those of their counterparts from monogamous families. In addition, the children from polygamous families reported significantly more problems in peer relationships than those from monogamous families. They also reported significantly poorer relationships with their fathers and poorer overall family functioning.

Furthermore, children from polygamous families showed lower school achievement than that of children from monogamous families. In short, the findings show that in every dimension—psychological, social, educational, and familial—children from polygamous families report more difficulty than their peers from monogamous families.

Mediating Factors for Children of Polygamous Families: Perceived Family Functioning

As presented earlier, the data show that children from polygamous families function more poorly than children from monogamous families. In an attempt to further explain these findings, we hypothesized that family functioning

Table 17.2   Psychological, Social, and Familial Functioning (means and standard deviations)

	Whole Sample (N = 352)	Polygamous (n = 178)	Monogamous (n = 174)
Mental health			
Somatization**	M = 0.85 (SD = 0.68)	0.96 (0.70)	0.75 (0.65)
Obsession-compulsion***	1.11 (0.76)	1.24 (0.82)	0.98 (0.68)
Depression**	1.00 (0.75)	1.11 (0.82)	0.90 (0.65)
Interpersonal sensitivity***	1.02 (0.81)	1.16 (0.85)	0.89 (0.75)
Anxiety	1.34 (0.68)	1.37 (0.71)	1.31 (0.66)
Hostility**	1.08 (0.79)	1.21 (0.84)	0.95 (0.72)
Phobic anxiety (panic)***	1,03 (0.79)	1,18 (0.81)	0.86 (0.73)
Paranoid ideation*	1.10 (0.76)	1.18 (0.78)	1.02 (0.73)
Psychotism***	1.05 (0.78)	1.19 (0.83)	0.91 (0.71)
GSI***	1.07 (0.59)	1.17 (0.61)	0.96 (0.56)
PST*	29.70 (11.74)	30.99 (11.60)	28.37 (11.76)
PSDI***	1.81 (0.53)	1.89 (0.56)	1.72 (0.49)
Self-esteem	2.98 (0.41)	2.95 (0.42)	3.01 (0.39)
Relationships with friends**	26.30 (16.23)	28.54 (16.44)	24.05 (15.75)
Relationships with the father***	32.03 (11.81)	34.12 (12.08)	29.95 (11.20)
Relationships with the mother	20.1 (14.15)	21.23 (13.36)	18.99 (14.83)
Family functioning**	2.16 (0.43)	2.23 (0.42)	2.097 (0.42)
Academic achievement**	72 (18.79)	68 (19.73)	76 (17.40)

*p < 0.05; **p < 0.01; ***p < 0.001 (based on a t-test analysis, 2-tail for differences between means).

Figure 17.1   Family Functioning Mediates the Effect of Family Structure on Psychological, Educational, and Social Functioning

would mediate the impact of the family structure on the children's psychosocial functioning as presented in Figure 17.1. We followed Baron and Kenny's four-step model for establishing the mediating effect of family functioning (Baron & Kenny, 1986; Kenny, Kashy, & Bolger, 1998):

Step 1: Our analyses began by trying to show that the independent variable (Family Structure) has a significant effect on the outcome variables (Psychological, Educational, and Social Functioning). This first step should establish that indeed, as hypothesized, the independent variable affects the dependent variables associated with the child's well-being.

Step 2: We next looked at whether the independent variable (Family Structure) has a significant effect on the mediating variable (Family Functioning).

Step 3: We went on to examine whether the mediating variable (Family Functioning) affects the outcome variables (Psychological, Educational, and Social Functioning) when the independent variable (Family Structure) is controlled for.

Step 4: Finally, we sought to establish whether there existed a mediation effect. For such an effect to exist, the independent variable's (Family Structure) effect should, ideally, lose its significance in relation to the outcome variables (Psychological, Educational, and Social Functioning) when the mediating variable (Family Functioning) is controlled for. The effects in Steps 3 and 4 are assessed in the same regression equation.

As noted, our first step was to establish a significant effect of the independent variable (Family Structure) on the outcome variables. Regression analysis was performed twice. First, the effect of family structure was assessed while controlling for different sociodemographic

variables (full model). Second, a stepwise regression was performed to achieve the best predictive model. As can be seen in Table 17.3, family structure is a significant predictor of peer relations and of six out of nine BSI dimensions, as well as the GSI. Thus, we conclude that children from polygamous families have poorer peer relations and poorer mental health functioning, compared with children from monogamous families.

The second step is to examine the effect of the independent variable on the mediating variable. Again, best and full regression analyses were performed. Table 17.3 presents the effects of family structure on general family functioning, controlling for sociodemographic variables. As expected, family structure was found to be a significant predictor of family functioning. Results indicate that children from polygamous families perceive more difficulties in their family's functioning than children from monogamous families.

The third step sought to show the effect of the mediating variable (Family Functioning) on the outcome variables (Social and Mental Health Functioning), while controlling for the independent variable (Family Structure). Table 17.4 presents the full and best regression models showing the effect of general family functioning while controlling for family structure and sociodemographic variables. As can be seen, family functioning is a major predictor of self-esteem, peer relations, academic achievement, and all the BSI dimensions, including the GSI.

Our fourth step was to show that the effect of the independent variable (Family Structure) on the outcome variables declines when the mediating variable (Family Functioning) is controlled for. As stated above, the findings presented in Table 17.3 show that family structure has a significant effect on children's psychological

Table 17.3 The Impact of Sociodemographic Factors on the Children's Social, Psychological, Educational, and Familial Functioning

	Age	Gender	SES	Father's Education	Family Structure	R^2 Full Model	R^2 Best Model
				Independent Variables in the Linear Regression Model (Betas)			
Family Functioning	−.03	−.02	−.18***	−.01	−.12*	.054*	.040[a]
Self-Esteem	−.06	.12*	.23****	.08	.01	.087****	.077[b]
Peers' Relations	.01	−.15*	−.11*	−.06	−.11*	.062***	.047[e]
Academic Achievement	−.08	.35***	.03	−.02	.09	.132***	.112[f]
Somatization	−.05	−.06	−.17**	−.03	−.12*	.063***	.040[a]
Obsessive Compulsive	−.01	−.02	−.17***	−.08	−.12*	.068***	.061[a]
Interpersonal Sensitivity	−.05	.05	−.18***	−.10	−.12*	.072***	.060[a]
Depression	.01	.10	−.21****	−.09	−.08	.079****	.055[c]
Anxiety	.01	.16*	−.16*	.01	−.01	.048*	.047[b]
Hostility	.05	−.11	−.17**	−.04	−.12*	.077***	.060[a]
Phobic Anxiety	−.08	.04	−.10	−.01	−.19***	.057**	.042[d]
Paranoid Ideation	.04	.08	−.15*	−.09	−.05	.045*	.027[c]
Psychotism	−.05	−.05	−.20***	−.04	−.13*	.076***	.069[a]
GSI	−.02	.01	−.21****	−.06	−.13*	.077***	.066[a]

NOTE: Age: age of respondents; Gender: 0 (male), 1 (female); Family Structure: 0 (polygamy), 1 (monogamy); Economic Status: 1 (very bad) to 6 (very good); Self–Esteem: 1 (low) to 4 (high); Peers' Relations: 0 to 100 higher value indicates more difficulties; BSI scales: 0 to 4 higher value indicates more difficulties; Academic Achievement: 0 to 100, higher value indicates higher academic achievement.

Best models: [a]Economic Status, Family Structure; [b]Economic Status, Gender; [c]Economic Status; [d]Family Structure; [e]Family Structure, Gender; [f]Gender.

*$p < .05$; **$p < .01$; ***$p < .005$; ****$p < .001$.

and social functioning, but the findings presented in Table 17.4 show that this effect is no longer significant when the impact of family functioning is controlled for. Thus, we conclude that family functioning mediates the impact of family structure on the psychological and social functioning of children from both monogamous and polygamous families.

Economic Status

The regression models presented in Tables 17.3 and 17.4 also point to the significant role that the family's economic status plays in the children's mental health and social functioning. Specifically, economic status has a significant effect on the children's self-esteem and all the BSI dimensions other than anxiety, as well as on

their peer relations and their perceptions of their family's functioning, beyond the effects of their family structure and other sociodemographic variables.

Discussion

Although, historically, a polygamous family structure was favored by the Bedouin-Arab of the Negev for the economic and social benefits it brought, this study shows that children from polygamous families have more mental health, educational, and social difficulties than their peers from monogamous families: They report higher levels of psychiatric symptoms, more problems in relating to their peers, poorer school achievement, and poorer relations with their

Table 17.4   Family Functioning as an Explaining Factor

	Independent Variables in the Linear Regression Model (betas)							
	Family Functioning	Age	Gender	SES	Father's Education	Family Structure	R^2 Full Model	R^2 Best Model
Self-Esteem	−.33****	−.06	.11*	.17***	.08	−.04	.191****	.181[b]
Peer Relations	.31****	.01	−.14*	−.05	−.06	−.07	.154****	.139[d]
Academic Achievement	−.14*	−.08	.35***	.00	−.02	.08	.149***	.134[d]
Somatization	.30****	−.04	−.06	−.12*	−.03	−.09	.146****	.133[a]
Obsessive-Compulsive	.32****	−.00	−.01	−.12*	−.08	−.09	.165****	.149[a]
Interpersonal Sensitivity	.23****	−.04	.05	−.14*	−.10	−.09	.123****	.101[a]
Depression	.27****	.01	.11	−.17***	−.09	−.04	.147****	.126[a]
Anxiety	.19***	.02	.16**	−.13*	.00	.02	.083***	.082[b]
Hostility	.16**	.06	−.11	−.14*	−.04	−.10	.102****	.075[a]
Phobic Anxiety	.23****	−.08	.05	−.06	−.01	−.16*	.105****	.096[c]
Paranoid Ideation	.21****	.04	.08	−.11	−.08	−.03	.087****	.071[a]
Psychotism	.24****	−.05	−.04	−.16**	−.04	−.10	.129*****	.113[a]
GSI	.31****	−.02	.02	−.15**	−.06	−.09	.165****	.153[a]

NOTE: General Family Functioning– higher value indicates more difficulties; Age– age of respondents; Gender: 0–male, 1–female; Family Structure: 0–polygamy, 1–monogamy; Economic status: 1–very bad to 6–very good; Self-Esteem: 1–low to 4–high; Peers' Relation: 0–100 higher value indicates more difficulties; BSI scales: 0–4 higher value indicates more difficulties; Academic achievement: 0–100 higher value indicates higher academic achievement.

Best models: [a]Family Functioning, Economic Status; [b]Family Functioning, Gender, Economic Status; [c]Family Functioning, Family Structure; [d]Family Functioning, Gender.

*$p < .05$; **$p < .01$; ***$p < .005$; ****$p < .001$.

fathers, although not with their mothers. Most of these findings are consistent with previous studies showing the same deleterious effects of polygamy on children's emotional and social adjustment (Al-Krenawi, Graham, & Slonim-Nevo, 2002; Al-Krenawi & Lightman, 2000). In fact the psychological condition of the children from polygamous families was not only worse than their counterparts in the monogamous families but were also worst than the norms of Israeli adolescents (Canetti et al., 1994).

How can these findings be interpreted? We suggest that there is a key mediating factor, family relations, and as a consequence we cannot dismiss entirely the potential benefits of a polygamous family structure. Specifically, our findings show that children in polygamous families suffer not because their fathers have two or more wives but because their families are more likely to experience conflicts among family members. Indeed, analysis using Baron and Kenny's (1986) four-step procedure for establishing mediation (Baron & Kenny, 1986; Kenny et al., 1998) suggests that family structure (polygamous or monogamous) influences children's mental health and peer relations *through* family functioning. These findings imply that polygamy is not in itself detrimental to children's adjustment. They suggest that when the family functions well, the children's adjustment will not be impaired.

We may wonder then what conflicts specifically arise in polygamous families that compromise their functioning? Our findings show that the children tend to perceive their relationships with their fathers as problematic. Indeed, the children's poorer relations with their fathers may be understood in the context of what usually happens in the polygamous father's relationship with his first wife and her children. As noted earlier, senior wives in polygamous Bedouin-Arab families are often rated as inferior to the subsequent wives, and the fate of the children follows suit. The father's emotional and economic resources are unevenly channeled to the second wife and her children. Thus, it is not surprising that children of senior wives do not take kindly to their fathers and rely, instead, on their mothers for love and caring (Adams & Mburugu, 1994; Al-Krenawi, 1998; Kilbride & Kilbride, 1990; Ware, 1979; Wittrup, 1990). Although we did not distinguish children from first and second wives in our analyses, it would be helpful in future research to do so. Other conflicts, although not analyzed here, are between the wives, the siblings from the different mothers, between members of the extended families, and of course, between the husband and his various wives. Feelings of jealousy, anger, and hurt are likely to be experienced when one has to compete for emotional and economic resources.

This certainly raises the question of how an indigenous family form such as polygamy and the rules surrounding the distribution of economic and emotional resources in a polygamous family serve the needs of children. It is common now to argue respectful tolerance for social differences based on a general agreement for a need for cultural sensitivity. However, in this case, where a family form appears to result in more family conflict and poorer mental health outcomes in children, one is left wondering as to the value of this diversity. In terms of resilience, we are puzzled whether by their nature nonconventional family structures that are indigenous to particular social groups such as the Bedouin-Arabs are in fact more likely to produce healthy children. Our findings hint at the need for a broader look at this problem. It is not that one family form or another meets children's needs better, but that the functioning of the family must be good enough to meet children's needs. These needs include a home environment without conflict. This nonconflictual home environment is conducive to fostering children's resilience. Although polygamy may once have contributed to raising healthy children and healthy communities, it seems questionable whether this is still the case, given the changes in where and how the Bedouin-Arab live.

Even when we look at economic status, we find again that a family's economic situation was a significant predictor of both family functioning and children's psychosocial condition. These findings are consistent with the studies noted earlier that link family functioning and economic status (Montgomery & Carter-Pokras, 1993; Starfield, 1991; Weinger, 1998) as well as with studies that show that children from families with a low economic status tend to have behavioral problems. Other family members in these families are also more likely to report a variety of psychological difficulties (Korenman et al., 1995). Our findings, however, also show that both the family functioning and economic status of polygamous families, as perceived by the children, were poorer than those of monogamous families. These findings support the view that although polygamy may once have been a useful and viable family form, it is no longer so in today's urban reality in which children are consumers of resources rather than producers. Although we may idealize romantic notions of certain family forms meeting children's needs and the needs of people's communities, such romanticism ignores the changes that have occurred in the specificity of the context in which families function. Arguably, the benefits of polygamy may no longer outweigh the costs to children's well-being and overall family functioning.

Implications for Interventions

Although this chapter focuses on the difficulties children in polygamous families experience, we think it is also important to emphasize the type of interventions and conditions that can assist these children in coping with their stressful life conditions. Namely, we need to ask not only what is wrong with this type of life but also what factors can help children survive and flourish living under the stressful life conditions that confront the sedentarized Bedouin-Arab in the Negev? We believe it is the role of social practitioners and social policymakers to work toward the provision of protective factors relevant to the lives of people such as the Bedouin-Arab of the Negev who have suffered forced settlement and significant changes in family structure. Specifically, we suggest a number of interventions that may occur at different levels.

On an individual level, social workers, teachers, psychologists, and health practitioners should view children living in polygamous families as children at risk. They should be aware of the potential for psychological, educational, and social difficulties and offer individual counseling and support that is sensitive to the heightened possibility that children are experiencing family discord, in particular conflict between parents and between children and their fathers. Such help should be given not only to children who already manifest symptoms but also to those who do not complain, as a matter of prevention. Counseling should focus on raising children's self-esteem, providing them with educational assistance, and discussing issues of family life. But counseling alone will not suffice. Children in polygamous families tend to suffer from poverty as well. Therefore, it is crucial that real assistance be given in the form of financial benefits, school materials, food, security, and health care.

At the familial level, social practitioners and family therapists should develop methods for treating polygamous families. They may use the polygamous children's difficulties as a strategy to enter Bedouin families, taking into account that entering Arab families through the problems associated with one wife or another is complicated and may affect the wife-husband relationship (Abu-Baker & Dwairy, 2003). Children in polygamous families could also be taught how to resolve conflicts with their fathers, how to build a coalition with other siblings (instead of competing with each other), and how to support each other. A similar process could take place among all siblings in the family; they could learn how to negotiate for

attention and resources, how to compromise, and how to build a successful, small community. The current methods of family therapy are based on nuclear Western families. New methods need to be developed for polygamous families, implemented, and then evaluated for their effectiveness. Issues of poverty, sharing of financial resources, and ways of improving the socioeconomic status of this small community, perhaps through economic initiatives, should be emphasized as well.

Much work needs to be conducted at the community level as well. First, the Bedouin-Arab people should be made aware of the negative side effects of polygamy, including the resulting low socioeconomic status, psychological difficulties, and social problems among children living in such families. Awareness could be raised via the local media, religious leaders, conferences, and the education system. Enhanced knowledge of the problems associated with polygamy could help men in deciding whether to consider creating a polygamous family structure despite cultural beliefs of its historical advantages. In addition, programs for children living in polygamous families should be developed to assist them in overcoming the potential difficulties related to their family structure. For example, a support group for children could be offered in the local schools, afternoon classes could be made available specifically for these children to increase their educational level, and children could find additional social supports through various after-school activities.

In Bedouin society, however, a problem exists regarding the use, availability, and access to psychological services. Children who suffer from psychological problems are often unaware of whom they can turn to or where they can find help. In addition to the fact that the accessibility and availability of formal services are limited in the Bedouin-Arab locales, approaching and using these services carries a negative stigma among the Bedouin-Arab population (Al-Krenawi & Graham, 2000). The question that needs to be asked, therefore, is, How do these children cope with their psychological problems? They may find solace in turning to the informal services available within their communities—for example, family, relatives, traditional healers, religious leaders, or other active members of society. Practitioners and policymakers must consider developing culturally competent services so that children who are suffering will not be ashamed or afraid to approach formal helpers when needed.

Finally, policymakers and political leaders in Israel must find ways to improve the economic condition of the entire Bedouin-Arab society by creating jobs and investing in the formal and informal educational system within this community. Opportunities for employment in this society are scarce, and there is a lack of counselors and educational psychologists in Bedouin-Arab schools. Clearly, only with substantial economic and educational development can real change in the conditions of children and families be expected. These changes, along with acknowledgment by the community of the need for a more mainstream family structure, are likely together to produce the most substantial improvements in the lives of Bedouin-Arab children. Creating the conditions for children to thrive depends on adapting to the social and contextual changes that have dramatically affected this formerly nomadic community. Although studies of resilience have shown that in most instances reinforcing cultural factors unique to a group of at-risk children buffer the effects of risk (see other chapters in this volume), this is not the case here. Instead, flexibility and a shift away from centuries-old family forms is more likely to result in healthier and more economically successful families capable of raising healthy children.

REFERENCES

Abu-Baker, K., & Dwairy, M. (2003). Cultural norms versus state law in treating incest: A suggested model for Arab families. *Child Abuse & Neglect, 27*, 109–123.

Adams, B., & Mburugu, E. (1994). Kikuyu bridewealth and polygyny today. *Journal of Comparative Family Studies, 25*(2), 159–166.

Al-Haj, M. (1987). *Social change and family processes: Arab communities in Shefar-A'm.* London: Westview Press.

Al-Krenawi, A. (1998). Family therapy with a multi parent/multi spousal family. *Family Process, 37*(1), 65–81.

Al-Krenawi, A. (1999). Explanation of mental health symptoms by the Bedouin-Arabs of the Negev. *International Journal of Social Psychiatry, 45*(1), 56–64.

Al-Krenawi, A. (2001). Women from polygamous and monogamous marriages in out-patients psychiatric clinic. *Transcultural Psychiatry, 38*(2), 187–199.

Al-Krenawi, A., & Graham, J. R. (1997). Social work and blood vengeance: The Bedouin-Arab case. *The British Journal of Social Work, 27*, 515–528.

Al-Krenawi, A., & Graham, J. R. (2000). Culturally sensitive social work practice with Arab clients in mental health settings. *Health and Social Work, 25*(1), 9–22.

Al-Krenawi, A., & Graham, J. R. (2001). Polygamous family structure and its interaction with gender: Effects on children's academic achievements and implications for culturally diverse social work practice in schools. *School Social Work Journal, 25*(3), 1–16.

Al-Krenawi, A., Graham, J. R., & Al-Krenawi, S. (1997). Social work practice with polygamous families. *Child & Adolescent Social Work Journal, 14*, 445–458.

Al-Krenawi, A., Graham, J. R., & Izzeldin, A. (2001). The psychosocial impact of polygamous marriages on Palestinian women. *Women and Health, 34*(1), 1–16.

Al-Krenawi, A., Graham, J. R., & Slonim-Nevo, V. (2002). Mental health aspects of Arab-Israeli adolescents from polygamous/monogamous families. *Journal of Social Psychology, 142*(4), 446–460.

Al-Krenawi, A., & Lightman, E. (2000). Learning achievements, social adjustment and family conflicts among Bedouin-Arab children from polygamous and monogamous families. *Journal of Social Psychology, 140*(3), 345–355.

Al-Krenawi, A., & Slonim-Nevo, V. (2003). *Psychosocial functioning in Bedouin-Arab society in the Negev: A comparison of polygamous and monogamous families.* Beer-Sheva, Israel: Ben-Gurion University of the Negev, Center for Bedouin Studies and Development.

Al-Sadawi, N. (1985). Growing up female in Egypt. In E. W. Fernea (Ed.), *Women and the family in the Middle East: New voices of change* (pp. 111–120). Austin: University of Texas Press.

Antonovsky, A. (1987). *Unraveling the mystery of health.* San Francisco: Jossey-Bass.

Antonovsky, A. (1993). The structure and properties of the sense of coherence scale. *Social Science and Medicine, 36,* 725–733.

Antonovsky, A. (1998). The salutogenic model as a theory to guide health promotion. *Megamot: Behavioral Science Quarterly, 39,* 170–182.

Baron, R. M., & Kenny, D. A. (1986). The moderator-mediator variable distinction in social psychological research: Conceptual, strategic and statistical considerations. *Journal of Personality and Social Psychology, 51,* 1173–1182.

Boettcher, A., Billick, S., & Burgert, W. (2001). Family functioning and depression in patients with medical illness. *Psychiatric Annals, 31*(12), 694–700.

Bradley, J. A. (2001). Evaluating the concept of the narcissistic family: Development of the childhood experiences questionnaire. *Dissertation Abstracts International, 61*(11-B), 6125.

Broude, G. J. (1994). *Marriage, family, and relationships. A cross-cultural encyclopedia.* Denver, CO: ABC-CLIO.

Canetti, L., Shalev, Y. A., & Kaplan-De-Nour, K. A. (1994). Israeli adolescents' norms of the Brief Symptoms Inventory (BSI). *Israel Journal of Psychiatry and Related Sciences, 29,* 150–158.

Chaleby, K. (1985). Women of polygamous marriage in inpatient psychiatric services in Kuwait. *Journal of Nervous and Mental Disease, 173*(1), 56–58.

Cherian, V. I. (1990). Academic achievement of children from monogamous and polygynous families. *Journal of Social Psychology, 130*(1), 117–119.

Derogatis, L., & Spencer, P. (1982). *The Brief Symptom Inventory: Administration, scoring and procedures, manual I.* Chevy Chase, MD: Johns Hopkins University School of Medicine.

D'Hondt, W., & Vandewiele, M. (1980). Attitudes of Senegalese secondary school students towards traditional African way of life and Western way of life. *Psychological Reports, 47,* 235–242.

Dorjahn, V. R. (1988). Changes in Temme polygyny. *Ethnology, 27,* 367–390.

Eapen, V., Al-Gazali, L., Bin-Othman, S., & Abou-Saleh, M. (1998). Mental health problems among schoolchildren in United Arab Emirates: Prevalence and risk factors. *Journal of American Academy Child and Adolescent Psychiatry, 37*(8), 880–886.

El-Islam, M. F. (1983). Cultural change and inter-generational relationship in Arabian families. *International Journal of Family Psychiatry, 4*(4), 321–329.

El-Islam, M. F., & Abu-Dagga, S. (1992). Lay explanation of symptoms of mental ill health in Kuwait. *International Journal of Social Psychiatry, 38*(2), 150–156.

Epstein, N. B., Baldwin, M. N., & Bishop, D. S. (1983). The McMaster family assessment device. *Journal of Marital and Family Therapy, 9,* 171–180.

Greenbaum, C. W., & Auerbach, J. G. (1992). The conceptualization of risk, vulnerability, and resilience in psychological development. In C. W. Greenbaum & J. G. Auerbach (Eds.), *Longitudinal studies of children at psychological risk: Cross-national perspectives* (pp. 9–28). Norwood, NJ: Ablex.

Hall, E. (1976). *Beyond culture.* New York: Doubleday.

Hudson, W. W. (1982). *The clinical measurement package: A field manual.* Chicago: Dorsey Press.

Kenny, D. A., Kashy, D. A., & Bolger, N. (1998). Data analysis in social psychology. In D. Gilbert, S. Fiske, & G. Lindzey (Eds.). *The handbook of social psychology* (4th ed., Vol. 1, pp. 233–265). Boston: McGraw-Hill.

Kilbride, P., & Kilbride, J. (1990). *Changing family life in East Kenya: Women and children at risk.* Philadelphia: University Park Press.

Korenman, S., Miller, J. E., & Sjaastad, J. E. (1995). Long term poverty and child development in the US: Results from the NLSY. *Child and Youth Service Review, 17*(1/2), 127–155.

Leadbeater, B., & Bishop, S. (1994). Predictors of behavior problems in preschool children of inner city Afro-American and Puerto Rican adolescent mothers. *Child Development, 65*(2), 638–648.

Low, B. S. (1988). Measures of polygyny in humans. *Current Anthropology, 29*(1), 189–194.

Macmillan dictionary of anthropology. (1986). London: Macmillan.

Marks, E. (1974). *The Bedouin society of the Negev* [in Hebrew]. Tel-Aviv: Reshafim Press.

McDermott, B. M., McKelvey, R., Roberts, L., & Davies L. (2002). Severity of children's psychopathology and impairment and its relationship to treatment setting. *Psychiatric Services, 53*(1), 57–62.

Montgomery, L., & Carter-Pokras, O. (1993). Health status by social class and/or minority status:

Implications for environmental equity research. *Toxicology and Industrial Health, 9*(5), 729–773.

Owuamanam, D. O. (1984). Adolescents' perception of the polygamous family and its relationship to self-concept. *International Journal of Psychology, 19*, 593–598.

Rosenberg, M. (1979). *Conceiving the self.* New York: Basic Books.

Sagy, S., & Antonovsky, A. (1998). The family sense of coherence: The salutogenic approach [in Hebrew]. *Megamot: Behavioral Science Quarterly, 39*, 80–96.

Starfield, B. (1991). Race, family income, and low birth weight. *American Journal of Epidemiology, 134*(10), 1167–1174.

Statistical year book of the Negev Bedouin. (in press). Beer-Sheva, Israel: Ben Gurion University of the Negev, Center for Bedouin Studies and Development.

Ware, H. (1979). Polygyny: Women's view in a transitional society, Nigeria 1975. *Journal of Marriage and the Family, 41*(1), 185–195.

Waysman, M., Solomon, Z., & Schwarzwald, J. (1998). Long-term positive change following traumatic stress among Israeli prisoners of war. *Megamot: Behavioral Science Quarterly, 39*, 31–55.

Weinger, S. (1998). Children living in poverty: Their perception of career opportunities. *Families in Society: The Journal of Contemporary Human Services, 3*, 320–330.

White, D. R. (1988). Causes of polygyny: Ecology, economy, kinship, and warfare. *American Anthropologist, 90*(4), 871–887.

Wittrup, I. (1990). Me and my husband's wife: An analysis of polygyny among Mandinka in the Gambia. *Folk, 32*, 117–142.

18

STRENGTHENING FAMILIES AND COMMUNITIES

System Building for Resilience

BARBARA J. FRIESEN

EILEEN BRENNAN

P arenting any child is a challenging, dynamic process. When a child's disability requires special care or places physical, economic, social, and emotional demands on the family, this challenge to family resources may in itself become a risk factor for the healthy development of that child and others in the family. However, Masten (2001) reminds us of the "ordinary magic" associated with the adaptive capacities of all children. She asserts that resilience is more common than not and concludes that

> very little evidence has emerged . . . to indicate that severe adversity has major or lasting effects on adaptive behaviors in the environment unless important adaptive systems, such as cognition and parenting, are compromised prior to or as a result of the adversity. (p. 232)

Given this, Masten suggests that we should emphasize strategies that protect or strengthen these basic protective systems.

In this chapter, we build on Masten's call to protect or restore basic protective mechanisms by focusing on (a) resilience and resilience building within the family, the system through which parenting is exercised, and (b) the community, which is both the ecological context within which families live and a source of direct influence on the lives of children. This examination is framed within what Farmer and Farmer (2001) describe as a developmental science perspective, wherein "the individual functions as an integrated organism and development arises from the dynamic interrelations among systems existing within and beyond the person" (p. 172). This conceptualization builds on Bronfenbrenner's (1986) synthesis

AUTHORS' NOTE: Preparation of the manuscript was supported in part by the Research and Training Center on Family Support and Children's Mental Health of the Regional Research Institute for Human Services, Portland State University, through NIDRR Grant H133B990025.

295

of evidence about the influence of the ecology, or external influences, on the family as the context for the development of children.

Figure 18.1 depicts this view of the relationships between children, their families, and their communities. Key assumptions about these relationships are that they are (a) embedded, meaning that children live within families, which are located within communities; (b) reciprocal, referring to the perspective that each system influences the other (child-family, family-community, and child-community); and (c) dynamic, meaning these relationships and influences change over time.

Family-child relationships, labeled 1 in Figure 18.1, include both the extensively researched influences of families on children, primarily exercised through parenting, as well as the influences of child characteristics and behaviors on family processes, including parents' behaviors. An example of the phenomenon of mutual interaction and influence between children and parents is described by Stoolmiller (2001). He focused on the relationship between boys' behavior and parental discipline practices and described a cycle that includes the caregiver's attempt to intervene in the child's behavior, followed by the child's resisting the attempt through a tantrum or other acting-out behavior. The caregiver responds by withdrawing the demand, and the child ceases the resistance. According to this framework, based on coercion theory, the child learns that such aversive behavior is effective at controlling the behavior of others. Many other examples of the reciprocal effects of child on parent and parent on child are presented in the research literature (see, e.g., Conger & Conger, 2002; Masten, 2001).

A second mutually influencing relationship is that between families and communities, labeled 2 in Figure 18.1. Sampson (2002) summarizes key research findings on the effects of neighborhoods on children and families, concluding that the ecological concentration of families and children affected by low income, racial isolation, and social problems has grown over the last two decades. Sampson emphasizes that economic stratification and social problems are powerful predictors of child outcomes,

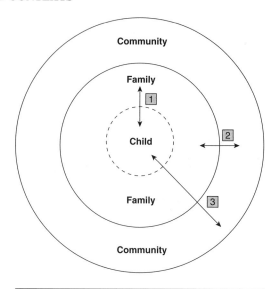

Figure 18.1   Relationships of Child, Family, and Community

particularly when considered together. In addition to the negative influences of community characteristics on families, however, there appears to be a cycle where families' responses to neighborhood conditions can exacerbate problems in the community. When families respond to neighborhood deterioration through withdrawal, demoralization, and retreat, they become less involved in setting and enforcing standards of behavior or engaging in mutual support. Brodsky (1996) describes a phenomenon of "resilient mothers" who act to protect their children from unsafe neighborhood conditions by restricting contact with neighborhood residents and events. Low community involvement does avoid exposure to negative community influences for individual children and families, but when many residents behave in this way, the cumulative result may be that fewer residents are engaged and available to contribute to neighborhood life. This, in turn, reduces the amount of collective social control that is correlated with decreased rates of delinquency and problem behaviors in children (Hann & Borek, 2001).

The phenomenon of collective social control (Hann & Borek, 2001) is illustrative of the third major relationship portrayed in Figure 18.1, that between the child and community. The child's entry into community life, including the educational system, provides the opportunity for youth to form relationships with peers and unrelated adults, engage in a variety of activities, and gain access to resources not available to them within their families. Entry into community life may also expose them to negative influences as well. Youth, however, can act as contributors to the collective good of their communities. Lerner (2003) describes a "developmental approach" that is reciprocal and interactive, with youth development and community development each influencing and building on the other.

Although their lives are closely linked to the health and well-being of their families and communities, our primary focus is on outcomes for children and youth, including those with disabilities. In the first section of this chapter we examine parenting within the context of the family, neighborhood, and community. The latter half of the chapter follows the child out of the family and into community settings.

FOCUS ON PARENTING: THE FAMILY IN CONTEXT

The child development and resilience literature contains much evidence about the importance of parenting to the development of children. In a resilience framework, attention is often given to the negative effects of poor parenting (risk factors) or the buffering effect of good parenting that protects children from an otherwise harsh environment. Baldwin, Baldwin, and Cole (1990) distinguish between stress-resistant children and stress-resistant families, those families that buffer or protect their children from a high-risk environment. They observe that if families successfully protect their children from adversity, perhaps the families, not the children, should be considered resilient.

Especially in the early years of a child's life, parents have the responsibility for creating the immediate environment in which their children grow and develop and for mediating the relationship between their children and the larger environment. Thus, it is not surprising that parenting emerges as a highly significant explanatory variable in outcomes for all children.

We have chosen to consider the elements of parenting by focusing on the developmental needs of children within Brazelton and Greenspan's (2000) framework of six "irreducible needs" of children: (a) physical protection, safety, and regulation; (b) ongoing nurturing relationships; (c) experiences tailored to individual differences; (d) developmentally appropriate experiences; (e) limit setting, structure, and expectations; and (f) stable supportive communities and cultural continuity. Each of the first five needs is examined in relation to elements of parenting quality, sources of threat to the capacity of the family system to meet the needs of children, and examples of some current and proposed interventions.

Physical Protection, Safety, and Regulation

Elements of parenting related to this set of children's needs include the ability to provide shelter, adequate nutrition, and physical protection, including supervision, either directly or through obtaining competent caregivers. Brazelton and Greenspan (2000) identify a range of challenges to children's safety and development, including toxic substances in the environment, extreme stress, chaotic home or child care environments, too much television watching, and inadequate supervision. A difficult challenge for families whose children have disabilities is finding competent child care or educational settings that will accept the child and accept responsibility for meeting his or her needs for physical safety and regulation while keeping the other children safe as well.

Threats to the capacity of the family to provide safety and supervision include family circumstances such as poverty and personal factors such as physical or mental illness of the parent or substance abuse that can compromise parenting ability. These threats are multiplied when the community in which the family lives is characterized by high rates of poverty, unsafe housing, violence, and crime. Poverty constitutes a major challenge to the capacity of the family to provide adequate safety. Issues related to poverty include poor-quality housing (with possible hazards such as lead-based paint, unsafe wiring, or rodents); unsafe neighborhoods; parents who work long hours, sometimes at several jobs; and the lack of affordable child care services that match parents' work schedules. In addition, there is evidence that children's challenging, aggressive behaviors may compromise the parents' ability to set limits or effectively supervise their children (Conger & Conger, 2002; Stoolmiller, 2001).

When the needs for physical protection, safety, and regulation are not met, the consequences for children may include physical injury, poor nutrition, vulnerability to becoming victims, and compromised growth and development. In addition to concerns about obvious physical injury, Brazelton and Greenspan (2000) emphasize the deleterious effects on central nervous system regulation associated with exposure to toxic substances, extreme stress, and chaotic environments.

When threats to children's safety are apparent, current interventions are most often aimed at addressing the needs of children within their families and may include removing children from family situations that are perceived as dangerous, either directly or because of child neglect. This is a very common strategy of child welfare systems. Interventions such as parent training designed to strengthen parents' ability to provide adequate supervision may be ineffective when families are overwhelmed by poverty or neighborhood violence or when affordable, high-quality child care is not available.

Ongoing, Nurturing Relationships

The second irreducible need of children identified by Brazelton and Greenspan (2000) is that of warm, caring relationships characterized by close emotional connections. Especially for young children, parents are the primary source of these relationships, although other caregivers are also critical when children spend long hours in a child care setting. The resilience literature is replete with evidence that a stable, caring relationship with a parent or other adult is characteristic of children who demonstrate the ability to cope and sometimes thrive in the face of adversity (Masten & Coatsworth, 1998; Rutter, 1987). Within the family, conditions that may challenge caregivers' abilities to provide nurturance

and emotional closeness include stress and exhaustion related to overwork, worry about finances and family problems (Conger & Conger, 2002), depression and other mental illnesses (Beardslee, Versage, Van de Velde, Swatling, & Hoke, 2002; Oyserman, Mowbray, Meares, & Firminger, 2000), physical illness or disability, substance abuse, or impaired cognitive skills. Caregivers' beliefs and child-rearing practices also shape parent-child relationships (Seigel, 1994; Stoiber & Houghton, 1993).

To intervene effectively to promote nurturing relationships, it is important to understand how barriers to good parent-child relationships may operate so that the interventions address critical targets of change. For example, a close examination of parental mental illness by Tebes, Kaufman, Adnopoz, and Racusin (2001) suggests that it is not the presence of psychiatric symptoms, per se, that are related to poor outcomes in children but, rather, family psychosocial processes that commonly accompany psychiatric disorder in parents. These five processes are diminished financial resources, constriction of social networks, impaired performance of parenting tasks, increased family stress, and disruption of the parent-child bond. The researchers found that these processes were a more consistent predictor of child adaptation than parental psychiatric disorder. Tebes et al. (2001) also demonstrate the importance of specifically targeting interventions. They found that reductions in family stress are likely to be associated with reductions in child symptoms and problem behaviors but that enhancements of parent-child bonds are more likely to be associated with increased child competencies. Tebes and his associates recommend that interventions for parents with mental illness should always include a focus on improving parenting and that it is critical that children's competence and well-being be assessed, not just their problem behaviors and symptoms.

Interventions developed by Beardslee and his colleagues (Beardslee et al., 2002) focus on helping children whose parents suffer from depression gain understanding about their parents' illness and develop coping skills that reduce their vulnerability to developing depression and other emotional disorders (i.e., build protective factors) through a child and family intervention that increases knowledge and fosters better parent-child relationships.

Any of the interventions that focus on improving parenting skills must also attend to the physical, economic, and social context in which parents and other caregivers operate. The primary public institution that directly intervenes with regard to parenting is the child welfare system. The primary tools of this system are removal of children for their protection, providing training and support for caregivers (such as parent training, and in some instances, homemaker services or respite care), and the provision of "substitute parents." Parents with mental health problems, substance abuse problems, or both are often enjoined to seek treatment. However, they face many obstacles to access. In addition, interventions by the child welfare system do not generally address underlying issues such as poverty or discrimination that may affect parents' effectiveness with their children.

Experiences Tailored to Individual Differences

This need identified by Brazelton and Greenspan (2000) refers to children's having the opportunity to learn, grow, and be challenged in ways that best fit their individual needs, capacities, and characteristics. To address this set of needs, parents and other caregivers must have both the capacity to assess and understand each child's temperament and characteristic ways of responding, and the ability to plan and carry out appropriate individualized plans and strategies. Challenges related to caregivers' knowledge and skills include lack of information about child development and differences in child temperament or a restricted range of parenting strategies. Other challenges include overcrowding at home or in child care settings such that there is an insufficient number of adults in relation to the number of children; stress, fatigue, or illness of caregivers; and child care settings that provide routinized care that can undermine parents' efforts to individualize.

Strategies that help parents and caregivers individualize responses to children include early intervention service planning for children with disabilities who qualify for a variety of early intervention services. In child care settings, child development and mental health consultants can help classroom teachers develop and implement individualized plans as well as work with parents to develop strategies tailored to their children's needs. Mental health consultation is available in all Head Start programs and in some other child care and preschool settings (Cohen & Kaufmann, 2000; Yoshikawa & Knitzer, 1997).

Interventions such as individualized service planning and mental health consultation, however, primarily address the content of planning and intervention needed by young children and do not generally address the circumstances when parents' lives are complicated by personal challenges such as substance abuse or mental illness, or the risks posed by unsafe housing or crime-ridden neighborhoods. Brazelton and Greenspan (2000) describe a concept they call the "vertical village," which is designed to ensure both the safety and nurturance of children while at the same time providing support for their parents. This approach calls for creating a supportive community within high-rise housing complexes that provides services directly supportive of the development of children (such as preschool and child care opportunities) and that also supports parents who are overwhelmed or challenged. What distinguishes this concept from ordinary social and mental health services is an emphasis on mutual support, collective responsibility, and community building.

Developmentally Appropriate Experiences

Closely aligned with the need for experiences that address individual differences is the need for developmentally appropriate experiences. Again, caregivers' abilities to provide developmentally appropriate experiences require that they have both the necessary knowledge and skills regarding child development and an environment that supports their use of these capacities. A basic requirement for addressing this need, of course, is that parents have information about child development, including a "road map" of the range of physical, perceptual, language, emotional, social, and cognitive milestones important for their children's healthy growth. This information can be gained informally, from relatives and friends, or through formal means such as reading, classes, or individual instruction. Parents who are isolated are less likely to gain child-rearing information through informal means and may also lack access to formal instruction. There are literally hundreds of published examples of parent training and information programs that focus on information and skill building, including services provided through pediatrician's offices (Minkovitz et al., 2003), parenting newsletters directed to urban families (Tineo, 2002), education classes for family members and child care professionals (Martinez, 2003), building parenting skills through addressing trauma in Lakota parents (Brave Heart, 1999), and a universal approach to promoting optimal child development for all families in selected school attendance areas in California (Goldstein, 1997). However, ensuring access for parents to appropriate and nonstigmatizing information and training is a major program challenge.

Even when parents have access to child development information, circumstances that may impede their use of this knowledge and these skills include personal challenges of caregivers—alone or in combination with various sources of family stress. Brazelton and Greenspan (2000) identify sufficient time spent by parents with their children and flexibility as children's needs change as key to meeting developmental needs. They also emphasize the importance of caregivers' having support from other adults in balancing the needs of their children and the demands of their work schedules, household duties, or other pressures on their time. These needs of parents for support from other adults may be partially met by various family support programs, but finding and setting aside sufficient parent-child interaction time is a challenge for many of today's families, especially those that do not have other adults to share in daily household duties or the means to purchase such help.

Lack of individualized or developmentally appropriate experiences for children is not likely to come to public attention except when the circumstances are extreme—for example, when parents are reported for child abuse because of inappropriate expectations and inappropriate discipline imposed on young children (Stoiber & Houghton, 1993). These needs of children and strategies to address them are less immediately obvious than the need for physical safety, protection, and supervision, but are no less crucial.

Limit Setting, Structure, and Expectations

Parents and other caregivers need to have the ability to develop and enforce appropriate limits, provide structure, and convey expectations for their children. Brazelton and Greenspan (2000) emphasize the importance of parents' spending adequate time with children to develop trusting relationships fundamental to establishing effective structure and limits.

As with the children's other needs, there are many programs designed to support parents in their abilities to provide effective structure and set appropriate limits. They include universal programs designed to prevent problems, promote health, or both, such as the use of schools as community centers and vehicles for parent education (Chung, 1993; Holtzman, 1992), and more commonly, those programs targeted at families defined as "at risk" (Culp, Culp, Blankemeyer, & Passmark, 1998; Miller, 1997; Wagner & Clayton, 1999). A third set of interventions target families whose young children are manifesting signs of behavior that put them at risk for future problems (Hann & Borek, 2001; Webster-Stratton, 1997).

It is important to understand that parental discipline practices and the responses of their children vary widely across cultures (Bradley, Corwyn, McAdoo, & Garcia-Coll, 2001; Lin & Fu, 1990). For example, Kotchick and Forehand (2002) point out that although authoritative parenting is often seen as the standard for effective parenting, authoritarian parenting has been found to have positive effects for African American and Asian youth. Therefore, both research that seeks to explain resilient responses in children and interventions designed to reduce risk, build protective factors, or both need to be fine-grained to account for the individual needs and responses of children. Recent studies of child-rearing practices and interventions among families from diverse backgrounds (e.g., Kolobe, 2004;

Shimoni, Este, & Clark, 2003) provide information that can be used to refine current practice.

This examination of parenting practices related to the developmental needs of children underlines the importance of understanding individual children and families in their ecological context. It is also apparent that interventions that seek to promote resilience through strengthening children's adaptive capacities or through changing the behavior of parents through direct intervention are necessary but not sufficient. Masten and Coatsworth (1998) characterize child-focused, skill-building approaches as "first-generation" competence research, noting that it is possible to change skills but that the consequences for subsequent adjustment are small. "Second-generation" research involves multi-causal ecological models that take into account the environments that have an impact on the child while also working to increase the adaptive capacity of the child. This same concept can be applied to parenting. First-generation change strategies are based on a host of intervention studies that demonstrate the effectiveness of parent training programs (Kazdin, 1997). Second-generation approaches to improving parenting must also take an ecological perspective.

The last irreducible need of children identified by Brazelton and Greenspan (2000) is the need for stable supportive communities and cultural continuity. The remainder of this chapter addresses the child-community relationship, first through settings and programs that directly affect the child through child care arrangements, after-school and mentoring programs, and community-centered youth development programs. Finally, we examine neighborhood and community strategies designed to increase their capacity to protect and support children and families.

CHILDREN IN NEIGHBORHOODS AND COMMUNITIES

As children develop, they need nurturing experiences beyond those available to them in their immediate families. They seek persons and environments that will challenge them to engage in more complex and sustained interactions; in the absence of these opportunities, the pace of their development will slow (Bronfenbrenner, 1995;

Bronfenbrenner & Morris, 1998). As the world of their experience opens to neighbors, peer groups, child care providers, teachers, mentors, and community members, children may engage in interactions that will build their resilience or that will expose them to further risks.

Unfortunately, in the current environment in which many children live, there is a "growing hecticness, instability and chaos in the principal settings in which human competence and character are shaped" (Bronfenbrenner & Morris, 1998, p. 995). The 24/7 nature of the workplace spills over into the family lives of children who are rushed from home to child care or who return to empty houses and spend hours in self-care (Heymann, 2000; Vandivere, Tout, Zaslow, Calkins, & Capizzano, 2003).

Much has been also written about the negative effects of poverty, violence, gangs, and urban hassles on the lives of children and youth and the risks and protective factors that they encounter in their communities (Duckworth, Hale, Clair, & Adams, 2000; DuRant, Cadenhead, Pendergrast, Slavens, & Linden, 1994; Egeland, Carlson, & Sroufe, 1993; Glodich, 1998; Van Soest & Bryant, 1995). For all children, but especially those with needs that have resulted in disability, developmental trajectories will be improved if sustained relationships with nurturing community members can be fostered, even in the midst of instability and chaos present in their society.

The Caring Community

Child care arrangements can profoundly affect outcomes for young children who have challenges by providing opportunities for social and emotional development and, in some cases, for intellectually challenging experiences that may be absent from the home environment (Knitzer, 2000; Shonkoff & Phillips, 2000; Yoshikawa, 1995). However, it is clear from a major longitudinal study of over 1,000 American children in child care that positive social, emotional, and cognitive outcomes are associated with high-quality care arrangements (Early Childcare Research Network, NICHD, in press). These children have been followed from their birth in 1991 to the present to examine care arrangements, parent-child interactions, and developmental outcomes. Even with maternal sensitivity and other family influences controlled, quality of care was a significant predictor of developmental outcomes in the first 7 years.

High-quality care that involves well-trained, stable care providers and safe and stimulating environments pays off in the form of young children who have higher levels of social competency and who are more ready to interact with peers and teachers in the school environment (Peisner-Feinberg & Burchanal, 1997).

Exposure to the enrichment of high-quality child care can also fulfill a key protective function for children who have been affected by disabilities, particularly those who have emotional or behavioral challenges. In a recent qualitative study of nine child care centers in the United States that successfully included children with emotional or behavioral disorders alongside their typically developing peers, parent interviews revealed that positive child outcomes including increased social skills and learning gains as well as reduced levels of stress in the family (Brennan, Bradley, Ama, & Cawood, 2003). These centers were characterized by experienced care providers, team approaches to problem solving, collaboration with other community agencies, and high levels of family support. They also all had access to knowledgeable mental health consultants who were well integrated into the centers' staffs.

Concerted efforts to support children with challenges in early childhood settings have paid off in communities that have invested in health and mental health consultation. Several recent studies of the effects of mental health consultation in child care environments have shown that consultation has been associated with increased staff self-efficacy and improved quality-of-care ratings in Northern California (Alkon, Ramler, & MacLennan, 2003); with retention of children in child care who otherwise would have been expelled in Cuyahoga County, Ohio (Albright, Brown, & Kelly, 2001); and with improvements in child social and emotional functioning and ability to engage in learning in San Francisco (Fong & Wu, 2002).

When children reach school age, a key concern becomes the way in which they spend their hours out of school. A surprisingly high proportion of children in the United States spend time alone or in the company of a sibling under 13 years of age—that is, in self-care. Vandivere et al.'s (2003) finding that 15% of children between the ages of 6 and 12 regularly spend time alone outside school hours is particularly troubling, because unsupervised afterschool hours may heighten the risk that children increase their use of tobacco and harmful drugs (Mott, Crowe, Richardson, & Flay, 1999; Mulhall, Stone, & Stone, 1996), lower social competence and school achievement (Pettit, Laird, Bates, & Dodge, 1997), and increase levels of externalizing behavior problems (Vandell & Posner, 1999). Particularly, self-care may act as a more serious risk factor for younger children and those from low-income families (Marshall et al., 1997; Vandivere et al., 2003).

Many working families cannot afford to have children spend their out-of-school hours in paid care and do not have family members available to provide the supervision and nurturing children need. To meet these needs for family support, safe and nurturing environments, and academic assistance, out-of-school care programs have been put into place through federal, state, and local efforts during the past decade in what the Afterschool Alliance has called the "great national awakening to the opportunity that afterschool offers" (Afterschool Alliance, 2004, p. 1). In fact, Capizzano and his co-workers found that 21% of all 6- to 9-year-olds with working mothers were in school-age care programs, and 10% of 10- to 12-year-olds were also enrolled in this community-based support (Capizzano, Tout, & Adams, 2000).

Some controlled systematic studies of the effectiveness of after-school programs have been conducted in the last 15 years. Four multi-site evaluations of major after-school programs have been summarized in a recent systematic review conducted by Kane (2004). Most of the study sites were in low-income communities and had a high proportion of children of color. The programs covered offered care at the end of the school day, usually 2 to 3 hours, for 4 or 5 days a week. They also provided academic supports, opportunities for sports and games, and training in social skills.

The evaluations found some support for higher grades in participants than in controls and consistent evidence that participants completed homework at greater rates than did controls and also had higher school attendance and less tardiness. Consistently, parents of children participating in the programs showed improved engagement in their children's schools. The proportion of time spent in self-care did not decrease but, rather, the after-school programs appeared to replace care by other adults in the community. The apparent lack of reduction in self-care may have been due to the types of measurements used or the reluctance of students to report that they were home alone (Kane, 2004).

In other extensive evaluations of out-of-school care programs, additional evidence was found for improved school attendance, higher achievement scores, perception of greater levels of safety at the program than in the home neighborhood, and fewer suspensions and expulsions for participants than for comparison children (Evaluation Services Center, 1999; Huang, Gribbons, Kim, Lee, & Baker, 2000; University of California at Irvine, 2001).

The positive child outcomes and family support available through out-of-school programs can also be available to children experiencing disabilities, although finding appropriate after-school environments may be challenging. A recent qualitative study of inclusive child care for children with emotional or behavioral challenges identifies organizational cultures and service provision structures that supported inclusion (Brennan, Bradley, & Siverson-Hall, 2003).

Mentoring as Intergenerational Community

One of the most consistent findings of studies of resilient children is that they have engaged in supportive long-term relationships with at least one caring adult in their community (Luthar & Zigler, 1991; Werner & Smith, 1982). Particularly for children whose families have not been able to provide them the support they need to navigate high-risk environments, the presence of a nonparental, caring adult can be crucial. Jean Rhodes (2002) defines mentorship as a "relationship in which the adult provides ongoing guidance, instruction, and encouragement aimed at developing the competence and character of the protégé" (p. 3).

Some children and youth connect with mentors naturally as they engage in family and community activities. Others are matched with mentors through formal programs designed to pair at-risk youth with stable, caring adults who volunteer their time. Finally, in an emerging model of mentoring, children identified as being particularly at risk are matched with paid mentors distinguished by their ability to build supportive connections.

Rhodes (1994, 2002) makes the case that youth may find their most effective mentors in their extended family, family friends, neighborhoods, faith groups, and educational settings or in organizations in which they participate. Natural mentors have been found to have positive effects on views that pregnant and parenting African American adolescents hold about their futures (Klaw & Rhodes, 1995), promoting optimism about their life chances and more favorable views about the opportunities and careers open to them. The presence of a natural mentor has also been linked to lower levels of high-risk behaviors such as carrying a weapon, having sex with multiple partners, illicit drug use, and heavy cigarette smoking (Beier, Rosenfeld, Spitalny, Zansky, & Bontempo, 2000).

Not every young person has access to mentors in the natural environment. It is especially difficult to establish strong bonds within communities that are low in social capital and for children at high risk (Rhodes, Bogat, Roffman, Edelman, & Galasso, 2002). Therefore, volunteer mentoring programs have been established in many communities. The most extensively studied of the many volunteer mentoring programs is Big Brothers/Big Sisters (BBBS), an organization that matches caring adult volunteers with youth from single-parent households. BBBS carefully screens adults and youth, orients and trains the volunteers, creates matches, and supervises the pairings using a case management approach. A carefully controlled study of 959 youth enrolled in BBBS revealed that those receiving mentoring were less likely to use drugs or alcohol, had higher evaluations of their own competence in school, had better attendance records and higher grades, and related better to parents and peers (Grossman & Tierney, 1998).

Perhaps the most convincing evidence of the protective effect of volunteer mentoring programs comes from an extensive meta-analysis conducted by DuBois, Holloway, Valentine, and Cooper (2002). The researchers investigated 55 studies of mentoring programs to determine the overall effect of these programs on youth and to examine the practices leading to the highest levels of success. Participation in mentoring had positive effects on all five types of youth outcomes in the studies: psychological and emotional development, problem or high-risk behaviors, social competence, academic indicators, and career or employment variables. The study also gave evidence that the greatest benefits of mentoring programs were reaped by youth affected by serious environmental risk factors, individual risk factors, or both.

Another innovative program serves at-risk youth in 11 American communities by providing paid mentors ("friends") for a long-term, intensive relationship. Friends of the Children pairs children from impoverished neighborhoods who are identified in 1st grade as having high individual risk factors, with extensively trained and supervised mentors who provide support through the 12th grade. Annual reports (Lucas, Furrer, Mackin, & Kobb, 2003) have documented high levels of social abilities in the children served, positive engagement in school, and improving levels of life skills.

YOUTH DEVELOPMENT THROUGH COMMUNITY-CENTERED APPROACHES

In communities where youth are seen as "resources to be developed rather than problems to be managed" (Roth & Brooks-Gunn, 2000, p. 4), community-based youth development approaches aim to foster thriving in youth and, consequently, prevent or curtail high-risk behaviors (Catalano, Berglund, Ryan, Lonczak, & Hawkins, 1999; Eccles & Gootman, 2002). In a study of factors that contributed to the success of youth development programs, Catalano and his co-workers found that 25 initiatives judged to be effective sought to strengthen the competency of youth in socioemotional, cognitive, and behavioral development and also improved the standards for social and personal behavior set by the family and community for the youth.

Since 1989, the Search Institute has been working on developing, testing, and disseminating an approach to youth development that focuses on key developmental assets—those "positive relationships, opportunities, competencies, values, and self-perceptions that youth need to succeed" (Scales & Leffert, 1999, p. 5). A total of 40 developmental assets have been identified by Peter Benson (1990) and his co-workers, which serve to both reduce high-risk behaviors and foster positive outcomes. This developmental framework includes both *external* assets (support, empowerment, constructive use of time, and setting of boundaries and expectations) and *internal* assets (commitment to learning, positive values, social competencies, and positive identity). This approach sought to increase developmental assets by strengthening individuals, families, and the community itself. In an extensive study of 99,462 youth in Grades 6 through 12, Leffert and his co-workers found an inverse relationship between the number of developmental assets the youth possessed and levels of alcohol use, depression, and violent behavior (Leffert et al., 1998). A more recent study has demonstrated that the relationship between possession of developmental assets and higher levels of positive behavior and lower levels of risk behavior holds across all racial, ethnic, and socioeconomic levels studied (Sesma & Roehlkepartain, 2003).

Lerner (2003) has called for a change in the social environments of the communities in which we are raising our young by developing long-term commitments to fostering developmental assets. Lerner's call is a real challenge, given that adults in the United States have been found to consider key developmental assets important for youth but report that they rarely engage in activities that provide assistance to unrelated youth in their own communities (Scales et al., 2001). To counteract this gap between cultural norms and actual practice, Benson (2003) has argued that we must move our communities closer to the ideal in which "developmental assets become a language of the common good, uniting sectors, citizens, and policy in the pursuit of shared goals for all children and adolescents" (p. 37). A current initiative called Healthy Communities-Healthy

Youth has linked communities in a supportive network dedicated to disseminating methods of strengthening developmental assets, focusing change on multiple sectors, and engaging youth in both leadership and implementation of asset building at the community level (Benson, 2003).

Neighborhood and Community Resources

As children develop, they live with their families in neighborhood settings that can either serve as ecologies that promote their successful development or add to their challenges. Considerable empirical evidence supports the view that neighborhood characteristics are related to children's experiences. Korbin and Coulton (1996) have conducted ethnographic studies in which neighborhood residents in areas with higher rates of child maltreatment and other adverse conditions perceived themselves as less able to control the behavior of children and youth in their areas. This lack of control was ascribed to the absence of a network of adults who would back each other up and who shared common goals.

The collective efficacy of neighborhoods, the extent to which neighbors share values and can count on each other to monitor children and youth and protect the social order, has also been shown to be related to levels of violence and victimization in urban settings, even controlling for social composition and past crime rates (Sampson, Raudenbush, & Earls, 1997). Children growing up in communities that have higher levels of social capital and generalized reciprocity (Breton, 2001), then, may have less exposure to maltreatment, be less frequently victimized, and have more opportunities for positive experiences.

As difficult economic times push more and more families and neighborhoods into stressful circumstances, how can the resilience of these sets of neighbors be strengthened? During the past decade, policymakers and researchers have been working on community- and neighborhood-level innovative approaches to enhance the life chances of children and youth. Connell and Gambone (1998) have proposed a community action framework addressing youth development and have identified two strategies that

can be carried out at the neighborhood level: (a) strengthen the capacity of community adults to support youth and (b) increase the quality and quantity of developmental opportunities for youth. Connell and Kubisch (2002) note that comprehensive community initiatives (CCIs) are attempting to revitalize communities by putting in place experiments that attempt to build the capacities of neighborhoods and communities to sustain social, economic, and physical improvements. These CCIs can be important forces for youth development, because adults become more able to support youth, and youth opportunities are opened up.

One notable urban experiment is the revitalization of Sheldon Park, a public housing community near downtown Pittsburgh, Pennsylvania (Feikema, Segalavich, & Jeffries, 1997). This neighborhood had high unemployment, a majority of households headed by single women, large numbers of young children, and isolation from other parts of the community. Using a seed grant, the local family service association worked with residents to establish Sheldon Park Pride, a multifaceted program designed to strengthen the neighborhood and establish ties with the local community. The initiative began with parenting supports and child screenings but grew to encompass leadership training, job training and development, community gardening, and literacy education. Evaluation revealed improved relationships among residents, higher levels of employment, reduced numbers of child abuse incidents, and child developmental gains.

An example of a community-based, universal intervention is described by Peters, Petrunka, and Arnold (2003). Located in Ontario, Canada, the Better Beginnings, Better Futures project provided three low-income communities with funds to develop a local prevention project designed to reduce emotional and behavioral problems and promote healthy development in children. A related goal was to strengthen the capacity of parents, families, and the neighborhood to address the needs of children. These goals were addressed through a participatory process that encouraged family agency and cross-agency partnerships. Although each of the three communities developed different approaches to improving their communities, many significant improvements were found across all sites, including lower rates of emotional and behavioral problems in children, better social functioning, and improved general health. Other areas of improvement included parents' health, housing conditions, and school-related variables. This ongoing project provides encouraging evidence that comprehensive, community programs that focus on strengthening families and supporting children can be successfully implemented and evaluated, and that they can be effective.

DISCUSSION

Our examination of family, neighborhood, and community circumstances related to the healthy development of children and youth suggests several implications for social programming and policy change.

First, parenting practices and their outcomes must be understood in the context of the family's culture, social and economic circumstances, and neighborhood/community in which they live, as well as in relation to the unique needs of the children involved. Because families are affected by myriad community and neighborhood influences, interventions designed to increase families' ability to protect their children from undesirable experiences and to promote competence must address that complexity. Specifically, evidence linking poverty to inadequate parenting practices is clear and strong; increasingly, we understand the mechanisms through which poverty influences parenting (e.g., parental stress, lack of time, depression, irritability, interparental and parent-child conflict). We have also noted the dilemmas associated with parents' seeking to protect their children through isolating them from people and events in the neighborhood.

Given this broadened understanding, it is clear that not only do social and clinical interventions need to consider the family's context, there is also a need for policy and programming that directly addresses the problems associated with poverty. As Seccombe (2002) suggests, "The ecosystemic perspective does not go far enough. It still places the primary responsibility upon individual versus structural-level conditions" (p. 389). Focusing on the United States,

Seccombe asserts that rather than studying how some children from impoverished circumstances manage to "beat the odds" (i.e., demonstrate resilience), we need national policy that changes the odds. She suggests an emphasis on policies that could strengthen the economic circumstances of families such as national health insurance, child support, a livable wage, and wage subsidies. Indeed, given clear evidence of links between children's experience of poverty and their mental health status (McLeod & Shanahan, 1996), as well as evidence that increasing family income alone can have a salutary effect on children's emotional and behavioral status (Costello, Compton, Keller, & Angold, 2003), we are tempted to suggest that all resources currently devoted to preventive and remedial interventions should be directly awarded to families with young children.

However, the evidence for the beneficial effects of family support and education is also strong, and we believe that families must be supported directly, as well as through neighborhood and community interventions. As Scales and Leffert (1999) have put it, "When we help families build their children's developmental infrastructure, we can help our most vulnerable young people rise above what may be a crumbling economic and physical infrastructure around them" (p. 220). Communities can support children in two ways: (a) directly, by supplying lively and healthy neighborhoods, quality care in the community, access to mentors who can guide them into adulthood, and enriching youth development programs and (b) indirectly, through supporting their families who provide the primary caregiving and basic sustenance that are part of their irreducible needs.

REFERENCES

Afterschool Alliance. (2004). *Afterschool Alliance backgrounder: Formal evaluations of afterschool programs.* Retrieved February 14, 2004, from www.afterschoolalliance.org/backgrounder.doc

Albright, L., Brown, S., & Kelly, D. (2001). Supporting young children with mental health needs. *Focal Point: A National Bulletin on Family Support and Children's Mental Health, 15*(1), 8–9.

Alkon, A., Ramler, M., & MacLennan, K. (2003). Evaluation of mental health consultation in childcare centers. *Early Childhood Education Journal, 31(2),* 91–100.

Baldwin, A. L., Baldwin, C., & Cole, R. E. (1990). Stress-resistant families and stress-resistant children. In J. Rolf, A. Masten, D. Cicchetti, K. Nuechterlein, & S. Weintraub (Eds.), *Risk and protective factors in the development of psychopathology* (pp. 257–280). Cambridge, UK: Cambridge University Press.

Beardslee, W. R., Versage, E. M., Van de Velde, P., Swatling, S., & Hoke, L. (2002). Preventing depression in children through resiliency promotion: The Preventive Intervention Project. In R. J. McMahon & R.D. Peters (Eds.), *The effects of parental dysfunction on children.* New York: Kluwer Academic/Plenum.

Beier, S. R., Rosenfeld, W. D., Spitalny, K. C., Zansky, S. M., & Bontempo, A. N. (2000). The potential role of an adult mentor in influencing high-risk behaviors in adolescents. *Archives of Pediatric and Adolescent Medicine, 154,* 327–331.

Benson, P. L. (1990). *The troubled journey: A portrait of 6th–12th grade youth.* Minneapolis, MN: Search Institute.

Benson, P. L. (2003). Developmental assets and asset-building community: Conceptual and empirical foundations. In R. M. Lerner & P. L. Benson (Eds.), *Developmental assets and asset-building communities* (pp. 19–46). New York: Kluwer Academic.

Bradley, R. H., Corwyn, R. F., McAdoo, H. P., & Garcia-Coll, C. (2001). The home environments of children in the United States: Part 1. Variations by ethnic and income group. *Child Development, 72(6),* 1844–1867.

Brave Heart (1999). Oyate Ptalyela: Rebuilding the Lakota nation through addressing historical trauma among Lakota parents. *Journal of Human Behavior in the Social Environment, 2(1–2),* 109–126.

Brazelton, T. B., & Greenspan, S. I. (2000). *The irreducible needs of children.* Cambridge, MA: Perseus.

Brennan, E. M., Bradley, J. R., Ama, S., & Cawood, N. (2003). *Setting the pace: Model inclusive childcare centers serving families of children with emotional or behavioral challenges* (Research monograph). Portland, OR: Portland State University, Research and Training Center on Family Support and Children's Mental Health.

Brennan, E. M., Bradley, J. R., & Siverson-Hall, B. (2003, October). *Including children with mental health challenges in before and after school care.* Paper presented at The Eighth National Conference on Advancing School-Based Mental Health, Portland, OR.

Breton, M. (2001). Neighborhood resiliency. *Journal of Community Practice, 9(1),* 21–36.

Brodsky, A. E. (1996). Resilient single mothers in risky neighborhoods: Negative psychological sense of community. *Journal of Community Psychology, 24(4),* 347–363.

Bronfenbrenner, U. (1986). Ecology of the family as a context for human development: Research perspectives. *Developmental Psychology, 22(6),* 723–741.

Bronfenbrenner, U. (1995). Developmental ecology through space and time: A future perspective. In P. Moen, G. H. Elder, Jr., & Luscher, K. (Eds.), *Examining lives in context: Perspectives on the ecology of human development* (pp. 619–647). Washington, DC: American Psychological Association.

Bronfenbrenner, U., & Morris, P. A. (1998). The ecology of developmental process. In R. M. Lerner (Ed.), *The handbook of child psychology: Vol. 1. Theoretical models of human development* (5th ed., pp. 993–1028). New York: Wiley.

Capizzano, J., Tout, K., & Adams, G. (2000). *Childcare patterns of school aged children with employed mothers.* Washington, DC: Urban Institute.

Catalano, R. F., Berglund, M. L., Ryan, J. A. M., Lonczak, H. S., & Hawkins, J. D. (1999). *Positive youth development in the United States: Research findings on evaluation of positive youth development programs.* Seattle: University of Washington, School of Social Work, Social Development Research Group.

Chung, M. J. (1993). Parent education for kindergarten mothers: Needs assessment and predictor variables. *Early Child Development & Care, 85,* 77–88.

Cohen, E., & Kaufmann, R. (2000). *Early childhood mental health consultation.* Washington, DC: Center for Mental Health Services of the Substance Abuse and Mental Health Services Administration and the Georgetown University Child Development Center.

Conger, R. D., & Conger, K. J. (2002). Resilience in midwestern families: Selected findings from the first decade of a prospective, longitudinal study. *Journal of Marriage and the Family, 64*(2), 361–373.

Connell, J. P., & Gambone, M. A. (1998). A community action framework for youth development: Rationale and early applications. In G. Walker, K. Pittman, & D. Watson (Eds.), *Directions for youth development.* Lawrence, KS: Conestoga Press.

Connell, J. P., & Kubisch, A. C. (2002). Community approaches to improving outcomes for urban children, youth, and families: Current trends and future directions. In A. Booth & A. C. Crouter (Eds.), *Does it take a village? Community effects on children, adolescents, and families* (pp. 177–202). Mahwah, NJ: Erlbaum.

Costello, E. J., Compton, S. N., Keller, G., & Angold, A. (2003). Relationships between poverty and psychopathology: A natural experiment. *Journal of the American Medical Association, 290*(15), 2023–2029.

Culp A. M., Culp R. E., Blankemeyer, M., & Passmark L. (1998). Parent education home visitation program: Adolescent and nonadolescent mother comparison after six months of intervention. *Infant Mental Health Journal, 19*(2), 111–123.

DuBois, D. L., Holloway, B. E., Valentine, J. C., & Cooper, H. (2002). Effectiveness of mentoring programs for youth: A meta-analytic review. *American Journal of Community Psychology, 30*(2), 157–197.

Duckworth, M. P., Hale, D. D. C., Clair. S., & Adams, S. E. (2000). Influence of interpersonal violence and community chaos on stress reactions in children. *Journal of Interpersonal Violence, 15*(8), 806–826.

DuRant, R. H., Cadenhead, C., Pendergrast, R. A., Slavens, G., & Linden, C. W. (1994). Factors associated with the use of violence among urban black adolescents. *American Journal of Public Health, 84*(4), 612.

Early Childcare Research Network, NICHD. (in press). The NICHD Study of Early Childcare: Contexts of development and developmental outcomes over the first seven years of life. In J. Brooks-Gunn & L. J. Berlin (Eds.), *Young children's education, health, and development: Profile and synthesis project report.* Washington, DC: Department of Education.

Eccles, J., & Gootman, J. A. (Eds.). (2002). *Community programs to promote youth development.* Committee on Community-Level Programs for Youth, Board on Children, Youth, and Families, Commission on Behavioral and Social Sciences and Education, National Research Council and Institute of Medicine. Washington, DC: National Academy Press.

Egeland, B., Carlson, E., & Sroufe, L. A. (1993). Resilience as process. *Development and Psychopathology, 5*(4), 517–528.

Evaluation Services Center. (1999). *1998–99 school-year program evaluation: Urban School Initiative School Age Childcare expansion.* Cincinnati, OH: University of Cincinnati, College of Education, Evaluation Services Center.

Farmer, T. W., & Farmer, E. M. Z. (2001). Developmental science, systems of care, and prevention of emotional and behavioral problems in youth. *American Journal of Orthopsychiatry, 71*(2), 171–181.

Feikema, R. J., Segalavich, J. H., & Jeffries, S. H. (1997). From child development to community development: One agency's journey. *Families in Society: The Journal of Contemporary Human Services, 78*(2), 185–195.

Fong, A., & Wu, R. (2002, July). *The San Francisco High Quality Childcare Mental Health Initiative and the Fu Yau project.* Paper presented at the Training Institutes on Developing Local Systems of Care for Children and Adolescents with Emotional Disturbances and Their Families, Washington, DC.

Glodich, A. (1998). Traumatic exposure to violence: A comprehensive review of the child and adolescent literature. *Smith College Studies in Social Work, 68*(3), 321–345.

Goldstein, H. M. (1997). *Santa Monica Infant and Family Support Project: Focusing on children's earliest years of development.* Unpublished doctoral dissertation, University of California at Los Angeles.

Grossman, J. B., & Tierney, J. P. (1998). Does mentoring work? An impact study of the Big Brothers Big Sisters program. *Evaluation Review, 22*(3), 403–426.

Hann, D. A., & Borek, N. (Eds.). (2001). *Taking stock of risk factors for child/youth externalizing behavior problems.* Bethesda, MD: National Institute of Mental Health.

Heymann, J. (2000). *The widening gap: Why America's working families are in jeopardy and what can be done about it.* New York: Basic Books.

Holtzman, W. H. (1992). Community renewal, family preservation, and child development through the school of the future. In W. H. Holtzman (Ed.), *School of the future* (pp. 3–18). Washington, DC: American Psychological Association and Hogg Foundation for Mental Health.

Huang, D., Gribbons, B., Kim, K. S., Lee, C., & Barker, E. L. (2000). *A decade of results: The impact of the LA's BEST after school enrichment program on subsequent student achievement and performance.* Los Angeles: University of California, Graduate School of Education and Information Studies, Center for the Study of Evaluation.

Kane, T. J. (2004). *The impact of after-school programs: Interpreting the results of four recent evaluations* (Working paper of the W. T. Grant Foundation). Los Angeles: University of California.

Kazdin, A. E. (1997). Parent management training: Evidence, outcome and issues. *Journal of American Academic Child and Adolescent Psychiatry, 36*(10), 1349–1356.

Klaw, E. L., & Rhodes, J. E. (1995). Mentor relationships and the career development of pregnant and parenting African-American teenagers. *Psychology of Women Quarterly, 19*(4), 551–562.

Knitzer, J. (2000). *Using mental health strategies to move the early childhood agenda and promote school readiness.* New York: Carnegie Corporation and the National Center for Children in Poverty.

Kolobe, T. H. A. (2004). Childrearing practices and developmental expectations for Mexican-American mothers and the developmental status of their infants. *Physical Therapy, 84*(5), 439–453.

Korbin, J., & Coulton, C. (1996). The role of neighbors and the government in neighborhood-based child protection. *Journal of Social Issues, 52*(3), 163–176.

Kotchick, B. A., & Forehand, R. (2002). Putting parenting in perspective: A discussion of the contextual factors that shape parenting practices. *Journal of Child and Family Studies, 11*(3), 255–269.

Leffert, N., Benson, P. L., Scales, P. C., Sharma, A. R., Drake, D. R., & Blyth, D. A. (1998). Developmental assets: Measurement and prediction of risk behaviors among adolescents. *Applied Developmental Science, 2*(4), 209–230.

Lerner, R. M. (2003). Developmental assets and asset-building communities: A view of the issues. In R. M. Lerner & P. L. Benson (Eds.), *Developmental assets and asset-building communities* (pp. 3–18). New York: Kluwer Academic.

Lin, C.- Y. C., & Fu, V. R. (1990). A comparison of child-rearing practices among Chinese, immigrant Chinese, and Caucasian-American parents. *Child Development, 61*(2), 429–433.

Lucas, L. M., Furrer, C., Mackin, J. R., & Kobb, J. A. (2003). *Friends of the Children—Portland: Annual evaluation report, September 2002—August 2003.* Portland, OR: NPC Research.

Luthar, S. S., & Zigler, E. (1991). Vulnerability and competence: A review of research on resilience in childhood. *American Journal of Orthopsychiatry, 61*(1), 6–22.

Marshall, N. L., Coll, C. G., Marx, F., McCartney, K., Keefe, N., & Ruh, J. (1997). After-school time and children's behavioral adjustment. *Merrill-Palmer Quarterly 43*(3), 497–514.

Martinez, J. C. (2003). Promoting the resiliency of child and families amidst chaos and uncertainty. *Journal of Developmental & Behavioral Pediatrics, 23*(6), 436–437.

Masten, A. S. (2001). Ordinary magic: Resilience processes in development. *American Psychologist, 56*(3), 227–238.

Masten, A. S., & Coatsworth, J. D. (1998). The development of competence in favorable and unfavorable environments. *American Psychologist, 53*(2), 205–220.

McLeod, J. D., & Shanahan, M. J. (1996). Trajectories of poverty and children's mental health. *Journal of Health and Social Behavior, 37*(3), 207–220.

Miller, D. B. (1997). Parenting against the odds: African-America parents in the child welfare system–A group approach. *Social Work with Groups, 20*(1), 5–17.

Minkovitz, C. S., Hughart, N., Strobino, D. Scharfstein, D., Grason, H., Hou, W., Miller, T., et al. (2003). A practice-based intervention to enhance quality of care in the first 3 years of life. *Journal of the American Medical Association, 290*(23), 3081–91.

Mott, J. A., Crowe, P. A., Richardson, J., & Flay, B. (1999). After-school supervision and adolescent cigarette smoking: Contributions of the setting and intensity of after-school self-care. *Journal of Behavioral Medicine, 22*(1), 35–58.

Mulhall, P. F., Stone, D., & Stone, B. (1996). Home alone: Is it a risk factor for middle school youth and drug use? *Journal of Drug Education, 26*(1), 39–48.

Oyserman, D., Mowbray, C. T., Meares, P. A., & Firminger, K. B. (2000). Parenting among mothers with a serious mental illness. *American Journal of Orthopsychiatry, 70*(3), 296–315.

Peisner-Feinberg, E. S., & Bruchinal, M. R. (1997). Relationships between preschool children's child-care experiences and concurrent development: The cost-quality, and outcome study. *Merrill-Palmer Quarterly 43*(3), 451–477.

Peters, R. D. V., Petrunka, K., & Arnold, R. (2003). The Better Beginnings, Better Futures Project: A universal, comprehensive, community-based prevention approach for primary school children and their families. *Journal of Clinical Child and Adolescent Psychology, 32*(2), 215–227.

Pettit, G. S., Laird, R. D., Bates, J. E., & Dodge, K. A. (1997). Patterns of after-school care in middle childhood: Risk factors and developmental outcomes. *Merrill-Palmer Quarterly, 43*(3), 515–538.

Rhodes, J. E. (1994). Older and wiser: Mentoring relationships in childhood and adolescence. *Journal of Primary Prevention, 14*(3), 187–196.

Rhodes, J. E. (2002). *Stand by me: The risks and rewards of mentoring today's youth.* Cambridge, MA: Harvard University Press.

Rhodes, J. E., Bogat, G. A., Roffman, J., Edelman, P., & Galasso, L. (2002). Youth mentoring in perspective: Introduction to the special issue. *American Journal of Community Psychology, 30*(2), 149–155.

Roth, J., & Brooks-Gunn, J. (2000). What do adolescents need for healthy development? Implications for youth policy. *Social Policy Report, 14*(1), 3–17.

Rutter, M. (1987). Psychosocial resilience and protective mechanisms. *American Journal of Orthopsychiatry, 57*(3), 316–331.

Sampson, R. J. (2002). How do communities undergird or undermine human development? What are the relevant contexts and what mechanisms are at work? In A. Booth & A. C. Crouter (Eds.), *Does it take a village? Community effects on children, adolescents, and families* (pp. 3–30). Mahwah, NJ: Erlbaum.

Sampson, R. J., Raudenbush, S. W., & Earls, F. (1997). Neighborhoods and violent crime: A multilevel study of collective efficacy. *Science, 277,* 918–924.

Scales, P. C., Benson, P. L., Roehlkepartain, E. C., Hintz, N. R., Sullivan, T. K., & Mannes, M. (2001). The role of neighborhood and community in building developmental assets for children and youth: A national study of social norms among American adults. *Journal of Community Psychology, 29*(6), 703–727.

Scales, P. C., & Leffert, N. (1999). *Developmental assets: A synthesis of the scientific research on adolescent development.* Minneapolis, MN: Search Institute.

Seccombe, K. (2002). Beating the odds vs. "changing the odds": Poverty, resilience, and family policy. *Journal of Marriage and the Family, 64*(2), 384–394.

Seigel, L. (1994). Cultural differences and their impact on practice in child welfare. *Journal of Multicultural Social Work, 3*(3), 87–96.

Sesma, A., Jr., & Roehlkepartain, E. C. (2003). Unique strengths, shared strengths: Developmental assets among youth of color. *Search Institute Insights & Evidence, 1*(2), 1–13.

Shimoni, R., Este, D. C., & Clark, D. E. (2003). Paternal engagement in immigrant and refugee families *Journal of Comparative Family Studies, 34*(4), 555–568.

Shonkoff, J. P., & Phillips, D. A. (Eds.). (2000). *From neurons to neighborhoods: The science of early childhood development.* Washington, DC: National Academy Press.

Stoiber, K. C., & Houghton, T. G. (1993). The relationship of adolescent mothers' expectations, knowledge, and beliefs to their young children's coping behavior. *Infant Mental Health Journal, 14*(1), 61–79.

Stoolmiller, M. (2001). Synergistic interaction of child manageability problems and parent-discipline tactics in predicting future growth in externalizing behavior for boys. *Developmental Psychology, 37*(6), 814–825.

Tebes, J. K., Kaufman, J., Adnopoz, J., & Racusin, G. (2001). Resilience and family psychosocial processes among children of parents with serious mental disorders. *Journal of Child and Family Studies, 10*(1), 115–136.

Tineo, W. (2002). *Impact of age-paced parenting newsletters on urban families with at-risk children.* Unpublished doctoral dissertation. Fordham University, New York.

University of California at Irvine, Department of Education. (2001). *Evaluation of California's After School Learning and Safe Neighborhoods Partnerships program: 1999–2000 preliminary report.* Irvine, CA: Author.

Vandell, D. L., & Posner, J. K. (1999). Conceptualization and measurement of children's after-school environments. In S. L. Friedman & T. D. Wachs (Eds.), *Assessment of the environment across the lifespan* (pp. 167–197). Washington, DC: American Psychological Association.

Vandivere, S., Tout, K., Zaslow, M., Calkins, J., & Capizzano, J. (2003). *Unsupervised time: Family and child factors associated with self-care* (Occasional paper No. 71). Washington, DC: Urban Institute.

Van Soest, D., & Bryant. S. (1995). Violence reconceptualized for social work: The urban dilemma. *Social Work, 40*(4), 549–557.

Wagner, M. M., & Clayton, S. L. (1999). The Parents as Teachers Program: Results from two demonstrations. *The Future of Children, 9*(1), 91–115.

Webster-Stratton, C. (1997). From parent training to community building. *Families in Society: The Journal of Contemporary Human Services, 78*(2), 156–171.

Werner, E. E., & Smith, S. (1982). *Vulnerable but invincible: A study of resilient children.* New York: McGraw-Hill.

Yoshikawa, H. (1995). Long-term effects of early childhood programs on social outcomes and delinquency. *The Future of Children, 5*(3), 51–57.

Yoshikawa, H., & Knitzer, J. (1997). *Lessons from the field: Head Start mental health strategies to meet changing needs.* New York: Columbia University, National Center for Children in Poverty.

19

PROFESSIONAL DISCOURSE AMONG SOCIAL WORKERS WORKING WITH AT-RISK ADOLESCENTS IN HONG KONG

Risk or Resilience?

KWAI-YAU WONG

TAK-YAN LEE

Hong Kong has made tremendous efforts in tackling problems with youth after riots in 1967 in which many young people were involved. The riots awakened policymakers to the hidden destructive power of young people and the social instability they can cause. The first comprehensive social welfare policy paper after the 1967 riots stated clearly that one function of a major service innovation for youth, the Youth Service Centre, was to offer legitimate release for young people's energy by channeling that energy into socially constructive activities (Social Welfare Department, 1973). At about the same time, a large-scale study by Ng (1975) found multiple factors leading to juvenile delinquency and recommended that new services be provided for young people as preventive measures. Following these recommendations, some nongovernmental organizations (NGOs) began to initiate services for both young people and their families. The government adopted most of Ng's recommendations and provided funding for Family Life Education Services, Outreaching Social Work Services, and School Social Work Services to tackle the alarming rates of problem youth. These efforts were meant to better address the needs of at-risk youth who until that time had been underserviced (Social Welfare Department, 1977).

This chapter provides a brief description of youth at risk in Hong Kong with a focus on changes that have occurred since 1967 and in particular, during the 1990s. It reports on a significant innovation in service delivery to address the problems youth face. That innovation, named the Understanding the Adolescent Project (UAP), involved the adoption of a screening mechanism in the school system for early identification of the most vulnerable youth, leading to intervention to meet their needs. The UAP was adapted from a similar program used with Canadian youth. Although reporting on this large-scale intervention program, this chapter first reviews the literature that supports the theoretical backbone for the UAP and identifies the inadequacies inherent in its theoretical framework—specifically, the lack of a cultural dimension. As a result of a critical review of the literature, both Western and Chinese, this chapter provides a cultural lens through which to reexamine the UAP, drawing on both the official evaluation report and front-line workers' experiences of the program. This reexamination will employ the concepts of resilience and protective factors to develop a more culturally appropriate foundation on which to base this kind of intervention strategy. In the process, we hope to articulate an alternative professional discourse for those who provide services to at-risk youth in Hong Kong, one that is focused on prevention and health from a Chinese perspective.

A BRIEF DESCRIPTION OF ADOLESCENTS AT RISK IN HONG KONG AND THE GOVERNMENT RESPONSE IN THE 1990s

Today, NGOs still provide these and other new services for youth in Hong Kong (e.g., Integrated Children and Youth Services Centres, Youth Night-drifters Service, etc.). However, these efforts have not been enough to stop the increase in problems involving adolescents over the past 10 years. A brief description of the situation is provided below.

Juvenile Delinquency

In 2000, the number of arrested young people under 16 was 6,229, representing a 13.5% rise in 1 year. Specifically, of that number, 1,873 young people under 21 were arrested for committing drug-related crimes

(Hong Kong Police Force, 2001). It was an alarming increase of 77.5% over the figure for 1999. According to the statistics released from the Narcotics Division of the Security Bureau, the year 2000 witnessed a continuing upward trend in the number of young drug abusers as well. A total of 4,000 drug abusers under the age of 21 were reported in 2000, compared with 2,481 in 1999, representing a 61% increase. Increases were also observed in cases of psychotropic substance abuse. Reported abusers of "ecstasy" rose from 343 in 1999 to 2,313 in 2000, and abusers of ketamine rose from 23 to 1,586 in the same period (Action Committee Against Narcotics, 2001).

Mental Health

Simultaneously, the mental health of young people also aroused public concern over the past decade. The prevalence of psychological and psychiatric problems among adolescents in Hong Kong was as high as 14% to 24% during the 1990s (Shek, 1996). The figures reflect only partly the extent of the seriousness of the problem. A telephone survey found that 43.6% of youth respondents claimed that they experienced significant stress in the past 3 months (Hong Kong Federation of Youth Groups, 1993). These results were also consistent with the findings of a study conducted by Ho (1995) for a major statutory consultation body, the Commission on Youth. In Ho's review of research on mental health among youth, he highlights Cheung and Lam's (1992) findings that the level of depression among Hong Kong students from Grades 5 to 8 was positively correlated with the number of stressful life events students experienced.

Suicide

Likewise, although adolescent suicide rates of the youth population from the 10- to 24-year-old age group in Hong Kong were relatively stable between 1980 and 2000, there was a gradual rising trend in adolescent suicide rates during the 1990s (mean = 5.96 per 100,000 for 1990–2000), which overall were higher than rates during the 1980s (mean = 4.4 for

1980–1989). There was also a gradual rising trend in adolescent proportional mortality rates for suicide throughout the 1990s (from 13.52% in 1990 to 28.28% in 2000) (Shek & Tang, 2003). The continuous rising numbers of suicide death within the youth population has caused public alarm in recent years. A study of 563 secondary school students aged 11 to 20 regarding their values and self-destructive behaviors found that 36.4% of the respondents reported suicidal ideations and 7.7% had actually attempted to harm themselves (Breakthrough, 1993). Of 168 (21.4%) known suicide cases in Hong Kong in 1998, 36 were those of youth under 19 (Coroner's Court, 1999). In another study, the prevalence rates of suicidal ideation and behavior among high school students in 2001 raised concerns that the problem was potentially widespread; 17.8% of students reported they had considered suicide, 5.4% had planned a suicide attempt, 8.4% had attempt suicide once or more, and 1.2% had required medical care as a result of an attempt (Hong Kong Jockey Club Centre for Suicide Research and Prevention, 2003).

From Reactive to Proactive: The Origin of a Large-Scale Resilience Promotion Program in Hong Kong

Although the social agenda in the 1970s and 1980s focused more on antisocial and delinquent young people, the social agenda for the 1990s shifted the focus to the risk factors in young people's lives and those who are most vulnerable. Clearly, there has been a shift to a strong preventive stance. Parallel to this development, there has been a growing interest among helping professionals and policymakers to tap the practical relevance of the concept of resilience for the development of social and educational interventions for vulnerable groups of young people.

In the early 1990s, with the return of Hong Kong's sovereignty to China in 1997 looming, the Hong Kong government expected a large number of young immigrants to come to the island from mainland China. Public attention to the needs of youth at risk was greatly increased during this time after a chain of alarming events, including the rising rates of suicide as noted above, murder, mental health problems, crime,

and delinquency, all of which became more prevalent during the lead up to the 1997 transition. For example, the incident of a teenage gang burning the corpse of a young victim not only attracted wide media coverage but also reinforced the call for extra efforts to provide services for adolescents at risk. In response to these public cries, the government set up a working group to overview and plan services.

In particular, a screening tool for early detection of adolescents with developmental needs who showed symptoms of being "potentially at risk" was developed in 1994 to 1996. This idea was imported from Canada, which had already experimented with the introduction of a screening mechanism in the school system for early identification of at-risk youth (Breakthrough Limited & The Centre for Clinical Trials and Epidemiological Research, 1998). Using a similar screening tool, it was estimated that between 14.6% and 18.7% (Breakthrough, 1997) of early adolescents in Hong Kong faced a variety of at-risk situations. In response, the UAP, a massive preventive program, was developed through the joint efforts of the Social Welfare Department, Breakthrough Limited (a Christian NGO specializing in youth services), the Chinese University, and four other Hong Kong NGOs. Interventions were planned and launched by phases to reach all Grade 7 students in Hong Kong.

The program demonstrates the great increase in interest to shift the attention of social welfare organizations from reactive to proactive measures. The theoretical framework and content behind such preventive interventions will be discussed next in parallel with an examination of the literature on adolescent resilience. Initiatives such as the UAP show clearly the incorporation of concepts associated with helping at-risk populations of youth achieve resilience and the changing professional discourse that now concentrates more efforts on promoting health rather than simply treating disease and disorder among young people.

THE CONCEPT OF RESILIENCE

Definitions of the concept of resilience vary among different authors. Masten, Best, and

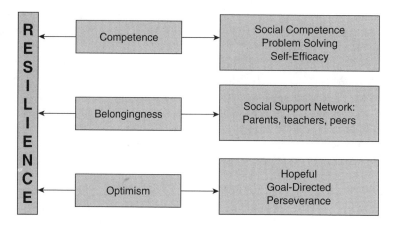

Figure 19.1   The Conceptual Grounding for the Understanding the Adolescent Project

Garmezy (1990) define resilience as a "process of, or capacity for, or the outcome of successful adaptation despite challenging and threatening circumstances" (p. 426). Werner and Smith (1982) consider resilience as the capacity to moderate internal (physiological) vulnerabilities (e.g., stress) as well as external stressors (e.g., family discord). Of particular relevance to the present discussion, research on risk and resilience (Clark, 1995; Connell, Spencer, & Alber, 1994; Grossman, Beinashowitz, & Anderson, 1992; Guetzloe, 1994; Rak & Patterson, 1996; Sagor, 1996; Weinreb, 1997; Worrell, 1996) identifies a number of preventive measures for avoiding negative outcomes in children and youth. Weinreb's findings (1997) show that resilience can shore up protective mechanisms in young children. Sagor (1996) emphasizes that resilience can be thought of as an antibody that enables young people to ward off attackers that might stop healthy development even among the most formidable of youth. Given many different dimensions to the concept of resilience, it is no surprise that Gordon and Song (1994) find it difficult to define resilience altogether. They speculate that it may not be a single construct but a complex of related processes that need to be separately identified and studied as discreet aspects of health. Thus, resilience, as it relates to youth, might best be understood as the combined preventive-promotive orientation of primary prevention efforts that have the potential to stop risk factors from affecting the behaviors of young people who are at risk.

Sharing similarities with findings from studies of resilience, three common elements were identified and adopted as the backbone for constructing the UAP—namely, competence (C), belongingness (B), and optimism (O), which together constitute the conceptual grounding for the design of interventions in the UAP. Figure 19.1 illustrates this conceptual grounding.

Personal Competence

Emphasis in the UAP is placed on the ability shown by youth to overcome problems and adversities within their family and school settings. To develop personal competence, four components are included—(a) self-acceptance skills, (b) problem-solving and stress-coping skills, (c) self-assertiveness skills, and (d) interpersonal skills.

Sense of Belonging

Research shows that students' successful development and transformative power rests on experiencing deeper levels of caring and supportive relationships (Lau, 2003). A sense of belonging can be developed within a network of protective factors, including when the conditions of empowerment are present. These factors involve interaction between young people and their families, schools, peer groups, and communities. Protective factors include caring and support, positive and high expectations, and opportunities for meaningful participation. The

UAP mobilizes the involvement of teachers and parents to provide this kind of caring and supportive environment.

Sense of Optimism

McMillan and Reed (1994) indicate that resilient students are optimistic about their future. Rutter (1987) also points out that optimism can protect people against psychological risks. An optimist is able to bounce back from personal defeat and knows how to talk to himself or herself while suffering that defeat (Seligman, 1995). The UAP aims to teach students a set of skills to enable them to speak to themselves about their setbacks in a way that is encouraging. This self-talk includes (a) being objective about the adversity one faces, (b) having positive beliefs that challenge negative interpretations of adversity, (c) recording all consequent positive feelings and actions concerning adversity, (d) setting a goal or plan to practice living in ways that demonstrate positive feelings and actions, and (e) providing recognition and rewards for strengthening youth's feelings of accomplishment and success.

UNDERSTANDING ADOLESCENT PROJECT (UAP): A SCHOOL-BASED PREVENTIVE PROGRAM TO PROMOTE ADOLESCENT RESILIENCE

The first phase of the UAP, completed in 1996, was to develop a valid and reliable screening tool for early identification of at-risk youth. The instrument (Hoh & Oborne, 1996; Oborne, 1994) was made up of the Hong Kong Student Information Form-Student Edition (HKSIF-S) and the Hong Kong Student Information Form-Teacher Edition (HKSIF-T). The instrument was tested and identified 29.8% of students as in need of early intervention (e.g., developmental and counseling services). The intervention phase of the project began in 1996 as an experiment and lasted 3 years. Each year, Grade 7 students whose scores on the HKSIF-S indicated they were in need of intervention were offered through the UAP a series of life-training activities to promote their resilience by fostering

the three core qualities discussed earlier: competence, belongingness, and optimism (CBO) (Lau, 2003). Workshops for parents and teachers were also organized to enhance the supportive network available to youth from both systems.

The experimental phase was succeeded by another round of experiments after refining the intervention activities that proved most useful during the first trials. This second phase of research began in 1999. Evaluation of this second phase was completed in 2001. In light of evidence of positive changes among the participants, the Social Welfare Department decided to fund the full-scale implementation of the UAP. It was suggested that it cover all secondary schools by the 2003–2004 school year (Lau, 2003).

Internal Assets

The UAP helps students accumulate their personal knowledge of how to sustain themselves as healthy people and firsthand experience putting this knowledge into practice through successive group experiential learning opportunities. The program is designed to build students' capacities associated with resilience within a network of protective factors that also create the conditions of empowerment. The program is intended to assist students in transforming their knowledge and experience into daily practices in their respective homes and schools.

The activities for students are grouped into a series of activity sets with specific objectives designated for each set. Of the eight activity sets, three involve parents and two involve teachers and school principals. Training activities are designed to strengthen students' personal competencies. Through experiential learning, skill training, self-reflection exercises, and a service-learning approach in which students are expected to make a contribution to their community, students' problem-solving skills, self-assertion skills, communication skills, and interpersonal skills are enhanced.

Feelings of competence stem from successful experiences related to solving problems (Reasoner & Dusa, 1991). Considering the social context in which Grade 7 students live, however, in particular the difficulty they experience dealing with stress associated with pressure from parents, teachers, peers, or themselves to behave in certain ways, it is not surprising that many do not feel they handle problems adequately. This growing group of students experiences stress negatively and reacts by taking drugs, withdrawing or denying their problems, avoiding contact with those who might help them, giving up, cutting class, or dropping out of school. Problem-solving skills that build a young person's capacity to deal effectively with these pressures can help him or her deal better with stressful situations through more socially acceptable behavior. The skills taught through the UAP intervention include effective communication with peers and adults, techniques for creating win-win situations, and the early identification of the elements of a stressful situation that can be most effectively addressed. Adolescents handle stress best when they feel supported and positive about themselves.

External Assets

In addition to personal competence training, the UAP encourages students to make a contribution to their communities. A sense of usefulness comes from actions of contribution. Sagor (1996) indicates that adolescents' sense of belonging can be built by showing them that they are valued members of a community. Adolescents participating in the UAP take actions in a safe and structured environment. They are also educated to use community resources to support their needs and development. Therefore, parents and teachers are also invited to participate in tailor-made workshops to learn the same set of skills being taught to their children that relate to resilience.

UAP workshops for parents and teachers promote simultaneous changes in significant others to help potentially at-risk adolescents change in positive ways. Such workshops assist participants to understand and master the concept and significance of resilience as well as the activities of the project so as to obtain their support and cooperation. Through workshops, parents are helped to build up their acceptance of their children and enhance parent-child communication skills. Teachers are helped to reinforce their skills in communicating with students and to enhance their acceptance of and support for

students. Other specially designed programs—for example, community service activities and parent-child camps—also improve the immediate social and family environment, thus creating the external conditions for children to realize the potential of internal resources.

Review of the Outcomes of the UAP: What Did We Learn?

An evaluation component built in to the UAP to examine its effectiveness has been part of the program since it started in 1996. According to Lau (2003), the project was well accepted by the students, parents, and teachers to whom it was offered. The involved parties found the project effective in promoting different aspects of students' resilience. In addition, positive changes in the relevant external systems, the school, and the family in particular, were identified. Also, students had some positive behavior changes in their anger management, conflicts resolution, communication with teachers, and social relationships. In terms of their overall experiences with the UAP, most students said that participation in the program had helped to boost their confidence in solving problems. They became more aware of the importance of teamwork and the need to provide mutual support and care to their friends. In particular, students were most impressed with the training camp and social service aspects of the program. Through participation in the activities of the camp, students reportedly recognized the importance of commitment to achieving the objectives of the activities. Many also said that they enjoyed the social service sessions, which included activities such as visiting the elderly. Youth found this activity provided them with an opportunity to help others while at the same time improving their social skills. However, although students highly valued the sense of satisfaction gained through participation in community services, the project overall did not help the students improve their family relationships and their sense of belonging to family and school—the protective factors for their growth and development.

There remain questions as to the effectiveness of the project. First, how much did the students get from the program in terms of anger management, conflict resolution, communication with teachers, and social relationship skills in less than 20 group sessions over 3 to 4 months? Did they internalize elements of the program meant to build their capacity for resilience? Second, was there an impact on the students' value or belief system, which is essential to any resilience-promoting program? Wolin and Wolin (1996) emphasize the importance of a change from a "risk mind-set" to a "challenge mind-set" in any resilience training. We speculate that a lack of change in the youth's value and belief systems may not be the fault in the UAP design. Instead, frontline social workers delivering the program may not have clearly understood the concept of resilience and may not have been skillful enough to work toward changes in students' mind-sets.

Third, how confident and competent are social workers in responding to the needs of the adolescents who report problems with their peers and their families? A lack of sufficiently skilled training may have resulted in some clients being harmed emotionally even though many had benefited greatly. How can we interpret the diversity of experiences in the client group? Clearly, such results call into question the preparedness of the social workers participating in such a large-scale project and the fidelity of program implementation.

Finally, we wonder about the low involvement and lack of impact on the teachers and the parents in the program. It is unreasonable to believe that the UAP induced dramatic changes in their perceptions and attitudes toward the adolescents in their care after only a few training sessions. Given these four drawbacks, we offer the UAP as a potentially helpful intervention but one that will require greater resources and further study to make it more effective. The launch of the UAP in Hong Kong did, however, show the commitment of the government to meet the needs of adolescents. The orientation to youth services has been changed from a focus on remediation (the medical model) to a focus on prevention (a challenge model). Despite the drawbacks noted above, the UAP is recognized for its contributions to the positive changes in skill and knowledge levels of the adolescent participants (Lau, 2003).

RETHINKING ADOLESCENT RESILIENCE: WHAT ROLE DOES CULTURE PLAY?

Although the above program may resemble others on which it was based, in particular those from Canada, there are considerations unique to Hong Kong that needed to be taken into account in its implementation. This need for adaptation raised a number of issues with regard to the generalizability of research on resilience across cultures. Specifically, there are four problems with the research on adolescent resilience and related conceptualizations of healthy functioning among at-risk populations when researchers and program designers think cross-culturally. First, because the corpus of research findings on resilience is derived from Western contexts, researching resilience and designing programs based on that research in the local context of a non-Western country should focus on the cultural dimensions of resilience as a major contextual variable. Consideration should be given to cultural values and family belief systems that influence a person's worldview and how that person makes sense of his or her experience. For instance, the Confucian code of conduct still influential in Hong Kong proscribes expression of negative affects and obliges people to fulfill their duty to their family. In the literature on adolescent resilience, there are no studies of which we are aware that situate all resilience processes or factors in the context of such specific cultural values and family beliefs, least of all the Chinese cultural context.

Second, the issues being examined by resilience researchers are not based on a clear conceptual framework. Moreover, there is a preoccupation with poverty as a risk factor. However, ecological models of human development suggest that we need to study issues pertaining to the personal, family, peer group, school, community, and cultural contexts as much or more than the simple economic status of the family. Furthermore, there is a developmental dimension in the study of resilience. We need to understand how resilience is developed in childhood and whether childhood resilience carries over into adolescence, especially in non-Western countries. Therefore, we argue that what Chinese parents regard as important to the well-being of

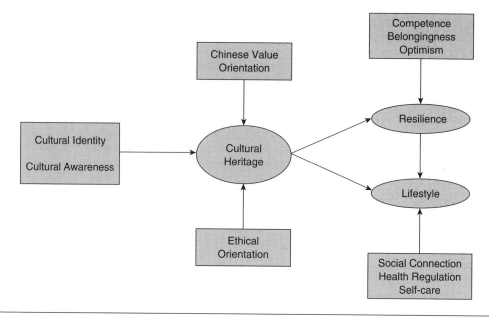

Figure 19.2 Choi's Cultural Heritage Model

their adolescent children should be included in the study of adolescent resilience. In a local study of Hong Kong families, Shek and Chan (1999) report that Chinese parents of adolescent children were mostly concerned about three things: academic achievement, the quality of family relationships (such as obedience), and proper behavior by young people, all factors with a uniquely Chinese flavor to their interpretation.

Third, cultural variations in childhood socialization are a significant factor in the development of adolescent resilience. In this regard, resilience research in a Chinese context should examine both behavioral and affective control; both play an important role in the success of children's interpersonal relationships and subsequent identity formation. Because both aspects of this control are an important part of how Chinese parents prepare their children for the future, it is likely that in this and other dimensions, Chinese families will differ from their counterparts in the West. We must, however, exercise caution that we do not overlook within-culture differences that may in fact be larger than cross-cultural differences (Chan, Cheung, Lee, Leung, & Liu, 1998a, 1998b).

We are not alone in advocating a cultural lens for the study of resilience. Choi (2003) who had been the driving force behind the UAP before

his retirement, proposed a model of cultural heritage as the basis for understanding adolescent resilience. In his model, the development of resilience is a result of cultural heritage that embraces Chinese values and ethics.

Choi's (2003) cultural heritage model (Figure 19.2) corroborates with our view that there is a cultural dimension to resilience. There are three reasons for this. First, resilience has been a virtue in the traditional Chinese culture, as evident in the dialectics that documented Confucian teaching. Second, Chinese parents these days still hold on to traditional values and beliefs, even though globalization has brought about substantial changes, which at least on the surface, appear to be changing their culture (Jose, Huntsinger, Huntsinger, & Liaw, 2000; Lee, 1999, 2002). In this connection, Chinese parents and adolescents may differ in their views on family functioning (Shek & Lai, 2000); the generational shift in values will be even more marked because the present generation of young people was raised in an era of affluence and smaller families. Third, Choi (2003) showed that cultural beliefs and folk notions supply a person with cognitive resources for coping with adversity.

Finally, as Ungar (2002, 2004) has argued, professionals should understand at-risk teenagers from a holistic point of view. The Child and Youth Resilience Measure (CYRM) currently under construction as part of an international research project (see Chapter 13), includes multiple dimensions—individual, interpersonal, community, and culture. This approach and others like it discussed throughout this volume have begun to address the shortcomings that thus far plague cross-cultural understandings of resilience.

A NEW CONCEPTION OF RESILIENCE

Although the concept of resilience is well-developed in Western societies, it is relatively new to local practitioners in Hong Kong. There is a discrepancy between what is meant by the concept and how initiatives to foster resilience are implemented and practiced.

Our experience showed that the competence component of the UAP seemed to have been better achieved than the optimism and the belongingness components (Lau, 2003). The program focused more on skill building than on fostering youth resilience as a whole. Further clarification of the concept of resilience is needed to continue development of services for youth at risk in Hong Kong specifically. In part, this means a critical examination of the concept must be based on the literature of the helping professions—namely, counseling, education, psychology, and social work (e.g., Carta, 1991; Garmezy, 1974, 1984, 1993; Kagan, 1990; Werner, 1989; Winfield, 1991) to construct working definitions of resilience applicable to practice settings within different cultures.

Common to most conceptualizations of resilience is the idea of human capacity to face, overcome, and even be strengthened by experiences of adversity (Grotberg, 1999). By this capacity, people can own their responses to adversity (Carver, 1998). The process is not static but dynamic as a process of trauma, thriving, and reorganization of the "self" takes place cyclically (Tedeschi & Calhoun, 1995). Therefore, resilience is the process and experience of adapting to disruptive, stressful, and challenging life events. It provides the individual with protective and coping skills and knowledge prior to the disruption (Richardson, Neiger, Jensen, &

Kumpfer, 1990). Through this process, young people regain functioning after exposure to adversity (Garmezy, 1993).

Resilience is a multidimensional construct with different meanings and imperatives, depending on disciplinary interpretations. The early resilience research focused on the identification of personal resources, skills, and competencies used to cope with the stress of a hostile environment. Resilience results from a transaction between environmental stressors and individual attributes. Recent research, particularly from a broader social work perspective, has focused attention on the interaction between individuals, family, and community resources (Ungar, 2001a, 2001b, 2002, 2003). Such research has examined resilience as a response by individuals to stressors, not as an individual trait. Social work researchers have tried to find solutions for children and families undergoing stress whose adaptation responses have been disruptive and nonproductive. As a result, resilience research has focused on the resilience of families (Silliman, 1998) and communities to assist them to change and adapt to crisis situations. This process of becoming resilient has cultural dimensions that have not been well explored. Choi's (2003) model helps to provide a conceptualization of resilience that includes a cultural dimension with implications for social work practice. This cultural dimension can be seen in work by researchers like Shek (2004) whose study on Chinese cultural beliefs about adversity found in a normal Hong Kong student population (not clinical samples) demonstrated that those who had a higher level of agreement with positive Chinese beliefs about adversity (or a lower level of agreement with negative Chinese beliefs about adversity) displayed a lower level of psychological symptoms as measured by their General Health Questionnaire scores. Furthermore, Shek found that identification with positive Chinese cultural beliefs about adversity was related to higher levels of adolescent mental health (including existential well-being, life satisfaction, self-esteem, and sense of mastery), better school adjustment, and fewer problem behaviors. The study shows that identification with traditional positive Chinese cultural beliefs regarding adversity is an important protective factor for adolescents facing economic disadvantage in Hong

Table 19.1   A Comparison of the Resilience Construct of the UAP and Choi's Cultural Heritage Model

Resilience Construct of UAP	Cultural Heritage Model (Choi, 2003)
	Need: Moving beyond fulfilling the wants of the parents, children, schools, and community to meeting the developmental needs of children
Optimism	**Hope:** Moving beyond the cognitive change of "learned optimism" to an inner transformation of mind and life goals
	Compassion: Moving beyond building personal resilience to cope with adversities to restoring compassion for other people who are suffering in the midst of adversity
Belongingness	**Identity:** Moving beyond rebuilding a sense of belonging to family, school and peers to rebuilding a sense of cultural identity
	Community: Moving beyond building up individual resilience to cultivating a resilient culture in families, schools, and community
Competence	**Meaning:** Searching the why of living in the midst of adversity because "he who has a why to live can bear with almost any how" (Frankl, 1984).

Kong. Table 19.1 shows the multidimensional nature of the concept of resilience and summarizes both the content of a cultural heritage model more appropriate to understanding the process that youth experience overcoming adversity in diverse settings and the inadequacy of the original conceptualization of the UAP.

Strength Base and Protective Factors

No matter which approach or theory of resilience we use, the emphasis remains on self-perceived strengths (Wolin & Wolin, 1996) and building protective processes rather than on removing risk factors (Braverman, 2001). Adolescents' perceptions of their experiences play a key role in determining the interplay between aspects of their vulnerability and the perceived strengths that result from their struggle with hardship (Wolin & Wolin, 1996). Therefore, the formation of a challenge mindset is important working with youth at risk. On the other hand, resilience skills may include the ability to form relationships (social competence), to solve problems (metacognition), to develop a sense of identity (autonomy), and to plan and hope for a sense of purpose and success in the future, what Richardson and his colleagues (Richardson et al., 1990) call a "self-righting mechanism."

Interestingly, categories of protective factors identified by many authors (e.g., characteristics of the child, relationships, cultural beliefs, and contexts) closely parallel the child, family, and school as sources of blame for problems. Locating resilience in a child or a family or a school is what has been called a "single-location discourse" (Pianta & Walsh, 1996). The three strands of a single-location discourse on risk and resilience create an "invidious triangle" of child, home, or school pathology (or success) in which attributions about failure and success rest on one of the points of this triangle. It is a serious mistake to conclude from the resilience literature that competence is a function (only) of an individual child's social skills or to expect that raising expectations in a school will raise achievement. Likewise, it is just as much a mistake to think that only improving a principal's leadership skills will produce an effective school. As has been cogently argued by Masten and Coatsworth (1995) and members of the Consortium on the School-Based Promotion of Social Competence (1994), competence—the factor we seek to promote in children exposed to harsh circumstances—is itself multifaceted and connected to a host of other factors in a broad social context.

Therefore, it is critical that efforts to promote resilience do not fall into the trap of single-factor explanations for success under conditions of risk, especially when we appreciate cultural variation among factors. As Egeland, Carlson, and Sroufe (1993) argue and convincingly demonstrate, success under conditions of adversity is clearly not reducible to a single set of circumstances and clearly not dependent solely on characteristics of individual children. Protective factors, including the temperament of the child, unexpected sources of support in the family and community, and self-esteem lead a majority of at-risk children to succeed in life. Furthermore, whereas Shek (2004) identifies the linkage between endorsement of cultural beliefs about adversity and adolescent adjustment, Choi's (2003) cultural heritage model draws on cultural dimensions of resilience and provides insights for turning our attention to aspects of healthy functioning such as needs, meaning, hope, identity, community, and compassion that are culture specific.

Intervention Strategy

The results of the evaluation of the UAP have shown that different parties involved have found the program useful in promoting some aspects of student resilience. In addition, positive changes in the school and family systems have also been identified. Concerning the effects of the UAP on students, clear and consistent observations have been obtained in certain areas (Lau, 2003). However, the program is questionable as to its effectiveness and efficiency in building student resilience in a short period of less than 20 sessions.

We speculate that problems with the program may have been further complicated by the cultural forces it had to contend with when adapted from its Canadian predecessor. The implications of a culturally sensitive read of the resilience literature, at least on the surface, appear straightforward. If high expectation is correlated with the success of high-risk adolescents in certain contexts, then we should raise expectations. If competence in high-risk adolescents is correlated with the lack of social skills, then we should teach them social skills appropriate to their cultural milieu. But this link between the correlates of success for high-risk adolescents and the translation of such factors into programming

that manipulates these factors is an oversimplification of a more complex process by which youth become resilient. Under scrutiny, such a simplified relationship between programming objectives and the research on resilience-related factors has not always held up. Too often, resilience has been defined solely in terms of isolated skills and the development of inner competencies, produced through short-term, add-on programs that educators can apply off-the-shelf (Pianta & Walsh, 1996, 1998).

Evaluation data suggest that, indeed, many adolescents do improve their skills in identified areas as a function of exposure to such programs. However, such skill-focused programs make sense mostly as parts of a package of interventions designed to enhance resilience among high-risk adolescents that includes multiple other components such as enhancing parenting skills or relationships with teachers, which themselves are best achieved with awareness of cultural norms unlikely to be built into prepackaged course designs. At their worst, programs that teach isolated skills or try to enhance child characteristics (e.g., self-esteem, affective expression) lack a strong empirical or theoretical basis for their goals and can be a waste of classroom time. Therefore, attempts to teach or build resilience through skill-focused approaches need to attend to the empirical and theoretical basis of the targeted skills and instructional methods. Furthermore, we must examine the extent to which these approaches address the functionality of the target skills and integration of these skills with existing patterns of behavior in different contexts (Pianta & Walsh, 1996, 1998).

Pianta and Walsh (1996) remind us that the concept of resilience, when applied in schools, requires careful consideration. The tendency for educators and policymakers to latch onto success stories may cause them to miss important issues relevant to how children actually succeed even when such programs are implemented in culturally homogeneous contexts. Has the success of these "resilient children" been achieved only in one domain? Has it been maintained over time? Is success located in the child, or is its systemic nature recognized? Are programs delivered in such a way so as to be well integrated with the child's behavioral repertoire and educational program? It is a good reminder for local social workers, educators, and others who intervene with at-risk youth to attend to these questions when implementing and evaluating the effectiveness of programming based on a conceptualization of resilience.

For example, resilience research has shown that successful development and personal transformation result not from programmatic approaches to enhancing children's well-being per se, but at the deeper level of relationship building, changes in beliefs and expectations, and a willingness among caregivers and other authority figures to share power with young people. Those in positions of authority in families and schools need to develop caring relationships not only between the parent and child but also between the teacher and student, students and students, teachers with other teachers, teachers and parents, and parents with other parents. Such relationships are evidently culturally based. Certain programmatic approaches, however, can provide the structure for developing these relationships and for providing opportunities for active student involvement: small-group process, cooperative learning, peer helping, cross-age mentoring, parent workshops, opportunities for parent-teacher interactions, and community service may all adapt to the Hong Kong context. Overall, schooling that has been a turnaround experience for stressed adolescents is described by them as being like "a family," "a home," "a community," and even "a sanctuary." Choi's model (2003) reminds us that it is imperative for social workers and others to build a culturally sensitive approach to practice to avoid inadvertently labeling variations in cultural expression, ways of navigating stress, and threat of harm or social oppression in negative or pathological terms.

CONCLUSION: IT TAKES A VILLAGE TO RAISE A CHILD

Not surprising to many professionals who work with high-risk children is that many of these children are exposed to a large number of services and programs within a given week of school (Pianta & Walsh, 1996). However, from a systems perspective, this piecemeal approach to service delivery in schools may, in fact, be a stressor for vulnerable children whose lives are already filled with discontinuity and lack of stability. A variety of alternative perspectives on service delivery argue for better use and integration of existing resources within a given classroom, school, family, or community to provide continuous support for children's development (Adelman, 1996; Melton, Limber, & Teague, 1999; Pianta & Walsh, 1998). Hawkins, Catalano, and Miller (1992) suggest that it is insufficient to focus on one social system (e.g., schools) if the goal is the enhancement of social skills. Rather, they reason that because the social world of young people is school, family, and community, there must be a coordinated effort among all three to be effective.

In traditional Chinese beliefs, the development of healthy individuals has been viewed as the primary responsibility of parents. However, recent disorganization of the family system in Hong Kong has resulted in a shift of this responsibility to the education, social welfare, and sometimes, the health care system with only ancillary roles accorded to the parents. This change has not been seen as positive, with the continuing belief that it is in the collective interest of society to ensure the well-being of all children by ensuring that the parent role remains well supported and intact. According to an African proverb, it takes a village to raise a child. The thought behind the phrase suggests that without the society, without help or assistance, a child cannot grow up successfully—in Africa or in Hong Kong. Resilience theory posits that the explanatory and predictive power of protective processes within the family, school, and community rests on their ability to meet basic human developmental needs for safety, connection, belonging, identity, respect, mastery, power, and ultimately, meaning (Benard, 2002; Choi, 2003; Werner & Smith, 1982). Resilient individuals have an ability to seek out people and environments that are good for their development, a kind of "niche seeking" behavior (Masten, 1997). Evidently, what they find will largely be related to what their context (including culture) provides.

The adaptation of the resilience concept to local practice in Hong Kong demonstrates there is room for improvement in conceptualizing and operationalizing the concept in theory and in practice globally. The preceding discussion contributes to the development of a comprehensive service construct and provides a direction for program planning that assists children to move from being at risk to being resilient through a change in individual and structural conditions. This understanding and application of the resilience concept in the context of Hong Kong has the potential to influence service ideologies elsewhere. However, as Benard (2002) has noted, "Fostering resilience . . . is a process and not a program." Building a caring and supportive cultural context and environment (however these are defined) is a more effective and efficient means to help youth grow and develop.

REFERENCES

Action Committee Against Narcotics. (2001). *Hong Kong narcotics report.* Hong Kong: Government Printer.

Adelman, H. S. (1996). Restructuring education support services & integrating community resources: Beyond the full service school model. *School Psychology Review, 25*(4), 431–445.

Benard, B. (2002). *The foundations of the resiliency framework: From research to practice.* Retrieved January 7, 2005, from www.resiliency.com/htm/research.htm

Braverman, M. T. (2001, Spring). Applying resilience theory to the prevention of adolescent substance abuse. *Focus.* Retrieved January 7, 2005, from http://ucce.ucdavis.edu/freeform/4hcyd/documents/CYD_Focus1190.pdf

Breakthrough. (1993). *A report of the study on the value orientation and the tendency to self-destroy among secondary school students in Hong Kong* [in Chinese]. Hong Kong: Breakthrough Limited.

Breakthrough. (1997). *The Understanding of the Adolescent Project: Research report.* Unpublished report of the Coordinating Committee for the Welfare of Adolescents and Youth at Risk, Health and Welfare, Hong Kong Government, Hong Kong.

Breakthrough Limited & the Centre for Clinical Trials and Epidemiological Research. (1998). *The Understanding the Adolescent Project: Pilot implementation and evaluation study: Report I.* Unpublished report of the Steering Group of Understanding the Adolescent Project—Pilot Implementation & Evaluation Study, Health and Welfare, Hong Kong Government, Hong Kong.

Carta, J. J. (1991). Education for children in inner-city classrooms. *American Behavioral Scientist, 34*(3), 440–453.

Carver, C. S. (1998). Resilience and thriving: Issues, models, and linkages. *Journal of Social Issues, 54,* 245–265.

Chan, W. T., Cheung, J. C. K., Lee, T. Y., Leung, K. K., & Liu, S. C. (1998a, October). *Hong Kong Youth Development Indices: Full report of the first survey.* Hong Kong: Hong Kong Youth Development Council. Retrieved January 7, 2005, from www.youthcouncil.org.hk

Chan, W. T., Cheung, J. C. K., Lee, T. Y., Leung, K. K., & Liu, S. C. (1998b). Moral values, judgments, and intentions of youths in Hong Kong. *Hong Kong Journal of Social Work, 32*(1), 105–111.

Cheung, S. K., & Lam, C. W. (1992). *Report on the Study of Adolescent Depression.* Hong Kong: Boys' and Girls' Clubs Association of Hong Kong.

Choi, P. Y. W. (2003). Resilience: Beyond skills. In *Proceedings of the Conference on Resilience: Fostering Children's Resilience.* Hong Kong: Save the Children Fund.

Clark, P. (1995). *Risk and resiliency in adolescence: The current status of research on gender differences.* Columbus: Ohio State University.

Connell, J. P., Spencer, M. B., & Aber, J. L. (1994). Educational risk and resilience in African-American youth: Context, self, action, and outcomes in school. *Child Development, 65,* 493–506.

Consortium on the School-Based Promotion of Social Competence. (1994). The school-based promotion of social competence: Theory, research, practice, and policy. In R. J. Haggerty, L. Sherrod, N. Garmezy, & M. Rutter (Eds.), *Stress, risk, and resilience in children and adolescents: Processes, mechanisms, and interventions* (pp. 268–316). New York: Cambridge University Press.

Coroner's Court. (1999). *Hong Kong Coroners report 1998.* Hong Kong: Government Printer.

Egeland, B., Carlson, E., & Sroufe, L. A. (1993). Resilience as process. *Development and Psychopathology, 5,* 517–528.

Frankl, V. E. (1984). *Man's search for meaning: An introduction to logotherapy,* (3rd ed.). New York: Simon & Schuster.

Garmezy, N. (1974). The study of competence in children at risk for severe psychopathy. In E. J. Anthony (Ed.). *The child in his family: Vol. 3. Children at psychiatric risk* (pp. 77–98). New York: Wiley.

Garmezy, N. (1984). Children vulnerable to major mental disorders: Risk and protective factors. Psychiatry Update: *American Psychiatric Association Annual Review, 3,* 91–103.

Garmezy, N. (1993). Children in poverty: Resilience despite risk. *Psychiatry, 56,* 127–136.

Gordon, E. W., & Song, L. D. (1994). Variations in the experience of resilience. In M. C. Wang & E. W. Gordon (Eds.), *Educational resilience in inner-city America* (pp. 27–43). Hillsdale, NJ: Erlbaum.

Grossman, F. K., Beinashowitz, J., & Anderson, L. (1992). Risk and resilience in young adolescents. *Journal of Youth and Adolescence, 21*(5), 529–550.

Grotberg, E. (1999). Countering depression with the five building blocks of resilience. *Reaching Today's Youth, 4*(1), 66–72.

Guetzloe, E. (1994). Risk, resilience, and protection. *Journal of Emotional and Behavioural Problems, 3*(2), 2–5.

Hawkins, J. D., Catalano, R. F., & Miller, J. Y. (1992). Risk and protective factors for alcohol and other drug problems in adolescence and early adulthood: Implication for substance abuse prevention. *Psychological Bulletin, 112,* 64–105.

Ho, J. K. M. (1995). *Help-seeking pattern & supportive network of young people in Hong Kong.* Hong Kong: Government Printer.

Hoh, Y., & Oborne, D. W. (1996, August). *Helping Asian refugee students: The Youth Entry Program and Five-Year Follow-up.* Paper presented at the 16th International Congress of Psychology, Montreal, Canada.

Hong Kong Federation of Youth Groups. (1993). *Youth and problem solving.* Hong Kong: Federation of Youth Groups.

Hong Kong Jockey Club Centre for Suicide Research and Prevention. (2003). *Suicidality among high school students in Hong Kong (*Research Report 2003–01). Hong Kong: University of Hong Kong.

Hong Kong Police Force. (2001). *Hong Kong police review.* Hong Kong: Government Printer.

Jose, P. E., Huntsinger, C. S., Huntsinger, P. R., & Liaw, F. R. (2000). Parental values and practices relevant to young children's social development in Taiwan and the United States. *Journal of Cross Cultural Psychology, 31*(6), 677–702.

Kagan, D. M. (1990). How schools alienate students at risk: A model for examining proximal classroom variables. *Educational Psychologists, 25*(2), 105–120.

Lau, J. (2003). *Report on evaluation of the Understanding the Adolescent Project (UAP) in secondary schools 2001/02.* Unpublished report. Hong Kong: Chinese University of Hong Kong, School of Public Health Faculty of Medicine, Centre for Clinical Trials and Epidemiological Research.

Lee, T. Y. (1999). Handling sibling disputes and conflicts [In Chinese]. In A. Kwan & G. Ko (Eds.), *Handbook of family crises* (pp. 25–40). Hong Kong: Cosmos Books.

Lee, T. Y. (2002). Process and outcome evaluation of youth empowerment practice [In Chinese]. In Editorial Committee (Eds.), *Youth empowerment in Hong Kong: Theory and practice* (pp. 13–42). Hong Kong: Chinese YMCA of Hong Kong.

Masten, A. (1997). Resilience in children at-risk. *Research Practice, 5*(1). Retrieved January 7, 2005, from http://education.umn.edu/CAREI/Reports/Rpractice/Spring97/resilience.htm

Masten, A., Best, K., & Garmezy, N. (1990). Resilience and development: Contributions from the study of children who overcome adversity. *Development and Psychopathology, 2*(4), 425–444.

Masten, A., & Coatsworth, D. (1995). Competence, resiliency, and psychopathology. In D. Cicchetti & D. Cohen (Eds.), *Developmental psychopathology: Risk, disorder, and adaptation* (pp. 715–752). New York: Wiley.

McMillan J. H., & Reed, D. F. (1994, January/February). At-risk students and resiliency: Factors contributing to academic success. *Clearing House, 67*(3), 137–140.

Melton, G. B., Limber, S. P., & Teague, T. L. (1999). Changing schools for changing families. In R. C. Pianta & M. J. Cox (Eds.), *The transition to kindergarten* (pp. 179–216). Baltimore: P. H. Brookes.

Ng, A. M. C. (1975). *The report on social causes of violent crime among young offenders in Hong Kong.* Hong Kong: Social Research Centre of the Chinese University of Hong Kong.

Oborne, D. W. (1994, May). *Receiving newcomers' families.* Paper presented in the Calgary Teachers Association Annual Conference, Calgary, Alberta, Canada.

Pianta, R. C., & Walsh, D. J. (1996). *High-risk children in schools: Constructing sustaining relationships*. New York: Routledge.

Pianta, R. C., & Walsh, D. J. (1998). Applying the construct of resilience in schools: Cautions from a developmental systems perspective. *School Psychology Review, 27*(3), 407–417.

Rak, C. L., & Patterson, L. E. (1996). Promoting resilience in at-risk children. *Journal of Counseling and Development, 74*(4), 368–373.

Reasoner, R. W., & Dusa, G. S. (1991). *Building self-esteem in the secondary schools*. Palo Alto, CA: Consulting Psychologists Press.

Richardson, G. E., Neiger, B., Jensen, S., & Kumpfer, K. (1990). The resiliency model. *Health Education, 21*(6), 33–39.

Rutter, M. (1987). Psychosocial resilience and protective mechanisms. *American Journal of Orthopsychiatry, 57*(3), 316–331.

Sagor, R. (1996). Building resiliency in students. *Educational Leadership, 54*(1), 38–43.

Seligman, M. (1995). *The optimistic child*. Boston: Houghton Mifflin.

Shek, D. T. L. (1996). Mental health of Chinese adolescents: A critical review. In S. Lau (Ed.), *Growing up the Chinese way* (pp. 169–199). Hong Kong: Chinese University Press.

Shek, D. T. L. (2004). Chinese cultural beliefs about adversity: Its relationship to psychological wellbeing, school adjustment and problem behavior in Hong Kong and adolescents with and without economic disadvantage. *Childhood, 11*(1), 63–80.

Shek, D. T. L., & Chan, L. K. (1999). Perceptions of the ideal child in a Chinese context. *Journal of Psychology, 133*(3), 291–302.

Shek, D. T. L., & Lai, M. F. (2000). Conceptions of an ideal family in Confucian thoughts: Implications for individual and family counseling. *Asian Journal of Counseling, 7*(2), 85–104.

Shek, D. T. L., & Tang, V. (2003). Adolescent suicide in Hong Kong during 1980–2000. *International Journal of Adolescent Medicine and Health, 15*(3), 245–265.

Silliman, B. (1998). Teaching resiliency to our children. *Human Development & Family Life Bulletin, 4*(1), 4–5.

Social Welfare Department. (1973). *Future development of social welfare in Hong Kong: A white paper*. Hong Kong: Government Printer.

Social Welfare Department. (1977). *The program plan on personal social work among young people*. Hong Kong: Government Printer.

Tedeschi, R. G., & Calhoun, L. G. (1995). *Trauma and transformation: Growing in the aftermath of suffering*. Thousand Oaks, CA: Sage.

Ungar, M. (2001a). Constructing narratives of resilience with high-risk youth. *Journal of Systemic Therapies, 20*(2), 58–73.

Ungar, M. (2001b). The social construction of resilience among problem youth in out-of-home placement: A study of health-enhancing deviance. *Child and Youth Care Forum, 30*(3), 137–154.

Ungar, M. (2002). *Playing at being bad: The hidden resilience of troubled teens*. East Lawrencetown, Nova Scotia, Canada: Pottersfield Press.

Ungar, M. (2003). Deep ecology and the roots of resilience: The importance of setting in outdoor experience-based programming for at-risk children. *Critical Social Work, 3*(1), 18–43.

Ungar, M. (2004). *Nurturing hidden resilience in troubled youth*. Toronto, Ontario: University of Toronto Press.

Weinreb, M. L. (1997). Be a resiliency mentor: You may be a lifesaver for a high-risk child. *Young Children, 52*(2), 14–20.

Werner, E. (1989). High-risk children in young adulthood: A longitudinal study from birth to 32 years. *American Journal of Orthopsychiatry, 59*(1), 72–81.

Werner, E., & Smith, R. (1982). *Vulnerable but invincible*. New York: McGraw-Hill.

Winfield, L. A. (1991). Resilience, schooling, and development in African-American youth. *Education and Urban Society, 24*(1), 5–14.

Wolin, S., & Wolin, S. J. (1996). The challenge model: Working with the strengths of children of substance abusing parents. *Child and Adolescent Psychiatric Clinics of North America, 5*(1), 243–256.

Worrell, F. C. (1996, August). *The risk-resiliency paradigm in research on dropping out*. Paper presented at the Annual Meeting of the American Psychological Association, Toronto, Canada.

20

RESILIENT YOUTH IN NORTH EAST INDIA

The Role of Faith-Based Organizations in Communities Affected by Violence

JERRY THOMAS

GEORGE MENAMPARAMPIL

India defies generalizations. Geographically, it provides a vast and varied landscape. Its human ecology is equally diverse, inhabited by over a billion people belonging to many linguistic, cultural, religious groups. The North East corner of the country, which this chapter is concerned with, itself showcases the social and cultural variety that India encompasses within it.

The North East, with Bangladesh on the west; Nepal, Bhutan, and China to the north; and Myanmar to the east, includes the states of Arunachal Pradesh, Assam, Manipur, Meghalaya, Mizoram, Nagalandm and Tripura. Generally referred to as "Assam" until the recent past, these states were created along ethnic lines, with one or two majority cultural communities in each state and a host of smaller distinct communities. The North East is a mosaic of tribes and ethnic groups spread over two river valleys (the Brahmaputra and the Barak) and the foothills of the great Himalayas (Hazarika, 1994). Although an integral part of India, this region is connected to the rest of the country by a mere 32-kilometer broad "chicken neck" of land between Bangladesh and Nepal.

Although its status as an integral part of India is now challenged by a number of insurgent groups, most Indians themselves are ignorant about this colorful part of their own country. It hits national headlines only when it is rocked by the now-routine violence or deluged by annual floods. The 2001 census reports a regional population of 37 million. It is estimated that youth between the ages of 15 and 35 compose a staggering 40% of the population.

In this chapter, we examine both the risk factors and resilience of the young people of the North East. Although their lives are frustrating and their exposure to violence and poverty extreme, they and their communities demonstrate many factors that help them to cope. We examine constellations of these factors and then look at faith-based organizations as an example of one type of social structure that can protect youth from the risks they face and build their resilience. Specifically, church-based community development initiatives of organizations such as Don Bosco have seldom been reviewed in the literature on resilience, although their importance to youth in the majority and minority worlds far exceeds their direct influence on parishioners. Such organizations, we will show, are a source of social, economic, and spiritual support in the lives of millions of youth, whether Christian or not.

THE YOUTH OF NORTH EAST INDIA

Although culturally diverse, youth in the region tend to favor adventure and activities that involve risk-taking behaviors. They find it easy to work in groups, and gender interactions are spontaneous and easy. Organizational skills are valued. The democratic traditions of their societies make them articulate and help them voice their opinions rather freely and fearlessly, although threats of politically motivated violence have now stymied that freedom.

Youth from the communities in the North East tend to exhibit pride in their communities and local cultural heritage, which makes them distinct as tribal peoples separate from the dominant Hindu and Moslem cultural groups elsewhere in India (Verghese, 1996). Most communities have never been subjugated and suppressed and therefore do not feel inferior to other groups as is the case with the lower castes and *dalits* in other parts of India. Increasingly, youth have become the voice of their communities, and youth groups articulate collective social, political, economic, and cultural aspirations. In most communities, the young people are the first or second generation to be educated. The elders in these communities, mostly illiterate, look on the educated youth as all knowing and all capable and have left them with much of the responsibility for securing their community's future. Every community has a youth group, in the form of either a student union or club or association that quite aggressively and vehemently voices the

grievances and demands of the community. The history of the region is replete with instances where these youth groups have assumed leadership. For example, the All Assam Students Union (AASU) led a 6-year-long agitation against the infiltration of people from Bangladesh. They later formed into a political party that swept the elections in the state and formed a government. The mushroom growth of militant and insurgent groups among youth of practically every ethnic group is another testimony to the power of young people in this region.

The difficult terrain, the struggle against the elements of nature to make a living, and the absence of most of the advantages of technological progress have all had their impact on the youth of the region. In particular, they are known for qualities such as resilience, readiness for sacrifice, a spirit of collaboration, courage, self-confidence, pride, and an ambitious nature. They are not easily overwhelmed by odds and take many problems in their stride as part of life.

On the negative side, however, a recent study of youth and youth work in the region (Thomas, 2001) found that youth lack self-discipline, a work ethic, and the patience to see projects through to their completion. High expectations lead to frustration. Even the uneducated and unskilled among them want the same lifestyle as their better-educated peers. Frustration often erupts into displays of anger and a willingness to become involved in armed revolts.

The Status of Youth Today

Young people of North East find themselves in a period of transition. Changes in the social, political, and economic conditions around them are experienced as destabilizing and stressful (Vattathara & Biju, 2002). We can describe these youth in several ways.

Youth in the North East Are
Members of a Society in Transition

Communities in the region have undergone rapid changes over a short span of time. As Menamparampil (in press) says,

In a place like Manipur where we have crammed centuries of normal change into a period of about two generations, and where even today people of different centuries seem to be living side by side, the contrasts among various sections of people are straining the society to the limits. The young are caught up in the trauma of this unprecedented turmoil in every aspect of life. The result is confusion, a tendency to look inward, a nostalgia for the past that is more mythical than real, since they have only heard or read about it, impatience with the society's inability to keep pace with the rest of the world, and uncertainty in the choice they have to make between the thrills and risks presented by the frenetic pace of ultramodern western culture and the secure but placid tempo of our rich, ancient civilization.

Breakdown of Social/Community Systems, Values, Attitudes. As educator Muslih-ud-Din explains, "Old value systems are crumbling. Alienation is increasing in this era of rapid social change" (Nishat, 2001, p. 3). Traditional social institutions for disciplining and grooming youth are fading away. With them is also being lost the system to transfer to the younger generations the ethos of a community working together. Instead, the value placed on play and informal socializing has been replaced by a competitive youth culture driven by schools in which the young are "urged to compete, win, excel, distinguish [themselves]" (Menamparampil, in press) The result, as some psychiatrists in the region say, has been the emergence of a "my world is me" syndrome (Nishat, 2001).

Affluence and Glamour Are Perceived as Key Indicators of Development. Even the rural illiterate are not free of the influence of the "Reebok shoes, Rayban glasses" attitude toward progress and development. The consequence has been what the UN Development Programme (UNDP, 1998) characterizes as "consumption" that has done little to help people in the region. The perception among youth is that the more you are able to "have," the more "developed" you become. Consumerism is taking its toll in the region. With development funds in the form of grants pouring in for various schemes from the central government and additional money coming in for counterinsurgency operations and maintenance of law and order, there is no dearth of cash available for some. However, as one

section of society rides the "development" (read affluence) wave, the others feel cheated. With legitimate means for affluence not always available, other means such as crime, extortion, and looting are increasingly common in communities where respect, hospitality, equity, and honesty were cherished values a generation ago.

Identity Crisis. In the wake of the social changes rapidly occurring, youth experience a confusion that has led to the mushrooming of nationalistic movements. "Who am I? Am I Khasi? A Northeasterner? An Indian? A Christian? What is my identity?" asked a young Khasi girl from Meghalaya, during a discussion in Guwahati on the problems faced by the youth in the North East.

Aggressive assertion of identity by many tribal and ethnic groups has become more common. Although awareness and assertion of one's identity is in itself a positive aspect of psychological development, competition between groups for resources such as land and water have prompted many groups to advocate armed militancy to protect their rights. Urged on by elders, politicians, and unions, youth increasingly are the ones who aggressively campaign for their community's rights.

Cultural Uprootedness. Aggravating the problem of identity is the feeling of a cultural uprootedness. Without placing blame on any single factor, changes in the way people live were brought about by exposure to the Christian church (which when first established in the region considered everything tribal as evil), modern education (which has devalued traditional knowledge), and transforming political and economic systems (that promote globalism rather than tribal communitarianism). Writing in a local Nagaland paper, *Nagaland Page,* Dutta (1999) complains,

> The youth of [the] North East are increasingly imbibing the crosscurrents of national and transnational cultures at the cost of roots. Television and other media are for increasing our mental vision. However the youth here are getting westernized with these without imbibing the work culture of the west. (p. 5)

Rapid Urbanization. Towns and cities hold the promise that dreams can be realized. Cities such as Guwahati and Shillong have attracted youth from the rest of the region with their educational institutions and the possibilities they offer. Beyond the region, cities such as Bangalore and Delhi have colonies of young people from the North East. A few successfully relocate. Most, however, must return home. The resulting stories of failure are having an impact on other youth considering their futures. There has been in the region a "three fold increase in truancy, drug intake and booze binges among youngsters, especially among the 10th and 11th graders" (Nishat, 2001, p. 3). Saikia, a Guwahati-based neuropsychiatrist has noted that "instances of stress and depression among youth have shot up considerably"; Dasgupta, a psychotherapist says, "More than 70% of my cases are troubled kids, unable to cope" (Nishat, 2001, p. 3).

Young People in the North East
Are Members of a Society in Conflict

The North East of India is well-known for the violence that has been occurring since independence. Armed insurgents started agitating in Nagaland after the British left the country. The Nagas declared their independence on August 14, 1947, one day before India's independence was celebrated. The Indian Army entered the Naga Hills to crush the insurgent movement in the 1950s. Finally, in 1997, the government of India entered into a cease-fire agreement with some of the factions fighting for independence, although fighting continues. Many of the insurgents have sophisticated weaponry and communication systems. Extortion of money from businesses, government servants, ordinary farmers, and educational and financial institutions fill their coffers. Kidnappings, revenge killings, factional fights, and random acts of violence are common occurrences.

Youth, like their families, are caught between the insurgents who force them at gunpoint to give the insurgents shelter and food and the security forces that arrest them for aiding the militants. Thousands of lives have been lost in the region through decades of violence. Daily realities and the power associated with joining the militants push many youth toward violent behavior even when they know it is not correct (Thomas, 2001). The legitimization, glamorization,

and induced callousness resulting from exposure to this violence provide a heady mixture, intoxicating young people who are on the lookout for opportunities to make a mark in life (Bok, 1999).

Young People in the North East
Experience Deep Frustration

There is a perception among youth exposed to the violence in the North East of a general deterioration in their communities with few prospects for change. In a study of youth in North East India coordinated by the Agency for Integral Development Action (AIDA), the development wing of the Salesian Province of Dimapur (Thomas, 2000) identified two groups of youth most susceptible to frustration. The first includes those who are educated but not skilled and who lack adult guidance. These youth are often unemployed and consequently easily enticed by the lure of money and power gained through association with the militant groups. The second group includes school dropouts who are without job skills, unemployed, and embarrassed to have to become laborers on farms. They, too, view participation in antisocial gangs and militant groups as a pathway to success.

Youth who fit with this second group are common. Figures released by the Ministry of Human Resources show the dropout rates in Classes 1 through 8 for the year 1999–2000 are above 64% in all parts of the region, except Manipur and Nagaland, where it is just below 45%. The state of Meghalaya has the second-highest dropout rate in the country, 77%. The success rate among students taking the high school leaving examination in most states of the North East does not exceed 40%. A staggering number of children have few prospects for the future.

It is estimated that the unemployment level among educated youth is over 40% in states across the region. In Assam, there are 1.5 million registered unemployed and as many or more unregistered ones. Unemployment figures remain high due to a number of factors: (a) Government positions are saturated, land-based employment is neither interesting nor appealing (although the situation is gradually changing), (b) youth are unwilling to do menial jobs, (c) youth possess minimal entrepreneurial skills, (d) there are few opportunities to work in industry, (e) there is a lack of access to modern technology, (f) youth lack self-discipline for sustained hard work, and (g) although there is a yearning for immediate gains, youth have shown a lack of willingness to plan for the future.

A study done by the National Institute of Advanced Studies conducted in-depth interviews with 600 16- to 25-year-olds and

> found them entangled in a web of frustration, anger, withdrawal and escapism. Half of them felt that people were justified in resorting to violence when there were no other ways to make the government listen. One third were willing to take to the gun to be heard and a fourth felt bloodshed was inevitable if the miserable conditions of the have-nots were not to change for the better. (quoted in Nishat, 2001, p. 3)

Anger at a lack of opportunities fuels criminal activity as well as participation in militancy. Police officials report a sharp rise in thefts and burglary by middle-class and lower-middle-class people.

Breakdown in Social and Personal Discipline. Traditional methods of social control are more or less absent from the lives of tribal youth in the North East today. For example, the system of bachelors' dormitories among a number of tribal groups in the region is rarely used any longer. Similarly, traditional patterns of disciplining children in which aunts and uncles assumed a great deal of responsibility have also been eroded, leaving parents to raise their children alone. Schools and churches have not filled the gap either. Parents complain that their children lack sufficient guidance and that too many children are overindulged. In a relatively secure community, this would be unhealthy. In a community where there is a high risk of violence and the likelihood that children will take up arms, the lack of elders providing direction to youth is having tragic consequences.

Youth in the North East
Experience Deep Insecurity

Camouflaged beneath an apparent aggressive self-confidence, youth speak of deep insecurities.

"Crack us open and darkness will flow out," says a young college student in a recent newspaper report by Nishat (2001) on youth. "We are a generation that breaks down easily; small things make us press the panic button," (p. 3) says a 22-year-old sales executive. The article goes on:

> Decisive, street-smart, competitive—that's the illusion. Burdened by the demands they make on themselves, today's youngsters seem to be in a vague kind of mourning: having lost something, of a sense of betrayal, insecurity, uncertainty, a gnawing frustration, loneliness and a feeling of being on the edge of a precipice. Candidly speaking—they are a troubled lot. (p. 3)

In a study by Thomas (2001) on the impact of violence on the personal and social lives of youth in Nagaland and Manipur, the majority of the 200 youth interviewed say they experience a tremendous sense of fear and insecurity in the wake of the violence in the region. They fear losing their lives or having their parents and other family members killed; they worry about being picked up by the security forces on suspicion of being insurgents, about being forced to join militant groups, and about being caught in the cross fire between militants and security forces. Living in communities that are engaged in long, drawn-out violence and conflict, they feel that they are not as good as their counterparts elsewhere in the country.

Furthermore, the tensions underlying these insecurities are increasing due to the emergence of a class system in what were once more egalitarian tribal societies. Youth are finding themselves in a society that is becoming more polarized, with greater distinctions being made between the rich and the poor, the educated and the uneducated, the influential and those without influence. Values, attitudes, and the nature of relationships are being defined by the parameters set by these distinctions.

Women's Status

Finally, and very importantly, there is a myth among people that women in the North East are empowered and enjoy equal rights. Although women in the North Eastern states do enjoy more freedom than in some communities across India and have demonstrated competence in handling the violence they face, many still face structural inequalities and are marginalized in social, economic, and political forums. There is a saying among the Mizos of Mizoram that goes, "A fence and a wife can be changed any time." Women do all the hard work in the field and at home.

Yet there is also evidence that women are exercising traditional rights as well. Many of them manage the economy of the family. In fact, Imphal, a large city in the province of Manipur, boasts one of Southeast Asia's largest markets managed by women, the Ima Keithel. Furthermore, a number of women have been actively resisting the actions of the army, which they accuse of perpetrating rights abuses against themselves, their children, and husbands.

Despite these select examples of empowerment, in most matters of public importance and decision making, women, old or young, are nowhere to be seen. Most tribes do not allow women to speak in their village councils. Very few women are in politics or hold government administrative posts. And when financial resources are limited, it is the boys in a family who get to go to school.

Factors That Help Youth to Cope

Despite this list of adversities, young people are determined to create a more friendly and positive community for themselves and their families, now and in the future. The factors listed below are taken from interviews conducted by Thomas with 37 youth. All youth included in these interviews were judged by professionals who work with them (teachers, clergy, and youth workers) to be coping well with the stress they experience.

Support From Family

Youth most often reported family support as the most important factor influencing their ability to cope well with the risks posed by their communities. Apart from the financial support that they receive, acceptance and emotional caring by the parents sustains youth. Youth describe

parents as most helpful when they take time to discuss issues that confront young people, exploring choices that they have, respecting the youth's opinion, trusting them and giving them responsibility, or setting reasonable limits when the youth want to do things that might place them further at risk. Encouraging youth to attend youth groups sponsored by their tribe or church, giving them the support to pursue their talents and interests, and cautioning them against certain groups and their influence were all aspects of the support youth found helpful from their families.

Community Support

Where community support complements the support offered by families, youth report doing well. Youth found it helpful when their communities consider the young person as capable and entrust him or her with responsibility. Youth gave examples of being given responsibility to organize community festivals, church events, cultural programs, and music and sports events. Youth felt that through the fulfillment of these responsibilities, they made a significant contribution to their community. Youth who were interviewed said it made them determined not to let down their community or village. Community involvement also gave youth the opportunity to meet more often with friends who were also eager to do well. Public occasions required them to develop social skills when greeting dignitaries and performing other social roles.

Faith and Religion

Among the youth interviewed in the North East, many are Christians. They speak of their faith as helping them to maintain balance and as being a tremendous source of strength. Prayer and church attendance mean much to them. Apart from the spiritual strength that comes from faith, youth say they meet through the church people who are ardently hope filled and willing to offer youth guidance. Being a member of a church makes a large multifaceted support system accessible to the youth for personal counseling, information about study and job opportunities, social networks, skills training, life orientation programs, meeting with elders, a forum in which to express their opinions and be heard, recreational facilities, and support during disasters, be they natural, economic, or personal. The church gives them, they said, a sense of belonging to a larger community.

Participation in Cultural Groups, Clubs, and Associations

Every village has its own clubs and social groups that offer youth acceptance for nonviolent behavior. In most instances, the groups and clubs are the only places that youth can "hang out" in the absence of any other recreational infrastructure and facilities. In Tripura, organizers of a theater troop for youth with whom Thomas works as a facilitator tell the story of the mother of one young man who pleaded with them to take her son into the troop, saying, "I know it will keep him away from bad friends and influence and from militancy." Even though the young man's contribution was not always helpful, leaders kept him in the troop: "We are not throwing him out from the drama troop because at least when he is with us he does not get into trouble. So we are keeping him even though he is not much of an actor." These groups offer youth a sense of purpose. Unfortunately, for many others, this same sense of purpose is being found among the militants. Communities are realizing they must present alternatives and are becoming more responsive to the demands of youth. As one young man explained, "We persuaded the school and church authorities to allow us [youth] to play in their playgrounds and to use some rooms for practicing music. Now there are fewer youth who are loitering around and getting into trouble in our small town. Some youth are also coming forward to help out in the school and in the program organized by the church."

Education and Prospects of Decent Jobs

Although on the one hand education has increased the frustration experienced by youth, it has also opened up for them avenues to move out of stifling surroundings and given them the confidence necessary to succeed. Employment opportunities in the North East are increasing, mostly in the service sector. The number of organizations and institutes coming forward to train the youth in job-oriented courses has increased as well.

Recognition of One's Own Capacity and Responsibility

Youth recognize that their government cannot fulfill its obligations to provide education and employment and to keep towns and villages functioning well. Youth experience the lack of a functional government in many sectors of society as a great disappointment. As a result, youth who rise above the frustration report awareness of their own capacities and the need to take responsibility for themselves and for their communities. This responsibility also includes organizing people to procure their rights, fight corruption and nepotism in the government, and make elected representatives more accountable to the people. Youth who participate in these communitarian initiatives report feeling better about themselves and their future prospects.

Development Initiatives by NGOs and Government Bodies

A large number of nongovernmental organizations (NGOs) and government agencies have sponsored youth initiatives that emphasize the role of youth in creating a better society. These initiatives also teach youth skills and provide the financial and technical support they need to invest themselves in economically productive and community development-oriented activities. One of the most effective government agencies is the National Bank for Agriculture and Rural Development (NABARD), which promotes sustainable and equitable agriculture and rural development through credit support and related services, trainings, research, monitoring, and evaluation. It is present in all states and has links in every district in India. Likewise, church-based social development organizations have gradually moved away from the charity approach to participatory development of communities. Young people are given prime importance in all their ventures. Among them the Rural Resource and Training Centre of Bosco Reach Out in Guwahati and AIDA in Dimapur have over the years helped change the mind-set of people about development and initiated a number of development programs in very remote areas of the region.

Personal Characteristics

Apart from those factors listed above, youth say they cope best with the vagaries of life in the region when they demonstrate certain characteristics and attitudes toward the multiple risks they face. These include, most important, a capacity to "grin and bear it." Life has always been tough in this region. At the time this chapter was being written, 18 of 23 districts in the state of Assam were reeling from the impact of devastating floods that inundated villages, fields, and roads. Landslides cut off entire states from the possibility of receiving outside help. Over the years, people have learned to accept such adversity. They take a pragmatic approach to life, learning to live with these disasters rather than putting much hope in the promises of politicians. In a rare example of candor, the chief minister of Assam appealed to the people to "learn to live with floods" ("Learn to Live With Floods," 2004, p. 1).

Similarly, a sense of humor and the capacity to laugh at one's self is also valued and contributes to people's capacity to cope. North Easterners are known for their sense of humor. Very often, they are laughing at their own idiosyncrasies. Their capacity to see the humorous side of life events makes an otherwise tough and routine life bearable and even enjoyable.

Not surprisingly then, people in the North East demonstrate the capacity to put up with great physical hardships. Traditionally, their lives consisted of hard work in the fields, two meals a day, a few mugs of homemade wine, enough clothes to protect their bodies, and a house to sleep in. A knife, a gun, a bow and arrow, and a spade formed the inventory of moveable property. Although times have changed, the needs, especially of people in rural areas, remain the same.

The Role Played by Faith-Based Organizations Helping Youth to Cope

The preceding list of hardships and people's capacities, at the individual, family, and community levels, demonstrates that people in the North East are both disadvantaged and determined to cope well with the adversity they face. Ensuring the resilience of youth in the region—and fostering the development of the resources, both structural and personal, that youth require to grow up well—is helped by a number of different organizations. As an exemplar of how a formal organization can assist the course of personal and community development, we examine the role of the Christian churches in the North East. These churches, like similar faith-based organizations worldwide, play a role in sustaining resilience among at-risk youth. That role, at least in the secular literature, has not been well articulated. Although resilience has been associated with church attendance in the West, there has been no examination to date of the more comprehensive role that churches might play in youth development.

Combined, the Christian churches of the North East have a relatively small membership. The various denominations together account for only 10% of the population. Yet the influence and reach of churches far outweighs their physical presence. In states such as Meghalaya, Mizoram, and Nagaland, the Church is the biggest and the most accepted NGO. Although much of its work may resemble that of other NGOs, the Church remains a faith-based organization that anchors all its interventions to its underlying mission. Paradoxically, despite the violence and grim realities of life, youth and adults have continued to participate in faith-based organizations that espouse values contrary to those of the militants. Both government officials and community members acknowledge the contribution of the Church in the fields of education, health care, and social services. In remoter areas where there are no government services, Church personnel provide the social safety net people require.

Specifically, we look at the impact of three major organizations of the Catholic Church that focus exclusively on youth in the region. These are the Don Bosco Youth Mission and Educational Services (DBYES) in Guwahati, the DBYES in Dimapur, and the North Eastern Regional Youth Commission (NERYC).

DBYES is the youth ministry wing of the Salesians of Don Bosco who have been present in the region since 1922. The Salesians of Don

Bosco is a group within the Catholic Church with a specific mission to educate and train youth. They are present in over 120 countries in the world. The group was founded by Don Bosco (1816–1888), an Italian priest, who as a young man had to overcome great poverty and ridicule to get himself educated and trained. One of his most famous sayings is, "It is enough that you are young for me to love you." The Salesians of Don Bosco operate, among many other programs, schools that have set the standard for English medium education in the region. They are known for their capacity to deal with youth, especially those living in difficult situations. Both branches of DBYES in Guwahati and Dimapur seek to provide education for all school-aged children, as well as for college and university students, school dropouts, those not able to attend school, and working youth in urban and rural settings, irrespective of their religious affiliations.

The NERYC is a third organization for youth, with activities covering the entire North East, including Guwahati and Dimapur. Every diocese has a Youth Commission headed by a youth director. Training and animation of personnel to carry on a youth ministry and advocacy on behalf of youth are NERYC's core activities.

These three organizations work in collaboration on a number of issues related to youth. Programs designed to help youth discover their potential talents and build their confidence are an important part of the services offered. The two branches of DBYES alone conduct more than 200 such programs every year for various groups of youngsters, both urban and rural. Programs vary from 3 to 7 days in duration, addressing a host of issues such as confidence building, how to fight shyness, discovering-accepting-appreciating oneself, discerning one's talents, establishing positive relationships, time management, decision making, setting realistic goals, friendship, and so on. Sessions are conducted in an interactive youth-friendly manner. Social analysis, which includes discussions of socially disturbing issues, village development, and health concerns, including the threat of HIV/AIDS, also form vital parts of these programs. Aiming primarily at personality development, they also emphasize making youth

socially fit adults concerned about the society in which they live.

Church leaders have also recognized that next to their parents, young people's teachers play an important role in a youngster's life. DBYES and, to a lesser extent, NERYC offer teacher training programs to the schools of the region. Apart from the knowledge and skills needed to manage a classroom and teach effectively, teachers are also trained to listen to the children in their classrooms and to facilitate their development from one life stage to another. Special course materials are offered to primary school teachers who have the responsibility of laying a strong foundation for children's intellectual and moral development.

Nonformal vocational training is offered for school dropouts to enable them to establish themselves and earn a decent living. Training in secretarial skills, modern office management, computer and desktop publishing, computer hardware, and TV and radio repair are just some of the programs offered to youth at very reasonable rates. Salesians also run nonformal centers to train youth in driving, repairing vehicles, carpentry, and land-based skills. Most of these programs are residential.

Training programs achieve other goals as well. Youth work is most effective when groups of youth are formed, nurturing youth leadership and providing structure for youth development interventions. Hence, each youth program ends with efforts to form one or more youth groups in the area in which it is offered, either in the form of a youth self-help group or a cultural and social club. These groups have shown themselves to be very successful at sustaining the changes youth make during programming. For example, in rural areas where youth self-help groups have been run, youth participants have followed up their participation with the creation of profitable income generation activities and entrepreneurial ventures that are helping to curb rural unemployment. Most important, these groups ensure that youth carry on in their communities as community leaders, themselves conducting peer training and establishing other youth groups that offer an alternative to the militant organizations that advocate armed conflict.

In line with these goals, the Church sponsors scout and guide troops. Scouts and guides and the scoutmasters and guide captains trained by DBYES have excelled at the national level. Furthermore, these scouts and guides are often the most valued students in school. Skilled and helpful, resourceful and prompt, they manifest the prospect for an active and reliable citizenry.

The Young Students' Movement (YSM) is another group promoted by NERYC in the schools of the region. YSM instills in youth social consciousness and encourages students to take up small issues at the local level with the help of their teachers and elders. The emphasis is on becoming service minded and to volunteer to assist those in need.

Intensive leadership training programs, of up to 2 weeks' duration, aimed to help young people who have already shown leadership help them to excel further. In communities where a gun culture prevails, these youth leaders present a healthy alternative for their communities to resolve conflict.

Still, the root causes of the violence need to be addressed. Unemployment is considered by many community leaders to be the root cause of the violence. Unemployment is associated with feelings of injustice. Therefore, DBYES funds career orientation programs for students in secondary schools. These programs outline career opportunities and give students the opportunity to take aptitude tests to help them orient themselves toward their possible future careers. DBYES also prepares interested educated youth to appear for competitive examinations for government positions through coaching, the provision of library and study facilities, mock interviews, sample tests, and building the student's confidence.

Exposure programs are also sponsored for youth and teachers. Teachers are taken on exposure trips to well-equipped schools in the country to update them on new educational technologies and to motivate them in their teaching. Youth groups from the different areas of the region have also been taken on exposure trips to show them how other communities have organized themselves with nonviolent solutions to social problems.

More locally, the church-based organizations have come to realize that the best way of speaking to groups of people is through their own indigenous cultural expressions. Church-sponsored theater, music, and art shows have been used to convey messages to youth and to the general public. Cultural expressions also make people proud of their heritage and roots, countering the pull toward problematic noncommunitarian behaviors. DBYES is presently organizing a mobile music and drama troop that will perform in schools and colleges of the region on themes relating to drug abuse, HIV-AIDS, reproductive health, and violence.

Exemplars of Church-Based Community Development

Literacy Centers

Many of the projects listed above are driven by a combination of church leaders, community elders, and youth themselves. New initiatives are constantly being developed as needs are identified. The churches of the North East are seen by their communities, both Christian and non-Christian, as a source of expertise on community development, education, and counseling.

For example, one of the authors (Menamparampil) has started a series of Don Bosco Literacy Centers in and around the city of Imphal for poor children who otherwise would have no opportunity or motivation to go to school because their parents are too poor to afford the minimal fees or they need the children at home to carry out work- and home-related tasks. Responding to the needs of this community of children, literacy centers take the school to the children rather than requiring children to come to the school. Started in October 2002, there are now 32 centers with over 800 children enrolled, most of whom are girls. In these centers, children are given basic linguistic and mathematical knowledge that enables them to join regular classes at government-run or private schools. As a result of this attachment to a daily educational regime, 238 of these children have convinced their parents to let them join a regular school. Many of these children continue to attend literacy programs in the later afternoon and early evening to catch up with students who have been attending regular school from Class 1. To further assist children move to the regular school system, members of the Church have sponsored 47 of the poorest children, providing the financial assistance required to participate in government schools, which charge annual fees and require students supply their own books and uniforms.

A team of 4 coordinators and 32 teachers are partners in this program. They undergo regular training in a variety of fields, including puppetry, storytelling, HIV/AIDS awareness, formation of self-help groups, financial management, and understanding children. Parents of the children are also provided with support and encouraged to form self-help groups and save money for income-generating activities. More than 10 such groups have formed and are functioning well.

Leadership Training

Recognizing the potential of youth and the dangers that come when that potential is not channeled, NERYC has launched a series of training sessions that help youth leaders play their role responsibly. Training is offered to youth who show leadership potential and are willing to invest some of their time every week animating their own peers. Selection for group participation is done by the Youth Commission in each diocese, keeping in mind the ethnic and linguistic diversity of the community. Eighty-eight youth are trained annually.

The training has five components, two of which are compulsory: training in facilitation skills and ethical living. These are 5-day residential programs. In the first, youth learn skills to facilitate workshops and training programs, such as event planning, understanding group dynamics, conducting group discussions, and communication skills. The second compulsory workshop, ethical living, helps young leaders to get in touch with themselves, identify their values and priorities, and spend time in reflective prayer. They are also offered the services of counselors if they need it. Working with youth in their communities is presented as a spiritual commitment.

Following completion of these two courses, youth leaders choose up to three other training programs to attend. These include (a) youth ministry skills training, which focuses on analyzing and understanding the situation of youth in the region and developing the skills necessary to work with youth groups and plan youth programs;

(b) introduction to social development, which raises awareness of development and how participants can lead villagers in local development initiatives; and (b) intensive training in rural technology, a 3-week course providing hands-on training in the skills and basic knowledge that would enable participants to make use of the region's abundant land resources. This program demonstrates the financial benefits of using the land well. Young people who have gone through these trainings assist the local youth directors in the dioceses in animating and training other youth.

Peace Education

Young people are the victims of violence and also in many cases perpetrators of violence. NERYC has shown that if youth can be trained by militant groups to be violent, then they can also be trained as advocates for peace—hence, the goal of creating a movement for peace with youth at the center. NERYC does not, however, see this initiative as an immediate solution but, instead, as an effort to build the political and social foundation for nonviolent solutions to social problems. Peace educators seek to equip youth with the skills needed to live with violence without taking to violence themselves. NERYC has focused on two sets of skills youth are trained in: resolving conflicts and valuing diversity. Youth are taught that conflicts are natural and that there are positive ways to deal with them when they occur on the streets, in the marketplaces, in schools, and in families. Similarly, NERYC trainers work with youth to value the great cultural diversity of the North East. In most cases, diversity has become a liability in the region. Youth are shown how to value that diversity in order to break down intergroup suspicions, prejudice, and fear.

The peace education program trains youth to be peace builders in their communities. Weeklong training programs are offered to youth where they learn the skills of analyzing conflicts, identifying connectors and dividers, enhancing communication, negotiating, and seeking consensus. Armed with the skills and the confidence gained during the program, young people return to their communities to hold meetings and organize programs that build on this peace theme. They are supported by NERYC staff and the diocesan Youth Commissions. More than 120 youth peace educators have been trained to date. The effect on communities is beginning to show. During the ethnic conflict between Karbis and Kukis in December 2003, one of the young peace educators who belong to the Karbi tribe said, "My people are killed, our villages are burned; I am angry, my friends are upset. But as peace educators, we shall not retaliate." Another youth peace educator who, as a result of the conflict between the Kukis and another tribe, the Paites, was left homeless, her parents jobless, and herself barred from being educated for 2 years, says that her training helped her to deal with her anger differently:

I now realize how important it is to see different situations from different perspectives and above all the need for reconciliation from thoughts like anger, fear. . . . I decided to help my community and people using all the knowledge I have about conflict resolution. I focused mainly on youth groups, allowing myself to help them to be aware of the crisis our community is going through. . . . I got a tremendous ability to see through different perspectives and empathize. Even though I have challenges that stand on my way, I have learned handling them skillfully, peacefully and successfully.

The power of theater and music is also used by NERYC to share the message of peace though a program called "Peace Spread" in the state of Tripura. Tripura has seen a demographic transition during the last few decades, with the majority tribal communities being reduced to a minority status by refugees from Bangladesh. The tribal peoples have resorted to militancy to redeem their rights. The refugees have responded with their own armed militancy to defend themselves. According to official figures, more than 1,400 civilians have been killed in extremist violence since 1993. Over 700 have been badly injured. Amidst an environment of mutual mistrust, anger, and suspicion, young boys and girls trained in the skills of street theater venture out into their communities' common spaces to show that peace is possible. Youth from the tribal communities perform in

Bengali-dominated localities sending a powerful message that not all tribals are militants and have taken to the gun; there are those among them who want peace. Their message is also shared with their own communities, despite the threat that artists like them run the risk of being kidnapped or killed.

Clearly, faith-based organizations and the individuals who work and volunteer with them do not claim to answer all the problems faced by youth of the region. They do, however, make a difference in the life of thousands of young people and provide an example of how NGOs can work on many different issues at one time in ways that involve young people in finding solutions to intransigent problems in their communities.

CONCLUSION

Apfel and Simon (1996) list a number of factors that contribute to children's capacity to build resilience:

Resourcefulness, or the gift of being able to extract even very small amounts of human warmth in the most dire circumstances and of knowing how to attract and use adult support outside the family if they cannot find it in their own family; curiosity, intellectual mastery, and the ability to relate one's own difficulties to others and to empathize with, say, seriously disturbed parents while keeping a safe distance and knowing how to find a safe place; a flexible array of emotional defenses including the ability to laugh even in the most trying circumstances and the possibility of delaying crying until a safer time; some goal for which to live; and models, among adults, of helpfulness to others along with instruction in how to do likewise. (quoted in Bok, 1999, p. 66)

The young people of North East India find themselves in a not very enviable position compared with their counterparts elsewhere. Although life can be frustrating under the given circumstances, some factors mentioned above are inherent in the communities that these youth belong to that help them to cope. Faith-based organizations in the region are one resource among many. Resilience among North East youth is expressed through many of the characteristics identified by authors such as Apfel and Simon. However, it takes access to the structural conditions and supports necessary to build and then use these characteristics to ensure healthy outcomes. The community development initiatives of church-based organizations such as Don Bosco in North East India are an example of a community-based initiative to address the risk factors youth face that also creates the conditions for resilience to emerge.

REFERENCES

Bok, S. (1999). *Mayhem.* Boston, MA: Perseus Books.

Dutta, D. (1999, August 27). Cultural decadence of youth. *Nagaland Page,* p. 5.

Hazarika, S. (1994). *Strangers of the mist: Tales of war and peace from India's northeast.* New Delhi, India: Viking.

Learn to live with floods. (2004, July 13). *The Telegraph* (Guwahati, India), p. 1.

Menamparampil, G. (in press). The youth. In Department of Human Development (Ed.), *Report on the status of youth in Manipur.* Imphal, Manipur: Department of Human Development.

Nishat, S. (2001, July 29). Living on the edge. *Assam Tribune,* p. 3.

Thomas, J. (Ed.). (2000). *Youth work: A design for the future: A study of youth work in north east India.* Dimapur, India: Agency for Integral Development Action.

Thomas, J. (2001). *Impact of violence on the social and personal life of young people of Nagaland and Manipur.* Unpublished doctoral research thesis, Mahatma Gandhi Kashi Vidyapith, Varanasi, India.

UN Development Programme. (1998). *Summary report from the HDR 1998 on Global Consumption Itanagar Workshop: The North-Eastern regions perspectives, Sept. 20–21.* Retrieved July 20, 2000, from www.undp.org.in/report/HDRKS98/wshitkey.htm

Vattathara, T., & Biju, M. (Eds.). (2002). *Youth vision.* Guwahati, India: Don Bosco.

Verghese, B. G. (1996). *India's northeast resurgent: Ethnicity, insurgency, governance, development.* New Delhi, India: Konark.

21

ALTERNATIVE APPROACHES TO PROMOTING THE HEALTH AND WELL-BEING OF CHILDREN

Accessing Community Resources to Support Resilience

KEN BARTER

Schools, mental health agencies, public health departments, judicial systems, child protection agencies, recreation services, and family resource centers are but a few of the Canadian public child-serving organizations that work with children and youth on a daily basis in attempts to promote their health and well-being. These organizations have in place policies, standards, procedures, working protocols, and professional practices to facilitate responding to the needs of children and youth. These public child-serving organizations tend to respond well to individuals and families who are deemed to be functioning adequately in society. People are educated in schools, they are born and die in hospitals, they are protected by law enforcement, and they receive a variety of public welfare services based on established eligibility criteria. However, once people are deemed to be malfunctioning, the response to the needs of individuals and families assumes different dimensions. Then these organizations are expected to engage in people-processing, people-sustaining, and people-changing functions (Hasenfeld, 1983). These functions are oftentimes carried out through legislative mandates that aim to protect, control, ameliorate, reduce, and remedy the barriers facing people who are experiencing difficulties.

It is well-known that child-serving organizations interface with millions of Canadian children and their families who are struggling with a number of significant difficulties associated with discrimination, poverty, few opportunities for employment and education, poor parenting, family violence, and parental psychopathology (Fraser, 1997). These difficulties or risk factors affect and significantly interfere with the health and well-being of children.

The presence of these factors in the lives of children and families, according to research in child growth and development, provides a knowledge base to predict outcomes. For example, it is well-known that people's health and well-being are related to socioeconomic factors such as income and level of education. Willms (2002) suggests that "the relationship between children's outcomes and family income is so firmly entrenched in our understanding of human development that the term 'children at risk' has almost become synonymous with 'children living in poverty'" (p. 8). Although it is easy to make this connection, many children from poor families still do well. In addition, children from families who are not poor can be vulnerable or at risk. Although having family income sufficient to respond to the needs of children is very important and desirable, income alone does not reduce vulnerability and poor outcomes. The benefits of good parenting, a supportive family, close relationships, a sense of belonging, and parents in good mental health have been demonstrated to outweigh the negative effects associated with poverty (Willms, 2002).

The challenge faced by public child-serving organizations is how to intervene with children, families, and communities to respond to known risk factors associated with undesirable outcomes for children and to promote protective factors that will facilitate desirable outcomes. This chapter explores this challenge and discusses barriers to promoting protective factors. The chapter also suggests alternatives to support that strengthen other protective factors to facilitate resilience and positive outcomes for children in terms of their health and well-being. It demonstrates that pathways to resilience must necessarily include pathways through the service systems mandated to support healthy children and families.

THE CHALLENGE

In Canada, the lack of opportunities for a significant number of children and families to realize their health and well-being is pervasive. Child and family poverty continues to be a critical problem; child abuse and neglect statistics are astounding; the number of children coming into the care of the state is increasing in significant numbers; substitute care resources are limited and in crisis; children and families relying on food banks are increasing in numbers; there continues to be little investment in prevention and early intervention; violence in families, schools, and communities is a real concern; power imbalances that have detrimental effects on women, children, youth, and minority groups continue to exist; and there continue to be negative public attitudes toward poor and disadvantaged citizens. These social injustices and the absence of political will and leadership to invest in Canada's children to meaningfully affect them are devastatingly sad and well documented in the literature (Barter, 2002, 2003; Campaign, 2000, 1998; Conway, 2001; Prilleltensky, Nelson, & Peirson, 2001; Pulkingham & Ternowetsky, 1997; Ross, Shillington, & Lochhead, 1994; Trocmé et al., 2001; Willms, 2002).

The persistence of the challenge is not due to lack of knowledge about the conditions in which children and families live. Enough is now known about the risk factors that children face and the "rotten outcomes" they experience (Schorr, 1988). Equally, enough is known about many of the antecedents associated with these factors and outcomes. For example, there are many who would suggest that Canadian society is in the midst of a social revolution as endeavors are underway to cope with and respond to the global economy, changing demographics, technological advances, environmental concerns, political upheaval and uncertainty, government reform and restructuring, and the reconfiguration of the Canadian welfare state. There exists controversy, often bitter controversy, in virtually every sphere of social welfare, from hospitals and schools to social welfare benefits, accessibility to services, and personal social services. Old structures, systems, and policies are crumbling before there is any clear indication of viable alternatives. Canadians remain unclear about what lies ahead (Barter, 2003).

Concomitant with this controversy is the unfortunate reality that millions of Canadians, who for reasons of abilities, age, gender, sexual orientation, culture, and race, find themselves in disadvantaged positions and are being denied the basic rights to justice and services. Despite the political rhetoric of fairness and equal opportunity, the gates of social justice seem to be sliding shut. For citizens who most require services, the implication of their growing disadvantage includes greater exposure to poverty, unemployment, unequal distribution of income and power, poor health, isolation, and a societal attitude of contempt for people who present challenges to structures of social control. For the organizations providing services, particularly child-serving organizations, the implications include limited or reduced funding, integration of services and programs with reduced human and financial resources, and organizational restructuring as governments shift responsibilities to community-based governance and systems of delivery. Professionals and paraprofessionals within these community-based organizations are coping with the uncertainty associated with displacement, increased workloads, and demands to develop new skills and competencies associated with their widening scope of responsibilities. For communities, the implication of this pattern among different levels of government to shed their responsibilities has contributed to a society where the gap between the haves and the have-nots is becoming more pronounced.

It is fair to say that Canadian society, like other minority-world nations, is characterized by increasing instability, whether ecological, economic, political, social, or cultural. In the opinions of some, this instability is viewed as crisis. For example, Ife (1997) suggests there is an ecological crisis as the limits to growth and industrialization in a finite world become evident; an economic crisis as the global economy develops to the point where nobody is able to control or understand the complexity of international trade and finance; a political crisis as politicians find it increasingly difficult to govern and solve issues within the parameters they have set for themselves; a social crisis as patterns of community and extended family break down in the name of economic progress; a cultural crisis as those specific cultural factors that give people a sense of identity and belonging are lost in a consumer culture; and a spiritual crisis as the rational secular worldview devalues spirituality or religious values and beliefs, anything that cannot be measured or counted.

Conway (2001) provides a plethora of evidence to suggest the serious and detrimental impact on families, children, and communities of this contemporary state of affairs in Canadian society. According to Conway, the Canadian

family is under strain. An example of the crises they face includes growing family poverty. In particular, there has been a dramatic increase in single-parent, female-headed families who are lacking sufficient income and supports to adequately attend to their parenting responsibilities. Poor families also face a lack of sufficient quality day care to support mothers in the labor force. Increasingly, many of these families have to use food banks. There is a concomitant increase in homelessness. Incidents of domestic violence toward women and children are also on the rise. Publications such as Murphy's (1999) *The Ugly Canadian: The Rise and Fall of a Caring Society* and Hurtig's (1999) *Pay the Rent or Feed the Kids: The Tragedy and Disgrace of Poverty in Canada* are indicative of what is taking place in Canada and the detrimental effects of shifting social policies on children.

The challenge is clear. The context in which children experience these crises and social injustices is equally clear. They are growing up with parents who are not only poor but isolated, impaired, and undermined by their surroundings. Parents are too drained to provide the consistent nurturance, structure, and stimulation that prepare children for school and for life. Many children experience themselves as failures, resulting from a lack of security, meaningful relationships, hope, a real sense of belonging, community supports, or opportunities to advance (Schorr, 1988). Although risk is ubiquitous in the lives of most children, and most risk factors, when considered in isolation, may have relatively weak effects (Willms, 2002), exposure to a number of risk factors increases exponentially the likelihood of poor outcomes (Kirby & Fraser, 1997; Prilleltensky et al., 2001).

Antecedents to undesirable outcomes for children are risk factors that are known to have certain predictive associations. According to Willms (2002) the term *predictive* is normally used to indicate a causal link between risk and an undesirable outcome. Causal links would suggest that if an individual's exposure to risk could be altered, then the likelihood of an undesirable outcome would change. On principle, if not in practice, causal links that have been established through research have been relied on to guide the design of interventions and primary prevention initiatives. However, the risk literature informs us of the complexities of relationships between risk factors and possible outcomes, given different types of risks (those internal or external to children). For example, Kirby and Fraser (1997) distinguish between "resilient" factors and "protective" factors. Resilient factors are those considered internal to the child, whereas protective factors are those considered external. All factors, according to Willms (2002) need to be understood in terms of being (a) unalterable, such as sex and ethnicity, and (b) those that can be changed with intervention, such as behavior and relationships with one's environment.

In many cases, unalterable factors dominate the list of risk factors related to life outcomes, perhaps because factors such as sex, ethnicity, and family structure are easier to measure than factors that capture the subtle processes associated with policy and practice. This shortcoming of risk and protective factor research may contribute to the pessimistic conclusion, shared by many people, that the life course of vulnerable children is largely predetermined by family background (Willms, 2002, p. 27).

Understanding risk from the perspective of unalterable and alterable factors suggests the importance of an ecological approach in working with children and families. Unfortunately, much of the emphasis has been at the individual micro level with limited attention to the meso or macro system levels (Prilleltensky et al., 2001). Evidence of this emphasis on the individual is clear with respect to interventions to protect children from risks. Child protection systems, for example, are primarily concerned with risk assessment and risk management, all geared toward protecting the child from further maltreatment. Although this is important, such interventions fail to take an ecological approach in considering that protection is only one key determinant of health for children. Consideration of other factors beyond the current mandate of protection services is also needed. These include external environmental issues that affect children and families, such as income and social status, social support networks, education, employment and working conditions, social environments, and physical environments (Guy, 1997).

Despite this understanding of risk factors and what is required to alter those factors to have more desirable outcomes, there are barriers that tend to get in the way of acting on research knowledge. Equally there are barriers to creating opportunities for a better balance between risk and protective factors to enhance resilience. These barriers can best be understood by asking critical questions: Why, despite our understanding of the social determinants of health, do interventions typically focus on the individual without due attention to changing pernicious environments? With all of today's knowledge about the benefits of prevention strategies, why do provincial ministries in Canada fail to balance investments in prevention with investments in treatment? Why is little attention paid to family planning and life skills in Canada's schools? Why do we have a high tolerance in Canadian society for social injustices? Why does child and family poverty remain, despite research that informs us of the detrimental effects of poverty on health and well-being?

Everyone has opinions and responses to these questions, particularly when it comes to what is in the best interests of children and families who require assistance and support. There is a consensus among most stakeholders that something should be done to fix the problems. However, what is lacking is a consensus on a comprehensive way to do this. Unfortunately, discussions on the "way to do this" generally deteriorate into complaints by one group toward another. As pointed out by Schorr (1988, 1998), it is not a question of knowledge, for we know what to do. Instead, as a society we have selected not to do it. Selecting not to act represents a significant barrier in creating opportunities to address the risk factors that prevent resilience from developing.

THE PROBLEM WITH INVESTMENT IN CHILD-SERVING ORGANIZATIONS

What society has done, in attempts to create these opportunities, is to invest in public child-serving organizations. These organizations are large bureaucracies that tend to emphasize legal rather than moral obligations. Information gathering and technical recording tend to overrule professional assessments. Client participation in policy and management decisions are limited or overlooked. Efficiency and productivity often take precedence over process and service quality. Professional autonomy and creativity are often not encouraged. Finally, there tends to be a lack of openness among managers of services to challenges to organizations' rules, policies, and procedures.

Field experiences, research, and the literature, particularly in regard to services to children, suggest that bureaucracies are not necessarily the right environment for creating opportunities where relationships, caring, investment in people, and compassion take place. Instead, service systems create an environment governed by policies and procedures—where power remains with high-level bureaucrats who are isolated from the grassroots; where thinking is compartmentalized and often reactive when fixing problems; where, at times, there is unwarranted political involvement; and where those who seek services or provide services are not seen as equal partners in the decisions that affect them. Bureaucratic environments tend to take the traditional top-down, programmatic, fix-it orientation to their work, what is referred to as a knowing-in-action (Fabricant & Burghardt, 1992) or categorical approach (Hooper-Briar & Lawson, 1994). In attempts to continue to try to fix things, an important dimension has been overlooked, that the many issues associated with the risk factors that bring about undesirable outcomes for children elude altogether bureaucratic intervention. Child-serving bureaucracies were never designed to appropriately respond to the complex issues, crises, and current realities facing contemporary children, families, and communities. In fact, the investment in bureaucracies has been such that it is said, "One of the most pervasive problems of modern society is the bureaucratization of work and relationships" (Schram & Mandell, 1997, p. 179).

Of significance as well, in terms of barriers to promoting protective factors to enhance resilience, is that these child-serving bureaucracies, similar to the children and families they are intended to serve, are under stress and in crisis (Adams & Nelson, 1995). Many have legal mandates in child welfare, welfare assistance, education, corrections, residential care, and mental health. The ever-growing emphases on efficiency, effectiveness, and accountability have created organizational environments where management and policy practices often serve to obstruct rather than facilitate social justice and empowerment of citizens.

It is known that in families where there are ongoing and persistent stresses, the family environment becomes one where hope fades into despair, affection withers into hostility, discipline turns into abuse, stability dissolves into chaos, and love becomes neglect. Risk factors are very much a part of these family environments and contribute to undesirable outcomes for children. Within bureaucracies, where there is ongoing and persistent stresses, the working environment becomes one where creativity withers into conformity, idealism turns into cynicism, collective sharing dissolves into protection of professional turf, and critical questions, challenges, and new ideas are oftentimes feared and avoided. These working environments contribute to ever-increasing emphasis on control, evidence-based practice, efficiency, accountability, and endeavoring to find clinical solutions to structural problems.

Persistent and ongoing crises within both families and child-serving organizations, juxtaposed with the contextual social, economic, cultural, and political realities of contemporary society, represent the extent of the challenges to shifting the balance between risk factors and protective factors in children's lives. These challenges are further enhanced by the negative attitudes about governments' and communities' abilities to make a difference in the lives of vulnerable children; the oftentimes reluctance on the part of child-serving organizations to engage in collaborative partnerships with the parents and families they serve for purposes of sharing power and resources; and the absence of a concerted effort on the part of the public to challenge society's tolerance for social injustices experienced by millions of Canadians, particularly those who are marginalized and disadvantaged.

ALTERNATIVES TO PROMOTING THE HEALTH AND WELL-BEING OF CHILDREN

The research is clear on risk and protective factors relating to family, school, neighborhood, and individual psychosocial and biological characteristics (Kirby & Fraser, 1997). The effects of poverty, inequality, racial discrimination, poor parental mental health, inadequate family support, family violence, isolation, and developmental delays are known risk factors associated with undesirable outcomes for children (Begun, 1993; Peirson, Laurendeau, & Chamberland, 2001; Werner, 1984). It is equally well-known that desirable outcomes are possible for children, despite one or several of these risk factors, if there are significant relationships with a caring adult, if there are opportunities available within the community and school for social connections, if there are good family and school support networks, and if a child has good thinking and problem-solving abilities (Benard, 1993; Garmezy, 1993).

Knowledge, grounded in research and experiences, makes clear how important it is for those who work with or on behalf of vulnerable children to create a manageable balance between risk and protective factors. Such a balance facilitates successful adaptation despite adversity. Hence, for vulnerable children, resilience is not so much the absence of risk factors or the presence of protective factors but the ability to cope with adversity, stress, and deprivation as risk and protective factors interact across multiple system levels. Kirby and Fraser (1997) suggest, "The nature of interactions of risk and protective factors that contribute to resilience are poorly understood and usually inconsistently described in the literature" (p. 17). These authors put forth two models of interaction—one additive, the other interactive.

The additive model proposes risk and protection as polar opposites. For example, high family stress is considered a risk factor, whereas low family stress is considered a protective factor. Children in families where stress is high will be at increased risk for social problems compared with children in families where stress is low. "In the additive models risk and protection are thought to counterbalance each other" (Kirby & Fraser, 1997, p. 18).

The interactive model better describes the relationship between risk and protective factors. In this model, "Protective factors have effect only in combination with risk factors" (Kirby & Fraser, 1997, p. 18). That is to say that the presence of protective factors has little effect when family stress is low but their effect emerges when stress is high. Within the interaction framework, the presence of protective factors can serve as a buffer to risk factors, can serve to interrupt cumulative effects of risk, and may intervene to prevent a risk factor from having an effect.

Both models suggest an appreciation of the many complexities associated with risk, protection, and resilience. As noted by Fraser and Galinsky (1997), most childhood problems are multidetermined. Embracing this multideterminism suggests shifting the promotion of children's health and well-being into a realm *beyond* the boundaries of current professional and organizational interventions. Alternatives, based on different thinking, are necessary.

In suggesting alternatives, it is important to avoid repeating past practices. It is well-known in Canada that efforts have already been made to change legislation, improve standards, hire more staff, engage in more training, heighten expectations, develop more policies, introduce more programs, and increase accountability. Albeit these are all worthwhile endeavors, the reality of how systems operate today suggests that such endeavors fall short of realizing their ultimate goals of dramatically improving the situation for disadvantaged children and families. Although laudable, these efforts have not been very clear with respect to tackling poverty and oppression and other social injustices.

Promoting the health and well-being of children with an emphasis on the key determinants of health raised earlier (protection, income and social status, social support networks, education) requires extending interventions beyond the family or individual levels to include interventions at the professional, organizational, and community levels. In other words, *risk and protective factors have to be considered beyond the four walls of parenting to embrace the social, economic, and political forces that affect families and communities.* Capturing this more holistic ecological approach implies approaching risk and protective factors based on different conceptual underpinnings. Before old concepts are changed or abandoned, new concepts must first be developed. These new concepts represent not only alternatives in promoting the health and well-being of children but equally suggest what is required in creating the necessary opportunities to facilitate resilience in children. Resilience in this context is "adaptive behaviour that produces positive social and health outcomes arising from the interplay of risk and protective factors" (Fraser & Galinsky, 1997, p. 265).

A suggested place to begin in bringing forth alternatives is by asking critical questions: Is it important to have collaboration among child-serving organizations (mental health, corrections, schools, recreation, family and community resource centers, child protection authorities) with respect to promoting the health and well-being of children? Is this collaboration in place? Are primary prevention and early intervention and outreach services given priority within child-serving organizations? Are structural dimensions (poverty, discrimination, violence, and other social injustices) an important aspect of the work being done in promoting the health and well-being of children? Is the status quo with respect to what is taking place in the lives of children and families who are marginalized and disadvantaged acceptable to Canadian society? Does the research and literature on children's well-being play a significant role in influencing policies and practices in work with vulnerable children? What interventions are necessary to help children cope with adversity? Is investment in alternative approaches to intervention being made?

Responses to these questions will vary. For some, it will be a matter of investing in more programs and services. For others, it will be getting the child-serving organizations to work more closely together or revamping current systems to take a completely new approach to working with vulnerable children and families. For still others, it might be a matter of getting the general community involved. Although responses vary, the research on children's services would suggest that the consensus is that change is required, given the evidence of what is known about risk factors that contribute to undesirable outcomes for children. There is also broad agreement that public child-serving organizations can no longer carry out their respective mandates and services without an investment in prevention and early intervention; that they can no longer assume responsibility for their mandates, roles, and responsibilities alone; that they

can no longer provide services in a framework of poverty; and that they can no longer present an image to the community and the children and families they serve that they have the power and influence to promote the health and well-being of children (Hooper-Briar, 1996; Schene, 1996).

There has to be a better way to assist children in coping with risk factors and promoting their health and well-being. There has to be a better way to act on and implement the proven attributes of successful programs: "Practitioners know that effective programs are characterized by flexibility, comprehensiveness, responsiveness, front-line discretion, high standards of quality and good management, a family focus, community rootedness, a clear mission, and respectful, trusting relationships" (Schorr, 1998, p. 18). Investments in prevention are equally well-known to be successful (Nelson, Laurendeau, Chamberland, & Peirson, 2001).

A reconceptualization embracing these attributes suggests alternatives with respect to redefining child welfare. These alternatives are found in the following definition proposed by Barter (in press):

> Child welfare is a collaborative process between community, families, and child serving organizations and professionals for purposes of reclaiming their strengths and capacities to develop the necessary preventative, supportive, supplementary, substitute and advocacy services that respect children's rights to health and well-being and actively seek to influence and change social, economic, and political policies that affect children and their families.

Several alternatives to promoting the health and well-being of children and to providing services to help children cope with adversity emerge from this definition.

First, services to children who are coping with risk factors demand a collaborative approach on the part of many stakeholders. Schools, mental health clinics, child protection authorities, and correctional services *are* public child welfare systems. They are all financed by the public purse and are mandated to serve children in accordance with legislation. However, within these various organizations, there is a perception that each is responsible for their respective mandates independent of the other. Yes, there are examples of coordination of services and communication across systems; however, examples of collaboration are less clear. Collaboration is distinct in that it requires a commitment to mutual goals; a common values orientation; a sharing of power, risks, and resources; mutual investment in end results; and a willingness to embrace change and to conduct business differently. These distinctive qualities are necessary dimensions in realizing the determinants of health for children and their families. A collaborative endeavor is not where you send individuals to be representatives. Instead, it is where individuals participate and represent a personal and organizational commitment to a shared process based on active and committed participation.

Prevention, Early Intervention, and Outreach

To suggest that services to children require a collaborative approach implies doing things differently based on a need to change the delivery and configuration of services (Barter, 1996; Graham & Barter, 1999). Doing things differently would mean moving into prevention, early intervention, and outreach. It would mean working at the community level to promote collaborative initiatives in providing comprehensive emergency services, establishing drop-in centers, heightening community awareness, involving volunteers, promoting family resource centers, and creating opportunities for parent and family involvement. Primary prevention initiatives would include legislative advocacy, parent education, public school education, community service networks, parent advocacy groups, and life and family planning. Combined, these initiatives by service delivery systems create the conditions necessary for resilience to be realized.

Beyond collaboration, the second quality of an alternative model of service delivery needed to promote child and family well-being is innovation in program design and delivery. Smale (1998) has characterized such innovation as second-order change. Innovation suggests introducing new practices, designing new methods of service delivery, approaching social problems differently, and developing models of best practice. Innovation also implies changing the rules by which systems operate at the level of structure and how relationships are organized. Being innovative emphasizes opportunities rather than problems; uses collective intelligence; builds on diversity and strengths; acts upon knowledge, experiences, and research; and supports the emergence of new systems that promote resilience among those at risk.

According to Hasenfeld (1983), innovation suggests the adoption of a direction, service, or method of service delivery that "becomes radical when its implementation requires changes in the allocations of resources, the distribution of power, and the internal structure of an organization" (p. 220). On the other hand, change refers to alterations in the allocation of resources to accommodate any shifts or adjustments within the organization. Change is not associated with doing business differently based on a rethinking of tasks, values, and priorities. Change alone is associated with the fix-it approach. Interventions to promote resilience in children suggest the appropriateness of radical innovation rather than changes that leave intact business-as-usual practices by staff and professionals in service delivery systems.

Radical innovation promotes moving services to children to the macro level (Baines, Evans, & Neysmith, 1993; Barter, 2003). Interventions at this level represent a shift in focus. The community becomes a primary client system with whom to engage for purposes of introducing innovation in practice that will support protective factors to enhance resilience and reduce clients' exposure to risk factors. Recognizing children in the context of the family and the family in the context of the larger social, economic, and political spheres highlights the importance of understanding "that many of the most critical problems that face families and their children are beyond individual control and reflect external conditions under which families live" (Goffin, 1983, p. 284). Making this shift is radical in that it is a direction intended to deal with the roots of the many issues underpinning risk.

Issues of poverty, oppression, distribution of power and income, and social injustices tend to remain in the background when working with disadvantaged families. Moving into the macro arena suggests the importance of connecting personal troubles and public issues. It is no longer acceptable to deal with symptoms alone (Carniol, 1995)—hence, the significance of advocacy as a third alternative in promoting the health and well-being of children. Advocacy is necessary for purposes of promoting organizational changes, community development, and education to ensure that programs and services are conducive to meeting the needs of children and their families (Herbert & Mould, 1992). Children have little power in society and a limited political voice. The rhetoric about children's best interests is not often followed by action. An active advocacy role that is collaboratively driven by all stakeholders will serve to provide children with a much-needed voice in political and policy arenas.

A fourth alternative is the recognition that services for vulnerable children must be provided in recognition of their rights as well as their needs. Until children are recognized as equal persons under the law, society will continue to have no obligation to provide for their needs. Economic, social, and cultural rights include the right to education, social supports, having basic needs met, and a sense of continuity and belonging in significant relationships. Endorsement of these rights is necessary to guide practices and policy. Such endorsement would mean agreement with a common value base and beliefs about vulnerable children. It would also help those concerned to acknowledge that children are persons with distinctive developmental needs and interests (Goffin, 1983; Ife, 1997). This agreement is not necessarily reflected in current practices, nor has the UN Convention on the Rights of the Child been placed front and center in children's services. Mitchell (2003) puts forth a valid argument that the convention is a framework from which to base theory and practice in working with children.

Talking about needs and rights in terms of the health and well-being of children promotes the determinants of health and well-being. Referring to these determinants suggests an ecological and social justice perspective to services to children. Where the ecological perspective is based on principles of holism, sustainability, diversity, and equilibrium, the social justice perspective recognizes structural disadvantage, empowerment, needs, rights, and participation (Ife, 1995). These principles connect personal difficulties and public issues contributing to a dual response to working with children, parents, and their communities.

A dual response promotes wellness. "Family wellness is more than the absence of discord: it is the presence of supportive, affectionate, and gratifying relationships that serve to promote the personal development of family members and the collective wellbeing of the family as a whole" (Prilleltensky et al., 2001, p. 8). Wellness is an ecological concept and suggests the importance of social and economic supports. Thinking wellness means that poverty and oppression, the two fundamental barriers that interfere with healthy development of individuals, do not remain hidden in terms of policies, practices, and planning. Wellness promotes the importance of ensuring that interventions are required at the child and family level, the professional and organizational levels, and the community level.

A final alternative is that of a new vision for promoting resilience and helping children cope with adversity. The new vision reflects the importance of family-centered practice and building community capacity. Family-centered interventions recognize parents as collaborative partners with strengths and capabilities in the context of their family and community. Such interventions are sensitive to culture, encourage the development of contextually specific coping mechanisms, emphasize the importance of parent-to-parent support, and involve parents in processes that affect them. A family-centered approach supports child-centered interventions while remaining more inclusive and participatory. Hooper-Briar and Lawson (1994) suggest that family-centered interventions connect children, parents, families, neighbors, and communities. They put forth the premise that if interventions do things to, and for, children and youth, things that parents could do themselves if they had the necessary supports and resources, then interventions are child-centered. By comparison, the family-centered approach offers a framework that assumes a more ecological and social justice perspective in working with children, families, and communities.

Building community capacity to promote children's health and well-being is a people-centered approach with emphasis on building capacity "of people," "by people," and "for people" (Barter, 2001). The phrase "of people" suggests strengthening and renewing people's personal skills and self-knowledge. This heightens capacity for self-determination by identifying needs and interests important to people based on their experiences. "By people" suggests commitment; engagement; application of enhanced capabilities, skills, and knowledge; participation; collaboration; self-governance; and ownership. "For people" implies mobilization of people's capacities to take action and work toward change, equal opportunities, and access to resources that are sustained in order to promote the collective good. Building capacities of people, by people, and for people means mutual investment and commitment on the parts of all stakeholders to work collaboratively together. This partnership is paramount to realizing an alternate vision of service delivery for children and families.

Community capacity building, as part of this new vision of services that foster resilience, is about bringing services to children and families out of a professional and bureaucratic paradigm into a citizen-family-community paradigm. It is no longer appropriate to throw money at problems that are only growing worse (Schorr, 1988). The evidence shows that simply spending more money will not help resolve either personal or social barriers to health or address the negative results of iatrogenic practices of human service professionals and their organizations. The citizen-family-community paradigm suggests that public services and programs be more community based, with communities assuming responsibility for governance based on the goals and priorities they see as important for the well-being of citizens. Expectations associated with community capacity building include partnership, interprofessional teamwork, client participation and involvement, staff empowerment, user-friendly services, primary prevention and promotion, community development, seamless systems of delivery, integrated programs and services, and community decision making and governance.

Community capacity building is about caring, respect, acceptance, and personal and social power. Instead of a knowing-in-action approach, community capacity building is a reflection-in-action approach (Fabricant & Burghardt, 1992). Reflection is a process of dialogue, analysis, and consciousness-raising that creates opportunities to challenge thinking, develop relationships, revisit assumptions and beliefs, and consider new approaches to service delivery.

SUGGESTIONS FOR PRACTICE

These alternatives sound the call for a new way of addressing risk and protective factors to promote the health and well-being of children. It means that professionals and paraprofesssionals must be supported and willing to cross traditional professional and bureaucratic boundaries to collaborate in creating opportunities for children and their families to avail themselves of needed supports. This perspective is growing as shown by contributors to this volume such as Armstrong and Boothroyd in Chapter 24, and MacDonald, Gloade, and Wein in Chapter 22 who address this same theme of collaboration. Within these collaborative initiatives, parents must be valued as both equal partners and resources for the strengths needed to address children's and families' specific challenges. As well, professionals must be prepared to venture away from familiar practices and move toward nontraditional settings and hours of work. Activities outside the bureaucracy are deemed essential. As such, roles and responsibilities will need to be redefined and understood. Emphasis on services being user-friendly, accessible, coherent, flexible, and responsive to the needs and rights of children is paramount.

Complexity and uncertainty permeate much of the terrain of risk and protective factors in working with vulnerable children. From a practice perspective, the current emphasis being placed on evidence-based and competency-based approaches to practice are not necessarily conducive to creating opportunities for change, particularly with families and children who are marginalized and excluded in their communities. Although the emphasis on evidence-based practice may have obvious attractions in terms of improving accountability and effectiveness of services, as well as having potential for cost-efficiency, its contribution to tackling poverty and oppression and other social injustices is less clear (Stepney, 2000). Of course, evidence-based practice is not new to child welfare work. Yet despite efforts to base interventions on evidence of best practices, the situation for children and families and for workers in child-serving organizations has not dramatically changed.

What seems to change, however, is the emphasis on rules, tools, techniques, conformity to procedures, and mechanisms for obtaining and measuring competencies. This emphasis seems to be an attempt to reduce the complex personal, professional, and social issues associated with risk and protective factors to problems related to the bureaucratic administration of social services. This approach reflects many of the criticisms and shortcomings of competency-based practice (Adams, 2002; Rossiter, 2002; Stepney, 2000). A suggestion for practice in terms of the alternatives being proposed is an understanding that in the uncertain and complex work of addressing risk and protective factors, it is relationships that bring about change. Creating opportunities to build these relationships between professionals, organizations, citizens, and families requiring or needing services is critically important. These relationships will stem from taking a community capacity-building approach, being innovative, taking a family-centered approach, and adopting a dual response in dealing with risk and protective factors.

SUMMARY

In spite of the many improvements in education, health, social services, and child protection, the quality of life for many Canadian children is being questioned and is of serious concern to multiple stakeholders. These concerns elude the traditional bureaucratic response. Alternative responses are required to deal with the known risk factors that children and families face. It is not so much a question of knowledge and research about what to do. The question is more one of, Why is this knowledge not being acted on? This chapter has identified several critical barriers and put forth alternatives for consideration

in working with vulnerable children to promote their health and well-being.

If there is genuine concern to reduce undesirable outcomes for many Canadian children, it is worthwhile to consider four key principles as put forth by Seita (2000): (a) connectedness—promoting close, positive relationships; (b) dignity—courtesy, respect, and safety; (c) continuity—continuous belonging to a group, family, or community; and (d) opportunity—capitalizing on one's strengths and forming a personal vision. These principles, if adopted, would make a major shift in how public child-serving organizations might promote the health and well-being of children. The alternatives and practice suggestions made in this chapter support these principles.

REFERENCES

Adams, P., & Nelson, K. (Eds.). (1995). *Reinventing human services: Community- and family-centered practice.* New York: Aldine De Gruyter.

Adams, R. (2002). Social work processes. In R. Adams, L. Dominelli, & M. Payne (Eds.), *Social work: Themes, issues and critical debates* (2nd ed., pp. 249–266). New York: Palgrave.

Baines, C., Evans, P., & Neysmith, S. (Eds.). (1993). *Women's caring: Feminist perspectives on social welfare.* Toronto, Ontario, Canada: McClelland & Stewart.

Barter, K. (1996). Collaboration: A framework for northern social work practice. In R. Delaney, K. Brownlee, & K. Zapf (Eds.), *Issues in northern social work practice* (pp. 70–94). Thunder Bay, Ontario, Canada: Centre for Northern Studies, Lakehead University.

Barter, K. (2001). *Capacity building as a core element of evaluation: A literature review.* Paper prepared for Population and Public Health, Atlantic Regional Office, Health Canada.

Barter, K. (2002, Spring). Enough is enough: Renegotiating relationships to create a conceptual revolution in community and children's protection. *Canada's Children,* pp. 28–29.

Barter, K. (2003). Strengthening community capacity: Expanding the vision. *Relational Child and Youth Care Journal, 16*(2), 24–32.

Barter, K. (in press). Re-conceptualizing services for the protection of children. In. J. C. Turner &

F. J. Turner (Eds.), *Canadian social welfare* (5th ed.). Toronto, Ontario, Canada: Pearson Education Canada.

Begun, A. L. (1993). Human behavior and the social environment: The vulnerability, risk, and resilience model. *Journal of Social Work Education, 29*(1), 26–35.

Benard, B. (1993). Fostering resilience in kids. *Educational Leadership, 51*(3), 44–48.

Campaign 2000. (1998). *Child poverty in Canada: Report card 1998.* Toronto, Ontario, Canada: Child Poverty Action Group.

Carniol, B. (1995). *Case critical: Challenging social services in Canada.* Toronto, Ontario, Canada: Between the Lines.

Conway, J. F. (2001). *The Canadian family in crisis* (4th ed.). Toronto, Ontario, Canada: James Lorimer.

Fabricant, M. B., & Burghardt, S. (1992). *The welfare state crisis and the transformation of social service work.* New York: M. E. Sharpe.

Fraser, M. W. (1997). The ecology of childhood: A multisystems perspective. In M. W. Fraser (Ed.), *Risk and resilience in childhood: An ecological perspective* (pp. 1–8). Washington, DC: NASW Press.

Fraser, M. W., & Galinsky, M. J. (1997). Toward a resilience-based model of practice. In M. W. Fraser (Ed.), *Risk and resilience in childhood: An ecological perspective* (pp. 265–275). Washington, DC: NASW Press.

Garmezy, N. (1993). Children in poverty: Resilience despite risk. *Psychiatry, 56*(1), 127–136.

Goffin, S. G. (1983). A framework for conceptualizing children's services. *American Journal of Orthopsychiatry, 53*(2), 282–290.

Graham J., & Barter, K. (1999). Collaboration: A social work practice method. *Families in Society: The Journal of Contemporary Human Services, 80*(1), 6–13.

Guy, K. A. (Ed.). (1997). *Our promise to our children.* Ottawa, Ontario, Canada: Canadian Institute of Child Health.

Hasenfeld, Y. (1983). *Human service organizations.* Englewood Cliffs, NJ: Prentice Hall.

Herbert, M. D., & Mould, J. W. (1992). The advocacy role in public child welfare. *Child Welfare, 71*(2), 114–130.

Hooper-Briar, K. (1996). Building new capacities for work with vulnerable children, youth, and families. In K. Hooper-Briar & H. A. Lawson (Eds.), *Expanding partnerships for vulnerable children, youth, and families* (pp. 352–361). Alexandria, VA: Council on Social Work Education.

Hooper-Briar, K., & Lawson, H. A. (1994). *Serving children, youth and families through interprofessional collaboration and service integration: A framework for action.* Oxford, OH: Danforth Foundation and Miami University, the Institute for Educational Renewal.

Hurtig, M. (1999). *Pay the rent or feed the kids: The tragedy and disgrace of poverty in Canada.* Toronto, Ontario, Canada: McClelland & Stewart.

Ife, J. (1995). *Community development: Creating community alternatives: Vision, analysis and practice.* Melbourne, Australia: Longman.

Ife, J. (1997). *Rethinking social work practice: Towards critical practice.* Melbourne, Australia: Longman.

Kirby, L. D., & Fraser, M. W. (1997). Risk and resilience in childhood. In M. W. Fraser (Ed.), *Risk and resilience in childhood: An ecological perspective* (pp. 10–33). Washington, DC: NASW Press.

Mitchell, R. C. (2003, August). *Ideological reflections on the DSM IV-R.* Paper presented at the 7th International Child and Youth Conference, University of Victoria, British Columbia.

Murphy, B. (1999). *The ugly Canadian: The rise and fall of a caring society.* Toronto, Ontario, Canada: J. Gordon Shillingford.

Nelson, G., Laurendeau, M. C., Chamberland, C., & Peirson, L. (2001). A review and analysis of programs to promote family wellness and prevent the maltreatment of preschool and elementary-school-aged children. In I. Prilleltensky, G. Nelson, & L. Peirson (Eds.), *Promoting family wellness and preventing child maltreatment: Fundamentals for thinking and action* (pp. 220–272). Toronto, Ontario, Canada: University of Toronto Press.

Peirson, L., Laurendeau, M. C., & Chamberland, C. (2001). Context, contributing factors, and consequences. In I. Prilleltensky, G. Nelson, & L. Peirson (Eds.). *Promoting family wellness and preventing child maltreatment: Fundamentals for thinking and action* (pp. 41–143). Toronto, Ontario, Canada: University of Toronto Press.

Prilleltensky I., Nelson, G., & Peirson L. (2001). *Promoting family wellness and preventing child maltreatment: Fundamentals for thinking and action.* Toronto, Ontario, Canada: University of Toronto Press.

Pulkingham, J., & Ternowetsky, G. (1997). The changing context of child and family policies. In J. Pulkingham & G. Ternowetsky (Eds.), *Child and family policies: Struggles, strategies, and options* (pp. 14–38). Halifax, Nova Scotia, Canada: Fernwood.

Ross, D. P., Shillington, R. E., & Lochhead, C. (1994). *The Canadian fact book on poverty.* Ottawa, Ontario, Canada: Canadian Council on Social Development.

Rossiter, A. (2002). The social work sector study: A response. *Canadian Social Work Review, 19*(2), 341–348.

Schene, P. (1996). Innovative directions in child welfare. In K. Hooper-Briar & H.A. Lawson (Eds.), *Expanding partnerships for vulnerable children, youth, and families* (pp. 25–30). Alexandria, VA: Council on Social Work Education.

Schorr, L. B. (1988). *Within our reach: Breaking the cycle of disadvantage.* Toronto, Ontario, Canada: Doubleday.

Schorr, L. B. (1998). *Common purpose: Strengthening families and neighborhoods to rebuild America.* New York: Anchor Books.

Schram, B., & Mandell, B. R. (1997). *Human services: Policy and practice* (3rd ed.). Toronto, Ontario, Canada: Allyn & Bacon.

Seita, J. R. (2000). In our best interest: Three necessary shifts for child welfare workers and children. *Child Welfare, 79*(1), 77–92.

Smale, G. G. (1998). *Managing change through innovation.* London: National Institute for Social Work.

Stepney, P. (2000). Implications for social work in the new millennium. In P. Stepney & D. Ford (Eds.), *Social work models, methods and theories* (pp. 9–19). Dorset, UK: Russell House.

Trocmé, N., MacLaurin, B., Fallon, B., Daciuk, J., Billingsley, D., Tourigny, M., Mayer, M., et al. (2001). *Canadian incidence study of reported child abuse and neglect.* Ottawa: Health Canada, Government of Canada.

Werner, E. E. (1984). Resilient children. *Young Children, 40*(1), 68–72.

Willms, J. D. (Ed.). (2002). *Vulnerable children: Findings from Canada's national longitudinal survey of children and youth.* Edmonton, Alberta, Canada: University of Alberta Press.

22

RESPECTING ABORIGINAL FAMILIES

Pathways to Resilience in Custom Adoption and Family Group Conferencing

NANCY MACDONALD

JOAN GLODE

FRED WIEN

E
ven a cursory examination of the history of relations between Aboriginal and non-Aboriginal peoples in Canada reveals a pattern of external control of virtually all aspects of Aboriginal life. This includes the imposition of mainstream approaches in many spheres of life, from governance to health education, under the guise of racial superiority and attempts at cultural assimilation. These patterns are especially evident with respect to family and child welfare practices. These practices have long and oppressive histories and continue today. We will examine these practices in an attempt to understand the structural conditions necessary for resilience to emerge among Aboriginal children. Far from dependent on individual characteristics, the most vulnerable of these children, those who require interventions by professionals or communities to keep them safe, have a much better chance to survive and

thrive when oppressive practices in child welfare are replaced with culturally relevant community-based approaches that allow individuals and families to heal.

In this chapter, we outline some of the history of child welfare practices in Aboriginal communities in Canada, concentrating especially on the post–World War II period when mainstream agencies intruded on the lives of persons living on First Nation reserves. We include a discussion of the "Sixties Scoop" when large numbers of Aboriginal children were taken away from their families and communities to be adopted in white homes. Reaction to this and other events resulted in the formation of Aboriginal child welfare agencies, developed to regain Aboriginal control over family and children's services.

Clearly, the approach that culminated in the Sixties Scoop was not one that respected Aboriginal families and community traditions of caring for those in need. Neither can one argue that these oppressive practices, reflected in other areas of social services such as education (residential schools), band governance, health service, and the criminal justice system, have served Aboriginal communities well.

Therefore, we discuss alternative approaches to family and children's services rooted in Aboriginal traditions but adapted to contemporary conditions. More specifically, we draw on literature about the resilience of families that takes into account the strengths of communities and their distinctive cultural traditions. We refer to parallel writing in the restorative justice domain, writing that emphasizes how communities can draw on their legal and customary traditions to care for themselves and others. We conclude the chapter by illustrating two approaches within family and child welfare that are more consistent with an Aboriginal worldview and that hold the promise of being both effective and legitimate in the eyes of Aboriginal peoples. Specifically, we refer here to family group conferencing and customary adoptions. We illustrate our argument by drawing on the culture, traditions, and experiences of the Mi'kmaq people in eastern Canada.

HISTORICAL BACKGROUND

In 1947, the Canadian Welfare Council and the Canadian Association of Social Workers submitted a joint presentation to a committee of the Senate and House of Commons appointed to consider changes to the Indian Act. Their presentation concluded that "Indian children who are neglected lack the protection afforded under social legislation available to white children in the community" and made recommendations regarding changes in relation to child welfare matters pertaining to First Nations people living on reserves. Johnston (1983), commenting on the impact of this report, notes that although the recommendations may have been made with the best intentions, "little attention was paid to the effect that extending provincial services would have on Indian families and communities. Nor did there appear to be any concern that provincial services might not be compatible with the needs of Indian communities" (p. 3).

Yet in 1951, major revisions were made to the Indian Act, which included a clause (Section 88) used to justify the extension of provincial child welfare services to Indians on reserve. Initially, these changes made little difference to people living on reserves because no additional funding was provided to the child welfare agencies to provide these newly recommended services. Section 88 of the Indian Act did not clarify the financial obligations of the federal government to the provinces, the consequence of which would be enduring conflict between the federal and provincial governments. As a result, in the decades to come, only some provincial child welfare programs were extended to residents of some reserves in some provinces. This ongoing confusion and conflict between the federal and provincial governments continued. In 1966, the disparity in child welfare services was acknowledged in the Hawthorn Report, which noted that the situation varies from "unsatisfactory to appalling" and recommended an extension of provincial child welfare services. The report also recommended that First Nations people be induced to accept provincial child welfare laws into their communities (Johnston, 1983).

Prior to the release of the Hawthorn Report, few provinces had formal or informal agreements with provincial child welfare authorities for on-reserve Aboriginal peoples. In Nova Scotia, however, there was a memorandum of agreement signed in 1964 by Canada and Nova Scotia that stipulated that Mi'kmaq people living on reserves in Nova Scotia would receive the same child welfare services provided to other residents. Included were assessment, counseling, child protection and placement services, homemaker and day care services, research, and evaluation. The federal government agreed to pay 100% of all costs incurred for the care and custody of "registered" children and 100% of related administrative costs. The same arrangement was extended to "status" children living off reserve.

This agreement may have been signed in good faith, but the end result was that children who were assessed to be in need of protection were removed from their families, homes, communities, and culture and placed in white foster and adoptive homes with little or no follow-up with the native family. Oddly, this was done in an effort to provide the mandated services required, but the services were provided away from the children's communities in a way that became punitive to Aboriginal families. In most provinces, there were few policies in place for the adoption of Aboriginal children, and many were adopted by families in the United States and in other parts of the world.

In 1983, Johnston termed the continuation of the colonization process in child welfare as the "Sixties Scoop," a process that began in the 1960s and went well into the 1980s. He noted that with some exceptions, child welfare services could still be described as varying from "unsatisfactory to appalling." In the early 1970s, Aboriginal leaders in a number of provinces, most notably Manitoba, began to express their anger about the high number of their children being placed for adoption outside of Canada. As a result, they instituted a moratorium on the placement of Aboriginal children in adoption homes outside of Canada. By 1982, there were policies or practices in effect in all jurisdictions in Canada prohibiting the placement of Aboriginal children in foster or adoption homes in the United States except in unusual circumstances. However, Johnston (1983) has noted many Aboriginal children continued to be "marketed" (p. 18) in the United States—and very likely in large numbers, even after this moratorium was implemented.

In 1983, a comprehensive study of Canada's Aboriginal child welfare policies and procedures was compiled by the Canadian Council on Social Development (Johnston, 1983). This was the first study in Canada to include a statistical overview of Aboriginal children in the care of child welfare agencies in Canada. The study found that Aboriginal children were highly over-represented in the child welfare system. For example, they represented 40% to 50% of the children in care in Manitoba. In addition, across Canada, Aboriginal children were 4 to 5 times more likely than non-Aboriginal children to be in the care of child welfare authorities. These findings reflected the concerns expressed by Aboriginal leaders in the 1970s, who put intense pressure on governments to stop what, in their view, amounted to cultural genocide.

By the mid-1970s, after further studies and reports, one began to see the first signs of child welfare programs controlled by Aboriginal people themselves. In Manitoba, for example, two tribal councils began to run their own child welfare services. The first was the Fort Alexander Band that in 1976 signed an agreement with the Department of Indian Affairs and initially began its child welfare services by employing three social worker trainees. The second tribal council was the Pas Band that followed with a similar initiative in 1977.

The Hurd Report in Manitoba, released in 1980, made major recommendations in relation to the preservation of Aboriginal identity, language, and culture and recommended that any child welfare service for Aboriginal people must involve Aboriginal people in its administration. The report also recommended that regional agencies for Aboriginal reserves be established by chiefs and councils. Indeed, throughout the 1980s, many Aboriginal child welfare agencies began to develop in various regions of the country. In the eastern region, for example, Mi'kmaw Family and Children's Services of Nova Scotia was established in 1985 and, after a lead-in period, began to provide all mandated child welfare services to the 13 bands in Nova Scotia by 1990.

There were and continue to be unique challenges for Aboriginal child welfare agencies. Cross (1986) noted that to make these services effective, they must be tailored to fit the unique cultural environment of Aboriginal communities. This has been a difficult challenge for Aboriginal child welfare agencies that are limited by funding based on children who are "in care" and by provincial legislation that has not been successful in providing culturally relevant services to Aboriginal peoples. Crichlow (2003) notes that "mainstream legal doctrine is dominated by a focus on individual rights, and this is not applicable or relevant to Aboriginal communities, where the rights of the community take precedence over the individual" (p. 94).

Other challenges for Aboriginal child welfare agencies include the racism evident in the child welfare system when it applies standards such as the "best interest of the child test," which is not culturally relevant to Aboriginal peoples in Canada. Socioeconomic factors such as poverty, overcrowded housing, and poor sanitary conditions were considered justifiable reasons for non-Aboriginal child welfare agencies to remove children from their families, communities, and cultures. Such conditions, although lamentable, were being judged by those who faced none of these structural barriers to raising their children.

To conclude, Phil Fontaine, National Chief of the Assembly of First Nations, recently told delegates to a National Child and Family Services Conference that "child welfare legislation for Aboriginal peoples in Canada is not acceptable, until we can exercise full control over our children, anything else is only an interim" (Fontaine, 2004). "Willy" Wilson Littlechild, a First Nations lawyer and the Chair of the Board for the newly established Yellowhead Tribal Custom Adoption Agency, said,

> The concepts of caring and sharing are provided to First Nations people by the Creator in the traditional form of *natural law,* giving authority to First Nations people to care for their own children. This form of authority is considered *natural authority* by Aboriginal people as the Creator is supreme, as opposed to the Parliament of Canada. (Littlechild, 2004)

He went on to say,

> Societies, in particular, child welfare societies, are foreign concepts to Aboriginal peoples, as collectively we care and share in the upbringing of our children. We have direct responsibility to our grandparents to share the care of our children and nowhere have we relinquished the "authority" to care for our own children. (Littlechild, 2004)

We agree with Crichlow (2003) who argues that Canada's child welfare system has become the new colonial exploiter of Aboriginal people in Canada. He describes the "Western colonization disease" as a racialization process that is never ending.

APPROACHES TO RESILIENCY

As Aboriginal people have sought to liberate themselves from colonial ideologies and approaches to child welfare practice, they have found support in the literature on individual and family resilience, in part because of its emphasis on strengths rather than weaknesses and because, in recent years, it has underlined the importance of culture and ethnicity in achieving resilience in the face of adversity (McCubbin, McCubbin, Thomson, & Thompson, 1998).

Tseng and Hsu (1991), for example, remind us that, over time, culture has influenced family functioning in many ways, such as marriage, choice of mates, postmarital residence, the family kinship system and descent groups, household and family structures, the primary axis of family obligations, family and community dynamics, and alternative family formations.

McCubbin and McCubbin (1993), in broadening our understanding of resilience to include issues of culture and ethnicity, introduced "the resiliency model of family stress, adjustment, and adaptation," which focused much more on interacting components such as the individual, the family, and the community rather than solely on the individualistic approach taken in earlier models of resiliency. McCubbin's work was unique in that it began to consider family strengths and capabilities, both intricately linked to aspects of culture and ethnicity. His model, discussed further in Chapter 2 of this volume, emphasizes the importance of identifying potential resources available to the family from the individual family members and their community. These resources provide a sense of mastery, self-esteem, and ethnic identity that counter the stressors families encounter. However, when the pileup of demands becomes too great, a failure of mastery occurs. This has been evident in the healing and recovery process for Aboriginal peoples, as the pileup of stress resulting from children being removed from their families, communities, and culture has been devastating over time.

McCubbin et al. (1998) also emphasized the importance of setting aside Eurocentric notions of the individual in favor of the adoption of an ecological or contextual perspective in which the individual family member, the family unit, nature, and the spiritual world are interconnected and interdependent. Using a Native Hawaiian example, the family is seen not only as an integral part of the social fabric of Native Hawaiian society but also as part of the consciousness or mind of the Native Hawaiian individual family member. All these units are "united and insepara-ble" from the larger social, natural, and spiritual forces in the world (see also Marsella, Oliveira, Plummer, & Crabbe, 1995). In this way, the notion of harmony (*Lakahi*) becomes the focal concept underlying adaptation and family well-being. "Adaptation, therefore, involves both har-mony and an energylike force (*mana*), which are interdependent and, in their presence, the family, the individuals, the spirit, and the social ecology or nature are one-unity" (McCubbin et al., 1998, p. 34).

McCubbin and his colleagues (1998) also noted that it is striking that the literature on both Native American Aboriginal peoples and the Native American Hawaiian peoples empha-size the importance of a relational perspective to understanding resiliency in families.

Along the same lines, Cross (1986) makes clear that the Native American Aboriginal rela-tional perspective to understanding resiliency in families must involve a focus on the family unit rather than the individual. He identifies four major forces or sets of factors that come into play in achieving adaptation of the entire family system. These include the context, the mind, the body, and the spirit. Contextual factors are identified as culture, community, family, peers, work, school, and social history. The mind is composed of the individual family member's cognitive processes such as feelings, defenses, and self-esteem. The body is described as encompassing all the physical aspects of the individual, such as genetic inheritance, gender, physical condition, nutrition, and substance use. The spiritual factor includes both positive and negative aspects of teachings, practices, and meta-physical or innate forces, a system that is in con-tinuous movement. Like Cross, McCubbin et al. (1998) write:

> The system is constantly balancing and rebalanc-ing itself as we change thoughts, feelings, our physical state and our spiritual state. Adaptation, therefore, is defined as a state of balance that con-tributes to the health of the members of the family and the family unit as a whole. In those situations where the family unit is out of balance, culture provides mechanisms to assist in the process of rebalancing. Native American Indians culturally maintain this balance in many ways, including

spiritual teachings, social skills and norms, dietary rules, and family roles. (p. 35)

Cross (1986) argues that, from a relational point of view, the resiliency of families emerges through an understanding of the holistic and complex interrelationships that come into har-mony and allow a family not only to survive but also to thrive. He states that the environments in which families function are filled with resour-ces that promote strength and harmony. For example, even though the impact of oppression is damaging to ethnic groups, it also fosters the development of survival skills, such as the development of a "sixth sense." He notes that parents and siblings teach children to recognize the subtle clues that may spell danger when they enter an environment in which they are not sure if they are welcome or not.

In an attempt to lessen the impact of racism and oppression in society, Aboriginal parents learn to cope with the dynamics of difference and pass their strategies on to their children. In the cognitive area, Cross notes that family resiliency is enhanced through the process of self-talk and by the stories Aboriginal peoples hear about how others have managed life events and change. In this way, family members learn proven strategies for using resources and adapt-ing to change. Through storytelling, families pass on stories of their lives and their skills and in doing so "are parenting for resiliency" (McCubbin et al., 1998, p. 36).

RESTORATIVE JUSTICE

In November 1997, then Minister of Justice Anne McLellan asked the Law Commission of Canada to report on the means for addressing the harm caused by physical and sexual abuse of children in institutions operated, funded, or sponsored by different levels of government. These schools included residential schools for Aboriginal children, schools for the deaf and blind, training schools, long-term mental health facilities, and sanatoria. Early on, Aboriginal members who were collaborating to write the report indicated that the issues for their group were different than for others because these schools had contributed to cultural genocide.

The Law Commission of Canada agreed to establish a separate group to deal with the Aboriginal concerns noting,

> The experience of Aboriginal children in residential schools was the result of a policy of assimilation sustained for several decades by the federal government, with the cooperation of many religious organizations. Deprived of their native languages, cultural traditions and religions, many Aboriginal children in residential schools were cut off from their heritage and made to feel ashamed of it. As a result, the residential schools system inflicted terrible damage not just on individuals but on families, entire communities and peoples. (Corbiere, Nawegahow, & Neheegahow, 1999, p. 2)

The commission made a number of general and specific recommendations and listed key principles that must be respected in all processes through which survivors of institutional child abuse seek redress.

For the Aboriginal participants, among the most significant outcomes of this study were two papers prepared by Aboriginal consultants with community collaboration (Corbiere et al., 1999; Jacobs, 1998). Both papers looked at how their authors' communities functioned prior to residential schools and the impact, intergenerationally, on the children who attended and on their families and communities. These included emotional deprivation, psychological and mental harm, physical harm, physical abuse and death, sexual abuse, unhealthy living conditions, and the destruction of spiritual beliefs. Because of the nature of the study, the issues of harm experienced by children who attended day school on reserve were mentioned but not documented, although their experiences were also horrific.

These studies also fueled hope because they documented the Aboriginal laws that were violated by the residential school experience. By doing so, they testified to the continuing existence and community knowledge of Aboriginal laws and codes of proper conduct. Inspired by these reports, the Atlantic Policy Congress of First Nations Chiefs commissioned a similar study that was completed in the summer of 1999. *Apoqonmaluktimk: Working Together to Help Ourselves* (Metallic & Young, 1999),

reported on traditional cultural principles and concepts of the Mi'kmaq and Maliseet people that could be used as a foundation for developing social policy and interventions. As a result, emphasis has now shifted to focus on community healing.

An early proponent of community healing in Canada was Connors, who is of Mohawk ancestry. Combining his academic learning with work with elders as he apprenticed in traditional approaches to healing, he came to see that

> in order to understand the process of healing social ills, such as sexual abuse, within First Nations communities we must first understand the root causes which have promoted the development of these dysfunctional relationships. This requires us to look at the connections between dysfunctional relationships and social structures. Abuse of people is related to the misuse of power against vulnerable members of society. (Connors, Oates, & Maurice, 1997, p. 3)

To develop and deliver any social service program in an Aboriginal community, there must be an intense period of dialogue with that community to develop a shared vision, agreement on the meaning and significance of common terms, and at least the beginnings of trust and respect among all participants. Because of the experiences of individuals, families, and communities after five or more generations of residential schools and other policies and practices of assimilation, many families and communities experience dysfunction in their lives. Restorative justice—a process to restore balance to the individual, family, and community— is now being used in many communities and in many program areas. Walker (2000) defines restorative justice as "an alternative approach to criminal justice which began evolving about 15 years ago in response to the ineffectiveness of our current justice system" (quoted in Pranis, 1996, p. 493). The current system is based primarily on retributive values where crime is a violation of the state, defined by lawbreaking and guilt. Justice determines blame and administers pain in a contest between the offender and the state directed by systematic rules. Restorative justice is based on values that hold that "crime is a violation of people and relationships.

It creates obligations to make things right. Justice involves the victims, the offender, and the community in a search for solutions that promote repair, reconciliation, and reassurance" (Zehr, 1990, p. 181). For many Aboriginal communities, restorative justice has become an experience of reclaiming customs and traditions, finding the kind of balance articulated by Cross and McCubbin. However, it must be understood that a program developed for one community cannot be implemented in another without a process of dialogue and adaptation to ensure a fit with the needs and worldview of that community.

Although approaches to restorative justice must be adapted to each community, they have fit well with the natural helping capacity available to members of Aboriginal communities. Waller and Patterson (2002) conducted a study in a Dine (Navajo) community with 25 individuals identified by their community. They found that

> helpers generally offered help before it was requested. . . . Dine natural helping differed from natural helping in other populations studied to the extent to which helping one's relations emerged as a central aspect of individual and community identity. Relationships between helpers and recipients were long-standing, . . . but were characterized by a greater degree of closeness and a stronger sense of commonality and reciprocity. Accordingly, there was little sense of social distance between helpers and recipients. Recipients were also more likely to ask for help. . . . Overall, findings suggest the importance of professionals and helpers recognizing community strengths, particularly informal helping, as a vital resource in Native American communities. (p. 73)

The Honorable Robert Yazzie, Chief Justice Emeritus of the Navajo Nation Supreme Court, describes historical events similar to those experienced by Canadian Aboriginals that have hindered both traditional peacekeeping practices as well as traditional child-rearing practices (Mirsky, 2004). He has worked to have both traditional practices revived and accepted by both his own community and mainstream society. Mirsky (2004), in documenting interviews with three Aboriginal justice practitioners of the southwestern United States, including Yazzie, notes:

> In healing, along with reintegrating individuals into their community, is more than punishment. . . . The Native peacekeeping process involves bringing together victims, offenders and their supporters to get to the bottom of the problem. In the Native world view there is a deep connection between justice and spirituality: in both, it is essential to maintain or restore harmony and balance. (p. 1)

The Wet'suwet'en Unlocking Aboriginal Justice Program is an example of restorative justice. The Wet'suwet'en, a group of First Nations communities in northwest British Columbia, have developed a program in response to the communities' dissatisfaction with the Canadian judicial system and the disproportionate number of Aboriginal people involved in the federal and provincial court systems. In the Wet'suwet'en approach, decisions are made by consensus among community members, aimed at restoring balance and harmony in a fair, just way when a crime has occurred. Through the process, kinship relationships are renewed, harmony and balance are restored, and traditional peacekeeping processes are reaffirmed (Mirsky, 2003).

To this point, we have recounted the historical background to contemporary issues in Aboriginal child welfare. We have also drawn on the literature pertaining to resilience and restorative justice to suggest the promise is inherent in taking a different approach to family and child welfare rooted in Aboriginal worldviews. We turn now to describing two, more specific, approaches to dealing with family and child welfare issues. Both place the Aboriginal extended family and community front and center as the locus of responsibility in resolving the issues that arise. The first of these approaches is family group conferencing.

FAMILY GROUP CONFERENCING

In many jurisdictions around the world, Aboriginal people have made sentencing circles a popular component of the criminal justice system. In many respects, family group conferencing (FGC) is an analogous approach for dealing with some, if not all, cases in the field of family and child welfare. The approach has its roots in

Aboriginal traditions in New Zealand and was pressed on the New Zealand government by the Maori as a preferred way of handling family and child welfare issues. After several years of experimentation and debate, the approach was adopted in legislation in 1989, when the Child, Young Persons and Their Families Act was passed. Since that time, the approach has spread to many different parts of the world, including Canada, the United States, and Europe. It has also been applied to cases that go well beyond the province of child welfare. Mirsky (2003), for example, delineates its use in the United Kingdom in cases involving youth justice, education, and family violence.

At its core, the FGC approach restores the central role and responsibility of the family, as well as the community, in dealing with issues that arise within the family. Professional personnel organize, facilitate, and provide information to move the process forward, but ultimately it is the extended family that comes together to resolve problems involving family members. The key steps in the process are as follows.

First, professional child welfare staff members take the lead in working with the client to identify all members of the family and significant others (such as a key friend, support person, elder, or priest) who might come together to discuss the particular child welfare issue that needs to be resolved. These persons are contacted by the social worker, invited to attend a family group conference, and given the necessary background information.

On a given day and at a location chosen by the client where he or she feels comfortable, the family and other invited members convene for a session that usually lasts several hours. The meeting is chaired by a coordinator who may be a social work supervisor or skilled facilitator, although other professional staff may also attend in addition to the family. After an opening prayer and introductions, information about the case at hand is shared with the group, and questions about different ways of resolving the issue, and about legal and other constraints, are addressed.

Members of the family are then invited to meet among themselves with or without professional staff present. The focus of this critical portion of the FGC is for the family to come to an agreement about how the particular family issue is to be resolved, to determine what specific steps need to be taken, and to allocate responsibility among family members and others for implementing the solution. A plan of action emerges, which is then taken back to the "plenary session."

When the wider group reconvenes, the plan of action is presented, discussed, and clarified. The professional staff assesses the plan to determine whether it is acceptable from the point of view of factors such as the safety of the child, legal, and other parameters. This assessment may be done on the spot and agreement given, or it may require consideration after the FGC has concluded.

In the months following the FGC, there is some monitoring of the implementation of the agreement and usually a follow-up meeting with the extended family to determine if the plan is on track, whether any adjustments need to be made, and how to deal with any steps that have not been implemented as planned.

From the description above, it becomes evident that the FGC approach departs in a number of respects from the mainstream approach to dealing with child welfare issues. In regular child welfare practice, the emphasis is usually on the caseworker and other professional staff playing a leading role in determining the process of intervention and its outcomes. Typically, meetings involve the client, one or two family members, and professional staff, with professional staff attending additional case conferences held among themselves. The process can become highly formal and adversarial, pitting family members against each other and leading to the need to mediate or initiate court proceedings to resolve family issues. The extended family is typically not directly involved in the proceedings.

In Nova Scotia, Mi'kmaw Family and Children's Services handles family and child welfare cases for all 13 Mi'kmaq communities in the province. During the past year, the agency has been offering the family group conferencing approach to a small number of families. Currently, a formal research project evaluating this approach in comparison with the approach normally used in Nova Scotia is being conducted. Early, unpublished results indicate that the experience of participants has so far been very positive.

One of the underlying reasons is that the FGC approach is more congruent with traditional Mi'kmaq culture. Although the historical record is incomplete on the question of how the Mi'kmaq handled family and child welfare issues in the distant past, Young (2004) argues that some hints can be found through an examination of key terms in the Mi'kmaq language and through the evidence provided by stories that have been passed on from one generation to the next through an oral tradition.

From these sources, one can draw a number of conclusions that help to explain why the FGC approach may resolve family and child welfare issues in a more satisfactory manner. The first and most obvious point to be made is that traditionally, of course, it was the family and the community that came together to resolve difficult issues. Kinship relations were and continue to be very important for individuals in the community, and as Young maintains, each person's destiny was linked to the family, group, or community. Many Mi'kmaq stories speak of the family, the community, or both coming together to restore balance or harmony if something untoward has happened or if it is necessary to reintegrate someone into the community or take some other action.

Indeed, there are particular words in the Mi'kmaq language that suggest that processes similar to family group conferencing would not have been unusual in the past. Young (2004) refers to the term *wikamou*, meaning "a request to meet, to come together, to gather" or "you are being summoned to participate in a discussion" (p. 47). During these family gatherings,

> Decision-making was by consensus and everyone had an opportunity to speak at these gatherings. One interesting concept that was used to ensure decisions would be reached by consensus was that if a person disagreed with the direction the wikamou was taking, that person had an obligation to withdraw from the discussion but abide by the consensus. This action ensured that any decision reached would be the result of consensus. (pp. 44–45)

Other relevant terms in the language include the following:

Mawiomi—a formal gathering: A *Mawiomi* may mean a traditional powwow, a religious (Christian) festival, feast, or political gathering. *Mawiomi* really means to bring the L'nu (Mi'kmaq) together in ceremony to discuss issues of concern.

Nujo'teket—witnessing: The contemporary meaning given to this term is a witness at a wedding ceremony, but the traditional meaning is that whenever agreement was made between parties, there had to be a formal witness present. The role of the witness was to formally record the event . . . and to recount . . . in stories for future generations.

Pokjimk—to deal harshly with someone: Another meaning of this is to send a person away, a type of banishment order. This was done when disagreement between individuals (usually closely related) could not be resolved because of the emotions through the disagreement. One of the parties left the immediate vicinity of the other (either voluntarily or by order) so that a healing space was allowed to develop.

Ntaqo'qon—shame or disgrace: A family member would use this phrase to illustrate the consequences of a particular action taken by another family member. In the L'nu worldview, there is no concept of individual guilt, but rather, there is the concept of collective guilt. When one family member is guilty of doing something, the entire family is seen as being guilty. Thus, the family has a vested interest in maintaining proper behavior among its members. (Young, 2004, pp. 40, 41)

Clearly, the family group conferencing approach reflects more of an Aboriginal worldview and represents a more promising approach to dealing with family and child welfare issues.

Approaches to Customary Care

A second innovative and culturally appropriate approach to child welfare practice in Aboriginal communities is customary care as a substitute for formal adoption. Farris-Manning and Zandstra (2003) note that although the overrepresentation of Aboriginal children in care is increasing each year, Canada does not have a national strategy to address issues of permanency, leaving many children in care in a state of "limbo." As well,

Dudding (quoted in Farris-Manning & Zandstra, 2003) has noted that not enough has been done to provide children, Aboriginal or non-Aboriginal, with the comfort and security of a permanent family.

In the Aboriginal context, however, the need is particularly acute because there has been a decline in the availability of foster homes and residential care facilities. Literature indicates that Aboriginal children have experienced higher rates of racism and discrimination while in the care of existing child welfare agencies in Canada (Palmer & Cooke, 1996). As Farris-Manning and Zandstra (2003) explain,

> When matching children to appropriate family-based care resources [there is] potential for children who are placed with families of different cultural/racial heritage to experience discrimination. Most provincial/territorial legislation does require cultural and racial consideration as part of placement matching, and placing agencies must make concerted efforts to match children with families appropriately. However, due to resource insufficiency, there is inadequate compliance with this requirement. (pp. 16–17)

Palmer and Cooke (1996) support these findings and further note that

> Caucasian foster carers or adoptive parents have no natural supports for FN [First Nations] children, and the children are vulnerable to internalizing ethnocentrism and prejudice. The records of Native children in foster and adoptive homes contain repeated stories of their efforts to scrub the brown color from their skins. (p. 719)

Currently, Aboriginal child welfare services in Canada are structured in such a manner that family reunification with adequate supports is not encouraged. Of particular concern is the fact that most government departments will provide funds for services only for those children who are in care. "This funding framework reflects a reduced emphasis on family preservation, and has a clear devaluation of the traditional roles of child welfare based on a reduction of risk indicators through community based prevention and support services to families" (Farris-Manning & Zandstra, 2003, p. 9).

In the Aboriginal context, recognition and support of custom adoption would be one effective way of addressing these issues. The Law Reform Commission of Nova Scotia (1995) released a report that defined custom adoption as occurring when a child's birth name is not changed and although the adoptive parent has care and custody, the natural mother and father have access and some rights. "It is akin to a trust arrangement, as the natural parent may retrieve the child if agreed upon by all parties" (p. 19).

In the report, it is noted that in Mi'kmaq communities, the adoptive parents would exercise most of the duties associated with the care and custody of the child(ren). However, the biological parent, usually the mother, would still have access to the child and some control over decisions made regarding the child. It was also noted that in Mi'kmaq communities, the mother may take back the custody of her child(ren) if agreed on by everyone involved. In addition, a child would in general retain his or her birth name, although he or she may also use the name of the adoptive parents in cases of custom adoption.

Daniel Paul (1993) a Mi'kmaq author, has provided a Mi'kmaq perspective on custom adoptions as practiced traditionally in Mi'kmaq communities:

> The children were raised in an atmosphere of benevolent devotion. They were loved and cherished by their parents and given loving care and attention by members of the Tribe. As a result of this ingrained attitude, MicMac children were never abandoned. They were considered extended family by adult members of the Tribe and were treated like one's own. If a child became homeless for any reason, he or she would be adopted by other members of the community and their life would soon return to normal. (p. 14)

In cases of custom adoption, the child is permanently with the adoptive parents, as long as they agree and the parents do not wish to retrieve the child(ren).

Bernie Francis (1995), a Mi'kmaq linguist, says that the Mi'kmaq language reflects the idea that "children are life and are not owned, they are the future" (quoted in Law Reform Commission of Nova Scotia, 1995, p. 12). The Mi'kmaq language uses terms pertaining to child-rearing responsibilities with no particular connection to ownership or familial ties. Francis notes that there is a word for being in the process of raising or rearing children and a term for the completion of that responsibility. Neither term distinguishes whether the child(ren) is biological or adopted. The point here is that the responsibility for the care of the child(ren) is accepted by the community as a whole. These views are based on the concept that the community cares for the children's *inherent right* to be taught the beliefs, values, customs, and traditions of their own family, community, and culture.

As with family group conferencing, we see how the Mi'kmaq language, stories, and ceremonies reflect a distinctive worldview that has evolved based on the experiences of a people over time. Again we find references supportive of an alternative child welfare practice. For example, the Mi'kmaq language stresses the importance of kin relationships. The word *Mi'kmaq,* itself, is derived from the word *Ni'kmaq,* which means *my Kin-Friends.* Tuma Young (2004), a Mi'kmaq lawyer, writes that in the Mi'kmaq worldview,

> The individual is not seen as a separate entity but as a component of a larger family unit. To show kindness to another person is showing kindness to your family and as a result, the two of you were connected to each other through the kinship system. (p. 49)

Other terms also refer to kinship relationships. We give two examples that pertain directly to custom adoptions:

> *Ankweak*—to take care of, to bring up as your own: This word is used to describe the concept of foster families in L'nu communities. The children are raised as one of the family members, treated no differently from the other children but always reminded who their kin relations are. There are no closed adoptions in L'nu communities; children know who the parents are and can have a relationship with the biological parent if they wish. The biological parents play a minimal role, whereas the foster parents are given a quiet but special recognition of their major role in the raising of the children.

> *Kekkunawet*—To become a godparent: The Kekkunet is a surrogate parent and has a special relationship with the child. If the Kekkunet has children of his or her own, then the godchild recognizes those children as godbrothers or godsisters. The kinship relationship system is also used to create alliances with individuals who are not part of the immediate or extended family. The Kekkunet can also be called on to help raise and counsel the child throughout its life. The power, authority, and persuasiveness of a Kekkunawet are legendary, and the role of the Kekkunawet needs to be examined fully when contemplating how L'nu Tplutaqan [customary laws] can be used in contemporary situations. (Young, 2004)

Although these kinds of adoptions are a customary practice of the Mi'kmaq and other Aboriginal groups, the formal recognition of this practice is limited. In particular, with the exception of the Northwest Territories and Quebec, all other jurisdictions in Canada do not officially recognize or sanction custom adoptions through their Aboriginal child welfare legislation. Indeed, it is fair to say that the practice of customary adoptions has been devalued by the dominant society, as the Law Reform Commission of Nova Scotia (2000) noted:

> Because some of the native Indian custom adoptions allow for continued contact with natural parents and for inheritance from natural parents, some persons have argued that it would be better to recognize a custom adoption as a type of guardianship rather than as an adoption. However, the majority of native persons indicated that they considered custom adoption as adoption, not guardianship. Furthermore, we note that the current concept of adoption, in white society, is a relatively new concept. In fact, adoption is as old as man. It has been practiced in many different cultures in many different ways. The North American white concept of adoption as a function of child welfare—involving the placing of children with strangers and the complete severing of natural parental ties, including the possibility of inheritance, is a relatively recent development in adoption and seems to reflect the realities of a highly mobile, nuclear-family-oriented, urban, industrial society.

> To impose this style of adoption on our own native Indian population and to call their custom

adoptions something less—i.e. guardianship would be, in our opinion, inappropriate. (p. 21)

On the positive side, at the international level, issues of customary laws and practices have been raised at the United Nations, where the Convention on the Rights of the Child supports recognition of the importance of Aboriginal practices and culture (Littlechild, 2004). As well, within Canada, there have been recent court petitions dealing with the issue of legal recognition of custom adoptions in which the courts have recognized this traditional practice under Section 35 (1) of the Constitution Act (Paul & Carrigan, 1993). However, in general, Canada has reserved the right not to apply the provisions of the articles of the UN Convention on the Rights of the Child, using a "statement of understanding," which means Canada is not bound by certain obligations because of a specific domestic situation. The domestic situation involves Article 21 of the Constitution Act that states, "Adoptions must be authorized only by competent authorities in accordance with applicable law and procedures" (Paul & Carrigan, 1993, p. 3). Because custom adoption may not comply with such requirements, Canada reserved the right *not* to comply with the provisions of Article 21: "To the extent that they may be inconsistent with customary forms of care among Aboriginal peoples in Canada" (Paul & Carrigan, 1993, p. 3).

However, in 1985 the federal Indian Act recognized custom adoption for the purposes of registering a person with the legal status as "Indian," as well as for the distribution of property on intestacy. It was at this time that a statutory recognition of custom adoption was extended to all matters falling within the scope of the Indian Act. Section 48(16) of the act has broadened the view of "child," and it now recognizes a child born in or out of wedlock, as well as a legally adopted child and a child adopted in accordance with Indian custom (Paul & Carrigan, 1993).

Thus, with respect to recognition for to custom adoptions. The first Aboriginal custom adoptions services agency began in 1999, with the establishment of the Yellowhead Tribal Services Agency, in Alberta. The Yellowhead Tribal Council members developed policies and procedures for the program based on the teachings of the Medicine Wheel, an ancient symbol that organizes the world into four colors, four elements, and four aspects of people. The program emphasizes that children are not parents' property but are considered gifts from the Creator.

> Respect is the key word in the relationship between Indian children and their parents. It lies at the center of a person's relationship to nature and to the Creator, respect for the elders, respect for the child, respect for all living things. (Yellowhead Tribal Council, 1999a, p. 1)

The mission statement for the agency reflects these values: "Our children are gifts from the Creator on loan to us on a daily basis. The primary right and responsibility for child rearing lies with parents, extended family, and community" (Yellowhead Tribal Council, 1999b, p. 1).

The Yellowhead Tribal Services Agency is the first federally funded Aboriginal child welfare agency in Canada to be recognized by provincial child welfare authorities and the first to include custom adoptions as a significant component of its mandate in the provision of services.

For the agency to maintain a nonpolitical, autonomous role in the various communities it serves, a Custom Care Executive Committee was established. The executive committee is composed of one community child welfare worker from each community who helps screen applicants for adoption from their own community. In addition, custom care workers also coordinate the use and maintenance of the local Child and Family Services Advisory Committee in each community, which assists in organizing, managing, and monitoring the customary care program at the community level. These are the various decision-making bodies involved in customary care placements, reflecting the consensus style decision making preferred by Aboriginal communities.

The Yellowhead Tribal Services Agency believes that the best permanent objective for a child is to grow up in his or her own family, extended family, or community. The agency's objective is to provide member band children with a sense of permanence in their family and community ties, as well as ties to their biological parents. Ongoing contact with their biological parents and children in out-of-home care is considered to be essential in the maintenance of continuity of relationships for the child. To date, the agency has custom adopted more than 30 children, children who would otherwise, in all likelihood, have been placed in non-Aboriginal foster or adoptive placement.

CONCLUSION

Custom adoptions and family group conferencing are traditional practices in Mi'kmaq communities, as well as in other Aboriginal communities in Canada. This needs to be recognized by provincial, territorial, and federal levels of government in Canada. Although these child welfare practices have not been consistently recognized by the provincial and territorial legislative authorities, the federal government has acknowledged customary practices in relation to child-rearing responsibilities with diverse Aboriginal communities. Furthermore, both child justice and child welfare bodies are understanding the importance of using interventions that reflect traditional worldviews of Aboriginal peoples.

Such recognition will help to remove a significant number of risk factors that have threatened Aboriginal children and families for decades. Such practices prevent the removal of Aboriginal people, adults and children, from their communities and their cultures. We believe that support for both family group conferencing and custom adoptions helps to establish conditions that support resilience. Structurally, these program innovations give Aboriginal communities a way to provide protection to their members without the compromises inherent in Eurocentric approaches to care and justice.

These practices carry with them great hope for people in the communities involved. As in the case of customary adoption, this is not just a replacement for legal guardianship. Custom adoption for the Mi'kmaq people, as well as other Aboriginal peoples, is nothing less than the expression of customary kinship law provided to them by the supreme spirit, the Creator. Likewise, family group conferencing returns to

communities the capacity to care for their own people, building on patterns embedded in their culture.

REFERENCES

Connors, E. W., Oates, J., & Maurice, L. B. (1997). The emergence of sexual abuse treatment models within First Nations communities. In D. A. Wolfe, R. J. McMahon, & R. D. Peters (Eds.), *Child abuse: New directions in prevention and treatment across the life span* (pp. 223–247). Thousand Oaks, CA: Sage.

Corbiere, D., Nawegahow, D., & Neheegahow, N. (1999). *Research report on Algonquin laws violated by the residential school process: The Mitchikanibkok Inuit experiences.* Ottawa, Ontario: Law Commission of Canada.

Crichlow, W. (2003). Western colonization as disease: Native adoption and cultural genocide. *Canadian Social Work, 5*(1), 88–107.

Cross, T. L. (1986). Drawing on cultural tradition in Indian child welfare practice. *Social Casework: The Journal of Contemporary Social Work, 67*(5), 283–289.

Farris-Manning, C., & Zandstra, M. (2003). *Children in care in Canada: A summary of current issues and trends with recommendations for future research.* Ottawa, Ontario: Child Welfare League of Canada. Retrieved January 10, 2005, from www.nationalchildrensalliance.com/nca/pubs/2003/Children_in_Care_March_2003.pdf

Fontaine, P. (2004, May 31). *Building a stronger future from our past: Through kinship care/permanency planning* [Opening plenary]. 5th Annual National Child & Family Services Conference, Calgary.

Jacobs, B. K. (1998). *Rekindled spirit.* Ottawa, Ontario: Law Commission of Canada.

Johnston, P. (1983). *The Canadian Council on Social Development Series: Native children and the child welfare system.* Toronto, Ontario, Canada: James Lorimer.

Law Reform Commission of Nova Scotia. (1995). *The legal status of the child born outside of marriage in Nova Scotia.* Halifax, Nova Scotia, Canada: Author.

Law Reform Commission of Nova Scotia. (2000). *Restoring dignity: Responding to child abuse in Canadian institutions, Executive Summary.*

Ottawa, Ontario, Canada: Minister of Public Works and Government Services.

Littlechild, W. (2004, May 31). *Building a stronger future from our past: Through kinship care/permanency planning* [Opening plenary]. 5th Annual National Child & Family Services Conference, Calgary.

Marsella, A. J., Oliveira, J. M., Plummer, C. M., & Crabbe, K. M. (1995). Native Hawaiian (Kanaka Maoli) culture, mind, and well-being. In H. I. McCubbin (Ed.), *Resiliency in Native American and immigrant families.* (pp. 93–115). Thousand Oaks, CA: Sage.

McCubbin, M. A., & McCubbin, H. I. (1993). Family coping with health crisis: The resiliency model of family stress, adjustment and adaptation. In C. Danielson, B. Hamel-Bissell, & P. Winstead-Fry (Eds.), *Families, health, and illness* (pp. 21–63). New York: Mosby.

McCubbin, H. I., McCubbin, M. A., Thompson, A. I., & Thompson, E. A. (1998). Resiliency in ethnic families: A conceptual model for predicting family adjustment and adaptation. In H. I. McCubbin (Ed.), *Resiliency in Native American and immigrant families* (pp. 1–46). Thousand Oaks, CA: Sage.

Metallic, F., & Young, T. (1999). *Apoqonmaluktimk: Working together to help ourselves.* Unpublished manuscript prepared for the Atlantic Policy Congress of First Nation Chiefs.

Mirsky, L. (2003). *The Wet'suwet'en Unlocking Aboriginal Justice Program: Restorative practices in British Columbia, Canada.* Retrieved October 21, 2003, from www.restorativepractices.org/library/wuaj.html

Mirsky, L. (2004). *Restorative justice practices of Native American, First Nation and other indigenous people of North America: Part Two.* Retrieved July 12, 2004, from www.restorativepractices.org/library/natjust2.html

Palmer, S., & Cooke, W. (1996). Understanding and countering racism with First Nations children in out-of-home care. *Child Welfare, 75*(6), 709–725.

Paul, D. (1993). *We were not the savages: A Micmac perspective on the collision of European and Aboriginal civilization.* Halifax, Nova Scotia, Canada: Nimbus.

Paul, V., & Carrigan, K. (1993). *The rights of the child: Custom adoption in Mi'kmaq communities in Nova Scotia.* Unpublished manuscript, prepared for the Law Reform Commission of Nova Scotia.

Pranis, K. (1996). A state initiative toward restorative justice: The Minnesota experience. In B. Galaway & J. Hudson (Eds.), *Restorative justice: International perspectives* (pp. 493–504). Monsey, NY: Criminal Justice Press.

Tseng, W. S., & Hsu, J. (1991). *Culture and family: Problems and therapy.* New York: Haworth Press.

Waller, M., & Patterson, S. (2002). Natural helping and resilience in a Dine (Navajo) community. *Families in Society, 83*(1), 73–84.

Yellowhead Tribal Council. (1999a). *Yellowhead tribal services manual.* Unpublished manuscript prepared for the Yellowhead Tribal Services Agency, Edmonton, Alberta, Canada.

Yellowhead Tribal Council. (1999b). *Yellowhead tribal services* [Pamphlet]. Edmonton, Alberta, Canada: Yellowhead Tribal Services Agency.

Young, T. (2004). *Comment.* Unpublished manuscript. Halifax, Nova Scotia, Canada.

Zehr, H. (1990). *Changing lenses: A new focus for crime and justice.* Scottdale, PA: Herald Press.

23

SOCIAL AND CULTURAL ROOTS OF RUSSIAN YOUTH RESILIENCE

Interventions by the State, Society, and the Family

ALEXANDER V. MAKHNACH

ANNA I. LAKTIONOVA

A dolescents and children are particularly vulnerable to chaos and conflict. The political upheaval experienced over the past decade in Russia provides a salient example of how youth struggle to cope with social change and instability. Economic instability and the loss of spiritual and moral values have meant that a number of dangerous tendencies have emerged in contemporary Russia. While some youth manage to thrive within this context of socioeconomic tension, many cope with their experiences and the opportunities perceived to be available to them by making choices that include vagrancy, alcohol and drug addiction, prostitution, crime, and suicide. In light of the personal, social, and economic costs of these trends, it is relevant to study patterns of resilience in today's adolescents. In Russia, the concept of resilience is a relatively new way to describe behavior. The Russian language has no word that is a direct translation of *resilience* but,

instead, the term «способность к преодолению неблагоприятных жизненных обстоятельств» (the ability to cope with adversity) is used.

To explore resilience in contemporary Russian youth, it is necessary to understand the personality characteristics that help them develop resilience, how their communities help form resilience and what social institutions and characteristics of familial and sociocultural environments serve to strengthen those qualities associated with resilient outcomes. This chapter will review the situation for youth in contemporary Russia, exploring some of the barriers to psychological and social well-being among young people. As an example of how the Russian State and families are coping with threats to their children's health, an examination of the Russian educational system is provided to explore one type of intervention intended to build resilience in young people during this time of great social change.

The Social Context of Contemporary Russia

The social instability of contemporary Russian society has led to a dearth of protective factors for children. This instability has been caused by political change, economic crises, and problematic interdenominational and ethnocultural relations. Some of the circumstances experienced by Russian children and adolescents include the following:

- Migration and related weakening of the traditional family and social support system
- New demands in technology, which require individuals to develop a new set of skills and abilities to succeed
- Mass media influence, which spreads ideas and values that are often incongruent with the ideas and values learned during upbringing and education
- Influence of changing social lives among young people, actively promoted and reinforced by the community
- Increased frequency of interpersonal, interethnic, and interdenominational interaction that has led to friction in and between communities

All these factors, both together and separately, threaten adolescents' feelings of security and confidence in their future. As one of the most vulnerable groups in the population, the sudden transitions that have taken place in Russia mean that youth often have a limited ability to cope with the effects of social change and the resultant ideological and interpersonal conflicts. These events have particularly influenced those adolescents who perceive themselves as having limited opportunities to affect change in their lives.

Some of the negative repercussions of the sociopolitical transformation experienced in contemporary Russia include changes for the worse in the quality of living conditions, vulnerability to life stressors, behavioral and social maladaptation, and mental health concerns. Various studies indicate a significant increase in mental health problems in all regions of the Russian Federation among all ages (Solokhina, 2003; Yastrebov, 1999). This increase in impaired mental health is affecting professional aspirations as well as social and familial interactions

among Russian youth. These circumstances combine to create an environment that is not conducive to the healthy development of children. As Nikitina (2003) suggests,

> These deformations are expressed in such negative tendencies of social development, as the increase in the number of social orphans and families that neglect their parenting duties, antipedagogical liberalization of social life norms, wider gaps between social classes, the growth and spread of potential hazards to one's life and to personal and social security, the establishing of strategies and scenarios of reaching personal success in life by any means, often immoral, which is unwanted for an adolescent's productive development. The social environment for raising children and adolescents in contemporary Russia could be described as harmful and in crisis. (p. 32)

Russian Youth: Who Are They?

Russian families are uniquely affected by the lack of continuity between Russian traditions and history and more recent shifts in ideology. In particular, changes in cultural beliefs since World War II have affected how children and their caregivers interact. Russian child rearing was commonly characterized by permissiveness and a tendency to delegate the task of establishing boundaries and teaching coping strategies to caregivers outside the family, such as teachers and other educators from social organizations. Contemporary Russian child rearing, however, although molded by traditional tenets of Russian culture and ideology, is now tempered by the more recent upheaval experienced by families in relation to their culture.

Lotman (1994) suggests that it has been characteristic of Russian culture throughout history to divide everything in the world into positive and negative. Furthermore, Shelina (2003) describes the organization of social structures in Russia as primarily based on one of two ideologies—individualism or communalism. Today, the traditional emphasis on one's connection to social groups, such as family and social class, has waned as each ceases to provide a sense of security. Furthermore, to many youth, the drawbacks of group decision making have become evident.

The concept of strict adherence to tradition is at the heart of the communal, more Eastern (as opposed to mistaken assumptions of Russia as a Western nation) type of society. In Russia, these "traditions" have now not only been repeatedly reformed but also discredited (Shelina, 2003).

Over the past 20 years, Russian children have been observed to be increasingly focused on their peers, more materialistic, and less respectful of authority (Fenko, 2000). Increasing antagonism toward the authority of the State and its institutions, including the education system, is often an impediment to healthy development. According to Hellinckx, Grietens, and Bodrova (1997), Russian teenagers display a wide variety of behavioral and emotional problems, characterized by symptoms such as withdrawal, psychosomatic problems, and delinquency. Gendered division of these symptoms has been noted, whereby girls are more likely to internalize their troubles and display symptoms such as anxiety, depression, and psychosomatic complaints, whereas boys more commonly externalize problems through behaviors associated with aggression and delinquency. Demographic factors also play a role in influencing adolescents' development of unhealthy behaviors or, conversely, in promoting their resilience. Diverse factors such as the family's monthly income, the parents' perception of their financial position, moving or changing schools frequently, whether adolescents have a room of their own, and mental illness in the family have all been noted to significantly influence the development of behavioral or emotional problems in Russian youth (Hellinckx et al., 1997).

The study of contemporary Russian adolescents requires an understanding of their values. Forming belief and value systems is an elaborate process influenced by the popular thinking of the era, class culture, familial attitudes, and the social environment. According to Sobkin (1997), the socialization of contemporary adolescents in Russia occurs not only within a context of socioeconomic instability but, more important, within a situation where values and norms are increasingly unclear. This lack of clarity is related most significantly to impairment of the mechanisms of value transmission from older generations to today's youth (Sobkin, 1997).

According to a Public Opinion Fund survey, when asked, "Would you personally want your children to have you as their role model?" 62% of all respondents answered "No," and 63% were either unable or unwilling to answer the question "What personality qualities would you want to see in your children?" (Petrova, 2002). This data suggests that many Russian parents are uncertain about how to help their children succeed in a modern society. Values that guided Russian adolescents in the 1940s or 1970s are radically different from the belief systems of the youth of the 1990s. Although the former prioritized community-based values, today the ideals of individualism dominate, creating a significant values gap between parents and their children.

Research conducted by Sobkin (1997) between 1991 and 1996 provides a closer look at the values of contemporary adolescents. When choosing from a list of possible priorities, "happy family life" was chosen by 73.5% of surveyed adolescents in 1991 shortly after perestroika (the period of dissolution of the USSR), although that declined to 60.2% in 1996. "Financial well-being" was chosen by 57.4% in 1991 and by 53.1% in 1996. "Successful career" was chosen by 49.0% in 1991 and by 42.2% in 1996. It is clear from this data that although a happy family life is still the most highly ranked priority for most high school students, traditional values of family, financial well-being, and career are in decline. It remains to be seen what will replace these priorities in the lives of Russian youth. More recent research data by Fenko (2000) showed that the factors most transformed during transitional economic periods are (a) family values and attitudes that children get from their parents in the form of "parent's messages"; (b) the macroeconomic situation, including economic crisis; (c) the allocative system in the society (market or socialism); and (d) day-to-day economic activity of children. We stress the necessity to take these factors into account in the process of education and psychological counseling of parents and teachers. The values reports from different age groups vary depending on the age of respondents. For example, those 35 years and younger chose values such as an "active life style" and "purposefulness" far more often than did respondents older then 55 years old who preferred values such as "strong will," "strong character," "independence," and "aim at success" (Petrova, 2004).

Analyses of gender-based differences reveal that these changing patterns in values among Russian youth affect boys and girls to varying degrees. For example, it is interesting to note that although the importance of raising children (for both boys and girls) remained stable over the period 1991 to 1996, the value of "happy family life" decreased drastically for girls, from 84.6% in 1991 to 66.3% in 1996, whereas for boys it remained constant. This suggests that contemporary girls have adopted more Western values, such as the desire for a career and self-fulfillment outside family life (Sobkin, 1997). It remains to be seen if such value shifts bring with them greater well-being among Russian youth or if they lead to social instability and concomitant health problems.

According to data gathered by Karpukhina (2000), the value of achieving material well-being deserves a separate analysis. Her studies of adolescents' and young adults' value systems suggest that financial success is a priority for many Russian young people. The desire to become rich and independent significantly influences the occupational goals of contemporary Russian youth. Nearly every fourth adolescent plans to start his or her own business after the completion of higher education. Achieving financial success also seems to be more important than the means by which wealth is accrued. The attitude that "any means are okay, even criminal ones, when achieving wealth" is becoming increasingly evident among today's youth (Karpukhina, 2000).

The results of research conducted by Borisova (2001) indicates similar priorities in the group of teenagers sampled, whereby 44.3% of boys and 11.1% of girls would "take something that's unaccounted for"; 62% of boys and 33.3% of girls would "get it through cheating"; 32.9% of boys and 11.2% of girls would "take money by force." This desire to get rich by any means is a sociopsychological phenomenon of contemporary teenager thinking. Most worrisome, it represents a real threat to lawfulness, indicating that Russian society can expect to see further criminalization in routine social relationships (Borisova, 2001).

Such a glorification of wealth and financial success also affects attitudes toward those who have not achieved these goals. Thus, according to 47.7% of adolescents surveyed, growth in the number of poor people in Russia is because "they have not adapted to life well"; 21% think that these people have "not gotten rid of the old ideals," and 18.2% see their inability to steal as the reason for their poverty (Karpukhina, 2000).

It is also interesting to look at the way in which adolescents view professional groups such as the police, who are expected to maintain social norms and instill a sense of legal responsibility and respect for the law. The most common descriptions presented by youth of an average police officer are cruel (59.7%), aggressive (57%), suspicious (51.8%), nontrusting (50.9%), authoritative (50%), angry (40.4%), heartless (37.7%), doesn't care (36%), unfair (35.1%), and gloomy (35.1%) (Rean, 2001). It is clear that police are perceived in wholly negative terms. It is difficult to explain such a negative image of "peacekeepers" by their occupation alone, even if we take into account that being suspicious and not trusting is an important part of performing the role of police officer. The negative impact of such stereotypes does, however, affect youths' respect for the law and social rules.

In addition to the prioritization of material success and an apparent breakdown in lawfulness, Russian youth tend to place a relatively low value on ideas such as becoming actively engaged with aspects of one's culture, knowing oneself, and developing one's abilities. It is evident that the views and attitudes that youth are coming to adopt are in many ways a reflection of the ideals of modern Western society. More cerebral values relating to culture and self seem often to be of secondary importance until basic material needs are met.

It is worthwhile noting, however, that other studies report a significant increase in religious awareness among Russian youth. This increase has occurred despite the trends noted above toward lawlessness and individualism. As many as 64% of 16- to 17-year-olds consider themselves religious, which is 1.5 times the overall national rate found among adults (Mchedlov, 1998). According to Mchedlov, who reports on a study conducted by researchers at the Moscow State University, 45% of 17-year-olds come to church at least once a year, although twice this number (84%) report regular attendance at dance clubs and parties. Adolescents usually come to church once or twice a year on major holidays (38–40%), and the number of those who attend church regularly (every month) is approximately 6% to 7%. Despite these numbers, only a minority of youth, 3%, actually keep up religious traditions in their homes on a daily basis, with 80% of these being girls (Rean, 2002). All this is a complex mosaic of values to understand. Researchers have shown that the value system of religious adolescents does not differ overall from that of nonbelievers, leading to the observation that religion and culture in postperestroika Russia is finding some convergence.

> The modern generation of adolescents accepts religion mostly as a part of the culture, as staying true to national traditions, as a part of their national identity. Such a state is caused by changes that are happening in our society. Atheism, which used to be a part of the national ideology, is now rejected, while the Church is being supported by the state. People start receiving spiritual images and ideas through mass media from an early age, and those images and ideas are presented as eternal cultural values. Our society, which has rejected all old ideals, has difficulty offering other alternatives which would be equal in value. (Rean 2002, p. 89)

The rise of both individualism and religious affiliation has not displaced entirely the high value placed on patriotism by Russian youth before perestroika. Patriotic education remains an important element of interventions with youth in contemporary Russian schools and more broadly in society as a whole. Although this aspect of contemporary youth culture has been neglected over the past decade, patriotism persists as a synonym for nationalism, which itself remains a vital part of youth culture. Research conducted by Rumyantseva (2003) examined high school students' understanding of the term *patriotism*. The following interpretations were offered by the students (listed in order of popularity):

1. Patriotism as love for your Motherland (associations: love, pride, Motherland, Russia, country, respect) (reported by 25% of adolescents).

2. Patriotism as a remnant of past history (associations: red, Lenin, USSR, partisans, Stalin, grandmother, World War II, Communist party, Comsomol) (reported by 10% of adolescents).

3. Patriotism as a moral characteristic of a person (associations: honesty, faithfulness, honor, dignity, responsibility, dedication, courage, faith, spirit, morality, patriot) (reported by 10% of adolescents).

Other understandings of patriotism included patriotism as militarism, as a State symbol, as an act of courage, as an emotional connection with family and close friends, as a national movement, as something that leads to public riots, as a feeling of unity with people, as love toward one's native city, and as debt. Among the actions identified as most patriotic were the following: trying to make life better for your country, working for the good of the country, not leaving the country even if you have a chance, obeying the laws of the Russian Federation, serving in the army, and loving your country (Rumyantseva, 2003). Findings such as these, when combined with those discussed earlier, paint a picture of Russian youth as both adapting to the realities of a new Russia while still somewhat rooted in its past traditions and historically nationalistic and moralistic ideology.

CULTURAL CHANGE AND ITS INFLUENCE ON THE PERSONALITIES OF RUSSIAN YOUTH

A person's experience of belonging to a certain culture is one of the most important environmental determinants of personality. Every culture has its own institutionalized and sanctioned behavior patterns, rituals, and beliefs. This means that most representatives of any given culture will have certain common personality characteristics. Cultural influences are therefore often invisible until we encounter representatives of another culture who see the world differently and, possibly, challenge beliefs native to our culture. Because we take cultural influences for granted, they pervasively shape our lives and the manner in which we identify our needs and find ways to satisfy them, our emotions and the way we express them, our relationships with other people and with ourselves, our ideas about what is sad or funny, our attitudes toward life and death, and what we consider healthy or a symptom of illness (Kitayama & Markus, 1994; Pervin & John, 1997).

Therefore, traditions play an important role in forming the character of the people of any given culture. Losing some of these traditions may well lead to the loss of distinctive character traits such as honesty, perseverance, hopefulness, and altruism. As Nalchajyan (2001) suggests, "We may witness the weakening of ethno-protective traditions and, therefore, of the adaptive mechanisms of the nation" (p. 58). Traditions, especially those that have the potential for developing positive character traits in children and adolescents, are an important means of socializing younger generations. Today in Russia, however, most of the traditions that were maintained during the Soviet era have been destroyed or discredited, and new traditions are not yet firmly established.

In contemporary Russia, the organizations that existed in the Soviet period, such as "Oktyabryata," "Pioneers," "Comsomolets," sport and military associations (similar to the "Boy Scouts" in the West), and student construction groups, have largely disappeared. These organizations commonly used initial probationary periods and rituals of acceptance for membership in unions, parties, and student or workers' groups. These rites of passage to adulthood served an important role in the psychosocial development of the youth of Russia. They have not been replaced in any formal or socially accepted way.

The disintegration of these social institutions has meant that the youth of Russia have lost a means of achieving a sense of status and belonging. With legitimate avenues thus thwarted, their need for status is expressed through the aggressive and antisocial behaviors of groups of adolescents who become sports and rock music hooligans or join criminal gangs. These groups often use rituals of initiation such as dividing and marking "their" territory, fighting with rival groups, affiliation signs such as tattoos, special clothing, "insider" slang, strict hierarchies in the group structure, and ceremonies of initiation into the "gang" that include painful tests (Shevchenko, 2001).

Thus, it is not surprising that, as with the disappearance of healthy avenues for youth association, the pedagogical potential of traditional cultural institutions, including literature and the arts, has also been weakened as a consequence of a changing society. Television in particular has assumed a disproportionately large role in the socialization of children. To understand the living conditions of children in modern society, their connection with their families, with school and with other children, we need to study the growing influence of the mass media on them.

The role of TV in children's lives has changed dramatically in the past 10 years, with television having now become a primary means of entertainment and often used as a "babysitter." Parents routinely play a secondary role in their child's life because they spend more of their time completing domestic chores or working outside the home than parenting and spending time with their children. The prevalence of violence on television serves to normalize aggressive behavior and can cause children to think that the world around them today is a place where such events commonly occur. Researchers studying the problem of aggression and violence emphasize the important role of the mass media, especially television, in spawning and reinforcing such behavior (Enikolopov, 2001). A researcher from the Public Opinion Foundation (FOM) writes,

> The share of broadcasting for children is no higher than 4% of overall broadcasting on the average among all mainstream TV channels in Russia in one year (TV broadcasting licenses clearly stipulates that this share is to be between 7% and 15% for different channels). American movies dominate on Russian TV (around 40% of all movies being shown), therefore for 70% of adolescents their favorite movie is made in the U.S.A. One hour of TV broadcasting shows an average of 4.2 scenes of violence or adult content. Every day a Russian adolescent sees at least 9 scenes of violence, aggression or adult content, and it encourages him [sic] to adopt a confrontational behavior model. (Presnyakova, 2002)

Technological changes have also increased the importance of computers as mechanisms of socialization. The computer is the primary source of entertainment for 25% of Russian adolescents (Petrova, 2002). Schools are also more and more being equipped with computers; State funding has enabled computers to be installed in over 30,000 schools in the rural areas of Russia. Students across Russia spend approximately 1.2 hours at computers daily. We can safely predict that by the time children from different social classes graduate, they will have had nearly equal opportunities to use computers. Although reports indicate that regular computer use has had a positive effect on students' academic performance, unbalanced virtual communication can cause children to develop a distorted perception of the world, destroy their intuition, and alienate them from their ethnic roots and the history of their nation.

Meanwhile, books specifically for children are unavailable to 80% of Russian children and adolescents. Libraries are a crucial institution in places where the population has a low purchasing capacity; up to 70% of children in rural areas are financially unable to buy books, and 28% of these children report libraries as their only source for books. The number of children who regularly read books has shrunk by half, as has the number of adolescents who attend entertainment facilities such as the theater. Although fine arts have not completely disappeared from the life of Russian society, the influence of the arts on the spiritual and social development of adolescents has diminished from the significant role they played a decade and a half ago (Nikitina, 2003).

Sports have also decreased in popularity for adolescents over the past decade, in part due to accessibility issues. Membership on most sports teams is no longer free of charge as it was in the former USSR. Today, even when there are no membership fees, the cost of equipment and uniforms must be assumed by parents, for whom the cost is often prohibitive.

It is apparent that the influence of activities rooted in Russian culture is waning, as arts, literature, and sports activities take second place to the virtual reality of television and computers. Not only is this a dangerously "unreal reality," but it also means that youth are disconnected in important ways from the world of their elders.

ADOLESCENT-PARENT RELATIONSHIPS

Relationships between adolescents and their parents are notoriously difficult. Statistical data about adolescent conflict with parents is quite consistent across different countries; most adolescents report some conflict, and a minority of youths feels misunderstood by parents, reporting intense conflict with their family (Claes, 1986; Craig, 1996). Russian data reinforces these trends, indicating that 3% of Russian adolescents are in constant conflict with their parents, 10% experience conflict often, 26% have conflicts rarely, and 22% of the surveyed population has no conflict with their family. Overall, however, most adolescents report having an emotionally positive attitude toward their family, feel safe and confident within their family, and enjoy talking to their family members (Yartsev, 1999).

Discord between youth and their parents is often rooted in poor communication. The cause of this breakdown in communication between adolescents and their parents is based, according to Kon (1989), on a parental "inability and unwillingness to hear them out, to understand what is going on in the complex world of a teenager" (p. 114) and a reluctance to accept the adolescent as an autonomous individual with valuable ideas. Adolescence is a stage when the need for respect and self-respect begins to manifest itself most intensively. As adolescents mature, their need increases for adults to interact with them in a more peerlike manner that reflects their near-adulthood. High school students report that their parents' level of understanding of how the adolescent sees the world is dramatically compromised by Grades 7 to 9. Adolescents therefore feel more at ease, understood, and respected when they speak with their peers than with their parents. The nature of adolescent-parent communication and relationships is also affected by cultural taboos, which lead to a hesitation on the part of many adolescents and their parents to have open discussions regarding sexual development and intimate relationships. The importance of this topic to adolescents means, however, that if this hesitation cannot be overcome, the relationship between youth and parent becomes less meaningful because crucial concerns of the child's life are left unspoken (Kon, 1989).

As children reach adolescence, their world widens and they begin to identify with people outside their families. Although their parents may not be their primary focus anymore, it is clear that parents continue to play an important role in the lives of their teenagers. Most Russian adolescents maintain an important emotional bond to their parents, especially their mothers (Shilshtein, 2002). In one Russian study (Kon, 1989), high school students ranked their preferences for spending their free time with parents, friends, with peers of the same gender, in a mixed group of peers, by themselves, and with other significant people in their lives. Parents were ranked in last place (sixth) for boys and in fourth place for girls. However, responses to the question, "Who would you confer with in a difficult situation?" revealed that both boys and girls most commonly would choose their mother in such circumstances. Fathers were the next choice for boys, whereas girls would choose a friend.

In this way, Russian youth resemble most other high school students across different cultures who tend to prefer to take all questions regarding personal, social, school, and even worldview problems to their mother rather than to their father (Kon, 1989; Rice, 1996). High school students, regardless of gender, are more open with their mother than they are with their father; they come to their mother for advice more often and treat her with more empathy. Fathers have an advantage in the "information area" and are engaged for discussion of topics such as politics and sports. Psychological reasons for this preference among adolescents may lie in a tendency for fathers to be more concrete and less flexible and empathetic, as well as the fact that fathers tend to spend much less time with adolescents.

Despite the changes in contemporary Russian society, it is reassuring to know that parents clearly remain significant figures in the lives of adolescents. Research by Rean (2001) indicates that teens describe their mothers more positively than they describe anyone else, including their peers. According to Rean (2001), people who are negative about their mothers are affected by a generally pessimistic and negative attitude toward all social relationships and events. In general, a negative attitude by a Russian youth toward his or her mother is considered to be an important indicator of overall poor personality development.

Adolescents commonly rely heavily on their family for the satisfaction of most needs, including that which they require financially and emotionally.

Families can ensure feelings of security by offering the unconditional love and support that instills confidence in youth, thus helping to relieve the anxiety faced by many adolescents in new or stressful situations. Adolescents also want to have parents who "give a good example to follow" and want to "be proud of their parents, to see them as people worthy to be admired" (Rice, 1996, p. 436). Role modeling and active assistance in positive problem resolution are therefore important ways in which Russian parents facilitate resilience in adolescents. Families who are unable to offer unconditional love and positive role modeling are thought to further jeopardize a youth's ability to cope with failure or other difficult circumstances.

Stressed families often have a difficult time coping with the problems of adolescence in an effective manner. Many Russian families suffer from a lack of competence in helping children form positive social attitudes and are also frequently unable to cooperate effectively with experts when the necessity arises for psychological, pedagogical, medical, social, or legal counseling. Teachers, school psychologists, and social workers encounter difficulties when working with such families, because methodical support for a competent approach to children's problematic behaviors is poorly developed in families under great stress (Vostroknutov, 2001). The state of Russian families today is therefore highly relevant to the development of resilience in adolescents.

RUSSIAN FAMILIES TODAY

The stress and conflict caused by social change have resulted in high rates of family breakdown and dysfunction in Russia, where a dramatic 114% increase has been recorded in the number of single-parent families between 1989 and 1995, and there has been a subsequent increase in the number of abandoned children from 113,913 in 1989 to 674,000 in 1999 (Vostroknutov, 2001). Although increases in adult mortality may explain some of this rise, the proportion of so-called social orphans accounts for most of the abandonments. A social orphan is a child who has biological parents who for some reason (alcoholism, mental illness, family violence, being refugees, or poverty) give up their child to the State. In some cases, the problem is not with the adults, but with the child. Children with special needs and mental illnesses are far more likely to be abandoned. In these cases, the government takes the responsibility to raise them (Galaguzova, 2000). Most adolescents in the care of the State are poor, disabled, or come from neglectful or abusive families.

According to the latest census data from 2002, of every 1,000 people aged 16 and older, 210 have never been married (compared with 161 in 1989), 572 are married (653 in 1989), 114 are widowed (110 in 1989), and 94 are divorced (72 in 1989). These numbers indicate that single-parent families are now increasingly common, and intact families are less of a social norm. These demographic changes reflect new forms of family behavior, which include "sexual, contraceptive and divorce revolutions" (State Committee of the Russian Federation on Statistics, 2002).

Dmitrieva and Polozhiy (2002) suggest that the social dynamics of contemporary Russian families are causing difficulties for the children. Some of the more troubling statistics include the reality that the number of children living in incomplete families (94% of which do not have a father in the home) continues to grow, and the number of children born outside of marriage has increased to 24.3% of all children. Physical and emotional abuse and neglect add to the statistics regarding problems that place children at risk. For example, the number of children removed from their parents' care and placed in the care of the State grew from 42,693 in 1998 to 46,515 in 1999.

The 1997 UNICEF report *Children at Risk in Central and Eastern Europe: Perils and Promises* has concluded that despite numerous internationally funded initiatives, the pressure on orphanages has not been alleviated, nor has a coherent system of community support for families been successfully developed. There is clearly an urgent need for a broad range of supportive resources, including legal, medical, and psychological services for Russian children (UNICEF, 1997).

Contemporary Changes in Family Law

Modern Russian legislation includes several new laws intended to protect children and clarify parental rights and responsibilities. According to

Article 56 of the revised Family Code of the Russian Federation (enacted December 29, 1995), children have legal recourse to protect their rights and privileges. Protection of the rights of children is the responsibility of parents, guardians, child protection institutions, and the courts. A child has the right under this legislation to be protected from parental exploitation, and children under the age of 14 years may seek protection for their rights from a child protection institution. Children aged 14 and older may approach the court directly. Anyone who is aware of a threat to a child's health or life or of an infraction on a child's rights is legally obliged to report this to his or her local child protection agency, which is mandated to protect the child.

Measures for protecting children who are abused by their parent(s) may include criminal sanctions and court-ordered restrictions, including the following:

- Limitation of parenting rights, according to Article 73 of the Family Code
- Deprivation of parenting rights, according to Article 69 of the Family Code
- Removal of the child from the parent(s) when there is a serious threat to the child's life or health, according to Article 77 of the Family Code
- Mother's (but not the father's) forced hospitalization when she poses danger to the child according to the Law About Psychiatric Help and the Rights of the Person Receiving It

Parental rights can be completely removed only through a court hearing. These legal provisions can be used only when parents abuse their children physically, emotionally, or sexually or if the parent suffers from an alcohol or drug addiction.

The Family Code of the Russian Federation also allows for a thorough psychological and psychiatric examination of children to be conducted when parents file for divorce. These assessments are used to determine custody and access agreements and are intended to protect the interests of children when their parents are in conflict. Although such assessments are currently rare, their use is increasing in divorce proceedings.

Russia's current legislation also provides for the social and legal protection of adolescents, including children who are no longer in the custody of their parents. Thus, according to the Civil Code, minors between the ages of 14 and 18 may be assigned a guardian to protect their rights and privileges as well as to perform a parenting role. Minors who have no parents or foster parents are not legally independent until the age of 18 and must have a guardian appointed for them to ensure that their interests are protected. The current Civil Code of the Russian Federation differs from former legislation primarily through Article 27, Emancipation. According to this article, minors over the age of 16 may be acknowledged as legally capable persons if they are employed or have a private business. A minor is announced legally capable (or emancipated) by a decision of a child protection institution and with the child's legal guardian's consent. This article applies to children who are residents of foster homes, orphanages, or educational institutions that are part of the child protection system. Usually children graduate from those institutions at age 16, sometimes having gone through an assisted-education program. When possible, they go on to reside in independent housing provided for them by the State. At the same time, because they live separately and lead an independent lifestyle, custody becomes annulled; sometimes extended family members who did not play an active role in the adolescent's life or who have no resources to help them become guardians (Kharitonova & Korolyova, 2001). Combined, these changes in law and practice have ensured that the most vulnerable of Russian youth, those without families to rely on, have in fact continued to be well protected. The result is adequate parenting by the State in efforts to bolster children's resilience prior to their being launched on their own. Although structurally these efforts are exemplary, it remains to be seen whether increasing demands on limited resources seriously diminish the effectiveness of the Russian social safety net's capacity to ensure minimal interventions for all at-risk children and youth.

Community Resources to Enhance Resilience

Raising children to become healthy members of society is a complex and difficult task even in optimal circumstances. This process is further complicated for children who grow up in dysfunctional families or orphanages, situations often characterized by social and emotional deprivation. The depth of the social, economic, psychological, and legal problems affecting Russian youth has become apparent as stressed families and State institutions struggle to offer guidance and opportunity for youth to develop into successful citizens of a changing society. The dramatic nature of social and ideological change in this society has meant that the experiences of parents and grandparents provide little guidance to the challenges of life in contemporary Russia. Although, traditionally, problems were resolved within Russian families, with older generations assuming an important mentoring and supportive function, this approach is no longer effective. The need for formal intervention has therefore been accepted on a State and community level and has resulted in the development of medical, social, and psychological centers to provide services to youth and families. A primary goal of these formalized services is to assist youth to develop the skills and attributes that will facilitate their success in contemporary Russia.

Modern Russian psychological theory and practice, however, is currently in a state of development and flux. Various trends have emerged and gained sporadic periods of popularity. However, the lack of overall organization and sustainability of resources such as counseling services and telephone hotlines has decreased the effectiveness and credibility of such services. This situation is further complicated by a lack of coordination between State-sponsored and private psychological services. Overall, it seems that the most effective assistance is offered through professional State-sponsored organizations rather than through the private sector.

Russian academics have also failed to provide effective links between theory and the informed practice of psychology and social work. Research and psychological testing is often performed by using poorly adapted versions of tests and questionnaires that commonly originated in the United States, without critique and consideration of their validity and utility for the Russian population. This failure to create culturally specific and relevant tools has greatly hindered the study and practice of psychology and social work in Russia.

A comprehensive listing of the problems in the delivery of mental health services would clearly be more extensive than that offered above. It is very important within this context to develop priorities and a methodical plan for the strategic delivery of services, with an emphasis on mental health services for children and adolescents that promote the development of resilience. Some recommendations for the improvement of the system of psychiatric and psychological services in Russia follow:

1. Developing interdepartmental cooperation between State institutions related to mental health care (Ministries of Health Care and Social Development, Education and Science, Internal Affairs)

2. Developing cooperation between State institutions, community-based services, and nongovernmental organizations

3. Organizing a system of consistent education for psychiatrists, psychologists, and social workers who specialize in the area of mental health services for children and adolescents

4. Developing a system of additional psychiatric, psychological, and psychotherapeutic training for general practitioners, targeting pediatricians, teachers, lawyers, social workers, and parents themselves

5. Encouraging research in the area of mental health services for children and adolescents

WHAT WORKS: EDUCATIONAL PROGRAMMING FOR PARENTS

Educational programming for parents is often one of the least developed components of working with the families of youth at risk. Parents frequently benefit from some basic information in areas such as psychology, psychiatry, and addictions that help them to understand their child's problems and enable them to consistently and effectively work together with professionals. One highly effective model of comprehensive work with "problem" children and their families is the School of Custodial Parents, established in Moscow in 1999 as a branch of a national charity organization called Pedagogical Search. This school was developed for foster parents, guardians, and people preparing to adopt children. However, the number of students at this school has been significantly increased to include the parents of children with physical and mental challenges, children with mental disorders, and children with severe forms of educational and social delays or disabilities. The curriculum has also been developed, tested, and improved over time. This parent education program consists of 90 to 100 hours of lectures, which include sessions provided by experts in different fields, including psychologists, special education teachers, psychiatrists, lawyers, addiction treatment specialists, and career counselors. In the course of these lectures, parents learn about children's different stages of development, age-related crises, effects of emotional and physical deprivation on the child's personality development, age-specific aspects of social experiences, criterion of social adaptation, and more broadly, the causes and manifestations of social and educational problems in children and adolescents. Parents also learn about the most common mental disorders in children and adolescents, with information provided on healthy sexual development of children and adolescents and how to prevent sexual disorders. Other topics covered include social orphans, preschool parenting for children with developmental disturbances, and the prevention of alcoholism, drug addiction, and adolescent criminal behavior. Counseling is available for both children and parents who participate in the educational aspects of the program. An interdisciplinary group of experts, working together—psychologists, social workers, psychiatrists, and defectologists (special education teachers)—counsel children at home. After discussing the assessments made by the various experts, specific recommendations are made for treatment, and other interventions are tailored to the needs of the children and their families (Iovchuk, Sherbakova, & Bezmenov, 2001).

METHODS OF INTERVENTION: RESILIENCE THROUGH EDUCATION

When we take into consideration the economic, political, and sociopsychological state of Russian families today, we can see the importance of developing a system of professional, social, and family education capable of developing resilience in future generations. In particular, in Russia today, the way forward to a healthier population of youth and families is believed to lie with the country's still well-functioning educational system. *Concepts of Modernization of Russian Education Through 2010*, developed by the Ministry of Education of the Russian Federation (the new title is Ministry of Education and Science of the Russian Federation) suggests that "all citizens of Russia, family and parenthood communities, federal and regional institutions of state power, local authorities, professional teaching community, scientific, cultural and commercial institutions should become active agents of educational policy" (Philippov, 2002).

Developing educational programming within the context of the systematic reform of the Russian State and individual communities requires an approach based on modern ideas and principles but one that also takes into account the Russian mentality and national, regional, and familial cultural traditions. Therefore, social and familial education is focused on achieving two related but separate goals—socializing young generations to be an integral part of a uniquely Russian modern society and the development of greater individuality. Educational programming, therefore, seeks to facilitate socialization and self-development, furthering children and adolescents' ability to respond in healthy ways to the chaotic and unhealthy nature of their social environment.

Despite financial and social barriers since perestroika, the Russian State remains determined to use all available resources to provide a State-funded educational system that will assist children and adolescents to develop the values and skills that will make them successful in modern Russia. Some of the principles on which this system of education is being renewed include the following:

1. *The principle of equal opportunities and social justice:* This principle emphasizes the recognition of social inequalities and other vulnerabilities among children and youth. It promotes State and community paternalism (which is seen as a positive characteristic) in regard to children in difficult situations.

2. *The principle of equality between educational territories across Russia:* This will be realized through the development of a national educational system, whereby standards and practices will be comparable throughout the country. The focus will be on national values. The society as a whole will be encouraged to further the spiritual, moral, and civic development of children and youth, with a primary focus on the reproduction of Russian culture.

3. *The principle of interdisciplinary cooperation and integration of formal and informal care providers in the care, education, and socialization of children:* This implies the consolidation of the efforts of different State and social institutions to create the proper conditions for the development and education of the youth of the country. This principle emphasizes the importance of interdisciplinary cooperation and strengthening the socialization and educational potential of social institutions and requires the effective participation of family, school, cultural and sports organizations, social welfare, social institutions, and the mass media. This principle serves to unite State, public, and familial structures that affect children's upbringing into a single system capable of flexible and effective change in the best interests of children and youth and their families, communities, and the State.

4. *The principle of democracy and decentralization when defining the role of the State in raising children and adolescents:* This principle is intended to prevent the excessive regulation of child development by the State or by children's caregivers. It implies that social institutions will use their freedom of choice in determining the best form and content of work done with children and adolescents. The principle also implies more responsibility on the part of State and social organizations for the transmission of ideals and values to youth (Nikitina, 2003).

THE EDUCATIONAL SYSTEM IN RUSSIA

As an illustration of how these principles are put into practice, one can examine the efforts by schools in Moscow to both maintain and build their capacity to educate children so that they are prepared for participation in the new Russia.

The primary challenge for the educational system is to guarantee that all children receive the level of education that will enable them to fulfill their potential. A total of 105 special educational institutions for children with different intellectual and psychophysical development levels have been established to meet this need in Moscow alone. In 28 educational institutions, adolescents with mental and physical challenges have the opportunity to complete their education and train in 1 of 14 careers. A program called Education and Health has developed a network of institutions known as "health schools." In such schools, children, besides getting a basic education, learn skills necessary for a healthy lifestyle, learn to make informed decisions that affect their well-being, learn ways to resolve conflicts both with adults and with peers, and learn how to keep themselves safe. Such schools exist in every district of the city.

In addition to these schools, educators recognized in the early 1990s the need to address the rise in adolescent criminality that had become evident in many communities. New types of educational institutions were established in Moscow in an attempt to contain this growing trend. These new institutions included 10 high schools with an emphasis on learning trades. The focus of these schools is to provide healthy options for youth with learning or behavioral difficulties or both, many of whom live in dysfunctional families and had dropped out of school before completing the required 9 years of high school. These schools were organized by representatives from 50 technical schools who developed a curriculum through which these youth could learn trade-related skills as well as complete their necessary basic education.

Moscow educators have developed many similar models of educational innovation. Schools have maintained their network of night schools that offer many adolescents an alternative opportunity to finish their education outside the regular school system. In over 500 schools, special education classes are offered to provide children with learning disabilities or developmental delays the opportunity to successfully complete high school. In addition, new educational and parenting techniques are currently being developed and taught to parents and others who live and work with at-risk youth. In many of these schools, teachers have experienced considerable success in their work, with about 70% of their students and the students' caregivers reporting healthier outcomes among the youth after graduation and with many former students pursuing postsecondary education. Presently, 27 educational support centers complement the city's educational system. These centers offer the opportunity for children of all ages to be assessed for developmental, behavioral, and learning problems. These centers also offer assistance to teachers and parents in developing individualized plans for furthering each child's development in accordance with his or her needs and resources. Assisting adolescents to achieve healthy outcomes requires a coordinated and scientifically sound approach on behalf of helping professionals. To this end, Moscow State Psychological and Pedagogical University has also started teaching classes on social work practice with adolescents, including adolescents with deviant behaviors (Selyavina, 2001).

This movement toward a comprehensive system of education and psychosocial development takes many forms. The Novorossiysk Center of Social-Psychological Adaptation, for example, focuses on helping adolescents develop resilient behaviors. Staff members at the center have identified four key principles in their work that they strive to promote: positive attitudes, being active, consistency, and willingness (Ashirova, 2001). The goal of the work done at the Novorossiysk Center seeks to develop positive attitudes and behavior among youth while challenging destructive decision-making processes. Group work has been chosen as the most effective way to accomplish this task and has proven an effective, culturally relevant way to help adolescents develop resilience. The main goals include receiving psychological support, learning social and other life skills, and developing a healthy lifestyle. In practice, interventions are done through training, whereby groups of adolescents develop personality resources (a better self-concept, self-respect, self-reliance) and learn behavioral skills, communication skills, and social competence. Besides achieving specific goals, the group work done at the center has the important "side effect" of an increase in personal and social maturity, activity, responsibility, and ability to dialogue with others. Thus, adolescents who have gained positive experiences of group interaction in training sessions become motivated and interested in voluntarily working on developing socially acceptable lifestyles.

Despite such innovative programs and attempts at structuring a school system that offers opportunities for all, significant problems still remain. It is evident that these challenges must be overcome before the education system is to fulfill its potential as a vehicle for building resilience in youth.

Challenges Within the Russian Educational System

Children in Russia commonly attend school for at least 10 years. The education system, therefore, has a potentially large influence on the development and socialization of children. Unfortunately, in most contemporary Russian schools, the emphasis is clearly on teaching a specific educational curriculum, with little attention paid to personal or social development. This limited focus is rooted in the individual and collective professional mind-set of teachers and is reflected in the pedagological practices employed during teaching and the structure of the school system itself (Rean, 2002). Education is, however, tied in important ways to the development of well-rounded and resilient students. Despite the challenges faced, Russian educators have historically been leaders in developing an education system that supports adolescent development and takes into account the developmental milestones relevant for each age group (see, e.g., Vygotsky, 1984, p. 262).

A number of developmental milestones among Russian children have, however, been found to be increasingly threatened. For example, children's ability to communicate with adults in a meaningful manner is becoming less and less developed (Dubrovina, 1995). Analysis of today's pedagogical process indicates a lack of healthy trusting relationships between adults and adolescent school students. This situation is associated with anxiety, insecurity, and low self-esteem among Russian youth. These problems hinder personal growth, problem-solving ability, and the development of relationships.

Such psychological threats to children's well-being have become more acute over the past 10 years, with the number of grade school children who feel inferior and insecure because of school problems increasing almost tenfold. The number of grade school students who feel anxious because of how they are treated by a teacher or fellow student has also increased by a factor of 8. One third of all children in Russian schools report feeling frustrated, insecure, and unsure of their strengths and abilities. Up to 60% of grade-school-aged children show a high level of disturbance in adaptational systems, including a weakened immune system. Approximately 70% to 80% of all children function in a state of overwork and maladaptation. All this means that there is the risk that an entire generation of "problematic" adolescents is now growing into adulthood, threatening to create a society of troubled individuals (Nikitina, 2003).

Overall, negative interactions between teachers and their students increases as children get older. Many teachers believe that adolescents are defined by undesirable character traits and behaviors. Such an attitude by individuals in positions of authority regarding youths who may already suffer from a lack of self-confidence has negative consequences for academic achievement. The potential for authority figures to positively influence youth and their ability to achieve will be realized only when they believe in the potential of the youth with whom they work (Prihozhan & Tolstikh, 1990).

The poor quality of teacher-student relationships is also reflected in adolescents' attitudes toward their teachers. A study by Rean (2001) revealed that students described their teachers with the following adjectives: *grungy* (57%), *responsible* (47.4%), *unfair* (47.4%), *authoritative* (39.5%), *neat* (39.5%), *hypocritical* (38.6%), *disciplined* (37.7%), *weak-willed* (36.8%), *wise* (36.8%), and *aggressive* (36.8%). Rean's work suggests a balance of negative and positive qualities associated with educators. This is important as teachers directly affect the quality of a student's education and socialization. Through teachers, students learn and internalize the norms and rules of their communities (Rean, 2001).

In many ways, schools do not seem to be fulfilling their potential to encourage the formation of resilient behaviors in children, do not always teach the skills necessary to solve difficult situations, and often reinforce the dysfunctional tendencies that exist among members of the child's family. Moreover, poor interpersonal interactions between teachers and adolescents cause or reinforce generational barriers, manifested through frequent conflicts and misunderstandings between teenagers and adults. Adolescents cannot overcome these barriers alone, especially because their immaturity often limits their ability to objectively reflect on and analyze their situation. Initiatives by well-intentioned educators discussed earlier are exactly what children and adolescents will need to overcome these and other barriers to a proper education. Providing quality education universally in ways tailored to the needs of high-risk individuals is one of the most likely pathways to resilience for Russian children and youth.

CONCLUSION

By virtue of their vulnerability and still-developing personalities, adolescents are among those most affected by social instability and dysfunction. It is therefore important to assist youth to develop the resilience that will enable them to find health and success within the context of modern-day Russia. This is therefore an important area of study and one that will better assist professionals to promote health among Russian youth. Further research is needed, however, to understand not only how education can better enhance resilience among youth but also how families and communities can conduct themselves in ways that ensure their children's healthy development as Russia continues to change.

REFERENCES

Ashirova, O. K. (2001). Principles of structuring preventive work in educational institutions of Novorossiysk [Abstract]. From *Adolescents and youth in a changing community* (pp. 21–22), the International Conference, Moscow, Novy Otschet.

Borisova, L. G. (2001). An adolescent in business: Socialization or deviation. *Sociological Studies,* Issue No. 9, 68–76.

Claes, M. (1986). *L'experience adolescente (Adolescent experience).* Bruxelle: Pierre Mardaga.

Craig, G. J. (1996). *Human development.* Upper Saddle River, NJ: Prentice Hall.

Dmitrieva, T. B., & Polozhiy, B. S. (2002). Mental health of Russians. *Man,* Issue No. 6, 21–32.

Dubrovina, I. V. (Ed.). (1995). *Psychological programs of personality development in adolescent and high school age.* Moscow: Pedagogika.

Enikolopov, S. N. (2001). Aggression and deviant behavior in adolescents and youth [Abstract]. From *Adolescents and youth in a changing community* (pp. 33–36), the International Conference, Moscow, Novy Otschet.

Fenko, A. B. (2000). Children and money: Characteristics of economic socialization in the market conditions. *Voprosy Psychologii,* No. 2, 94–101.

Galaguzova, M.A. (Ed.). (2000). *Social pedagogy.* Moscow: Vlados.

Hellinckx, W., Grietens, H., & Bodrova, V. (1997). Prevalence and correlates of problem behavior in 12- to 16-year-old adolescents in the Russian Federation. *International Journal of Child & Family Welfare, 2*(2), 86–112.

Iovchuk, N. M., Sherbakova, A. M., & Bezmenov, P. V. (2001). Educational aspects of interdisciplinary work with a "problematic" child family [Abstract]. From *Adolescents and youth in a changing community* (pp. 128–130), the International Conference, Moscow, Novy Otschet.

Karpukhina, O. I. (2000). Youth of Russia: Specificities of socialization and self-determination. *Sociological Studies,* Issue No. 3, 124–128.

Kharitonova, N. K., & Korolyova, E. V. (2001). Legislation and major aspects of legal protection of children [Abstract]. From *Adolescents and youth in a changing community* (pp. 152–164), the International Conference, Moscow, Novy Otschet.

Kitayama, S., & Markus, H. (Eds.). (1994). *Emotion and culture.* Washington, DC: American Psychological Association.

Kon, I. S. (1989). *Early youth psychology.* Moscow: Prosveshenie.

Lotman, U. M. (1994). *Tarus-Moscow semiotic school.* Moscow: Gnozis.

Mchedlov, M. P. (1998). About religious values of Russian youth. *Sociological Studies,* Issue No. 6, 107–112.

Nalchajyan, A. A. (2001). *Ethnic characterology.* Yerevan, Armenia: Hogeban.

Nikitina, L. E. (2003). Current state and problems of contemporary upbringing: Ideology and principles of development. *Issues of Children's and Adolescents' Mental Health,* No. 2, 32–37.

Pervin, L. F., & John, O. P. (1997). *Personality theory and research.* New York: John Wiley.

Petrova, A. S. (2002). *Parents' opinion on the free time of the adolescent.* Retrieved June 22, 2002, from www.fom.ru

Petrova, A. S. (2004). *Russians value industry and honesty.* Retrieved April 26, 2004, from www.fom.ru

Philippov, V. M. (2002). *Concepts of modernization of Russian education through 2010.* Retrieved February 11, 2002, from www.philippov.ru/news/27/224

Presnyakova, L. (2002). *Abandoned children.* Retrieved June 27, 2002, from www.fom.ru

Prihozhan A. M., & Tolstikh, N. N. (1990). *Adolescents in textbook and in real life.* Moscow: Znanie.

Rean, A. A. (2001). *Practical psychodiagnostics of personality.* Saint Petersburg, Russia: Saint Petersburg State University Publishing House.

Rean, A. A. (Ed.). (2002). *Psychology of a man from birth till death.* Moscow: Olma-Press.

Rice, F. P. (1996). *The adolescent: Development, relationships, and culture* (8th ed.). New York: Allyn & Bacon.

Rumyantseva, P. V. (2003). Ideas of high school students about patriotism and patriotic behavior. *Yearly Journal of the Russian Psychology Society. Abstracts from the III Russian Congress of Psychologists, 6,* 578–581.

Selyavina, L. K. (2001). The strategy of management departments and educational institutions in Moscow in preventing antisocial behavior in adolescents [Abstract]. From *Adolescents and youth in a changing community* (pp. 69–71), the International Conference, Moscow, Novy Otschet.

Shelina, S. L. (2003). About tasks, goals and means of upbringing children in an era of changes. *Yearly Journal of the Russian Psychology Society. Reports from the III Russian Congress of Psychologists, 8,* 409–414.

Shevchenko, U. S. (2001). Using ethological mechanisms of initiation in adolescent psychotherapy [Abstract]. From *Adolescents and youth in a changing community* (pp. 246–248), the International Conference, Moscow, Novy Otschet.

Shilshtein, E. S. (2000). Peculiarities of presentation of self in adolescents. *Voprosy Psychologii,* Issue No. 2, 69–78.

Sobkin, V. S. (1997). *Dynamics of value orientations in high school age adolescents.* Doctoral dissertation, Moscow Psychological Institute of the Russian Academy of Education.

Solokhina, T. A. (2003). The management of the quality of psychiatric assistance. *Psychiatria,* Issue No. 4, 63–70.

State Committee of the Russian Federation on Statistics. (2002). *Main data (summary) of the population census in Russia.* Retrieved December 22, 2002, from www.perepis2002.ru

UNICEF. (1997). *Children at risk in Central and Eastern Europe: Perils and promises* (MONEE Project Regional Monitoring Report, 4). Florence, Italy: UNICEF International Child Development Centre.

Vostroknutov, N. V. (2001). Family and problems of deviant behavior in contemporary society [Abstract]. From *Adolescents and youth in a changing community* (pp. 109–124), the International Conference, Moscow, Novy Otschet.

Vygotsky, L. S. (1984). The problems of age. In A. R. Luria & M. G. Yaroshevsky (Eds.), *Selected papers of L. S. Vygotsky* (Vol. 4, pp. 244–268). Moscow: Pedagogika.

Yartsev, D. V. (1999). Specificities of socialization of a contemporary adolescent. *Voprosy Psychologii,* Issue No. 6, 54–59.

Yastrebov, V. S. (1999). The management of psychiatric assistance. In A. S. Tiganov (Ed.), *Manual on psychiatry* (pp. 329–356). Moscow: Meditsina.

24

INTERCEPTS OF RESILIENCE AND SYSTEMS OF CARE

MARY I. ARMSTRONG

BETH A. STROUL

ROGER A. BOOTHROYD

The purpose of this chapter is to explore the concepts of systems of care and of child resilience and to examine the ways in which these concepts intersect. The chapter begins with a review of the concepts of systems of care and resilience, providing a brief background, a summary of key elements, and a review of recent clarifications of each of these concepts. Intercepts, or points of agreement, between the two concepts are then outlined, as well as divergences. The chapter concludes with a set of recommendations regarding how a synthesis of the two concepts can lead to improved systems of treatment services and supports for at-risk children and their families.

SYSTEMS OF CARE

Background and Definition

Calls for reform in children's mental health in the United States date back to the 1960s. In nearly all the reports and documents advocating system change, the major themes were the same, documenting that not enough children in need were accessing services and that the services provided were not effective (President's Commission on Mental Health, 1978; U.S. Congress, 1986). Specifically, the themes noted the following:

- Most children in need simply were not getting mental health services.
- Those served were often in excessively restrictive settings.
- Services were limited to outpatient, inpatient, and residential treatment. Few, if any, intermediate, community-based options were available.
- Various child-serving systems sharing responsibility for children with mental health problems rarely worked together.
- Typically, families were blamed and were not involved as partners in their child's care (Friesen & Huff, 1996).
- Agencies and systems rarely considered or addressed cultural differences in the populations they served (Isaacs-Shockley, Cross, Bazron,

Dennis, & Benjamin, 1996; U.S. Department of Health and Human Services, 2001).

The proposed solution to these systemic problems was comprehensive, community-based systems of services and supports, which eventually became known as "systems of care." Systems of care were originally defined (Stroul & Friedman, 1986) as "a comprehensive spectrum of mental health and other necessary services which are organized into a coordinated network to meet the multiple and changing needs of children and their families" (p. 3).

Over the past 20 years, the framework of systems of care has been extensively used by states and communities in the United States and by other countries in the development of networks of supports and services for children with mental health problems as well as other at-risk populations, such as children in the child welfare and juvenile justice systems. There has been a great deal of progress in developing systems of care (Stroul & Friedman, 1996), including the creation of a federal program (the Comprehensive Community Mental Health Services for Children and Their Families Program) to support the development of systems of care across the United States (U.S. Department of Health and Human Services, 2001).

Key Elements

Values and Principles

The systems of care concept is based on a set of core values, including that services should be community based, child centered and family focused, and culturally competent. In addition, guiding principles for systems of care specify that services should be comprehensive; individualized to each child and family; provided in the least restrictive, clinically appropriate setting; coordinated at both system and service delivery levels; involve families and youth as full partners; and emphasize early identification and intervention (Stroul & Friedman, 1986, 1996).

Systems of Care Framework

The systems of care concept recognizes that children and families have needs in many domains and promotes a holistic approach in which *all* life domains and needs are considered when serving children and their families rather than addressing mental health treatment needs in isolation. Accordingly, the systems of care framework is organized around eight overlapping dimensions, each representing an area of need for the child and family (Stroul & Friedman, 1986, 1996).

The mental health dimension is emphasized because of its obvious importance for children with emotional disorders and includes a range of both nonresidential and residential services and supports. However, for children exposed to other forms of trauma, other components of the systems may be of greater importance. Experience has demonstrated the need to expand the definition of mental health services and has shown that additional services, such as respite care, school-based mental health services, mental health consultation, behavioral aides, and case management, are also essential.

All the components of the mental health dimension are interrelated, and so the effectiveness of any one component is related to the availability and effectiveness of all other components. In addition, an appropriate balance between the components of a service system is important, particularly between the more restrictive and the less restrictive services. Finally, the concepts of treatment intensity, treatment restrictiveness, and treatment setting are frequently confused—intensive treatment interventions (even the *same* treatment interventions) can be offered in a variety of settings and service programs.

Recent Clarifications

Recently, there have been renewed calls for reform in the delivery of children's mental health services, including a conference sponsored by the surgeon general of the United States that resulted in a "national action agenda" (U.S. Public Health Service, 2000); a Carter Center symposium on the subject, resulting in action steps for reform; and most recently, the President's New Freedom Commission on Mental Health, which examined mental health services for both children and adults and issued a set of recommendations in 2003 (New Freedom Commission on Mental Health, 2003).

Table 24.1   Systems of Care Values and Principles

Core Values

1. The system of care should be child centered and family focused, with the needs of the child and family dictating the types and mix of services provided.

2. The system of care should be community based, with the locus of services as well as management and decision-making responsibility resting at the community level.

3. The system of care should be culturally competent, with agencies, programs, and services that are responsive to the cultural, racial, and ethnic differences of the populations they serve.

Guiding Principles

1. Children with emotional disturbances should have access to a comprehensive array of services that address their physical, emotional, social, and educational needs.

2. Children with emotional disturbances should receive individualized services in accordance with the unique needs and potentials of each child and guided by an individualized service plan.

3. Children with emotional disturbances should receive services within the least restrictive, most normative environment that is clinically appropriate.

4. The families and surrogate families of children with emotional disturbances should be full participants in all aspects of the planning and delivery of services.

5. Children with emotional disturbances should receive services that are integrated, with linkages between child-serving agencies and programs and mechanisms for planning, developing, and coordinating services.

6. Children with emotional disturbances should be provided with case management or similar mechanisms to ensure that multiple services are delivered in a coordinated and therapeutic manner and that they can move through the system of services in accordance with their changing needs.

7. Early identification and intervention for children with emotional disturbances should be promoted by the system of care to enhance the likelihood of positive outcomes.

8. Children with emotional disturbances should be ensured smooth transitions to the adult service system as they reach maturity.

9. The rights of children with emotional disturbances should be protected, and effective advocacy efforts for children and adolescents with emotional disturbances should be promoted.

10. Children with emotional disturbances should receive services without regard to race, religion, national origin, sex, physical disability, or other characteristics, and services should be sensitive and responsive to cultural differences and special needs.

SOURCE: Stroul and Friedman (1986, p. 17).

As the field has begun to consider the action steps needed to improve children's mental health services in today's environment, much consideration is also being given to examining how the systems of care concept has evolved and how it remains useful as a framework for reform.

Current discussions of needed reforms in children's mental health focus on asking how children and adolescents with emotional disorders (including those at risk) and their families can be better served and supported. Improvements in many areas of service systems and treatment interventions are sought, including improved access to mental health services, engagement of children and families in care, cost-effectiveness of services, efficacy of treatment interventions, integration of care across systems, involvement

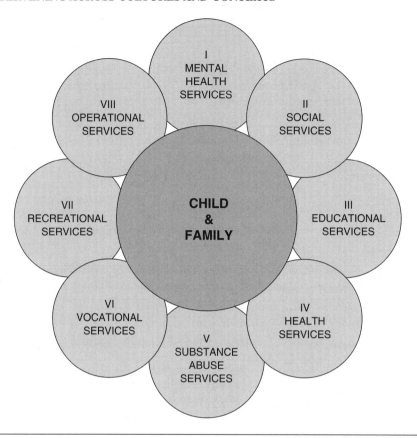

Figure 24.1   Systems of Care Framework

of families and youth, and attention to cultural differences. Calls for increased investment of resources in children's mental health services reflect the current reality of insufficient service capacity to meet the needs (Stroul, Pires, & Armstrong, 2001). In identifying needed improvements in services and service systems, many have arrived at similar conclusions to those reached by earlier reformers—that children with emotional disorders and their families need a range of comprehensive, individualized, coordinated services and supports; that all key partners must come together to plan for and deliver these services; that families must be full partners; and that cultural competence in service delivery is critical. These are the fundamental elements of the systems of care concept and philosophy that emerged in the 1980s. This concept continues to offer a framework for system reform in children's mental health, although the field's understanding of the concept and how it is

implemented has changed through ongoing system development activities and will continue to evolve as reforms progress.

The term *systems of care* has been interpreted as referring to a "model," and people have tried to "replicate" it, to "operationalize" it, to measure it, to evaluate it, and to compare it to "traditional" services. In addition, a number of inaccurate interpretations of the meaning of the systems of care concept have emerged over time. Stroul (2002) clarified the concept by emphasizing that first and foremost, systems of care are *a range of treatment services and supports guided by a philosophy and supported by an infrastructure.*

In another effort to clarify the meaning of the systems of care concept, Friedman and Hernandez (2002) recently wrote that developing a system of care is neither a specific nor a simple intervention and that it could be seen as a general statement of "policy" indicating a desire to establish a complex system targeted at a specific

Table 24.2	Mental Health Dimensions

Nonresidential services

Prevention
Early intervention
Assessment
Outpatient treatment
Home-based services
Day treatment
Crisis services

Residential services

Therapeutic foster care
Therapeutic group care
Therapeutic camp services
Independent living services
Residential treatment
Crisis residential services
Inpatient hospitalization

Other essential services

Case management
Respite services
School-based mental health services
Behavioral aides
Mental health consultation

population of children and families based on a widely agreed-on set of principles and values. Hernandez and Hodges (2003) wrote that systems of care may be better thought of as a cluster of organizational change strategies based on a set of values and principles intended to shape policies, regulations, funding mechanisms, services, and supports. These interpretations emphasize the complexity of the system of care concept.

Stroul (2002) emphasized that it is essential to recognize that developing a system of care is a *multifaceted, multilevel* process, involving (a) making changes in state policies, financing mechanisms, training, and other structures and processes to support systems of care; (b) making changes at the local system level needed to plan, implement, manage, and evaluate the system; and (c) making changes at the service delivery level to provide a broad array of effective, state-of-the-art treatment services and supports to children and families in an individualized and coordinated manner.

CONSTRUCT OF RESILIENCE

Leaders in the field of resilience research such as Luthar, Cicchetti, and Becker (2000a), Masten (2001), and Rutter (1990) have all proposed that the construct of child resilience includes two essential factors: (a) the presence of serious threats to adaptation or development and (b) the achievement of positive adaptation and good outcomes. The need to use a developmental perspective is a common theme in theoretical frameworks for child resilience. A developmental perspective takes into account the child's developmental level and functioning, the multiple levels of influence on a child's developmental pathways, and reciprocity between the risk and protective factors and the child's adjustment. Resilience in children occurs through normal human adaptive processes, including the development of cognition, regulation of behavior, and interactions with caregivers and the environment (Masten, 2001).

Key Elements

Risk Factors

As noted above, the concept of resilience includes the judgment that serious threats to child development are present. The phenomenon of resilience emerged from the study of risk factors in disciplines such as epidemiology and developmental psychopathology (Cicchetti & Toth, 1997; Masten, Morison, Pellegrini, & Tellegen, 1990; Rutter, 1990). Risk factors describe those circumstances that increase the likelihood that a child will experience negative outcomes and problem behaviors. There is considerable agreement that risk factors can be found within the child, the family, the neighborhood, and in societal structures.

Rutter (1979) conducted a study to identify family risk factors for child psychiatric disorders and found that more than one risk factor needed to be present to affect child outcomes. He also found that the presence of two risk factors resulted in a fourfold increase in risk for psychiatric disorder, and so on. In a study using data from the Ontario Child Health Study, risk factors from the child's environment as well as child attributes classified as protective factors were examined to determine which protective factors, holding risk constant, predict absence of child psychiatric disorders (Rae-Grant, Thomas, Offord, & Boyle, 1989). For both children (4- to 11-year-olds) and adolescents (12- to 16-year-olds), the risk factor with the highest relative odds for presence of a child psychiatric disorder was family problems. The National Institute of Mental Health (Hann & Borek, 2001) recently convened an expert panel to conduct an extensive literature review of family risk factors for children's externalizing behavior problems. The evidence-based, malleable risk factors identified were lower levels of parental engagement, greater use of invalidation, and harsh and inconsistent discipline.

Better understanding is needed regarding how risk factors and risk processes operate in person-environment interactions. There is some evidence, for example, that boys are more vulnerable to stressors in the first decade of life; in the second decade, girls are more susceptible to risks; and males are more vulnerable in the third decade (Werner & Smith, 1992).

Protective Factors

The other core characteristic of child resilience is the process that mediates the relationship between stress and competence. There is disagreement regarding the nature of these processes, except for the belief that they are related to the presence of protective factors or mechanisms. There are two basic models to explain the interaction between stressors (i.e., risk factors) and protective factors—the main effect and the buffering effect. Substantial main effects have been found for parenting qualities, intellectual functioning, socioeconomic status, and positive self-perceptions (Masten, 2001). Kirby and Fraser (1997) reviewed three variations of the buffering effect model. First, protective factors may operate as a buffer to risk factors, reducing the possible negative effects of a stressor. Second, protective factors break the cycle of a chain of risk factors. Finally, the presence of a protective factor may prevent the initial onset of risk.

Rak and Patterson (1996) reviewed several studies and identified a number of protective factors within the child and the family. At the child level, protective factors included an active

approach to problem solving, the ability from infancy on to gain the positive attention of others, an ability to be alert and autonomous, the tendency to seek out novel experiences, and an optimistic view even in the face of distressing experiences. At the family level, protective factors included the age of the opposite sex parent, consistent nurturing during the first year of life, alternative caretakers who step in when parents are not present, a multi-age network of relatives, the presence of sibling caretakers, and structure and rules during adolescence.

Recent Clarifications

Luthar and Zelazo (2003), as well as numerous other authors, point out the ambiguity and lack of clarity regarding the construct of resilience because theorists and researchers use the term in varying ways. Their position is that resilience is a process or phenomenon rather than an individual trait or personal attribute. The belief is that the term should not be used as an adjective describing a person but rather as a description of positive adaptation or child trajectories (Luthar, Cicchetti, & Becker, 2000b). There are at least two reasons for defining resilience as a process. First, we do not want to "blame the victim," with the victim being either the child or the family, or both. Second, we do not want to infer that some children are unable to overcome adversity.

INTERCEPTS OF THE SYSTEMS OF CARE AND RESILIENCE CONSTRUCTS

Given that both constructs developed during the same historical period, it is not surprising that their theoretical foundations and many assumptions are similar. On the other hand, there are a number of differences between the two concepts.

Theoretical Grounding in Systems Theory

Based on a review of the seminal literature for both concepts, it is evident that both systems of care and child resilience use social systems theory as their theoretical foundation. Social systems theory recognizes that different parts of a whole, functioning entity are interrelated and interdependent (Bertalanffy, 1981). Performance of any one part not only affects other parts but also may depend on those parts for its survival (Berrien, 1968; Robbins, Chatterjee, & Canda, 1998). Systems theory encompasses the individual as well as his or her social environment. From a systems perspective, the goal of helping professions is to help individuals perform life tasks, alleviate distress, and achieve aims and positions that are important to them. Systems that may help people are informal or natural systems, formal systems, and social institutions.

There are at least two areas where we can identify the influence of systems theory on both systems of care and child resilience. First, both concepts recognize and incorporate the belief that a child lives within and is affected by the social environment. The roles of the family, the community, and social institutions, especially schools, in the promotion of child competence are acknowledged by both constructs. Second, both concepts are premised on the belief that child characteristics and behavior affect the systems in which they are engaged. In other words, in a system, each component can operate as either a dependent or an independent variable. A number of studies have demonstrated that a reciprocal relationship exists between the quality of parenting and a child's personality and behavior (Crockenberg, 1981; Crowley & Kazdin, 1998; Grolnick & Ryan, 1989; Steinberg, Elmen, & Mounts, 1989). Using a system of care framework, McDonald, Gregoire, Poertner and Early (1997) developed a model of caregiving for children with emotional problems. Their research found only three latent variables that made a significant direct contribution to caregiver stress. The latent variable with the highest contribution to caregiver stress was the child's externalizing problem behaviors.

Ecological Approach

One type of systems theory, ecology systems theory, constructs the individual system as part of a larger ecological system, with which the individual must negotiate so as to accommodate, adjust, and survive. Ecological systems theory views individuals as constantly adapting in an interchange with many different aspects of their environment. Adaptation is believed to be reciprocal; people are able to develop through change and are supported by the environment (Payne, 1991).

The family ecological model is one theoretical framework used to explain the relationship between families and the contributing factors to their well-being (Bronfenbrenner, 1986). Rather than focusing on intrafamilial processes and characteristics, the focus is on external factors that may contribute to a family's capacity for parenting. Bronfenbrenner identified three external systems that affect the family: meso-systems, exosystems, and chronosystems. A mesosystem, for example, refers to the influences that operate between the primary settings in which child development takes place, such as home and school. It assumes that effects occur in both directions; that is, school affects home, and home affects what occurs in school. Exosystem models identify the influences in settings in which parents function but where children do not enter, such as the parents' work environment. Chronosystem models analyze the dynamic relationships between changes and continuities over time, both within the person and within the environment.

Both systems of care and child resilience use an ecological approach. For example, the explicit goal of systems of care is that children will be able to live and function well at home with their family, in school, and their own community (Brannan, Baughman, & Reed, 2002). In addition, systems of care take an ecological approach to child development. A child is viewed ecologically as an individual who interacts with others in a number of life domains.

Early research studies on child resilience were focused on the personal characteristics and attributes of children. In the last two decades, we have seen a shift to a more comprehensive focus on three sets of factors: attributes of children, of families, and of wider social environments (Luthar et al., 2000a). Today, there is general agreement that both risk and protective factors and processes can be identified at multiple levels; studies of child resilience identify and examine risk and protective factors and processes in all areas of a child's life (Fraser & Galinksy, 1997; Werner & Smith, 1992; Wyman, Sandler, Wolchik, & Nelson, 2000). Many of the chapters in this volume do likewise.

Multilevel Perspective and Causation

As is indicated by the term *systems of care*, inherent in this framework is the recognition that families, communities, and social institutions affect at-risk children both positively and negatively. Values and principles specify that both treatment and support services should be community based, that families should be integrally involved in all aspects of service delivery, and that services should be coordinated among those agencies and systems that share responsibility for children with emotional disorders.

Through a review of several research studies, Kirby and Fraser (1997) proposed a multilevel model of common risk and protective factors for many childhood problems. At the system level, common risk factors are poverty; lack of education, employment options, or both; and racial discrimination. Protective factors include opportunities for education, employment, and achievement. At the family and neighborhood level, risk factors include child abuse or neglect, parental conflict (believed to be a barrier to effective parenting), parental mental health and substance abuse problems, and poor parenting skills. Social support for parents and youth, the presence of a caring, supportive adult, positive parent-child relationship, and effective parenting skills are identified as protective factors. At the individual child level, risk factors include biomedical problems and gender (a marker for certain conditions). Individual-level protective factors are easy temperament, self-efficacy, competence in normative roles, self-esteem, and intelligence. The assumption is that individual, family, and neighborhood protective factors and processes can mediate risk factors at any level.

Target Population: Children at Risk

Another convergence of both concepts is their roots in child psychopathology, with its focus on children who are at risk for a variety of psychosocial problems. According to Cicchetti and Garmezy (1993), growth of the developmental perspective in child psychopathology led to a growing interest in resilience. There was recognition that an understanding of the mechanisms and processes that lead to positive outcomes in the face of adversity increases knowledge of both normal and abnormal development (Luthar, Burack, Cicchetti, & Weisz, 1997). The systems of care concept was developed to address the needs of children with serious emotional disturbances and their families, although its application has been expanded to include children at risk.

Strengths-Based Focus

Despite the shared roots in psychopathology, a focus on strengths can be found in both concepts. Although not part of the early writings on systems of care, the systems of care values and principles created a service-planning process characterized as "individualized service planning" or a "wraparound approach." In the wraparound process, both the child and the family are active members of the treatment planning team. The first phase of service planning has to do with the identification of both strengths and challenges in the child and family's life. The assumption is that strengths are present in every family and that child and family strengths should be used in the development and implementation of the child's service plan (Burchard, Bruns, & Burchard, 2002).

As noted, child resilience likewise assumes the presence of strengths, referred to as protective factors and processes. Several theories have been proposed to explain how protective factors increase resilience in children. Rutter (1987) distinguished between protective factors and protective processes. He defined protective factors as those variables and mechanisms that modify a person's response to a risk situation, and protective processes as successful engagement with risk that involves a change from risk to adaptation. Rutter (1990) identified four mediating mechanisms in protective processes: (a) mechanisms that directly reduce the impact of risk exposure, (b) mediating factors that stop or reduce the impact of risk chains, (c) the development of a child's self-esteem, and (d) turning points and the opening up of new opportunities. More recently, Rutter added four more protective mechanisms: (a) protective processes that reduce sensitivity to risk, (b) an increase of positive chain reactions, (c) compensatory positive experiences that counter the effects of risk, and (d) positive cognitive processing of negative events (Rutter, 1995). A related phenomenon in child resilience is the ability of some children to actively generate and create experiences that foster competence (Masten et al., 1990). Both Murphy and Moriarty (1976) and Werner (1993) in their landmark studies identified the ability of resilient children to evoke help and positive responses, as well as their capacity to identify resilient caregivers.

The shared focus on strengths has parallels with new understandings in related fields that approach human functioning with assumptions of active human agency, prevention, and health promotion (Windle, 1999). In the field of health care, the salutogenic model emphasizes the concept of coherence, a person's belief that the environment is structured and predictable, that resources are available to meet whatever challenges are present, and that the challenges are worthy of engagement (Antonovsky, 1990). This approach to well-being contends that the strength of resistant resources is far more important than strength avoidance. Healing, a related concept from the field of holistic health, is described as a process that makes the patient better able to cope with new situations rather than as simply the return to the state of health previous to the disease (Dubos, 1990).

Challenge of Definitional Ambiguity and Drift

Over time, a number of inaccurate interpretations of the meaning of the systems of care concept have emerged. Some of the "myths and misconceptions" about systems of care include the following:

- They are primarily designed to improve service coordination and integration.
- They do not focus on clinical interventions but mostly focus on system infrastructure.
- The philosophy is primarily focused on family involvement and cultural competence.
- They are different from and/or do not involve evidence-based interventions.
- No "traditional" services are included in them.
- They primarily involve providing "wraparound" services.
- They place greater value on nonprofessional service providers and natural supports than on other clinicians, providers, and treatment modalities.

However, systems of care *do* involve clinical interventions, and they involve "traditional" services such as outpatient, inpatient, and residential treatment, as well as more recently developed service modalities, such as home-based services, therapeutic foster care, multisystemic therapy (MST), intensive case management, and others, many of which have an emerging evidence base from research in community settings (Burns & Hoagwood, 2002; Burns, Hoagwood, & Mrazek, 1999). Wraparound is an *approach* to planning and providing highly individualized services and supports of all types that is used extensively within systems of care. Using the wraparound approach leads to the development of a comprehensive, holistic, individualized service plan for a child and family that brings to bear all the needed treatment services and supports. The wraparound approach is also an *element* of the systems of care concept and philosophy. Furthermore, systems of care involve highly trained clinicians of all disciplines, as well as paraprofessionals, families as providers, and other creative staffing strategies to meet different needs. Systems of care involve *all* these things.

Many theorists and researchers have similarly identified issues related to definitional ambiguity regarding child resilience. A recent review identified major areas of concern (Luthar et al., 2000a). First, there is little consensus regarding definitions. For example, the term *resilience* is used in reference to at least three groups: (a) at-risk children who show better than expected outcomes, (b) youth who maintain positive adaptation despite stressful experiences, and (c) children who demonstrate good recovery from a traumatic event or situation. A second discrepancy is in the conceptualization of resilience as a personal trait versus a dynamic process. In addition, there is little consensus regarding major terms such as *protective factors* or *vulnerability*. For example, the term protective factor is used to reference both main effect models and those involving interactive processes.

COMPLEXITY OF THE CONSTRUCTS

Research on both systems of care and resilience is challenged methodologically by limitations in the precision of measurement. With respect to the study of resilience, Luthar and her colleagues (Luthar et al., 2000a) note that children exposed to various types of adversity are often treated analytically as a homogeneous group. Researchers frequently fail to take into account potentially important aspects of the adversity children experience, such as severity, duration, or protective factors, that might explain variability in child outcomes. Other investigators argue the need for increased complexity. Curtis and Cicchetti (2003), for example, indicate that research on resilience has focused almost exclusively on psychosocial variables as explanatory factors in differential outcomes. They argue that researchers need to include potential biological factors such as neural plasticity as potential predictors of resilience.

Similarly, Friedman and Hernandez (2002) note the complexity associated with systems of care studies and the challenge facing evaluators in "determining how to describe and measure it" (p. 68). There are a number of reasons for this. First, as Manteuffel, Stephens, and Santiago (2002) explain, communities develop programs tailored to their needs. Second, studying systems of care is complex because the interventions provided to children served within the same system of care are intended to be individualized (Farmer, 2000). Third, Farmer also noted that different service providers provide interventions to children at different times. Fourth, the children and adolescents served by local systems are as diverse as are the environments in which the systems are located (Friedman & Hernandez, 2002). These multiple sources of variability, many by design, create enormous challenges for researchers attempting to determine which systems of care components are most effective and for whom.

Lack of Definitional Consensus and Clarity

Research on both systems of care and resilience share a lack of definitional consensus, clarity, and operationalization related to both the independent and dependent variables frequently examined. Despite the existence of a set of guiding principles (Stroul & Friedman, 1986, 1996), there exists no single set of agreed-on, operationally defined criteria for

determining whether or not a system of care exists. As a result, variability exists regarding the degree to which existing systems of care conform to these guiding principles, which are likely partly responsible for variability in the relative effectiveness of these systems of care. A study conducted by Brannan et al. (2002) found that funded systems of care were more likely to adhere to the guiding principles compared with unfunded child mental health systems. However, they also found meaningful variability across sites in their adherence to these principles as well as principles in which sites' adherence was generally lacking. A challenge to researchers is that "communities develop programs according to their own unique circumstance within the system-of-care framework" (Manteuffel et al., 2002, p. 17). Rosenblatt (1998) characterized this issue as "the problem of the independent variable: what is a system of care?" (p. 330).

Similar challenges exist in identifying and measuring the dependent or outcome variables. Because of the varied goals within a systems of care framework, researchers have employed a variety of child-level outcome measures across various domains and using different measures (Rosenblatt, 1998). The domains most relevant for systems of care research are probably best articulated by Hoagwood, Jensen, Petti, and Burns (1996) as (a) child symptoms and diagnoses, (b) child adaptive functioning, (c) consumer perspectives such as satisfaction, (d) environments, and (e) systems outcomes. One approach in systems of care research has been to include a wide variety of measures across these domains in their attempts to assess system effectiveness. A problem with this approach was noted by Boothroyd, Banks, Evans, Greenbaum, and Brown (2004), who indicate that given that these individually tailored interventions have goals for children and families that can focus on a wide range of outcomes such as improving child functioning, improving family communication skills, or increasing the family's social support network, the use of a broad array of outcome measures results in children and families being assessed on a number of measures for which their intervention was not intended to have an impact. This decreases the likelihood that positive changes will be observed for the group.

There exists wide variation in the definitions and operationalization among researchers studying resilience. Researchers focus on various domains to identify children who are resilient or show competence. These domains include areas such as clinical symptoms, academic attainment, and personality traits (Heller, Larrieu, Dimperio, & Boris, 1999). Even when researchers focus within the same domains, the standard used to define resilience often differs. For example, high school graduation might define competence in one study, whereas above-average grades might be the standard in another. The general recommendation is that risk factors and competence should be assessed in similar domains (Luthar & Zelazo, 2003). For example, the resilience or competence of children who are at risk because of factors such as low parental educational attainment levels or having learning disabilities should be examined in terms of some form of academic or school success.

In terms of the measurement of risk (and protective) factors, Windle (1999) argued that research on resilience lacks a conceptual framework as various investigators assess risk using a broad range of characteristics spanning from low birth weight to poverty to child maltreatment to psychiatric disorders and substance abuse.

In summary, researchers in both systems of care and resilience face challenges in terms of having agreed-on definitions and indicators of the independent variables (i.e., risk and protective factors and system of care) as well as the dependent variables of interest (resilience/competence and child outcomes).

DIVERGENCE OF THE TWO CONSTRUCTS

There are also areas where the two constructs lack agreement with one another and have different foci or areas of emphasis.

System Level Versus Individual Child Level

For child resilience, the starting point and focus is children at risk. In this regard, child resilience has stayed close to its roots in developmental psychopathology. For systems of care, the focus has been, and continues to be, both the child at risk and system-level factors and processes. As noted earlier, the concept of systems of care was developed to address systemic issues and problems, such as insufficient funds and a lack of trained, qualified staff, in efforts to serve children with serious emotional problems and their families.

Research on systems of care and research on resilience share a multilevel perspective (i.e., person, family, environment); however, historically, both areas of inquiry evolved into this multilevel perspective from opposite ends of the continuum (Luthar et al., 2000a; Masten et al., 1990; Rosenblatt, 1998; Rosenblatt & Woodbridge, 2003; Werner, 1993; Werner & Smith, 1992). Systems of care research began with various system redesign and integration strategies such as alternative funding strategies, multidisciplinary treatment teams, and cross-agency memoranda of understandings (MOUs) (Rosenblatt & Woodbridge, 2002). As noted by Farmer (2000), the early focus of these system redesign strategies was clearly on system-level changes (see, e.g., Behar, 1985; Burchard & Clarke, 1990). Over time, however, the focus shifted in response to increasing demands for individual-level outcomes as measures of system effectiveness (Farmer, 2000). Given this, increased emphasis emerged within systems of care research focused on provider behaviors and child and family outcomes. For example, a recent study of children's in-home emergency psychiatric services that used a systems of care framework identified outcomes at the family level (increases in social supports, caregiver self-efficacy, and family adaptability and cohesion), at the child level (higher self-esteem, higher levels of functioning at home and school), and at the service delivery level (reduced provider burnout, higher levels of provider cultural competence) (Evans, Boothroyd, & Armstrong, 1997). Despite this multilevel research approach, it is unclear whether system-level change is a necessary condition to affect child-level outcomes (Farmer, 2000), although some investigators argue that researchers should focus on individual-level outcomes, examining processes and factors such as therapeutic alliance (Bickman, Noser, & Summerfelt, 1999; Bickman, Smith, Lambert, & Andrade, 2003).

In contrast, the study of resilience historically began at the individual level—attempting to determine why children exposed to adversity differed with respect to their subsequent "competence" or "resilience" (Luthar et al., 2000a; Masten & Garmezy, 1985; Werner & Smith, 1992). As Luthar et al. (2000a) discuss, over time, researchers expanded their search for explanatory protective factors and mechanisms, moving away from simply examining qualities associated with the child to a broader focus on aspects of their families and the characteristics of the environments in which they resided. For example, a recent study of resilience in children with serious emotional problems focused on the role of parental social supports and their relationship with family well-being, quality of parenting, and the child's resilience (Armstrong, 2003). This book, and the questions it raises, takes this exploration even further, looking at broader systems of care, cultural factors, and other aspects of the environment that influence individual outcomes, the traditional focus of resilience research.

Formal Versus Informal Supports and Services

Perhaps because the initial target population for systems of care was children and youth with serious emotional disturbances, systems of care tend to emphasize treatment supports and services offered by providers, both agency-based and individual practitioners. Although systems of care opened up the service array from inpatient and outpatient services to a broader array of community-based services and supports, and encouraged in-home and school-based services, the base continues to be human service providers. The introduction of individualized service planning included some emphasis on the use of informal supports, but implementation has been challenging. For example, one of the stated values of the wraparound process is that natural supports should outnumber professionals at service-planning meetings. However, a recent study that included observations of 72 service-planning meetings found that about 60% of the team meetings included no natural supports (Walker, Koroloff, & Schutte, 2003). Only 7 meetings had more than one natural support person who attended the planning meeting.

The construct of child resilience, on the other hand, tends to be "blind" to the distinction between formal and informal support services. The schema of risk and protective factors and processes, for example, tends to emphasize characteristics and attributes of the community, the family, and the child and is silent about the role of the formal service delivery network (for more on this, see Barter's and MacDonald, Glode, and Wein's contributions detailing community-based approaches to child welfare in Aboriginal and non-Aboriginal settings, Chapters 21 and 22, respectively).

Developmental Tasks Versus Here and Now

A review of the framing literature for both systems of care and child resilience indicates that the importance of developmental tasks and critical periods in a child's formation is stressed much more in child resilience. The construct of child resilience has its roots in developmental psychopathology, and many early writings on child resilience emphasize the importance of using a developmental perspective for understanding adaptation in children (Cicchetti & Garmezy, 1993; Masten et al., 1990; Sroufe & Rutter, 1984). Child adaptation is viewed within the context of developmental periods. Characteristics of a developmental perspective, including holism, directedness, differentiation, and the coherence of an individual's development, are presented as the framework for understanding child resilience (Sroufe & Rutter, 1984). The developmental perspective is used to explain why resilience is not static and that new vulnerabilities, new strengths, or both may emerge during developmental transitions throughout the life course (Cicchetti & Garmezy, 1993). In a discussion of how to operationalize social competence, Luthar et al. (1997) emphasize that competence equates with behaviors that indicate success at meeting expectations associated with a specific developmental stage.

Action Versus Theory

Since its inception, the concept of system of care has been action oriented because it was developed as an organizing framework for the delivery of children's mental health services. The focus was, and continues to be, on "How?"—how to organize services and supports so that these youth have positive outcomes, are able to live and grow as members of their family and school community, and can become productive young adults who can make a contribution to their community?

For child resilience, the operative question has been and continues to be "Why?"—why do some children who experience high levels of trauma overcome the odds?

Family and Youth Involvement

One of the guiding principles for systems of care has been that families should be full participants in the planning and delivery of services (Stroul & Friedman, 1986). Child resilience does not address the issue of family or youth partnerships, probably because its focus is not on intervention.

Importance of Culture and Context

As noted earlier, the core values of systems of care are that services should be community based, child centered and family focused, and culturally competent. The final value, cultural competence, specifies that agencies and the services they provide, need to be responsive to cultural, racial, and ethnic differences (Stroul & Friedman, 1986). Although implementation has been challenging, the importance of culture in the planning and provision of a service network has been, and continues to be, a consistent theme in the systems of care literature (Isaacs-Shockley et al., 1996; Stroul & Friedman, 1996).

The construct of child resilience has placed less emphasis on culture. For example, research studies typically have not included race and culture as a variable to be examined. Some investigators have begun to more closely examine issues of culture within the context of child resilience (McCubbin, McCubbin, Thompson, & Thompson, 1998). In their chapter in this volume (Chapter 2), McCubbin and McCubbin describe how the resiliency model of family stress, adjustment, and adaptation (McCubbin & McCubbin, 1993) is particularly well suited for identifying and understanding how sociocultural factors influence children's and families' responses to stressful events. Ungar and his colleagues, in this volume and elsewhere (see Chapter 13; Ungar, Lee, Callaghan, & Boothroyd, in press), describe an international study of resilience among adolescents facing war, violence, cultural disintegration, and structural inequalities across five continents. Central to this study is an innovative approach to cross-cultural research in efforts to better understand the phenomenon of resilience.

FUTURE INTERCEPTS

Facing the challenge of definitional ambiguity has resulted in the recognition of the complexity of both systems of care and child resilience. Both theoretical frameworks may benefit from embracing the system theory's concept of equifinality, meaning that many trajectories can lead to child competence. There is a growing body of research supporting the premise that child development and well-being depends on reciprocal transactions between the child and his or her environment over time. Researchers in both systems of care and child resilience need to understand the multiple trajectories that can lead to positive outcomes, such as school readiness and successful transition to adulthood.

Another potential intercept is between individualized care planning and protective processes. From the child resilience literature, it is now clear that efforts to promote competence in children at risk need to focus on strategies that protect or restore the effective functioning of basic adaptational processes (Masten, 2001). Although one of the assumptions of a wraparound approach is to build on child and family strengths, an additional benefit would be to consciously seek and facilitate protective processes and mechanisms in a child's life, including making use of natural turning points, such as high school graduation or entering middle school, creating new opportunities for a child, and providing compensatory experiences that can counteract previous traumas.

In the area of treatment services and supports, a reciprocal transaction could benefit both concepts. Systems of care have tended to place less emphasis on the informal and naturally occurring protective factors and mechanisms in a child's life, including natural helpers, turning points, and normal developmental and adaptational processes. Individualized care planning, as well as system-level and organizational-level reforms, could make better use of these concepts. Child resilience, on the other hand, could pay greater attention to the formal service system as a protective factor.

The study of child resilience could benefit from embracing the systems of care value placed on culture and context. A family's cultural heritage often includes traditions, values, and beliefs that can play a protective role for children at risk. Cultural institutions, such as churches and social organizations, need to be viewed as protective factors and included in every child's assessment.

Both areas of inquiry could profit from applying and sharing advances in multilevel analytic strategies to simultaneously examine person, family, and community influences on the outcomes of children served in systems of care as well as in interventions that promote child competence in response to traumatic events.

In this chapter, we have attempted to highlight the founding principles of the systems of care movement in the United States over the past 20 years and to summarize the research base that has emerged. In addition, we presented a brief historical overview of the resilience literature and then contrasted the similarities and differences in the constructs of systems of care and child resilience. We concluded by highlighting the areas in which we believe policymakers, planners, and researchers examining systems of care or child resilience can benefit through increased awareness of each other's work as well as through joint policy, planning, and research efforts.

REFERENCES

Antonovsky, A. (1990). The Salutogenic Model of Health. In C. Swencionis (Ed.), *The healing brain: A scientific reader* (pp. 231–243). New York: Guilford Press.

Armstrong, M. I. (2003). *An empirical study: A model of the pathways between social support, family wellbeing, parenting quality, and child resilience.* Unpublished Doctoral Dissertation, Memorial University of Newfoundland, St. John's, Newfoundland.

Behar, L. (1985). Changing patterns of state responsibility: A case study of North Carolina. *Journal of Clinical Child Psychology, 14*(3), 188–195.

Berrien, F. K. (1968). *General and social systems.* New Brunswick, NJ: Rutgers University Press.

Bertalanffy, L. V. (1981). *A systems view of man.* Boulder, CO: Westview Press.

Bickman, L., Noser, K., & Summerfelt, W. T. (1999). Long-term effects of a system of care on children and adolescents. *Journal of Behavioral Health Services & Research, 26*(2), 185–202.

Bickman, L., Smith, C. M., Lambert, E. W., & Andrade, A. R. (2003). Evaluation of a congressionally mandated wraparound demonstration. *Journal of Child and Family Studies, 12*(2), 135–156.

Boothroyd, R. A., Banks, S. M., Evans, M. E., Greenbaum, P. E., & Brown, E. (2004). Untangling the web: An approach to analyzing the impacts of individually tailored, multi-component treatment interventions. *Mental Health Service Research, 6*(4), 143–153.

Brannan, A. M., Baughman, L. N., & Reed, E. D. (2002). System-of-care assessment: Cross-site comparison of findings. *Children's Services: Social Policy, Research, and Practice, 5*(1), 37–56.

Bronfenbrenner, U. (1986). Ecology of the family as a context for human development: Research perspectives. *Developmental Psychology, 22*(6), 723–742.

Burchard, J. D., Bruns, E. J., & Burchard, S. N. (2002). The wraparound approach. In K. Hoagwood (Ed.), *Community treatment for youth: Evidence-based interventions for severe emotional and behavioral disorders* (pp. 69–90). New York: Oxford University Press.

Burchard, J. D., & Clarke, R. T. (1990). The role of individualized care in a service delivery system for children and adolescents with severely maladjusted behavior. *Journal of Mental Health Administration, 17*(1), 48–60.

Burns, B. J., & Hoagwood, K. (2002). *Community treatment for youth: Evidence-based interventions for severe emotional and behavioral disorders.* New York: Oxford University Press.

Burns, B. J., Hoagwood, K., & Mrazek, P. J. (1999). Effective treatment for mental disorders in children and adolescents. *Clinical Child and Family Psychology Review, 2*(4), 199–254.

Cicchetti, D., & Garmezy, N. (1993). Prospects and promises in the study of resiliency. *Development and Psychopathology, 5*(4), 497–502.

Cicchetti, D., & Toth, S. L. (1997). Transactional ecological systems in developmental psycho-pathology. In J. R. Weisz (Ed.), *Developmental psychopathology: Perspectives on adjustment, risk, and disorder* (pp. 317–349). Cambridge, UK: Cambridge University Press.

Crockenberg, S. B. (1981). Infant irritability, mother responsiveness, and social support influences on the security of infant-mother attachment. *Child Development, 52*(3), 857–865.

Crowley, M. J., & Kazdin, A. E. (1998). Child psy-chosocial functioning and parent quality of life among clinically referred children. *Journal of Child and Family Studies, 7*(2), 233–251.

Curtis, W. J., & Cicchetti, D. (2003). Moving research on resilience into the 21st century: Theoretical and methodological considerations in examining the biological contributors to resilience. *Development and Psychopathology, 15*(3), 773–810.

Dubos, R. (1990). Self-healing: A personal history. In C. Swencionis (Ed.), *The healing brain: A scientific reader* (pp. 135–146). New York: Guilford Press.

Evans, M. E., Boothroyd, R. A., & Armstrong, M. I. (1997). Development and implementation of an experimental study of the effectiveness of intensive in-home crisis services for children and their families. *Journal of Emotional and Behavioral Disorders, 5*(2), 93–105.

Farmer, E. M. Z. (2000). Issues confronting effective services in systems of care. *Children and Youth Services Review, 22*(8), 627–650.

Fraser, M. W., & Galinsky, M. J. (1997). Toward a resilience-based model of practice. In M. W. Fraser (Ed.), *Risk and resilience in childhood* (pp. 265–276). Washington, DC: NASW Press.

Friedman, R. M., & Hernandez, M. (2002). The national evaluation of the Comprehensive Community Mental Health Services for Children and Their Families Program: A commentary. *Children's Services: Social Policy, Research, and Practice, 5*(1), 67–74.

Friesen, B. J., & Huff, B. (1996). Family perspec-tives on systems of care. In B. A. Stroul (Ed.), *Children's mental health. Creating systems of care in a changing society* (pp. 41–68). Baltimore, MD: Brookes.

Grolnick, W. S., & Ryan, R. M. (1989). Parent styles associated with children's self-regulation and competence in school. *Journal of Educational Psychology, 81*(2), 143–154.

Hann, D. M., & Borek, N. (Eds.). (2001). *Taking stock of risk factors for child/youth externalizing behavior problems*. Rockville, MD: Department of Health and Human Services, Public Health Service, National Institutes of Health, National Institute of Mental Health.

Heller, S. S., Larrieu, J. A., Dimperio, R., & Boris, N. W. (1999). Research on resilience to child maltreatment: Empirical considerations. *Child Abuse & Neglect, 23*(4), 321–338.

Hernandez, M., & Hodges, S. (2003). Building upon the theory of change for systems of care. *Journal of Emotional and Behavioral Disorders, 11*(1), 19–26.

Hoagwood, K., Jensen, P. S., Petti, T., & Burns, B. J. (1996). Outcomes of mental health care for children and adolescents: A comprehensive conceptual model. *Journal of the American Academy of Child and Adolescent Psychiatry, 35*(8), 1055–1063.

Isaacs-Shockley, M., Cross, T., Bazron, B., Dennis, K., & Benjamin, M. (1996). Framework for a culturally competent system of care. In B. A. Stroul (Ed.), *Children's mental health: Creating system of care in a changing society* (pp. 23–40). Baltimore: Brookes.

Kirby, L. D., & Fraser, M. W. (1997). Risk and resilience in childhood. In M. W. Fraser (Ed.), *Risk and resilience in childhood: An ecological perspective* (pp. 10–33). Washington, DC: NASW Press.

Luthar, S. S., Burack, J. A., Cicchetti, D., & Weisz, J. R. (1997). Preface. In J. R. Weisz (Ed.), *Develop-mental psychopathology: Perspectives on adjust-ment, risk, and disorder* (pp. xv-xxi). Cambridge, UK: Cambridge University Press.

Luthar, S. S., Cicchetti, D., & Becker, B. (2000a). The construct of resilience: A critical evaluation and guidelines for future work. *Child Develop-ment, 72*(3), 543–562.

Luthar, S. S., Cicchetti, D., & Becker, B. (2000b). Research on resilience: Response to commen-taries. *Child Development, 71*(3), 573–575.

Luthar, S. S., & Zelazo, L. B. (2003). Research on resilience: An integrative review. In S. S. Luthar

(Ed.), *Resilience and vulnerability: Adaptation in the context of childhood adversities* (pp. 510–550). Cambridge, UK: Cambridge University Press.

Manteuffel, B., Stephens, R. L., & Santiago, R. (2002). Overview of the national evaluation of the Comprehensive Community Mental Health Services for Children and Their Families program and current findings. *Children's Services: Social Policy, Research, and Practice, 5*(1), 3–20.

Masten, A. S. (2001). Ordinary magic: Resilience processes in development. *American Psychologist, 56*(3), 227–238.

Masten, A. S., & Garmezy, N. (1985). Risk, vulnerability, and protective factors in developmental psychopathology. In A. E. Kazdin (Ed.), *Advances in clinical child psychology* (Vol. 8, pp. 1–52). New York: Plenum Press.

Masten, A. S., Morison, P., Pellegrini, D., & Tellegen, A. (1990). Competence under stress: Risk and protective factors. In S. Weintraub (Ed.), *Risk and protective factors in the development of psychopathology* (pp. 236–256). Cambridge, UK: Cambridge University Press.

McCubbin, H. I., McCubbin, M. A., Thompson, A. I., & Thompson, E. A. (1998). Resiliency in ethnic families: A conceptual model for predicting family adjustment and adaptation. In I. Hamilton & M. McCubbin (Eds.), *Resiliency in Native American and immigrant families* (pp. 3–47). Thousand Oaks, CA: Sage.

McCubbin, M. A., & McCubbin, H. I. (1993). Families coping with illness: The resiliency model of family stress, adjustment and adaptation. In C. Danielson, B. Hamel-Bissel, & P. Winstead-Fry (Eds.), *Families, health and illness* (pp. 21–63). New York: Mosby.

McDonald, T. P., Gregoire, T. K., Poertner, J., & Early, T. J. (1997). Building a model of family caregiving for children with emotional disorders. *Journal of Emotional and Behavioral Disorders, 5*(3), 138–148.

Murphy, L. B., & Moriarty, A. E. (1976). *Vulnerability, coping, and growth from infancy to adolescence.* New Haven, CT: Yale University Press.

New Freedom Commission on Mental Health. (2003). *Achieving the promise: Transforming mental health care in America* (Publication No. SMA-03–3831). Rockville, MD: Department of Health and Human Services.

Payne, M. S. (1991). Systems and ecological perspectives. In M. S. Payne (Ed.), *Modern social work theory: A critical introduction* (pp. 137–156). Chicago: Lyceum Books.

President's Commission on Mental Health. (1978). *Report of the sub-task panel on infants, children and adolescents.* Washington, DC: Author.

Rae-Grant, N., Thomas, B. H., Offord, D. R., & Boyle, M. H. (1989). Risk, protective factors, and the prevalence of behavioral and emotional disorders in children and adolescents. *Journal of the American Academy of Child and Adolescent Psychiatry, 28*(2), 262–268.

Rak, C. F., & Patterson, L. E. (1996). Promoting resilience in at-risk children. *Journal of Counseling and Development, 74*(4), 207–221.

Robbins, S. P., Chatterjee, P., & Canda, E. R. (1998). Systems theory. In *Contemporary human behavior theory: A critical perspective for social work.* Needham Heights, MA: Allyn & Bacon.

Rosenblatt, A. (1998). Assessing the child and family outcomes of systems of care for youth with severe emotional disturbance. In A. Duchnowski (Ed.), *Outcomes for children and youth with emotional and behavioral disorders and their families* (pp. 329–362). Austin, TX: Pro-Ed.

Rosenblatt, A., & Woodbridge, M. W. (2003). Deconstructing research on systems of care for youth with EBD. *Journal of Emotional and Behavioral Disorders, 11*(1), 27–37.

Rutter, M. (1979). Protective factors in children's responses to stress and disadvantage. In M. W. Kent & E. Rolf (Ed.), *Primary prevention of psychopathology:* Vol. 3. *Social competence in children* (pp. 49–74). Hanover, NH: University Press of New England.

Rutter, M. (1987). Psychosocial resilience and protective mechanisms. *American Journal of Orthopsychiatry, 57*(3), 316–331.

Rutter, M. (1990). Psychosocial resilience and protective mechanisms. In S. Weintraub (Ed.), *Risk and protective factors in the development of psychopathology* (pp. 181–214). Cambridge, UK: Cambridge University Press.

Rutter, M. (1995). Psychosocial adversity: Risk, resilience and recovery. *South African Journal of Child and Adolescent Psychiatry, 7*(2), 75–88.

Sroufe, L. A., & Rutter, M. (1984). The domain of developmental psychopathology. *Child Development, 55*(1), 17–29.

Steinberg, L., Elmen, J. D., & Mounts, N. S. (1989). Authoritative parenting, psychosocial maturity, and academic success among adolescents. *Child Development, 60*(6), 1424–1436.

Stroul, B. A. (2002). *Issue brief—-System of care: A framework for system reform in children's mental health.* Washington, DC: Georgetown University Child Development Center, National Technical Assistance Center for Children's Mental Health.

Stroul, B. A., & Friedman, R. M. (1986). *A system of care for severely emotionally disturbed children and youth.* Washington, DC: Georgetown University, CASSP Technical Assistance Center.

Stroul, B. A., & Friedman, R. (1996). The system of care concept and philosophy. In B. A. Stroul (Ed.), *Children's mental health: Creating systems of care in a changing society* (pp. 591–612). Baltimore: Brookes.

Stroul, B. A., Pires, S. A., & Armstrong, M. I. (2001). *Health care reform tracking project: Tracking state health care reforms as they affect children and adolescents with behavioral health disorders and their families—2000 State Survey* (No. 183). Tampa: Research and Training Center for Children's Mental Health, Department of Child and Family Studies, Division of State and Local Support, Louis de la Parte Florida Mental Health Institute, University of South Florida.

Ungar, M., Lee, A. W., Callaghan, T., & Boothroyd, R. A. (in press). An international collaboration to study resilience in adolescents across cultures. *Journal of Social Work Research and Evaluation.*

U.S. Congress, Office of Technology Assessment. (1986). *Children's mental health: Problems and services: A background paper.* Washington, DC: Author.

U.S. Department of Health and Human Services. (2001). *Mental health: Culture, race, and ethnicity—A supplement to Mental Health: A report of the Surgeon General.* Rockville, MD: U.S. Department of Health and Human Services, Public Health Office, Office of the Surgeon General.

U.S. Public Health Service. (2000). *Report of the Surgeon General's Conference on children's mental health: A national action agenda.* Washington, DC: Author.

Walker, J. S., Koroloff, N., & Schutte, K. (2003). *Implementing high-quality collaborative individualized service/support planning: Necessary conditions.* Portland, OR: Portland State University, Research and Training Center on Family Support and Children's Mental Health.

Werner, E. E. (1993). Risk, resilience, and recovery: Perspectives from the Kauai Longitudinal Study. *Development and Psychopathology, 5*(4), 503–515.

Werner, E. E., & Smith, R. S. (1992). *Overcoming the odds: High risk children from birth to adulthood.* Ithaca, NY: Cornell University Press.

Windle, M. (1999). Critical conceptual and measurement issues in the study of resilience. In J. L. Johnson (Ed.), *Resilience and development: Positive life adaptations* (pp. 161–176). New York: Kluwer Academic/Plenum.

Wyman, P. A., Sandler, I. N., Wolchik, S., & Nelson, K. (2000). Resilience as cumulative competence promotion and stress protection: Theory and intervention. In R. P. Weissberg (Ed.), *The promotion of wellness in children and adolescents* (pp. 133–184). Washington, DC: CWLA Press.

25

YOUTH CIVIC ENGAGEMENT

Promise and Peril

SCOT EVANS

ISAAC PRILLELTENSKY

Recent interest in youth civic engagement (YCE) parallels the growing attention being paid to social capital (Putnam, 2000; Putnam & Feldstein, 2003). Like social capital, YCE poses promises as well as perils. The promise of YCE lies in enhanced wellness for participating youth, for their interpersonal connections, and for the community at large. The perils lie in accentuating the virtues of participation at the expense of changing structural inequalities and power differentials that ultimately undermine the goods associated with democratic participation (Nelson & Prilleltensky, 2004). These threats may prove unfounded if YCE addresses inequality, injustice, and power differentials. However, if YCE is primarily about supporting the structures that uphold the status quo, we should proceed with caution. Participation can easily create an impression of progress, when in fact such engagement may reinforce only models of charity as opposed to models of justice. Such is the case with many social capital efforts that have proliferated in response to Putnam's calls to revive community (Putnam, 2000; Putnam & Feldstein, 2003). In a thinly veiled

cautionary note, Muntaner, Lynch, and Davey Smith (2003) have characterized the flock around social capital as "Communitarians of the world unite! ignoring the class, gender, and race structure" (p. 292).

Our condemnation may be premature. After all, it can be argued that before youth can engage in any kind of social justice, they have to learn how to participate. Young people first need to experience what it feels like to move beyond the negative roles of "clients" or "adults-in-waiting" into the empowering roles of participants and valued "community members" (Ungar, Langlois, & Hum, 2004). Perhaps, it can be argued, what we are witnessing today is the first developmental phase of a long process designed to engage youth in civic action. However, before we render a judgment on the promises and perils of civic engagement, we first offer criteria for what might constitute a positive or negative outcome from YCE. Our criteria are based on the achievement of two desirable outcomes: wellness and resilience. We then continue with a three-part argument to demonstrate the advantages and disadvantages of youth becoming involved in their communities. In the first part of this chapter, we show that as youth master the skills of participation, they are able to move beyond the reinforcement of unjust social structures. In the second part, we examine the strengths of a YCE approach. Then in the third part, we turn our attention to shortcomings of the YCE movement to address injustice and power inequalities. As we will show, although engagement is a part of wellness and resilience leading to social justice, YCE is not isomorphic with positive outcomes. History is replete with cases of people becoming engaged in social movements that support discrimination and exclusion of the "other."

WELLNESS AND RESILIENCE

Wellness is a positive state of affairs, brought about by the simultaneous and balanced satisfaction of personal, relational, and collective needs. Cowen (1991, 1994, 1996), a leading theorist of wellness, defined the construct as

> the positive end of a hypothetical adjustment continuum—an ideal we should strive continually to approach. . . . Key pathways to wellness, for all of us, start with the crucial needs to form wholesome attachments and acquire age-appropriate competencies in early childhood. Those steps, vital in their own right, also lay down a base for the good, or not so good, outcomes that follow. Other cornerstones of a wellness approach include engineering settings and environments that facilitate adaptation, fostering autonomy, support and empowerment, and promoting skills needed to cope effectively with stress. (Cowen, 1996, p. 246)

Although Cowen asserts that health and wellness derive from multiple sources, internal and external to the child, including opportunities for empowerment, his definition is psychocentric in its focus on the individual and family. A broader view of health has been proposed in the Canadian federal government report *Mental Health for Canadians: Striking a Balance* (Epp, 1988). According to the Epp report, health involves not only individual well-being but equality and social justice as well. We concur with Wiley and Rappaport (2000), who argue that neither wellness nor resilience can be explained in the absence of a power analysis.

Wellness emerges from the synergistic interaction of multiple forces that affect how needs at three levels are met (Nelson & Prilleltensky, 2004; Prilleltensky & Nelson, 2002; Prilleltensky, Nelson, & Peirson, 2001a, 2001b). At the personal level, individuals have to meet needs for a sense of control, hope, optimism, physical and psychological growth, stimulation, health, meaning, and spirituality. At the next level, relationships, individuals need to satisfy requirements for mutual respect, appreciation for diversity, caring, and compassion. Finally, at the third level, communities seek to promote a fair and equitable distribution of power and resources, democratic means to make decisions, adequate access to health services, decent housing and employment, a clean environment, accessible transportation, and food security (Nelson & Prilleltensky, 2004; Prilleltensky & Nelson, 2002). Although not an exhaustive list, combined, these needs represent some of the basic requirements of wellness. Maximal wellness may be said to occur when both individuals and their communities as a whole benefit from the satisfaction of their needs at all levels. For example, as a private citizen, the resident of a community derives tangible benefits from access to universal health care, high-quality schools, and safe communities. Communities, as collective entities, benefit from institutions that promote participation, employment, and health and from individuals who support these health-enhancing entities (Nelson & Prilleltensky, 2004; Putnam, 2000).

But how do we meet these needs? The fulfillment of needs depends on individual and collective values, resources, programs, and policies. Values are primordial because they determine priorities for the generation and distribution of resources, programs, and policies. Parallel to these three levels of wellness, values may be organized along a continuum that ranges from the personal to the collective (Prilleltensky & Nelson, 2002). At one end, people require freedom and self-determination to exercise control over their lives. In the middle of the range, people require respect, participation, and a sense of community. This is reflected in the values of solidarity and fraternity. At the collective end, communities that promote justice, fairness, and equality are those most likely to meet the health needs of their members.

Individual and collective values serve people best when they achieve equilibrium. Too much emphasis on self-determination diminishes fraternity and solidarity, whereas too much emphasis on the collective thwarts individual uniqueness. A delicate balance is required among values for personal, relational, and collective wellness.

Resources, which translate into programs and policies such as day care, health care, unemployment insurance, and public education, are often determined by the values of the dominant class. When self-determination is heralded as the ultimate value and individualism reigns in resource distribution, policies typically emphasize the need for people to solve their own problems, in large disregard for the social conditions that lead to problems in the first place. In contrast, when the collective is privileged over all other values, personal sacrifice is bound to ensue (Prilleltensky, 1997, 2001).

Unlike wellness, which is a satisfactory state of affairs, resilience is associated with the ability to cope under adverse circumstances. This is the case when needs at one or more levels of wellness are inadequately met. In such situations, the individual, family, or community is called on to cope under less than ideal circumstances. As we note below, various coping and compensating mechanisms have been shown to support processes and outcomes of resilience. Resilience is not a personality characteristic, nor is it a static or permanent state of affairs; rather, it is a dynamic process, associated with—but not identical to—personality features. Furthermore, as this volume makes abundantly clear, it is a quality found at all levels of analysis, from the personal to the relational to the collective.

Resilience and wellness are theoretically linked, but distinct. Under conditions of adversity, resilience must precede the promotion of wellness. Under optimal circumstances, health and wellness are more readily achieved. But wellness, as much as resilience, relies on values, resources, programs, and policies influenced by dynamics of power. Those in power usually impose their values and will onto the people, determining priorities that suit their particular interests. Values do not exist in a political vacuum, nor do organizations that support children and youth. It is our contention, therefore, that neither concept, wellness or resilience, can be fully grasped without accounting for power differentials.

BENEFITS OF YOUTH CIVIC ENGAGEMENT FOR PERSONAL WELLNESS

One of the important developmental and protective factors to consider related to YCE is self-efficacy—the perception that one can achieve desired goals through one's action (Bandura, 1989). To foster development, youth need opportunities to be efficacious and to make a difference. They have a need for "mattering" (Eccles & Gootman, 2002). Opportunities to do things that make a real difference build self-efficacy.

Like Cowen (1996), we believe that wellness and self-efficacy hinge on experiences and feelings that promote competence and skills. Children and youth can develop mastery and a sense of control in family, school, and community settings. As they mature into youth and young adulthood, they may also expand their competencies through participation in social and civic affairs (Pancer & Pratt, 1999). It is important to young people's definition of self as resilient to experience opportunities that not only enhance their personal skills and competencies but also their political competence (Ungar, 2004). Competencies and self-efficacy develop through participation in different settings, especially when children and youth have a voice in the governance of those settings and can influence decision-making processes. As personal and political competence increase, so too does their sense of control over the institutions and structures in which they find themselves. Although many settings provide children and youth with opportunities for participation, opportunities that develop political competence, power, and self-determination are often limited.

Community participation and prosocial activities also appear to offer young people valuable opportunities to work on important developmental tasks. Researchers have documented how opportunities for meaningful involvement contribute to the development of protective factors (Benson, 1997; Catalano, Berglund, Ryan, Lonczak, & Hawkins, 2002; Lerner, 2004; Lerner

& Benson, 2003; Scales & Leffert, 1999). With sufficient opportunities for involvement in meaningful activities, and adequate supports, young people may overcome negative experiences and even thrive. Ungar (2004), in his research with high-risk teens, found that "experiences that enhance capacities, promote self-determination, increase participation, and distribute power and justice" (p. 285) have the potential to promote wellness-enhancing alternate discourses youth associate with experiences of resilience.

Ongoing exposure to positive experiences, settings, and people enhances the acquisition of assets that youth assert they need for healthy development. Adolescents who spend time in communities that offer rich developmental opportunities experience less risk and show evidence of higher rates of positive development in a variety of domains, including school achievement, employment, family life, relationships, and life satisfaction in general (Eccles & Gootman, 2002; Lerner, 2004).

As young people enter adolescence, they have a need to experience control over events and a say in decisions that affect their lives. Evidence suggests that a strong sense of self, confidence in their ability to cope with challenges, and experiences of task completion are all protective factors (Rutter, 1987). Mastery over a difficult situation reinforces efforts to take action, which, in turn, precipitates positive chain reactions, including social acceptance. Acceptance, in turn, leads to new opportunities and expanded roles within the community (Bandura, 1989; Rutter, 1987; Wyman, Sandler, Wolchik, & Nelson, 2000).

Evans (2004) witnessed just such a positive chain reaction as it was unfolding. In a study of youth empowerment, he documents the story of a group of young people who, after learning how much check-cashing outlets in their neighborhood were charging their customers, was eager to spread the information among members of their community. These teenagers from low-income families researched neighborhood economic issues as part of a summer youth civic engagement program. The youth reported feeling empowered (and energized) by the information they gained. When they shared the information with others, they were treated as experts, which

in turn contributed to their self-efficacy. After the first public presentation of the results of the research the youth themselves had conducted, they were asked to present to other groups, businesses, and organizations from their community and beyond. One group participant described the experience as follows:

> At first I got up there and was thinking that they weren't going to be interested, we're a bunch of kids that don't really know what adults have to go through. People were really listening and saying yeah, that's true. They were really listening to us and saying like "Wow that's wild 313% [interest rate on money paid]. I can't believe that these youth really know stuff like that; they know more than I know." They were really asking us questions. Man that's really touching people. (Evans, in press)

These young people have been rewarded for their work. They have been invited to share their knowledge across their community, to lead a class at their school on the subject, and to present their material to a national youth organization in the nation's capital. Opportunities like this, that stretch and challenge youth with demanding tasks, have been shown to protect against current and future adversity (see Masten, Best, & Garmezy, 1990; Prilleltensky et al., 2001b; Rutter, 1987; Werner, 1995).

In addition to skills, control, and self-efficacy, voice and decision-making power are also correlated with positive developmental outcomes. Voice and choice define our sense of agency and contribute to positive psychosocial development. Simply put, young people feel important and part of something bigger than themselves—part of a community.

Young people speak of embracing opportunities to contribute in a variety of settings. These opportunities, it seems, appear to be reinforcing. The more youth experience opportunities to have a voice, the more they find their voice and want to contribute. They also begin to see how much value their voice can have for their community (Catalano et al., 2002). One young person described how it felt to be included in organizational decisions as follows:

> It makes you feel like a person, like you're an equal. Teens can have a good idea or an opinion

and it's important. Adults need to know. It makes you feel important to know that you can have a say. It's important to have a say so cause we are the one's who will be in charge soon. (Evans, in press).

Accounts of youth experiences like this demonstrate that power and control are determinants of voice and choice. At times, power and control are accomplished through collaborative means, whereas at other times, they are achieved through conflict. In either case, they support voice and choice (Prilleltensky et al., 2001a, 2001b).

Intellectual, social, and cognitive skills are also correlated with resilience (Garmezy, 1985; Masten et al., 1990; Werner, 1995). Handling complex interpersonal and social situations requires thinking on different levels. Developing these capacities is a gradual and ongoing process that requires extensive experience and exposure to community conflict (Clark, 1988; Keating, 1990). Unfortunately, we often expect young people to develop these competencies without providing *in vivo* opportunities in a supportive climate. Studies support the notion that opportunities for participation and problem-solving promote responsibility and lead to positive developmental outcomes for young people (Catalano et al., 2002; Rutter, 1987). Experiences of this sort foster empowerment, perceptions of control, and self-efficacy (Lord & Hutchison, 1993; Prilleltensky et al., 2001ba; Rutter, 1987).

Empowering opportunities often grow from voluntary structured activities and service to others. Studies indicate that participation in well-designed activities during nonschool time is associated with development of positive identity, increased initiative, positive relationships with diverse peers and adults, better school achievement, reduced rates of dropping out of school, reduced delinquency, and more positive outcomes in adulthood (Barber, Eccles, & Stone, 2001; Youniss & Yates, 1997; Youniss, Yates, & Su, 1997). Werner and Smith (1992) found that participants in their study of a birth cohort of children born on the Hawaiian Island of Kauai in 1955 who were the most resilient as adults tended to have taken on various kinds of helping responsibilities as adolescents, whether this was paid work or a more informal contribution such as caring for ailing family members.

As in Werner and Smith's (1992) study, community service, volunteering, and service learning have all been associated directly or indirectly with a wide range of positive developmental outcomes (see Scales & Leffert, 1999, for a thorough review of this literature). The learning benefits and potential positive outcomes are magnified when the activities take place in quality settings and when an intentional reflective component is built into the structure of the experience (Eyler & Giles, 1999). Furthermore, there is some evidence to suggest that young people can benefit by looking more critically at the broader society and at the barriers facing their families and communities in regard to control over the services they require (Lewis-Charp, Yu, Soukamneuth, & Lacoe, 2003). Therefore, as we would expect, youth organizing and civic activism offer new ways of working with young people. Young people benefit by learning how to participate in a group action process, build consensus, and set aside personal interests to consider those of the collective (Lewis-Charp et al., 2003). With this approach, youth are assets and agents capable of transforming their toxic environments, not simply individuals who need to develop resilience and resistance (Ginwright & James, 2002).

BENEFITS OF YOUTH CIVIC ENGAGEMENT FOR COLLECTIVE WELLNESS

Adolescents are potential agents of change in their own lives and in their communities. Through meaningful civic and political involvement, young people can develop the skills and capacities that foster resilience and help transform communities at the same time. Youth can play important roles in educating, organizing, and taking action on issues of social justice. Families, schools, neighborhoods, and community- and faith-based organizations can facilitate youth and community development by creating opportunities for teenagers to play meaningful roles, influence decisions, help others, and partner with adults in addressing the root causes of suffering in their communities (Lerner, 2004).

For example, John (2003) describes the role of youth in establishing the Devon Youth Council in England. Among other things, the council was charged with promoting the UN Convention on the Rights of the Child. This successful initiative led to the establishment of similar councils throughout England and other countries. In related work, John (2003) reports on the remarkable efforts of the Children's Parliament in rural Rajasthan, India. With help from a social work institute, the parliament was set up to influence government policies affecting children, from literacy to the hiring and firing of teachers, to access to potable water. The many contributions reported by John make it abundantly clear that children can readily surpass our current expectations of them. Another notable contribution of a youth movement is the work of Free the Children. Started by Craig Kielburger, a Canadian teen in the early 1990s, Free the Children seeks to liberate young laborers from bondage in India. Since its inception, however, its mandate has grown to include the construction of schools in developing nations and other humanitarian projects. Completely run by young people, this organization is another exemplar of what youth can accomplish and contribute to the community at large.

In the United States, a recent study of marginalized youth engaged in civic activism by Lewis-Charp and colleagues (2003) witnessed the impact youth organizing groups can have on their communities. In one case example, youth organizing groups helped to close down a cement plant that was a problem for those living nearby, created a recreational skate park for teens, and initiated the creation of a sexual discrimination policy for their school district. One of these local groups was also able to secure funds for a cleanup of the Bronx River and for the development of the Bronx greenway. As these examples illustrate, young people, if given the opportunity and support, can help change communities.

These examples also demonstrate that youth can play meaningful leadership roles at all levels of their community, from families to schools and civic organizations. If given active roles on committees, governing boards, and other decision-making bodies, young people can learn how to work effectively, take responsibility for important decisions, and find their voice and power. Through participation in social and civic affairs, young people have an opportunity to develop and expand their competencies (Pancer & Pratt, 1999). Youth who are involved in these institutions are not only less likely to violate social norms but also more likely to reinforce community norms through their participation (Youniss et al., 1997).

CHALLENGES TO MEANINGFUL PARTICIPATION

A major barrier to the healthy development of young people is the absence of opportunities to participate meaningfully in the contexts that affect their lives. This is especially the case for disadvantaged and marginalized youth—those who have most to gain from participation. Just as young people are becoming ready and able to contribute to community, they are being denied the opportunities and supports they need for full participation (Ginwright & James, 2002).

Well-meaning attempts often relegate youth to token participants, with no power and no preparation for their role as decision makers. For example, we are aware of a school board charter that was recently changed to create two positions for high school students on the board. These positions, however, did not come with voting privileges. Students can have a say but have no power to influence decisions.

Other organizations are also creating slots on governing councils for young people but often neglect to prepare them to serve effectively in these roles. The culture of these bodies and the structure of the meetings remain largely adult centered. In addition, meetings are held at locations and times inconvenient for youth. Furthermore, the content and format of meetings is not adjusted to meet the needs of youth participants.

Organizations that want increased youth participation in decision making must be willing to alter their processes so that youth can play an authentic role (Lewis-Charp et al., 2003). If our aim is to promote youth engagement in civic matters, for their personal development and for community well-being, we must do more to better facilitate full participation by youth.

NEGATIVE ENGAGEMENT

Although we have been discussing youth participation as a desirable event in young people's lives, many risks are faced by youth who join fanatical groups that meet their needs for belonging through indoctrination into belief systems that promote hatred. History is replete with examples of young people joining fascist groups or religious extremists bent on ethnic cleansing. The bonding created by such organizations decimates any shred of possible bridging across ethnic, religious, or sexually diverse groups.

We raise this caution because we do not wish to romanticize involvement in civic engagement. Like other associations, engagement may establish negative dynamics that can potentially damage self-esteem and exclude young people from full participation. Joining a civic association is only the first step. What happens once a young person has joined depends on many factors, including leadership, sense of community, and social support.

In *Bowling Alone,* Putnam (2000) describes the perils of people bonding together to create a sense of belonging at the expense of providing bridging opportunities for others to join in. Although a sense of cohesion is a desirable quality in communities, it can breed exclusion. When exclusion is combined with intolerance, dangerous outcomes are possible, as in discrimination, oppression, exploitation, and in more extreme instances, extermination. These are not exaggerated claims. The many ethnic wars that have taken place over the last century and that continue today prove that this is no idle threat. The ultimate question is, engagement for what? In the absence of freedom, respect for diversity, equality, and justice, the bonding generated by civic associations may lead to dogmatism, racism, sexism, and xenophobia.

CHALLENGES TO THE IDEALISM OF YCE

As noted in the introduction to this chapter, the promise of YCE is threatened by the peril of idealism. Unless the engagement we promote for youth includes a critical analysis of the power dynamics that exclude them from full participation, the peril may outweigh the promise. We should remember that many of the injustices perpetrated against the poor and the marginalized are carried out by the very institutions we want youth to join: schools, local governments, and social services. How can we ensure that the type of engagement we foster in youth is different from mere reinforcement of the status quo? These doubts should cause us to pause (Nelson & Prilleltensky, 2004). Unless engagement is accompanied by social change, YCE, as much as social capital, can limit its contribution to the promotion of person-centered capacities that are ultimately undermined by the presence of overwhelming environmental and social problems facing youth.

In their extensive review of programs for positive youth development, Catalano et al. (2002) recognize an extensive list of positive personal, relational, and collective outcomes. However, there is no mention of injustice, inequality, or power differentials. Most of the outcomes may be safely designated as "apolitical." Of 25 evaluated programs with strong research designs,

> nineteen effective programs showed positive changes in youth behavior, including significant improvements in interpersonal skills, quality of peer and adult relationships, self-control, problem solving, cognitive competencies, self-efficacy, commitment to schooling, and academic achievement. Twenty-four effective programs showed significant improvements in problem behaviors, including drug and alcohol use, school misbehavior, aggressive behavior, violence, truancy, high risk sexual behavior, and smoking. (Catalano et al., 2002, Executive Summary section, final para.)

As can be seen, most of the positive outcomes reported deal with personal and interpersonal skills, none of which call for critical thinking or sociopolitical development. This is not surprising, given that by definition, positive youth development programs have been characterized by the following features:

1. Promote bonding

2. Foster resilience

3. Promote social competence

4. Promote emotional competence

5. Promote cognitive competence

6. Promote behavioral competence

7. Promote moral competence

8. Foster self-determination

9. Foster spirituality

10. Foster self-efficacy

11. Foster clear and positive identity

12. Foster belief in the future

13. Provide recognition for positive behavior

14. Provide opportunities for prosocial involvement

15. Foster prosocial norms (Catalano et al., 2002)

Although the last two features address social norms, the scope of the programs reviewed by Catalano and his colleagues is both narrow in its focus and decidedly apolitical.

CONCLUSION

There is some evidence that civic activism can be a pathway to well-being and resilience for youth and for communities (Ginwright & James, 2002; John, 2003; Lerner, 2004; Lewis-Charp et al., 2003; Morsillo & Prilleltensky, in press). However, much more attention has been paid to the personal skills that accrue through YCE. Opportunities for participation also hold the potential to contribute to community well-being in three primary ways: (a) analyzing power in social relationships, (b) promoting social change, and (c) acting collectively (Ginwright & James, 2002). Traditional after-school and youth development organizations and programs can better foster both individual youth and community wellness by shifting their activities toward youth organizing and civic activism. This shift will not be easy however. There are powerful internal and external barriers for organizations to do this. Many adults lack the critical awareness of how social and political factors influence positive outcomes and regard political activism as incongruous with organizational purpose.

How do we enable positive individual and community outcomes, and how do we thwart negative ones? How do we prevent co-optation of YCE, and how do we merge the lessons of participation with the insights of injustice? Efforts are under way to merge hitherto fragmented roles: the helping role with the change agent role, the ameliorative role with the transformative role, the clinical role with the community builder role, and the caring role with the justice role (Prilleltensky & Nelson, 2002; Prilleltensky & Prilleltensky, 2003). For as long as we envision the contribution of YCE as merely ameliorative, enhancing personal capacities without linking competencies to social justice, YCE will fare no better than many programs that limit their contributions to person-centered outcomes. Arguably, resilience, like health, is not a strictly individual experience but one that depends on social and political structures to be achieved.

Territorialism, parochialism, and acquired ignorance have prevented the creation of new roles for helpers and youth workers that might address this more politicized understanding of power and participation. It is unacceptable to delegate social change to politicians alone who, in the United States, have been unable to provide universal health care and ratify the UN Convention on the Rights of the Child; in Australia and Canada, have been unable to improve the quality of life for Aboriginal people; and who the world over, ignore the plight of youth and the poor. Adults working with youth, and youth themselves, need to join hands in learning how to address personal, relational, and collective wellness at the same time. Splitting roles into "fixers" and "changers" is inconceivable. Humans and societies require integrative roles for citizens. It is a chimera to believe that once adults and youth "put their house in order" they will be in a position to contribute to the common good. The common good cannot wait. In fact, part of putting their own house in order is to enhance collective well-being. The personal good is inextricably tied to the common good. YCE cannot afford to go the path of personal skills only. Personal and relational wellness are essential but insufficient parts of overall health. Without collective wellness, and without YCE actively contributing to it, personal and relational wellness are bound to suffer. Youth workers and allied professionals have a responsibility to merge strategies for personal and collective well-being.

It is interesting to note the stark contrast between multiple personal outcomes and scant community outcomes in youth programs (Catalano et al., 2002; Lerner, 2004). This discrepancy reflects the very strategies and aims of initiatives targeting youth. Judging from the available evidence, most youth programs designed to improve positive and civic development concentrate on personal, cognitive, and social skills to the detriment of political understanding of the conditions that lead to youth exclusion, discrimination, and poverty. Most programs reviewed by Lerner (2004) and Catalano et al. (2002) look remarkably didactic, person-centered, and wedded to charity models of well-being. Few programs strive to challenge the status quo (Morsillo & Prilleltensky, in press) or address injustice.

In our programs and in our general interactions with youth, it seems clear that the aim should be to support young people in building capacities and to create opportunities for youth to work alongside adults to address harmful conditions. In so doing, we simultaneously foster resilience and promote human and community development by equipping youth with skills and by providing them with opportunities to use those skills in ways to challenge inequality. This is a dynamic, experiential, and self-reinforcing process. Youth gain skills, a sense of belonging, and a deeper understanding of themselves and their world through social action. Youth are more inclined to act as they develop skills, interpersonal competencies, and sociopolitical awareness.

But programs are only one way to foster participation and social conscience. We need to look beyond programs and services as we create ways to build capacities and opportunities for healthy development. Developmental theory might suggest that programs and services should be the fallback position and a sure sign that the natural facilitation of development has broken down (Kegan, 1982). Parents and families surely play a crucial role. However, the community, not the family alone (as Winnicott, 1965, proposed), may be the most important

holding environment for thriving (Kegan, 1982; Lerner, 2004). As a culture, we need to do a better job supporting the developing young person as he or she strives toward self-sufficiency, competence, identity, and political agency. Adults across a community can look for ways to give young people the opportunity to have a voice in public contexts and in the decisions that affect their lives.

We agree with McKnight (1995) who suggests a community vision where the marginalized are not treated as clients but instead are "incorporated into community to experience a network of relationships, work, recreation, friendship, support, and the political power of being a citizen" (p. 169). The aim is to create communities where resources facilitate personal power and control as well as collective well-being. It is incumbent, therefore, on adults to join with youth to create more supportive structures to confront injustice and oppression.

REFERENCES

Bandura, A. (1989). Human agency in social cognitive theory. *American Psychologist, 44*(9), 1175–1184.

Barber, B. L., Eccles, J. S., & Stone, M. R. (2001). Whatever happened to the jock, the brain, and the princess? Young adult pathways linked to adolescent activity involvement and social identity. *Journal of Adolescent Research, 16*(5), 429–455.

Benson, P. L. (1997). *All kids are our kids: What communities must do to raise caring and responsible children and adolescents*. San Francisco: Jossey-Bass.

Catalano, R. F., Berglund, M. L., Ryan, J. A. M., Lonczak, H. S., & Hawkins, J. D. (2002, June 24). Positive youth development in the United States: Research findings on evaluations of positive youth development programs. *Prevention and Treatment, 5,* Article 15. Retrieved March 29, 2004, from www.journals.apa.org/prevention/volume5/pre0050015a.html

Clark, R. M. (1988). *Critical factors in why disadvantaged students succeed or fail in school*. New York: Academy for Educational Development.

Cowen, E. (1991). In pursuit of wellness. *American Psychologist, 46,* 404–408.

Cowen, E. (1994). The enhancement of psychological wellness: Challenges and opportunities. *American Journal of Community Psychology, 22,* 149–179.

Cowen, E. (1996). The ontogenesis of primary prevention: Lengthy strides and stubbed toes. *American Journal of Community Psychology, 22,* 235–249.

Eccles, J. S., & Gootman, J. A. (2002). *Community programs to promote youth development.* Washington, DC: National Academy Press.

Epp, J. (1988). *Mental health for Canadians: Striking a balance.* Ottawa, Ontario, Canada: Minister of Supplies and Services.

Evans, S. D. (in press). Youth sense of community: Voice and power in community contexts. *Journal of Community Psychology.*

Eyler, J., & Giles, D. (1999). *Where's the learning in service-learning?* San Francisco, CA: Jossey-Bass.

Garmezy, N. (1985). The NIMH-Israeli high-risk study: Commendation, comments, and cautions. *Schizophrenia Bulletin, 11*(3), 349–353.

Ginwright, S., & James, T. (2002). From assets to agents of change: Social justice, organizing, and youth development. In B. Kirshner (Ed.), *Youth participation: Improving institutions and communities* (pp. 27–46). San Francisco, CA: Jossey-Bass.

John, M. (2003). *Children's rights and power.* London: Jessica Kingsley.

Keating, A. E. (1990). Adolescent thinking. In S. S. Feldman & G. R. Elliot (Eds.), *At the threshold: The developing adolescent* (pp. 54–89). Cambridge, MA: Harvard University Press.

Kegan, R. (1982). *The evolving self: problem and process in human development.* Cambridge, MA: Harvard University Press.

Lerner, R. (2004). *Liberty: Thriving and civic engagement among America's youth.* London: Sage.

Lerner, R. M., & Benson, P. L. (2003). *Developmental assets and asset-building communities: Implications for research, policy, and practice.* New York: Kluwer Academic/Plenum.

Lewis-Charp, H., Yu, H. C., Soukamneuth, S., & Lacoe, J. (2003). *Extending the reach of youth development through civic activism: Outcomes of the Youth Leadership for Development Initiative.* Oakland, CA: Social Policy Research Associates.

Lord, J., & Hutchison, P. (1993). The process of empowerment: Implications for theory and practice. *Canadian Journal of Community Mental Health, 12*(1), 5–22.

Masten, A. S., Best, K. M., & Garmezy, N. (1990). Resilience and development: Contributions from the study of children who overcome adversity. *Development and Psychopathology, 2*(4), 425–444.

McKnight, J. (1995). *The careless society: Community and its counterfeits.* New York: Basic Books.

Morsillo, J., & Prilleltensky, I. (in press). Social action with youth: Interventions, Evaluation, and psychopolitical validity. *Journal of Community Psychology.*

Muntaner, C., Lynch, J., & Davey Smith, G. (2003). Social capital and the third way in public health. In R. Hofrichter (Ed.), *Health and social justice* (pp. 285–304). San Francisco: Jossey-Bass.

Nelson, G., & Prilleltensky, I. (2004). *Community psychology: In pursuit of liberation and well-being.* New York: Palgrave Macmillan.

Pancer, S. M., & Pratt, M. (1999). Social and family determinants of community and political involvement in Canadian youth. In M. Yates & J. Youniss (Eds.), *Community service and civic engagement in youth: International perspectives.* Cambridge, UK: Cambridge University Press.

Prilleltensky, I. (1997). Values, assumptions, and practices: Assessing the moral implications of psychological discourse and action. *American Psychologist, 52*(5), 517–535.

Prilleltensky, I. (2001). Value-based praxis in community psychology: Moving towards social justice and social action. *American Journal of Community Psychology, 29*(5), 747–777.

Prilleltensky, I., & Nelson, G. (2002). *Doing psychology critically: Making a difference in diverse settings:* Toronto, Ontario, Canada: Macmillan.

Prilleltensky, I., Nelson, G., & Peirson, L. (Eds.). (2001a). *Promoting family wellness and preventing child maltreatment.* Toronto, Ontario, Canada: University of Toronto Press.

Prilleltensky, I., Nelson, G., & Peirson, L. (2001b). The role of power and control in children's lives: An ecological analysis of pathways toward wellness, resilience and problems. *Journal of Community and Applied Social Psychology, 11*(2), 143–158.

Prilleltensky, I., & Prilleltensky, O. (2003). Reconciling the roles of professional helper and critical agent in health psychology. *Journal of Health Psychology, 8,* 243–246.

Putnam, R. (2000). *Bowling alone: The collapse and revival of American community.* New York: Simon & Schuster.

Putnam, R., & Feldstein, L. (2003). *Better together: Restoring the American community.* New York: Simon & Schuster.

Rutter, M. (1987). Psychosocial resilience and protective mechanisms. *American Journal of Orthopsychiatry, 57*(3), 316–331.

Scales, P. C., & Leffert, N. (1999). *Developmental assets: A synthesis of the scientific research on adolescent development.* Minneapolis, MN: Search Institute.

Ungar, M. (2004). *Nurturing hidden resilience in troubled youth.* Toronto, Ontario, Canada: University of Toronto Press.

Ungar, M., Langlois, M., & Hum, M. (2004, May). *Mistaken identities: Canadian youth and their search for a place in their communities.* Keynote presentation to the International Conference on Youth Empowerment: A Cross-Cultural Exchange, Hong Kong.

Werner, E. E. (1995). Resilience in development. *Current Directions in Psychological Science, 4*(3), 81–85.

Werner, E. E., & Smith, R. S. (1992). *Overcoming the odds: High risk children from birth to adulthood.* Ithaca, NY: Cornel University Press.

Wiley, A., & Rappaport, J. (2000). Empowerment, wellness, and the politics of development. In D. Cicchetti, J. Rappaport, I. Sandler, & R. Weissberg (Eds.), *The promotion of wellness in children and adolescents* (pp. 59–100). Washington, DC: Child Welfare League of America.

Winnicott, D. W. (1965). *Maturational processes and the facilitating environment.* New York: International Universities Press.

Wyman, P. A., Sandler, I., Wolchik, S., & Nelson, K. (2000). Resilience as cumulative competence promotion and stress protection: Theory and intervention. In D. Cicchetti, J. Rappaport, I. Sandler, & R. P. Weissberg (Eds.), *The promotion of wellness in children and adolescents* (pp. 133–184). Thousand Oaks, CA: Sage.

Youniss, J., & Yates, M. (1997). *Community service and social responsibility in youth.* Chicago: University of Chicago Press.

Youniss, J., Yates, M., & Su, Y. (1997). Social integration: Community service and marijuana use in high school seniors. *Journal of Adolescent Research, 12*(2), 245–262.

26

Resilience in the Palestinian Occupied Territories

Toine van Teeffelen

Hania Bitar

Saleem Al-Habash

A focus on resilience is an extremely useful way of looking at the mental health of children and adults in the Occupied Palestinian Territories (OPT: includes the West Bank, Gaza, and East-Jerusalem). On the one hand, Palestinians are dealing with a broad range of adversities and psychological stressors that, especially during the latest intifada (Palestinian uprising), have tested them and their health to the limit; on the other hand, they possess individual, social, and national assets that help the majority continue to live on despite the many problems they face. In this chapter, we detail both the adversities Palestinians face and the consequences of those adversities to their mental health. We also examine evidence of the resilience of Palestinian youth in the OPT. In particular, we consider how a development organization, the Palestinian Youth Association for Leadership and Rights Activation (PYALARA), a Palestinian youth nongovernmental organization (NGO) in the West Bank, creates conditions that bolster resilience among Palestinian youth.

This discussion will show that resilience is as dependent on how, structurally, organizations respond to the needs of youth, providing them opportunities for meaningful participation in their communities, as it is the individual qualities each youth has when confronting adversity.

The Challenges Faced

Palestinians in the West Bank, Gaza, and East-Jerusalem presently find themselves in a crisis of dramatic proportions. Strict border closures and a system of Israeli checkpoints and roadblocks, initiated during the first half of the 1990s, have reached an unprecedented level during the second intifada (from September 2000 to the present). Travel has become full of obstacles and hazards—not only traveling from the OPT into Israel but also between Palestinian cities or districts inside the West Bank and Gaza. As a result, there has been a steep decline in employment opportunities, trade movements, and the provision of services. In a recent study, the International Labour Organization (*Unemployment, Poverty Grips,* 2004) noticed an expanded unemployment rate of 35.3%, "a number which would be even higher if women confined to their homes by necessity and not by choice were included." In their report on poverty, Christian Aid (2003) indicated that almost three quarters of Palestinians in the OPT now live on less than $2 a day, the official UN poverty line.

The majority of Palestinians in the OPT—over 3 million—are young, below 24 years of age, and confronted with little hope that their situation will get better in the near future. There has been a tendency among youth and adults to focus on the deficits they routinely experience. They can barely meet others outside their community, so important for adolescents who want to enjoy a normal social life, engage in social experimentation and adventuring, or test their competencies. Youth also know that they will face difficulty in finding appropriate vocational or academic study opportunities after high school. Furthermore, given the stagnation in the search for political solutions to the Palestinian-Israeli conflict, we observe present-day Palestinian youth to be generally pessimistic about the duration of the occupation or whether a viable Palestinian state will ever emerge. The recent Israeli policy of building the separation wall/fence, the political-military measure that attracted a great deal of international attention in 2003 and 2004, is generally perceived as an instrument of annexation, making the establishment of a viable Palestinian state impossible. Many Palestinians, including the youth, talk daily of their struggle to confront a policy of national fragmentation and "silent transfer" (the emigration of Palestinians from the OPT to countries abroad as a way to cope with the economic and social obstacles they face in the OPT). Youth perceive that, gradually, Israel is trying to test the resolve of Palestinians to induce them to give up on their project of nation building.

Although youth experience their individual opportunities to be very limited and the political track to be blocked, they also face a great many, often recurrent, crises in daily life. From September 28, 2000, to July 20, 2004, 3,209 Palestinians were killed as a result of the violence, an average of over 2.3 per day. From that total, an estimated 23.5% were children (age 18 and under) (*Palestine Monitor*, 2004). The number of unarmed people killed so far in the West Bank and Gaza during the second intifada is over 2,000.

Thousands of Palestinian youth have become emotionally handicapped as a result of clashes with the army. In a study conducted among 10- to 19-year-olds in the OPT in 2003, the Gaza Community Mental Health Program discovered that 94.6% had experienced a funeral, 83.2% had witnessed shooting incidents, 62% had seen a relative being hurt or killed, and 36% had been teargassed (quoted in Shahade, 2004). A psychosocial assessment of Palestinian children in August 2002 by Arafat and Boothby (2003) showed 93% "not feeling safe and exposed to attack" (p. 5), and almost half of the children "personally experienced violence owing to the ongoing Palestinian-Israeli conflict or . . . witnessed an incident of such violence befalling on an immediate family member" (p. 5). "One out of five children (21%) . . . had to move out of their homes, temporarily or permanently, overwhelmingly for conflict related reasons" (p. 5). Witnessing relatives or friends being imprisoned, especially when they are older and carry authority, is an additional stressor on young people. During the direct occupation of the Palestinian cities by the Israeli army, from spring 2002 on, tens of thousands of arrests have been made, and Palestinian youth have been imprisoned or seen their fathers or brothers being imprisoned.

Such violent happenings cause fear and anxiety in children. During intifada clashes, a great many children and youth were forced to lay on the ground for several hours in their homes or to hide in kitchens and stairwells to avoid stray bullets. Even then, many witnessed bullets coming into the homes, family members escaping death, or soldiers entering and sometimes occupying their homes for the purpose of using them as lookout posts. Some young people have witnessed the demolition of their houses after they were considered illegally built or in retaliation for a family member being involved in violent action against the Israelis or for the purposes of Israeli construction projects (e.g., the building of settlement roads or the separation wall/fence).

Less dramatically, but also significantly affecting people's mood, are the humiliations people routinely witness or experience at checkpoints. People aimlessly waiting at checkpoints for many hours has become commonplace. Each community has countless stories about soldiers mocking them or asking people to perform irrelevant and humiliating tasks in order to pass. Related to these barriers to free movement, a stressor that usually goes unobserved but that has a pervasive influence on Palestinians is the continuous uncertainty experienced organizing daily life. Whole communities often do not know in the early morning what the day will bring, whether the children and youth can go to school, which route to take to work, or whether there will be work tomorrow. During the months of December 2002 to February 2003, it appeared to be a purposeful policy of the military to keep the inhabitants of Palestinian cities such as Bethlehem uncertain about whether a curfew would be installed that day or lifted, with word coming only the morning on which the curfew was to take effect. This uncertainty led to stressful situations inside families who did not know whether to work or send their children to school. "You cannot plan for tomorrow," has become a common complaint heard in the OPT.

These obstacles should be viewed in a more general context of personal and collective vulnerability. Due to the violence, there is a basic lack of safety in public life, and many parents do not allow their children to leave home in the evening. The lack of safety is also keenly felt at the economic level. The OPT do not have an institutional safety net associated with welfare states, such as unemployment or retirement allowances. What many experience in such a risky situation is an accumulation of adversities in daily life, such as when a child has a handicap, a father is unemployed, and family members cannot reach the places they need to go, including medical and educational facilities, because of hazards and restrictions when traveling. Characteristic of Palestinian life in the OPT is an accumulation of interlocking obstacles that make nearly all aspects of daily life an uphill struggle, a continuing experience of exponential risks resulting from multiple stressors (Small & Memmo, 2004).

Although everybody is at risk, there are those whose exposure to multiple risks is particularly acute, including those in lower socioeconomic strata, the refugee camps, on the peripheries of the West Bank, in the Gaza Strip as a whole (with its large refugee camps), near the Israeli settlements (where clashes with settlers may be frequent), and near the separation wall/fence. Groups at special risk include the disabled, who are often already secluded from public life but are now further affected by financial constraints and travel obstacles. Girls and young women are also affected disproportionately; they cannot easily leave home alone because of unsafe streets and traditional conventions against their travel in the late afternoon and evening. Arguably, political and military circumstances affect them more than they affect boys and young men.

MENTAL HEALTH ISSUES

How does this situation of interlocking adversities affect the mental health and behavior of young people in the OPT? First, it has been documented by mental health organizations and psychologists that the emotional behavior of individual youth display many direct symptoms of trauma and anxiety, such as nightmares and bed-wetting, increased aggressiveness and hyperactivity, and a decrease in attention span and capacity to concentrate (Arafat & Boothby, 2003). World Vision, a leading foreign aid organization working in the OPT, speaks in a recent report about the psychosocial syndromes and trauma that Palestinian children face (Albina, 2002). That report includes results from an unpublished study by Tamar Lavi from Tel Aviv University that showed a 70% prevalence rate of posttraumatic stress disorder (PTSD) among Palestinian children from the West Bank and Gaza Strip, compared with a 20% to 60% prevalence of such syndromes in international studies on children in war zones (Albina, 2002). It has been suggested by Palestinian spokesperson Hanan Ashrawi that the term *PTSD* is not appropriate in the case of the OPT, because Palestinians do not face just *post*traumatic stress disorders but rather *ongoing* trauma disorders (personal communication, March 2004).

PYALARA's own experiences as a youth development NGO in the OPT point to how the reality of risk and vulnerability negatively affects youths' sense of self-efficacy, especially for the estimated 95% of youth who are not actively involved in the present intifada (unlike the previous one during the end of the 1980s and the beginning of the 1990s in which many youth participated, largely because of its nonviolent character). PYALARA staff members hear youth in workshops say frequently that they do not feel in control of their lives, nor do they experience control over the general political developments around them or over the events that take place at the level of their family and community. It is very common to hear youth implicitly or explicitly speak about their lack of power; for instance, they feel subject to political "conspiracies," or they say that "it doesn't really matter what we are doing, the Israelis do what they want anyway" or that the Palestinian National Authority is "not doing anything." Moreover, although they often see democracy at work in other societies, including Israel, they don't see many opportunities to have their own voices heard.

Against this background of powerlessness and frustration, one problematic health response is the withdrawal by many youth from active participation in their families and communities. Many youth are inactive, staying at home, watching television (several music video satellite stations have become available in the Arab world, attracting huge youth audiences). Youth lack both a role and a voice. The result is a kind of generalized frustration turning inward—not an explosion but an *im*plosion. Their withdrawal is sometimes a reaction to the gravity of events. After prolonged periods of curfew in the Palestinian cities, it was not uncommon to observe people being confused, not concentrating and rather forgetful, overcome by an overall loss of orientation as they ventured to reconstruct regular routines.

Another specific response to the political situation is a compensatory identification with suicide bombers, as documented by the Gaza Community Mental Health Program (quoted in Shahade, 2004). This identification results from the absence of powerful and inspiring persons in youths' social environments. Because Arab society and culture place special importance on a strong father figure, children and youth are deeply affected by the diminished authority of fathers who have become unemployed, humiliated at checkpoints by young Israeli soldiers, or put in custody. At the national level, until his recent death, Yasser Arafat, considered by many to be the father of the Palestinian national movement for five decades, was imprisoned in his headquarters in Ramallah, making him a leader without the physical opportunity to lead. The Palestinian police, part of the Palestinian Authority, have become a symbol of powerlessness as well, because they are usually perceived to comply with Israeli army commands. In this void of leadership, the suicide bomber takes on the role of a substitute, seemingly powerful figure, expressing in a single, spectacular and deadly act the frustration and rage of those victimized. A small but significant number of parents (5%–8%) reported that "their children have become fixated on thoughts of death and revenge" (Arafat & Boothby, 2003, p. 6).

Withdrawal, anger, and feelings of revenge go hand in hand with a pervasive despair about both the larger political context and the hassles of daily life. Feelings of hopelessness have deepened. In the streets, it is common to hear expressions such as, "For Palestinians yesterday is always better than today." Informally, many youth are ambiguous about the official Palestinian "story" of a progressive struggle leading to independence. Even though people in general subscribe to the legitimacy of Palestinian national rights and regard Palestinian spokespersons as expressing their collective rights in the conflict with Israel, it is also often said that the struggle goes from one "debacle" to another. Such pronouncements speak to people's sense of being abandoned by their leaders and misguided by social institutions.

Overall, the mental health situation of youth and adults is characterized by a pervasive sense of the obstacles faced rather than a focus on opportunities. It is difficult to challenge this view when it appears grounded in a reality that indeed effectively blocks development, personally and economically. "Nothing is easy here," people say. Many identify with the painting of the Palestinian artist Suleiman Mansour that depicts the Palestinian people's identity as an old man carrying the globe on his back. Daily talk is full of images of being "closed up" or about how one is living in a "coffin," "cage," or "prison." The visibility of the newly constructed and well-guarded separation wall/fence adds to this sense that one's life is buttressed, immobile. "Traveling [from the southern or middle West Bank to the northern part] to a city like Jenin is in people's experience almost like traveling to the moon," a development worker recently commented to one of the authors.

The constant awareness of one's confinement and a sense of waiting without knowing the future generate feelings of boredom among youth, especially outside school hours and on holidays. Diaries written by older students in the OPT (see the compilation by Atallah & van Teeffelen, 2004) display a remarkable swing between, on the one hand, a basic nervousness, sense of vulnerability, and uncertainty because of the hazards of daily life, and on the other, routine boredom of living in an environment that lacks the presence of spatial and temporal "horizons."

SOURCES OF RESILIENCE

Given this gloomy picture, Palestinians continue to possess a range of significant resources, a resilience that presents a balance to the threats to their mental health and a way out of their desperate situation. After all, the academic and developmental interest in concepts such as resilience has precisely sprung from a need to correct the pervasive image of helpless and traumatized victims that puts responsibility for change on psychosocial professionals or policymakers, with few expectations of the affected persons themselves (Newman, 2004). To their own misfortune, Palestinians have long been confronting, in the media and politics, the bipolar stereotypes of victimized refugees and victimizing terrorists (van Teeffelen, 2004). Under the gaze of an international audience, their resilience is overlooked. Resources for resilience among Palestinians do exist, however, and include social opportunities, supportive networks, and spiritual, cultural, or value-based strengths.

Of these, their national and cultural identity is the most ubiquitous resource they possess. Palestinians have as cultural traits stubbornness and the enduring capacity to cope, a capacity

perhaps founded on the traditional mentality of the peasant (the majority of Palestinians before the 1948 war were peasants) who are strongly attached to their lands. Rooted in a centuries-old history of collective resilience (and resistance) forged during confrontations with rulers and landlords and of fighting subjugation by successive military and political rulers, talk of despair is neutralized by a spoken, or unspoken, collective will not to have their spirits broken. Palestinians will say, "While we suffer more, the Israelis suffer too, and this will in the end break their spirit rather than ours."

This spirit, however, is not one-dimensional, limited to one or two expressions of emotion (anger and despair, for instance) but rather can manifest in a range of interpretative and emotional repertoires helpful for coping with the uncertainties of life as it is. Combined with this is a willingness to accept suffering while celebrating at the level of the human spirit, warmth and a certain "lightness" characteristic of Mediterranean culture. Visitors to Palestine may be struck by the ability of Palestinians to laugh and enjoy the quiet rhythm of life interrupted by impatient but friendly bursts of social interaction.

Much of Palestinian cultural resilience is a way of coping with suffering, a survival strategy that allows them to "hang on." In local discourse, this daily strategy for living is sometimes called *sumud* or steadfastness, a concept close to but not exactly the same as resilience. Stretched over a period of three decades, the Palestinian lawyer Raja Shehadeh (1982, 1992, 2003) has written a series of diaries in which he gave personal meaning to *sumud,* or what he initially called "the third way"—neither allowing oneself to be subjugated by the occupation (through withdrawal or inactivation) nor making a choice for armed struggle. The third way was to stay put, not to leave the country or to become resigned to the occupation but to remain attached to living a normal life.

As a concept, *sumud* has not been unproblematic. It initially was employed as a top-down concept by Arab and Palestinian leaders to express politically a desired steadfastness during the national struggle. But staying put became a sometimes impossibly rigid demand, not linked to the demands of daily life, when for instance youth were advised to stay in the country while study or work possibilities elsewhere were much better—possibilities that would in fact allow them later to provide a greater contribution to the national cause. Also, the *sumud* concept—sometimes metaphorically likened in Palestinian arts and popular culture to the ineradicable desert cactus or the long-living olive tree with its roots deep in the soil—was criticized for not being flexible enough to meet the challenges of modern life and identity. This life is after all characterized by mobility, by "routes" rather than "roots" (Woodward, 2002). Perhaps the term *resilience* has more "flexible" connotations than *sumud* can provide. Yet somehow *sumud* captures the essential elements of endurance and refusal to give up without which no account or analysis of Palestinian society can be valid.

A factor relevant to the cultural *sumud* of Palestinians is the importance of religion as a source of faith, spiritual commitment, guidance, and consolation. Observers during the intifada have often equated the increase in Islamic religious observance with an increase in political radicalism and despair, resulting in support for militant paramilitary groups like Hamas and Islamic Jihad. Yet such observations, although satisfying media stereotypes of Islam, give reductive meaning to a complex phenomenon. During uncertain and seemingly hopeless times, many persons and families consider faith as a beacon for spiritual orientation in a world lacking leadership and values. For instance, in the diaries of Palestinian youth (Atallah & Van Teeffelen, 2003), several Christian and Moslem girls at a private school in Bethlehem mentioned as their main inner source of strength the inspiring example of religious personalities, Palestinian and non-Palestinian, who devoted themselves to the improvement of the world. In this sense, religion may well contribute to an inner, spiritual resilience. At the same time, it is also true that religion can contribute to a crippled form of resilience when it incorporates youth into hierarchical relations that block initiative and independence and when religion feeds fanaticism. To what extent religion contributes to mental health is therefore a complex and contradictory subject that certainly, in the Palestinian context, awaits study and research.

Resilience is further supported by educational opportunities. In the study by Arafat and Boothby (2003), education was felt to be the single most important resource for healthy development. Despite the odds of gaining access to education, when it is available at all, 96% of Palestinian children saw education as their main means to improve their situation. Commitment to education is very strong among Palestinian families for historical reasons. After losing much of their land in 1948, Palestinian families inculcated values of education into their children because education was perceived as a way of opening horizons for alternative routes in life. It helped to develop their resilience, a resilience understood not only as psychic strength and the capacity to endure adversities over a prolonged period of time ("steeling" one's self to adversity, as it is appropriately described in the resilience literature; Small & Memmo, 2004) but also in terms of tactical inventiveness, problem-solving capacities, and survival techniques that enable one to meet the requirements of an adventurous journey through life. Understood this way, the resilient person should not only be steadfast but also make detours before coming on course again to find solutions that ensure survival (Cyrulnik, 2002).

When referring to flexible problem-solving skills and tactical resilience, we should not only think about the influence of formal organizations for youth such as the educational system but also of informal daily survival techniques such as supportive sociality, which includes sharing the many tricks needed to cross checkpoints, the informal and impromptu release of thoughts and feelings between family members at the morning break, and the pervasive dark humor that helps anybody, including youth, rise above their situation and look at it in a lighter way. In our experience, mutually supportive discussion about the small moments of daily life is a major factor in explaining Palestinian resilience, combining and valorizing the influence of cultural values and social networks.

Crucial supportive networks for social resilience are the extended family and the community. The family is considered a moral pillar in Palestinian society and takes a central place in Palestinian popular culture. Traditionally, and now most especially in the refugee camps, the Palestinian families' ability to endure, successfully recover from wars, and reorganize the social fabric after dislocation is critical to the survival of its members (Sayigh, 1976). In Palestinian society it is still common—even though to a somewhat lesser extent than in the past, because of globalization and the influence of the media—to take care of each other, emotionally and financially; to create a feeling of togetherness during feasts and celebrations; and to lend each other support during times of crisis such as curfews or illness in the family. Hospitality, generosity, and sociability are values that underpin social life to an extent unknown in the West. A friend of ours said that after she had a car accident, she was so warmly and promptly surrounded by families and friends that for some moments she completely forgot about the accident! Social occasions on the balcony and in the garden or strolls in the street in good weather are common and form natural resting points in Palestinian life, providing relaxation as well as moments to reenergize the spirit and experience a gay, uplifting friendliness. This spirit endured even during the few hours of permitted movement following long curfews in Palestinian cities. As people rushed to buy their amenities, it was still common to see people supporting each other by giving walkers a ride or making purchases for the elderly. In addition, it has to be noted that it is uncommon to see persons begging on Palestinian streets. The effective welfare safety net is not created by formal institutions but by extended families. Based on values and practices of mutuality, there is an informal involvement in neighborhood or community voluntary work, the last being another traditional custom among Palestinians, perhaps, we speculate, rooted in ancient practices of cooperative work among the peasantry.

Guided by these principles, a great many Palestinian NGOs have contributed over the years to enhancing the resilience of youth. Although the history of Palestinian NGOs in relation to the Palestinian National Authority is beyond the scope of this chapter, it should be noted that prior to the signing of the Oslo agreement,[1] the role of NGOs in the OPT was more focused on relief and aid for crisis-affected Palestinian citizens, in addition to acting as referral organizations substituting for the lack of a ruling government. After a new future was envisioned with the semiresolution of the

Palestinian-Israeli conflict (proven a failure after almost 7 years), the role of the nongovernmental organizations started to evolve as an important component in the development of Palestinian society into a proto-state. The collapse of the peace process and the reescalation of violence and conflict during the second intifada have meant that NGOs have had to change their course once again, providing opportunities for dealing with the emergency situation resulting from the violence. With regard to youths' role in these NGOs, they organized and facilitated leisure activities, training and workshops, nonviolent actions, and community work. Specific activities have included the following:

Activation and Awareness Raising

- Summer camps
- Discussion meetings
- Club activities
- Local journeys
- International journeys

Skills Related

- Skill-enhancing courses and workshops for youth (arts, computer, etc.)

Expressive, "Voice" Activities

- Diary writing
- International computer exchanges
- Counseling workshops
- Youth media
- Theater and film
- Participation in international meetings

Community Actions

- Voluntary community work (e.g., rebuilding demolished houses or supporting patients)
- Advocacy campaigns for issues such as people's right and access to education
- Support to victims of violence
- Nonviolent direct or indirect actions in protest against the occupation or the separation wall/fence

A major task of youth development NGOs in Palestine has been to look for ways to bring about healing through activities such as those listed above, counter despair, and challenge negative thinking, all part of efforts to strengthen *sumud*. PYALARA, as one of the organizations founded to address these issues, has developed an innovative model of intervention and social action in which media, counseling techniques, and the establishment of new social relationships among youth have been strategically combined to create a deeper and broader health effect.

THE STORY OF PYALARA

PYALARA was established in 1999, initially with the aim to serve a Palestinian youth audience as a youth media and communications-oriented NGO. It was an initiative by a group of young journalists who were determined to give Palestinian youth a voice through the establishment of a youth paper. This paper became *The Youth Times,* a 24-page monthly bilingual newspaper produced by and for youth. Before the establishment of *The Youth Times,* only a few young people could publish their writing in the daily newspapers in the OPT. During several brainstorming sessions with young people from different Palestinian locations, it became clear to the founders of *The Youth Times* that young people needed to have a louder voice in their community. Hindering this expression was a Palestinian media that lacked cultural identity, professionalism, and a comprehensive vision about its role as a tool for change. Moreover, the print media were politically one-sided, boring, semiofficial, and did not meet the social, political, educational, and entertainment needs of their readers. In this context, *The Youth Times* was a fruit hard to harvest. People were not accustomed to a youth paper by and for youth. At the time, the Palestinian media did not feature any youth papers, pages, or magazines, and those that were available in the shops—youth magazines from the Arab world—were all made by adults and usually directed themselves toward young people in a patronizing manner.

Circumstances have obliged *The Youth Times* to adopt a much broader view of the needs of Palestinian youth. A few months after PYALARA's establishment as a registered NGO in October

2000 with the intent to produce both print and television reports about issues of concern to young people in the OPT, the second intifada erupted. A sense of paralysis, uncertainty, fear, and helplessness prevailed throughout the territories. The energized, active, and enthusiast youth associated with PYALARA suddenly felt powerless and lost their sense of direction. In response, a youth conference organized by PYALARA, Palestinian Youth Vision, and the YWCA took place in Jerusalem in November 2000 with more than 200 young Palestinians in attendance. The conference was titled "The Role of Young People in Times of Conflict." Youth participants mapped out their role for the stressing times ahead. The ideas and recommendations agreed on constituted the action plan on which PYALARA started to strategize its role during the second intifada.

In the presence of Bertrand Bainvel, UNICEF's program officer, PYALARA's members shared their deep feelings of anxiety, frustration, and despair. "I am really scared," said Lana, a 14-year-old from Jerusalem. "When I was going to PYALARA's office, the Israeli soldiers body-searched me, my school bag. . . . They humiliated me to the extent that I wished I had anything with me to defend myself." She started crying and continued: "I was ready to do a real crazy thing at that moment." Nisreen, a 15-year-old, gently interrupted: "What would you gain if you do something stupid? . . . You should control yourself and think of better ways to express your anger."

The level of frustration and helplessness expressed at the meeting was great. The young people participating repeatedly said that they felt terrible about being unable to do anything about the escalation of violence and the worsening political situation. We had witnessed this frustration daily before the meetings. Those who could make it through checkpoints, invasions, and curfews were coming to our offices to talk, some of them expressing their frustration through writings, whereas others could not speak or write at all, so fearful had they become.

Those youth who made it to PYALARA-supported meetings came together to find a way out of their situation by helping others far more affected by the invasions and curfews than they were to express themselves. Saleem Habash, managing editor of PYALARA's *The Youth Times* recounts,

> At the start of the Intifada when Mohammed al-Dura was killed [a small Gaza boy killed while in the arms of his father, an event accidentally filmed and repeatedly shown on all Palestinian and Arab TV stations], we realized that most young people were unable to express themselves and that this would lead to an explosion. I wanted to spread the word that youth could do something.

The initiative of what later became the We Care project evolved from these brainstorming sessions.

Young people and PYALARA subsequently advocated and lobbied with the Jerusalem office of UNICEF to support a new initiative. UNICEF gave the green light for launching a project that aimed to alleviate the pressure that Palestinian adolescents experience. A cadre of Palestinian university students (specializing in sociology, psychology, and social work) were trained to become mentors and psychosocial supports for their peers. The training included psychosocial intervention methods, conflict resolution techniques, communication, and leadership skills.

After training, the mentors of the We Care project headed to the field to meet with school pupils in a selected number of underprivileged areas in the West Bank and Gaza. In pairs, they conducted a series of workshops aimed at alleviating the pressures of the crisis affecting their peers. Through a series of 8 to 10 youth-to-youth sessions, youth mentors helped adolescents by listening to their problems, giving them advice, providing them with information, and making them aware that there were people who cared about them. In the beginning, the young people and mentors had to deal with the psychological barriers between them and create trust and a sense of mutual solidarity. The fact that the mentors were only a few years older than the pupils greatly facilitated interaction.

After the ice was broken between the mentors and school pupils, the mentors encouraged the pupils to relieve their inner feelings about the problems they were suffering. The issues that the young people related to the mentors at first had most to do with the political situation—about how the violence affected them; how

some of them faced nightmares, nervousness, sadness, or anger over the loss of a relative or a friend; concerns about their inability to socialize due to the inability to travel; and general feelings of fear, insecurity, despair, and revenge.

After young people expressed their problems and feelings, they discussed with the mentors ways to cope with these problems. Several youth talked about how they reacted violently to their feelings. Wael, a 13-year-old from the Qalandia refugee camp near Ramallah, felt relieved only when he could throw stones at the jeep of soldiers patrolling the streets adjacent to the camp. When asked why he threw stones at a fully protected jeep, Wael said, "Those Israelis have to know that we will not allow them to steal more Palestinian land." In another of the We Care sessions, a 16-year-old girl from the Nablus area said that she envied the boys who could throw stones at Israeli jeeps and soldiers. "I wish to have the courage to go to the streets and also throw stones at the occupiers." Despite the fact that less than 1% of Palestinian youth resort to stone throwing, face-to-face interviews conducted at the time by PYALARA revealed that those youngsters who expressed their anger and frustration against the occupation by throwing stones, by demonstrating, burning tires, or writing slogans in the streets were in fact less prone to think of suicidal acts or bombings. Interviews also showed that the more silent and less expressive the youth were, the more inclined they were to carrying out suicide bombings.

Interestingly, after a number of sessions with We Care mentors, many of the young people showed indifference to the political problems they were facing, at least as they had first perceived and understood them. Once given a platform on which to express themselves, they chose instead to focus on normal teen problems, such as difficulties with relationships between boys and girls; sexual problems; social problems (such as domestic violence and violence in school, early marriage, and the use of drugs); problems related to their local communities including social, interpolitical, and family problems; or study- and work-related problems, all complicated by the political realities of their lives but nevertheless common to teenagers globally.

Mentors were asked not to give any prescriptions for action. Many of the students described the mentors as "having become our friends." Fifteen-year-old Mohammed from Ar-Ram, an area near Jerusalem well-known for drug abuse, violence, and prostitution and an area particularly badly affected by the intifada, told us, "The mentors were like my friends. I could tell them anything. They did not solve any of my problems, but helped me in solving them." Hana from Ramallah said that working with PYALARA and being involved in its activities had given her the self-confidence and self-esteem to become active in her society. "When I started to attend the We Care sessions with PYALARA, I started to feel that there were people who cared about me and my problems." Before attending, she said her life was "black," but that that blackness began to decrease the more she became involved with PYALARA. Crucial to the success of the We Care sessions was helping youth to find roles and activities in specific fields such as journalism or community work, which made them perceive themselves as proactive participants in the political process, which boosted their self-confidence. We Care thus carried young Palestinians from a state of isolation and frustration into a more nourishing environment that not only catered to their needs for inclusion and power but also channeled their energies in a creative and sustainable manner.

In summary, the We Care project addressed a need to make available a refuge for youth where they could find people who listened to them, gave them appropriate advice, and assisted them to realize their potential. But beyond helping individual kids, the project also had a broader social dimension. It followed the long-valued tradition of volunteer work among Palestinians, encouraged hand-in-hand cooperation between universities and schools, between NGOs and ministries, between older and younger youth, and between those empowered and those less advantaged adolescents.

Despite these many positive outcomes, the approach was criticized nonetheless. The bulk of the critique was focused on a single issue that reflected the widespread acceptance of traditional mental health models of caring, which relied on experts. How could young people talk with their peers effectively about their problems, especially during such a severe situation, without any real professional help? The youths'

enthusiastic endorsement of the project was an effective answer to its critics. The dogmatic assertions by the experts only hardened the determination of PYALARA staff and the youth they served to continue their work.

Even though the level of interaction between the mentors and adolescents was high, some of the youth demanded more sessions as well as a private environment more conducive to talk about personal problems. In 2002, a youth-to-youth hotline was established after an intensive training of the mentors. Many calls were received from young people seriously affected by the intifada. The callers felt that it was easier for them to speak to an "invisible friend" whom they could tell anything without being shy. As a tool to listen to youth, the hotline does not provide prescriptions for how callers can solve their problems. Instead, operators are taught to help youth express their anger in healthy ways. In case of serious problems, callers are referred to more professional helpers.

Through both these initiatives, it has become apparent that the frustrations felt in general by young Palestinians are multiplied in the case of those who also cope with physical disability in a society where few specialized resources are available. Eighteen-year-old Hamdan has never been able to walk without support. His early childhood was a profoundly unhappy time because his family lacked understanding of his particular needs. According to him, "I was always alone, always crying; I didn't feel human." A chance encounter in 2000 led to an invitation from PYALARA for Hamdan to attend a journalism course in Jordan, which Hamdan felt "was the first time people treated me with respect." Since then, he has been an active participant in all activities at PYALARA's office north of Jerusalem, traveling from his home in Bethlehem along a route made tortuous by the Israeli Army roadblocks. In early 2002, Hamdan negotiated with PYALARA to take responsibility for the production of a four-page special feature in *The Youth Times* focusing on disability issues. He explained his motivation for this as follows: "I don't want others to live a hard life like me. I have a message in my life, which I must offer. Even if I die, I must paint a smile on handicapped people's faces." With the confidence and skills acquired through activities with PYALARA, Hamdan has taken a lead role in local initiatives to support disabled young people in his area. He explains that "it has helped to make me part of society."

A Televised Voice

Participants in the We Care groups moved from reflection to action as they became more involved with PYALARA and each other. Groups were provided with an opportunity to share their ideas in *The Youth Times* and to make use of PYALARA's weekly television program *Alli Sotak* [Speak Up] to voice their issues and concerns. It has to be emphasized that there continues to be very little attention paid in the Palestinian media, schools, and among care-givers to the health and lifestyle questions Palestinian youth face. PYALARA's work has brought a new level of awareness to the experi-ence of Palestinian youth. Until this work began, it was uncommon to find the perspectives of teenagers represented during political discus-sions conducted in the media or in public places, even though youth have been the main street actors in the intifada and are the main victims of restrictions on mobility prevalent in the OPT.

Established in 1999, PYALARA was selected by UNICEF to help celebrate, for the first time in Palestine, the International Broadcasting Day for Children. A series of television episodes were produced by young Palestinians that became the base for regular television programming by 2002. Young people now not only present but also produce the televised episodes. *Alli Sotak* has become a weekly 2-hour program broadcast by Palestine TV that tackles both light and serious issues of concern for youth. According to estimates based on polls conducted by the Palestine Bureau of Statistics, over the period of its 5-year existence *Alli Sotak* has been regularly viewed by as many as 300,000 people. The relatively high number of viewers, combined with the 90,000 to 100,000 readers of *The Youth Times* demonstrates how collectively oriented Palestinian society is. Episodes are watched and the newspapers read in a communal setting with multiple family members and visitors present or among peers at school or university.

The television programming by PYALARA is owned by the youth themselves, as is their newspaper. Through both mediums, although most especially the television, PYALARA participants are able to reach almost every household in the West Bank and Gaza. Even more important, they are also able to address the concerns of youth who because of a handi-cap or because of family restrictions and social conventions are unable to leave their homes.

Participants in PYALARA's production work routinely comment on the impact their partici-pation has had on their lives. Ahmed, a 17-year-old from Jerusalem, considers PYALARA's media as a door to his future, allowing him to express his worries and those of his peers. Eighteen-year-old Lana said that her experi-ence producing a television program helped her to deal better with the bitter outcomes of the Palestinian-Israeli conflict, making her experi-ences of value to others: "Through *Alli Sotak,* I can express myself. I can communicate with my peers from all over Palestine. I can share their pains and touch their souls." This same impact is felt by media consumers. In research by Birzeit University's Department of Mass Communi-cation (2004), 77.3% of young people who read *The Youth Times* said that they thought that it both activated and empowered Palestinian youth. Almost 80% believed that it raised their awareness of their rights and responsibilities, and 30% felt that the newspaper changed their views and attitudes toward a variety of issues.

The results reflect PYALARA's commitment to focus on issues relevant to youth, producing programming and journalistic accounts that can make even the most modest individuals heroes and heroines in their underprivileged communi-ties. For example, when a group of young girls from Biddo near Ramallah tackled the issue of early marriage, their whole village watched the special TV episode they produced. Such initia-tives make adolescents role models for their peers who watch the shows or read what they write in *The Youth Times.*

Saleem Habash, Age 22: My Experience

In 1997 I got to know about a new idea of a newspaper for young people—all made by young people. Since I loved writing, and I could not find a place to publish my writings but my notebooks and computer, I was excited to get involved. At that time, during the years after the

Oslo agreement was signed, it was a duty to help develop Palestinian society. A whole new bunch of creative and fruitful ideas were evolving, and the process of development was being remolded into a more vibrant momentum.

At that time I was in high school, a 15-year-old who had lots of energy but nowhere to express myself or a forum to speak through. I started getting involved with the preparatory meetings held in the Jerusalem Times office. Afterward, I became a correspondent for The Youth Times. I remember the first time I had an article published in the newspaper, with my personal photo beside it, I was returning back from school, and people were pointing at me saying that they had seen my picture in the newspaper.

After that, I became very active with The Youth Times and PYALARA. In 2001, I became a PYALARA staff and then managing editor for The Youth Times.

My experience with PYALARA has changed a lot about who I am without changing my principles and beliefs. PYALARA has given me the space and tools to grow, yet without being forced into a certain shape. Having the tools for change, you end up in a cycle of creating change: not only do you create change amongst others, but further, they exert change within your life as well; it is a cycle.

Being involved with PYALARA has given me the strength to become an activist in my society and an advocate for the rights of children and young people. There is not just one experience that makes all the difference, which teaches the person fully and makes him or her to become more resilient. Rather, the experiences between the ups and downs are the ones that really educate the individual and make of him or her a new person. I remember, once, I was excited to cover a musical festival in Ramallah. We contacted the organizers and convinced them to give us a press pass to enter and view all the shows. Apparently, mine was taken away because I was, then, too young to be at the show. I became almost furious about this unjust treatment. It did not stop right there, but I was urged to write about what happened, and I did. I wrote about it in the paper from all my heart and soul. Everyone read it, and I felt that although I missed being treated like the other journalists, I was the gatekeeper for the freedom of the press.

Now, everything is different. My role has developed greatly. I am responsible for urging other young people to write and express themselves. The uniqueness of PYALARA stems from the fact that we do it differently. Everything is developmental; we develop ourselves to help develop other young people.

PYALARA has played a major role in my life. Having worked with PYALARA has urged me to become a journalist and has unleashed various sides of my personality that have not been touched before. Even in the darkest days, I found my shelter in PYALARA.

Lessons Learned

Our experience with PYALARA has shown that promoting resilience requires the abandonment of an overly medical and individualistic approach to health promotion. We must look instead for a holistic way to intervene that places emphasis on the context in which social relationships take place.

Furthermore, disadvantaged youth need opportunities to become fully involved participants in their society. Youth need a voice, a respected role, and a meaningful cause to sustain health, especially during bewildering times such as this intifada. Such involvement helps them to develop psychological protection, self-esteem, and confidence. Through the act of tackling issues collectively, youth develop a sense of competence and political and self-efficacy. What PYALARA demonstrates is that participation by youth should not be a form of tokenism but should involve youth at the very first steps in the development of programming. They should be involved in designing, implementing, and monitoring the projects in which they are engaged. In fact, We Care and the youth media projects have all been youth initiatives in which adults played only a distant role.

PYALARA's success also teaches us that successful trauma projects do more than provide skills training and discussion groups. Any training PYALARA gives is always linked to action and field implementation. Any investment put in training and empowering young persons helps them to become leaders, providers of services, and role models for their peers. In this way, PYALARA guarantees a sustained engagement with, and the participation of, groups of young people even as institutions build their capacity through the efforts of the youth.

Resilience is realized through the structures provided, specifically how support is provided and accessed and resources and opportunities for personal and collective development organized. The development of peer-to-peer relationships as part of projects promoting resilience has been shown to be particularly helpful, especially when older competent youth such as university students support younger youth at school. These mentoring relationships can sometimes provide better support than family members to youth in crisis (Newman, 2004), especially in a traditionally hierarchical society such as that of the Palestinians. We fully endorse Gilligan's (1999) plea to make use of nonprofessional mentors who, with only a modest allowance, can offer quality time, enthusiasm, and commitment to their younger peers. Furthermore, when these mentors do not come from the community where school students live, they may in fact be trusted with more intimate information than is the case of those who are part of the local community. In a sense, these mentors are both indigenous and external members of the youths' communities (Gilligan, 1999), combining the advantages of both. This is even more the case for youth who help to operate the hotline at PYALARA's offices.

In PYALARA's experience, youth media constitute a strategic social resource for the development of resilience, for several reasons. First, a healthy youth media help youth to express themselves and to relay in creative ways the issues they face. Resilience is greatly enhanced when traumatized youth have the opportunity to express themselves through genres with which they are familiar. PYALARA's media projects give room to various forms of expression, including music, popular song, text, and poetry, as well as more standard types of journalistic reporting. Second, making and watching media reports about situations or events that leave traumatic scars (such as long curfews and being a witness to violence in the streets or at school) help youth to better understand their problems. Furthermore, a vibrant youth media helps to put youth issues into a broader context so that it becomes possible for youth to look at

and understand those issues with perspective and depth. Exemplary cases of coping, resilient, or transformative behavior in response to adverse or challenging situations, documented as part of these media expressions, inspire viewers and readers alike. Third, making media products gives participating youth active roles that are interesting, challenging, prestigious, and skill based. These roles include journalist, cameraman, soundman, interviewer, program producer, editor, and writer. By fulfilling such roles, youth demonstrate their interests and abilities and develop their skills and a sense of competence and self-esteem. Skill development is enhanced through exposure to the work of other media professionals as well. In fact, recently, local journalists of the satellite station Al-Jazeera, several of them female, have become role models for PYALARA participants. These journalists have reported, not without danger, about daily events from the West Bank and Gaza, inspiring PYALARA's youth to do the same. Enacting media-related roles is a source of self-worth and prestige for youth and provides opportunities to participate in a modern and adventurous-looking vocation. Their role as journalists also makes it possible for them to approach decision makers and experts for their opinions on issues that affect youth. Fourth, media projects provide publicity to particular youth issues and thus allow local community projects to find a much larger following nationwide. Fifth, developing media products about youth helps Palestinian youth to consider how they want to be seen even because images of them are being broadcast locally and abroad by others. Because Palestinian youth are well aware of the bipolar images of violent activism and helpless suffering that others have of them, critical reflection through the production of their own images has helped to open up space for more nuanced portrayals of youth in Palestine.

The combination of peer-to-peer activities and media projects is characteristic of the overall philosophy of PYALARA. Combined, the effect is particularly felicitous: The first type of activities help youth to work through issues on an interpersonal, face-to-face level, and the second, media-based interventions make it possible to disseminate the perspectives of youth to a much wider public, leading to activism and empowerment among young people. This dual approach builds on traditional sources of cultural resilience in Palestinian society such as *sumud* while also contributing to a climate in which can be negotiated cultural notions of steadfastness and community.

Like many other Palestinian NGOs, PYALARA works hard at making itself a nurturing "family" for the youth who participate, providing a sense of belonging and participation in a supportive group conducive to personal growth.

Of course, the focus of PYALARA is not just the youth themselves. Much energy is expended to network with the larger community at local, district, and national levels. PYALARA's projects provide opportunities for youth to relate directly with decision makers, schools, educational and health services, churches, mosques, professionals, businesses, music groups, and community clubs. Media and social interventions open up avenues for youth who want to relate to various community services and activities while simultaneously making community institutions responsive to the needs of youth. This "community capacity building," whereby communities are identified and mobilized to support common goals, is increasingly seen as facilitating resilience among children (Kretzman & McKnight, 1993).

Thus, PYALARA's emphasis on promoting children's rights does not unfold in an abstract, decontextualized, or rhetorical way. In all its projects, PYALARA focuses on the local concrete community issues faced by youth, linking these local concerns to issues of general rights and international law to build among youth a sense of (in)justice as experienced in their own daily lives. This focus on rights has been especially important because it has helped to anchor PYALARA's work to moral values relevant to daily living. In the Palestinian context, resilience is not the same as adaptation to an unjust system such as an occupation, nor does an emphasis on resilience mean that the need to pursue larger social change is forgotten (see the critical remarks about resilience as an approach in Small & Memmo, 2004). Rather, youth are encouraged to examine their lives from a perspective of equity, justice, and human rights. Such a perspective cannot be guaranteed under conditions of occupation and ongoing Israeli noncompliance with principles of international law.

NOTE

1. Signed on May 4, 1994, outlining the first stage of Palestinian autonomy—in Gaza and Jericho—including Israeli redeployment and the establishment of a Palestinian self-governmental authority. Israel remained in control of the settlements, military locations, and security matters. The stipulated interim period ended on May 4, 1999.

REFERENCES

Albina, M. (2002, October 8). *Palestinian children show signs of trauma.* Report prepared for World Vision, Jerusalem. Retrieved January 13, 2005, from www.reliefweb.int/w/rwb.nsf/s/D4EDE 6E172BBCB1FC1256C4C00517A78

Arafat, C., & Boothby, N. (2003). *A psychosocial assessment of Palestinian children.* Jerusalem: Secretariat of the National Plan of Action for Palestinian Children (NPA) and Save the Children.

Atallah, S., & van Teeffelen, T. (2004). *Diaries from Palestine 2000–2004: The wall cannot stop our stories.* Bethlehem: Terra Sancta School/Sisters of St Joseph.

Birzeit University's Department of Mass Communication. (2004). *The impact of youth media on Palestinian youth: The* Youth Times *as a case study.* Unpublished manuscript.

Christian Aid. (2003). *Losing ground: Israel, poverty and the Palestinians.* London: Author.

Cyrulnik, B. (2002). *Les Vilains Petits Canards* [Ugly ducklings]. Paris: Editions Odile Jacob.

Gilligan, R. (1999). Enhancing the resilience of children and young people in public care by mentoring their talents and interests. *Child and Family Social Work, 4,* 187–196.

Kretzman, J., & McKnight, J. (1993). *Building communities from inside out.* Chicago: ACTA.

Newman, J. (2004, March). *Protection through participation.* Paper presented to the Voices Out of Conflict: Young People Affected by Forced Migration and Political Crisis conference, London.

Palestine Monitor. (2004, July). [Fact sheet]. Retrieved January 13, 2005, from www.palestine monitor.org/new_web/palestinian_killed.htm

Sayigh, R. (1979). *Palestinians: From peasants to revolutionaries.* London: Zed Press.

Shahade, A. (March 29, 2004). A quarter of Palestinian children . . . Seek martyrdom (Translated by T. van Teeffelen). *Al-Wasat supplement, Al-Hayat,* Jerusalem. Retrieved in English translation January 13, 2005, from www.geocities.com/raph_co/press/children

Shehadeh, R. (1982). *The third way: A journal of life in the West Bank.* London: Quartet.

Shehadeh, R. (1992). *The sealed room.* London: Quartet.

Shehadeh, R. (2003). *When the Bulbul stopped singing: A diary of Ramallah under siege.* London: Profile Books.

Small, S., & Memmo, M. (2004). Contemporary models of youth development and problem prevention: Toward an integration of terms, concepts, and models. *Family Relations, 53*(1), 3–11.

Unemployment, poverty grips Palestinian workers [Press release]. (2004). Geneva: International Labour Organization, Department of Communication. Retrieved January 13, 2005, from www.ilo.org/public/english/bureau/inf/pr/2004/ 24.htm

van Teeffelen, T. (2004). (Ex)communicating Palestine: From bestselling terrorist fiction to real-life personal accounts. *Studies in the Novel, 36*(3), 438–458.

Woodward, K. (2002). *Understanding identity.* London: Arnold.

27

Resiliency and Young African Canadian Males

Wanda Bernard

David Este

In the preface to his book "*Nurturing Young Black Males*", Ronald Mincy (1994b) recollects about growing up in his neighborhood, poignantly sharing how he and his brothers eluded behaviors that would have hindered their future as African Americans:

> The Patteson Projects provided many opportunities for us (young Black males) to make other choices (other than becoming young absent fathers) that would ruin our long-term prospects. Cocaine trafficking was rising and many of our friends were committing petty crimes. Violence was already increasing in our neighborhoods. (p. 2)

> My mother forbade us to "hang out" at night. On warm nights I would see a group of boys or young men hanging out under my window, laughing, smoking, drinking or gambling. My brothers and I wanted to join them but if we were not in the house before dark the punishment was swift, sure, and humiliating. (p. 2)

> Today, most of the young men who regularly hung out below my window are dead, physically debilitated, or incarcerated. My brothers and I were

spared this fate by my mother's convictions, courage, and wisdom. (pp. 2–3)

Mincy's experiences substantiate a critical question that serves as a catalyst for academics, practitioners, policymakers, and families interested in youth resiliency; that is, what factors or forces enable some youth to overcome hostile environments and become productive contributors to society, whereas others remain trapped, destined to become members of what Glasgow (1981) describes as the underclass? Of particular concern are minority groups such as young African American males as described by Lee (1994):

> Social and economic indicators for Black male youth in America today provide a profile of a group whose quality of life is in serious jeopardy. It has become increasingly apparent that adolescent Black males are confronted with a series of obstacles in their attempts to attain academic, professional, and personal success. (p. 33)

Mincy (1994b) was writing during a period when grave concerns emerged that African

American males were at high risk: "Young black men are disproportionately represented among labor force non-participants, victims, perpetrators of violence, general assistance recipients, and inmates of prisons and mental health institutions" (p. 196).

Numerous writers have stressed the need to develop, implement, and evaluate programs and services to foster the social and economic empowerment of young black males.

Several studies over the last 15 years (Barbarin, 1993; Brodsky, 1999; McCubbin et al., 1998; Reynolds, 1998) have focused on African American youth and their families who, despite living in a socially and economically marginalized society, have achieved success. Hill (1998) provides an insightful list of questions to investigate resiliency within African American communities and specific populations within the community:

- Why do sizeable numbers of black teenage mothers have successful outcomes as adults?
- Why do black adolescents living in inner cities have lower rates of smoking cigarettes, drinking alcohol, and drug abuse than white adolescents living in the suburbs?
- Why are single black parents likely to have more positive developmental outcomes for their children than single white parents? (p. 50)

Adolescent resiliency persistently garners attention by researchers. In comparison with their American counterparts (see Chapter 3), however, there is little literature that encapsulates the challenges of young African Canadian males. Increasingly, members of this group must cope with severe forms of "everyday racism," defined by Essed (1991) as follows:

A process in which (a) socialized racist notions are integrated into meanings that make practices immediately definable and manageable, (b) practices with racist implications become in themselves familiar and repetitive, and (c) underlying racial and ethnic relations are actualized and reinforced through these routine or familiar practices in everyday situations. (p. 52)

Racism and discrimination toward young African Canadian males is even more prevalent

in Canadian institutions such as the educational, legal, and social service systems where members of this group are likely to be victims of racial profiling.

Institutional or systemic racism is present when the established policies, rules, and regulations reflect and support differential treatment of various groups within the organization or society (James, 2003) and are used to maintain social control and the status quo of the dominant group:

It refers to the way in which the rooted inequalities of society operate to justify the allocation of racial groups to particular categories and class sites. It explains how the ideas of inferiority and superiority based on socially selected physical characteristics, and which are found in society's norms and values, operate to exclude racial minority group members from accessing and participating in major social and cultural institutions. (pp. 137–138)

In its comment on racism in Canada, the African Canadian Legal Clinic said:

As a result of the anti-Black racism that pervades Canada's body politics, racism is entrenched in Canadian institutions, policies, and practices, so much that its institutionalized and systemic forms are either functionally normalized or rendered invisible to dominant White society. This contemporary form of racism nonetheless replicates the historical and de facto substantive conditions and effects of spatial segregation, economic disadvantage, and social division. It involves discrimination in the immigration and refugee system, the criminal justice system, employment, education, health, and other spheres in society. (Smith, Lawson, Chen, Parsons, & Scott, 2002, p. 21)

This chapter is divided into three sections. The first establishes the context within which young African Canadians navigate and the challenges they may face as adults in Canadian society, particularly in the areas of education and employment. In the second section, definitions and conceptions of resiliency and other critical aspects are provided along with a summary of Hill's resiliency model developed for African Americans. The chapter concludes with reflections on resiliency from 30 African

Nova Scotian males and the factors that contributed to their success in a society that continues to marginalize people of African descent. Through their stories, the strength of individuals, families, friends, and community organizations is realized and the significance of resiliency revealed.

THE CANADIAN CONTEXT

Service providers, educators, and researchers have become increasingly aware of the suffering by young African Canadian males triggered by the manifestation of everyday and institutional racism that in turn severely limits educational and employment opportunities. Este and Bernard (2003) maintain:

> Poverty, high unemployment, underemployment, and lack of education and marketable skills are symptomatic of the reality of the social, economic, and political exclusion experienced by African Canadians. The unemployment rate for Canadians of African origin is one and a half times higher than that for the total population. This community has the lowest rate of self-employment of all racial groups. (p. 326)

Issues confronting the African Canadian community are not recent developments but rooted in historical experiences since their arrival in Canada during the 17th and 18th centuries. Although the majority either attempted to integrate into the mainstream society or expressed a desire to do so, the presence of the "color line," described by scholars such as Walker (1980) and Tulloch (1975) as subtle racism, effectively excluded the majority of African Canadians from becoming members of the broader society. When they protested their secondary status, they were battling racist attitudes that could not be destroyed. Rejected by and alienated from the dominant group, African Canadians turned inward and created their own institutions that resulted in the formation and consolidation of a distinct culture (Walker, 1980, 1995).

Canadian governments have invested minimally in African Canadians. In addition to a dramatic downsizing of government and the public sector, economic policies have focused on decreased government intervention and increased power for big business. There appears to be no understanding of the need to redress systemic discrimination with effective policies and procedures. Este and Bernard (2003) describe the economic status of African Nova Scotians as follows:

> There is a lack of support for Black businesses and the low business–participation is tied to high unemployment. Although the youth unemployment rate in Canada is high, the rate for African Canadian youth is even higher, particularly for males, who continue to drop out (or be pushed out) of public school at an alarming rate (Dei, Mazzucca, McIsaac, & Zire, 1997). No business sector exists in the African Nova Scotian community to assist youth who are unemployed and unskilled. (p. 326)

Bernard and Bernard (2002) argue that the history of marginalization and oppression, in addition to the systemic barriers to social and economic resources and power, has had a devastating impact on the emotional and psychological well-being of African Canadian people. Christensen (1998) refers to these phenomena as the cycle of unequal access and argues that extraordinary interventions are required if the cycle of psychological trauma that results from such limitations is to be broken. Christensen further contends that this cycle leads to low self-esteem, a sense of hopelessness, internalization of oppression and racism, anger, anxiety, and the destruction of self and others.

Mensah (2002), in his work *Black Canadians: History, Experiences, Social Conditions,* states the following:

> Given the high unemployment rate for Canadian Blacks, together with their acute underrepresentation in high occupations, it is hardly surprising that they have relatively lower employment incomes for both full- and part-time workers and lower average annual income. Moreover . . . excepting the province of Quebec and the Northwest Territories, Blacks have higher unemployment rates than the average person in all Canadian provinces and territories. (p. 146)

A recent report by Statistics Canada (Milan & Tran, 2004) titled "Blacks in Canada: A Long History" presents recent data that describe the employment and economic status of African Canadians:

> Unemployment rates in 2001 were substantially lower than they were in 1991, but rates for Blacks were higher than those for all prime working age adults. In 1991, Canadian-born and foreign-born Blacks of prime working age both had a 12.5% age standardized unemployment rate. . . . the unemployment rate of Canadian-born Blacks dropped more than that of foreign-born Blacks. In 2001, Canadian-born Blacks had a 7.9% unemployment rate compared with 9.6% for foreign-born Blacks. (p. 7)

Flegel (2004) maintains that limited job opportunities for black youth in Montreal contribute to the high levels of poverty as age and racial discrimination result in disproportionately high levels of unemployment in the workforce (p. 49). Unemployment rates convey only a partial picture of the situation for African Canadians; there is no statistical information on the number who are underemployed. For those who are employed, some critical questions emerge, such as what types of jobs they are obtaining, whether the work is full-time or part-time, and what opportunities exist for occupational advancement. Highly educated newcomers, in particular, are subjects of this phenomenon when the educational credentials acquired in their country of birth or another nation are not recognized in Canada.

Milan and Tran (2004) also speculate about the reasons why African Canadians have lower employment rates and employment income and higher rates of unemployment:

> According to the Ethnic Diversity Survey [2003], Blacks are more likely to feel that they have been discriminated against or treated unfairly because of their ethnicity, culture, race, skin colour, language, accent or religion. Nearly one-third (32%) of Blacks aged 15 and over said they had had these experiences sometimes or often in the past five years compared with 20% of all visible minorities and 5% of those who were not a visible minority. Another 17% of Blacks rarely reported these experiences, compared with 15% for all visible minorities and 5% of those who were not a visible minority. (p. 7)

Several writers (e.g., Bernard & Bernard, 2002; Mensah, 2002) strongly contend that despite their origins, African Canadians are marginalized in terms of income and occupational status. In their description of the realities of African Nova Scotians, Este and Bernard (2003) claim that the impact of exclusion is far-reaching: "African Nova Scotians are at greater risk for major health problems such as diabetes and hypertension; family and social problems, including violence and abuse; identity and self-esteem problems; and mental health challenges" (p. 326). The same authors assert that systemic racism is manifested by the overrepresentation of African Canadians in mandated services such as child welfare and by underrepresentation in voluntary services such as counseling.

African Canadian Youth and the Education System

> Learning to read and write are basic skills that are needed if one is to work and be a fully productive citizen. These skills are not taught to most black males. Educational systems fail to impart or inspire learning in black males of all ages. (bell hooks 2004, pp. 40–41)

One of the obvious societal institutions where antiblack racism is prevalent is the education system. This is not a new phenomenon for people of African descent; historically, African Canadians were either denied access to educational opportunities or the education provided was not equivalent to that of white children. Segregated schools operated in Ontario and Nova Scotia well into the 1950s and 1960s, respectively. However, as indicated in the Black Learners Advisory Committee Report on Education (1994), members of the African Canadian community did not passively accept the status quo:

> Many lessons have been learned as one examines the history of education and the Black community in Nova Scotia. The lessons also demonstrate centuries of incredible fortitude as Black Nova Scotians, especially in their role as parents, struggled

in vain to gain access to an education system that prepared the dominant population for a wide variety of roles in society while excluding Black children. (p. 1)

Scott (2004) quotes a parent who describes how teachers treat African Canadian students:

> Teachers take it out on the Black kids. If they do well, they are wrong. If they do it right, they are wrong. When the kids do good, nobody believes them. My son did a great assignment. The teacher did not believe that he did [it] himself. His self-esteem dropped. (p. 8)

Several writers (Braithwaite & James, 1996; Henry, 1994; Kelly, 1998) have examined the experiences of African Canadian youth in the school system. Henry (1994), in her book dealing with the Caribbean Diaspora in Toronto, maintains that adolescents from this community encounter challenges that may affect their educational experience, including adjusting to family reunifications, family expectations, a heterogeneous society, and the school system. Based on interviews and discussions with Caribbean immigrants, Henry contends that the most pressing issues for Caribbean students are the structural and attitudinal behaviors that prevail: "Systemic racism and the differential treatment of Caribbean students, administrators, and other students is a significant problem that directly contributes to the lack of achievement and high dropout rates in some regions" (p. 134). She states that the following practice is one of several examples of the structural and systemic barriers for Caribbean students:

> Differential treatment begins when students are assessed for placement into the system. This issue has a long history and sufficient time has already elapsed for the building of stereotypes about Caribbean and especially Jamaican students. They are already perceived to be slow learners and are often routinely put back by at least one year. (p. 134)

Regardless of their origin, Henry's words are applicable to African Canadian adolescents in general.

An example of the attitude of white teachers and students is revealed in the following comment by a student involved in Kelly's (1998) study that focused on the experiences of African Canadian students in Edmonton:

> Last year, I had a teacher for social studies, and I said, "Let's do something about Black people," and he got mad at me. And all these [classmates] were saying I hate teachers . . . and that I am racist because I asked for a class on Black stuff. (p. 132)

In a more recent document, *Anti-Black Racism in Canada: A Report on the Canadian Government's Compliance With the International Convention on the Elimination of All Forms of Racial Discrimination* prepared by the African Canadian Legal Clinic (Smith et al., 2002), issues and practices are identified that perpetuate antiblack racism in educational institutions: "Institutional and individual racist practices that push Black students out of schools occurs in subtle and overt ways, done through teacher attitudes that convey low expectations and disrespect for African Canadian students and their culture" (p. 6).

One of the most serious concerns centers on the educational achievements of African Canadian students and the number of students who are forced out of the school system:

> A Toronto Board of Education study . . . [over] two decades showed that Black students were second to Aboriginal people in being most highly represented in basic levels of programs of study and a 1991 school survey of a Toronto area Board of Education revealed that African Canadian youth were not accumulating credits as well as other students. (Smith et al., 2002, p. 7)

The report compiled by the African Canadian Legal Clinic provides statistical information related to the achievement of African Canadian students:

> The . . . survey showed that 36% of Black students were at risk of dropping out or failure to gather sufficient credits to graduate in six years. This compared with 20% for Whites and 18% for Asians, . . . high school students who had enrolled in 1987 also showed that by 1991, 42% of African Canadian students compared to 33% of the overall population had dropped out of school. (Smith et al., 2002, p. 7)

These statistics echo the concerns raised in 1992 in Toronto:

> The African Canadian community has been crying out in anguish over the poor performance of its youth in the Ontario school system. The dropout rate, the truancy rate, the failure rate, the basic streaming rate—all these pointed inexorably to the fact, where Black kids are concerned, something is terribly wrong. (*Towards a New Beginning*, 1992, p. 77)

A participant in Dei's (1993) study provided reasons for the school dropout rate of African Canadian youth:

> I know of students who drop out because when they look at the issue of educational aspiration and how that is linked to employment, and they look within society and see that their own people are not attaining jobs—they are unemployed, and they themselves have got an education—they feel that the educational system is not just, and regardless of whether or not they have an education, they will not gain employment . . . they've reached the point that they do feel "pushed out." (p. 51)

In the view of both parents and students, a combination of practices and behaviors within the school system contributes to the negative experiences of African Canadian students, particularly males. Henry (1994) summarized the factors to "include low self-esteem; the lack of Black teachers as role models; the persistent invisibility of Black studies and Black history within the curriculum" (p. 124). The report by the African Canadian Legal Clinic (Smith et al., 2002) included similar factors and additional practices such as the following:

> Streaming . . . is the process whereby African Canadian youth are pushed into high school vocational programs rather than encouraged and supported to enter the academic stream. This practice is based on the belief that Black students do not possess the intellectual ability to succeed in the more academic program. (p. 2)

According to the Royal Commission on Learning (Begin & Caplan, 1995), black students, who make up 9% of the Toronto population, were significantly overrepresented (18%) in the lower "basic" academic stream. More than 1 in 3 black students (36%) were at risk of leaving high school without a diploma based on their marks and credit accumulation in the core subjects of English and math (quoted from Simmons & Plaza, 1998, p. 103).

The absence of role models and teachers who are sensitive to the educational concerns of the African Canadian community is usually highlighted as another major deficiency of the education system. James and Braithwaite (1996) quote UN Ambassador Stephen Lewis in his letter to Bob Rae, Premier of Ontario in 1992, where he identified this concern, "Where are the visible minority teachers? Why are there so few role models?" Solomon (1996) quotes S. H. King whose work centers on the lack of African American teachers and stresses the importance in having instructors with this background to serve as an inspiration to young males who are often led to believe that they are not able to excel academically:

> African American teachers are of critical importance, not just because children need to see that teachers of colour exist or that people of colour can assume leadership positions. They are needed because of their many other roles, perspectives, and practices. (p. 217)

The exclusion of African heritage programs and curriculum is frequently cited as a factor that contributes to the lack of connection between African Canadian students and the education system. From the perspective of African Canadians, the curriculum is too Eurocentric, it negates black history and culture, and it imparts a very negative message that their worldview is not valued:

> The balance and perspective effectively maintains the status quo and perpetuates a worldview that places Caucasian achievement at the centre and the achievements, beliefs, and cultural practices of other people, including Black people and other people of colour, at the margin. (Henry, 1994 p. 141)

In her personal reflections on being an African Canadian student, Kong (1996) quotes James Walker:

In the Anglo-dominated schools they [Black students] have been taught that the heroes are white, the accomplishments have been attained by whites, the nation was built by whites, all of which leaves Blacks as intruders, or at best, hangers-on in a flow of history that ignores them. (p. 63)

The omission of the contributions by people of African descent to Canadian society negatively affected Kong's racial and national identity. Ironically, African Canadians who are considered a "visible minority" group within the curriculum become the "invisible people." Roberts-Fiati (1996) contends that giving validation to the world of African Canadian children and youth in the classroom can have a positive impact on these individuals and that teachers should make a concerted effort to incorporate material that reflects the lives and experiences of these children in the class.

The hostile environments of schools and classrooms present additional obstacles for African Canadian youth in their quest to obtain a quality education. Dei (1996) stresses that for black students, "The low teacher expectations represent deeply held beliefs about people who are non-white" (p. 46). He also notes that students in his study stated that certain teachers made fun of black students, thereby making them "feel dumb." Some black students also suffer after being told by teachers that they will "never amount to much" or the best program for them would be the vocational education route, thus facilitating and supporting the streaming process.

As part of the Racism, Violence, and Health Project, African Canadian parents who attended the first annual community forum in Calgary explicitly spoke about the racism experienced by school-aged children:

The perception is that a Black person is not bright enough. The teacher will block your child from entering the matriculation stream. It is up to the parents to take the responsible position to help your child succeed.

Our children are placed in vocational schools. We do not know the system so our kids are affected. We keep telling our children that they have to rise above the racism by students and teachers.

I took the children out of the school system and teach them at home. The white kids are not suspended when bullying takes place. Only Black kids are suspended and are always supposed to be guilty. (Este, 2003, p. 11)

The parents further described how their children are affected by their experiences at school:

Our children experience racism at schools and we as parents are left to pick up the pieces. The psychological damage to our children is immense. We need to educate people about the harmful effects of racism. (p. 9)

I am deeply concerned about the welfare of young school-aged children and what they experience at school. There is definitely a lack of role models for these children and this may hurt their motivation. (p. 7)

Summarizing the experiences of African Canadian youth in the education system, James and Braithwaite's (1996) comments capture the essence of the range of issues:

Indeed, racism is a theme of Black students' school experience and the source of their disenchantment with it. It is an integral part of the course content, classroom atmosphere, discipline procedures. . . . It is the most serious barrier to their progress in that it affects their self-esteem and sets up limitations around them in the form of expectations which, as self-fulfilling prophecy, they meet. (p. 19)

Education in Western society is still viewed as the pathway to employment opportunities and economic security. The message that they must work hard to succeed in Canadian society has been repeatedly imparted to many black youth. James and Braithwaite (1996) comment on this phenomenon: "Most [Black youth] believed that education was important to their success in this society and that racism and discrimination were merely 'obstacles' that they would be able to overcome through their high level of education" (p. 21). However, as Flegel (2002) remarks, "An increasing number of youths are wondering whether the pursuit of post-secondary education has any worth given the possibility that they will not be able to find jobs" (p. 41).

Flegel (2002) highlights a major finding from the study titled "The Evolution of the Black Community in Montreal: Change and Challenge," which was that a black university graduate is more likely to be unemployed than a black person who has not graduated from high school (p. 41). For African Canadian students and their parents, the struggle for an education system that addresses the needs of the youth will continue to be a protracted one. As a result, some members of this community have advocated for the development of African-centered or Africentric schools that would foster the social and academic learning of all students.

Racial Profiling

> The past three decades have been marked by expressions from African Canadian communities about police surveillance and attacks on African Canadian community leaders. In particular, the African Canadian community has expressed concern on several occasions about such issues as over-policing as well as police harassment and brutality. (Smith, 2004, p. 3)

There are numerous definitions for racial profiling. Fredrickson and Siljander (2002) define it as follows:

> Racial profiling is a term that is generally understood to mean enforcement action on the part of police officers that is motivated more by racial bias than by any reasonable suspicion or probable cause that may exist under the circumstances. (p. 15)

Gold (2003) also describes this practice:

> Racial profiling is thus profiling (i.e., identification of target criminals) based on one characteristic: race. It is an attempt to identify previously undetected criminals based upon the single factor of race (p. 394)
>
> It describes a practice in which a person's race or ethnicity influences police decisions to stop citizens, search them, or make an arrest. (p. 391)

Wortley and Tanner (2003), who have written extensively on the practice of racial profiling in Toronto, provide this definition of the term:

> Racial profiling . . . is typically defined as a racial disparity in police stop-and-search practices, racial differences in customs searches at airports and border crossings, increased police patrols in racial minority neighbourhoods and undercover activities, or sting operations that selectively target particular ethnic groups. (pp. 369–370)

Other factors that would be taken into consideration include age (young), dress (hooded sweatshirt, baggy pants), time of day (late evening), and geography (in the wrong neighborhood).

In a study conducted by the Committee to Stop Targeted Policing in 2000 in Toronto, it was found that two of three interviewees (of the 167 interviews, many of them were African Canadians from low-income neighborhoods) reported they were assaulted or threatened by police, which ranged from being beaten, slapped, punched, and maced. Threats included threats of death (37%). Other intimidation tactics included police demanding names and identification of people who had done nothing wrong (79%), being harassed (74%), being threatened with arrest (59%), being searched without good cause (54%), being issued false tickets for jaywalking (49%), being arrested on false or improper charges that were eventually thrown out (35%), and being photographed on the street without their consent.

Both James (1998) and the authors of the report published by the African Canadian Legal Clinic (Smith et al., 2002) present highlights from the 1995 study titled *Report of the Commission on Systemic Racism in the Ontario Criminal Justice System* that depicted the daily lived experience of African Canadians. The study noted the following:

- Police stop blacks twice as often as whites, particularly black males.
- The pattern of differential treatment extends from policing on the streets into halls of justice where blacks are detained more often and for longer periods. Whites are less likely (23%) to be detained before trial than blacks (30%), particularly if they are up on a drug charge (10%, against 31% for blacks). (Commission on Systemic Racism, 1995, p. 6)

The material also cites statistics by Wortley that reinforce the manifestation of antiblack racism within the criminal justice system. Wortley reported:

- 42.7% black males report being stopped by police in the past 2 years compared with 22.1% whites and Asians.
- 28.7% black males report being stopped twice in the past 2 years compared with whites and Asians. (Smith et al., 2002, p. 7)

A quote by one of James's (1998) research participants clearly illustrates a typical experience for the African Canadian male:

Once we were stopped by the police because they said that we fit the descriptions of robbery suspects. The description was that the robbers were Black. The cops asked us to open up our bags and they took everything out. (p. 167)

James contends that young black men in Canada are portrayed as potential criminals who should be feared. He also adds that the characterization of these men, combined with the perception that they are listless or hanging out on the streets, contributes to the assumption that they, indeed, are potential criminals.

Kelly (1998) cites two African Canadian male students whose words express the reality most black men in Canada experience or fear in relation to police:

One time I was pretty much pissed off. I had come from a party and got dropped off and then I hear this car screech to a halt. I felt a hand and this cop putting me into this car. They kept saying, "I know you're lying. . . ." Then they heard over the radio that they had caught the person. They didn't apologize; they just took off the cuffs and let me go. (p. 18)

One time I was walking with a Caucasian girl and a cop pulled up . . . beside me and said, "Are you okay, Miss? Is this guy giving any trouble to you?" (pp. 18–19)

The participants in Kelly's study also stated that if they walked into a store, someone watched them to make sure they were not stealing. Hence, a strong stereotype exists that perpetuates the notion that black youth, especially males, are troublemakers or "criminals" (Kelly, 1998).

In a recent report released by the Ontario Human Rights Commission (2003), the following conceptualization of racial profiling was articulated: "It includes any action undertaken for reasons of safety, security, or public protection that relies on stereotypes about race, colour, ethnicity, ancestry, religion, or place of origin, rather than on reasonable suspicion, to single out an individual for greater scrutiny or different treatment" (p. 6). This report describes the effects of racial profiling, including compromising the futures of African Canadians, creating mistrust of institutions, feeling alienated and having a diminished sense of citizenship, a negative impact on communities, changes in behavior of community members, the unseen toll, the physical effects, and the cost to society from the practice of this behavior. Many African Canadians quoted in the report commented on their lack of trust with societal institutions due to racial profiling:

I do not go to the police when I have a problem. I will not do so in the future either. However, if there is a problem that absolutely requires police assistance and I can request help on the phone anonymously, so they can't see that I'm Black, then I will. (p. 27)

Now I feel very afraid for my two boys. I'm afraid for them to go out. I'm scared when they go out with Black friends. They're like a magnet. It's not fair that four Black kids can't walk around. (p. 25)

Others felt excluded and that they did not belong in Canadian society:

[Being stopped because I was driving a car registered to a union] tells me I'm not good enough to work for a union, because I am Black. And this made me feel less than a human being. And this shows that my contribution to Canadian society is not valued. (p. 31)

Examples of the experiences of African Canadian youth and their treatment by the police force in Toronto are provided by James (1998):

I think that if you are Black and wearing a suit, they think that you did something illegal to get the suit. They don't think that Black people have money. (p. 166)

A bald head is a message. If you are white and you have a bald head, you are probably seen as a skinhead. If you are Black and have a bald [head], you will probably be [seen as] a gang member. (p. 166)

The following is typical for African Canadian males:

There was a robbery in the area. The cop pulled me over and all of a sudden a whole swarm of cops came. It was eight cops. I was with three guys. The cops said that we fit the description of the robbers who were five in number but we fit the description of three. They surrounded us and asked us to lie on the ground and they had their guns out. (p. 167)

In the fall of 2002, the *Toronto Star* published a series of articles that examined the treatment of African Canadians by the police and legal system. The data assessed information on 480,000 incidents where an individual was charged with a crime or ticketed for a traffic offense. It also reviewed the total population of criminal charges (approximately 800,000) from 1996 to 2002. Some of the salient findings included the following:

- Although only 8.1% of Toronto's population, African Canadians comprise 34% of the drivers charged with out-of-sight traffic offenses (e.g., driving without a license, driving with a suspended license, and driving without proper insurance).
- After being taken into custody, African Canadians were held for court appearance 15.5% of the time compared with 7.3% for whites.
- For cocaine possession (over 2,000 cases), 41.5% of African Canadians were released at the scene compared with 63% of the whites. (Smith, 2004, p. 73)

Smith (2004) concluded that based on the *Star*'s evidence, racial profiling is an "alarming reality."

Wortley and Tanner (2003) report on their recent study that provides some insight regarding racial profiling and the experiences of African Canadian high school students in Toronto:

Over 50% of the black students in the study (survey sample of approximately 3,400 high school students) reported that they had been stopped and questioned by police on two or more occasions in the two previous years, compared to only 23% of whites, 11% of Asians, and 8% of South Asians. Similarly, over 40% of black students claimed that they had been physically searched by the police in the two previous years compared to only 17% of their white and 11% of their Asian counterparts. (p. 371)

This type of treatment undoubtedly contributes to the mistrust of African Canadians toward societal institutions such as the police. It is important to stress that racial profiling is not limited to the legal and educational systems but extends to other societal domains. Kelly (1998) maintains that shopping malls are sites where African Canadian youths are also profiled:

The students perceive that the mall security guards often seek them out as a group to ask them to "move on" or to remove articles of clothing that signify perceived gang membership and therefore potential violence. (p. 18)

One of Kelly's participants commented:

They just look at you . . . the way you dress, and stuff like that. . . . Black people dress different from White people. . . . and the way we dress they always look at us and say that we are in a gang. . . . It's like we walk around as friends but they take it the wrong way. We just move with the crowd. (p. 20)

Barlow (2001) argues that racial profiling will continue to exist as long as cultural stereotypes about criminal offenders, particularly those responsible for violence and drugs, are linked with race (p. 13). Consequently, there is a need for strong and effective antiracism initiatives to deal with the pain caused by racial profiling and to eradicate this severe form of systemic racism.

RESILIENCY: A CONCEPTUAL REVIEW

Within the literature, a number of definitions are associated with the term *resiliency*. At a basic level, the ability to bounce back, recover, or successfully adapt in the face of obstacles and adversity is a common theme. For example, McGloin and Widom (2001) refer to resiliency as describing "those [individuals] who demonstrate a good outcome in spite of high risk, sustained competence under stress, and recovery from trauma" (p. 1021). Similarly, Garmezy (1991) maintains that the qualities of resilience include the tendency to rebound, recoil, or spring back and the power of recovery. Fraser, Richman, and Galinsky (1999) describe aspects of resilience as follows:

- Overcoming the odds—being successful despite exposure to high risk
- Sustaining competence under pressure—adapting successfully to high risk
- Attitudes (such as optimism bias), beliefs (such as commitment to conventional lines of action), and dispositional characteristics (such as an easygoing temperament) (p. 137)

A detailed definition of resilience is provided by Walsh (2003):

It [resilience] involves dynamic processes fostering positive adaptation within the context of significant adversity. These strengths and resources enable individuals and families to respond successfully to crises and persistent challenges and to recover and grow from these experiences, . . . resilience involves key processes over time that foster the ability to struggle well, surmount obstacles, and go on to live and love life fully. (p. 1)

Michael Rutter (cited in Hill, 1998), a British psychiatrist who is one of the leading resilience writers, stresses that resilience should be viewed as a positive phenomena—healthy responses to stressful circumstances or risk situations at various points of time in an individual's life. He contends that resilience can be enhanced in response to situations involving stress or risk or by facilitating the operation of protective mechanisms or processes.

The literature describing the characteristics of resilient youth is rich. McWhirter, McWhirter, McWhirter, and McWhirter (2003) provide the following attributes:

- An active approach to life's problems, including a proactive problem-solving perspective that enables the child to negotiate emotionally hazardous experiences
- An optimistic tendency to perceive pain, frustration, and other distressing experiences constructively
- The ability to gain positive attention from others both in the family and elsewhere
- An ability to be alert and autonomous with a tendency to seek novel experiences
- Competence in school, social, and cognitive areas (p. 82)

Rak, Patterson, and Lewis (1996) describe the personal characteristics of resilient children as (a) an active evocative approach toward problem solving that enables the children to negotiate an array of emotionally dangerous experiences, (b) an ability from infancy on to gain the positive attention of others, (c) exhibiting an optimistic view of their experiences even when encountering difficult situations, and (d) having the ability to maintain a positive vision of a meaningful life. However, several other factors contribute to the resiliency of youth. Within the literature, there appears to be consensus that the family milieu is a critical influence. Lee (1996) describes the significance of the family in adolescent development:

The family is the chief socializing influence on adolescents. Home atmosphere, parental involvement, and family relationships shape adolescent personality and instill modes of thought and behavior important for impending adult life. Important role modeling from parents and other family members can promote socially responsible behavior and contribute to the acquisition of values and ethics. (p. 34)

A positive family environment, including lack of physical crowding, consistently enforced rules with strict but fair supervision, and well-balanced discipline, contributes to the development of resilient adolescents (Rak et al., 1996). Fraser and his colleagues (1999) claim that families may require resources such as parenting, training, financial, and other forms of support that enhance their ability to contribute to the resiliency of their adolescents. An important goal of intervention at the family level should be the enhancement of coping abilities by the parents, which, ideally, will lead to the reduction of stress in their lives (Smith & Carlson, 1997).

Writers such as Werner (1984) and Rutter (1990) contend that there also are individuals such as teachers, school counselors, coaches, mental health workers, clergy, and good neighbors in the environment who may contribute to resilient adolescents' positive outcomes. Such persons are well situated to work with youth and to convey the message that these adolescents will succeed in life.

HILL'S RESILIENCY FRAMEWORK

Several frameworks provide insight and explanations related to resiliency at the individual, family, and community levels. A summary of Hill's (1998) comprehensive framework is presented here along with a discussion that incorporates the work of other writers that complement his work. Following the work of Rutter (1990), Hill's conceptual framework identifies protective mechanisms or processes that can increase the resiliency of low-income individuals and families of color. These protective mechanisms are described at three levels—individual, family, and community. Although Hill's work is based on the experiences of African Americans, it may also be useful in helping to understand the process of resiliency associated with young African Canadian males.

Individual Level

At the individual level, Hill (1998) explicates internalizing positive values, enhancing social competencies, and fostering academic orientation as three protective mechanisms that foster resiliency.

Internalizing Positive Values

Hill's (1998) examination of the research articulating the strengths of people of color showed that resilient youth are more likely to have positive values:

Respect for family, high regard for the elderly, strong religious orientation, personal responsibility

and concern about the welfare for others . . . Resilient children and youth place a high priority on satisfying the wishes and desires of their parents and other family members. (p. 53)

Social Competencies

Hill (1998) maintains that youth who are resilient exhibit strong social competencies and that self-esteem or self-concept is an important factor in resilient youth. In direct relation to black children, he states, "Most contemporary research in this field [resiliency] reveals that the self-esteem of black children is often equal to and sometimes higher than the self-esteem of white children" (p. 54).

Those youth who are able to resist negative influences from their peers in areas such as poor school performance, substance abuse, and delinquent activities have more positive outcomes than do less resilient youth.

Promoting Academic Orientation

Not surprisingly, Hill (1998) asserts that individuals who display a strong commitment to academic success have more resilient outcomes. He contends that these youth spend more time than less resilient youth completing their homework, attending classes on a regular basis, responding to questions from their teachers, and engaging in a variety of extracurricular activities.

Family Level

Like other writers (Lee, 1994; Mincy, 1994), Hill (1998) asserts that the family plays a critical role in fostering resiliency in African American children and youth through the following five processes.

Instilling Family Values

Parents who inculcate their children with strong family values such as respect for parents and reverence for the elderly while stressing and demonstrating the importance of children, the provision of mutual support and the need for reciprocity in social relations, are those parents most likely to establish a strong foundation on which resilience in children is based (Hill, 1998).

Communications and Social Interactions

According to Hill (1998), primary protective mechanisms for facilitating resilience in African American families are effective communication patterns and positive interactions. Mincy (1994) also contends that these are critical processes.

Control and Discipline. Mincy (1994) emphasizes the importance for African American parents to maintain control and discipline over their children. Hill (1998) describes what is required: "Discipline goes beyond correcting undesirable behavior to providing emotional nurturance for strong character development. Control also involves monitoring the in-home and out-of-home activities of children" (p. 56).

Provision of Academic Support

The provision of supports to enhance the academic achievements of African American children is another element critical to their resiliency. According to Hill (1998), these may encompass frequent contact with their children's teachers, attending meetings with teachers, and serving as a volunteer for school-related activities. Such activities send a clear message that the parents are active participants in ensuring that their children succeed academically.

Garibaldi (1992) asserts that there is an urgent need for African American male students, their teachers, and their parents to work together in a cooperative manner. He suggests the following strategies to encourage academic achievement:

- Students who perform well should not be ostracized, ridiculed, intimidated, physically assaulted, or belittled by their peers.
- There is a need to minimize the social and psychological stresses that academically talented African American students must confront on a daily basis.
- Teachers must challenge the young Black intellectually and . . . provide them with immediate, continuous, and appropriate reinforcement as well as positive feedback for their academic accomplishments.
- Parents must motivate, encourage, and reinforce their sons so that they will use their talents and

ability to perform successfully in the classroom. More specifically, parents need to acknowledge and, if possible, reward their sons' academic accomplishments and stress the value of learning.
- Parents need greater interaction with the teachers in order to find out how their sons are performing and areas where they require assistance.
- Teachers need to learn how to communicate effectively with the parents of young African male students and share with the parents their children's academic strengths as well as weaknesses.
- There is an urgent need to change the negative perceptions teachers possess related to the academic capabilities of young African American males. (pp. 8–9)

Flexible Family Role

Another mechanism for facilitating resiliency in African American families is to have flexible family roles. Hill (1998) argues that the adaptability of roles in these families is demonstrated by the following: equalitarian patterns in work and household activities, shared parenting, surrogate parenting, and the functionality of single-parent families. In relation to the latter, Hill states, "Studies consistently reveal that children of black female-headed families have higher educational aspirations, higher rates of college attendance, and lower levels of high school dropouts, anti-social behavior, and substance abuse than children reared in white female-based families" (p. 56).

He also contends that the value of taking care of each other when assistance is required is another value within African American families. Este and Bernard (2003) maintained that in the context of African Nova Scotian families, there appears to be this type of reverence for the elderly who have survived a hostile environment where educational and employment opportunities were limited.

Community Protective Mechanisms

Hill (1998) identifies two processes that contribute to resiliency. These include using the talents of individuals who are labeled (e.g., as "low income") and enhancing the role of mediating structures such as informal and formal groups. Congruent with the strengths perspective advocated by Salabeey (1997), Hill (1998) recognizes that in economically challenged communities, all residents possess talent, capacity, and strength. The use of these assets is an important contribution to the facilitation of resiliency of inner-city children and youth.

Informal groups such as neighbors, extended families, and peers are viewed as mechanisms to buffer or reduce the impact of stressful circumstances or negative risk factors such as racism, poverty, and limited education. According to Hill (1998) and Mincy (1994), more formal groups such as schools, social services, and youth-serving organizations are instrumental in fostering resiliency. In particular, from historical and contemporary perspectives, African American churches are viewed as a major contributor to enhancing the resiliency of African American families and children: "The historical role of churches as major contributors to the stability and resilience of African American families has been widely documented. Black churches provide regular social and economic support to black individuals at all stages of their life cycle" (Hill, 1998, p. 59).

Writers such as Walker (1979, 1995), Hill (1981), and Pachai (1990) make clear that the black church was a pillar of strength within these communities. The following excerpts from Walker (1979) and Hill (1981), respectively, reinforce this viewpoint:

> The Black church has harboured and succoured a distinct view of life that is rich and satisfying to its members. It is, of course, a Christian definition of the meaning of life, a gospel oriented definition that has survived despite the increasing materialization of mainstream society. If Blacks hold values that are distinct from white society's, those distinctions can be traced to the central importance of the Gospel in the Black community life, as preserved and transmitted by the Black church. (Walker, 1979, pp. 86–87)

> Early in the 19th century, when some religious groups—particularly the Quakers—undertook to combat slavery by the Underground Railway movement, Blacks began to come into Canada,

first in small numbers, later in thousands. Their churches, which had been an important part of their life before they fled from the USA, were quickly transplanted to Canadian soil and carried on their ministry there. The earliest and most important institutions in all Black Upper Canadian communities were the churches. (Hill, 1981, p. 130)

Summary

Conceptually, and from a practice perspective, it is necessary to examine adolescent resiliency as interactions between the individual and his or her environment. Walsh (2003), in capturing this viewpoint, states, "Resilience came to be viewed in terms of an interplay of multiple risk and protective processes over time involving individual, family, and large sociocultural influences" (p. 2). Fraser et al. (1999) echo Walsh's words:

> Although resilience is ipso facto an individual response, it is not an individual trait. It is conditioned on both individual and environmental factors. It must be viewed ecologically. . . . Resilience emerges from heterogeneity of individual and environmental influences that conspire to produce exceptional performance in the face of significant threat. (p. 138)

The reflections of 30 African Nova Scotian males and their experiences living in a society where racism prevails on a daily basis constitute the balance of this chapter. These narratives clearly illustrate the interplay between individual and environmental factors that not only enable these men to survive in a hostile and demeaning environment but that also facilitate their success. The lessons extracted from their experiences may be helpful for young African Canadian males who are challenged on a regular basis in Canadian society.

AFRICAN NOVA SCOTIAN MEN'S REFLECTIONS ON RESILIENCY

The critical questions explored next in this chapter are these: What are the strategies that enable black boys to survive in societies where they are expected to fail? What conditions enable them to move beyond survival to achieve success? We report here on exploratory research conducted by Bernard (1996) with African Canadian men. A reflexive analysis of that data is used to capture reflections on resiliency of African Canadian boys as self-defined after their journey into manhood. We begin with a description of the research study methodology.

The Research Study

The research, *Survival and Success: As Defined by Black Men in Sheffield, England, and Halifax, Canada* (Bernard, 1996), was a participatory action research project. It involved two groups of black men, called research working groups (RWGs), one in each site, in an exploratory study of the strategies they used to survive and succeed in societies where they were expected to fail. Beginning from the standpoint of black men in Halifax and how they defined success, the research used a number of data-gathering methods. There were 20 individual interviews and focus groups with 10 men in each site. In addition, a conference in each site allowed for a wider community of black men and their allies to be involved in the research. This chapter reports only on the experiences of the African Canadian men who participated. Also included are data gathered in follow-up focus groups with the Halifax participants.

A thematic analysis of the data was initially done by the RWGs and further developed by focus group and conference participants, thus allowing for inquiry audits and member checks (Lather, 1991). These authors conducted a secondary reflective analysis of the data. We report here on the survival strategies that emerged in the research. Black men in the two sites shared the experiences of living with everyday racism (Essed, 1991) and also shared the following survival strategies that not only helped them to survive but also to succeed: (a) positive racial identity, (b) having positive role models and mentors, (c) having a strong racial and political consciousness, (d) having positive personal values and supportive relationships with family and friends, (e) the ability to set and to work toward goals, (f) attaining education and marketable skills, (g) finding and maintaining employment or creating self-employment, and (h) spirituality.

A secondary analysis of the data was done to further understand those strategies that were specifically used by the men as they negotiated the journey through adolescence to manhood. The following strategies were identified: (a) positive racial identity; (b) having positive role models and mentors; (c) having strong supportive relationships with parents, grandparents, and extended family and community; and (d) getting an education. The men's stories are used to explore the factors that helped them make positive choices as they confronted the many challenges and barriers that black boys have to overcome to become positive, productive men in Canadian society. We begin with a discussion of what survival and success means to these men, then move on to discuss those strategies that helped them to get there.

Defining Survival and Success

As one of our participants stated, "It is a wonder that we have survived at all, considering all of the obstacles that we have had to overcome. So many doors have been closed to us." Yet, despite the obstacles, black men have survived and do succeed, as they self-define it. Although we recognize that there are both positive and negative habits of survival, our focus is on positive habits or strategies. Scott (1991) asserts that positive habits include taking action to transcend, empower, love, and confront injustice. The men who have managed to survive and are perceived as successful have used a variety of strategies, which we call strategies of survival. These are strategies of mind, will, feeling, and action and are evidenced in the workplace, in schools, and in the black and women's liberation movements (Scott, 1991), as well as in the home and in social interactions.

This exploratory investigation into strategies that black men use to survive began with a definition of a "successful black man" as one who had achieved or was working toward a set goal (or set of goals) using positive, constructive means that he maintained over time. Furthermore, a successful black man was considered to be one who had overcome obstacles, had managed to survive, and used his success to help bring others along. Black men were invited to tell their stories of survival and success, to explore the strategies that helped them not only to cope but also to overcome individual and systemic barriers and to achieve a modicum of success. These men tell a story of survival at the most basic level. One man says,

> Survival means being able to wake up everyday, going out and trying to make it, without letting the stress of racism and racial pressure get you down. . . . part of surviving is dealing with racism every day of your life with your dignity intact.

Another says,

> Survival . . . is not to be suppressed by all the negative connotations that society imposes on black men. . . . surviving means reclaiming the ability to be self-sufficient and claiming a structure that will enable black people to have a voice.

Black men also comment on the need not only to survive but to succeed, and they define what they mean by success as indicated above. One participant said, "Success is not about how much money you have, the type of car you drive, or the type of work you do! It is about how you live your life."

Similar themes emerged at the conference, "Black Men Surviving the 90's," where David Divine gave a keynote address titled "Successful Black Men." According to Divine (1994),

> Keys to success are not related to money or influence or sexual conquest, but to common, taken-for-granted values such as respect, time for self and others, integrity, being open to others, and loving oneself and others. A measure of one's success is the degree of positive influence that you bring to someone else's life, as well as your own. (p. 23)

Being successful is partly determined by how to give back to the community. One participant clearly articulates this point: "When a black man makes it, he must not, should not, and cannot forget where he came from." Black men are seen as successful if they are using their success to help uplift the race. As one man said, "Even the smallest action can work wonders for someone's soul, in building someone's ability to dream and to carry out those dreams" and "successful black men must give back and be visible in the community."

These may appear to be lofty ideals for black boys to aspire to. One might ask how any young person could reach such goals. In the next section, we share the strategies that black adolescent males discussed during this study, beginning with the development of a positive racial identity.

Positive Racial Identity

The majority of the participants in the study indicated that the development of a positive racial identity created by connecting with African principles and beliefs and with others in the Diaspora was a survival strategy used by black men. This includes the development of love and respect for oneself and others, a positive value system, and a connection with a black, African community and culture. The necessity of having a positive sense of self as a black person was also stressed in the focus groups, where participants argued that the maintenance of this, once success in white society is achieved, is vital to collective identity and survival. For many, developing a positive sense of self and a positive racial identity is the very essence of survival as Africans in the Diaspora. Having a strong sense of who they are is a necessary first step to being able to cope with everyday racism and racial profiling. One man tells it this way: "Our major source of strength is embracing our African roots, history, and culture. . . . it is important to know our history. . . . if we don't know our history it is difficult to plan our future."

Another says,

> My parents taught me to love and respect myself and others. However, they also taught me that I could never forget that I am black, and therefore that I must be strong in order to survive. That is one of the most essential things about being black.

Finally, one of the participants said:

> I was taught at an early age to be proud of being a black Nova Scotian. Growing up in the 60s and hearing James Brown sing, "Say it loud—I'm black and I'm proud," brought new meaning to

black pride here in Nova Scotia. It gave me a very solid foundation from which to fight and resist the racism that was all around me. Today I pass on the same message to my children.

Clearly, having a positive racial identity is a strategy that helps black boys negotiate their space and location in society as they journey to manhood. This is consistent with Hill's (1998) thesis that enhancing social competencies is a core skill for young, poor people of color to master to achieve success and resiliency. The impact of negative images and stereotyping can be overwhelming, and some internalize these messages, despising themselves and rejecting their ethnicity. However, the black men participating in this research suggest that the development of a positive racial identity—that is, a positive perception and acceptance of oneself as a black person, an African-descended person—is a vital survival strategy.

Positive Role Models and Mentors

Equally important in the study was the presence of role models and mentors. Linked to the development of positive identity is one's access to a wide range of roles with which to identify. Moving through the life cycle, young people are exposed to a range of people and institutions as they define their individual identities. Black young people have limited access to positive black images and role models, whether in the education system, in society, or through the media and mass culture. Yet the accessibility and availability of positive role models, mentors, or both was identified as a successful survival strategy in this study. Black men want role models who they can emulate; however, they need to be within one's reach. As one Halifax participant said, "A role model is someone whose *principles* I can copy." The emphasis here is on principles, as stressed by the respondent, suggesting that the values and morals that one displays are most important. The young men in our study recognized the importance of having positive role models and mentors in their lives and are committed to the principle of giving back to the next generation. The significance of role models and mentors is illustrated in some of the men's stories.

I looked at our forefathers from slavery. They had to bear the brunt of the struggle. . . . I looked at the black men [in my community] who were still out there doing things, making changes while maintaining a positive outlook, and I saw them progress. . . . they help brothers like me keep going, keep moving forward.

Another says, "The opportunity to see different black men that are making a living and providing for their families . . . made me want to strive to be all that I could be."

And another asserts, "I think of the endless contributions that have been made and are still being made . . . it gives me strength and pride . . . and helps me to keep going.

Finally, the story of this man summarizes the important role that black men play in helping black youth resist and survive.

Black men have taught me how to cope with and deal with life . . . they also showed me that I could succeed, as I modeled myself after people who were positive success stories. I was able to disregard the negative men in my life.

Having access to role models and mentors was clearly a positive strategy for resilience for these young African Canadian men. This is consistent with Hill's (1998) assertion that having formal and informal community supports serves as a protective mechanism. Similarly, Werner (1984) and Rutter (1990) emphasize the significance of coaches, teachers, and other community members as sources of support for at-risk youth.

Family and Community

Equally important is the role of family, extended family, and community, which was identified by all the participants. It is an extra bonus when one's parent(s) can also be role models and mentors. All participants in this study stressed the importance and significance of family and community support. The role of mothers in particular was seen as central in recounting contributions made to the individual and collective survival of African Canadian men. However, the role of fathers and the issue of father responsibility were also noted as a significant factor that helped black men to succeed. In addition, the role of grandparents and extended family and community supports were identified as positive factors that helped adolescent boys navigate their way through to adulthood. Some of the men talked about the significance of their parents and grandparents:

> My parents and grandparents were all strong, stable people. I could count on them to be there . . . and to challenge me on the negative things. . . . I did not want to do anything bad to disgrace them, or lose their support and respect.

> My mother provided me with all the positive advice and experiences possible. . . . She was a good role model as a parent . . .

> I never got into trouble with the law, thanks to my mother . . . I was always more afraid of disappointing her than I was scared of the police. I had such respect for her that I would never do anything to bring her shame or distress. . . .

> My father was there even when I did not know it. His presence, though limited, made me realize how much we counted on him in the family for all sorts of things. Now that I am a father myself, I realize some of the things that he did, he did because he wanted to protect us from harm. He died before I could thank him for his contributions to my survival, but I tell my children about him every day in my words and my actions.

Some of the strengths and ability to make positive choices can be traced back to early teachings in the family.

> My grandmother influenced me greatly by teaching me the value of life is something we find in ourselves . . . and that helped me to always make good choices.

> My grandparents . . . paved . . . a pattern of lifestyle that I could follow. My grandmother taught me about human emotions; everyone can cry. My grandfather taught me to be strong. These values have taught me to say no to certain things instead of yes and kept me out of trouble.

These views are consistent with what other researchers such as Hill (1998), Lee (1994), and Rak et al. (1996) have stressed, that flexible family roles and family and community supports help facilitate resiliency.

The notion of communities sharing responsibility for child rearing and helping young black people negotiate the barriers on their journeys also emerged in this research. For example, one participant who grew up in a small semi-urban community said, "Black communities always offer a sense of comfort, support, and love. . . . the community has been an integral part of the black man's life, a place where love is not denied."

Another offered a similar perspective:

> People from the community offered a lot of support, encouragement, and guidance . . . some who were able to see the potential in me and others . . . when every parent in the community had high expectations of their children. . . . There were so many community-based groups and organizations that gave us a place to develop our skills and to grow and mature.

For many black youth, their homes and communities are not only sites of love, resistance, and support, they are also the first teachers. In Halifax in particular, the role of the Church and church-led organizations has been instrumental in the survival of the community in general and for African Nova Scotian young men in particular. Of the participants, 85% stated that the Church has been instrumental in the survival of black men and black people in general in Nova Scotia. All participants in Halifax believe that the Church also has a role in the future survival of black men; furthermore, this role has to be more proactive and radical in the spiritual and social development of black men and the black community as a whole.

Education as Key to Survival

In addition to the role of the Church and community, participants noted the importance of both formal and informal education. This is similar to Hill's (1998) finding that formal and informal groups in low-income communities are vital to their members' survival and success. A responsive education system is seen as one of the most important influences on black youth because education is key to survival. However, the findings in this study indicate that black men's experiences in education have been largely negative. Participants repeatedly defined their experience as one of miseducation because of Eurocentric curriculum and racist educational practices. Although the majority of this sample have attained higher levels of education, most have done so at great personal sacrifice. Many returned to education after leaving school early, and those who stayed did so in an atmosphere that discouraged and demotivated them. As black men in this study reflected on their educational journey, they shared stories about the people who helped influence them and helped to keep them in school. For many, the involvement of their parents was key. One man explains:

> My parents encouraged us and showed us the advantages of a good education in preparing for . . . one's future, . . . they influenced me to achieve an education . . . to develop leadership qualities and responsibilities . . . and to be the best that I could be.

Another man further elaborates on the theme of informal education:

> My survival, and that of my brothers and sisters depended on a good solid foundation, which was provided by our family. Our parents instilled in all of us positive values, strong moral values, and a sense of responsibility . . . thus providing us with a better opportunity to survive. . . . we all did well in school because we knew we had to, as tough as it was to constantly fight the negativity.

Hill (1998) also maintains that resiliency is more readily attained when parents help facilitate an academic orientation.

In this study, education was seen as a tool for empowerment, a survival strategy that could not be taken from black men, even though the literature is replete with examples of the many challenges that black youth experience in education. So how is it that some black youth survive? In addition to the supports provided by parents, siblings, and positive role models and mentors, many of the black men in this study shared stories of the positive influences that some of their teachers had been. For some, it was simply having someone who believed in them, whereas for others, it was being motivated

by teachers who appeared to care. This is consistent with Werner's (1984) and Rutter's (1990) thesis that teachers have the potential to be contributing factors in youth's resiliency. The following stories are illustrative:

> Early in my life I did have one teacher that was influential. She showed that she was concerned and it didn't matter what my color was. She was the first white woman that helped me to understand the ability that I had to do well if I applied myself and filtered out the negativity.
>
> I recall a white male teacher who was positive and encouraging. He helped me to believe in myself and to understand that I could achieve goals if I set them and stayed on target regardless of what others said or did.

For some others, the drive to succeed is motivated by the negativity one experiences from those in authority. For example, one participant talked about the difficult transition from segregated to integrated schooling.

> I was at the top of the class in my local community school where all my teachers and classmates looked like me. But when I went to the integrated high school, I quickly learned to hate school. I remember a teacher telling me that I was going nowhere, and that is when I decided to hit the books and prove him wrong.

DISCUSSION

African Canadian men are victims of cultural pain and disenfranchisement brought on by institutional, systemic, individual, and cultural racism and sexism. This is a shared phenomenon, based on their everyday experiences and realities. Those who survive and succeed do so against incredible odds. They are not alone. The stories in this chapter reveal some of the influences of family and community that help black boys successfully negotiate their passage to manhood.

What are the implications for families, social workers, and health care professionals who are working with at-risk African Canadian youth today? Communities could offer "rites of passage" programs that help black youth navigate their way through life transitions. Such programs would help empower youth and their caregivers as they create collective strategies of resistance and resilience. Parents and grandparents could apply the Africentric principles in their daily lives. Living the principles of Africentricity could serve as a buffer from the harsh realities of a racist and race-conscious society.

The lessons learned from these men's reflections could serve young black men today as they negotiate their space in society. The value of positive racial identity, strong role models and mentors, formal and informal education, and family and community supports could be developed as road maps for young African Canadian youth as they face today's challenges.

We have identified problems in the education system, the legal system, and the society at large, all of which create barriers for African Canadian youth. The struggle to challenge these structural barriers needs to continue. More allies are needed in the struggle. Social workers and health care professionals could advocate for structural change within their agencies and within the wider community. African people need to reclaim their space in society. Africentricity allows us to step back to our origins, in order to move forward.

REFERENCES

Barbarin, O. A. (1993). Coping and resilience: Exploring the inner lives of African American children. *Journal of Black Psychology, 19,* 478–492.

Barlow, H. (2001). Driving while black: Observations on the practice and future of racial profiling in the U.S. *Journal of Intergroup Relations, 38*(3), 3–15.

Begin, M., & Caplan, G. (1995). *For the love of learning: Report of the Royal Commission on Learning.* Toronto, Ontario, Canada: Royal Commission on Learning.

Bernard, C., & Bernard, W. T. (2002). Learning from the past/visions for the future: The black community and child welfare in Nova Scotia. In B. Wharf (Ed.), *Community work approaches to child welfare* (pp. 116–130). Toronto, Ontario, Canada: Broadview Press.

Bernard, W. T. (1996). *Survival and success: As defined by black men in Sheffield, England and Halifax, Canada.* Unpublished doctoral dissertation, University of Sheffield, Sheffield, UK.

Black Learners Advisory Committee. (1994). *BLAC report on education—redressing inequity: Empowering black learners: Vol. 1. Summary.* Halifax, Nova Scotia, Canada: Author.

Braithwaite, K., & James, C. (Eds.). (1996). *Educating African Canadians.* Toronto, Ontario, Canada: James Lorimer.

Brodsky, A. (1999). Making it: The components and process of resilience among urban, African-American single mothers. *American Journal of Orthopsychiatry, 69*(2), 148–160.

Christensen, C. P. (1998). Social welfare and social work in Canada: Aspects of the black experience. In V. D'Oyley & C. James (Eds.), *Re/Visioning: Canadian perspectives on the education of Africans in the late 20th century* (pp. 36–55). North York, Ontario, Canada: Captus Press.

Commission on Systemic Racism in the Ontario Criminal Justice System. (1995). *Report of the Commission on Systemic Racism in the Ontario Criminal Justice System.* Toronto, Ontario, Canada: Queen's Printer for Ontario.

Dei, G. S. (1993). Narrative discourses of black/ African parents and the Canadian public school system. *Canadian Ethnic Studies, 3,* 49–64.

Dei, G. S. (1996). Listening to voices: Developing a pedagogy of change from the narratives of African Canadian students and parents. In K. Braithwaite & C. James (Eds.), *Educating African Canadians* (pp. 32–57). Toronto, Ontario, Canada: James Lorimer.

Divine, D. (1994). Successful black men. In W. T. Bernard (Ed.), *Black men surviving the 90's conference proceedings* (pp. 12–26). Sheffield, UK: University of Sheffield.

Essed, P. (1991). *Understanding everyday racism: An interdisciplinary theory.* Newbury Park, CA: Sage.

Este, D. (2003). *Racism, violence, and health project: Report on the community forum held January 29, 2003.* Unpublished report.

Este, D., & Bernard, W. T. (2003). Social work practice with African Canadians: An examination of the African Nova Scotian community. In A. Al-Krenawi & J. Graham (Eds.), *Multicultural social work in Canada: Working with diverse ethno-racial communities* (pp. 306–337). Don Mills, Ontario, Canada: Oxford University Press.

Flegel, P. (2002, February). Challenges to Canadian multiculturalism: The case of the black Montreal. *Canadian Issues,* pp. 39–41.

Flegel, P. (2004). Intersecting oppressions in urban Montreal: A hip-hop perspective. *Canadian Diversity, 3*(1), 47–49.

Fraser, M., Richman, J., & Galinsky, M. (1999). Risk, protection, and resilience: Toward a conceptual framework for social work practice. *Social Work Research, 23,* 131–142.

Fredrickson, D., & Siljander, R. (2002). *Racial profiling: Eliminating the confusion between racial and criminal profiling and clarifying what constitutes discrimination and persecution.* Springfield, IL: Charles C Thomas.

Garibaldi, A. (1992). Educating and motivating African American males to succeed. *Journal of Negro Education, 61*(4), 4–11.

Garmezy, N. (1991). Resilience in children's adaptation to negative life events and stressed environments. *Pediatric Annals, 20*(9), 459–466.

Glasgow, D. (1981). *The black underclass: Poverty, unemployment and entrapment of ghetto youth.* New York: Random House.

Gold, A. (2003). Media hype, racial profiling, and good science. *Canadian Journal of Criminology and Criminal Justice, 45*(3), 391–399.

Henry, F. (1994). *The Caribbean diaspora in Toronto: Learning to live with racism.* Toronto, Ontario, Canada: University of Toronto Press.

Hill, D. (1981). *The freedom seekers: Blacks in early Canada.* Agincourt, Ontario, Canada: Book Society of Canada.

Hill, R. (1998). Enhancing the resilience of African American families. *Journal of Human Behaviour in the Social Environment, 1*(2/3), 49–61.

hooks, bell. (2004). *We real cool: Black men and masculinity.* New York: Routledge.

James, C. E. (1998). Up to no good: Blacks on the streets and encountering police. In V. Satzewich (Ed.), *Racism and social inequality in Canada* (pp. 157–176). Toronto, Ontario, Canada: Thompson.

James, C. E. (2003). *Seeing ourselves: Exploring ethnicity, race, and culture* (3rd ed.). Toronto, Ontario, Canada: Thompson.

James, C. E., & Braithwaite, K. (1996). The education of African Canadians: Issues, contexts, expectations. In K. Braithwaite & C. E. James (Eds.), *Educating African Canadians* (pp. 13–31). Toronto, Ontario, Canada: James Lorimer.

Kelly, J. (1998). *Under the gaze: Learning to be black in white society.* Halifax, Nova Scotia, Canada: Fernwood.

Kong, N. H. (1996). Confronting a history of exclusion: A personal reflection. In K. Braithwaite & C. E. James (Eds.), *Educating African Canadians* (pp. 58–68). Toronto, Ontario, Canada: James Lorimer.

Lather, P. (1991). *Getting smart: Feminist research and pedagogy with/in the post modern.* New York: Routledge.

Lee, C. (1994). Adolescent development. In R. Mincy (Ed.), *Nurturing young black males* (pp. 33–44). Washington, DC: Urban League of America.

McCubbin, H., Fleming, W., Thompson, A., Neitman, P., Elver, K., & Savas, S. (1998). Resiliency and coping in "at risk" African-Canadian youth and their families. In H. McCubbin, E. Thompson, A. Thompson, & J. Futrell (Eds.), *Resiliency in African American families* (pp. 287–328). Thousand Oaks, CA: Sage.

McGloin, J. M., & Widom, C. S. (2001). Resilience among abused and neglected children grown up. *Development and Psychopathology, 13,* 1021–1038.

McWhirter, J., McWhirter, B., McWhirter, E., & McWhirter, R. (2003). *At-risk youth: A comprehensive response* (3rd ed.). Belmont, CA: Brooks/Cole-Thompson Learning.

Mensah, J. (2002). *Black Canadians: History, experience, social conditions.* Halifax, Nova Scotia, Canada: Fernwood.

Milan, A., & Tran, K. (2004, Spring). Blacks in Canada: A long history. *Canadian Social Trends, 72,* Statistics Canada Catalogue No. 11–008–2.7.

Mincy, R. (1994a). Conclusions and implications. In R. Mincy (Ed.), *Nurturing young black males* (pp. 187–203). Washington, DC: Urban League of America.

Mincy, R. (1994b). Why this book? In R. Mincy (Ed.), *Nurturing young black males* (pp. 1–5). Washington, DC: Urban League of America.

Ontario Human Rights Commission. (2003). *Paying the price: The human cost of racial profiling: Inquiry report.* Toronto, Ontario, Canada: Author.

Pachai, B. (1990). *Beneath the clouds of the promised land: The survival of Nova Scotia's blacks: Vol. 2, 1800–1989.* Halifax, Nova Scotia, Canada: Black Educators' Association.

Rak, C., Patterson, L., & Lewis, E. (1996). Promoting resilience in at-risk children. *Journal of Counseling and Development, 74*(4), 368–373.

Reynolds, A. (1998). Resilience among black urban youth: Prevalent, intervention effects, and mechanisms of influence. *American Journal of Orthopsychiatry, 68,* 84–100.

Roberts-Fiati, G. (1996). Assessing the affects of early marginalization on the education of African Canadian children. In K. Braithwaite & C. E. James (Eds.), *Educating African Canadians* (pp. 69–80). Toronto, Ontario, Canada: James Lorimer.

Rutter, M. (1990). Psychosocial resilience and protective mechanisms. In J. Rolf, A. S. Masten, D. Cicchetti, K. H. Nuechterlein, & S. Weintraub (Eds.), *Risk and protective factors in the development of psychopathology* (pp. 181–214). New York: Cambridge University Press.

Salabeey, D. (1997). *The strengths perspective in social work.* New York: Longmans.

Scott, J. (2004). *English language and communication issues for African and Caribbean immigrant youth in Toronto.* Retrieved January 14, 2005, from http://ceris.metropolis.net/Virtual%20Library/ education/scott1.html

Scott, Y. K. (1991). *The habit of surviving.* New York: Ballantine Books.

Simmons, A., & Plaza, D. (1998). Breaking through the glass ceiling: The pursuit of university training among African-Caribbean migrants and their children in Toronto. *Canadian Ethnic Studies Journal, 30*(3), 99–120.

Smith, C. (2004). *Crisis, conflict, and accountability.* Toronto, Ontario, Canada: African Canadian Community Coalition on Racial Profiling.

Smith, C., & Carlson, B. (1997). Stressing, coping, and resilience in children and youth. *Social Science Review, 71*(2), 231–256.

Smith, C. C., Lawson, E., Chen, M., Parsons, M., & Scott, S. (2002). *Anti-black racism in Canada: A report on the Canadian government's compliance with the international convention on the elimination of all forms of racial discrimination.* African Canadian Legal Clinic. Retrieved January 14, 2005, from www.aclc.net/antiba_table.html

Solomon, R. P. (1996). Creating an opportunity structure for Blacks and other teachers of colour. In K. Braithwaite & C. E. James (Eds.), *Educating African Canadians* (pp. 216–233). Toronto, Ontario, Canada: James Lorimer.

Towards a new beginning: The report and action plan of a four-level government/African Canadian community working group. (2003). Toronto, Ontario, Canada: City of Toronto.

Tulloch, H. (1975). *Black Canadians: A long line of fighters.* Toronto, Ontario, Canada: NC Press.

Walker, J. W., St. G. (1979). *Identity: The black experience in Canada.* Toronto, Ontario, Canada: Ontario Educational Communications Authority.

Walker, J. W., St. G. (1980). *A history of blacks in Canada: A study guide for teachers and students.* Hull, Quebec, Canada: Minister of State for Multiculturalism.

Walker, J. W., St. G. (1995). African Canadians. In P. Magocsi (Ed.), *Encyclopedia of Canada's peoples* (pp. 139–176). Toronto, Ontario, Canada: University of Toronto Press.

Walsh, F. (2003). Family resilience: A framework for clinical practice. *Family Process, 42*(1), 1–18.

Werner, E. E. (1984). Resilient children. *Young Children, 40*(1), 68–72.

Wortley, S., & Tanner, J. (2003). Data, denials, and confusion: The racial profiling debate in Toronto. *Canadian Journal of Criminology and Criminal Justice, 45*(3), 367–389.

28

Violence Prevention Programming in Colombia

Challenges in Project Design and Fidelity

Luis F. Duque

Joanne Klevens

Michael Ungar

Anna W. Lee

For the past several years, violence has ranked first as the major cause of mortality in Colombia (Colombia Ministerio de Salud, 1994a) and is one of the most frequent causes for hospitalization, emergency care, and disability, generating nearly 25% of the burden of disease (Colombia Ministerio de Salud, 1994b). Although the burden for disease for intentional injury at the world level is 3.4% (World Health Organization, 2000), this figure stands at 44.8% in the case of Medellín, Colombia's second largest city with 2 million inhabitants. If one counts all types of violent injuries, the figure rises to 56.6% (Londoño, Grisales, Fernández, & Cadena, 1999). In other words, in Medellín, the healthy years lost for injuries resulting from intentional violence are nearly equal to that for all other causes of death

or injury combined. Of the 10 Colombian cities with the largest population, Medellín has the second highest rate of violent deaths (Colombia. Instituto Nacional de Medicina Legal y Ciencias Forenses, 1999, 2000), currently amounting to 60 homicides per 100,000 inhabitants per year. Of all kidnappings in the world, 60% occur in Colombia, and 1 of every 5 kidnappings in the world takes place in the province of Antioquia (whose capital is Medellín).

Unlike what many people believe, violence generated by leftist or rightist armed groups does not constitute the major violence problem in Colombia. It is estimated that only between 5% and 20% of total homicides in the country can be attributed to the armed insurgence (Colombia. Instituto Nacional de Medicina Legal y Ciencias Forenses, 2000; Comisión de Estudios sobre la

Violencia, 1987). Guerrilla violence accounts for only one third of all violence-related costs in the country; two thirds of these attacks are the result of urban violence related to daily conflicts or organized crime (Colombia. Departamento Nacional de Planeacion, 1998).

VIOLENCE PREVENTION IN DEVELOPING WORLD CONTEXTS

Several longitudinal studies have been conducted to determine what factors predict violence and delinquency. Still others have examined factors that prevent violence. However, almost all these have taken place in developed countries with the resources to support alternatives to violence, as well as the structural supports to deliver programs and ensure their fidelity. A program's fidelity refers to the degree of adherence the program shows to the principles and procedures of the program model as it is implemented across different settings.

Early violence prevention programs, then, are almost exclusively designed to fit contexts that are different from communities with levels of violence unheard of in the developed world. To date, the majority of these types of programs have been experimental or have been implemented among limited subgroups of the populations in the United States and Canada. The best known exception is the Head Start project initiated in 1965, which has included over 15 million children from many different cultural backgrounds in United States and which has undergone notable changes since its beginning (General Accounting Office, 1997). Such programs typically target one or two behaviors such as prevention of future violence and criminality, alcohol abuse, or drug abuse, or improved prosocial behavior and academic performance. Few have simultaneously targeted multiple behavioral problems, measured impact, or shown successful outcomes (Shonkoff & Meisels, 2000).

Positive outcomes, as other chapters in this volume demonstrate, are associated with resilience among those vulnerable to the influence of violence. These health-enhancing behaviors have the potential to influence the transgenerational transmission of violence by addressing personal, familial, and community factors that propel cycles of violence.

The challenge is to conceptualize a violence prevention program that can adapt to the exigencies of a developing country facing the enormous challenges brought about by violence. If such a program is to have a meaningful impact on the ability of children in the developing world to overcome the adversity they experience related to their exposure to violence, then the program must be adaptable to the contexts in which the majority of the world's children live.

For the past 5 years, community and academic stakeholders in Medellín have designed and implemented the Early Prevention of Aggression Project, which is, as far as we know, the first such initiative undertaken on a large scale in a Latin American country. The project targeting individual and family risk factors seeks the early identification of children with high probabilities of developing aggression in public schools and day care centers and works with their teachers and families to prevent violent behavior. Its efforts are intended to create the conditions children aged 3 to 9 need to grow up psychologically well and without the threat of violence. As cornerstones of everyday resilience (Masten, 2001), it is reasonable to assume that violence-free homes and communities, the provision of alternative coping strategies and resources that make violence unnecessary among children and their caregivers, and education about violence and its impact that sensitizes educators and their communities to the need to address the root causes of violence would combine to create the conditions necessary for more children to achieve positive outcomes associated with resilience. These outcomes would be expected even if other adversities associated with living in a country struggling to develop economically persist.

In this chapter, we explore the Early Prevention of Aggression Project design, and we address some of the challenges it has faced in its implementation. Specifically, this chapter explores some of the findings from the first stages of a longitudinal evaluation of the project currently underway. It addresses shortcomings in the fidelity of the project and raises questions regarding expectations that violence prevention programs like it can be imported from developed country contexts. More broadly, experiences implementing the project attest to the barriers that professionals and communities encounter when attempting to create structural supports such as safer communities that are foundational to children's resilience.

THE PROBLEM OF AGGRESSION IN CHILDREN

Several studies, including two recent Colombian studies, reveal that the population of serious aggressors globally (those involved in theft, armed assault, or sexual assault) is small (Duque & Klevens, 2000; Duque, Klevens, & Ramírez, 2003a, 2003b; Farrington, 1995; Farrington & West, 1993), although they generate a high volume of victims. Studies conducted in various developed countries also reveal that aggression and antisocial behavior in children is one of the best predictors of aggression and criminality in adulthood, particularly among male children, who present with more serious and earlier manifestations (Brame, Nagin, & Tremblay, 2001; Keenan & Shaw, 1994; Loeber, 1982; Nagin & Tremblay, 1999; Olweus, 1979). It has been reported that approximately 14% to 17% of all children have behavior problems (Campbell, 1995). The proportion found in Itagüí, a municipality next to Medellín, Colombia, is 23% (Duque & Klevens, 2001). Depending on the measurement of "behavior problems" used and the time of application, the population under study (high risk versus community samples), time of follow-up, and study design (prospective or retrospective), between 30% and 84% of children with these behavior problems in preschool persist with behavior problems through adolescence and adulthood (Campbell, 1995; Farrington, 1992; Farrington & Maughan, 1999; Kratzer & Hodgins, 1997; Stattin & Magnusson, 1991). There is a significant continuity between childhood aggression and adolescent aggression (Brame et al., 2001) and adult violence (Eron & Huesmann, 1990; Farrington, 1991; Thornberry & Krohn, 2003).

Aggression in a child generates a "snowball" effect (Patterson, Capaldi, & Bank, 1991; Patterson, DeBaryshe, & Ramsey, 1989; Pepler & Slaby, 1996). His or her behavior generates rejection from parents, who resort to increasingly more severe disciplinary methods. It also produces rejection from teachers, which, coupled with the child's impulsiveness and hyperactivity, hampers learning, elevating the risk of failure and school dropout. Likewise, it causes rejection among schoolmates (Coie & Kupersmidt, 1983). These aggressive children, once isolated, tend to seek out peers with similar problems (Cairns & Cairns, 1994). During adolescence, these children have a higher risk of early use of alcohol and drugs, alcohol-related problems, premature and promiscuous sexuality, possession of weapons, affective and occupational instability, and violence against women (Caspi, Elder, & Bem, 1987; Farrington, 1995). Whether these problems are consequences of early aggression or other underlying common risk factors remains to be determined. They do underscore, however, the need to intervene early and comprehensively. Arguably, sustainable interventions that target these multiple negative behavioral outcomes need to be developed and evaluated for developing countries such as Colombia.

Risk Factors for the Appearance or Persistence of Early Aggression

The appearance of early aggression and a high persistence of aggression in a subgroup of children lead some to believe that its roots are found in early childhood or prior to birth. Factors that might be significant prior to birth include a family history of criminality, which becomes particularly important when coupled with an inadequate environment for upbringing (Cadoret, Yates, Troughton, Woodworth, & Stuart, 1995), "in-uterus" exposure to alcohol (Streissguth, Sampson, & Barr, 1999), perinatal complications (Kandel & Mednick, 1991), and certain temper traits (Chess & Thomas, 1992). Gender is perhaps one of the most influential factors in violent behavior. Males, particularly youths, predominate in both victims and aggressors of all types of violence, with the exception of verbal or indirect violence. Such predominance appears during the preschool years (Tremblay et al., 1999) and cannot be attributed completely to biological factors but, instead, must also be accounted for by children's socialization processes (Kruttschnitt, 1994; Pepler & Slaby, 1996). The family is the first place in which the child observes and learns his or her initial behavior. Families with children having behavior problems are characterized by high levels of conflict, stress (Campbell, 1995; Loeber & Stouthamer-Loeber, 1986), and violence (Klevens, Restrepo, Roca, & Martinez, 2001; Tolman & Bennett, 1990). Parents of aggressive children tend to use coercive upbringing strategies more frequently (Rothbaum & Weisz, 1994). Maltreatment is, in particular, one of the most frequent factors singled out as a determinant of aggression, although the majority of maltreated children do not become aggressors themselves (Widom, 1989). A greater tendency to tolerate the child's coercive behavior (e.g., disobedience, fits, or aggression toward others) and ignore prosocial behaviors has also been observed in these families (Patterson et al., 1991). Both child abuse and witnessing family violence (Klevens et al., 2001), as well as a lack of clarity in norms, poor parental supervision, and a family history of crime and interpersonal violence are factors associated with aggression in Colombian studies of violent behavior (Duque, Klevens, & Ramírez, 2003a, 2003b). Some studies, including those conducted in Colombia, have reported that the perception of having a mother overwhelmed by problems is significantly more frequent among delinquent populations (Klevens et al., 2001; Klevens & Roca, 1999). This might constitute another factor that could disrupt interactions between a mother and her son and her capacity to supervise or correct him adequately. It has been reported that in communities of low socioeconomic status, family traits account for 53% of the variation in aggressive behavior, whereas in high-socioeconomic status communities, family characteristics are responsible for a mere 3% of the variance (Pagani, Boulerice, & Tremblay, 1997).

Retrospective studies of resilient men in Colombia compared with men who became involved in crime or substance abuse showed that resilient men perceived stronger support from families and described their mother as a strong person who had taken charge of the situation, introducing stability amid life stressors, and stressing the importance of education and work; they also showed greater degrees of control and coherence in their lives and had fewer and more selective friends. Resilient men also reported less arbitrary and physical punishments and more affection, acceptance, and supervision from their caregivers than did aggressive persons (Klevens, Restrepo, & Roca, 2000; Klevens &

Roca, 1999). Another Colombian study on the interrelationships between individual, family, peer, and societal factors has shown the importance of family in promoting resilience. The availability of drugs, low familial contact, and low identification with one's heritage were offset by a close parent-child relationship, thereby leading to less marijuana use. In addition, all cultural and ecological factors related to violence were buffered by a close parent-child mutual attachment. Important to our discussion here, the protective effect of family appeared to be more important in Colombia than among youth in the United States (Brook et al., 1998; Brook, Brook, De la Rosa, Whiteman, & Montoya, 1999).

Prevention Possibilities

Fortunately, there exist various effective alternatives to prevent or modify the course of early aggression. In a systematic review of literature on successful experiences for early prevention conducted for the Medellín Violence Prevention Program (Klevens, Tremblay, & Corporación Presencia Colombo Suiza, 2000), 21 programs were found that complied with the following parameters: (a) based on a sample of 50 or more children under 12 years of age, (b) used a control group for comparison, and (c) using standardized instruments, measured results in terms of aggression or antisocial behavior at least 1 year following the intervention.[1] Unfortunately, as noted above, all these programs took place in developed countries. There is a dearth of research on violence prevention efforts in developing countries.

Seven types of activities were identified through this review, with the following results:

1. Interventions promoting cognitive skills generate a high impact when carried out during preschool age and when combined with the development of other types of skills in the child, such as planning. It is not clear if parental involvement in educational activities constitutes an essential component.

2. Workshops for children that consolidate social interaction skills are effective for children with behavior problems as well as for high-risk children, but the cognitive content should be adapted to children under the age of 7.

3. Workshops for parents in the contingent and consistent management of child behavior reveal 60% to 75% reductions on a short-range basis in aggressive and antisocial behavior among children aged 3 to 8. The impact is lower in children whose families are low income or without social support and in which there exists violence or intrafamily conflict. These workshops alone will not generalize the results to other contexts such as school, and hence intervention in two environments is recommended: family and school.

4. Training of educators in the contingent and consistent management of behavior of the child decreases problems in the classroom, but it will not suffice to decrease the incidence of delinquency.

5. Home visits during the early years of life are effective, particularly when they succeed in modifying the course of life of the mother and mobilizing her support network.

6. Administration of medication to aggressive children contributes to the performance of children with hyperactivity and attention disorder in such a way that they can profit more from school activities or any other type of intervention.

7. Linking high-risk children with mentors seems to have a positive impact, but existing evidence is still weak given the limited number of evaluations conducted on this intervention.

A review of the literature reveals other results that can be expected from these types of programs (Barnett, 1995, 1998; Karoly et al., 1998; Kellermann, Fuqua-Whitkey, Rivara, & Mercy, 1998; Miller, 1994; Webster-Stratton, 1991; Yoshikawa, 1995):

- *Decreased criminal activity and enhanced social behavior:* Projects in which this effect was measured revealed positive results in the sense that, once reaching adolescence or adulthood, children who participated in the early prevention of violence projects had a lower incidence and less serious violations of legal norms and better social behavior standards than did children in control groups.
- *Better cognitive and emotional development:* A favorable effect was observed on children's IQ during the intervention or immediately following it; however, this effect tends to fade a few years after the intervention is completed. Only some very high-quality interventions conducted during the early years tend to present positive, long-lasting effects in IQ level.
- *Improved educational results:* In the majority of the projects, groups participating in the programs showed better academic performance, less repetition of grade levels, fewer dropouts, and a higher high school graduation rate than did the comparison groups. These effects are even higher when the intervention has a longer duration and when it takes place at the preschool and elementary school level.

Given the multiple causes of the early appearance of aggression and antisocial behavior, combined interventions are recommended to modify various factors simultaneously in the child's different contexts and expand their influence over several years (Tremblay & Craig, 1995; Wasserman & Miller, 1998). Such multilevel intervention addressing individual, familial, community, and cultural factors associated with the risks that predict violence in children is typical of scores of other initiatives targeted at enhancing functioning among populations under stress. As other chapters in this volume demonstrate, however, we have seldom understood the complexity of multilevel intervention in contexts other than those of developed countries. Despite the fact that many communities in developed countries may resemble those in the developing world in terms of systemic prejudice, marginalization, and poverty, arguably, the proximity of these communities to others of privilege makes their situation distinct from that of environments such as Medellín, which lacks national resources equal to those of the developed nations on which it seeks to model its interventions.

THE MEDELLÍN VIOLENCE PREVENTION PROGRAM

One of the authors (Duque) directed the team that designed and initiated the implementation of the Program for Peaceful Coexistence in Medellín, funded by the city with an international loan. This program had six components: (a) promoting nonviolence among children and youth,

(b) bringing justice closer to communities, (c) social communication as a promoter of nonviolence, (d) violence surveillance, (e) institutional modernization, and (f) community participation in monitoring and evaluation (Duque, 2000). The Early Prevention of Aggression Project, designed by the second author (Klevens), was one of the projects in the first component, "Promoting Nonviolence Among Children and Youth," of the Program for Peaceful Coexistence. At the center of the Early Prevention Project are interventions for children in public schools and day care centers. By 2005, the project should reach half of all children aged 4 to 9 in the city of Medellín—that is, nearly 107,000 children in 452 schools and 56 day care centers located in marginal areas, with high rates of violence and scarce social and economic resources. With this project, the municipality hopes to prevent aggression and delinquency, use of psychoactive substances, and low school performance and dropout in children from these communities, to ensure social and economic progress. The Early Prevention of Aggression Project was designed in response to the alarming violence figures for the municipality of Medellín (Duque, 2000). To our knowledge, this project is the first of its kind to be conducted on a large-scale basis in Latin America or other developing country—hence, the importance of establishing the effectiveness of this program with a child population. In the following sections, we will describe the original design, the changes introduced to the design, and the problems observed in the preliminary evaluation to extract some of the lessons learned along the way.

Design and Implementation of the Project

The Early Prevention of Aggression Project, once designed, went through extensive consultations with local experts and municipal servants to adjust the design to the local context. Through the various discussions with these participants, it became clear that there was discomfort with the theoretical base (conductive social learning) instead of a psychodynamic orientation, which was the orientation further adopted by the secretary of education of the Medellín municipality. There was also discomfort with a foreign intervention model. Unfortunately, there were no rigorously evaluated Colombian experiences or experiences based in psychodynamic theory from which to draw.

The Early Prevention of Aggression Project was proposed to do two things: (a) train teachers to teach and promote prosocial skills in the classroom and manage children's behavior contingently, consistently, and nonviolently and (b) provide support and skills to parents of children already manifesting behavior problems to help them manage their child's behavior contingently, consistently, and nonviolently. In this way, the total population of children in selected schools and classrooms participates in the project, but only those children with behavior problems receive *additional* support in their homes.

For the school intervention, a manual was adapted from existing sources (McGinnis & Goldstein, 1990, 1997; Shure, 1994; Slaby, Roedell, Arezzo, & Hendrix, 1995; Slaby, Wilson-Brewer, & Dash, 1994; Sobel, 1983) to provide teachers with a basic understanding of the strategies proposed and activities for the classroom. Teachers volunteered to participate in the program. They were trained by faculty members of the University of Antioquia and a nongovernmental organization whose mandate is to address violence. In the initial design, groups of 10 to 12 teachers would attend a 2-hour workshop facilitated by a trained professional once a week for 17 consecutive weeks. During this time, the professional trainer would visit each teacher in his or her group twice a month and provide on-the-job feedback. After the 17 weeks of training, the trainer would continue to meet monthly with each teacher's group for 6 more months to provide support and troubleshoot problems.

The purpose of the training was to encourage teachers to do the following:

- Establish clear norms and routines as well as clear and predictable procedures in their classrooms to create a predictable, safe, and nurturing school climate
- Modify the physical and programmatic environment of their classrooms and schools to reduce opportunities for conflict and promote opportunities for cooperation and sharing
- Shape prosocial behaviors and strategies for the pacific resolution of conflicts

- Favor encouragement of positive behavior over punishment for the negative
- Teach nearly 40 prosocial skills, which include courtesy norms, understanding of one's feelings and those of others, assertive communication, and strategies for the peaceful management of conflict

The manual prepared for the teachers included a series of specific activities to be conducted. It was also expected that teachers would address aggression in students in a contingent and consistent manner and acquire the habit of shaping prosocial behavior in children during all classroom and playground activities. In fact, some of these modifications in the classroom and school have been nothing short of a cultural shift in emphasis among some educators. The project's message was that teachers can greatly affect the patterns of violence among students and that their work will create conditions that buffer children's exposure to violence and offer alternatives that may seed resilience. The goal, then, was that the project would influence (a) the incidence of aggressive behaviors among students, (b) the initiation of psychoactive substance (alcohol, illicit drugs) and tobacco use, (c) the initiation of risky and delinquent behaviors, and (d) school performance and dropout.

Determining Level of Risk

As part of an ecological intervention, simultaneously with work done in the schools with educators, support was to be provided for the families of children with more serious behavior problems. These children were identified through an instrument adapted and normed for the Medellín population, known as the COPRAG, a measure of children's prosocial and aggressive behavior (Agudelo et al., 2002). The instrument, which is completed by parents or teachers of the children, includes 45 questions using a 3-point Likert scale, covering four subscales: prosocial skills, proactive aggression, reactive aggression, and attention deficit hyperactivity disorder. One additional question asks about the child's school performance. To develop this measure, 53 items representing conceptual definitions for "prosocial behavior" and "aggressive behavior" were selected from

Tremblay et al.'s (1996) National Longitudinal Survey of Children and Youth, Achenbach's (1991) Child Behavior Checklist, and Correa and Olaya's (1999) Pediatric Symptom Checklist. Other scales were developed from work by Apodaca, Lopez, and Etxebarria (1998). Items in English were translated and back translated to ensure comparability. The original 53-item measure (filled out by teachers) was tested in a sample of 83 school-aged children from three different schools in Bello (part of metropolitan Medellín but excluded from the intervention).

The revised measure was applied to another sample of students ($N = 714$) from 20 schools in Medellín. Resulting data were factor-analyzed using principal components factor analysis. A five-factor solution was selected based on eigenvalues, the proportion of variance explained by the factor, and the meaningfulness of the items in each scale. The resulting factors appeared to represent aggression (14 items), prosocial behavior (11 items), hyperactivity and attention deficit (8 items), depression and anxiety (7 items), and indirect aggression (5 items). The scale appeared to be internally consistent with a Cronbach's alpha of .934, for the complete measure, ranging from .88 to .937 for each of the subscales. The subscales were significantly correlated with each other, with coefficients ranging from .076 (between prosocial behavior and indirect aggression) to .67 (between physical aggression and indirect aggression). A score of 30 on the aggression subscale, which corresponded to the 90th percentile, was considered the cutoff point for aggressive behavior, while a score of 31, which corresponded to the 25th percentile, was taken as the cutoff point for lack of prosocial behavior.

To establish interrater reliability, the primary caregiver of a subsample (from the previous sample) of children ($n = 165$), was also asked to respond to the measure. Concordance between teachers and caregivers was low, with a kappa of 0.24. However, the teachers' reports were strongly associated with caregivers' reports of a perceived "behavior problem" for the child.

Information on domestic violence, family alcohol and drug use, and parent discipline techniques as well as the child's social information processing deficits was also gathered. The Conflict Tactics Scale (Strauss, 1979) was proposed to measure violence among adults in the family, and a modified version was proposed to measure violence toward the index child. A measure for social information-processing deficits was designed based on work by Slaby and Guerra (1988) and Dodge and Coie (1987). Twelve pictures depicting social interactions were developed. Separate pictures were made for girls and boys so that the characters in each picture were of the same gender as the respondent. Three vignettes represented accidental situations (e.g., a boy rushes by and knocks things off your desk), three represented prosocial situations (e.g., you are on the floor and another child asks you if you need help), three represented ambiguous situations (e.g., you ask a child sitting on a bench with a ball if he'll lend you his ball and he says "no"), and three represented aggressive situations (e.g., a child cuts in line in front of you). Children were asked (a) to describe the problem, and responses were coded on the number of hostile interpretations given; (b) what they would do in this situation, with probing for alternatives by interviewers; and (c) what the consequences would be if they chose to carry out the most aggressive response they had proposed.

Shortly after the beginning of the academic calendar year, teachers participating in the project completed the COPRAG instrument on all students in their classes. COPRAG test score determination was calculated by university faculty members rather than by teachers, to avoid stigma in the school environment.

Family-Based Interventions for Children at Highest Risk of Aggression

The second component of the proposed intervention consisted of training professionals to act as advisers to families of those children identified with scores at or above the 90th COPRAG test percentile. The design called for weekly home visits and monthly parent group workshops during 1 year, with the parents advancing to a new learning module once they showed that they could apply the knowledge gained in a daily situation. Based on adult learning principles (Knowles, 1980), family advisers were expected to facilitate critical analysis among parents of their interaction and communication patterns with their child, including their

discipline and supervision techniques, and model these practices for parents.

The manual for family advisers adapted material from various sources (Dinkmeyer & McKay, 1989; Garber, Garber, & Spizman, 1987; Patterson, 1976; Slaby et al., 1995) that was judged to be socially and culturally appropriate in these communities. Parents were to be encouraged to (a) clearly communicate their expectations with regard to positive or negative behaviors expected of their child, (b) adequately supervise the child's behavior, (c) praise the child's positive behavior, and (d) provide negative consequences, with no aversion ("time-out" or loss of privileges) in response to aggressive behavior.

The institutions in charge of the different components of the intervention (School of Humanities and Social Sciences of the University of Antioquia for elementary school teacher training, Colombian Society for Psychoanalytic Care (ODRES) for preschool teacher training, and the Catholic Bolivarian University for training of family advisers) were selected competitively after a public announcement.

The intervention as described was presented to officials from the Secretary of Education Office and various universities in Medellín. At this presentation, it became evident that the social cognitive model on which the intervention is based was not the theoretical orientation accepted by the participants, who favored a more psychodynamic approach. Thus, the objectives of the project were reformulated so that instead of reducing aggressive behavior and promoting prosocial behavior, it would promote insight into current child-rearing and child management practices among teachers and parents. A psychodynamic orientation (i.e., assumption that aggression is innate and that promoting insight will lead to behavior change) was adopted for the project implementation (Domínguez, 2002).

Further changes included modification of the 2-week training of trainers that we proposed reduced to 2 days by the municipality because of costs. The quantitative measures proposed to collect data for follow-up and evaluation were deemed too burdensome and culturally inappropriate and were replaced with qualitative data (interviews and field diaries). In addition, the institutions selected for training the family advisers negotiated with the municipality a reduction in the number of home visits (from weekly to two meetings overall) and parent group workshops (from monthly to six sessions in total). To replace the home visits and workshops families were to receive, family advisers offered each family two family counseling sessions at the advisers' offices. The institutions training the teachers also negotiated reductions in their component: instead of 17 workshops spaced over 17 weeks, they would do 10 concentrated in 10 days, with no bimonthly on-the-job training sessions, although they would do bimonthly workshops.

As the implementation began, family advisers were allowed to include families with children with scores less than the 90th percentile on the COPRAG, once they completed service for the children falling within the 90th percentile and above, to use available funds in their contract. During the first year of intervention, the institutions in charge of training teachers adapted the manual to give it a psychodynamic orientation. Finally, in 2003, a group of consultants recommended that the crux of the intervention shift from children and families to schools to deal with culture and school climate instead of individual behavior (Montoya, Montoya, Pardo, & Alvarez, 2003).

To date, the project has been implemented continuously for 3 years with the following community coverage (see Table 28.1).

Evaluation

In total, 8,900 children from child care centers and schools participated in the first cohort of implementation in 2001. Of these, 579 scored above the 90th percentile on the COPRAG and were initially eligible for the family-based

Table 28.1 Coverage of the Early Prevention of Aggression Project, Medellín, Colombia

Phase	Teachers and Caregivers	Schools and Day Care Centers
Pilot, 2001	361	57
Second, 2003	1,394	163
Third, 2004	338	46
Total	**1,778**	**266**

intervention. Because there was room in the budget to fund interventions with more families, 1,853 additional families received direct support from the project. To examine the effectiveness of the project, 339 youth were selected from the first cohort of the project in 2001 and are now being studied by the University of Antioquia and Dalhousie University. Of these 339 children, 115 scored above the 90th percentile on the two aggression subscales of the COPRAG, 154 between the 75th and 89th percentiles, and 107 below the 75th percentile. A control group of 339 youth was matched by age, gender, and socioeconomic status to those children in the intervention cohort.

Initial data from this evaluation show great variation in program participation during implementation of the project. Although some sites had shown great enthusiasm and included the participation of directors, teachers, and caregivers, others implemented the program only partially or hardly at all. Similar variations of participation were found among the families who received the additional support and training. Thus, based on the qualitative data collected, schools, day care centers, teachers, caregivers, and families were classified as A (good), B (fair), and C (poor or not participating). The classification criteria and breakdown of ratings are as detailed in Tables 28.2 and 28.3.

Implementation in day care centers and with day care workers was very positive: Educators working with preschool children adhered to the program closely, with all 138 educators from 22 day care centers participating well in most aspects of the intervention. However, the poor participation rates of elementary school teachers were disconcerting; 56% demonstrated poor levels of participation.

Our results contrast sharply with expected levels of participation for programs on which the Medellín Project were based. For example, in their report on rates of participation for a comparable program, Tremblay and his colleagues (Tremblay, Pagani-Kurtz, Mâsse, Vitaro, & Pihl 1995; Vitaro, Brendfen, & Tremblay, 1999) report that 87% of the teachers in the schools involved completed the initial rating of aggression among their students.

The differences in implementation may be explained by variation in expectations by school

Table 28.2   Fidelity Criteria for the Early Prevention of Aggression Project

Fidelity	School or Day Care Center	Teacher, Day Care Giver	Family
A	Principal trained and committed $\geq 80\%$ teacher participation Accomplished three program phases	Attended 9–10 of 10 training sessions	≥ 1 parent attended 9–10 of 10 training sessions
B	50%–79% teacher participation Accomplished two or three program phases	Attended 8 of 10 training sessions	≥ 1 parent attended 6, 7, or 8 of 10 training sessions
C	Less than 50% teacher participation Accomplished two or three program phases	Attended ≤ 7 of 10 training sessions	≥ 1 parent attended 5 or fewer of 10 training sessions

Table 28.3   Fidelity to the Early Prevention of Aggression Project

		Fidelity			
		A	B	C	Total
Institutions					
Schools	Number	4	7	22	33
	Percentage	12	21	67	100
Day care centers	Number	22	2	0	24
	Percentage	92	8	0	100
Total institutions	Number	26	9	22	57
	Percentage	46	16	39	100
Teachers					
Teachers	Number	72	19	132	223
	Percentage	32	9	59	100
Day care givers	Number	138	0	0	138
	Percentage	100	0	0	100
Total teachers	Number	210	19	132	361
	Percentage	58	5	37	100
Families	Number	531	513	1.398	2.442
	Percentage	22	21	57	100

and day care administrators regarding their staff's participation. In the elementary schools, only those teachers who wanted to participate were trained, meaning that the project may have been implemented in only one or two classrooms within each school. In contrast, all the teachers in the preschools were trained, along with support staff. This degree of saturation appears to have made a significant difference in the quality of project implementation. The reluctance among schoolteachers to participate may, however, be related to the overcrowded conditions in many teachers' classrooms, with teachers responsible for 40 to 45 students each. Day care group sizes are much smaller. Furthermore, no incentives were given to the teachers to add these violence prevention activities to their already full workload.

Even more troubling, however, is that of the 2,242 families involved in the more intensive intervention, only 22% were considered to have participated at a "good" level. Another 21% had "fair" levels of participation, and the majority (57%) showed "poor" levels of participation. These numbers also contrast with reports of participation by Tremblay (Tremblay et al., 1995; Vitaro et al., 1999) who found that 35.9% of families of aggressive children in the program they initiated refused to participate in the intervention, and another 8.4% dropped out before the end of the intervention. Although this is a notably high rate of poor participation, our experience in a developing-world context shows that families are even more likely than families in developed countries to avert participation in such programs. Staff members who were tasked with contacting families report that the main barrier they experienced in engaging parents in the project was finding an adult caregiver of the identified child with whom to work. Frequently, caregivers were absent from their homes during the hours that family advisers were willing and able to visit the families. Advisers were limited in the number of hours they could safely move around the communities, given the level of violence present in the communities in which they provided outreach.

In addition, as noted earlier, the implementation team was allowed to conduct only a 2-day workshop to explain the project in general to those professionals contracted through partner institutions to train teachers. This gave the implementation team only enough time to present the empirical support for the project and its content. Team members could not discuss the theoretical orientation in detail or use strategies to better engage staff and families.

Lessons Learned

Implementing a large-scale violence prevention project in a community such as Medellín where there are significant stressors necessarily requires adaptation. Addressing risk through structural change and community-wide support is a noteworthy ambition, but the practicalities of implementation in a developing-world context make success less ensured. Looking back, ideally, we would have begun with a pilot project to test the feasibility and efficacy of the proposed intervention in this new setting, with members of the core pilot project team doing the intervention to ensure initial fidelity and philosophical congruence rather than taking this intervention to such a large scale and hoping that third parties would implement it appropriately. Although a pilot phase was proposed, pressure by the municipality to increase coverage forced us to carry out the work initially with 57 schools (hardly a "pilot").

We also learned the importance of identifying and working with allies. As previously explained, the two institutions hired to train the teachers and day care workers did not agree with the social cognitive orientation from the start. Finding partners who shared the theoretical orientation of the proposed project probably would have ensured better rates of participation and fidelity. In addition, we feel strongly that trainers would have needed at least 2 weeks (instead of 2 days) of training to become adequate project instructors. Better skill development and a lengthier orientation for trainers would have increased their buy-in to the project goals as well as increased the likelihood that they acquired the skills needed to model and provide appropriate feedback to the teachers they trained.

There were, of course, reasons why the project was implemented so quickly. Although we enjoyed ample community and institutional participation, culminating in an initially large number of project sites, it was still a very long and drawn-out process that seriously delayed implementation and ran the risk of failing altogether when the government changed and threatened to end the project.

Given the adjustments made to the project during the multiple discussions with high levels of participation by community members and school administrators, we expected that the project was feasible and acceptable in the local context in which it would be implemented. However, such contextualization did not occur, and many of the better aspects of the intervention were watered down or lost during the constant give and take among stakeholder groups.

Initial outcomes that have been documented show that these problems have influenced the project's effectiveness. Qualitative analyses of field diaries suggested that teachers had changed in their ways of thinking about children's aggressive behavior and had clear ideas of how to intervene in conflict situations, but their actions remained unchanged. We believe that it is possible that, given the psychodynamic orientation of the revised intervention, trainers spent a great deal of time promoting "insight" or awareness of inappropriate teaching practices but did not model or practice the specific skills that were to be implemented as part of the original project design. Even if teachers had wanted to do the intervention in the ways intended, they may not have gained the skills needed to do so during their training.

The most important lesson learned is that a large city, such as Medellín, is able to invest substantial sums of money and resources in a long-term preventive intervention and is able to persist in its implementation despite all the difficulties we have observed in these first few years of a project such as ours. The Peaceful Coexistence Program was designed and planned with the participation of 500 experts from 80 entities: experts from the Mayor's Office, officials from various government offices (Police Department, Army, Forensic Medicine, the Attorney General's Office, Child Services, etc.), representatives from private foundations and nongovernmental organizations, academics and researchers from the main universities, and community and church leaders. This ample participation in the initial design of the Peaceful Coexistence Program may have contributed to its sustainability. Support from the mayor elected in 2000 who was deeply committed to social change and who made available sufficient resources to fund the project through the negotiation of a loan from the Inter-American Development Bank also ensured the project's long-term viability.

Although a project of this magnitude is a huge undertaking for any community, it is particularly so for one plagued by an epidemic of violence such as Medellín. This intervention is allowing us to investigate the impact of an early violence prevention program on children in a developing country. The structure, having borrowed program elements from developed countries, will allow us to compare findings across settings. As such, the project has shown many strengths from which we can learn much about what is required to conduct violence prevention work in the developing world. The project has been implemented in very dangerous neighborhoods. It has managed to include an evaluation component. There has been a high degree of local commitment by the municipality and business and education leaders, as well as an international team of experts and researchers who assist with the project. However, even with these strengths, demonstrating the effectiveness of the project over time will be difficult. The validity of many of the items borrowed for inclusion in the COPRAG has not been established in Spanish. Finally, like many such programs, issues of fidelity in program implementation have raised concerns about measures of the program's effectiveness. These drawbacks, not unique to this program, highlight the difficulties in implementing comprehensive violence prevention programs in developing countries and the challenges of demonstrating their effectiveness.

Although initial participation rates are disappointing, we feel the work is still valuable, not only for those children whose caregivers do participate fully but to investigate what are feasible and effective practices for other developing countries, countries in transition, and even economically developed countries that have communities with high rates of violence. In this way, efforts to implement this project are enhancing our understanding of the cultural specificity necessary to implement violence prevention programs that create the structural conditions necessary to create and sustain resilience among child populations in the developing world.

NOTE

1. Programs reviewed included Abikoff (1991); Conduct Problems Prevention Research Group (1999a, 1999b); Durlak, Furhman, and Lampman (1991); Graziano and Diament (1982); Greenberg, Kusche, Cook, and Quamma (1995); Guerra, Eron, Huesmann, Tolan, and VanAcker (1996); Hawkins et al. (1992); Hinshaw, Klein, and Abikoff (1998); Kazdin (1987, 1997); Kazdin, Siegel, and Bass (1992); Kolvin et al. (1981); Lochman (1992); Long, Forehand, Wierson, and Morgan (1994); McCarton

et al. (1997); Miller (1994); O'Donnell, Hawkins, Catalano, Abbott, and Day (1995); Olds et al. (1998); Schweinhart, Weikart, and Larner (1986); Seitz, Rosenbaum, and Apfel (1985); Soloman, Watson, Deluchi, Schaps, and Battistich (1997); Spencer et al. (1996); Strayhorn and Weidman (1991); Tierney and Grossman (1995); Tolan and MacKay (1996); Tonry and Farrington (1995); Tremblay, Masse, Pagani, and Vitaro (1996); Wasserman and Miller (1998); Webster-Stratton (1985, 1991); Webster-Stratton and Hamond (1997); Webster-Stratton, Kolpacoff, and Hollinsworth (1988).

REFERENCES

Abikoff, H. (1991). Cognitive training in ADHD children: Less to it than meets the eye. *Journal of Learning Disabilities, 24,* 205–209.

Achenbach, T. (1991). *The child behavior checklist.* Burlington, VT: University of Vermont.

Agudelo, S. L. M., Giraldo, C. A., Gaviria, L. M. B., Sandoval, C. C. A., Rodríguez, M. A., Gómez, C. J. F., Gallon, L. A., et al. (2002). *Características de las familias y escuelas relacionadas con los comportamientos agresivos y prosociales en niños y niñas de 3 a 11 años.* [Characteristics of the families and schools related to the aggressive and prosocial behaviors in children 3 to 11 years old]. Medellín, Colombia: Universidad de Antioquia, Colciencias, CES.

Apodaca, P., Lopez, F., & Etxebarria, I. (1998). Conducta prosocial en preescolares. [Prosocial conduct in pre-schoolers]. *Infancia y Aprendizaje, 82,* 45–61.

Barnett, W. S. (1995). Long-term effects of early childhood programs on cognitive and school outcomes. *The Future of Children, 5,* 25–50.

Barnett, W. S. (1998). Long-term cognitive and academic effects of early childhood education on children in poverty. *Preventive Medicine 27,* 204–207.

Brame, B., Nagin, D. S., & Tremblay, R. E. (2001). Developmental trajectories of physical aggression from school entry to late adolescence. *Journal of Child Psychology and Psychiatry, 42,* 503–512.

Brook, J. S., Brook, D. W., De la Rosa, M., Duque, L. F., Rodriguez, E., Montoya, I., & Whiteman, M. (1998). Pathways to marijuana use among adolescents: Cultural/ecological, family, peer and personality influences. *Child Adolescence and Psychiatry, 37,* 759–766.

Brook, J. S., Brook, D. W., De la Rosa, M., Whiteman, M., & Montoya, I. (1999). The role of parents in protecting Colombian adolescents from delinquency and marijuana use. *Archives of Pediatric Adolescent Medicine, 153,* 457–465.

Cadoret, R. J., Yates, W. R., Troughton, E., Woodworth, G., & Stuart, M. A. (1995). Genetic-environmental interactions in the genesis of aggressivity and conduct disorders. *Archives of General Psychiatry, 52,* 916–924.

Cairns, R. B., & Cairns, B. D. (1994). *Lifelines and risks: Pathways of youth in our times.* New York: Cambridge University Press.

Campbell, S. B. (1995). Behavior problems in preschool children: A review of recent research. *Journal of Child Psychology and Psychiatry, 36,* 113–149.

Caspi, A., Elder, G., & Bem, D. (1987). Moving against the world: Life-course patterns of explosive children. *Developmental Psychology, 23,* 308–313.

Chess, S., & Thomas, A. (1992). Dynamics of individual behavioral development. In M. D. Levine, W. B. Carey, & A. C. Crocker (Eds.), *Developmental-behavioral pediatrics.* Philadelphia: Saunders.

Coie, J., & Kupersmidt, J. (1983). A behavioral analysis of emerging social status in boys' groups. *Child Development, 54,* 1400–1416.

Colombia. Departamento Nacional de Planeacion. (1998). *La paz: El desafío para el desarrollo* [La Paz: The challenge for development]. Bogotá, Colombia: Tercer Mundo Edit.

Colombia. Instituto Nacional de Medicina Legal y Ciencias Forenses. Centro de Referencia Nacional sobre Violencia. (1999). *Lesiones de causa externa, Colombia 1998* [Injuries of external origin, Colombia 1998]. Bogotá, Colombia: Author.

Colombia. Instituto Nacional de Medicina Legal y Ciencias Forenses. Centro de Referencia Nacional sobre Violencia (2000). *Forensis 1999 Datos para la vida.* Instituto Bogotá, Colombia: Author.

Colombia. Ministerio de Salud. (1994a). *La Salud en Colombia. Diez Años de Información* [Health in Colombia. Ten years of information]. Santa Fe de Bogotá, Colombia: Litografía ARCO.

Colombia. Ministerio de Salud (1994b). *La Carga de la Enfermedad en Colombia* [The load of the disease in Colombia]. Santa Fe de Bogotá, Colombia: Litografía ARCO.

Comisión de Estudios sobre la Violencia. (1987). *Colombia: Violencia y democracia* [Colombia: Violence and democracy]. Bogotá, Colombia: Universidad Nacional de Colombia.

Conduct Problems Prevention Research Group. (1999a). Initial impact of the fast track prevention trial for conduct problems: I. The high risk sample. *Journal of Consulting and Clinical Psychology, 67,* 631–647.

Conduct Problems Prevention Research Group. (1999b). Initial impact of the fast track prevention trial for conduct problems: II Classroom effects. *Journal of Consulting and Clinical Psychology 67,* 648–657.

Correa, M. L., & Olaya, A. (1999). *Validacion del Pediatric Symptom Checklist para detectar riesgos psicosociales en escolares* [Validation of the Pediatric Symptom Checklist to detect psychosocial risks in students]. Unpublished masters thesis, University of Antioquia, Medellín, Colombia.

Dinkmeyer, D., & McKay, G. D. (1989). *STEP (Systematic Training for Effective Parenting): The parent's handbook.* Circle Pines, MN. American Guidance Service.

Dodge, K. A., & Coie, J. D. (1987). Social-information-processing factors in reactive and proactive aggression in children's peer groups. *Journal of Personality and Social Psychology, 53,* 1146–1158.

Domínguez, F. (2002). *Observaciones al proceso de aplicación del modelo de prevención temprana de la agresión. Pautas de educación y crianza* [Observations of the process of application of the model of early prevention of aggression. Guidelines for education and child-rearing]. Medellín, Colombia: Secretaria de Educación, Alcaldía de Medellín.

Duque, L. F. (2000). *El Programa de Convivencia Ciudadana de Medellín* [Program for peaceful coexistence in Medellín]. Medellín, Columbia: Cargraphics.

Duque, L. F., & Klevens, J. (2000). La Violencia en Itagüí, Antioquia (I): Prevalencia y Distribución [Violence in Itagüí, Antioquia (I): Prevalence and distribution]. *Biomédica, 20,* 151–68.

Duque, L. F., & Klevens, J. (2001). La Violencia en Itagüí, Antioquia (II): Factores asociados [Violence in Itagüí, Antioquia (I): Associated factors]. *IQEN, 6*(11), 161–170.

Duque, L. F., Klevens, J., & Ramírez, C. (2003a). Cross sectional survey of perpetrators, victims, and witnesses of violence in Bogotá, Colombia. *Journal of Epidemiology Community Health, 57,* 355–360.

Duque, L. F., Klevens, J., & Ramírez, C. (2003b). Overlap and correlates of different types of aggression among adults: Results from a cross-sectional survey in Bogotá, Colombia. *Aggressive Behaviour, 29,* 191–201.

Durlak, J. A., Furhman, T., & Lampman, C. (1991). Effectiveness of cognitive-behavior therapy for maladapting children: A meta-analysis. *Psychological Bulletin, 110,* 202–214.

Eron, L. D., & Huesmann, L. R. (1990). The stability of aggressive behavior. In M. Lewis & S. M. Miller (Eds.), *Handbook of developmental psychopathology* (pp. 147–156). New York: Plenum.

Farrington, D. P. (1991). Childhood aggression and adult violence: Early precursors and later life outcomes. In D. J. Pepper & K. H. Rubin (Eds.), *The development and treatment of childhood aggression* (pp. 5–29). Hillsdale, NJ: Erlbaum.

Farrington, D. P. (1992). Criminal career research in the United Kingdom. *British Journal of Criminology, 32,* 521–536.

Farrington, D. P. (1995). The Twelfth Jack Tizard Lecture. The development of offending and antisocial behavior from childhood: Key findings from the Cambridge Study in Delinquent Development. *Child Psychology and Psychiatry, 360,* 929–964.

Farrington, D. P., & Maughan, B. (1999). Criminal careers in two London cohorts. *Criminal Behavior and Mental Health, 9,* 91–106.

Farrington, D. P., & West, D. J. (1993). Criminal, penal and life histories of chronic offenders: Risk and protective factors and early identification. *Criminal Behavior and Mental Health, 3,* 492–523.

Garber, S. W., Garber, M. D., & Spizman, R. F. (1987). *Good behavior.* New York: St. Martin's Press.

General Accounting Office. (1997). *Head Start: Research provides little information on impact of current program* (GAO/HEHS-97–59). Washington, DC: Government Printing Office.

Graziano, A. M., & Diament, D. M. (1982). Parent behavioral training: An examination of the paradigm. *Behavior Modification, 16,* 3–38.

Greenberg, M. T., Kusche, C. A., Cook, E. T., & Quamma, J. P. (1995). Promoting social competence in school-aged children: The effects of the PATHS curriculum. *Development and Psychopathology, 7,* 117–136.

Hawkins, J. D., Catalano. R. F., Morrison, D. M., O´Donnell, J., Abbott, R. D., & Day, L. E. (1992). The Seattle Social Development Project: Effects of the first four years on protective factors and problem behaviors. In J. McCord & R. E. Tremblay (Eds.), *Preventing antisocial behavior: Interventions from birth to adolescence* (pp. 139–161). New York: Guilford Press.

Hinshaw, S. P., Klein, R. J., & Abikoff, H. (1998). Childhood attention deficit disorder: Nonpharmacologic and combination treatments. In P. Nathan & J. Gorman (Eds.), *A guide to treatments that work* (pp. 3–24). New York: Oxford University Press.

Kandel, E., & Mednick, S. A. (1991). Perinatal complications predict violent offending. *Criminology, 29,* 519–530.

Karoly, L. A., Greenwood, P. W., Everingham, S. S., Hoube, J., Kilburn, M. R., Rydell, C. P., Sanders, M., et al. (1998). *Investing in our children: What we know and don't know about the costs and benefits of early childhood interventions.* Santa Monica, CA: RAND.

Kazdin, A. E. (1987). Treatment of antisocial behavior in childhood: Current status and future directions. *Psychological Bulletin, 102,* 187–203.

Kazdin, A. E. (1997). Parent management training: Evidence, outcomes and issues. *Journal of the American Academy of Child and Adolescent Psychiatry, 36,* 1349–1356.

Kazdin, A. E., Siegel, T. C., & Bass, D. (1992). Cognitive problem solving skills training and parent management training in the treatment of antisocial behavior in children. *Journal of Consulting and Clinical Psychology, 60,* 733–747.

Keenan, K., & Shaw, D. S. (1994). The development of aggression in toddlers: A study of low-income families. *Journal of Abnormal Psychology, 22,* 53–77.

Kellermann, A. L., Fuqua-Whitkey, D. S., Rivara, F. P., & Mercy, J. (1998). Preventing youth violence: What works. *Annual Review of Public Health, 19,* 271–292.

Klevens, J., Restrepo, O., & Roca, J. (2000). Some factors for explaining resilience among young men in Colombia. *Revista de Salud Publica, 2,* 165–172.

Klevens, J., Restrepo, O., Roca, J., & Martinez, A. (2001). Risk factors for adult male criminality in Colombia. *Criminal Behavior and Mental Health, 11,* 73–85.

Klevens, J., & Roca, J. (1999). Nonviolent youth in a violent society: Resilience and vulnerability in the country of Colombia. *Violence and Victims, 14,* 311–322.

Klevens, J., Tremblay, R., & Corporación Presencia Colombo Suiza. (2000). *Prevención temprana de la violencia: Estrategias de Intervención* [Early prevention of violence: Strategies for intervention]. Medellín, Colombia: Alcaldía de Medellín.

Knowles, M. (1980). *The modern practice of adult education: From pedagogy to androgogy.* Chicago: Follett.

Kolvin, I., Garside, R. F., Nicol, A. R., MacMillan, A., Wolstenhome, F., & Leitch, I. M. (1981). *Help starts here.* New York: Tavistock.

Kratzer, L., & Hodgins, S. (1997). Adult outcomes of child conduct problems: A cohort study. *Abnormal Child Psychology, 1,* 65–81.

Kruttschnitt, C. (1994). Gender and interpersonal violence. In A. J. Reiss & J. A. Roth (Eds.), *Understanding and preventing violence: Vol. 3. Social influences* (pp. 293–376). Washington, DC: National Academy Press.

Lochman, J. E. (1992). Cognitive-behavioral intervention with aggressive boys: Three-year follow up and preventive effects. *Journal of Consulting and Clinical Psychology 48,* 1181–1209.

Loeber, R. (1982). Stability of antisocial behavior: A review. *Child Development, 53,* 1431–1446.

Loeber, R., & Stouthamer-Loeber, M. (1986). Family factors as correlates and predictors of juvenile conduct problems and delinquency. In N. Tonry & M. Norris (Eds.), *Crime and justice: An annual review of research* (Vol. 7, pp. 29–150). Chicago: University of Chicago Press.

Londoño, J. L., Grisales, H., Fernández, S. J., & Cadena, E. (1999). Años de vida saludables perdidos por la población de Medellín.[Lost years of healthy life among the population of Medellín]. *Rev. Facultad Nacional de Salud Pública, 17*(1), 63–92.

Long, P., Forehand, R., Wierson, M., & Morgan, A. (1994). Does parent training with young noncompliant children have long term effects? *Behavioral Research Therapy, 32,* 101–107.

Masten, A. (2001). Ordinary magic: Resilience processes in development. *American Psychologist, 56*(3), 227–238.

McCarton, C. M., Brooks-Gunn, J., Wallace, I. F., Bauer, C. R., Bennett, F. C., Berbaum, J. C.,

Broyles, S., et al. (1997). Results at age 8 years of early intervention for low birth weight premature infants. The infant health and development program. *JAMA, 277,* 126–132.

McGinnis, E., & Goldstein, A. P. (1990). *Skill-streaming in early childhood. Teaching prosocial skills to the preschool and kindergarten child.* Champaign, IL: Research Press.

McGinnis, E., & Goldstein, A. P. (1997). *Skill-streaming the elementary school child.* Champaign, IL: Research Press.

Miller, L. S. (1994). Preventive interventions for conduct disorder: A review. *Child and Adolescent Psychiatric Clinics of North America, 3,* 405–419.

Montoya, E. M., Montoya, M., Pardo, V. M., & Alvarez, B. (2003). Una memoria reflexiva sobre el proceso de asistencia técnica en la implementación de un modelo de prevención temprana de la agresividad, pautas de educación y crianza 2000–2003 [A reflective memory on the process of technical attendance in the implementation of a model of early prevention of aggressiveness, guidelines for education and childrearing 2000–2003]. Medellín: Corporación Colombo Suiza.

Nagin, D., & Tremblay, R. E. (1999). Trajectories of boys' physical aggression, opposition, and hyperactivity on the path to physically violent and nonviolent juvenile delinquency. *Child Development, 70,* 1181–1196.

O'Donnell, J., Hawkins, J. D., Catalano, R. F., Abbott, R. D., & Day, L. E. (1995). Preventing school failure, drug use, and delinquency among low income children: Long term intervention in elementary schools. *American Journal of Orthopsychiatry, 65,* 87–100.

Olds, D., Henderson, C. R., Cole, R., Eckonode, J., Kilzman, H., Luckey, D., Pettit, L., et al. (1998). Long-term effects of nurse home visitation on children's criminal and antisocial behavior. *JAMA, 280,* 1238–1244.

Olweus, D. (1979). Stability of aggressive reaction patterns in males. A review. *Psychological Bulletin, 86,* 852–875.

Pagani, L., Boulerice, B., & Tremblay, R. E. (1997). The influence of poverty on children's classroom placement and behavior problems. In G. Duncan & J. Brooks-Gunn (Eds.), *Consequences of growing up poor* (pp. 311–339). New York: Russell Sage.

Patterson, G. R. (1976). *Living with children: New methods for parents and teachers.* Champaign, IL: Research Press.

Patterson, G. R., Capaldi, D., & Bank, L. (1991). An early starter model for predicting delinquency. In D. J. Peplar & K. H. Rubin (Eds.), *The development and treatment of childhood aggression.* Hillsdale, NJ: Erlbaum.

Patterson, G. R., DeBaryshe, B. D., & Ramsey, E. (1989). A developmental perspective of antisocial behavior. *American Psychologist, 41,* 432–444.

Pepler, D. J., & Slaby, R. G. (1996). Theoretical and developmental perspectives on youth and violence. In L. D. Eron, J. H. Gentry, & P. Schlegel (Eds.), *Reason to hope: A psychological perspective on violence and youth* (2nd ed., pp. 27–58). Washington, DC: American Psychological Association.

Rothbaum, F., & Weisz, J. (1994). Parental caregiving and child externalizing behavior in non-clinical samples: A meta-analysis. *Psychological Bulletin, 116,* 55–74.

Schweinhart, L. J., Weikart, D. P., & Larner, M. B. (1986). Consequences of three preschool curriculum models through age 15. *Early Child Research Quarterly, 1*(33), *35,* 37–38.

Seitz, V., Rosenbaum, L. K., & Apfel, N. H. (1985). Effects of a family support intervention: A ten-year follow up. *Child Development, 56,* 376–391.

Shonkoff, J. P., & Meisels, S. M. (Eds.). (2000). *Handbook of early childhood intervention* (2nd ed.). Cambridge, MA: Cambridge University Press.

Shure, M. (1994). *Raising a thinking child: Help your young child resolve conflicts and get along with others.* New York: Pocket Books.

Slaby, R. G., & Guerra, N. G. (1988). Cognitive mediators of aggression in adolescent offenders: Assessment. *Developmental Psychology, 24,* 580–588.

Slaby, R. G., Roedell, W. C., Arezzo, D., & Hendrix, K. (1995). *Early Violence Prevention: tools for Teachers of Young Children.* Washington, DC: National Association for the Education of Young Children.

Slaby, R. G., Wilson-Brewer, R., & Dash, K. (1994). *Aggressors, victims and bystanders.* Newton, MA: Education Development Center.

Sobel, J. (1983*). Everybody wins: 393 non-competitive games for young children.* New York: Walker.

Soloman, D., Watson, M. S., Deluchi, K. L., Schaps, E., & Battistich, V. (1997). Enhancing children's prosocial behavior in the classroom. *American Journal of Educational Research, 24,* 527–554.

Spencer, T., Biederman, J., Willens, T., Harding, M., O'Donnell, D., & Griffin, S. (1996). Pharmacotherapy of attention-deficit hyperactivity disorder across the life cycle. *Journal of the American Academy of Child and Adolescent Psychiatry, 35,* 409–432.

Stattin, H., & Magnusson, D. (1991). Stability in change in criminal behaviour up to age 30. *British Journal of Criminology, 31,* 327–346.

Strauss, M. A. (1979). Measuring intrafamily conflict and violence: The Conflict Tactics Scales. *Journal of Marriage and the Family, 41,* 75–88.

Strayhorn, J. M., & Weidman, C. S. (1991). Follow up one year after parent-child interaction training: Effects on behavior of preschool children. *Journal of the American Academy of Child and Adolescent Psychiatry, 30,* 138–143.

Streissguth, A. P., Sampson, P. D., & Barr, H. M. (1999). Neurobehavioral dose-response effects of prenatal alcohol exposure in humans from infancy to adulthood. *Annals of New York Academy of Sciences, 562,* 145–158.

Thornberry T. P., & Krohn M. D. (Eds.). (2003). *Taking stock of delinquency. An overview of findings from contemporary longitudinal studies.* New York: Kluwer Academic/Plenum.

Tierney, J. P., & Grossman, J. B. (1995). *Making a difference: An impact study of big brothers/big sisters.* Philadelphia: Public/Private Ventures.

Tolan, P. H., & MacKay, M. M. (1996). Preventing serious antisocial behavior in inner-city children: An empirical based family intervention program. *Family Relations, 45,* 148–155.

Tolman, R. M., & Bennett, L. W. (1990). A review of quantitative research on men who batter. *Journal of Interpersonal Violence, 5,* 87–118.

Tonry, M., & Farrington, D. P. (Eds.). (1995). *Building a safer society: Strategic approaches to crime prevention.* Chicago: University of Chicago Press.

Tremblay, R. E., & Craig, W. M. (1995). Developmental crime prevention. In M. Tonry & D. P. Farrington (Eds.), *Building a safer society: Strategic approaches to crime prevention* (pp. 151–236). Chicago: University of Chicago Press.

Tremblay, R. E., Japel, C., Pérusse, D., Boivan, M., Zoccolillo, M., Montplaisir, J., & McDuff, P. (1999). The search for age of "onset" of physical aggression: Rousseau and Bandura revisited. *Criminal Behavior and Mental Health, 9,* 24–39.

Tremblay, R. E., Masse, L. C., Pagani, L., & Vitaro, F. (1996). The Montreal prevention experiment. In R. de V. Peters & R. J. McMahon (Eds.), Preventing *Childhood Disorders, Substance Abuse & Delinquency.* Thousand Oaks, CA. Sage.

Tremblay, R. E., Pagani-Kurtz, L., Mâsse, L. C., Vitaro, F., & Pihl, R. O. (1995). A bimodal preventive intervention for disruptive Kindergarten boys: Its impact through mid-adolescence. *Journal of Consulting and Clinical Psychology, 63,* 560–568.

Vitaro, F., Brendfen, M., & Tremblay, R. E. (1999). Prevention of school dropout through the reducation of disruptive behaviors and school failure in elementary school. *Journal of School Psychology, 37,* 205–226.

Wasserman, G. A., & Miller, L. S. (1998). The prevention of serious and violent juvenile offending. In R. Loeber & D. P. Farrington (Eds.), *Serious and violent juvenile offenders: Risk factors and successful interventions* (pp. 197–247). Thousand Oaks, CA. Sage.

Webster-Stratton, C. (1985). The effects of father involvement in parent training for conduct problem children. *Journal of Child Psychiatry and Psychology, 26,* 801–810.

Webster-Stratton, C. (1991). Annotations: Strategies for helping families with conduct disordered children. *Journal of Child Psychiatry and Psychology, 32,* 1047–1062.

Webster-Stratton, C., & Hamond, M. A. (1997). Treating children with early onset conduct problems: A comparison of child and parent training interventions. *Journal of Consulting and Clinical Psychology, 65,* 93–19.

Webster-Stratton, C., Kolpacoff, M., & Hollinsworth, T. (1988). Self administered video tape therapy for families with conduct problem children. Comparison of two cost-effective treatments and control group. *Journal of Consulting and Clinical Psychology, 56,* 558–566.

World Health Organization. (2000). *World health report 2000: Statistics annex.* Geneva: Author.

Widom, C. (1989). The cycle of violence. *Science, 244,* 160–166.

Yoshikawa, H. (1995). Long-term effects of early childhood programs on social outcomes and delinquency. *The Future of Children, 5,* 51–75.

AUTHOR INDEX

SUBJECT INDEX

ABOUT THE EDITOR

Michael Ungar is both a social worker and marriage and family therapist with experience working directly with children and adults in mental health, educational, and correctional settings. Now Associate Professor in the School of Social Work at Dalhousie University, Halifax, Canada, he continues to supervise and consult extensively with educators, guidance counselors, and other professionals in Canada, the United States, and overseas. He has conducted many workshops internationally on resilience-related themes relevant to the treatment and study of at-risk youth and has published dozens of peer-reviewed articles on resilience and work with children and their families. He is also the author of two books: *Playing at Being Bad,* a book for parents, and *Nurturing Hidden Resilience in Troubled Youth,* for family therapists. Dr. Ungar holds numerous research grants from national funding bodies and is a collaborator on several international research projects as well. Currently, he leads a study titled Methodological and Contextual Challenges Researching Childhood Resilience: An International Collaboration that includes researchers from 10 countries on five continents.

About the Contributors

Laura S. Abrams is Assistant Professor of Social Work in the School of Social Work at the University of Minnesota, Twin Cities. She is interested in social context influences on youth identity, self-perceptions, and risk behaviors. Her current project is an ethnographic study of cultures of correctional institutions for youthful male offenders. This project explores how these institutions construct masculine identities, how offenders view their treatment, and how these institutions prepare youth for transitions home.

Saleem Al-Habash was born in 1982 and is now the managing editor of the *Youth Times*. He was one of the founding members of the Palestinian Youth Association for Leadership and Rights Activation (PYALARA), where he has volunteered and worked since 1998. He is completing his bachelor degree in journalism and political Science from the University of Birziet and is a freelance writer for the Al-Ayyam daily newspaper. He lives in Ramallah.

Alean Al-Krenawi is Associate Professor in and Chairman of the Spitzer Department of Social Work at Ben-Gurion University of the Negev, Israel. His area of research is multicultural social work and mental health with particular interest on indigenous peoples. He has published over 50 peer-reviewed journal articles in the area of social work and mental health with the Arab societies in the Middle East, over 20 book chapters, and several books. His most recent project is the preparation of a book on Islam and social work.

Lewis Aptekar is currently Professor of Counselor Education at San Jose State University. Some of his academic awards include Fulbright scholarships (Colombia, Swaziland, Honduras), a position as Nehru Visiting Professor, and a scholarly residency at the Bellagio Rockefeller Foundation Study and Conference Center (Italy). His has written two books, *Street Children of Cali* and *Environmental Disasters in Global Perspective,* and more than 50 articles and chapters. He is currently working on a manuscript titled *Human Rights and Survival in an Ethiopian Refugee Camp.*

Mary I. Armstrong has over 20 years experience in children's behavioral health, public sector managed care, children's health insurance, and child welfare and social services. She is currently Assistant Professor and Director of the Division of State and Local Support, Department of Child and Family Studies at the Louis de la Parte Florida Mental Health Institute, University of South Florida. She is responsible for the administration of the Division of State and Local Support and of evaluation and research activities. Her current activities include a national study of public sector managed care and its effects on children with serious emotional problems, child welfare privatization, the impact of welfare reform on the adolescent daughters of enrollees, and financing mechanisms for systems of care. During 2002, she was appointed as a member of the national Outcomes Roundtable for Children and Families. She has many publications in both professional journals and textbooks.

Ken Barter is Professor and former Chair in Child Protection with the School of Social Work, Memorial University of Newfoundland. His research has been in the field of public child welfare, child protection, administration, and social work. He has published numerous book chapters, journal articles, research reports, and conference proceedings and presented to audiences at provincial, national, and international conferences.

William H. Barton is Professor and Director of Research Services at the Indiana University School of Social Work in Indianapolis. Following 8 years of postdoctoral research at the Institute for Social Research and the Center for the Study of Youth Policy, both at the University of Michigan, he joined the faculty of the Indiana University School of Social Work where he has worked since 1993. He teaches courses in juvenile justice policy, program evaluation research methods, and the philosophy of science. His research interests include juvenile justice, delinquency prevention and youth development issues, and the applied methodologies of program evaluation and needs assessment. In addition to several journal articles and book chapters, his publications include two books—*Reforming Juvenile Detention* (coedited with Ira Schwartz) and *Closing Institutions for Juvenile Offenders* (with Denise Gottfredson).

Wanda Thomas Bernard is Associate Professor and Director of the School of Social Work, Dalhousie University. She has a particular interest in antiracist and anti-oppressive social work theory and practice. Much of her professional study and work pursuits have focused on race, racism, and racial uplift. She and her colleague, David Este, are currently undertaking a major research project on the intersection of violence, racism, and health, a 5-year, multisite, national project funded by the Canadian Institutes of Health.

Fred H. Besthorn is Associate Professor of Social Work at the University of Northern Iowa, Cedar Falls, Iowa. He has written extensively on the development of a framework for integrating deep ecological awareness with social work policy and strengths-based practice. This involves research on the relationship between environmental degradation and its social, economic, and spiritual impact on disadvantaged populations. He is the creator of the Global Alliance for a Deep-Ecological Social Work. This unique organization unites social workers around the world sharing a commitment to incorporating deep environmental awareness into traditional social work practice and the founder of *Earth Consciousness: The Journal of Environmental Social Work and Human Services*—the first online journal of its kind devoted exclusively to the creative works of social workers and human service professionals who care deeply for the natural world.

Hania Bitar is the founder and Director General of the Palestinian Youth Association for Leadership and Rights Activation (PYALARA). In 1997, she established and edited the *Youth Times*—the first Palestinian youth newspaper—which developed into a 24-page monthly with an outreach of 200,000 youth readers. With a background in literature from the Catholic University (USA), she started her professional career as a teacher of English language at Bethlehem University and at the YAWCA in Jerusalem. She was awarded a Fulbright scholarship in 1992, was nominated as a Global Leader for Tomorrow in 2002 and Young Arab Leader in 2003. She is the author of several articles and has been a keynote speaker at a number of international conferences.

Cindy Blackstock is Executive Director, First Nations Child and Family Caring Society and Codirector of the Center of Excellence for Child Welfare. A member of the Gitksan Nation, she has worked in the field of child and family services for over 20 years. Key research interests include exploring the etiological drivers of child maltreatment in First Nations communities and the role of the voluntary sector and philanthropic organizations in expanding the range of culturally and community-based responses to child maltreatment.

Roger A. Boothroyd is Associate Professor in the Department of Mental Health Law and Policy at Louis de la Parte Florida Mental Health Institute at the University of South Florida. His background is in the field of educational psychology, specializing in measurement, evaluation, and research design. His current research interests include examining the impact of health care financing arrangements on members' access, outcomes and quality of care, welfare reforms and its effects on mothers and children, and research ethics. He has been a coprincipal investigator on grants funded by the National Institutes of Health and the Substance Abuse and Mental Health Services Administration.

Jo Boyden is a social anthropologist and senior research officer at the Refugee Studies Centre, University of Oxford. For many years, she worked internationally as a social development consultant to a broad range of development and humanitarian relief agencies, governmental, nongovernmental and intergovernmental. This involved a mix of primary and secondary research, advocacy, training, planning, monitoring, and evaluation. Drawing mainly on fieldwork in South Asia, she is currently researching children's and adolescent's experiences of armed conflict and forced migration. The focus of this research is the development of theory and empirical evidence regarding risk, resilience, and coping in childhood; young people's economic, political, and social roles and responsibilities; intergenerational relations; and social and cultural constructions of childhood and youth.

Eileen M. Brennan is an applied psychologist with specialized training in human development. She has concentrated her recent scholarship on investigations of family support and the ways in which employed parents of children with emotional disorders fit work and family responsibilities together. She is Professor and Associate Dean of Social Work at Portland State University. For the last 10 years, she has also served as a principal investigator with the Research and Training Center on Family Support and Children's Mental Health for studies of work-life integration and of inclusion of children with mental health disorders in child care settings. She has written and presented widely on the topics of social support, family support, and work-life issues and is currently coauthoring a book on family support and work-life integration with Julie M. Rosenzweig.

Marion Brown is a PhD student (social work) at Memorial University of Newfoundland and a lecturer at the School of Social Work, Dalhousie University. Her social work practice has focused on community-based programming with youth populations. Her research interests include exploring gender identity negotiations and constructs of aggressive behaviors among young women in residential care through qualitative methods.

Laura Camfield is Research Officer for the UK ESRC-funded Research Group on Well-Being in Developing Countries (WeD) at the University of Bath. She is a qualitative researcher who also uses quantitative and participatory techniques to explore people's experiences. Her primary research interest is conceptualizing and measuring quality of life, but she has also published on narrative approaches to chronic illness and disability. She completed her PhD on measuring the quality of life of people with dystonia. Since the mid-1990s, she has also been engaged in research into the experiences of people living with multiple sclerosis, dystonia and intellectual disabilities, and the treatment and care of people with HIV/AIDS and imprisoned female foreign nationals.

Marc Colbourne is a master of social work student in the School of Social Work, Dalhousie University. He worked for 10 years as Coordinator of Support Services at the Lesbian, Gay and Bisexual Youth Project and has recently begun a position with Canada World Youth, facilitating community development projects in Nova Scotia and Latin America.

Philip Cook is the founder and current Executive Director of the International Institute for Child Rights and Development. The Institute is part of the Centre for Global Studies at the University of Victoria and a recognized Canadian leader in community-based, national, regional, and international applications of the UN Convention on the Rights of the Child. Since 1995, he has overseen the institute's growth as a leader in linking children's healthy development to broad issues of human development and participatory governance across diverse cultures and situational contexts.

Wendy M. Craig is Associate Professor in the Department of Psychology at Queen's University, Kingston, Ontario, Canada. Her research program focuses on bullying and victimization and on the development of aggression in young females. In recognition of her work on bullying and victimization, she recently won an Investigator Award from the Canadian Institute of Health Research. She has published widely in the area, including topics of bullying and victimization, peer processes, sexual harassment, and aggression in girls. Also, she is editor of a volume on childhood social development.

Luis F. Duque is a physician with a background in public health who taught epidemiology and research methods for nearly 15 years at two Colombian universities. He has conducted research projects on the epidemiology of violence in several Colombian cities, and he directed the first National Household Survey on Psychoactive Substance Use in Colombia. He also directed the design and preparation of the City of Medellín's Early Violence Prevention Program and was its first Director. He was also formerly the President of the University of Antioquia, Dean of its National School of Public Health, a Deputy Minister of Health, and Director of the National Institute of Health. He currently works as a researcher of the National School of Public Health, University of Antioquia and is President of the Direction Council of the Colombian Health Association.

Lesley du Toit is the Founder and Executive Director of the Child and Youth Care Agency for Development, a South African nongovernmental organization promoting children's full and healthy development. Her work has mainly been in the residential child care field and youth work where she has done direct care work, therapeutic work with troubled children, teaching and supervising of child care workers, curriculum development for degree programs in child and youth care, and more recently, policy and legislative reform for the South African Government from 1995 to 2001. She has received numerous national and international awards for her programming and policy work with children and has advised various national governments on issues of child welfare and HIV/AIDS.

Dave Este is an Associate Professor in the Faculty of Social Work, University of Calgary. His teaching and research interests include social work practice with immigrants and refugees, management of nonprofit organizations, qualitative research methods, and mental health.

Scot D. Evans is a doctoral student in the Community Research and Action program at Peabody College of Vanderbilt University. He has extensive practical experience in community-based organizations as a youth development worker, family counselor, youth program developer, program evaluator, and organizational consultant. Currently, his research is focused on the role of human service organizations in promoting social change, in particular one community-based human service organization that is attempting to shift its practice paradigm from amelioration to transformation. Scot's community work with Isaac Prilleltensky and others at Vanderbilt has attracted the attention of the local United Way who have asked them to begin working closely with four other community-based organizations on a similar process of change.

Barbara Friesen is Director of the Research and Training Center on Family Support and Children's Mental Health, Portland, Oregon, and a Professor of Social Work at Portland State University. She brings substantial experience to the understanding and improvement of services for children and their families through her role as the principal investigator of the Center's Family Participation Project. She has authored publications on a number of mental health topics, including community practice, family-centered services, prevention, professional training, family support, and family views of residential treatment. She has worked in both clinical and administrative positions in a number of mental health settings, including state institutions, adult and children's psychiatric day treatment programs, and therapeutic classrooms in the public schools.

James Garbarino is Professor in and Director of the Department of Human Ecology at Cornell University in Ithaca, New York, as well as the Director of the acclaimed "Just for Kids!" program. He is an internationally recognized expert in issues dealing with child abuse, specializing in psychological maltreatment. His research focuses on the impact of violence and trauma in the family and community on child and youth development, and it examines interventions to deal with these effects. He has authored and edited numerous books; serves as a consultant to television, magazine, and newspaper reports on children and families; and has been a consultant or adviser to a wide range of national and international organizations concerned with the health and well-being of children, including the American Medical Association, the National

Science Foundation, and Childwatch International Research Network.

Jane F. Gilgun is Professor in the School of Social Work at the University of Minnesota, Twin Cities. She has done research for many years and published widely in the areas of how persons overcome adversities, the meaning of violence to perpetrators, strengths-based assessments and child and family treatment programs, and capacities of parents adopting children with special needs. Her current research projects are on the development of violent behaviors and a project on parenting adoptive children with special needs. She has presented widely on resilience, violence, and treatment approaches that build on client strengths. She is the author of workbooks for children and their families where the children have a variety of adjustment issues associated with histories of adversity.

Joan Glode is a Mi'kmaq woman from Nova Scotia, Canada. Joan has worked both on- and off-reserve in a variety of programs involving social services for both urban Aboriginal and on-reserve First Nations peoples. She worked as a Human Rights Officer with the Nova Scotia Human Rights Commission, as Executive Director of the Friendship Center in Halifax, and as a middle manager with the Department of Indian Affairs. She is now the Executive Director of Mi'kmaw Family & Children's Services, a mandated child welfare agency that also operates two Family Healing Centers that provide shelter and safety to women and children and outreach counseling to men.

Wanjiku Kironyo is a social psychologist with a specialization in marriage and family counseling. She has taught at the University of Nairobi in the Department of Social Work. Through a student placement, she learned about the dire needs of women and children in the slums of Nairobi. This experience led to the development of the Maji Mazuri Center for social and economic development in the late 1980s of which she is Director. She also directed the African Family Development Program for 4 years and chaired the Breastfeeding Information Group. She has traveled widely giving lectures to formal and informal institutions in different parts of the world. She also helps various Kenyan-based

organizations establish community-based organizations like the one she directs.

Joanne Klevens is a physician and former head of the Community Health Department of Javeriana University in Colombia. She currently works for the U.S. Centers for Disease Control, National Center for Injury Prevention and Control. She, along with Luis F. Duque, directed the design of the Medellín Early Violence Prevention Project and conducted several research projects on violence epidemiology in Colombia.

Anna I. Laktionova is Director of the Counseling Center at the Institute of Psychology and Psychotherapy, Moscow, where she works with adolescents. She is also a half-time senior researcher at the Moscow State Psychological and Pedagogical University Research Laboratory. Her work examines the psychological and social problems of orphans in Moscow. Concurrently, she is pursuing doctoral studies at this same university with research focused on coping mechanisms of youth, social adaptation of adolescents, and resilience. She worked previously as a high school vice principal.

Avital Laufer is a health sociologist. Her doctoral dissertation examined violence among Israeli youth and won the Bar-Ilan President and Dean prize for excellence. Her studies focus on youth violence and the effects of terror on youth. She completed her postdoctoral studies at the Adler Research Center at Tel Aviv University. Currently, she is a lecturer at the College of Judea and Samaria in Israel.

John C. LeBlanc is Assistant Professor of Pediatrics, Psychiatry, and Community Health and Epidemiology at Dalhousie University, Halifax, Nova Scotia, Canada. He is based at the IWK Health Centre, a teaching hospital for children and women's health. He holds an IWK Health Centre Investigatorship award that allows him to devote 75% of his time to research. His research interests are in the early identification of disruptive behaviors in children and the evaluation of school-based interventions to reduce these.

Anna W. Lee is currently a postdoctoral associate in the Department of Neurobiology and Behavior at the Rockefeller University in

New York. Her current research investigates how estrogen modulates adrenergic facilitation of reproductive behavior on a molecular level. Her excitement in research, however, lies in linking the brain and behavior, encompassing aspects from psychology, animal behavior, neuroscience, and biophysics. During her Ph.D. work at Dalhousie University, she was involved in the initial stages of the International Resi-Lience project.

Lee Tak-yan is Associate Professor and concurrently Fieldwork Coordinator of the Department of Applied Social Studies, City University of Hong Kong. His research covers civic awareness and civic education, youth development indices, parenting styles and parent-child conflict, adolescent gambling behavior, sociocultural beliefs, moral values and behavior, and effectiveness of parent-teacher associations. He has recently published on topics including handling sibling conflicts, adolescent moral behavior, social worker performance planning, learning strategies as predictors for fieldwork outcomes and performance, youth empowerment, adolescents facing problems in the cyber era, and factors in successful relapse prevention of drug addicts. He has published over 50 journal articles, monographs, and book chapters.

Linda Liebenberg is a South African doctoral student, now managing the International Resilience Project in Halifax, Canada. She has previously managed research projects relating to out-of-school youth in informal settlements surrounding Cape Town and women on farms in the West Coast/Winelands region of South Africa. With a background in psychology and sociology, her main focus is the use of visual methods in varied research contexts. Her interests also include mixed methodologies and how they relate to our understanding of women and children in developing countries.

Nancy MacDonald is Assistant Professor in the School of Social Work, Dalhousie University, Halifax, Nova Scotia. Previously, she worked with Mi'kmaq Family and Children's Services of Nova Scotia and has more than 15 years of direct child welfare practice experience with the Mi'kmaq communities in Nova Scotia. She has been a member of the Mi'kmaq Health Research Group since October 2000, where there are ongoing research projects developed and completed by this group. Nancy has developed and delivered elective courses for the BSW program called Social Work With Aboriginal Populations and Child Welfare With Aboriginal Peoples. Other courses include Cross Cultural Issues for Social Work Practice and Beginning Social Work Practice. She is a Planning Group Member of Aboriginal Women's Health and Healing Research Group. She is lead author of "Managing Institutional Practices to Promote and Strengthen Diversity: One School's Journey," in *Anti-Oppressive Social Work Practice*, edited by Wes Shera and is lead author of "Respecting Aboriginal Families: Pathways to Resilience in Custom Adoption and Family Group Conferencing," in *Pathways to Resilience,* edited by Michael Ungar.

Alexander V. Makhnach is a psychologist and Rector at the Institute of Psychology, Russian Academy of Sciences, Moscow, a leading institute of psychology in Russia. In 1994–1995 he worked on the development of the international program The Challenge of Foster Care under the auspice of Christian Solidarity International (Switzerland) and the Russian Ministry of Education that designed a system of foster families in Russia. From 1997 to 1998 he served as scientific secretary for the working group for development of the federal program Development of Philosophical, Clinical and Applied Psychoanalysis. More recently he has been on the Board of Experts and then as Scientific Vice-Director of the Assistance to Russian Orphans–ARO Program. He teaches basic skills in counseling, family therapy, foundations of supervision, and assessment in several state universities in Moscow and Tomsk. He is the author of more than 60 papers on issues such as psychodiagnostics, methodology of supervision, personality, and youth issues.

Gillian Mann has a background in anthropology and education. She has worked for more than 10 years in the field of policy and programs for children living in adversity, as both a practitioner and a researcher. Her interests lie in children's social competencies and relationships at the household, family, and community levels. Recently, her work has focused on the experiences of separated boys and girls in particular, including those children who live without their parents as a result of war, HIV/aids, or both. She is currently engaged in an ethnographic study of the cognitive and emotional development of Congolese refugee children living in Dar es Salaam, Tanzania.

Jacqueline McAdam-Crisp has degrees in child and youth care and for the past 20 years has worked with children in need of protection in Canada, Kenya, Rwanda, and Ethiopia. Her MA work was done in Nairobi, Kenya, with the assistance of a Canadian International Development Agency (CIDA) award and in cooperation with Wanjiku Kironyo. Her research focused on the development of an alternative form of education for street youth. She is presently working on her PhD in human development at the Fielding Graduate Institute in Santa Barbara, California. Her research focuses on the experiences of children following situations of war and their coping abilities, mental health, and resiliency.

Hamilton I. McCubbin is Professor at the Center on the Family, University of Hawaii at Manoa, and Director, Institute for the Study of Resilience in Families and Center on the Family, University of Wisconsin–Madison. Formerly the Chancellor and CEO, Kamehameha Schools, Honolulu, Hawaii, he has also held posts as the Dean of the School of Human Ecology and Child and Family Studies, University of Wisconsin–Madison, and as Head, Family Social Science, University of Minnesota. His scholarly interests include family stress, coping, and resilience with an emphasis on multi-ethic families, development, and change over the life cycle.

Laurie ("Lali") D. McCubbin is Assistant Professor, in the department of Educational Leadership and Counseling Psychology, Washington State University, in Pullman, Washington. Her research interests and expertise include risk and protective factors and resilience across the life span, cultural identity development, multicultural counseling, and career development. She is also Associate Director of the Stress, Coping and Resilience Project: Individuals, Families and Communities in collaboration with the University of Hawaii at Manoa.

Allister McGregor is Director of the UK ESRC-funded Research Group on Well-Being in Developing Countries (WeD) and is Senior Lecturer in the Department of Economics and International Development at the University of the Bath. The WeD research group is developing a conceptual and methodological framework for understanding the social and cultural construction of well-being in developing countries. The group is working with research partners in Bangladesh, Ethiopia, Peru, and Thailand to carry out detailed empirical research in rural and urban communities in each country. He has a disciplinary background in economics and social anthropology and has extensive experience of primary fieldwork in South and Southeast Asia.

George Menamparampil, a Catholic priest and Salesian of Don Bosco, pioneered the nonformal education of the young in North East India and Bhutan. From 1988 to 1997 he was the adult adviser to MIJARC, an international youth organization based in Brussels. In this capacity, he conducted training programs for youth in grassroots and international forums. From 1998 to 2002, he was a member of the national youth animation team of the Salesians in India. Since March 2002, he has been based at Imphal in Manipur, India, offering a variety of services to underprivileged youth.

Isaac Prilleltensky is the author or editor of five books in the field of community psychology. In addition to these books, he has published approximately 60 articles in refereed journals and 20 book chapters. He has been an invited speaker in many countries, including Argentina, Canada, England, Scotland, the United States, New Zealand, Australia, Venezuela, Spain, Cuba, Norway, and Israel. He is a member of the editorial board of several journals, including the *Journal of Community Psychology* and the *Journal of Community and Applied Social Psychology*. He is a fellow of the American Psychological Association and of the Society for Community Research and Action. He is currently the Director of Graduate Studies in Human and Organizational Development at Vanderbilt University, where he also directs the doctoral program in Community Research and Action.

Ora Prilleltensky is a psychologist, who from 2000 to 2002 taught in the counseling program at Victoria University in Melbourne, Australia. She now teaches counseling in the Department of Human and Organizational Development in Peabody College at Vanderbilt University. Ora is a mother with a physical disability and the author of *Motherhood and Disability: Children and Choices* published by Palgrave/MacMillan in 2004.

Vered Slonim-Nevo is Associate Professor in the Spitzer Department of Social Work, Ben Gurion University of the Negev, Israel, where she has taught advanced clinical courses since 1989. Her research areas include family relations, polygamy, immigration, AIDS prevention, and treatment evaluation. She is also a clinical social worker who counsels families and individuals.

Zahava Solomon is Professor of Psychiatric Epidemiology and Social Work at the Tel-Aviv University and the Head of the Adler Research Center for Child Welfare and Protection. She joined the Israeli Defense Force (IDF) in 1981 and served as Head of the Research Branch in the Medical Corps from 1981 to 1992. In 1990 she joined the Tel-Aviv University and since May 1997 has been Head of the Adler Center for the Study of Child Welfare and Protection. She is internationally known for her research on traumatic stress and especially on the psychological sequel of combat stress reactions, war captivity, and the Holocaust. She has published five books on psychic trauma-related issues and over 200 articles and more than 50 chapters. She was member of the *DSM-4* Advisory Subcommittee for PTSD and has earned numerous Israeli and international awards and research grants.

Joyce West Stevens is Professor Emeritus at Boston University School of Social Work. Prior to her tenure there, she spent many years in both the public and private sectors serving inner-city populations in child welfare, mental health, hospital, and private practice settings. Her investigative studies have been in the area of adolescent health-compromising behaviors, including adolescent pregnancy and substance abuse. Her book *Smart and Sassy: the Strengths of Inner City Black Girls* examines adolescent

developmental issues within the context of daily life, which she argues is necessary when providing direct services. She has been the recipient of both service and research grants and was Principal Investigator for the African American Women's Study, a 3-year NIDA-funded project that investigated the generational transmission of substance use and nonuse among African American women and daughter pairs.

Beth A. Stroul is Vice-President and co-founder of Management & Training Innovations, Inc., a consulting firm in McLean, Virginia, and serves as a consultant in the area of mental health policy. She has completed numerous research, evaluation, policy analysis, and technical assistance projects related to service systems for children and adolescents with emotional disorders and their families. She has been a consultant to the National Technical Assistance Center for Children's Mental Health at Georgetown University since its inception in 1984. Her projects have included coauthoring a widely circulated monograph that presents a conceptual framework and philosophy for a system of care titled, *A System of Care for Children and Adolescents With Severe Emotional Disturbances.* She has published extensively in the field of children's mental health.

Pamela J. Talbot is a graduate student in the master of science program in community health and epidemiology at Dalhousie University. She is focusing on mental health and mental health promotion as part of a holistic model of health. Currently, she is an honorary Killam scholar.

Eli Teram is Professor, Faculty of Social Work, Wilfrid Laurier University, Waterloo, Ontario, Canada. He teaches policy, research, and organization and management courses in the master's and doctoral programs. His research interests relate to the organizational context of social work practice, including professional power and the processing of clients, teamwork, organizational control, and multiculturalism. His current research projects include an action-oriented study of ethical issues in social work practice (with Marshall Fine) and an exploration of the experience of childhood sexual abuse survivors with health professionals (with Candice Schachter and Carol Stalker). He is on the editorial board of the

Canadian Journal of Community Mental Health. He started his professional career working with street gangs in Israel.

Jerry Thomas is a member of the Salesians of Don Bosco, a religious order working with youth. He has been working with youth in North East India for the past 20 years. He recently completed a youth survey for the Salesian province of Dimapur, and studies on youth work in Northeast India, on the ULFA—an insurgent group in Assam. His work has examined the impact of violence on youth. Currently as Director of the North Eastern Regional Youth Commission at Guwahati, he facilitates and coordinates youth activities in the 11 Catholic dioceses in the region.

Nico Trocmé is Professor in the Faculty of Social Work, University of Toronto, and the Director of Centre of Excellence for Child Welfare (CECW). He is the principal investigator for the Canadian Incidence Studies of Reported Child Abuse and Neglect, a periodical survey of investigated maltreatment conducted in Canada. Additional research activities include pilot testing a national framework for tracking outcomes for children receiving child welfare services, analysis of child welfare service trends in Ontario, examination of rates of maltreatment related injuries, and an analysis of child welfare service responses to corporal punishment.

Toine van Teeffelen is Director of Development at the Arab Educational Institute in Bethlehem and member of the board of Palestinian Youth Association for Leadership and Rights Activation (PYALARA). He studied sociology at the University of Rotterdam and social anthropology at the University of Amsterdam, completing his master's thesis with a study of Israeli anthropology.

In the late 1980s and the beginning of the 1990s, he conducted his PhD studies with a discourse analysis of the images of Palestine and Israel in Western popular literature. Articles based on this study appear in various international volumes and journals. He has also authored English and Dutch books about the Palestine-Israel conflict.

Fred Wien is Professor in the School of Social Work, Dalhousie University. He served as the school's Director between 1981 and 1986 and on an acting basis more recently. He is also the Director of the Atlantic Aboriginal Health Research Program, established in the fall of 2002 to strengthen the health research capacity of Aboriginal people in Atlantic Canada. He served as Deputy Director of Research with the Royal Commission on Aboriginal Peoples with particular responsibility for managing the commission's research program in the area of employment and economic development. He has published many books and articles arising from research on the subject of the socioeconomic development of disadvantaged communities.

Wong Kwai-Yau is a social work supervisor with the Boys' and Girls' Clubs Association of Hong Kong. His work experience is with children and youth, including gangs, developmental and preventive programs, and moral education. In addition, his work also addresses problems of child and family poverty. Recently, he and his colleagues started a pilot project, Project Chance, to eradicate child poverty among children in the association. Projects he has led were granted the Outstanding Program Award for his association and recognized by colleagues in the social work field. He has been actively involved in childhood and adolescent resilience work in Hong Kong.